Thirteenth edition

INTRODUCTION TO
GEOGRAPHY

Arthur Getis
San Diego State University

Judith Getis

Mark D. Bjelland
Gustavus Adolphus College

Jerome D. Fellmann
University of Illinois, Urbana–Champaign

WITH CONTRIBUTIONS BY

Victoria L. Getis
Ohio State University

Connect
Learn
Succeed™

INTRODUCTION TO GEOGRAPHY, THIRTEENTH EDITION

Published by McGraw-Hill, a business unit of The McGraw-Hill Companies, Inc., 1221 Avenue of the Americas, New York, NY 10020. Copyright © 2011 by The McGraw-Hill Companies, Inc. All rights reserved. Previous editions © 2009, 2008, and 2006. No part of this publication may be reproduced or distributed in any form or by any means, or stored in a database or retrieval system, without the prior written consent of The McGraw-Hill Companies, Inc., including, but not limited to, in any network or other electronic storage or transmission, or broadcast for distance learning.

Some ancillaries, including electronic and print components, may not be available to customers outside the United States.

This book is printed on acid-free paper.

Printed in the United States of America.

3 4 5 6 7 8 9 0 QDB/QDB 1 0 9 8 7 6 5 4 3 2 1

ISBN 978–0–07–352287–6
MHID 0–07–352287–2

Vice President, Editor-in-Chief: *Marty Lange*
Vice President, EDP: *Kimberly Meriwether David*
Senior Director of Development: *Kristine Tibbetts*
Executive Editor: *Margaret J. Kemp*
Executive Marketing Manager: *Lisa Nicks*
Senior Project Manager: *Sandy Wille*
Buyer II: *Sherry L. Kane*
Lead Media Project Manager: *Stacy A. Vath*
Manager, Creative Services: *Michelle D. Whitaker*
Cover/Interior Designer: *Elise Lansdon*
Cover Image: © *Royalty-Free/CORBIS*
Senior Photo Research Coordinator: *Lori Hancock*
Photo Research: *LouAnn K. Wilson*
Compositor: *Laserwords Private Limited*
Typeface: *10.5/12 Adobe Caslon Regular*
Printer: *Quad/Graphics*

Geography & Public Policy box: Map background: © Nova Development; Globe: © Image by Reto Stockli, NASA/Goddard Space Flight Center. Enhancements by Robert Simon; Mountains: © Getty Images; Sailboats: © MedioImages/Getty Images; Women: © GOODSHOOT/Alamy; Chicago skyline: © IMS Communications Ltd/Capstone Design. All Rights Reserved.; Crowd: © Punchstock/Digital Vision

All credits appearing on page or at the end of the book are considered to be an extension of the copyright page.

Library of Congress Cataloging-in-Publication Data

Introduction to geography / Arthur Getis . . . [et al.] —Thirteenth ed.
  p. cm.
  Includes index.
  ISBN 978–0–07–352287–6 — ISBN 0–07–352287–2 (hard copy : alk. paper) 1. Geography. I. Getis, Arthur, 1934-
  G128.G495   2011
  910—dc22

                                                                2010013747

www.mhhe.com

Brief Contents

PART 1

The Earth Science Tradition 49

PART 2

The Culture-Environment Tradition 159

PART 3

The Location Tradition 311

PART 4

The Area Analysis Tradition 433

Contents

The Earth Science Tradition 49

CHAPTER FOUR
Physical Geography: Weather and Climate 80

CHAPTER FIVE
The Geography of Natural Resources 118

The Culture-Environment Tradition 159

The Location Tradition 311

The Area Analysis Tradition 433

Preface

"If you build it, they will come" was the message that inspired the character played by Kevin Costner in the movie *Field of Dreams* to create a baseball field in his Iowa cornfield. A similar hope encouraged us when we first began to think about writing *Introduction to Geography* in 1975. At that time, very few departments of geography in the United States and Canada offered a general introductory course for students—that is, one that sought to acquaint students with the breadth of the entire field. Instead, most departments offered separate courses in physical and human or cultural geography.

Recognizing that most students will have only a single college course and textbook in geography, we wanted to develop a book that covers all of the systematic topics that geographers study. Our hope, of course, was that the book would so persuasively identify and satisfy a disciplinary instructional need that more departments would begin to offer a general introductory course to the discipline, a dream that has been realized.

APPROACH

Our purpose is to convey concisely and clearly the nature of the field of geography, its intellectual challenges, and the logical interconnections of its parts. Even if students take no further work in geography, we are satisfied that they will have come into contact with the richness and breadth of our discipline and have at their command new insights and understandings for their present and future roles as informed adults. Other students may have the opportunity and interest to pursue further work in geography. For them, we believe, this text will make apparent the content and scope of the subfields of geography, emphasize its unifying themes, and provide the foundation for further work in their areas of interest.

The content is structured around the major research traditions of the discipline. Chapter 1 introduces students to the four organizing traditions that have emerged through the long history of geographic thought and writing: earth science, culture-environment, locational, and area analysis. Each of the four parts of this book centers on one of these geographic perspectives. Within each of the first three parts are chapters devoted to the subfields of geography, each placed with the tradition to which we think it belongs. Thus, the study of weather and climate is part of the earth science tradition; population geography is considered under the culture-environment tradition; and urban geography is included with the locational perspective. The tradition of area analysis—of regional geography—is presented in a single final chapter, which draws on the preceding traditions and themes and is integrated with them by cross-references. A fuller discussion of the book's organization is offered in Chapter 1, pp. 17 to 18.

Of course, our assignment of a topic may not seem appropriate to all users, since each tradition contains many emphases and themes. Some subfields could logically be attached to more than one of the recognized traditions. The rationale for our clustering of chapters is given in the brief introduction to each part of the text.

A useful textbook must be flexible enough in its organization to permit an instructor to adapt it to the time and subject matter constraints of a particular course. Although designed with a one-quarter or one-semester course in mind, this text may be used in a full-year introduction to geography when employed as a point of departure for special topics and amplifications introduced by the instructor or when supplemented by additional readings and class projects.

Moreover, the chapters are reasonably self-contained and need not be assigned in the sequence presented here. The "traditions" structure may be dropped and the chapters rearranged to suit the emphases and sequences preferred by the instructor or found to be of greatest interest to the students. The format of the course should properly reflect the joint contribution of instructor and book, rather than be dictated by the book alone.

NEW TO THIS EDITION

Although we have retained the framework of presentation introduced in the previous edition of this book, we have revised, added, and deleted material for a variety of reasons.

- Current events always mandate an updating of facts and analyses and may suggest discussion of topics hitherto slighted. Such things as the 2010 earthquake in Haiti, changes in the production and consumption of natural resources, changes in spatially variable patterns of population growth and decline, and changes in the populations of major urban areas require updating in each new edition of our textbook. Every table and figure in the book has been reviewed for accuracy and currency and has been replaced, updated, or otherwise revised where necessary.

- Continuing changes in technology and in social, economic, political, and environmental structures and relationships also require revision of previously published material. Among the topics that merited new or revised treatment in this thirteenth edition are the covert use of GPS technology to track criminal suspects (Chapter 2), fuel economy standards (Chapter 5), illegal immigration across the U.S./Mexico border (Chapter 8), and technological innovation (Chapter 10).

- As always, we rely on reviewers of the previous edition to offer suggestions and to call our attention to new emphases or research findings in the different topical areas of geography. Our effort to incorporate their ideas is reflected not only in the brief text modifications or additions that occur in nearly every chapter but also in more significant alterations.

New Figures

To reflect the most recent data, many figures have been revised or newly drawn for the thirteenth edition of *Introduction to Geography*. They include:

- All maps, graphs, charts, and tables related to natural resource use that required updating (Chapter 5)
- New map of the U.S. regions that use the terms *pop, soda,* or *coke* for a soft drink (Chapter 7)
- Updated map of the world's principal religions (Chapter 7)
- New map of Darfur (Chapter 9)
- Updated map of legislative women (Chapter 9)
- New map of global centers of technological innovation (Chapter 10)
- New map of the Great Pacific Garbage Patch (Chapter 12)
- New Appendix 3 using 2009 world population data

New/Revised Boxes

The boxed elements in the book have been updated if necessary or replaced with new discussion texts.

- Updated box "Red States, Blue States," with two new cartograms showing the results of the U.S. presidential election of 2008 (Chapter 2)
- New Geography & Public Policy box, "An Invasion of Privacy," discussing the legal and ethical questions of privacy rights and public safety raised by the covert use of GPS technology to track criminal suspects (Chapter 2)

- Revised Geography & Public Policy box, "Fuel Economy and CAFE Standards" (Chapter 5)
- Completely revised "The Matter of Race" box to reflect recent scholarships (Chapter 7)
- Expanded "Terrorism & Political Geography" box, with a new case study of Darfur (Chapter 9)
- Updated and revised "Legislative Women" box (Chapter 9)
- New Geography & Public Policy box, "Mountaintop Removal: Good or Bad?" (Chapter 12)

New/Revised Topical Discussions

- New opening vignette about the January 2010 earthquake in Haiti
- "Climate Regions" section completely revised and condensed
- All resource-use data updated to reflect the most recent production, consumption, and reserve figures
- Population data and projections updated to reflect the latest available world, regional, and country information from UN population agencies, the Population Reference Bureau, and the U.S. Census Bureau
- New table of the world's 10 most populous countries in 2009 with projections for 2050
- New discussion and photographs of architectural styles
- Terrorism and political geography
- New opening vignette about the Great Pacific Garbage Patch
- Substantial revision of the case study of the Everglades ecosystem region

To respond to suggestions from reviewers and/or to make room for new material, some discussions and figures have been deleted from the previous edition. They include:

- The Geologic Timescale (Chapter 3)
- Box on permafrost (Chapter 3)
- Material on soils (Chapter 4)
- Shortening of the "El Niño" box (Chapter 4)
- "Sports and National Identity" box (Chapter 9)

ACKNOWLEDGMENTS

A number of reviewers have greatly improved the content of this and earlier editions of *Introduction to Geography* by their critical comments and suggestions. Although we could not act upon every helpful suggestion, or adopt every useful observation, all were carefully and gratefully considered. In addition to those acknowledgments of assistance detailed in previous editions, we note the thoughtful advice provided by the following individuals.

Anthony Amato, *Southwest Minnesota State University*

Bruce Boland, *Fairmont State*

Jeff Bradley, *Northwest Missouri State University*

Adrienne Domas, *Michigan State University*

Linda Fair, *Binghamton University*

Chad Garick, *Jones County Junior College*

Mark Gunn, *Meridian Community College*

Molly McGraw, *Southeastern Louisiana University*

Jean Parker, *Boise State University*

William Porter, *Elizabeth City State University*

Christa Smith, *Clemson University*

We gratefully express appreciation to these and unnamed others for their help and contributions and specifically absolve them of responsibility for decisions on content and for any errors of fact or interpretation that users may detect.

Finally, we note with deep appreciation and admiration the efforts of the publisher's "book team," separately named on the copyright page, who collectively shepherded this revision to completion. We are grateful for their highly professional interest, guidance, and support.

Arthur Getis

Judith Getis

Mark Bjelland

Jerome D. Fellmann

FEATURES

Every effort has been made to gain and retain student attention, the essential first step in the learning process.

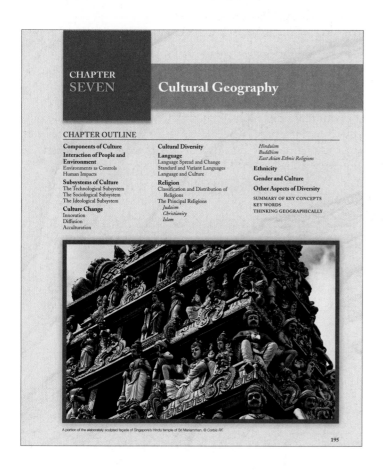

Chapter outlines clarify the organization of the chapters.

Chapter-opening vignettes capture student interest in preparation for the subject matter to follow.

More than 450 full-color maps, charts, and photographs, along with information and explanations, serve as an extension of the text, not just identification or documentation of the figure. World maps have been put on the Robinson projection, and colors have been chosen to accommodate most color-blind readers. **The foldout world maps** at the back of the text can be easily referenced from any chapter in the text.

---

196   PART TWO   The Culture-Environment Tradition

The Gauda's[1] son is 18 months old. Every morning, a boy employed by the Gauda carries the Gauda's son through the streets of Gopalpur. The Gauda's son is clean; his clothing is elegant. When he is carried along the street, the old women stop their ceaseless grinding and pounding of grain and gather around. If the child wants something to play with, he is given it. If he cries, there is consternation. If he plays with another boy, watchful adults make sure that the other boy does nothing to annoy the Gauda's son.

Shielded by servants, protected and comforted by virtually everyone in the village, the Gauda's son soon learns that tears and rage will produce anything he wants. At the same time, he begins to learn that the same superiority which gives him license to direct others and to demand their services places him in a state of danger. The green mangoes eaten by all of the other children in the village will give him a fever; coarse and chewy substances are likely to give him a stomachache. While other children clothe themselves in mud and dirt, he finds himself constantly being washed. As a Brahmin [a religious leader], he is taught to avoid all forms of pollution and to carry out complicated daily rituals of bathing, eating, sleeping, and all other normal processes of life.

In time, the Gauda's son will enter school. He will sit motionless for hours, memorizing long passages from Sanskrit holy books and long poems in English and Urdu. He will learn to perform the rituals that are the duty of every Brahmin. He will bathe daily in the cold water of the private family well, reciting prayers and following a strict procedure. The gods in his house are major deities who must be worshipped every day, at length and with great care.[2]

The Gauda and his family are not Americans, as references and allusions in the preceding paragraphs make plain. The careful reader would infer, correctly, that they are Indians—and if one were to read more of the book from which this excerpt is taken, it would become evident that the Gauda lives in a village in southern India. The class structure, the religion, the language, the food, and other strands of the fabric of life mentioned in the passage place the Gauda, his family, and his village in a specific time and place. They bind the people of the region together as sharers of a common culture and set them off from those of other areas with different cultural heritages. The approximately 7 billion people who were the subject of Chapter 6 are of a single human family, but it is a family differentiated into many branches, each characterized by a distinctive *culture*.

To some writers and commentators, *culture* means the arts (literature, painting, music, etc.). To a social scientist, **culture** is the specialized behavioral patterns, understandings, and adaptations that summarize the way of life of a group of people. In this broader sense, culture is as much a part of the regional differentiation of the earth as are topography, climate, and other aspects of the physical environment. The visible and invisible evidences of culture—buildings and farming patterns, language and political organization—are elements in the spatial diversity that invites and is subject to geographic inquiry. Cultural differences in area result in human landscapes with variations as subtle as the differing "feel" of urban Paris, Moscow, and New York or as obvious as the sharp contrasts of rural Zimbabwe and a cash grain farm in America's Midwest (Figure 7.1).

Because such differences exist, cultural geography exists, and one branch of cultural geography addresses a whole range of "why?" and "what?" and "how?" questions. Why, since humankind constitutes a single species, are cultures so varied? What are the most pronounced ways in which cultures and culture regions are distinguished? What are the origins of the different culture regions we now observe? How, from whatever limited areas in which single culture traits and amalgams developed, were they diffused over a wider portion of the globe? Why do cultural contrasts between recognizably distinct people persist even in such presumed "melting pot" societies as that of the United States or in the outwardly homogeneous, long-established countries of Europe? How is knowledge about cultural differences important to us today? These and similar questions are the concerns of the present chapter and, in part, of Chapters 8 and 9.

COMPONENTS OF CULTURE

Culture is transmitted within a society to succeeding generations by imitation, instruction, and example. It is learned, not biological, and has nothing to do with instinct or with genes. As members of a social group, individuals acquire integrated sets of behavioral patterns, environmental and social perceptions, and knowledge of existing technologies. Of necessity, we learn the culture in which we are born and reared. But we need not—indeed, cannot—learn its totality. Age, sex, status, and occupation dictate the aspects of the cultural whole in which we become fully indoctrinated.

A culture displays a social structure—a framework of roles and interrelationships of individuals and established groups. Despite overall generalized and identifying characteristics and even an outward appearance of uniformity, a culture is not homogeneous. The "American" culture, for example, contains innumerable complex, composite, and often competing subgroups: farmers and city dwellers; males and females; teenagers and retirees; liberals and conservatives; owners and employees; members of different religious, political, social, or other formal organizations; and the like. Each individual learns and is expected to adhere to the rules and conventions not only of the culture as a whole but also specific to the subgroups to which he or she belongs. And those subgroups may have their own recognized social structures.

Culture is a complexly interlocked web of behaviors and attitudes. Realistically, its full and diverse content cannot be appreciated, and in fact may be wholly misunderstood, if we concentrate our attention only on limited, obvious traits.

[1]Gauda = village headman.
[2]Excerpt from *Gopalpur: A South Indian Village*, by Alan R. Beals, copyright © by Holt, Rinehart and Winston, Inc., and renewed 1990 by Alan R. Beals, reprinted by permission of the publisher.

195

---

198   PART TWO   The Culture-Environment Tradition

differences, varied food preferences, and a host of other internal differentiations, may nonetheless share enough joint characteristics to be recognizably distinctive cultural entities to themselves and others. Certainly, citizens of "melting pot" United States would identify themselves as *Americans*, together constituting a unique culture system on the world scene.

Culture traits, complexes, and systems have spatial extent. When they are plotted on maps, the regional character of the components of a culture is revealed. Geographers are interested in the spatial distribution of these individual elements, but their usual concern is with the **culture region**, a portion of the earth's surface occupied by people sharing recognizable and distinctive cultural characteristics. Examples include the political organizations societies devise, their religions, their form of economy, and even their clothing, eating utensils, and housing. There are as many such culture regions as there are separate culture traits and complexes of population groups.

Finally, a set of culture regions showing related culture complexes and landscapes may be grouped to form a **culture realm**. The term recognizes a large segment of the earth's surface having fundamental uniformity in its cultural characteristics and showing a significant difference in them from adjacent realms. Culture realms are, in a sense, culture regions at the broadest scale of generalization. In fact, the scale is so broad and the diversity within the recognized realms so great that the very concept of realm may mislead more than it informs.

Indeed, the current validity of distinctive culture realms such as those suggested in Figure 7.3 has been questioned in light of an assumed globalization of all aspects of human society and economy. The result of that globalization, some observers maintain, is a homogenization of cultures as economies are integrated and uniform consumer demands are satisfied by standardized commodities produced by international corporations. Others insist, however, that the world is far from homogenized and observe that globalization continues to be countered by powerful forces of regionalism, place identity, and ethnicity. One of the many possible divisions of human cultures into realms is offered in Figure 7.3. Culture realms, regions, systems, complexes, and traits are all elements in the spatial hierarchy of cultural geography. Direct and indirect reference to them will be encountered throughout this chapter.

INTERACTION OF PEOPLE AND ENVIRONMENT

Culture develops in a physical environment that, in its way, contributes to differences among people. In premodern subsistence societies, the acquisition of food, shelter, and clothing—all parts of culture—depends on the utilization of the natural resources at hand. The interrelations of people with the environment of a given area, their perceptions and use of it, and their impact on it are interwoven themes of geography. They are the special concerns of those geographers and anthropologists exploring **cultural ecology**, the study of the relationship between a culture group and the natural environment it occupies.

Cultural ecologists see evidence that subsistence pastoralists, hunter-gatherers, and gardeners adapted their productive activities—and, by extension, their social organizations and relationships—to the specific physical limitations of their different local habitats. Presumably, similar natural environmental conditions influenced the development of similar adaptive

FIGURE 7.3 Culture realms of the modern world. Culture realms, regions, systems, complexes, and traits are all elements in the spatial hierarchy of cultural geography. This map proposes just one of many possible subdivisions of the world into multifactor culture regions.

Boxed inserts (three to five per chapter) are written to further develop ideas and enhance student interest in the material. Most chapters include a box on gender-related issues, including **Chapter Six:** *Millions of Women Are Missing* and **Chapter Nine:** *Legislative Women.*

"**Geography & Public Policy**" boxes highlight an important or controversial issue, encouraging students to think about the relevance of geography to real-world concerns. Critical thinking questions at the end of each box prompt students to reflect upon and form an opinion about the issue and can serve as catalysts for class discussion.

GEOGRAPHY & Public Policy

Mountaintop Removal: Good or Bad?

As its name suggests, mountaintop removal (MTR)—also called mountaintop mining, or MTM—is a type of coal mining that requires the removal of a mountaintop to get at the coal seams lying beneath. The first step is to clear-cut upper-elevation forests and strip off the topsoil. The lumber is burned or sold, and the topsoil is supposed to be removed and set aside for later reclamation. Once the area is cleared, miners use explosives to blast away the overburden (rock and subsoil) to expose the coal seams beneath. Enormous machines scrape away the rubble and dump it down the sides of the mountain into valleys and streambeds. As much as 240 meters (800 ft) of mountaintop may be removed, leading critics of the practice to call it strip mining on steroids.

Federal law requires that, after active mining has been completed and the mountaintop has been regraded, most sites must be reclaimed to the land's premining contour and use, but waivers can be granted so that reclamation creates a level plateau or a gently rolling contour. Topsoil or a substitute is placed on top and grass seed is spread in a mixture of seed, fertilizer, and mulch. Trees may be planted, or the land can be reclaimed to be used for other purposes if a greater use than natural restoration can be found for it. Most reclamation efforts have focused on stabilizing rock formations and controlling for erosion, not on reforestation of the affected area. Fast-growing, non-native grasses planted to quickly provide vegetation compete with native tree seedlings, and trees have difficulty establishing root systems in compacted landfill.

Mountaintop mining began in the Appalachian Mountains in the 1970s as an extension of conventional strip-mining techniques. It occurs primarily in West Virginia and eastern Kentucky; other sites are in Virginia, Tennessee, and Ohio. It received an impetus from the shortages of petroleum in 1973 and 1979, when energy prices soared and increased the demand for coal in the United States. MTR expanded further in the 1990s as a method of retrieving relatively low-sulfur coal, made desirable by amendments to the U.S. Clean Air Act.

Mountaintop mining has two distinct advantages for coal companies. Highly mechanized, it requires relatively few workers, significantly reducing the labor costs of a company. Second, many of the coal seams mined in the MTR method are too thin to be mined

using more conventional techniques. Because miners can repeat the blasting process over and over again, MTR makes it economically feasible to mine the seams, which often exist in multiple stratified layers on a single mountain. This allows for almost complete recovery of coal from a single mountain.

Critics of MTR contend that it has such substantial environmental, water, and health impacts and is so destructive that the government should stop giving out new permits for it. "The science is so overwhelming that the only conclusion one can reach is that mountaintop mining needs to be stopped," says a leading environmental scientist. According to studies by the Environmental Protection Agency, mining operations have permanently altered stream flows and wildlife habitats in the watersheds. More than 2400 kilometers (1500 mi) of streams across central Appalachia have been buried by valley fills. Removal of the forests, which used to support several endangered species, leads to a loss of biodiversity.

MTR also causes water pollution. When rainwater falls on the rubble dumped down the mountainside, it picks up pollutants from the rocks that came from deep underground. The water that emerges is polluted with metals and chemicals called sulfates, which can be toxic to the insects and fish in Appalachian streams.

Communities near mining sites have a host of health problems. Exposed to airborne dust and debris, to contaminated water wells, and to fish tainted with toxins, people show increased rates of mortality, lung cancer, and chronic heart, lung, and kidney diseases. In addition, residents are forced to contend with continual blasting from mining operations that can take place up to 92 meters (100 yds) from their houses and operate 24 hours a day.

Considering the Issues

1. The president of the West Virginia Coal Association contends that MTR is only an "interim disruption to the existing environment" and that it provides much needed flatter areas that offer new opportunities for development, such as an airport,

IMPACT ON PLANTS AND ANIMALS

People have affected plant and animal life on the earth in several ways. When human impact is severe enough, a species can become *extinct*; that is, it no longer exists. Although fossil records show that extinction is a natural feature of life on Earth, scientists estimate that in recent history the rate of extinction has increased exponentially—an increase due to human activity. *Endangered* species are those that are present

in such low numbers that they are in immediate jeopardy of becoming extinct in the wild if the causes of endangerment continue, while *vulnerable* species have decreasing populations and are likely to become endangered within the foreseeable future. Both endangered and vulnerable species are termed *threatened.*

Certain kinds of species have a greater probability than others of becoming extinct. They usually exhibit one or more of the following characteristics. They exist in small populations

414

Chapter Summaries of Key Concepts bring together and reinforce the major ideas of the chapter.

A **Key Words** list with page references makes it easy for students to verify their understanding of the most important terms in the chapter.

Thinking Geographically questions enable students to check their grasp of chapter material.

Appendix 1: Map Projections includes a discussion of methods of projection, globe properties and map distortion, and classes of projections.

Appendix 2: Climate, Soils, and Vegetation supplements Chapter 4 by providing information about soil formation, soil profiles and horizons, soil taxonomy, and natural vegetation regions.

El Niño

El Niño is a term coined years ago by fishermen who noticed that the normally cool waters off the coasts of Ecuador and Peru were considerably warmer every 3 or 4 years around Christmastime, hence the name El Niño, Spanish for "the child," referring to the infant Jesus. If fishermen had been able to identify the scientific associations that present-day oceanographers and climatologists make, they would have recognized a host of other effects that follow from El Niño.

During the winter of 1997–1998, an unusually severe El Niño caused enormous damage and hundreds of deaths. The West Coast of the United States, especially California, was inundated with rainfall amounts double, triple, and even quadruple

normal. For the November to March winter period, San Francisco received 102.24 centimeters (40.25 in.) of rain—normal is 41.63 centimeters (16.39 in.). The 38 centimeters (15 in.) in February 1998 was the most for that month in the 150 years of record keeping in San Francisco. The resort city of Acapulco, Mexico, was badly battered by torrential rains and high, wind-blown tides. Parts of South America, especially Ecuador, Peru, and Chile, were ravaged by floods and mud slides, while droughts and fires scorched eastern South America, Australia, and parts of Asia, especially Indonesia. A stronger than usual southern branch of the jet stream generated by El Niño spawned dozens of tornadoes, which killed more than 100 people in Alabama, Georgia, and Florida.

The top diagram shows normal circumstances in the southern Pacific Ocean. Trade winds blow warm surface water westward and allow cold water to come to the surface along the South American coast. The bottom diagram shows that, during El Niño, winds from near Australia blow warm water eastward to the coast of South America.

Air is said to be *supersaturated* when it contains so much water vapor that the vapor condenses (changes from a gas to a liquid) and forms droplets if fine particles, called *condensation nuclei*, are present. These particles, mostly dust, pollen, smoke, and salt crystals, nearly always exist. At first, the tiny water droplets are usually too light to fall. As many droplets coalesce into larger drops, and become too heavy to remain suspended in air, they fall as rain. When temperatures below the freezing point cause water vapor to form ice crystals instead of water droplets, snow is created (Figure 4.19).

Large numbers of rain droplets or ice crystals form clouds, which are supported by slight upward movements of air. The form and altitude of clouds depend on the amount of water vapor in the air, the temperature, and wind movement. Descending air in high-pressure zones usually yields cloudless skies. Whenever warm, moist air rises, clouds form. The most dramatic cloud formation is probably the *cumulonimbus*, pictured in Figure 4.20. This is the anvil-head cloud that often

accompanies heavy rain. Low, gray *stratus* clouds appear more often in cooler seasons than in warmer months. The very high, wispy *cirrus* clouds that appear in all seasons are made entirely of ice crystals. *Cumulus* clouds are often called fair-weather clouds.

Relative humidity is a percentage measure of the moisture content of the air, expressed as the amount of water vapor present relative to the maximum that can exist at the current temperature. As air gets warmer, the amount of water vapor it can contain increases. If the relative humidity is 100%, the air is completely saturated with water vapor. A relative humidity value of 60% on a hot day means the air is extremely humid and very uncomfortable. A 60% reading on a cold day, however, indicates that, although the air contains relatively large amounts of water vapor, it holds, in absolute terms, much less vapor than on a hot, muggy day. This example demonstrates that relative humidity is meaningful only if we keep air temperature in mind.

Summary of Key Concepts

- The term *spatial interaction* refers to the movement of people, goods, information, and ideas between one place and another. Many factors influence how individuals view and use space. The concepts of spatial perception and spatial cognition are helpful in considering how individuals view their environment. Other important variables are the nature of the information available, people's age, their past experiences, and their values.
- The concept of activity space helps us understand differences in the extent of space people use. The age of an individual, his or her degree of mobility, and the availability of opportunities all play a role in defining the limits of individual activity space.
- *Distance decay* refers to the decline of interaction with increasing distance between places. The concept of critical distance identifies the distance beyond which the decrease in familiarity with places begins to be significant. Unfamiliarity with distant points outside one's normal activity space affects space evaluations, interaction flows, and travel patterns.

- How space is used is a function of all of these factors, but certain factors having to do with the diffusion of innovations indicate what opportunities exist for individuals living in various places. Contagious and hierarchical diffusion influence the geographic direction that cultural change will take. Effort and cost are among the barriers to diffusion.
- A special type of human interaction is migration. When strong enough, various push and pull factors motivate a long-distance, permanent move. Migration fosters the spread of culture by means of a relocation diffusion process. The ability of many to make well-reasoned, meaningful decisions is a function of the utility they assign to places and the opportunities at those places.
- Economic, political, and cultural patterns and processes are becoming more integrated and people more interdependent as a result of globalization, the increasing interconnection of all parts of the world.

Key Words

activity space 247	hierarchical migration 267	spatial diffusion 251
chain migration 261	mental map 248	spatial interaction 244
channelized migration 267	migration 256	stage in life 250
contagious diffusion 252	migration field 266	step migration 261
critical distance 244	place utility 261	territoriality 247
distance decay 244	pull factor 259	transnational corporation
globalization 268	push factor 259	(TNC) 269
hierarchical diffusion 253	return migration (countermigration) 267	

Thinking Geographically

1. What is the role of distance in helping us understand spatial interaction?
2. Think of the various conflicts that have taken place in the world in the past century. Does the concept of distance decay bear on the location of adversaries? Why?
3. On a blank piece of paper, and without any maps to guide you, draw a map of the United States, putting in state boundaries wherever possible; this is your mental map of the country. Compare it with a standard atlas map. What conclusions can you reach?
4. What is meant by *activity space*? What factors affect the spatial extent of the activity space of an individual? What is your activity space?
5. Recall the places you have visited in the past week. In your movements, were the distance-decay and critical-distance rules operative? What variables affect an individual's critical distance?

6. Briefly distinguish between *contagious diffusion* and *hierarchical diffusion*. In what ways, if any, were these forms of diffusion in operation in the culture hearths discussed in Chapter 7?
7. What considerations affect a decision to migrate? What is *place utility* and how does its perception induce or inhibit migration?
8. What common barriers to migration exist? Why do most people migrate within their own country?
9. Define the term *migration field*. Some migration fields show a *channelized* flow of people. Select a particular channelized migration flow (such as the movement of Scandinavians to the United States, people from the Great Plains to California, or southern blacks to the North) and explain why a channelized flow developed.
10. Identify the effects of globalization on your lifestyle and the patterns of trade in your urban area.

Appendix 3: 2009 World Population Data Sheet of the Population Reference Bureau (a modified version) includes basic demographic data and projections for countries, regions, and continents, as well as selected economic and social statistics helpful in national and regional comparisons. The comparative information in the appendix data is useful for student projects, regional and topical analyses, and study of world patterns.

TEACHING AND LEARNING SUPPLEMENTS

McGraw-Hill offers various tools and technology products to support *Introduction to Geography*. Students can order supplemental study materials by contacting their local bookstore or by calling 800-262-4729. Instructors can obtain teaching aids by calling the Customer Service Department at 800-338-3987, visiting the McGraw-Hill website at www.mhhe.com, or contacting their local McGraw-Hill sales representative.

Teaching Supplements for Instructors

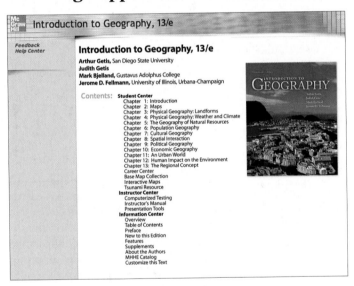

Introduction to Geography **website at http://www.mhhe.com/getis13e**

The *Introduction to Geography* website offers a wealth of teaching and learning aids for instructors. In addition to all of the student assets available, instructors will appreciate:

- A password-protected Instructor's Manual
- Access to the online **Presentation Center,** including illustrations, photographs, and tables from the text in convenient jpg and PowerPoint® format
- PowerPoint Lecture Outlines®
- Online activities, such as multiple choice and matching quizzes, interactive map exercises, Internet exercises, and critical thinking questions

Presentation Center

Build instructional materials whereever, whenever, and however you want!

Accessed through the website, the **Presentation Center** is an online digital library containing assets such as art, photos, tables, PowerPoints, and other media types that can be used to create customized lectures, visually enhanced tests and quizzes, compelling course websites, or attractive printed support materials.

Access to your book, access to all books!

The **Presentation Center library** includes thousands of assets from many McGraw-Hill titles. This ever-growing resource gives instructors the power to utilize assets specific to an adopted textbook as well as content from all other books in the library.

Nothing could be easier!

Presentation Center's dynamic search engine allows you to explore by discipline, course, textbook chapter, asset type, or key word. Simply browse, select, and download the files you need to build engaging course materials. All assets are copyrighted by McGraw-Hill Higher Education but can be used by instructors for classroom purposes.

Instructors will find the following digital assets for *Introduction to Geography:*

- **Color Art** Full-color digital files of illustrations in the text can be readily incorporated into lecture presentations, exams, or custom-made classroom materials.
- **Photos** Digital files of photographs from the text can be reproduced for multiple classroom uses.
- **Tables** Every table that appears in the text is provided in electronic format.
- **PowerPoint Lecture Outlines** Ready-made presentations that combine art and photos and lecture notes are provided for each of the 13 chapters of the text. These outlines can be used as they are or tailored to reflect your preferred lecture topics and sequences.

- **PowerPoint Slides** For instructors who prefer to create their lectures from scratch, all illustrations, photos, and tables are preinserted by chapter into blank PowerPoint slides for convenience.

Klett-Perthes World Atlas
(ISBN 978–0–07–329073–7; MHID 0–07–329073–4)

This high-quality world atlas by well-known mapmaker Klett-Perthes features over 300 pages of detailed climate, physical, political, population, regional, and thematic maps as well as statistical information for all countries. Also included is a glossary of important terms, an extensive index, and instructions on how to read a map—a must for all introductory geography students! Ask your McGraw-Hill sales representative for further details on how to receive a discount and package this outstanding atlas with *Introduction to Geography*. Explore the many products and resources available from Klett-Perthes by visiting their website at www.klettmaps.com.

Computerized Test Bank Online

A comprehensive bank of test questions is provided within a computerized test bank powered by McGraw-Hill's flexible electronic testing program EZ Test Online (www.eztestonline.com). EZ Test Online allows you to create paper and online tests or quizzes in this easy to use program!

Imagine being able to create and access your test or quiz anywhere, at any time, without installing the testing software. Now, with EZ Test Online, instructors can select questions from multiple McGraw-Hill test banks or write their own, and then either print the test for paper distribution or give it online.

Test Creation

- Author/edit questions online using the 14 different question type templates.
- Create printed tests or deliver online to get instant scoring and feedback.
- Create question pools to offer multiple versions online—great for practice.
- Export your tests for use in WebCT, Blackboard, PageOut, and Apple's iQuiz.
- Compatible with EZ Test Desktop tests you've already created.
- Sharing tests with colleagues, adjuncts, TAs is easy.

Online Test Management

- Set availability dates and time limits for your quiz or test.
- Control how your test will be presented.
- Assign points by question or question type with drop-down menu.
- Provide immediate feedback to students or delay until all finish the test.
- Create practice tests online to enable student mastery.
- Your roster can be uploaded to enable student self-registration.

Online Scoring and Reporting

- Automated scoring for most of EZ Test's numerous question types.
- Allows manual scoring for essay and other open-response questions.
- Manual re-scoring and feedback are also available.
- EZ Test's grade book is designed to easily export to your grade book.
- View basic statistical reports.

Support and Help

- User's guide and built-in page-specific help.
- Flash tutorials for getting started on the support site.
- Support website—www.mhhe.com/eztest
- Product specialist available at 1-800-331-5094
- Online training: http://auth.mhhe.com/mpss/workshops/

Electronic Textbook

CourseSmart is a new way for faculty to find and review eTextbooks. It's also a great option for students who are interested in accessing their course materials digitally and saving money. CourseSmart offers thousands of the most commonly adopted textbooks across hundreds of courses from a wide variety of higher education publishers. It is the only place for faculty to review and compare the full text of a textbook online, providing immediate access without the environmental impact of requesting a print exam copy. At CourseSmart, students can save up to 50% off the cost of a print book, reduce their impact on the environment, and gain access to powerful web tools for learning including full text search, notes and highlighting, and email tools for sharing notes between classmates. **www.CourseSmart.com**

Course Delivery Systems

With help from WebCT, Blackboard, and other course management systems, professors can take complete control of their course content. Course cartridges containing website content, online testing, and powerful student tracking features are readily available for use within these platforms.

Learning Supplements for Students

Introduction to Geography website at
http://www.mhhe.com/getis13e

The website for *Introduction to Geography* is a great place to review chapter material and enhance your study routine. Visit this site for access to the following online study tools:

- Chapter quizzing
- Critical thinking questions
- Interactive maps
- Web links to chapter related material
- Selected references

Additional Teaching/Learning Tools

McGraw-Hill offers a multitude of reference materials providing valuable geography-related materials at a discounted price when packaged with your text. Students of geography and other disciplines, as well as the general reader, will find these unique materials invaluable to their understanding of current world countries and events. Ask your McGraw-Hill sales representative about the following.

Annual Editions

The **Annual Editions** series is designed to provide students with convenient, inexpensive access to current, carefully selected articles from the public press. They are updated on

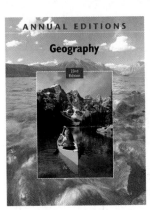

a regular basis through a continuous monitoring of over 300 periodicals. Each volume presents articles written for a general audience by experts and authorities in their fields. Organizational features include an annotated listing of selected World Wide Web sites; an annotated table of contents; a topic guide; a general introduction; brief overviews for each section; and an online Instructor's Resource Guide with testing materials. *Using Annual Editions in the Classroom* is offered as a practical guide.
www.mhhe.com/annualeditions

(ISBN 978–0–07–805072–5; MHID 0–07–805072–3)
Annual Editions: Developing World 11/12 by Griffiths
(ISBN 978–0–07–351551–9; MHID 0–07–351551–5)
Annual Editions: Geography, 23/e by Pitzl
(ISBN 978–0–07–805084–8; MHID 0–07–805084–7)
Annual Editions: Global Issues 11/12 by Jackson
(ISBN 978–0–07–805093–0; MHID 0–07–805093–6)
Annual Editions: World Politics 11/12 by Purkitt

Taking Sides

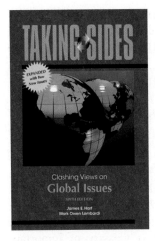

The **Taking Sides** volumes present current issues in a debate-style format designed to stimulate student interest and develop critical thinking skills. Each issue is thoughtfully framed with an issue summary, an issue introduction, and a postscript or challenge questions. The pro and con essays—selected for their liveliness and substance—represent the arguments of leading scholars and commentators in their fields. **Taking Sides** readers feature annotated listings of selected World Wide Web sites. An online Instructor's Resource Guide with testing materials is available for each volume. *Using Taking Sides in the Classroom* (available in print and online) is an excellent resource that offers practical suggestions for fostering critical thinking in the classroom when using the **Taking Sides** readers.
www.mhhe.com/takingsides

(ISBN 978–0–07–805008–4; MHID 0–07–805008–1)
Taking Sides: Clashing Views on African Issues, 4/e by Moseley
(ISBN 978–0–07–738192–9; MHID 0–07–738192–0)
Taking Sides: Clashing Views on Global Issues, 6/e Expanded by Harf/Lombardi
(ISBN 978–0–07–351504–5; MHID 0–07–351504–3)
Taking Sides: Clashing Views on Latin American Issues by DeGrave et al.
(ISBN 978–0–07–805010–7; MHID 0–07–805010–3)
Taking Sides: Clashing Views in World Politics, 15/e by Rourke

Global Studies

Global Studies is a unique series designed to provide comprehensive background information and selected world press articles on the regions and countries of the world. Each **Global Studies** volume includes an annotated listing of World Wide Web sites. **Global Studies** readers are supported by an online Instructor's Resource Guide with an extensive question bank for use in discussion and testing.
www.mhhe.com/globalstudies

(ISBN 978–0–07–352776–5; MHID 0–07–352776–9)
Global Studies: Africa, 13/e by Krabacher et al.
(ISBN 978–0–07–337987–6; MHID 0–07–337987–5)
Global Studies: China, 13/e by Zhu

(ISBN 978–0–07–337976–0; MHID 0–07–337976–X)
Global Studies: Europe, 10/e by Frankland
(ISBN 978–0–07–802617–1; MHID 0–07–802617–2)
Global Studies: India and South Asia, 10/e by Norton
(ISBN 978–0–07–337985–2; MHID 0–07–337985–9)
Global Studies: Japan and the Pacific Rim, 10/e by Collinwood
(ISBN 978–0–07–352777–2; MHID 0–07–352777–7)
Global Studies: Latin America and the Caribbean, 14/e by Goodwin
(ISBN 978–0–07–352775–8; MHID 0–07–352775–0)
Global Studies: The Middle East, 13/e by Layachi
(ISBN 978–0–07–340147–8; MHID 0–07–340147–1)
Global Studies: Russia and the Near Abroad, 12/e by Ioffe

Student Atlas

The **Student Atlas** series combines full-color maps and data sets to introduce students to the importance of the connections between geography and other areas of study, such as world politics, environmental issues, and economic development. These thematic atlases will give students a clear picture of the recent agricultural, industrial, demographic, environmental, economic, and political changes in every world region. Each **Student Atlas** is supported by an online Instructor's Resource Guide with testing materials.
www.mhhe.com/studentatlas

(ISBN 978–0–07–352760–4; MHID 0–07–52760–2)
Student Atlas of World Geography, 6/e by Allen
(ISBN 978–0–07–340148–5; MHID 0–07–340148–X)
Student Atlas of World Politics, 9/e by Allen/Sutton

Related Titles of Interest

McGraw-Hill offers many different related titles of interest that provide students with valuable geography-related information. Contact your McGraw-Hill sales representative for information about the following products.

Cartography: Thematic Map Design, Sixth Edition by Dent/Torguson/Hodler. www.mhhe.com/dent6e
ISBN 978–0–07–294382–5; MHID 0–07–294382–3
Contemporary World Regional Geography, Third Edition by Bradshaw/White/Dymond/Chacko. www.mhhe.com/bradshaw3e
ISBN 978–0–07–305150–5; MHID 0–07–305150–0
Essentials of World Regional Geography, Second Edition by Bradshaw/White/Dymond/Chacko.
www.mhhe.com/Whiteessentials2e
ISBN 978–0–07–336933–4; MHID 0–07–336933–0
Physical Geography Laboratory Manual, First Edition by Lemke/Ritter/Heywood. www.mhhe.com/lemke1e
ISBN 978–0–07–727603–4; MHID 0–07–727603–5
Human Geography: Landscapes of Human Activities, Eleventh Edition by Fellmann/Bjelland/Getis/Getis.
www.mhhe.com/fellmann11e
ISBN 978–0–07–352285–2; MHID 0–07–352285–6

Arthur Getis received his B.S. and M.S. degrees from Pennsylvania State University and his Ph.D. from the University of Washington. He is the co-author of several geography textbooks as well as several books dealing with spatial analysis. He has published widely in the areas of infectious diseases, spatial analysis, and geographic information systems. He is honorary editor of *The Journal of Geographical Systems* and serves on the editorial boards of *Geographical Analysis* and *Annals of Regional Science*. He has held administrative appointments at Rutgers University, the University of Illinois, and San Diego State University (SDSU), where he held the Birch Chair of Geographical Studies. In 2002 he received the Association of American Geographers Distinguished Scholarship Award. Professor Getis is a member of many professional organizations and has served as an officer in, among others, the Western Regional Science Association and the University Consortium for Geographic Information Science. Currently he is Distinguished Professor Emeritus at SDSU.

Judith Getis earned her B.A. and a teaching credential from the University of Michigan and her M.A. from Michigan State University. She has co-authored several geography textbooks and wrote the environmental handbook *You Can Make a Difference*. In addition to numerous articles in the fields of urban geography and geography education, she has written technical reports on topics such as solar power and coal gasification. She and her husband, Arthur Getis, were among the original unit authors of the High School Geography Project, sponsored by the National Science Foundation and the Association of American Geographers. In addition, Mrs. Getis was employed by the Urban Studies Center at Rutgers University; taught at Rutgers; was a social science examiner at Educational Testing Service, Princeton, New Jersey; developed educational materials for Edcom Systems, Princeton, New Jersey; and was a professional associate in the Office of Energy Research, University of Illinois.

Mark Bjelland earned his B.S. degree from the University of Minnesota and an M.S. from the University of Washington. He worked for six years as an environmental consultant on projects dealing with environmental justice, pollution cleanup, urban redevelopment, and water supply planning. He then earned a Ph.D. in geography from the University of Minnesota, writing his dissertation on abandoned, contaminated industrial lands in U.S. and Canadian cities. He is associate professor and chair of geography at Gustavus Adolphus College. Students in his advanced urban geography course use geographic information systems to do research for community organizations. He has led geography field courses around the Midwest and to the Pacific Northwest and Great Britain. He has been granted two Fulbright awards to study urban environmental planning in Europe. His research has been published in the *Research Journal of the Water Pollution Control Federation*, the *Journal of Environmental Engineering*, *The Professional Geographer*, *Urban Geography*, and a number of book chapters.

Jerome D. Fellmann received his B.S., M.S., and Ph.D. degrees from the University of Chicago. Except for visiting professorships at Wayne State University, the University of British Columbia, and California State University/Northridge, his professional career has been spent at the University of Illinois at Urbana-Champaign. His teaching and research interests have been concentrated in the areas of human geography in general, and urban and economic geography in particular, geographic bibliography, the geography of Russia and the CIS, and geographic education. His varied interests have been reflected in articles published in the *Annals of the Association of American Geographers*, *Professional Geographer*, *Journal of Geography*, the *Geographical Review*, and elsewhere. He is the co-author of McGraw-Hill's *Human Geography: Landscapes of Human Activity*. In addition to teaching and research, he has held administrative appointments at the University of Illinois and has served as a consultant to private corporations on matters of economic and community development.

In Memory of

JUDITH M. GETIS

JEROME D. FELLMANN

*Both of whom passed away during
the final preparation of this book.*

CHAPTER ONE

Introduction

CHAPTER OUTLINE

This Italian valley village with its fields forms a cultural landscape in sharp contrast to the natural landscape of the background Dolomite Alps. © *Creatas/Jupiter Images RF.*

1

On January 12, 2010, the world's attention turned to Haiti, where a magnitude 7.0 earthquake struck near the capital city of Port-au-Prince (Figure 1.1). The quake occurred along the Enriquillo-Plaintain Garden fault, which had been locked for decades, building up stress as the Caribbean plate shifted 20 mm eastward each year relative to the North American plate. With an epicenter just 25 km (16 mi) west-southwest of the capital city of Port-au-Prince and relatively shallow at just 13 km (8.1 mi) below the surface, the quake affected the country's most populated areas. By overlaying maps of population and maps of earthquake intensity, it was estimated that 3.5 million of Haiti's 9 million people experienced powerful shaking capable of moderate to very heavy damage. In the capital city, the devastation was astounding. As bodies were pulled from the rubble, the estimated death toll climbed to over 250,000, while the true number will never be known. After the quake, inadequate food supplies, untreated injuries, and disease outbreaks raised the death toll even higher. Key structures were destroyed or seriously damaged, including the presidential palace, the national assembly building, the national penitentiary, the main cathedral, the United Nations headquarters for Haiti, the airport control tower, port docks and cranes, luxury hotels, hospitals, and schools. The destruction and loss of life hit rich as well as poor. Near the epicenter in the fishing village of Leogane, nearly every building was destroyed. Long after the world's media attention moved on, Haitians continue to work resiliently to rebuild their country's government buildings, schools, churches, businesses, homes, roads, and utilities, as well as to rebuild their lives, institutions, and economy.

News reports often refer to catastrophes such as these as "natural disasters," but the devastating human consequences of the earthquake were not due to nature alone. The study of geography, by combining the study of earth systems and human societies, sheds important light on such events. Natural disasters, such as hurricanes, floods, landslides, and earthquakes, that hit poor, developing countries have death tolls many times higher than those that hit rich, developed countries. While the Haitian earthquake was powerful and hit in a highly populated area, poverty and its consequences were also to blame for the earthquake's huge toll and the ensuing problems encountered during rescue, relief, and recovery work. Haiti is the poorest country in the Western Hemisphere and like other developing countries has undergone a massive migration from rural areas to the crowded city of Port-au-Prince. Haiti is burdened by large international indebtedness for loans taken out by previous, corrupt governments but, in the years prior to the earthquake, had made substantial progress in stabilizing government institutions and renegotiating its international debts. At academic conferences, geologists had warned of the extreme earthquake risk in Haiti as seismic pressures built up along the fault. But in a poor, indebted country where many houses are makeshift slum dwellings and day-to-day survival is a challenge for much of the population, updating and enforcing building codes, creating disaster preparation plans, and earthquake proofing even key public buildings were not a priority. The earthquake was a tragic setback for a country with few resources to draw upon.

FIGURE 1.1 A street scene in Port-au-Prince, Haiti, after the January 12, 2010, earthquake, showing the destruction and displacement of people. © *Damon Winter/The New York Times/Redux.*

Partly to blame for the many deaths were the lack of building codes specific to Haiti's earthquake hazards and poor construction materials and techniques that could not withstand the forces of earthquakes. Limited financial resources meant little or no government inspection and the temptation for builders to skimp on the amount of cement in their concrete and reduce or leave out the expensive reinforcing steel bars that are necessary to enable masonry (brick or concrete block) and concrete buildings to resist the sideways forces of earthquakes. Ironically, the traditional rural dwelling constructed with a wood frame and tin roof was usually safer than newer concrete or masonry buildings.

Relief and recovery efforts were complicated by poor infrastructure systems, the lack of backup or alternate infrastructure systems, and the lack of emergency services. Damaged port facilities and roads, inadequate water systems, and a lack of reliable electricity hindered recovery efforts. Extreme poverty meant there was no insurance claim or bank account to fall back upon for many Haitians who had lost homes, jobs, and family members. The Haitian earthquake is a tragic reminder that human actions take place within the context of the environment. It is also a reminder that, just as maps and satellite images were essential tools in the rescue, relief, and recovery processes, many of the world's pressing problems require a geographic understanding that takes in earth systems, the locational aspects of human activities, and the relationships between human societies and their environment—all important themes in the discipline of geography.

WHAT IS GEOGRAPHY?

Many people associate the word *geography* simply with knowing *where* things are: whether they be countries, such as Myanmar and Uruguay; cities, such as Timbuktu or Almaty; or deposits of natural resources, such as petroleum or iron ore. Some people pride themselves on knowing which rivers are the longest, which mountains are the tallest, and which deserts are the largest. Such factual knowledge about the world has value, permitting us to place current events in their proper spatial setting. When we hear of an earthquake in Turkey or an assault in Chechnya, we at least can visualize where they occurred. Knowing *why* they occurred in those places, however, is considerably more important.

Geography is much more than place names and locations. It is the study of spatial variation, of how and why things differ from place to place on the surface of the earth. It is, further, the study of how observable spatial patterns evolved through time. Just as knowing the names and locations of organs in the human body does not equip one to perform open-heart surgery, knowing where things are located is only the first step toward understanding why things are where they are, and what events and processes determine or change their distribution. Why are earthquakes common in Turkey but not in Russia, and why is Chechnya but not Tasmania wracked by insurgency? Why are the mountains in the eastern United States rounded and those in the western states taller and more rugged? Why do you find a concentration of French speakers in Quebec but not in other parts of Canada?

In answering questions such as these, geographers focus on the interaction of people and social groups with their environment—planet Earth—and with each other; they seek to understand how and why physical and cultural spatial patterns evolved through time and continue to change. Because geographers study both the physical environment and human use of that environment, they are sensitive to the variety of forces affecting a place and the interactions among them. To explain why Brazilians burn a significant portion of the tropical rain forest each year, for example, they draw on their knowledge of the climate and soils of the Amazon Basin; population pressures, landlessness, and the need for more agricultural area in rural Brazil; the country's foreign debt status; midlatitude markets for lumber, beef, and soy beans; and Brazil's economic development objectives. Understanding the environmental consequences of the burning requires knowledge of, among other things, the oxygen and carbon balance of the earth; the contribution of the fires to the greenhouse effect, acid rain, and depletion of the ozone layer; and the relationships among deforestation, soil erosion, and floods.

Geography, therefore, is about earth space and the content of that space. We think of and respond to places from the standpoint of not only where they are but, what is more important, what they contain or what we think they contain. Reference to a place or an area usually calls up images about its physical nature or what people do there, and this often suggests to us, without our consciously thinking about it, how those physical things and activities are related. "Bangladesh," "farming," and "flooding" or "Colorado," "mountains," and "skiing" are examples. The content of an area, that is, has both physical and cultural aspects, and geography is always concerned with understanding both (Figure 1.2).

EVOLUTION OF THE DISCIPLINE

Geography's combination of interests was apparent even in the work of the early Greek geographers who first gave structure to the discipline. Geography's name was reputedly coined by

FIGURE 1.2 Aspen, Colorado, demonstrates changing interactions between physical environment and human activity. Mineral resources, mountainous terrain, and abundant snowfall have made different specialized human uses attractive and possible. The brick buildings in the foreground are the legacy of its original settlement as a silver mining town, peaking with over 5000 residents in 1890 but declining to about 700 by 1930. The groomed ski slopes in the background represent the town's current identity as a premier ski resort, year-round tourist destination, and home to celebrities. © *Punchstock RF.*

the Greek scientist Eratosthenes over 2200 years ago from the words *geo,* "the earth," and *graphein,* "to write." From the beginning, that writing focused both on the physical structure of the earth and on the nature and activities of the people who inhabited the various lands of the known world. To Strabo (c. 64 B.C.–A.D. 20), the task of geography was to "describe the several parts of the inhabited world, . . . to write the assessment of the countries of the world [and] to treat the differences between countries." Even earlier, Herodotus (c. 484–425 B.C.) had found it necessary to devote much of his writing to the lands, peoples, economies, and customs of the various parts of the Persian Empire as necessary background to an understanding of the causes and course of the Persian wars.

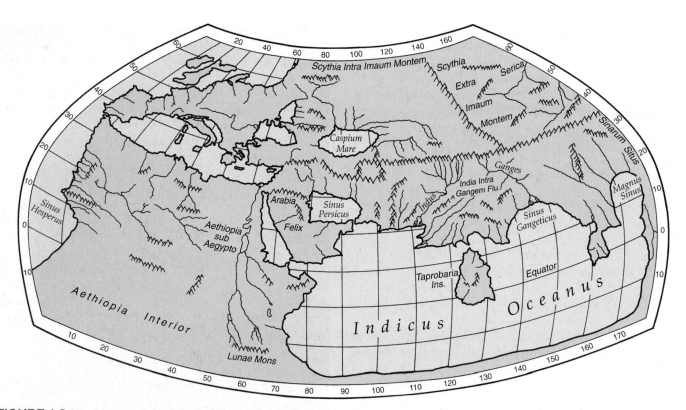

FIGURE 1.3 World map of the 2d-century A.D. Greco-Egyptian geographer-astronomer Ptolemy. Ptolemy (Claudius Ptolemaeus) adopted a previously developed map grid of latitude and longitude based on the division of the circle into 360°, permitting a precise mathematical location for every recorded place. Unfortunately, errors of assumption and measurement rendered both the map and its accompanying six-volume gazetteer inaccurate. Ptolemy's map, accepted in Europe as authoritative for nearly 1500 years, was published in many variants in the 15th and 16th centuries. The version shown here summarizes the extent and content of the original. Its underestimation of the earth's size convinced Columbus a short westward voyage would carry him to Asia.

Greek (and, later, Roman) geographers measured the earth, devised the global grid of parallels and meridians (marking latitudes and longitudes; see p. 22), and drew upon that grid surprisingly sophisticated maps of their known world (Figure 1.3). They explored the apparent latitudinal variations in climate and described in numerous works the familiar Mediterranean Basin and the more remote, partly rumored lands of northern Europe, Asia, and equatorial Africa. Employing nearly modern concepts, they described river systems, explored cycles of erosion and patterns of deposition, cited the dangers of deforestation, described variations in the natural landscape, and noted the consequences of environmental abuse. Against that physical backdrop, they focused their attention on what humans did in home and distant areas—how they lived; what their distinctive similarities and differences were in language, religion, and custom; and how they used, altered, and perhaps destroyed the lands they inhabited. Strabo, indeed, cautioned against the assumption that the nature and actions of humans were determined by the physical environment they inhabited. He observed that humans were the active elements in a human-environmental partnership.

The interests guiding the early Greek and Roman geographers were and are enduring and universal. The ancient Chinese, for example, were as involved in geography as an explanatory viewpoint as were westerners, though there was no exchange between them. Further, as Christian Europe entered its Middle Ages between A.D. 800 and 1400 and lost its knowledge of Greek and Roman geographic work, Muslim scholars—who retained that knowledge—undertook to describe and analyze their known world in its physical, cultural, and regional variation.

In the 15th and 16th centuries, European voyages of exploration and discovery put geography at the forefront of the scientific revival. Modern geography had its origins in the surge of scholarly inquiry that, beginning in the 17th century, gave rise to many of the traditional academic disciplines we know today. In its European rebirth, geography from the outset was recognized—as it always had been—as a broadly based integrative study. Patterns and processes of the physical landscape were early interests, as was concern with humans as part of the earth's variation from place to place. The rapid development of geology, botany, zoology, climatology, and other natural sciences by the end of the 18th century strengthened regional geographic investigation and increased scholarly and popular awareness of the intricate interconnections of things in space and between places. By that time, accurate determination of latitude and longitude and scientific mapping of the earth had made assignment of place information more reliable and comprehensive. A key figure during this period of geographic research was Alexander von Humboldt. Humboldt, for whom Humboldt University in Berlin, Germany, is named, led ambitious scientific expeditions to distant places and synthesized vast amounts of geographic data in his famous writings.

Subfields of Geography

During the 19th century, national censuses, trade statistics, and ethnographic studies gave firmer foundation to human geographic investigation. By the end of the 19th century, geography had become a distinctive and respected discipline in universities throughout Europe and in other regions of the world where European academic examples were followed. The proliferation of professional geographers and geography programs resulted in the development of a whole series of increasingly specialized disciplinary subdivisions, many represented by separate chapters of this book. Political geography, urban geography, and economic geography are examples of some of these subdivisions.

Geography's specialized subfields are not isolated from one another; rather, they are closely interrelated. Geography in all its subdivisions is characterized by three dominating interests. The first is in the spatial variation of physical and human phenomena on the surface of the earth; geography examines relationships between human societies and the natural environments that they occupy and modify. The second is a focus on the systems that link physical phenomena and human activities in one area of the earth with other areas. Together, these interests lead to a third enduring theme, that of regional analysis: geography studies human-environmental (or "ecological") relationships and spatial systems in specific locational settings. This areal orientation pursued by some geographers is called *regional geography*.

Other geographers choose to identify particular classes of things, rather than segments of the earth's surface, for specialized study. These *systematic geographers* may focus their attention on one or a few related aspects of the physical environment or of human populations and societies. In each case, the topic selected for study is examined in its interrelationships with other spatial systems and areal patterns. *Physical geography* directs its attention to the natural environmental side of the human-environmental structure. Its concerns are with landforms and their distribution, with atmospheric conditions and climatic patterns, with soils or vegetation associations, and the like. The other systematic branch of geography is *human geography*. Its emphasis is on people: where they are, what they are like, how they interact over space, and what kinds of landscapes of human use they erect on the natural landscapes they occupy.

Why Geography Matters

There are three good reasons people study geography. First, it is the only discipline concerned with understanding why and how both physical and cultural phenomena differ from place to place on the surface of the earth. Each chapter in this book is designed to give you a basic knowledge of the many processes that shape our world. Chapter 3, for example, introduces you to the tectonic forces that warp, fold, and fault landforms; create volcanoes; and cause earthquakes and tsunami. The discussion of cultural geography in Chapter 7 will give you a framework for understanding the technological, sociological, and ideological components of culture and an awareness of the forces that bring about changes in a culture over time.

Second, a grasp of the broad concerns and topics of geography is vital to an understanding of the national and international problems that dominate daily news reports. Global climate change, the diffusion of AIDS and other diseases, international trade imbalances, inadequate food supply and population growth in developing countries, turmoil in Africa and the Middle East—all of these problems have geographic dimensions, and geography helps explain them. To be geographically illiterate is to deny oneself not only the ability to comprehend local and world problems but also the opportunity to contribute meaningfully to the development of policies for dealing with them.

Finally, because geography is such a broad field of study, a great diversity of job opportunities await those who pursue college training in the discipline. Geographic training opens the way to careers in a wide array of fields (see "Careers in Geography"). Geographical techniques of analysis are used for interpreting remotely sensed images, determining the optimum location for new businesses, monitoring the spread of infectious diseases, delineating voting districts, and a host of other tasks.

SOME CORE GEOGRAPHIC CONCEPTS

The topics included within the broad field of geography are diverse. That very diversity, however, emphasizes the reality that all geographers—whatever their particular topical or regional interests—are united by the similar questions they ask and the common set of basic concepts they employ to consider their answers. Of either a physical or cultural phenomenon, they will inquire: What is it? Where is it? How did it come to be what and where it is? Where is it in relation to other physical or cultural realities that affect it or are affected by it? How is it part of a functioning whole? How does its location affect people's lives and the content of the area in which it is found?

These and similar questions are rooted in geography's concern with earth space and are derived from enduring central themes in geography. In answering them, geographers draw upon a common store of concepts, terms, and methods of study that together form the basic structure and vocabulary of geography. Geographers believe that recognizing spatial patterns is the essential starting point for understanding how people live on and shape the earth's surface.

Geographers use the word *spatial* as an essential modifier in framing their questions and forming their concepts. Geography, they say, is a *spatial science*. It is concerned with the *spatial distribution* of phenomena, with the *spatial extent* of regions, the *spatial behavior* of people, the *spatial relationships* between places on the earth's surface, and the *spatial processes* that underlie those behaviors and relationships. Geographers use *spatial data* to identify *spatial patterns* and to analyze *spatial systems, spatial interaction, spatial diffusion,* and *spatial variation* from place to place.

The word *spatial* comes, of course, from *space*, and to geographers it always carries the idea of the way things are distributed, the way movements occur, and the way processes operate over the whole or a part of the surface of the earth. The geographer's

Careers in Geography

Geography admirably serves the objectives of a liberal education. It can make us better-informed citizens, more able to understand the important issues facing our communities, our country, and our world and better prepared to contribute solutions.

Can it, as well, be a pathway to employment for those who wish to specialize in the discipline? The answer is "yes," in a number of different types of jobs. One broad cluster is concerned with supporting the field itself through teaching and research. Teaching opportunities exist at all levels, from elementary to university postgraduate. Teachers with some training in geography are in increasing demand in elementary and high schools in the United States, reflecting geography's inclusion as a core subject in the federally adopted *No Child Left Behind Act* and the national determination to create a geographically literate society (see "The National Standards," p. 17). At the college level, specialized teaching and research in all branches of geography have long been established, and geographically trained scholars are prominently associated with urban, community, and environmental studies; regional science; locational economics; and other interdisciplinary programs.

Because of the breadth and diversity of the field, training in geography involves the acquisition of techniques and approaches applicable to a wide variety of jobs outside the academic world. Modern geography is both a physical and social science and fosters a wealth of technical skills. The employment possibilities it presents are as many and varied as are the public and private agencies and enterprises dealing with the natural environment, with human economic and social activities, and with the acquisition and analysis of spatial data.

Many professional geographers work in government at the federal, state, and local levels and in a variety of international organizations. Indeed, geographers have made careers in essentially all of the many bureaus and offices of the executive departments of the U.S. national government—Agriculture, Commerce, Education,

Health and Human Services, Homeland Security, Housing and Urban Development Interior, and others—and in their counterparts at the state level. Such major independent federal agencies as the Central Intelligence Agency (CIA), National Aeronautics and Space Administration (NASA), Federal Trade Commission, National Geospatial-Intelligence Agency (NGA), Federal Aviation Agency, and many others have steady need for geographically trained workers.

Although many positions do not carry a geography title, physical geographers serve as water and other natural resource analysts, weather and climate experts, soil scientists, and the like. Areas of recent high demand include environmental managers and technicians and geographic information specialists. Geographers who have specialized in environmental studies find jobs in both public and private agencies. Their work may include assessing the environmental impact of proposed development projects on such things as air and water quality and endangered species, as well as preparing the environmental impact statements required before construction can begin.

Human geographers work in many different roles in the public sector. Jobs include data acquisition and analysis in health care, transportation, population studies, economic development, and international economics. Many geography graduates find positions as planners in local and state governmental agencies concerned with housing and community development, park and recreation planning, and urban and regional planning. They map and analyze land use plans and transportation systems, monitor urban land development, make informed recommendations about the location of public facilities, and engage in basic social science research.

Most of the same specializations are found in the private sector. Geographic training is ideal for such tasks as business planning and market analysis; factory, store, and shopping center site selection; and community and economic development programs for banks, public utilities, and railroads. Publishers of maps,

---

space, then, is earth space, the surface area occupied or available to be occupied by humans. Spatial phenomena have locations on that surface, and spatial interactions occur among places, things, and people within the earth area available to them. The need to understand those relationships, interactions, and processes helps frame the questions that geographers ask.

Those questions have their starting point in basic observations about the location and nature of places and about how places are similar to or different from one another. Such observations, though simply stated, are profoundly important to our comprehension of the world we occupy.

- Places have location, direction, and distance with respect to other places.
- A place has size; it is large, medium, or small. Scale is important.
- A place has both physical structure and cultural content.
- The attributes, or characteristics, of places develop and change over time.

- The content of places is structured and explainable.
- The elements of places interrelate with other places.
- Places may be generalized into regions of similarities and differences.

These basic notions are the means by which geographers express fundamental observations about the earth spaces they examine and put those observations into a common framework of reference. Each of the concepts is worth further discussion, for they are not quite as simple as they seem.

Location, Direction, and Distance

Location, direction, and *distance* are everyday ways of assessing the space around us and identifying our position in relation to other things and places of interest. They are also essential in understanding the processes of spatial interaction that figure so importantly in the study of both physical and human geography.

atlases, news and travel magazines, and the like employ geographers as writers, editors, and mapmakers.

The combination of a traditional, broad-based liberal arts perspective with the technical skills required in geographic research and analysis gives geography graduates a competitive edge in the labor market. These field-based skills include familiarity with geographic information systems (GIS, explained in Chapter 2), cartography and computer mapping, remote sensing and photogrammetry, and competence in data analysis and problem solving. In particular, students with expertise in GIS, who are knowledgeable about data sources, hardware, and software, are finding they have ready access to employment opportunities. The following table, based on the booklet "Careers in Geography,"[a] summarizes some of the professional opportunities open to students who have specialized in one (or more) of the various subfields of geography. Also, be sure to read the discussion of geography careers accessed on the homepage of the Association of American Geographers at www.aag.org. Additional links on the topic of geography careers can be found in the Online Learning Center for this text. The link can be found in the Preface.

Geographic Field of Concentration	Employment Opportunities
Cartography and geographic information systems	Cartographer for federal government (agencies such as Defense Mapping Agency, U.S. Geological Survey, or Environmental Protection Agency) or private sector (e.g., Environmental Systems Research Institute, ERDAS, Intergraph, or Bentley); map librarian; GIS specialist for planners, land developers, real estate agencies, utility companies, local government; remote-sensing analyst; surveyor
Physical geography	Weather forecaster; outdoor guide; coastal zone manager; hydrologist; soil conservation/agricultural extension agent
Environmental studies	Environmental manager; forestry technician; park ranger; hazardous waste planner
Cultural geography	Community developer; Peace Corps volunteer; health care analyst
Economic geography	Site selection analyst for business and industry; market researcher; traffic/route delivery manager; real estate agent/broker/appraiser; economic development researcher
Urban and regional planning	Urban and community planner; transportation planner; housing, park, and recreation planner; health services planner
Regional geography	Area specialist for federal government; international business representative; travel agent; travel writer
Geographic education	Elementary/secondary school teacher; general geography college professor; overseas teacher

[a]"Careers in Geography," by Richard G. Boehm. Washington, D.C.: National Geographic Society, 1996. Previously published by Peterson's Guides, Inc.

Location

The location of places and things is the starting point of all geographic study, as well as of our personal movements and spatial actions in everyday life. We think of and refer to location in at least two different senses, *absolute* and *relative*.

Absolute location is the identification of place by a precise and accepted system of coordinates; therefore, sometimes it is called *mathematical location*. We have several such accepted systems of pinpointing positions. One of them is the global grid of parallels and meridians—that is, latitude and longitude (discussed in Chapter 2, pages 22–24). With it, the absolute location of any point on the earth can be accurately described by reference to its degrees, minutes, and seconds of *latitude* and *longitude*.

Other coordinate systems are also in use. Survey systems such as the township, range, and section description of property in much of the United States give mathematical locations on a regional level, and street address precisely defines a building according to the reference system of an individual town. Absolute location is unique to each described place, is independent of any other characteristic or observation about that place, and has obvious value in the legal description of places, in measuring the distance separating places, or in finding directions between places on the earth's surface.

When geographers—or real estate agents—remark that "location matters," however, their reference is usually not to absolute but to **relative location**—the position of a place or thing in relation to that of other places or things (Figure 1.4). Relative location expresses spatial interconnection and interdependence and may carry social (neighborhood character) and economic (assessed valuations of vacant land) implications. On an immediate and personal level, we think of the location of the school library not in terms of its street address or room number but where it is relative to our classrooms, the cafeteria, or another reference point. On the larger scene, relative location tells us that people, things, and places exist not in a spatial vacuum but in a world of physical and cultural characteristics that differ from place to place.

New York City, for example, may in absolute terms be described as located at (approximately) latitude 40°43′N (read

FIGURE 1.4 The reality of *relative location* on the globe may be strikingly different from the impressions we form from flat maps. The position of Russia with respect to North America when observed from a polar perspective emphasizes that relative location properly viewed is important to our understanding of spatial relationships and interactions between the two world areas.

FIGURE 1.5 Travel times from downtown San Diego, 2002, in minutes. Lines of equal travel time (*isochrones:* from Greek *isos,* equal, and *chronos,* time) mark off the different linear distances accessible within given spans of time from a starting point. The fingerlike outlines of isochrone boundaries reflect variations in road conditions, terrain, traffic congestion, and other aids or impediments to movement. Note the effect of freeways on travel time.

as 40 degrees, 43 minutes north) and longitude 73°58′W. We have a better understanding of the meaning of its location, however, when reference is made to its spatial relationships: to the continental interior through the Hudson-Mohawk lowland corridor or to its position on the eastern seaboard of the United States. Within the city, we gain understanding of the locational significance of Central Park or the Lower East Side not solely by reference to the street addresses or city blocks they occupy but also by their spatial and functional relationships to the total land use, activity, and population patterns of New York City.

In view of these different ways of looking at location, geographers make a distinction between the *site* and the *situation* of a place. **Site,** an absolute location concept, refers to the physical and cultural characteristics and attributes of the place itself. It is more than mathematical location, for it tells us something about the specific features of that place. **Situation,** on the other hand, refers to the external relations of the place. It is an expression of relative location with particular reference to items of significance to the place in question. Site and situation in the city context are further examined in Chapter 11.

Direction

Direction is the second universal spatial concept. Like location, it has more than one meaning and can be expressed in absolute or relative terms. **Absolute direction** is based on the cardinal points of north, south, east, and west. These appear in all cultures, derived from the obvious "givens" of nature: the rising and setting of the sun for east and west, the sky location of the noontime sun and of certain fixed stars for north and south.

We also commonly use **relative,** or *relational,* **directions.** In the United States, we go "out West," "back East," or "down South"; we worry about conflict in the "Near East" or economic competition from the "Far Eastern countries." Despite their reference to cardinal compass points, these directional references are culturally based and locationally variable. The Near East and the Far East locate parts of Asia from the European perspective; they are retained in the Americas by custom and usage, even though one would normally travel westward across the Pacific, for example, to reach the "Far East" from California, British Columbia, or Chile. For many Americans, "back East" and "out West" are reflections of the migration paths of earlier generations for whom home was in the eastern part of the country, to which they might look back. "Up North" and "down South" reflect our accepted custom of putting north at the top and south at the bottom of our maps.

Distance

Distance joins *location* and *direction* as a commonly understood term that has dual meanings for geographers. Like its two companion spatial concepts, distance may be viewed in both an absolute and a relative sense.

POPULATION DENSITIES

Midwestern States

Density per Square	
Mile	Kilometer
1280 or more	494 or more
640–1279	247–493
320–639	124–246
160–319	62–123
80–159	31–61
40–79	16–30
20–39	8–15
19 or less	7 or less

(a)

Illinois Counties

(b)

FIGURE 1.6 Population density and map scale. "Truth" depends on one's scale of inquiry. Map **(a)** reveals that the maximum year 2000 population density of midwestern states was no more than 123 people per square kilometer (319 per sq mi). From map **(b),** however, we see that population densities in three Illinois counties exceeded 494 people per square kilometer (1280 per sq mi) in 2000. If we were to reduce our scale of inquiry even further, examining individual city blocks in Chicago, we would find densities reaching 2500 or more people per square kilometer (10,000 per sq mi). Scale matters!

Absolute distance refers to the spatial separation between two points on the earth's surface measured by an accepted standard unit—such as miles or kilometers for widely separated locales, feet or meters for more closely spaced points. **Relative distance** transforms those linear measurements into other units more meaningful to human experience or decision making.

To know that two competing malls are about equidistant in miles from your residence is perhaps less important in planning your shopping trip than is knowing that, because of street conditions or traffic congestion, one is 5 minutes and the other 15 minutes away (Figure 1.5). Most people, in fact, think of time distance rather than linear distance in their daily activities; downtown is 20 minutes by bus, the library is a 5-minute walk. In some instances, money rather than time is the distance transformation. An urban destination might be estimated to be a $10 cab ride away, information that may affect either the decision to make the trip at all or the choice of travel mode to get there. As a college student, you already know that rooms and apartments are less expensive at a greater distance from campus.

A *psychological* transformation of linear distance is also frequent. A solitary late-night walk back to the car through an unfamiliar or dangerous neighborhood seems far longer than a daytime stroll of the same distance through familiar and friendly territory. A first-time trip to a new destination frequently seems much longer than the return trip over the same path. Nonlinear distance and spatial interaction are further considered in Chapter 8.

Size and Scale

When we say that a place may be large, middle size, or small, we speak both of the nature of the place itself and of the generalizations that can be made about it. Geographers are concerned with **scale,** though we may use that term in different ways. We can, for example, study a problem such as population or landforms at the local scale or on a global scale. Here, the reference is purely to the size of unit studied. More technically, scale tells us the relationship between the size of an area on a map and the actual size of the mapped area on the surface of the earth. In this sense, as Chapter 2 makes clear, scale is a feature of every map and is essential to recognizing what is shown on that map.

In both senses of the word, *scale* implies the degree of generalization represented (Figure 1.6). Geographic inquiry may be broad or narrow; it occurs at many different size-scales. Climate may be an object of study, but research and generalization focused on climates of the world will differ in degree and kind from study of the microclimates of a city. Awareness of scale is very important. In geographic work, concepts, relationships, and understandings that have meaning at one scale may not be applicable at another.

For example, the study of world agricultural patterns may refer to global climate patterns, cultural food preferences, levels of economic development, and patterns of world trade. These large-scale relationships are of little concern in the study of crop patterns within single counties of the United States, where topography, soil and drainage conditions, farm size, ownership, and capitalization, or even personal management preferences, may be of greater explanatory significance.

FIGURE 1.7 This Landsat satellite image reveals contrasting cultural landscapes along the Mexico-California border. Move your eyes from the Salton Sea (the dark patch at the top of the image) southward to the agricultural land extending to the edge of the picture. Notice how the regularity of the fields and the bright colors (representing growing vegetation) give way to a marked break, where irregularly shaped fields and less prosperous agriculture are evident. Above the break is the Imperial Valley of California; below the border is Mexico. © *NASA*.

Physical and Cultural Attributes

All places have individual physical and cultural attributes distinguishing them from other places and giving them character, potential, and meaning. Geographers are concerned with identifying and analyzing the details of those attributes and, particularly, with recognizing the interrelationship between the physical and cultural components of area: the human-environmental interface.

The physical characteristics of a place are such natural aspects as its climate, soil, water supplies, mineral resources, terrain features, and the like. These **natural landscape** attributes provide the setting within which human action occurs. They help shape—but do not dictate—how people live. The resource base, for example, is physically determined, though how resources are perceived and utilized is culturally conditioned.

Environmental circumstances directly affect agricultural potential and reliability; indirectly, they may affect such matters as employment patterns, trade flows, population distributions, national diets, and so on. The physical environment simultaneously presents advantages and disadvantages with which humans must deal. Thus, most places offer trade-offs in terms of climate favorability, natural hazards, farming and fishing productivity, natural resources, and natural scenery. For example, a scenic volcano may someday erupt, or a mild, coastal location may be vulnerable to hurricanes and so forth. Physical environmental patterns and processes are explored in Chapters 3 and 4 of this book.

At the same time, by occupying a given place, people modify its physical attributes. The visible imprint of that human activity is called the **cultural landscape.** It, too, exists at different scales and at different levels of visibility. Contrasts in agricultural practices and land use between Mexico and southern California are evident in Figure 1.7, whereas the signs, structures, and people of Los Angeles's Chinatown leave a smaller, more confined imprint within the larger cultural landscape of the metropolitan area itself.

The physical and human characteristics of places are the keys to understanding both the simple and the complex interactions and interconnections between people and the environments they occupy and modify. Those interconnections and modifications are not static or permanent but are subject to continual change.

The existence of the United States Environmental Protection Agency (and its counterparts elsewhere) is a reminder that humans are the active and frequently harmful agents in the continuing interplay between the cultural and physical worlds (Figure 1.8). Virtually every human activity leaves its imprint on the earth's soil, water, vegetation, animal life, and other resources, as well as on the atmosphere common to all earth space, as Chapter 12 makes clear.

Attributes of Place Are Always Changing

The physical environment surrounding us seems eternal and unchanging but, of course, it is not. In the framework of geologic time, change is both continuous and pronounced. Islands form and disappear; mountains rise and are worn low to swampy plains; vast continental glaciers form, move, and melt away, and sea levels fall and rise in response. Geologic time is long, but the forces that give shape to the land are timeless and relentless.

Even within the short period of time since the most recent retreat of continental glaciers—12,000 or 13,000 years ago—the environments occupied by humans have been subject to change. Glacial retreat itself marked a period of climatic alteration, extending the area habitable by humans to include vast reaches of northern Eurasia and North America formerly covered by thousands of feet of ice. With moderating climatic conditions came changes in vegetation and fauna. On the global scale, these were natural environmental changes; humans were as yet too few in number and too limited in technology to alter materially the course of physical events. On the regional scale, however, even early human societies exerted an impact on the environments they occupied. Fire was used to clear forest undergrowth, to maintain or extend grassland for grazing animals and to drive them in the hunt, and later to clear openings for rudimentary agriculture.

With the dawn of civilizations and the invention and spread of agricultural technologies, humans accelerated their management and alteration of the now no longer "natural"

FIGURE 1.8 Sites such as this Anacortes, Washington, oil refinery are major emitters of potentially toxic chemicals to the atmosphere, land, and water. Pollution control technologies have significantly reduced, but not eliminated, their negative impacts on the environment. However unsightly or smelly they may be, oil refineries provide the gasoline, diesel, heating oil, jet fuel, and asphalt products that are necessary to economic activity and everyday life in industrialized countries.© *Walter Siegmund.*

environment. Even the classical Greeks noted how the landscape they occupied differed—for the worse—from its former condition. With growing numbers of people, and particularly with industrialization and the spread of European exploitative technologies throughout the world, the pace of change in the content of area accelerated. The built landscape—the product of human effort—increasingly replaced the natural landscape. Each new settlement or city; each agricultural assault on forests; and each new mine, dam, or factory changed the content of regions and altered the temporarily established spatial interconnections between humans and the environment.

Characteristics of places today are the result of constantly changing past conditions. They are the forerunners of differing human-environmental balances yet to be struck. Geographers are concerned with places at given moments of time. But to understand fully the nature and development of places, to appreciate the significance of their relative locations, and to understand the interplay of their physical and cultural characteristics, geographers must view places as the present result of past operation of distinctive physical and cultural processes (Figure 1.9).

You will recall that one of the questions geographers ask about a place or thing is "How did it come to be what and where it is?" This is an inquiry about process and about becoming. The forces and events shaping the physical and explaining the cultural environment of places today are an important focus of geography and are the topics of most of the chapters of this book. To understand them is to appreciate the changing nature of the spatial order of our contemporary world.

Interrelations between Places

The concepts of relative location and distance that were introduced earlier lead directly to another fundamental spatial reality: places are interrelated with other places in structured and comprehensible ways. In describing the processes and patterns of that **spatial interaction,** geographers add *accessibility* and *connectivity* to the ideas of location and distance.

Tobler's First Law of Geography tells us that, in a spatial sense, everything is related to everything else but relationships are stronger when things are near one another. Our observation, therefore, is that interaction between places diminishes in intensity and frequency as distance between them increases—a statement of the idea of "distance decay," which we explore in Chapter 8. Are you more likely to go to a fast-food outlet next door or to a nearly identical restaurant across town? Our decision making sometimes is unpredictable, but in this case you can see that most people would probably more often choose the nearer place.

Consideration of distance implies assessment of **accessibility.** How easy or difficult is it to overcome the "friction of distance"? That is, how easy or difficult is it to overcome the barrier of the time and space separation of places? Distance isolated North America from Europe until the development of ships (and aircraft) that reduced the effective distance between the continents. All parts of ancient and medieval cities were accessible by walking; they were "pedestrian cities," a status lost as cities expanded in area and population with industrialization. Accessibility between city districts could be maintained only by the development of public transit systems whose fixed lines of travel increased ease of movement between connected points and reduced it between areas not on the transit lines themselves.

Accessibility, therefore, suggests the idea of **connectivity,** a broader concept implying all the tangible and intangible ways in which places are connected: by physical telephone lines, street and road systems, and pipelines and sewers; by unrestrained walking across open countryside; by radio and TV broadcasts; by cell phone service areas; and in nature even by movements of wind systems and ocean currents. Where routes are fixed and flow is channelized, *networks*—the patterns of routes

FIGURE 1.9 The process of change in a cultural landscape. **(a)** Miami, Florida, in 1913 was just a small settlement on the banks of the Miami River amid woodlands and wetlands. **(b)** By the end of the 20th century, it had grown from a few thousand inhabitants to some 350,000, with buildings, streets, and highways completely transforming its natural landscape. *Sources: (a) © Historical Museum of Southern Florida; (b) © South Florida Water Management District.*

FIGURE 1.10 An indication of one form of spatial interaction and *connectivity* is suggested by this "desire line" map recording the volume of daily work trips within the San Francisco Bay area to the Silicon Valley employment node. The ends of the desire lines define the outer reaches of a physical interaction region defined by the network of connecting roads and routes. The region changed in size and shape over time as the network was enlarged and improved, the Valley employment base expanded, and the commuting range of workers increased. The map, of course, gives no indication of the global reach of the Valley's *accessibility* and interaction through other means of communication and interchange. Redrawn with permission from Robert Cervero, Suburban Gridlock. *© 1986 Center for Urban Policy Research, Rutgers, the State University of New Jersey.*

connecting sets of places—determine the efficiency of movement and the connectedness of points. Demand for universal instantaneous connectivity is common and unquestioned in today's advanced societies. Technologies and devices to achieve it proliferate, as our own lifestyles show. Cell phones, e-mail, broadband wireless Internet, instant messaging, and more have erased time and distance barriers formerly separating and isolating individuals and groups and have reduced our dependence on physical movement and on networks fixed in the landscape.

There is, inevitably, interchange between connected places. **Spatial diffusion** is the process of dispersion of an idea or a thing (a new consumer product or a new song, for example) from a center of origin to more distant points. The rate and extent of that diffusion are affected, again, by the distance separating the origin of the new idea or technology and other places where it is eventually adopted. Diffusion rates are also affected by such factors as population densities, means of communication, advantages of the innovation, and importance or prestige of the originating node. Further discussion of spatial diffusion is found in Chapter 8.

Geographers study the dynamics of spatial relationships. Movement, connection, and interaction are part of the social and economic processes that give character to places and regions (Figure 1.10). The increasingly global reach of those spatial interactions is expressed in the term *globalization*. **Globalization** implies the increasing interconnection of more and more peoples and parts of the world as the full range of social, cultural, political, economic, and environmental processes becomes international in scale and effect. Promoted by continuing advances in worldwide accessibility and connectivity, globalization encompasses other core geographic concepts of spatial interaction, accessibility, connectivity, and diffusion. More detailed implications of globalization will be touched on in Chapters 8 and 10.

Place Similarity and Regions

The distinctive characteristics of places—physical, cultural, locational—immediately suggest two geographically important ideas. The first is that no two places on the surface of the earth can be *exactly* the same. Not only do they have different absolute locations, but—as in the features of the human face—the precise mix of physical and cultural characteristics of place is never exactly duplicated. The inevitable uniqueness of place would seem to impose impossible problems of generalizing spatial information.

That this is not the case results from the second important idea, that the natural and cultural characteristics of places show patterns of similarity in some areas. For example, a geographer doing fieldwork in France may find that all farmers in one area use a similar, specialized technique to build fences around their fields. Often, such similarities are striking enough for us to conclude that spatial regularities exist. They permit us to recognize and define **regions,** earth areas that display significant elements of internal uniformity and external differences from surrounding territories. Places are, therefore, both unlike and like other places, creating patterns of areal differences and coherent spatial similarity.

The problems of the historian and the geographer are similar. Each must generalize about items of study that are essentially unique. The historian creates arbitrary but meaningful and useful historical periods for reference and study. The "Roaring Twenties" and the "Victorian Era" are shorthand summary names for specific time spans, internally quite complex and varied but significantly distinct from what went before or followed after. The region is the geographer's equivalent of the historian's era: a device to classify the complex reality of the earth's surface into manageable pieces. Just as historians focus on key events to characterize certain historical periods, geographers focus on key unifying elements or similarities to determine the boundaries of regions. By identifying and naming regions, a complex set of interrelated environmental or cultural attributes can easily be conveyed through a simpler construct.

Spatial Distributions

Regions are not "given" in nature any more than "eras" are given in the course of human events. Regions are devised; they are spatial summaries designed to bring order to the infinite diversity of the earth's surface. At their root, they are based on the recognition and mapping of *spatial distributions*—the spatial arrangement of environmental, human, or organizational features selected for study. For example, the location of Welsh speakers in Great Britain is a distribution that can be identified and mapped. As many spatial distributions exist as there are imaginable physical,

cultural, or connectivity elements of area to examine. Those that are selected for study, however, are those that contribute to the understanding of a specific topic or problem.

Let us assume that we are interested in studying burglary rates in the United States. We see from Figure 1.11 that some states have significantly higher rates than others. A resident of Arizona is roughly three times as likely to be a victim of a burglary as a resident of North Dakota. Does the distribution of rates appear random, or do the states with the highest rates appear to be clustered along the southern border and the West Coast? Mapping a spatial distribution is just the first step; now we must try to explain it. In the case of burglaries, we would ask what factors account for the observed pattern. Is the pattern similar to that for other types of crimes, such as murder and aggravated assault? Do largely rural states have lower burglary rates? It is commonly assumed that big cities and poverty are associated with crime, and that young people commit more crimes than older people. We would want to ascertain whether any of those distributions are correlated with burglary rates.

Types of Regions

Regions may be *formal, functional,* or *perceptual.* A **formal** (or **uniform**) **region** is an area of essential uniformity regarding a single physical or cultural feature or a limited combination of physical or cultural features. Your home state is a precisely bounded formal political region within which uniformity of law and administration is found; the name *Corn Belt* suggests a region based on farm economy and crop characteristics. Later in this book we will encounter formal (homogeneous) cultural regions with standardized characteristics of language, religion, ethnicity, or economy. Figure 1.12 and the front-paper foldout maps of landform regions and country units show other formal regional patterns. The formal region is based on objective, often statistically derived identifiers. Whatever the basis of its definition, the formal region is a sizeable area over which a valid generalization of uniformity may be made with respect to some attribute or attributes—that is, the attribute holds true for the entire region.

A **functional** (or **nodal**) **region,** in contrast, may be visualized as a spatial system. Its parts are interdependent, and throughout its extent the functional region operates as a dynamic, organizational unit. Like the formal region, a functional region is objectively defined; but a functional region has unity in the manner of its operational connectivity, not in the sense of static content. The defining characteristics of interaction and connection of a functional region are most clearly recognized at its node or core and lessen in dominance toward its margins. As the degree and extent of control and interaction in an area change, the boundaries of the functional region change in response; that is, a nodal region's boundaries remain constant only as long as the interchanges that establish it remain unaltered. Examples are the trade areas of towns, the circulation area of a newspaper, the area that receives a television station's signal, and the territories subordinate to the financial, administrative, health care, retail, and service functions of regional capitals, such as Chicago, Atlanta, or Minneapolis (Figure 1.13).

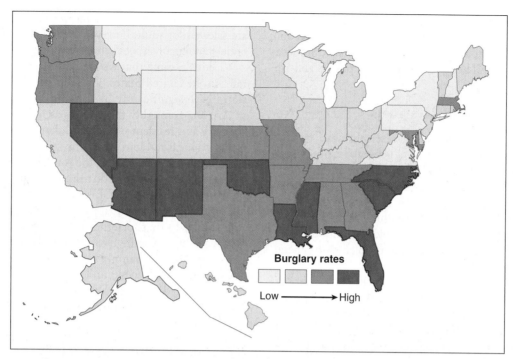

FIGURE 1.11 Comparative burglary rates per 100,000 people, 1998. As this simplified example suggests, all spatial data can be mapped, revealing regional patterns that invite analysis. Here, the higher incidence of burglaries in southern and western states is clearly evident. The question is "Why?" At a different scale, an attempt to explain burglary rates would require gathering data not at the state level but for smaller spatial units, such as counties or census tracts. One would also consider many possible relationships between crime rates and such factors as the sex, income, and age of convicted offenders. *Source: U.S. Department of Justice,* Crime and Justice Atlas 2000, *p. 55.*

FIGURE 1.12 This generalized **land use map of Australia** is composed of *formal regions* whose internal economic characteristics show essential uniformities, setting them off from adjacent territories of different condition or use.

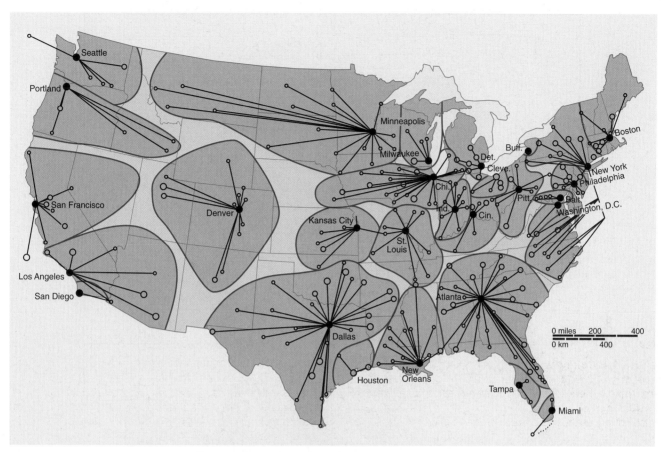

FIGURE 1.13 The *functional regions* shown on this map were based on linkages between large banks of major central cities and the "correspondent" banks they formerly served in smaller towns. Although the rise of nationwide banks has reduced their role, the regions once defined an important form of *connectivity* between principal cities and locales beyond their own immediate metropolitan area. *Redrawn by permission from* Annals of the Association of American Geographers, *John R. Borchert, vol. 62, page 358, Association of American Geographers, 1972.*

Perceptual (or **vernacular** or **popular**) **regions** are less rigorously structured than the formal and functional regions geographers devise. They are regions that exist and have reality in the perceptions of their inhabitants and the general society. As composites of the mental maps of ordinary folk, they reflect feelings and images rather than objective data. Because of that, perceptual regions may be more meaningful in individuals' daily lives than the more objective regions of geographers.

Ordinary people have a clear idea of spatial variation and employ the regional concept to distinguish between territorial entities. People individually and collectively agree on where they live. The vernacular regions they recognize have reality in their minds and are reflected in regionally based names employed in businesses, by sports teams, or in advertising slogans. The frequency of references to "Dixie" in the southeastern United States represents that kind of regional consensus and awareness, as does "Midwest" in popular understanding and literary reference (Figure 1.14). The boundaries of vernacular regions, of course, vary on the mental maps of different groups both within and outside the recognized area, but the regions themselves reflect the way people view space, assign their loyalties, and interpret their world. At a different scale, such urban ethnic enclaves as "Little Italy" and "Chinatown"

have comparable regional identity in the minds of their inhabitants. Less clearly perceived by outsiders but unmistakable to their inhabitants are the "turfs" of urban clubs or gangs. Their boundaries are sharp, and the perceived distinctions between them are paramount in the daily lives and activities of their occupants.

As you read the chapters of this book, notice how many examples of regions and regionalism are presented in map form and discussed in the text. Note, too, how those depictions and discussions vary between the three different regional types as the subjects and purposes of the examples change. Chapter 13 contains additional special regional studies, primarily of formal and functional regions, illuminating specific topics that are the subjects of Chapters 3 to 12.

GEOGRAPHY'S THEMES AND STANDARDS

The core geographic concepts discussed so far in this chapter reflect both the "fundamental themes in geography" and the "National Geography Standards." Together, the "themes" and "standards" have helped organize and structure the study

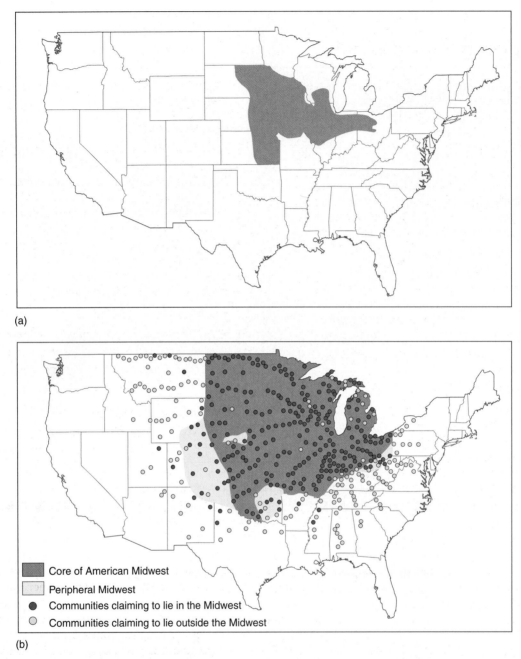

(a)

(b)

- ■ Core of American Midwest
- ▢ Peripheral Midwest
- ● Communities claiming to lie in the Midwest
- ○ Communities claiming to lie outside the Midwest

FIGURE 1.14 The vernacular Midwest. The extent and shape of vernacular regions can be as varied as the unique mental maps of ordinary individuals or be summed up from the collective judgments of sampled groups. **(a)** A survey of state-based popular literature revealed an author's consensus core Midwest region that was less extensive than its core based on questionnaire responses **(b)** from postmasters in 536 communities who were asked whether, in their opinion, their village was in the Midwest. See also Figure 13.1. *Sources: (a) From James R. Shortridge,* The Middle West: Its Meaning in American Culture. *Lawrence: University of Kansas Press, 1989. Figure 6.1, p. 98. Redrawn with permission. (b) From Joseph W. Brownell, "The Cultural Midwest" in* Journal of Geography. *Vol. 59, Figure I, p. 82. Redrawn with permission.*

of geography over the past several years at all grade and college levels. Both focus on the development of geographic literacy. The former represent an instructional approach keyed to identification and instruction in the knowledge, skills, and perspectives students should gain from a structured program in geographic education. The latter—"standards"—codify the essential subject matter, skills, and perspectives of geography essential to the mental equipment of all educated adults.

The *five fundamental themes,* as summarized by a joint committee of the National Council for Geographic Education

and the Association of American Geographers, are those basic concepts and topics that recur in all geographic inquiry and at all levels of instruction:

- **location:** the meaning of relative and absolute position on the earth's surface;
- **place:** the distinctive and distinguishing physical and human characteristics of locales;
- **relationships within places:** the development and consequences of human-environmental interactions;

The National Standards

The inclusion of geography as a subject area to be assessed under the *No Child Left Behind Act* reflects the conviction that a grasp of the skills and understandings of geography is essential in an American educational system "tailored to the needs of productive and responsible citizenship in the global economy." Along with the "basic observations" reviewed in the text, the National Geography Standards 1994 help frame the kinds of understanding we will seek in the following pages and suggest the purpose and benefit of further study of geography.

The 18 geography standards tell us the following: *The geographically informed person knows and understands:*

The World in Spatial Terms

1. How to use maps and other geographic tools and technologies to acquire, process, and report information from a spatial perspective.
2. How to use mental maps to organize information about people, places, and environments in a spatial context.
3. How to analyze the spatial organization of people, places, and environments on Earth's surface.

Places and Regions

4. The physical and human characteristics of places.
5. That people create regions to interpret Earth's complexity.
6. How culture and experience influence people's perceptions of places and regions.

Physical Systems

7. The physical processes that shape the patterns of Earth's surface.

8. The characteristics and spatial distribution of ecosystems on Earth's surface.

Human Systems

9. The characteristics, distribution, and migration of human populations on Earth's surface.
10. The characteristics, distribution, and complexity of Earth's cultural mosaics.
11. The patterns and networks of economic interdependence on Earth's surface.
12. The processes, patterns, and functions of human settlement.
13. How the forces of cooperation and conflict among people influence the division and control of Earth's surface.

Environment and Society

14. How human actions modify the physical environment.
15. How physical systems affect human systems.
16. The changes that occur in the meaning, use, distribution, and importance of resources.

The Uses of Geography

17. How to apply geography to interpret the past.
18. How to apply geography to interpret the present and plan for the future.

Source: *Geography for Life: National Geography Standards 1994.* Washington, D.C.: National Geographic Research and Exploration, 1994.

- movement: patterns and change in human spatial interaction on the earth;
- regions: how they form and change.

The National Geography Standards were established as part of the nationally adopted *Goals 2000: Educate America Act* (see "The National Standards"). Designed specifically as guidelines to the essential geographic literacy to be acquired by students who have gone through the U.S. public school system, the standards address the same conviction underlying this edition of *Introduction to Geography*—that being literate in geography is a necessary part of the mental framework of all informed persons.

ORGANIZATION OF THIS BOOK

The breadth of geographic interest and subject matter, the variety of questions that focus geographic inquiry, and the diversity of concepts and terms geographers employ require a simple, logical organization of topics for presentation to students new to the field. Despite its outward appearance of complex diversity, geography should be seen to have a broad consistency of purpose achieved through the recognition of a limited number of distinct but closely related "traditions." William D. Pattison, who suggested this unifying viewpoint, and J. Lewis Robinson (among others), who accepted and expanded Pattison's reasoning, found that four traditions are logical and inclusive ways of clustering geographic inquiry. Although not all geographic work is confined by the separate traditions, one or more of them are implicit in most geographic studies. The unifying categories—the four traditions within which geographers work—are

1. the earth science tradition;
2. the culture-environment tradition;
3. the locational (or spatial) tradition;
4. the area analysis (or regional) tradition.

The mutual interdependence of the four traditions is suggested by Figure 1.15, as are their common individual and collective ties to the full range of research and study techniques that geographers employ: maps, of course, but also remote sensing, statistical tools, geographic information systems, and other spatial analysis techniques.

FIGURE 1.15 The four traditions of geography do not stand alone. Rather, each is interconnected with the others and all together depend on unifying research skills and tools. As the diagram indicates, the chapters of this text are grouped by reference to the "traditions" to help you recognize the broad divisions of geography as well as its underlying and unitary nature. To avoid diagram clutter, lines connecting each box to every other have not been drawn but should be understood.

We have used the four traditions as the device for clustering the chapters of this book (from Chapter 3 onward), hoping they will help you recognize the unitary nature of geography while appreciating the diversity of topics studied by geographers. They are, in a sense, introduced by Chapter 2, which views maps (and related tools and techniques) as essential, distinctive, and unifying tools of geographers.

The **earth science tradition** is the branch of the discipline that addresses itself to the earth as the habitat of humans. It is the tradition that in ancient Greece represented the roots of geography, the description of the physical structure of the earth, and of the natural processes that give it detailed form. In modern terms, it is the vital environmental half of the study of human-environmental systems, which together constitute geography's subject matter. The earth science tradition prepares the physical geographer to understand the earth and its resources as the common heritage of humankind and to find solutions to the increasingly complex web of pressures placed on the earth by its expanding, demanding human occupants. Consideration of the elements of the earth science tradition constitutes Part One (Chapters 3 to 5) of this text.

Part Two (Chapters 6 to 9) details some of the content of the **culture-environment tradition.** Within this theme of geography, consideration of the earth as a purely physical entity gives way to a primary interest in how people *perceive* the environments they occupy. Its focus is on culture. The landscapes that are explored and the spatial patterns that are central are those that are cultural in origin and expression. People in their numbers, distributions, and diversity; in their patterns of social and political organization; and in their spatial perceptions and behaviors are the orienting concepts of the culture-environment tradition. The theme is distinctive in its thrust but tied to the earth science tradition, because populations exist, cultures emerge, and behaviors occur within the context of the physical realities and patternings of the earth's surface.

The **locational tradition**—or, as it is sometimes called, the *spatial tradition*—is the subject of the chapters of Part Three (Chapters 10 to 12). It is a tradition that underlies all of geographic inquiry. As Robinson suggested, if we can agree that geology is rocks, that history is time, and that sociology is people, then we can assert that geography is earth space. The locational tradition is primarily concerned with the distribution of cultural phenomena or physical items of significance to human occupance of the earth. It explores as well the spatial patterns of interaction between humans and the ecosystems that sustain them.

Part, but by no means all, of the locational tradition is concerned with distributional patterns. More central are scale, movement, and areal relationships. Map, statistical, geometric, and systems analysis research are among the techniques employed by geographers working within the locational tradition. Irrespective, however, of the analytic tools used or the sets of phenomena studied—economic activities, city systems, or the impact of cultural impositions on the physical landscape—the underlying theme of the locational tradition is the distribution of the phenomenon discussed and the flows and interconnections that unite it to related physical and cultural occurrences.

The **area analysis tradition** is considered in Chapter 13, which makes up Part Four of *Introduction to Geography*. Again, the roots of this tradition may be traced to antiquity. Strabo's *Geography* was addressed to the leaders of Augustan Rome as a summary of the nature of places in their separate characters and conditions—knowledge deemed vital to the guardians of an empire. Imperial concerns may long since have vanished, but the study of regions and the recognition of their spatial uniformities and differences remain. Such uniformities and differences, of course, grow out of the structure of human–environmental systems and interrelations that are the study of geography. To illustrate the role and diversity of regional studies in geography, much of Chapter 13 consists of special regional investigations and models illuminating specific topics that are the themes of topical Chapters 3 to 12 of this book.

The identification of the four traditions of geography is not only an organizational convenience but also a recognition that, within that diversity of subject matter called geography, unity of interest is ever-preserved. The traditions, though recognizably distinctive, are intertwined and overlapping. We hope their use as organizing themes—and their further identification in short introductions to the separate sections of this book—will help you grasp the unity in diversity that is the essence of geographic study.

Key Words

absolute direction 8
absolute distance 9
absolute location 7
accessibility 11
area analysis tradition 18
connectivity 11
cultural landscape 10
culture-environment tradition 18
earth science tradition 18

formal (uniform) region 13
functional (nodal) region 13
globalization 12
locational tradition 18
natural landscape 10
perceptual (vernacular, popular) region 15
region 13
relative direction 8

relative distance 9
relative location 7
scale 9
site 8
situation 8
spatial diffusion 12
spatial interaction 11

Thinking Geographically

1. In what two meanings and for what different purposes do geographers refer to *location?* When geographers say "location matters," what aspect of location commands their interest?

2. What does the term *cultural landscape* imply? Is the nature of the cultural landscape dictated by the physical environment?

3. What kinds of distance transformations are suggested by the term *relative distance?* How is the concept of *psychological distance* related to relative distance?

4. How are the ideas of *distance, accessibility,* and *connectivity* related to processes of *spatial interaction?*

5. Why do geographers concern themselves with *regions?* How are *formal* and *functional* regions different in concept and definition?

6. What are the *four traditions* of geography? Do they represent unifying or dividing approaches to geographic understanding?

FIGURE 2.3 The latitude and longitude of Hong Kong are 22°17′N, 114°10′E. What are the coordinates of Hanoi?

FIGURE 2.4 A portion of the Vincennes, Indiana–Illinois, topographic quadrangle showing evidence of original French long-lot survey. Note the importance of the Wabash River in both long-lot and Vincennes street-system orientations. This 1944 U.S. Geological Survey map was originally published at the fractional scale of 1:62,500. *Source: U.S. Geological Survey.*

meridian in some places in order to avoid having two different dates within a country or an island group. Thus, the International Date Line zigzags so that Siberia has the same date as the rest of Russia and the Aleutian Island and Fiji Island groups are not split. New days begin at the date line and proceed westward, so that west of the line is always 1 day later than east of the line.

By citing the degrees, minutes, and, if necessary, seconds of longitude and latitude, we can describe the location of any place on the earth's surface. To conclude our earlier example, the center of Chicago is located at 41°52′50″N, 87°38′28″W. Hong Kong is at 22°17′40″N, 114°10′26″E (Figure 2.3).

Land Survey Systems

The geographic grid of parallels and meridians is one way to describe location. In North America, three other types of land-identification systems have been employed, and each has left its mark on the landscape.

Early French settlers used the *long-lot* system for claiming and allotting farmland in North America. The system was introduced into the St. Lawrence Valley and followed French settlers wherever they established colonies: Quebec, the Mississippi Valley, Louisiana, and elsewhere. The long lot was a surveyed elongated holding typically about 10 times longer than wide, stretching far back from a narrow river frontage. The back of the lot was indicated by a roadway roughly parallel to the line of the river, marking the front of a second and perhaps a third series of long lots. The system provided each settler with a fair access to fertile land along the floodplain, with lower-quality river terrace land and remote poorer-quality back areas on the valley slopes serving as woodlots. Dwellings were built at the front of the holding, where access was easy

and the neighbors were close. By 1760, long lots extended for more than 400 kilometers (250 mi) along both shores of the St. Lawrence River, and areas settled by the French retain the imprint of these early land concessions (Figure 2.4).

English settlers in the colonies brought with them a system of property description known as *metes and bounds*. The system utilized physical features of the local geography, along with directions and distances, to define and describe in sequence the boundaries of a parcel of land. A typical description might read, "From the point at the junction of Salt and Indian Fork Creeks, south for 100 yards, then southeast to the large boulder, northeast to the old oak tree, north toward Salt Creek, then down the center of the creek to the starting point." Based in part on such temporary landscape elements as prominent trees, unusual rocks, streams that might dry up or change course, and human-made features such as roads and fences, the metes and bounds system led to boundary uncertainty and dispute. It also resulted in road patterns, such as those found in

Pennsylvania and other eastern states, where routes are often controlled by the contours of the land rather than the regularity of a geometric survey.

When independence from Great Britain was achieved, the federal government decided that the public domain should be surveyed and subdivided before being opened for settlement. The Land Ordinance of 1785 established a systematic survey known as the *township and range* system. It was based on survey lines oriented in the cardinal directions: *base lines* that run east-west and *meridians* that run north-south (Figure 2.5). A grid of lines spaced at 6-mile (9.7-km) intervals divided the land into a series of squares. A *township* consisted of a square 6 miles (9.7 km) on a side; this was further divided into 36 *sections* 1 mile (1.6 km) on a side. Every section of 640 acres (259 hectares) was subdivided into quarter-sections of 160 acres (64.8 hectares), and these quarter-sections—considered the standard size for a farm—were originally designated the minimum area that could be purchased for settlement. That minimum was later reduced to 80 acres (32.4 hectares) and then to 40 acres (16.2 hectares). Each parcel of land had a unique identification.

The township and range rectangular survey system was first used in eastern Ohio and later extended across most of the United States, as far west as the Pacific Ocean and as far north as Alaska. The Canada Land Survey System is similar to that developed in the United States, employing base lines and meridians and dividing land into townships, ranges, sections, and subdivisions of sections. The rectangular survey system significantly affected the landscape of the central and western United States and Canada, creating the basic checkerboard pattern of minor civil divisions, the regular pattern of section-line and quarter-line country roads, the block patterns of fields and farms, and the gridiron street systems of towns and cities.

MAP PROJECTIONS

The earth can be represented with reasonable accuracy only on a globe, but globes are not as convenient as flat maps to store or use, and they cannot depict much detail. For example, if we had a large globe with a diameter of 1 meter, we would have to fit the details of over 100,000 square kilometers of earth surface in an area a few centimeters on a side. Obviously, a globe of reasonable size cannot show the transportation system of a city or the location of very small towns and villages.

In transforming a globe into a map, we cannot flatten the curved surface and keep intact all the properties of the original. **Globe properties** are as follows:

1. All meridians are of equal length; each is one-half the length of the equator.
2. All meridians meet at the North and South Poles and are true north-south lines.
3. All parallels of latitude are parallel to the equator and to each other.
4. Parallels decrease in length with distance from the equator.

5. Meridians and parallels intersect at right angles.
6. The scale on the surface of the globe is everywhere the same in all directions.

Only the globe grid itself retains all of these characteristics. To project it onto a surface that can be laid flat is to distort some or all of these properties and consequently to distort the reality the map attempts to portray.

The term **map projection** designates the way the curved surface of the globe is represented on a flat map. All flat maps distort, in different ways and to different degrees, some or all of the four main properties of actual earth surface relationships: area, shape, distance, and direction. Figure 2.6 shows how distortion occurs.

Area

Some projections, such as the Mollweide and cylindrical equal-area projection (Figure 2.6a, b), enable the cartographer to represent the *areas* of regions in correct or constant proportion to earth reality. That means that any square inch on the map represents an identical number of square miles (or of similar units) anywhere else on the map. As a result, the shape of the portrayed area is inevitably distorted. A square on the earth, for example, may become a rectangle on the map, but that rectangle has the correct area. Such projections are called **equal-area** or **equivalent projections**. *A map that shows correct areal relationships always distorts the shapes of regions.*

Equal-area projections are used when a map is intended to show the actual areal extent of a phenomenon on the earth's surface. If we wished to compare the amount of land in agriculture in two parts of the world, for example, it would be very visually misleading to use a map that represented the same amount of surface area at two different scales.

Shape

Although no projection can provide correct shapes for large areas, some accurately portray the shapes of small areas by preserving correct angular relationships (Figure 2.6c). These true-shape projections are called **conformal projections,** and the importance of *conformality* is that regions and features "look right" and have the correct directional relationships. They achieve these properties for small areas by assuring that parallels of latitude and meridians of longitude cross each other at right angles and that the scale is the same in all directions at any given location. Both these conditions exist on the globe but can be retained for only relatively small areas on maps. Because that is so, the shapes of large regions—continents, for example—are always different from their true earth shapes, even on conformal maps. *A map cannot be both equivalent and conformal.*

Distance

Distance relationships are nearly always distorted on a map, but some projections maintain true distances in one direction or along certain selected lines. Others, called **equidistant projections,**

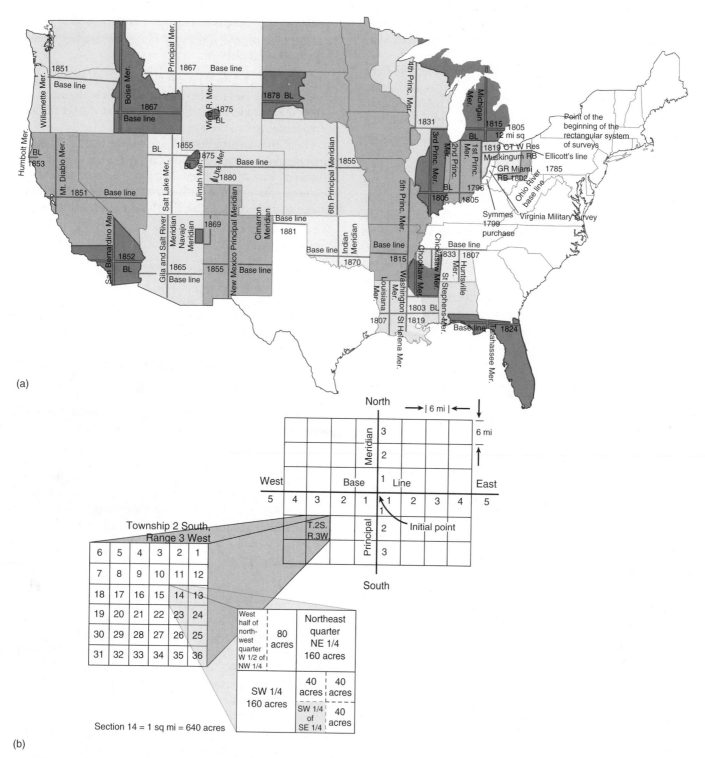

FIGURE 2.5 (a) Principal base lines and meridians governing the U.S. Public Land Survey (USPLS). (b) Township, section, and further divisions of the USPLS. The township and range survey system gives each parcel of land a unique identification. *Townships* are numbered by rows (called tiers) and columns (called ranges). In the example shown here, the township in the second tier south of the base line and in the third range west of the principal meridian is labeled T.2S, R.3W. Every township is divided into sections 1 mile (1.6 km) on a side and numbered from 1 to 36, beginning at the northeast corner of the township. *Sections* can be divided into quarters, eighths ("half-quarters"), and sixteenths ("quarter-quarters"). The Land Office code for the shaded area in the lower right diagram would be SW 1/4 of the SE 1/4 of Sec. 14, T.2S, R.3W. *(a) From U.S. Department of the Interior, Bureau of Land Management,* Surveying Our Public Lands. *Washington, D.C.: U.S. Government Printing Office, 1980.*

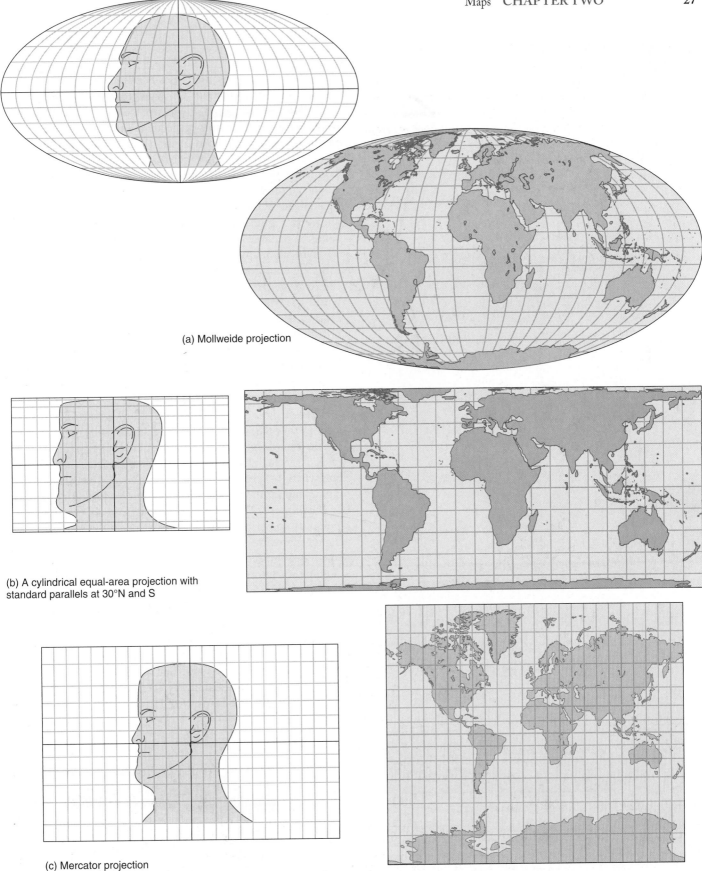

(a) Mollweide projection

(b) A cylindrical equal-area projection with standard parallels at 30°N and S

(c) Mercator projection

FIGURE 2.6 This figure illustrates the distortion inherent in three different map projections. A head drawn on one projection (Mollweide) has been transferred to two other projections, keeping the latitude and longitude the same as they are found on the first. This does *not* mean the first projection is the best of the three. The head could have been drawn on any one of them and then plotted on the others.

Source: Arthur Robinson et al., Elements of Cartography, *5th ed., Fig. 5.6, p. 85. New York, Wiley, © 1984.*

show true distance in all directions, but only from one or two central points (Figure 2.7a). Distances between all other locations are incorrect and, quite likely, greatly distorted. A planar equidistant map centered on Detroit, for example, shows the correct distance between Detroit and the cities of Boston, Los Angeles, and any other point on the map. But it does *not* show the correct distance between Los Angeles and Boston. *A map cannot be both equidistant and equal-area.*

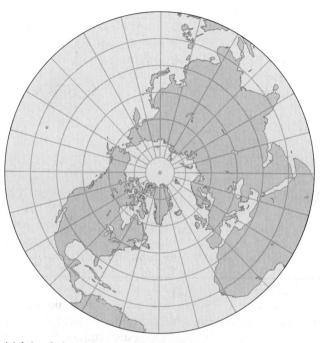

(a) Azimuthal equidistant projection, polar case

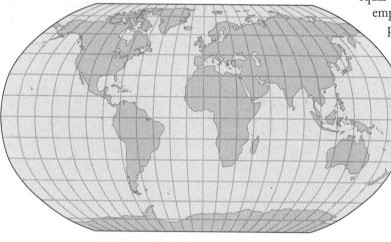

(b) Robinson projection

FIGURE 2.7 **(a)** On this *equidistant projection,* distances and directions to all places are true only from the center (North Pole). No flat map can be both equidistant and equal-area. **(b)** The Robinson projection, a compromise between an equal-area and a conformal projection, gives a fairly realistic view of the world. The most pronounced shape distortions are in the less-populated areas of the higher latitudes, such as northern Canada, Greenland, and Russia. On the map, Canada is 21% larger than in reality, while the 48 contiguous states of the United States are 3% smaller than they really are.

Direction

As is true of distances, directions between all points cannot be shown without distortion. On **azimuthal projections,** however, true directions are shown from one central point to all other points. (An *azimuth* is the angle formed at the beginning point of a straight line, in relation to a meridian.) Directions or azimuths from points other than the central point to other points are not accurate. The azimuthal property of a projection is not exclusive—that is, an azimuthal projection may also be equivalent, conformal, or equidistant. The equidistant map shown in Figure 2.7a is, as well, a true-direction map from the same North Pole origin.

Not all maps are equal-area, conformal, or equidistant; most are compromises. One example of such a compromise is the *Robinson projection,* which was designed to show the whole world in a visually satisfactory manner and which is used for most of the world maps in this textbook (Figure 2.7b). It does not show true distances or directions and is neither equal-area nor conformal. Instead, it permits some exaggeration of size in the high latitudes in order to improve the shapes of landmasses. Size and shape are most accurate in the temperate and tropical zones, where most people live.

Mapmakers must be conscious of the properties of the projections they use, selecting the one that best suits their purposes. If a map shows only a small area, the choice of a projection is not critical—virtually any can be used. The choice is more important when the area to be shown extends over a considerable longitude and latitude; then the selection of a projection depends on the purpose of the map. Some projections are useful for navigation. If numerical data are being mapped, the relative sizes of the areas involved should be correct, so that one of the many equal-area projections is likely to be used. Display maps usually employ conformal projections. Most atlases indicate which projection has been used for each map, thus informing the map reader of the properties of the maps and their distortions. More information about map projections can be found in Appendix 1.

Selection of the map grid, determined by the projection, is the first task of the mapmaker. A second decision involves the scale at which the map is to be drawn.

SCALE

The **scale** of a map is the ratio between the measurement of something on the map and the corresponding measurement on the earth. Scale is typically represented in one of three ways: verbally, graphically, or numerically as a representative fraction (Figure 2.8). As the name implies, a *verbal* scale is given in words, such as "1 inch to 1 mile" or "10 centimeters to 1 kilometer." A *graphic* scale, sometimes called a *bar* scale, is a line or bar placed on the map that has been subdivided to show the map lengths of units of earth distance.

(a) **Verbal scale**

(b) **Graphic scale**

(c) **Representative fraction scale**

FIGURE 2.8 Map scales relate a map distance to a distance on the earth's surface. **(a)** A *verbal scale* is given in words. **(b)** A *graphic scale* divides a line into units, each unit representing the distance between two points on the earth's surface. The graphic scale is the only kind of scale to remain correct if the map is reproduced as a different size, *provided that* the scale is enlarged or reduced by the same percentage. **(c)** A *representative fraction (RF) scale* is a simple fraction or ratio. The units of distance on both sides of the scale must be the same; they need not be stated.

A *representative fraction (RF)* scale gives two numbers, the first representing the map distance and the second indicating the ground distance. The fraction may be written in a number of ways. There are 5280 feet in 1 mile and 12 inches in 1 foot; 5280 times 12 equals 63,360, the number of inches in 1 mile. The fractional scale of a map at 1 inch to 1 mile can be written as 1:63,360 or 1/63,360. On the simpler metric scale, 1 centimeter to 1 kilometer is 1:100,000. The units used in each part of the fractional scale are the same; thus, 1:63,360 could also mean that 1 foot on the map represents 63,360 feet on the ground, or 12 miles—which is, of course, the same as 1 inch represents 1 mile. Numerical scales are the most accurate of all scale statements and can be understood in any language.

The map scale, or ratio between the map dimensions and those of reality, can range from very large to very small. A *large-scale map*, such as a plan of a city, shows an area in considerable detail. That is, the ratio of map to ground distance is relatively large—for example, 1:600 (1 inch on the map represents 600 inches, or 50 feet, on the ground) or 1:24,000. At this scale, features such as buildings and highways can be drawn to scale. Figure 2.10 on page 31 is an example of a large-scale map. *Small-scale maps*, such as those of countries or continents, have a much smaller ratio. Buildings, roads, and other small features cannot be drawn to scale and must be magnified and represented by symbols to be seen. Figures 2.2 and 2.3 are small-scale maps. Although no rigid numerical limits differentiate large-scale from small-scale maps, most cartographers would consider large-scale maps to have a ratio of 1:50,000 or less, and maps with ratios of 1:500,000 or more to be small-scale.

Each of the four maps in Figure 2.9 is drawn at a different scale. Although each is centered on Boston, notice how scale affects both the area that can be shown in a square that is 2 inches on a side and the amount of detail that can be depicted. On map (a), at a scale of 1:25,000, about 2.6 inches represent 1 mile, so that the 2-inch square shows less than 1 square mile. At this scale, one can identify individual buildings, highways, rivers, and other landscape features. Map (d), drawn to a scale of 1 to 1 million (1:1,000,000, or 1 inch represents almost 16 miles), shows an area of almost 1000 square miles. In this map, only major features, such as main highways and the location of cities, can be shown, and even the symbols used for that purpose are generalized and occupy more space on the map than would the features depicted if they were drawn true to scale.

Small-scale maps like (c) and (d) in Figure 2.9 are said to be very *generalized*. They give a general idea of the relative locations of major features but do not permit accurate measurement. They show significantly less detail than do large-scale maps and typically smooth out such features as coastlines, rivers, and highways.

TYPES OF MAPS

Out of the many features that can be shown on a map, geographers must first select those that are relevant to the problem at hand and then decide how to display them in order to communicate their message. In that effort, they can choose from among different types of maps.

General-purpose, reference, or *location* maps make up one major class of maps familiar to everyone. Their purpose is simply to display one or more natural and/or cultural features of an area or of the world as a whole. Common examples of the natural features shown on maps are water features (coastlines, rivers, lakes, and so on) and the shape and elevation of terrain. Cultural features include transportation routes, populated areas, property-ownership lines, political boundaries, and names.

The other major type of map is called the *thematic*, or *special-purpose*, map, one that shows a specific spatial distribution or category of data. Again, the phenomena being mapped may be physical (climate, vegetation, soils, and so on) and/or cultural (e.g., the distribution of population, religions, diseases, or crime). Unlike reference maps, the features on thematic maps are limited to just those that communicate the specific spatial distribution.

Topographic Maps and Terrain Representation

As we noted, some general-purpose maps depict the shape and elevation of the terrain. These are called **topographic maps.** They usually portray the surface features of relatively small areas, often with great accuracy (Figure 2.10). They not only show landforms, streams, and other natural features but may also display things that people have added to the natural landscape. These include transportation routes, buildings, and such land uses as orchards, vineyards, and cemeteries. Many types of boundaries, from state borders to field or airport limits, are also depicted on topographic maps.

The U.S. Geological Survey (USGS), the chief federal agency for topographic mapping in this country, produces several topographic map series, each on a standard scale. Complete topographic coverage of the United States is available at scales of 1:250,000 and 1:100,000. Maps are also available at various other scales. Scales used for state maps depend on the size of the state and range from 1:125,000 (Connecticut) to 1:500,000 (Alaska).

A single map in one of these series is called a *quadrangle.* Topographic quadrangles at the scale of 1:24,000 exist for the entire area of the 48 contiguous states, Hawaii, and territories, a feat that requires about 57,000 maps. Each map covers a rectangular area that is 7.5 minutes of latitude by 7.5 minutes of longitude. As is evident from Figure 2.10, these 7.5-minute

quadrangle maps provide detailed information about the natural and cultural features of an area. Because of Alaska's large size and sparse population, the primary scale for mapping that state is 1:63,360 (1 inch represents 1 mile). The Alaska quadrangle series consists of more than 2900 maps.

In Canada, the responsibility for national mapping lies with Survey and Mapping and Remote Sensing, Natural Resources (NRCAN). Maps at a scale of 1:250,000 are available for the entire country; the more heavily populated southern part of Canada is covered by 1:50,000-scale maps. Provincial mapping agencies produce detailed maps at even larger scales.

The USGS produces a list of the symbols it uses on topographic maps (Figure 2.11), and some older maps provide legends on the reverse side. Separate symbols are used to depict types of roads and highways. There are four symbols for dams and four more for types of bridges. On maps of cities, where it would be impossible to locate every building separately, the built-up area is denoted by special tints, and only streets and public buildings are shown.

FIGURE 2.9   The effect of scale on area and detail. The four maps all show Boston, but at different scales. The larger the scale, the greater the number and kinds of features that can be included. Among other things, at a scale of 1:25,000, map **(a)** shows streets, street names, and some buildings. Map **(d)**, at the smallest scale, shows only major cities, highways, and water bodies. The area shown in map **(a)** is indicated by the pink square on map **(b)**, the area covered in **(b)** by the pink square on map **(c)**, and the area of map **(c)** by the square on map **(d)**.

FIGURE 2.10 **A portion of the La Jolla, California, 7.5-minute series of U.S. Geological Survey topographic maps.**
The fractional scale is 1:24,000 (1 inch equals about one-third of a mile), allowing considerable detail to be shown. The pink tint denotes built-up areas, in which only schools, churches, cemeteries, parks, and other public facilities are shown. *Source: U.S. Geological Survey.*

BUILDINGS AND RELATED FEATURES

Building	■ □ ▨ ▨
School; church	♪ ♪
Built-up area	
Racetrack	◯ ▭
Airport	✕ ✕
Landing strip	⊏⊐⊏⊐⊏⊐
Well (other than water); windmill	○ ¥
Tanks	● ⊘
Covered reservoir	⊘ ▨
Gaging station	๑
Landmark object (feature as labeled)	⊙
Campground; picnic area	⊥ ⊼
Cemetery: small; large	⊞ Cem

ROADS AND RELATED FEATURES

Roads on Provisional edition maps are not classified as primary, secondary, or light duty. They are all symbolized as light duty roads.

Primary highway	
Secondary highway	
Light duty road	
Unimproved road	
Trail	
Dual highway	
Dual highway with median strip	
Road under construction	U. C.
Underpass; overpass	
Bridge	
Drawbridge	
Tunnel	

FIGURE 2.11 Some of the standard symbols used on topographic maps published by the U.S. Geological Survey.
Source: U.S. Geological Survey.

As noted earlier, topographic maps depict the surface of the earth. Cartographers use a variety of techniques to represent the three-dimensional surface of the earth on a two-dimensional map. The easiest way to show relief, or variation in elevation, is to use numbers called *spot heights* to indicate the elevation of selected points. A *bench mark* is a particular type of spot height that is used as a reference in calculating elevations of nearby locations (see "Geodetic Control Data").

The principal symbol used to show elevation on topographic maps, however, is the **contour line,** along which all points are of equal elevation above a datum plane, usually mean sea level. Contours are imaginary lines, perhaps best thought of as the outlines that would occur if a series of parallel, equally spaced horizontal slices were made through a vertical feature. Figure 2.12 shows the relationship of contour lines to elevation for an imaginary island.

FIGURE 2.12 Contours drawn for an imaginary island. The intersection of the landform by a plane held parallel to sea level is a contour representing the height of the plane above sea level.

The **contour interval** is the vertical spacing between contour lines, and it is normally stated on the map. The more irregular the surface, usually, the greater is the number of contour lines that will need to be drawn; the steeper the slope, the closer are the contour lines rendering that slope. Contour intervals of 10 and 20 feet are often used, though in relatively flat areas the interval may be only 5 feet. In mountainous areas, the spacing between contours is greater: 40 feet, 100 feet, or more.

Although contour lines represent terrain, giving the map reader information about the elevation of any place on the map and the size, shape, and slope of all relief features, most map readers find it difficult to visualize the landscape from contour lines. To heighten the graphic effect of a topographic map, contours are sometimes supplemented by the use of *shaded relief.* An imaginary light source, usually in the northwest, can be thought of as illuminating a model of the area, simulating the appearance of sunlight and shadows and creating the illusion of three-dimensional topography. Additionally, bands of color for elevation ranges can be used to "color between" the contour lines. These are called elevation, or *hypsometric*, tints.

The tremendous amount of information on topographic maps makes them useful to engineers, regional planners, land use analysts, and developers, as well as to hikers and casual users. Given such a wealth of information, the experienced map reader can make deductions about both the physical character of the area and the cultural use of the land.

Thematic Maps and Data Representation

The study of the spatial patterns and interrelationships of things, whether people, crops, or traffic flows, is the essence of geography. Various kinds of symbols are used to record

Geodetic Control Data

The horizontal position of a place, specified in terms of latitude and longitude, constitutes only two-thirds of the information needed to locate it in three-dimensional space. Also needed is a vertical control point defining elevation, usually specified in terms of altitude above sea level. Together, the horizontal and vertical positions constitute *geodetic control data.* A network of more than 1 million points whose latitude, longitude, and elevation have been precisely determined, recorded, and marked covers the entire United States.

Each point is indicated by a bronze marker fixed in the ground. You may have seen some of the vertical markers, called *bench marks,* on mountaintops, hilltops, or even city sidewalks. The marker indicates which agency put it in place, its elevation, and sometimes the date it was put in place. Every U.S. Geological Survey (USGS) map shows the markers in the area covered by the map, and the USGS maintains Geodetic Control Lists containing the description, location, and elevation of each marker. A bench mark is indicated on the map by the letters *BM,* a small *x,* and the elevation.

These lists were revised in 1987 when, after 12 years' effort, federal scientists completed the recalculation of the precise location of some 250,000 bench marks across the country. In using a satellite locating system for the first national resurvey of control points since 1927, the National Oceanic and Atmospheric Administration (NOAA) found, for example, that New York's Empire State Building is 36.7 meters (120.4 ft) northeast of where it formerly officially stood. The Washington Monument has been moved northeast by 28.8 meters (94.5 ft), the dome of California's state capitol in Sacramento has been relocated 91.7 meters (300.9 ft) southwest, and Seattle's Space Needle now has a position 93 meters (305.1 ft) west and 20 meters (65.6 ft) south of where maps formerly showed it. The satellite survey provides much more accurate locations than did the old system of land measurement of distances and angles. The result is more accurate maps and more precise navigation.

© Roger Scott.

the location or numbers of these phenomena on thematic maps. The symbols and maps may be either *qualitative* or *quantitative.*

The principal purpose of the qualitative map is to show the distribution of a particular class of information. The world location of producing oil fields, the distribution of national parks, and the pattern of areas of agricultural specialization within a country are examples. The interest is in where these things are, without reporting about, for example, barrels of oil extracted, number of park visitors, or value of crops produced.

In contrast, quantitative thematic maps show the spatial characteristics of numerical data. Usually, a single variable, such as population, income, or land value, is chosen, and the map displays the variation of that feature from place to place. Multivariate maps show two or more variables at once.

Point Symbols

Features that occur at a particular point in space are represented on maps by *point symbols.* Thousands of types of such features exist on the earth: churches, schools, cemeteries, and historical sites, to name a few. Symbols used to represent them include dots, crosses, triangles, and other shapes. On a qualitative thematic map, each such symbol records merely the location of that feature at a particular point on Earth.

Sometimes, however, our interest is in showing the variation in the number of things that exist at several points—for example, the population of selected cities, the tonnage handled at certain terminals, or the number of passengers at given airports.

There are two chief means of symbolizing such distributions, as Figures 2.13 and 2.14 indicate. One method is to choose a symbol, usually a dot, to represent a given quantity of the mapped item (such as 50 people) and to repeat that symbol as many times as necessary. Such a map is easily understood because the dots give the map reader a visual impression of the pattern. Sometimes pictorial symbols—for example, human figures or oil barrels—are used instead, to mimic the phenomenon being mapped.

If the range of the data is great, the geographer may find it inconvenient to use a repeated symbol. For example, if one country has 500 times the population of another, or one port handles 50 or 100 times as much tonnage as another, that many more dots would have to be placed on the map and could begin to coalesce. To circumvent this problem, the cartographer can choose a second method and use graduated symbols. The size of the symbol is varied according to the quantities represented. Thus, if squares or circles are used, the *area* of the symbol ordinarily is proportional to the quantity shown (Figure 2.14).

There are occasions, however, when the range of the data is so great that even circles or squares would take up too much room on the map. In such cases, symbols such as spheres or cubes are used, and their *volume* is proportional to the data.

• One dot equals 10,000 people

FIGURE 2.13 Dot map of the distribution of the population in California, by county. In a dot-distribution map, all of the dots have the same value, which is stated in the map legend. The placement of dots on this map does not indicate precise locations of people within the county but simply their total number. Dot maps can provide a good visual impression of the distribution and relative density of a phenomenon—in this case, how the number of people varies from county to county.

Unfortunately, many map readers fail to perceive the added dimension implicit in volume, and most cartographers do not recommend the use of such symbols.

Area Symbols

Features found within defined areas of the earth's surface are represented on maps by *area symbols.* As with point symbols, such maps fall into two general categories: those showing differences in kind and those showing differences in quantity. Atlases contain numerous examples of the first category, such as patterns of religions, languages, political entities, vegetation, or types of rock. Normally, different colors or patterns are used for different areas, as shown in Figure 2.15.

One way to show how the *amount* of a phenomenon varies from area to area is by using **choropleth maps.** The term is derived from the Greek words *choros* ("place") and *pleth* ("magnitude" or "value"). The quantities shown may be absolute numbers (e.g., the population of counties) or derived values, such as percentages, ratios, rates, and densities (e.g., population density by county). The data are grouped into a limited number of classes, each represented by a distinctive color, shade, or pattern. Figure 2.16 is an example of a choropleth map. In this case, the areal units are states. Other commonly used subdivisions are counties, townships, cities, and census divisions.

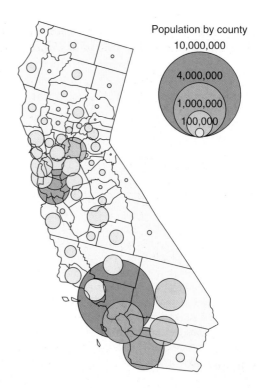

Population by county
10,000,000
4,000,000
1,000,000
100,000

FIGURE 2.14 Graduated-circle map of the distribution of population in California, by county. On this map, the area of a circle is proportional to the number of people within each county. The scale at the top of the map helps the reader interpret the map.

As Figures 2.15 and 2.16 reveal, three main problems characterize maps (whether qualitative or quantitative) that show the distribution of a phenomenon in an area:

1. They give the impression of uniformity to areas that may actually contain significant variations.
2. Boundaries attain unrealistic precision and significance, implying abrupt changes between areas, when, in reality, the changes may be gradual.
3. Unless colors are chosen wisely, some areas may look more important than others.

A special type of area map is the **area cartogram,** or **value-by-area map,** in which the areas of units are drawn proportional to the data they represent (Figure 2.17). Population, income, cost, or another variable becomes the standard of measurement. Depending on the idea that the mapmaker wishes to convey, the sizes and shapes of areas may be altered, distances and directions may be distorted, and contiguity may or may not be preserved (see "Red States, Blue States, p. 37").

Line Symbols

As the term suggests, *line symbols* represent features that have length but insignificant width. Some lines on maps do not have numerical significance. The lines representing rivers, political boundaries, roads, and railroads, for example, are not quantitative. They are indicated on maps by such standardized symbols as those that follow and those shown in Figure 2.11.

Often, however, lines on maps do denote specific numerical values. Contour lines that connect points of equal elevation above mean sea level are a kind of **isoline,** or line of constant value. Other examples of isolines are *isohyets* (equal rainfall), *isotherms* (equal temperature), and *isobars* (equal barometric pressure).

Flow-line maps are used to portray linear movement between places. They may be qualitative or quantitative. Examples of *qualitative* flow maps are those showing ocean currents or airline routes. The lines are of uniform thickness and generally have arrowheads to denote direction of movement. On *quantitative* flow maps, on the other hand, the flow lines are scaled so that their widths are proportional to the amounts they represent. Migration, traffic, and commodity flows are usually portrayed this way. The location of the route taken, the direction of movement, and the volume of flow can all be depicted. The amount shown may be either an absolute or a derived value—for example, the actual traffic flows or a per mile figure. In Figure 2.18, the width of the flow lines is proportional to the number of interstate migrants in the United States. Another flow-line map appears in Figure 5.7.

Map Misuse

Most people have a tendency to believe what they see in print. Maps are particularly persuasive because of the implied precision of their lines, scales, symbol placement, and information content. It is useful to remember that all maps are abstractions and inevitably distort reality. As in all forms of communication, the message conveyed by a map reflects the intent and, perhaps, the biases of its author. Maps can subtly or blatantly manipulate the message they impart or intentionally contain false information.

Sometimes the cause of cartographic distortion has been ignorance, as when the cartographers of the Middle Ages filled the unknown interiors of continents with mythical beasts. Other times the motivation for distortion has been to promote a cause or to thwart foreign military and intelligence operations. Cartographers use various techniques to make such maps.

- Lack of a scale: a scale may be absent and the sizes of some areas diminished while others are enlarged.
- A simple design that omits data or features that would make the map more accurate.

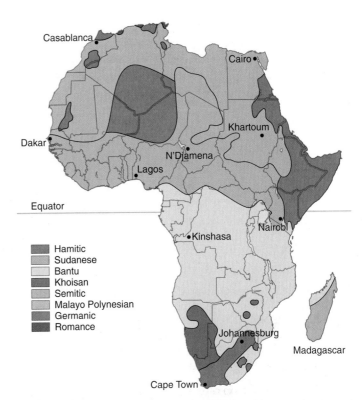

FIGURE 2.15 Language regions of Africa. Maps such as this one may give the false impression of uniformity within a given area—for example, that only Bantu is spoken over much of southern Africa. Such maps are intended to represent only the predominant language in an area.

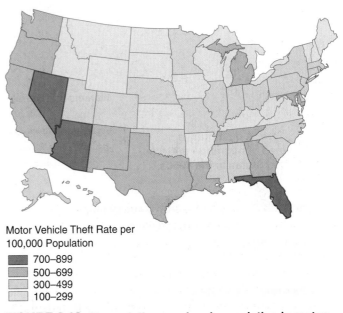

Motor Vehicle Theft Rate per 100,000 Population

- 700–899
- 500–699
- 300–499
- 100–299

FIGURE 2.16 Choropleth map showing variation in motor vehicle theft rates by state, 1998. Quantitative variation by area is more easily visualized in map than in tabular form. *Source: Redrawn from* Crime and Justice Atlas 2000, *U.S. Department of Justice, p. 55.*

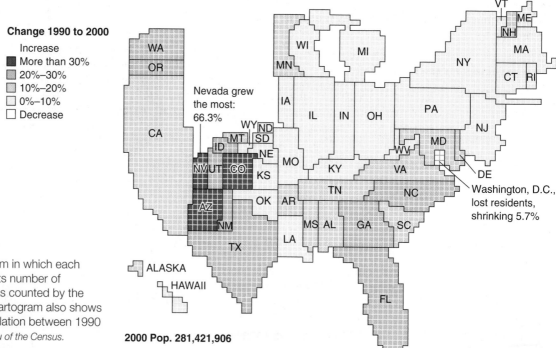

Change 1990 to 2000

Increase
- More than 30%
- 20%–30%
- 10%–20%
- 0%–10%
- Decrease

Nevada grew
the most:
66.3%

Washington, D.C.,
lost residents,
shrinking 5.7%

2000 Pop. 281,421,906

FIGURE 2.17 A cartogram in which each state is sized according to its number of residents in the year 2000 as counted by the U.S. Census Bureau. The cartogram also shows the percent change in population between 1990 and 2000. *Source: U.S. Bureau of the Census.*

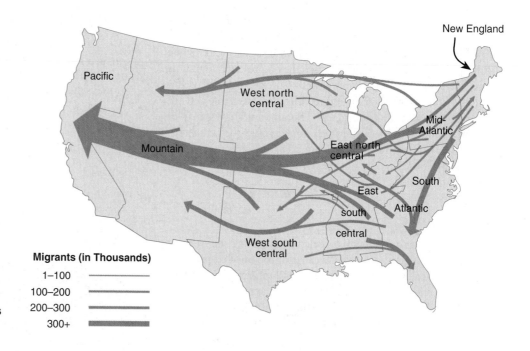

Migrants (in Thousands)

1–100	
100–200	
200–300	
300+	

FIGURE 2.18 A quantitative flow-line map of migration patterns in the United States in the 1950s.

- Colors that have a strong psychological impact.
- Bold, oversized, and/or misleading symbols.
- Action symbols, such as arrows to indicate military invasions or repulsions and pincers to show areas threatened by encirclement (Figure 2.19).
- Selective omission of data: many governments, for example, do not indicate the location of military installations on their maps; the hub maps in airline magazines typically show lines radiating from the hub to the cities the airline serves, giving the impression that the flights are nonstop.

- Inaccuracies or "disinformation" for military opponents. The chief cartographer of the USSR acknowledged in 1988 that for 50 years the policy of the Soviet Union had been to deliberately falsify almost all publicly available maps of the country. The types of cartographic distortions on Soviet maps included the displacement and omission of features and the use of incorrect grid coordinates. The routes of highways, rivers, and railroads were sometimes altered by as much as 10 kilometers (6 mi). A city or town might be shown on the east bank

Red States, Blue States

Every map has a purpose. The mapmaker's decision of what data to represent and how to represent them can affect our view of reality. The media discussed the results of the U.S. presidential election of 2008 in terms of "red" states and "blue" states. Red were those where a majority of voters voted for the Republican candidate, John McCain, while blue states favored the Democratic candidate, Barack Obama. On both maps shown here, the 48 contiguous states are colored accordingly: red and blue to indicate Republican and Democratic majorities, respectively.

Nationwide, the Democrats won by a substantial margin—53% for Obama, 46% for McCain. Map (a), however, gives the impression that the Republican candidate won the election, since there is more red than blue on the map. While the map is accurate, it is misleading in that most red states have small populations, whereas most blue states have large ones. Three researchers at the University of Michigan's Center for the Study of Complex Systems devised an area cartogram, map (b), that reconfigures the states based on the size of their population rather than their land area. On this map, there is clearly more blue than red. States with more people appear larger than states with fewer people. Rhode Island, for example, with its 1.1 million inhabitants, appears about twice the size of Wyoming, which has half a million—even though Wyoming has 60 times the acreage of Rhode Island.

The researchers created a number of other maps depicting the results of the election. Some show election results by county, others the sizes of states proportional to their number of electoral votes; on others red and blue are joined by a third color, purple, to indicate a nearly balanced percentage of Democratic and Republican votes. They can be viewed at www.personal.umich.edu/~mejn/election/.

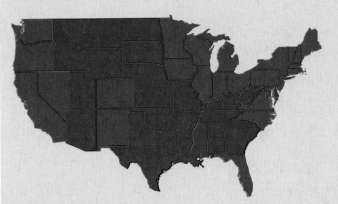

(a) Conventional view. This map of the November 2008 presidential election shows state-by-state results, colored red and blue to indicate Republican and Democratic majorities.

(b) Population cartogram. Election results are shown on a cartogram where state sizes are based on population rather than land area.

(a)   (b)

FIGURE 2.19 The Nazis, who ruled Germany from 1933 to 1945, used maps as tools of propaganda. The maps shown here were designed to increase sympathy for Germany by showing it threatened by encirclement. **(a)** Arrows represent pressure on Germany from all sides. **(b)** Pincers signify pressure against Germany from France and Poland. *Source: Karl Springenschmid,* Die Staaten als Lebewesen: Geopolitisches Skizzenbuch *(Leipzig: Verlag Ernst Wunderlich, 1934).*

The Peters Projection

Developed and promoted by Arno Peters, a German journalist-historian, the Peters projection purports to reflect concern for the problems of the Third World by providing a less European-centered representation of the world. Because it is an equal-area map, Peters claimed that it shows the densely populated parts of the earth and the countries of the Third World in proper proportion to one another. He persuaded a number of socially concerned agencies with special interest in the Third World, including the World Council of Churches, the Lutheran Church of America, and UNESCO and several other United Nations organizations, to adopt the map.

Presented in 1973 as a "new invention," the projection aroused a storm of controversy. Critics pointed out that, by saying his projection was fairer and more accurate than the Mercator,

Peters used the latter as a meaningless foil, a "straw man" to knock down. If Peters wanted to demonstrate that the less-developed countries deserve a larger share of our attention and resources, he might better have used an area cartogram (see Figure 2.17) in which each country is scaled according to its number of inhabitants, which would do more to call attention to enormous populations of Third World countries, such as India, China, and Indonesia. Detractors also noted that the Peters projection badly distorts shapes in the tropics and at high latitudes and that many equal-area projections yield a world map with less distortion of shapes. In addition, distances and directions cannot be measured except under very limited conditions. Finally, the projection was not new but, in fact, a very slight modification of an equal-area projection developed by James Gall in 1855.

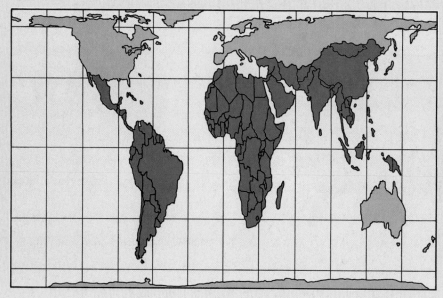

of a river, when, in fact, it was on the west bank. Even when features were shown correctly, the latitude and longitude grid might be misplaced.

- An inappropriate projection. For more than a decade, the John Birch Society and other political groups concerned about the "Red Menace" used the Mercator projection, which grossly exaggerates the sizes of areas in the higher latitudes, to magnify the Communist threat, and China and Russia were colored red. The Peters projection was developed to promote social justice (see "The Peters Projection").

In summary, maps can distort and lie as readily as they can convey verifiable spatial data or the results of scientifically valid analyses. The more that map users are aware of those possibilities and the more understanding they possess of map projections, symbolization, and common forms of thematic and reference mapping standards, the more likely they are to reasonably question and clearly understand the messages maps communicate.

GEOGRAPHIC INFORMATION TECHNOLOGIES

The latter half of the 20th century saw a revolution in the ways geographic data are collected, stored, and analyzed; in the ways maps are produced; in the number and kinds of maps that can be made; and in the applications to which maps are now put. Two of the important new technologies involve remote sensing and global positioning satellites.

Remote Sensing

When topographic maps were first developed, it was necessary to obtain the data for them through fieldwork, a slow and tedious process that involved relating a given point on the earth's surface to other points by measuring its distance, direction, and altitude. Much fieldwork has now been replaced by **remote sensing,** detecting the nature of an object and the content of an area without direct contact with the ground. In the early 20th century, fixed-wing aircraft provided a platform for

(a)

(b)

FIGURE 2.20 **(a) Wavelengths of the electromagnetic spectrum in micrometers.** One micrometer equals 1 one-millionth of a meter. Sunlight is made up of different wavelengths. The human eye is sensitive to only some of these wavelengths, the ones we see in the colors of the rainbow. Although invisible, near infrared wavelengths can be recorded on special sensitized film and by scanners on satellites. The scanners measure reflected light in both the visible and near infrared portions of the spectrum. Wavelengths longer than 4.0 micrometers characterize terrestrial radiation. **(b)** A color-infrared aerial photograph of Washington, D.C. *(b) U.S. Geological Survey.*

the camera and the photographer, and by the 1930s aerial photographs from planned positions and routes permitted reliable data gathering for mapping purposes.

Although there are now a variety of sensing devices, aerial photography employing cameras with returned film remains a widely used remote-sensing technique. Mapping from the air has certain obvious advantages over surveying from the ground, the most evident being the bird's-eye view that the cartographer obtains. Using stereoscopic devices, the cartographer can determine the exact slope and size of features such as mountains, rivers, and coastlines. Areas that are otherwise hard to survey, such as mountains and deserts, can be mapped easily from the air. Furthermore, millions of square miles can be surveyed in a very short time.

Standard photographic film detects reflected energy within the visible portion of the electromagnetic spectrum (Figure 2.20a). It can be supplemented by special sensitized infrared film that has proved particularly useful for

the recording of vegetation and hydrographic features. Color-infrared photography yields what are called *false-color images*—"false" because the film does not produce an image that appears natural (Figure 2.20b). For example, leaves of healthy vegetation have a high infrared reflectance and are recorded as red on color-infrared film, while unhealthy or dormant vegetation appears as blue, green, or gray. Clear water appears as black, but sediment-laden water may appear light blue.

For wavelengths longer than 1.2 micrometers (a micrometer is 1 one-millionth of a meter) on the electromagnetic spectrum, sensing devices other than photographic film must be used. Nonphotographic imaging sensors include thermal scanners, radar, and lidar.

- *Thermal scanners* record the longwave radiation emitted by water bodies, clouds, and vegetation, as well as by buildings and other structures and are used to produce images of thermal radiation (Figure 2.21). Unlike conventional photography, thermal sensing can be employed during nighttime as well as daytime, giving it military applications. It is widely used for studying various aspects of water resources, such as ocean currents, water pollution, surface energy budgets, and irrigation scheduling.

- Operating in a different band of the electromagnetic spectrum, *radar* (short for *ra[dio] d[etecting] a[nd] r[anging]*) systems also can be used day or night. Because radar can penetrate clouds and vegetation as well as darkness, it is particularly useful for monitoring the locations of airplanes, ships, and storm systems and for mapping parts of the world that are perpetually hazy or cloud-covered (Figure 2.22).

- *Lidar* (short for *li[ght] d[etection] a[nd] r[anging]*) is a relatively new remote-sensing technology that utilizes an airborne laser to transmit light out to an object. Some of the light is reflected back to the instrument, where it is analyzed to yield information about the target. Lidar is ideal for any kind of mapping that requires a precise depiction of the ground surface (see Figure 2.26).

Since the 1970s, both manned and unmanned spacecraft have supplemented the airplane as the vehicle for imaging earth features. Many images are now taken either from continuously orbiting satellites or from manned spacecraft flights, such as those of the *Apollo* and *Gemini* missions. Among the advantages of satellites are the speed of coverage and the fact that views of large regions can be obtained.

In addition, satellites are equipped to record and report back to the earth digitized information from multiple parts of the electromagnetic spectrum that are outside the range of human eyesight. Satellites enable us to map the invisible, including atmospheric and weather conditions, in addition to providing images with applications in agriculture and forest inventory, identification of geologic structures and mineral deposits, and monitoring of a variety of environmental phenomena, including water pollution

(a)

(b)

FIGURE 2.21 Thermal radiation images of the World Trade Center site in New York City, 2001. Following the collapse of the twin towers on September 11, 2001, fire-fighting and rescue teams relied on daily thermal images of the site to detect fire patterns in the rubble and underground. Based on the patterns revealed, the teams decided where to work that day. **(a)** A few days after the attack, a nearly constant field of heat (shown in red) covered most of the 16-acre site. **(b)** A month later, the underground blaze was confined largely to where the two towers once stood. *New York State Office of Cyber Security and Critical Infrastructure Coordination (CSCIC) © 2001.*

FIGURE 2.22 A SLAR mosaic of Los Angeles, California. Side-looking airborne radar (SLAR) instruments on aircraft or satellites transmit microwave energy to the ground. The portion of the signal that returns to the sensor is recorded as digital values that can be represented on photographic film. The "side-looking" aspect produces shadows of varying lengths, enhancing subtle features of the terrain. This mosaic was compiled from many radar image strips. *Source: U.S. Geological Survey.*

into photo-like images for use in both long-term scientific research and in current-condition mapping programs.

Landsat images have a variety of research applications, including the following:

- tracing ocean currents
- assessing water quality in lakes
- mapping snow cover, glaciers, and polar ice sheets
- analyzing soil and vegetation conditions
- monitoring global deforestation
- monitoring strip-mining reclamation
- identifying geologic structures and associated mineral deposits
- mapping population changes in metropolitan areas

Some Landsat data are utilized not for long-term scientific research but for immediately monitoring, mapping, and responding to natural and human-caused disasters, such as storms, floods, earthquakes, volcanoes, wildfires, and oil spills (Figure 2.23).

The Global Positioning System

In recent years, the **Global Positioning System (GPS)** has made the determination of location significantly easier than it used to be. This navigation and positioning system was conceived in the 1970s and is maintained by the U.S. Department of Defense (DoD). The technology uses a network of DoD satellites that orbit some 20,000 kilometers (12,500 mi) above the earth, passing over the same spot every 24 hours. As they orbit, the satellites continuously transmit their positions, time signals, and other data. A GPS receiver records the positions of a number of the satellites simultaneously, then determines its latitude, longitude, and altitude and the time (Figure 2.24).

and the effects of acid rain. Military applications of remotely sensed images include better aircraft navigation, improved weapons targeting, and enhanced battlefield management and tactical planning, which raises the question of who should have access to the information (see "Civilian Spy Satellites").

Perhaps the best known remote-sensing spacecraft are the **Landsat satellites,** the first of which was launched in 1972. The different sensors of the Landsat satellites are capable of resolving objects between 15 and 60 meters (50 and 200 ft) in size. Even sharper images are yielded by the French SPOT satellite; its sensors can show objects that are larger than 10 meters (33 ft). Satellite imagery is relayed by electronic signals to receiving stations, where computers convert the signals

GEOGRAPHY & *Public Policy*

Civilian Spy Satellites

Although remote-sensing satellites have been orbiting the earth for about three decades, only since 1999 have detailed satellite images such as that shown here become available to the general public. Until recently, images from commercial satellites were considerably fuzzier and less detailed than those from military satellites. That is no longer the case. In 1994, the federal government lifted technical restrictions on private companies, permitting them to build a new generation of civilian "spy" satellites and to sell the images to any buyer. Space Imaging Corporation, based in Denver, Colorado, launched the first high-resolution commercial satellite, *Ikonos 1* (after the Greek word for "image") in 1999. Two other U.S. firms launched similar satellites the following year. The new imaging technology is so powerful that it can detect and record objects on the ground as small as 1 meter wide: cars, houses, even hot tubs.

Military planners are finding high-resolution images from commercial satellites invaluable, capable of providing up-to-date information and a higher level of detail and precision than conventional maps. Adding multiple layers of data, such as information from a topographic map, current weather conditions, and reports from soldiers in the field, to the images facilitates the planning of missions. Army commanders in Iraq, for example, have used the images to pinpoint tall structures that might be used by snipers, to determine whether bridges have been destroyed, and to identify alleys that could be ambush routes.

The new imagery also has been welcomed by clients such as geologists, city planners, and disaster-relief officials. Nongovernmental public interest groups use the images for such activities as pressuring governments to live up to environmental laws and treaties, tracking refugee movements, detecting illegal waste dumps, and monitoring arms control agreements. At the same time, the sharp visual detail and widespread availability of the images provided by the satellites have raised fears about national security. "Any time a powerful new technology is introduced, there's a battle over the uses to which it's put," one intelligence official noted. "Here, the potential for beneficial uses is very high, on balance. But the potential for abuse certainly exists and we'll no doubt see some of that."

One of the chief concerns is that the images, which rival military reconnaissance in sharpness and accuracy, can be purchased by those who would threaten the national welfare. In wartime, for example, foes could use them to track the location of military troops and equipment. Terrorists could use the imagery to plan surprise attacks. General Richard B. Myers, head of the U.S. Space Command, warns that the government must decide what to do in times of armed conflict. "There's going to be risk in operations like this when you're selling what can be used against you."

A satellite image of San Francisco International Airport. Only recently have detailed, accurate, high-quality images such as this one been taken from commercial satellites and made available to the general public. © *2000 Space Imaging. All Rights Reserved.*

American companies, however, operate under a number of security restrictions. They are forbidden to sell images to customers in several countries, including Cuba and North Korea. And in the interests of national security, the government can put any area off limits. Soon after September 11, 2001, for example, the Pentagon purchased exclusive rights to all satellite images of Afghanistan and Pakistan from Space Imaging.

Considering the Issues

1. Do you think that the availability of the new, detailed satellite images is a potential threat to national security? Might access to images of their enemies make belligerent countries more dangerous than they already are? Why or why not?

2. In what ways might access to satellite imagery stem the tides of environmental and social destabilization?

3. Should the federal government, which licenses the satellites, be allowed to exercise "shutter control," cutting off image sales during wartime? Defend your answer.

41

FIGURE 2.23 Three major clusters of fires are evident in this satellite image of southern California taken on October 22, 2007: near Los Angeles, in the San Bernardino Mountains, and in San Diego. Data from remotely sensed images can be used to keep track of the extent and intensity of fires and to update maps of active fires several times a day. They assist fire managers on the ground in determining where best to position firefighters to contain a blaze, to assess damage after a fire is contained, and to plan recovery efforts. *© Images courtesy of MODIS Rapid Response Project at NASA/GSFC.*

GPS technology was originally designed for military applications, particularly naval and aerial navigation. The technology has facilitated the development of precision-guided weapons, the so-called smart bombs that home in on a target. Other government applications include the use of GPS receivers for monitoring geologic fault lines and ocean currents, the sensing of global warming in the atmosphere, firefighting, and mapping disaster scenes.

Seeking clues as to why the space shuttle *Columbia* broke apart upon its reentry into the atmosphere on February 1, 2003, for example, federal government investigators used GPS technology to define the debris field, which covered portions of Texas, Louisiana, and several other states. As hundreds of volunteers and law enforcement officers found and collected thousands of pieces of debris, their precise locations were fed into a computer equipped with special mapping software. Just a few days after the tragedy, the Federal Emergency Management Agency's Disaster Field Office in Lufkin, Texas,

FIGURE 2.24 This handheld GPS receiver shows latitude, longitude, and a map on a small liquid crystal display screen. Sales of stand-alone GPS devices such as this one have fallen recently as "smart phones" (e.g., BlackBerry and Apple's iPhone) have added GPS to their other features. *Courtesy Garmin Corporation.*

was printing more than 1000 maps a day. The maps helped emergency workers focus on the areas they needed to search in order to retrieve more of the shuttle debris.

As GPS receivers have become smaller, lighter, and less expensive, civilian applications have multiplied (see "Geocaching). Several automobile manufacturers make in-car navigation systems an option in their new cars, and some rental car agencies provide them in their vehicles. The systems tap GPS signals to monitor the car's exact location, comparing it with a computerized atlas stored on a compact disc. The car's location, constantly updated, appears on a computer screen mounted on the dashboard. The navigation systems enable motorists to find out where they are and how to reach their destination. For example, the driver can give a street address or the name of a movie theater, a hospital, or another building and the system displays it on the screen, indicates how far away it is, and tells how long it should take to drive there. The system also gives turn-by-turn directions on the screen map or directions "spoken" by an electronic voice. Car navigation systems are particularly popular among sales representatives, real estate agents, and repair people, who frequently drive to unfamiliar places.

In the past few years, systems have been developed for building miniaturized GPS receivers into all kinds of things, such as watches, bracelets, cell phones, and even dog collars, in order to ascertain their locations. A number of states use GPS monitoring

Geocaching

Geocaching has been variously described as high-tech hide-and-seek, a new twist on an old-fashioned scavenger hunt, and the hottest new leisure activity. The rules are simple. An individual goes outside and in a publicly accessible place hides a waterproof container containing a few items—pens, key chains, small toys, or other inexpensive trinkets—as well as a logbook. This is the *cache.* Having hidden it, the individual goes online to *geocaching .com* or another website to post the latitude and longitude of the hidden treasure, and perhaps some clues to help searchers find it.

Now it's your turn. You go to one of the websites where the coordinates of caches are posted, pick a site in your area, program the coordinates into your portable GPS device, and use the device to find the cache. If successful, you enter your name, the date, and the time in the logbook; take an item out of the cache; leave something in return; and then replace the cache exactly where you found it.

Geocaching got its start in 2000, when the U.S. government allowed civilian GPS devices to have the same degree of accuracy as military devices, and almost immediately the hobby caught on around the globe. Coordinates of hundreds of thousands of caches have been posted on the Web. Enthusiasts say

the hobby gives them exercise, an incentive to explore new areas, and experience in orienteering.

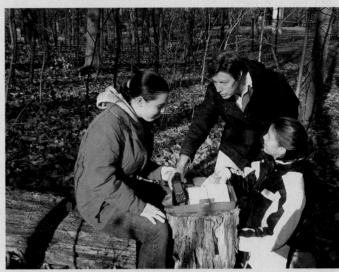

Courtesy of Arthur Getis.

devices as a surveillance system to track the movements of people on parole and probation. The law enforcement use of GPS technology to track suspects is raising legal and ethical questions about privacy rights and public safety (see "An Invasion of Privacy?").

Virtual and Interactive Maps

Since its establishment in 1993, the World Wide Web has been instrumental both in disseminating geographic information and in fostering the integration of geospatial data. Maps are easily, freely, and widely available on the Internet, and online mapping systems enable users to view images of nearly any place on Earth. Google is one of the best known of the companies that produce maps on the Web; others are Microsoft and Yahoo.

Google Earth (earth.google.com) combines aerial photographs, satellite images, and maps with street, terrain, and other data. (Google Earth is free; professionals can purchase more sophisticated versions of the software, such as Plus and Pro, from the company.) The program gives the user an aerial view of a place. This can be accessed by entering the name of the place or its longitude and latitude or simply by scrolling across the virtual globe and zooming in on a particular location. The accuracy and sharpness of the images vary. Most of the aerial photographs and satellite images will have been taken within the last 3 years, and Google periodically updates them. For some major cities, the resolution is high enough to provide clear three-dimensional images of individual buildings and the color of cars on the street. Special features enable the user to zoom in and out of an image as well as to tilt or rotate it.

The digital maps produced by Google, Microsoft, and some other Internet companies can be merged with data from other sources to create what are called *mashups,* Web applications that combine data from more than one source into an integrated experience—an example of *interactive mapping.* Now anybody with modest programming skills, not just professional cartographers, can make maps, and people have created millions of them. Mashups can be simple or complex. Some people simply overlay the locations of things—crime statistics, for example—onto an online street map of their area. The user can search for crimes by type, location, or the date they were committed. Other types of information that have been combined with maps are bicycle trails, gas stations with low prices, and school rankings; the list is virtually endless. Some people have annotated digital maps and/or photo images with text (e.g., recent news events, reviews), photographs, sound, and even videos. You can see samples of mashups by entering "mashups" into your search engine. To get an idea of the number, kinds, and variety of interactive websites, search for "interactive maps" on the Web.

INTEGRATING TECHNOLOGY: GEOGRAPHIC INFORMATION SYSTEMS

The technologies just described would not be possible without computers. They have become an integral part of almost every stage of the cartographic process, from the collection

GEOGRAPHY
& Public Policy

An Invasion of Privacy?

Police investigating a series of burglaries in Latham, New York, in 2005 attached a GPS receiver under the bumper of a suspect's car and left it there for 65 days. Based on the tracking information, police charged the suspect with burglarizing two stores. In another case, someone was attacking women in northern Virginia, grabbing them from behind and molesting them before running away. After logging 11 cases in 6 months, police identified a suspect. They had put a GPS device on the suspect's van, allowing them to track his movements, and soon caught him dragging a woman into a wooded area. In neither case did the police obtain a search warrant.

Law enforcement agents have also used GPS technology embedded in cell phones to link suspects to crime scenes by analyzing their phone records. Such records show a phone's approximate location at the beginning and end of a call. In a murder case in New York City, they were used to convict a nightclub bouncer in the death of a female graduate student whom he had met at the bar. The phone records showed that he had made several calls as he drove from his house in Queens to a deserted street in Brooklyn to dump the body.

In hundreds and perhaps thousands of cases, police have used GPS to catch killers, car thieves, drug dealers, sexual predators, burglars, and robbers, often without obtaining a warrant or court order. Does the covert use of GPS technology to track suspects violate the Fourth Amendment rights of protection against unreasonable searches and seizures? Should the government be required to obtain a search warrant by showing probable cause for connecting a cell phone user to criminal activity?

Existing laws do not provide clear or uniform guidelines. Some jurisdictions allow law enforcement agencies to track the location of cell phone users without search warrants; others do not. Phone companies wish that Congress would clarify the laws, so that they are clear about their legal responsibilities. The U.S. Supreme Court has not addressed the issue, and as of 2009 a few states had reached varied conclusions. In New York, Washington, and Oregon, police may not use GPS receivers to track an individual's movements without a warrant, but the Wisconsin Court of Appeals ruled that GPS tracking does not violate Fourth Amendment rights—that police can attach receivers to cars without obtaining search warrants, even if an individual is not a crime suspect.

Considering the Issues

1. Advocates of the warrantless use of GPS technology argue that GPS tracking is essentially the same as having an officer trail someone; it's just cheaper and more accurate. As one attorney said, "It helps cut down on the number of police officers who would have to be out tracking someone." On the other hand, another attorney contended that, "While it may be true that police can conduct surveillance of people on a public street without violating their rights, tracking people everywhere they go and keeping a computer record of it for days or even months without them knowing is a completely different type of intrusion." With which side, if either, do you agree?

2. A district attorney in Queens said, "People who obey the law have nothing to fear from cell phone tracking. Law enforcement has a responsibility to keep pace with the latest advances in technology in order to improve its efficiency in combating crime." Privacy advocates, however, contend that people have a reasonable expectation of privacy regarding their physical location. As one judge wrote, "Most Americans don't know that their cell phones create a record of their movements and would be appalled to learn that the government can access it without showing probable cause." If you have a cell phone, do you care if your movements can be tracked as long as the phone is turned on? Do you know what information your phone is sending about your movements and where that information is going? If locational information is to be collected, should people be given advance notice and the opportunity to opt out?

3. GPS devices give the government and corporations access to much extraneous information about individuals, including the clubs and restaurants they go to, whose houses they visit, and what political meetings they attend. Should the cost of carrying a cell phone include the loss of one's personal privacy, or do you believe citizens do not expect their every move to be continuously and indefinitely monitored by a technical device without their knowledge, except where a warrant has been issued based on probable cause?

and recording of data to the production and revision of maps. Although the initial cost of equipment is high, the investment is repaid in the more efficient and more accurate production and revision of maps.

Computers are at the heart of what is known as a **geographic information system (GIS),** a computer-based set of procedures for assembling, storing, manipulating, analyzing, and displaying geographically referenced information. Any data that can be located spatially can be entered

into a GIS. The five major components of a GIS are the following:

1. a data input component that converts maps and other data from their existing form into digital or computer-readable form

2. a data management component used to store and retrieve data

3. data manipulation functions that allow data from disparate sources to be used simultaneously

4. analysis functions that enable the extraction of useful information from the data

5. a data output component that makes it possible to visualize maps and tables on the computer monitor or as hard copy (such as paper)

While the use of computers and printers in map production permits increases in the speed, flexibility, and accuracy of many steps in the mapmaking process, that use in no way reduces the obligation of the mapmaker to employ sound judgment in the design of the map or the communication of its content.

The Geographic Database

The first step in developing a GIS is to create a **geographic database,** a digital record of geographic information from such sources as maps, field surveys, aerial photographs, and satellite imagery. As long as every item in the database is tied to a precise geographic location, a GIS can use information from many different sources and in many different forms. The purpose of the study will determine the data to be entered into the database. For a physical geographer studying the sensitivity of wetlands to damage in a particular area, the source data might include maps of rainfall amounts at different points, soil types, vegetative cover, originating points of water pollution, contours, and direction of stream flow. An urban geographer or regional planner, on the other hand, might use a GIS data set that contains the great amount of place-specific information collected and published by the U.S. Census Bureau, including political boundaries, census tracts, population distribution, a building inventory, race, ethnicity, income, housing, employment, and so on.

Once geographic information is in the computer in digital form, the data can be manipulated, analyzed, and displayed with a speed and precision not otherwise possible. Because computers can process millions of facts in seconds, they are particularly useful for researchers who need to analyze many variables simultaneously. The development of geographic information systems has deemphasized the use of maps to store information and has enabled researchers to concentrate on using maps for analyzing and communicating spatial information. With the appropriate software, a computer operator can display any combination of data, showing the relationships among variables almost instantly (Figure 2.25). In this sense, a GIS allows an operator to generate maps or perform spatial analyses that were virtually impossible to create or perform only a few decades ago.

GIS operations can produce several types of output: displays on a computer monitor, listings of data, or hard copy. When a map is to be produced, the specialist can quickly call up the desired data. Geographic information systems are particularly useful for revising existing maps because outdated

Terrain Models

Network
- Street center lines
- Drainage network

Utilities
- Sanitary sewer lines
- Water lines
- Telephone
- Gas/electric

Lots/Ownership
- Lot lines
- Property lines

Zones/Districts
- Comprehensive plan
- Municipal zoning
- Voting precincts
- School districts
- Census tracts/blocks

Base Mapping
- Road pavement
- Buildings/structures
- Fences/parking lots
- Drainage
- Wooded areas
- Spot elevation
- Contour lines
- Recreational facilities

FIGURE 2.25 A model of a geographic information system. Information layering is the essence of a GIS. Map information that has been converted to digital data is stored in the computer in different data "layers." A GIS enables the user to combine just the layers that are desired to produce a composite map and to analyze how those variables relate to each other. In this example, the different layers of information are to be used in different combinations for city planning purposes. What sorts of layers might you need if you were asked to locate a new Starbucks in an urban area? *Reprinted by permission of Shaoli Huang.*

data—for example, population sizes—can be modified or replaced easily. Additionally, a GIS facilitates exploratory analysis by enabling an operator to quickly change variables and/or model parameters and to use multiple spatial scales.

Applications of GIS

Who uses geographic information systems? Tens of thousands of people in a variety of fields use them for a variety of purposes. Every issue of *ArcNews,* a monthly publication of the

Environmental Systems Research Institute, Inc., describes numerous examples of "GIS in Action" from many fields. In human geography, the vast and growing array of spatial data has encouraged the use of GIS to explore models of regional economic and social structure, to examine transportation systems and urban growth patterns, to study patterns of voting behavior, and so on. For physical geographers, the analytic and modeling capabilities of GIS are fundamental to the understanding of processes and interrelations in the natural environment.

In addition to geographers, researchers in fields ranging from archaeology to zoology use geographic information systems, as a few examples indicate.

- Biologists and ecologists use GIS to study numerous environmental problems, including air and water pollution, landscape conservation, wildlife management, and the protection of endangered species.
- Epidemiologists need accurately mapped information to study both the diffusion of diseases, such as malaria, SARS, AIDS, and dengue fever, and entomological risk factors.
- GIS software has made it possible for political scientists to evaluate existing legislative districts using criteria such as compactness and contiguity and to suggest ways the boundaries of the districts might be redrawn.
- Sociologists have used GIS to identify clusters of segregation and to examine the changing structures of segregation over time.

Many companies in the private sector also use computerized mapmaking systems. Among others, oil and gas companies, restaurant chains, soft-drink bottlers, and car rental companies rely on GIS systems to perform such diverse tasks as identifying drilling sites, picking locations for new franchises, analyzing sales territories, and calculating optimal driving routes.

Many bureaus and agencies at the local, regional, state, and national levels of government employ geographic information systems. These include such departments as highway and traffic control, public utilities, and planning. Law enforcement agencies use spatially based software packages to analyze patterns of crime, identify "hot spots" of criminal activity, and redeploy police resources accordingly.

Government officials also use GIS to help plan emergency response to natural and human-induced disasters, such as tornadoes, hurricanes, earthquakes, floods, and wildfires. Because disasters usually occur suddenly, threatening people and structures, they create chaos and panic. Increasingly, GIS technology is being used to help communities prepare for disasters and create response plans. By merging information on the types of roads, the locations of fire stations, the anticipated response times of fire and rescue squads, and other data, for example, planners can produce maps depicting evacuation zones, evacuation routes, and shelter locations. When disaster strikes, whether it is a wildfire in Arizona or a tornado in Oklahoma, maps produced using GIS have proved invaluable in tasks such as locating houses, identifying property ownership, helping responders decide where to send field crews or rescue workers, and siting field hospitals and paramedic bases. In the wake of a disaster, maps have been used to locate damaged structures, assess property damage, and prepare for debris removal.

One of the most dramatic examples of GIS applications occurred in the days immediately following the attacks on the World Trade Center on September 11, 2001. Response and recovery teams needed to know such things as the stability of the rubble and the remaining buildings, which subway lines were damaged, where watermains were located, and where there were utility outages. With fires still burning at the site of the attack, and the mayor's planning office destroyed, GIS experts immediately began gathering the data needed to provide highly accurate maps of the site. The maps, continually updated, helped emergency managers track the expansion or abatement of the underground fires and enabled them to determine how rescue equipment could gain access to the site, where to safely position large recovery equipment, and by what route debris could be removed (Figure 2.26).

FIGURE 2.26 A three-dimensional lidar image of the site of the World Trade Center. Accurately mapping the wreckage of the World Trade Center using a combination of remote sensing, GPS, and GIS was invaluable in recovery and cleanup efforts after the attacks of 9/11. The GPS system was used to position both ground and airborne mapping sensors. Aircraft outfitted with three kinds of sensors collected high-resolution aerial photography, thermal imagery, and lidar (light detection and ranging) data. Within hours after the data were collected, GIS professionals from government, industry, and academia merged the digital data to produce large, high-resolution images of the building structures and the surrounding area. The three-dimensional models created by the lidar system enabled engineers to calculate the volume of the rubble piles, track their movement and change, and determine the reach needed by cranes to remove it. *NOAA/U.S. Army JPSD.*

The career opportunities for people skilled in GIS techniques are excellent. A variety of private industries, including insurance, marketing, real estate, epidemiology, health care, environmental resource management, transportation, homeland security, disaster preparedness and response, use geospatial information technologies. GIS professionals are also widely employed by federal, state, and local government departments that deal with regional and community planning and such services as water, police, fire, sewer, transportation, health, education, and welfare.

Summary of Key Concepts

- Maps are as indispensable to the geographer as are words, photographs, and quantitative techniques of analysis. Also relying on maps are people involved in the analysis and solution of many of the critical issues of our time, such as climate change, pollution, national security, and public health—all issues that call for the accurate representation of elements on the earth's surface.
- The geographic grid of longitude and latitude is used to locate points on the earth's surface. Latitude is the measure of distance north and south of the equator, while longitude is the angular distance east or west of the prime meridian.
- All systems of representing the curved earth on a flat map distort one or more earth features. Any given projection will distort area, shape, distance, and/or direction.
- Among the most accurate and most useful large-scale maps are the topographic quadrangles produced by a country's chief mapping agency. They contain a wealth of information about both the physical and the cultural landscape and are used for a variety of purposes.
- Remote sensing from aircraft and satellites employing a variety of sensors is an important source of spatial data. The need to store, process, and retrieve the vast amounts of data generated by remote sensing has spurred the development of geographic information systems, which provide a way to search for spatial patterns and processes.

As you read the remainder of this book, note the many different uses of maps. For example, notice in Chapter 3 how important maps are to your understanding of the theory of continental drift; in Chapter 7, how maps aid geographers in identifying cultural regions; and in Chapter 8, how behavioral geographers use maps to record people's perceptions of space.

Key Words

area cartogram (value-by-area map) 34
azimuthal projection 28
cartography 21
choropleth map 34
conformal projection 25
contour interval 32
contour line 32
equal-area (equivalent) projection 25
equidistant projection 25

flow-line map 35
geographic database 45
geographic grid 22
geographic information system (GIS) 44
Global Positioning System (GPS) 40
globe properties 25
International Date Line 23
isoline 35

Landsat satellite 40
latitude 22
longitude 23
map projection 25
prime meridian 23
remote sensing 38
scale 28
topographic map 29

Thinking Geographically

1. What important map and globe reference purpose does the *prime meridian* serve? Is the prime, or any other, meridian determined in nature or devised by humans? How is the prime meridian designated or recognized?

2. What happens to the length of a degree of longitude as one nears the North and South Poles? What happens to a degree of latitude between the equator and the poles?

3. From a world atlas, determine, in degrees and minutes, the locations of New York City; Moscow, Russia; Sydney, Australia; and your hometown.

4. List at least five globe properties.

5. Briefly make clear the differences in properties and purposes of *conformal, equivalent,* and *equidistant* projections.

Give one or two examples of the kinds of map information that would best be presented on each type of projection.

6. Give one or two examples of how maps can be misused.

7. In what different ways can *map scale* be presented? Convert the following map scales into their verbal equivalents.

   1:1,000,000   1:63,360   1:12,000

8. What is the purpose of a *contour line?* What is a *contour interval?* What landscape feature is implied by closely spaced contours?

9. What kinds of data acquisition are suggested by the term *remote sensing?* To what uses are remotely sensed images put?

10. What are the basic components of a *geographic information system?* What are some of the applications of GIS?

PART
ONE

The Earth Science Tradition

For nearly a month the mountain had rumbled, emitting puffs of steam and flashes of fire. Within the past week, on its slopes and near its base, deaths had been recorded from floods, mud slides, and falling rock. A little after 8:00 in the morning of May 8, 1902, the climax came for volcanic Mount Pelée and the thriving port of Saint Pierre on the island of Martinique. To the roar of one of the biggest explosions the world has ever known and to the clanging of church bells aroused in swaying steeples, a fireball of gargantuan size burst forth from the upper slope of the volcano. Lava, ash, steam, and superheated air engulfed the town, and 29,933 people met their death.

More selective, but for those victimized just as deadly, was the sudden "change in weather" that struck central Illinois on December 20, 1836. Within an hour, preceded by winds gusting to 70 miles per hour, the temperature plunged from 40°F to −30°F. On a walk to the post office through slushy snow, Mr. Lathrop of Jacksonville, Illinois, found, just as he passed the Female Academy, that "the cold wave struck me, and as I drew my feet up the ice would form on my boots until I made a track . . . more like that of [an elephant] than a No. 7 boot." Two young salesmen were found frozen to death along with their horses; one "was partly in a kneeling position, with a tinderbox in one hand, a flint in the other, with both eyes open as though attempting to light the tinder in the box." Others died, too—inside of horses that had been disemboweled and used as makeshift shelters, in fields, woods, and on roads both a short distance and an eternity from the travelers' destinations.

Fortunately, few human environmental encounters are as tragic as these. Rather, the physical world in all its spatial variation provides the constant and generally passive background against which the human drama is played. It is to that background that physical geographers, acting within the earth science tradition of the discipline, direct their attention. Their primary concern is with the natural rather than the cultural landscape and with the interplay between the encompassing physical world and the activities of humans.

The interest of those working within the earth science tradition of geography, therefore, is not necessarily in the physical sciences as an end in themselves but in physical processes as they create landscapes and environments of significance to humankind. The objective is not solely to trace the physical and chemical reactions that have produced a piece of igneous rock or to describe how a glacier has scoured the rock; it is the relationship of the rock to people. Geographers are interested in what the rock can tell us about the evolution of the earth as our home or in the significance of certain types of rock for the distribution of mineral resources and fertile soil.

The questions that physical geographers ask do not usually deal with the catastrophic, though catastrophe is an occasional element of human–earth-surface relationships. Rather, they ask questions that go to the root of understanding the earth as the home and the workplace of humankind. What does the earth as our home look like? How have its components been formed? How are they changing, and what changes are likely to occur in the future through natural or human causes? How are environmental features related to past, present, and prospective human use of the earth? These are some of the basic questions that geographers who follow the earth science tradition attempt to answer.

The three chapters in Part One of our review of geography deal, in turn, with landforms, weather and climate, and natural resources. Although the subject matter of each clearly identifies it with the fundamental earth science background of the discipline, a brief word about the content and purpose of each chapter is appropriate.

The treatment of so vast a field as landforms (Chapter 3) must be highly selective within an introductory text. The aim here is simply to summarize the great processes by which landforms are created and to depict the general classes of features resulting from those processes without becoming overly involved in scientific reasoning and technical terms.

In Chapter 4, "Physical Geography: Weather and Climate," the major elements of the atmosphere—temperature, precipitation, and air pressure—are discussed, and their regional generalities and associations in patterns of world climates are presented. The study of weather and climate adds coherence to our understanding of the earth as the home of people. Frequent reference will be made to the climatic background of human activities in later sections of our study.

Part One concludes with Chapter 5, "The Geography of Natural Resources." Here, we first explore the renewable and nonrenewable energy and nonfuel mineral resources that are the bases of today's diversified industrial and service economies. Later in the chapter, we discuss the land resources supporting all human life and activity and review the strategies of resource management to achieve environmentally sustainable economies.

The focus of Part One, therefore, is on the earth as the environment and habitat of humans. Both the diversity and reciprocal nature of human-environmental interactions are recurring themes not only of the following three chapters but in all geographic inquiry.

Opposite page: Lake Josephine with the Grinnell Glacier in the distant background, Glacier National Park, Montana. © *PictureQuest RF.*

CHAPTER THREE

Physical Geography: Landforms

CHAPTER OUTLINE

Mt. Moran as seen from Oxbow Bend, Grand Teton National Park, Wyoming. © *Corbis RF.*

Although too early for sunbathers and snorkelers, the Hawaiian Islands will have a new island to add to their collection, which contains such scenic beauties as Oahu, Maui, and Kauai. It is Loihi, 0.8 kilometer (0.5 mi) below sea level, just 27 kilometers (17 mi) from the big island of Hawaii. Because the speed of its ascent must be measured in geologic time, it probably will not appear above the water surface for another million or so years. It is a good example, however, of the ceaseless changes that take place on the earth's surface. As the westernmost of the islands erode and sink below sea level, new islands arise at the eastern end. In Loihi's most recent explosion in 1996, scientists feared that a giant wave would be set off at the surface that could devastate the islands, including the city of Honolulu and popular Waikiki Beach. Fortunately, this was not the case.

Humans on their trip through life continuously are in touch with the ever-changing, active, moving physical environment. Most of the time, we are able to live comfortably with the changes, but when a freeway is torn apart by an earthquake, or floodwaters force us to abandon our homes, we suddenly realize that we spend a good portion of our lives trying to adapt to the challenges the physical environment has for us.

For the geographer, things just will not stand still—not only little things, such as icebergs or new islands rising out of the sea, or big ones, such as exploding volcanoes changing their shape and form, but also monstrous things, such as continents that wander about like nomads and ocean basins that expand, contract, and split in the middle like worn-out coats.

Geologic time is long, but the forces that give shape to the land are timeless and constant. Processes of creation and destruction are continually at work to fashion the seemingly eternal structure upon which humans live and work. Two types of forces interact to produce those infinite local variations in the surface of the earth called *landforms:* (1) forces that push, move, and raise the earth's surface and (2) forces that scour, wash, and wear down the surface. Mountains rise and are then worn away. The eroded materials—soil, sand, pebbles, rocks— are transported to new locations and help create new landforms. How long these processes have worked, how they work, and their effects are the subject of this chapter.

Much of the research needed to create the story of landforms results from the work of geomorphologists. A branch of the fields of geology and physical geography, *geomorphology* is the study of the origin, characteristics, and development of landforms. It emphasizes the study of the various processes that create landscapes. Geomorphologists examine the erosion, transportation, and deposition of materials and the interrelationships among climate, soils, plant and animal life, and landforms.

In a single chapter, we can only begin to explore the many and varied contributions of geomorphologists. After discussing the contexts within which landform change takes place, we consider the forces that are building up the earth's surface and then review the forces wearing it down.

EARTH MATERIALS

The rocks of the earth's crust vary according to mineral composition. Rocks are composed of particles that contain various combinations of such common elements as oxygen, silicon, aluminum, iron, and calcium, together with less abundant elements. A particular chemical combination that has a hardness, density, and definite crystal structure of its own is called a **mineral.** Some well-known minerals are quartz, feldspar, and micas. Depending on the nature of the minerals that form them, rocks are hard or soft, more or less dense, one color or another, or chemically stable or not. While some rocks resist decomposition, others are very easily broken down. Among the more common varieties of rock are granites, basalts, limestones, sandstones, and slates.

Although one can classify rocks according to their physical properties, the more common approach is to classify them by the way they formed. The three main groups of rock are igneous, sedimentary, and metamorphic.

Igneous Rocks

Igneous rocks are formed by the cooling and solidification of molten rock. Openings in the crust give molten rock an opportunity to find its way into or onto the crust. When the molten rock cools, it solidifies and becomes igneous rock. The name for underground molten rock is *magma;* above ground, it is *lava. Intrusive* igneous rocks are formed below ground level by the solidification of magma, whereas *extrusive* igneous rocks are created above ground level by the solidification of lava (Figure 3.1).

The composition of magma and lava and, to a limited extent, the rate of cooling determine the minerals that form. The rate of cooling is mainly responsible for the size of the crystals. Large crystals of quartz—a hard mineral—form slowly beneath the surface of the earth. When combined with other minerals, quartz forms the intrusive igneous rock called *granite.*

The lava that oozes out onto the earth's surface and makes up a large part of the ocean basins becomes the extrusive igneous rock called *basalt,* the most common rock on the earth's surface. If, instead of oozing, the lava erupts from a volcano crater, it may cool very rapidly. Some of the igneous rocks formed in this manner contain cavities and are light, such as *pumice.* Some may be glassy, as is *obsidian.* The glassiness occurs when lava meets standing water and cools suddenly.

Sedimentary Rocks

Some **sedimentary rocks** are composed of particles of gravel, sand, silt, and clay that were eroded from already existing rocks. Surface waters carry the sediment to oceans, marshes, lakes, or tidal basins. Compression of these

(a) Basalt (igneous)

(b) Limestone (sedimentary)

(c) Shale (sedimentary)

(d) Gneiss (metamorphic)

FIGURE 3.1 Various rock types. *(a) © The McGraw-Hill Companies, Inc./Photo by Bob Coyle; (b) Photo by I. J. Witkind, USGS Photo Library; (c) The McGraw-Hill Companies, Inc./Photo by Bob Coyle; (d) The McGraw-Hill Companies, Inc./Photo by Jacques Cornell.*

materials by the weight of additional deposits on top of them and a cementing process brought on by the chemical action of water and certain minerals cause sedimentary rock to form.

Sedimentary rocks evolve under water in horizontal beds called *strata* (Figure 3.2). Usually one type of sediment collects in a given area. If the particles are large and rounded—for instance, the size and shape of gravel—a gravelly rock called *conglomerate* forms. Sand particles are the ingredient for *sandstone,* whereas silt and clay form *shale* or *siltstone.*

Sedimentary rocks also derive from organic material, such as coral, shells, and marine skeletons. These materials settle into beds in shallow seas, forming *limestone.* If the organic material forms mainly from decomposing vegetation, it can develop into a sedimentary rock called *bituminous coal. Petroleum* is also a biological product, formed during the millions of years of burial by chemical reactions that transform some of the organic material into liquid and gaseous compounds. The oil and gas are light; therefore, they rise through the pores of the surrounding rock to places where low-permeability rocks such as shale block their upward movement. Sedimentary rocks vary considerably in color (from coal black to chalk white), hardness, density, and resistance to chemical decomposition.

Large parts of the continents contain sedimentary rocks. For example, nearly the entire eastern half of the United States is overlain with these rocks. Such formations indicate that, in the geologic past, seas covered even larger proportions of the earth than they do today.

Metamorphic Rocks

Metamorphic rocks are formed from igneous and sedimentary rocks by earth forces that generate heat, pressure, or chemical reaction. The word *metamorphic* means "changed shape." The internal earth forces may be so great that heat and pressure change the mineral structure of a rock, forming new rocks. For example, under great pressure, shale, a sedimentary rock, becomes *slate,* a rock with different properties. Limestone, under certain conditions, may become *marble,* and granite may become *gneiss* (pronounced nice). Materials metamorphosed at great depths and exposed only after overlying surfaces have been slowly eroded away are among the oldest rocks known on Earth. Like igneous and sedimentary rocks, however, their formation is a continuing process.

Rocks are the constituent ingredients of most landforms. The strength or weakness, permeability, and mineral content control the way rocks respond to the forces that shape and reshape them. Two principal processes alter rocks: (1) the forces that tend to build landforms up and (2) the gradational processes that wear landforms down. All rocks are part of the *rock cycle* through which old rocks are continually transformed into new ones by these processes. No

FIGURE 3.2 The sedimentary rocks of the Grand Canyon in Arizona are evident in this photograph. © *Digital Vision RF.*

a) Cementation and compaction (lithification)
b) Heat and pressure
c) Weathering, transportation, deposition
d) Cooling and solidification

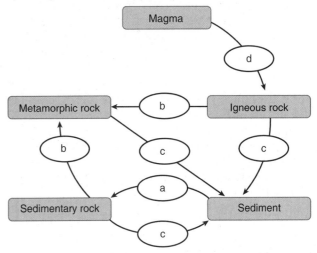

FIGURE 3.3 The rock cycle. *Source: Adapted from McConnell et al., The Good Earth, p. 209, Checkpoint 7.22, © McGraw-Hill, 2008.*

rocks have been preserved unaltered throughout the earth's history. Figure 3.3 shows the rock cycle and the processes that shaped it.

GEOLOGIC TIME

The earth was formed about 4.5 billion years ago. When we think of a person who lives to be 100 years old as having had a long life, it becomes clear that the earth is incredibly old indeed. Because our usual concept of time is dwarfed when we speak of billions of years, it is useful to compare the age of the earth with something more familiar.

Imagine that the height of the Sears Tower in Chicago represents the age of the earth. The tower is 110 stories, or 412 meters (1447 ft), tall. In relative terms, even the thickness of a piece of paper laid on the rooftop would be too great to represent an average person's lifetime. Of the total building height, only 4.8 stories represent the 200 million years that have elapsed since the present ocean floors began to form.

At this moment, the landforms on which we live are ever so slightly being created and destroyed. The processes involved have been in operation for so long that any given location most likely was the site of ocean and land at a number of different times in its past. Many of the landscape features on Earth today can be traced back millions of years. The processes responsible for building up and tearing down those features are occurring simultaneously, but usually at different rates.

Since the 1960s, scientists have developed a useful framework within which one can best study our constantly changing physical environment. Their work is based on the early 20th-century geologic studies of Alfred Wegener, who proposed the theory of **continental drift.** He believed that all landmasses were once united in one supercontinent, which Wegener named Pangaea ("all Earth"), and that over many

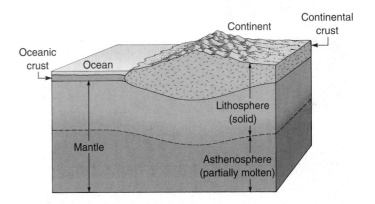

FIGURE 3.4 The outer zones of the earth (not to scale). The *lithosphere* includes the crust. The *asthenosphere* lies below the lithosphere.

millions of years the continents broke away from each other, slowly drifting to their current positions. Although Wegener's theory was initially rejected outright, new evidence and new ways of rethinking old knowledge have led to wide acceptance in recent years by earth scientists of the idea of moving continents. Wegener's ideas were a forerunner of the broader **plate tectonics** theory, which is explained in the next section, "Movements of the Continents."

MOVEMENTS OF THE CONTINENTS

The landforms mapped by cartographers are only the surface features of a thin cover of rock, the earth's *crust* (Figure 3.4). Above the earth's interior is a partially molten layer called the

asthenosphere. It supports a thin but strong solid shell of rocks called the **lithosphere,** of which the outer, lighter portion is the earth's crust. The crust consists of one set of rocks found below the oceans and another set that makes up the continents.

The lithosphere is broken into about 12 large and many small, rigid plates, each of which, according to the theory of plate tectonics, slides or drifts very slowly over the heavy, semimolten asthenosphere. A single plate often contains both oceanic and continental crust. Figure 3.6a shows that the North American plate, for example, contains the northwest Atlantic Ocean and most, but not all, of North America. The peninsula of Mexico (Baja California) and part of California are on the Pacific plate.

Scientists are not certain why lithospheric plates move. One reasonable theory suggests that heat and heated material from the earth's interior rise by convection into particular crustal zones of weakness. These zones are sources for the divergence of the plates. The cooled materials then sink downward in subduction zones. In this way, the plates are thought to be set in motion. Strong evidence indicates that, about 225 million years ago, the entire continental crust was connected in one supercontinent, which was broken into plates as the seafloor began to spread. The divergence came from the widening of what is now the Atlantic Ocean. Figure 3.5 shows four stages of the drifting of the continents.

Materials from the asthenosphere have been rising along the mid-Atlantic Ocean fracture and, as a result, the seafloor has continued to spread. The Atlantic Ocean is now 6920 kilometers (4300 mi) wide at the equator. If it diverges by a bit less than 2.5 centimeters (1 in.) per year, as scientists have estimated, one could calculate that the separation of the

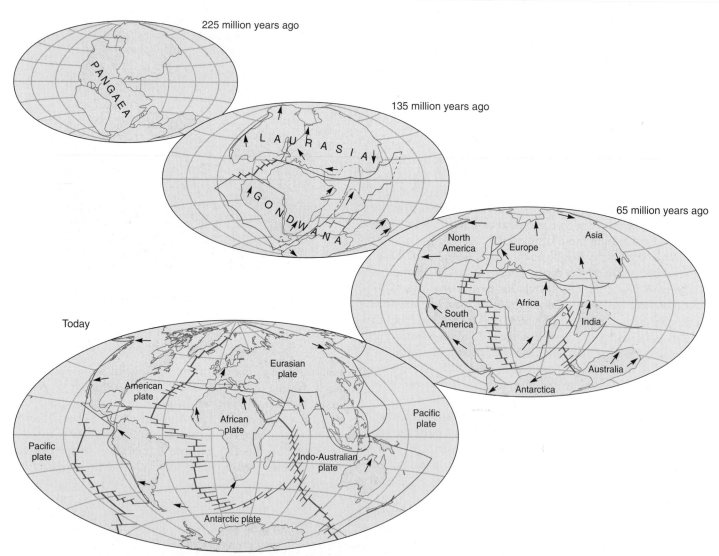

FIGURE 3.5 Reconstruction of plate movements during the past 225 million years. The northern and southern portions of Pangaea are called Laurasia and Gondwana, respectively. Some 225 million years ago, the continents were connected as one large landmass. After they split apart, the continents gradually moved to their present positions. Notice how India broke away from Antarctica and collided with the Eurasian landmass. The Himalayas were formed at the zone of contact. *Source: American Petroleum Institute.*

continents did, in fact, begin about 225 million years ago. Notice on Figures 3.6a and 3.7 how the ridge line that makes up the axis of the ocean runs parallel to the eastern coast of North and South America and the western coast of Europe and Africa.

Boundaries where plates move away from each other are called *divergent plate boundaries. Transform boundaries* occur where one plate slides horizontally past another plate, whereas at *convergent boundaries* two plates move toward each other (Figure 3.6b). Collisions sometimes occur as the lithospheric plates move. The pressure exerted at the intersections of plates can cause earthquakes, which over periods of many years change the shape and features of landforms. Figure 3.8 shows the location of near-surface earthquakes for a recent time period. Comparison with Figure 3.6a illustrates that the

areas of greatest earthquake activity are at plate boundaries. An example of this is the Haitian earthquake of January 12, 2010, (see p. 2 in Chapter 1). The capital city of Haiti, Port-au-Prince, lies close to the boundary between the Caribbean and North American plates.

The famous San Andreas fault in California is part of a long fracture separating two lithospheric plates, the North American and the Pacific. Earthquakes occur along **faults** (fractures in rock along which there has been movement) when the tension or compression at the junction becomes so great that only an earth movement can release the pressure.

Despite the availability of scientific knowledge about earthquake zones, the general disregard for this danger is a difficult cultural phenomenon with which to deal (see the

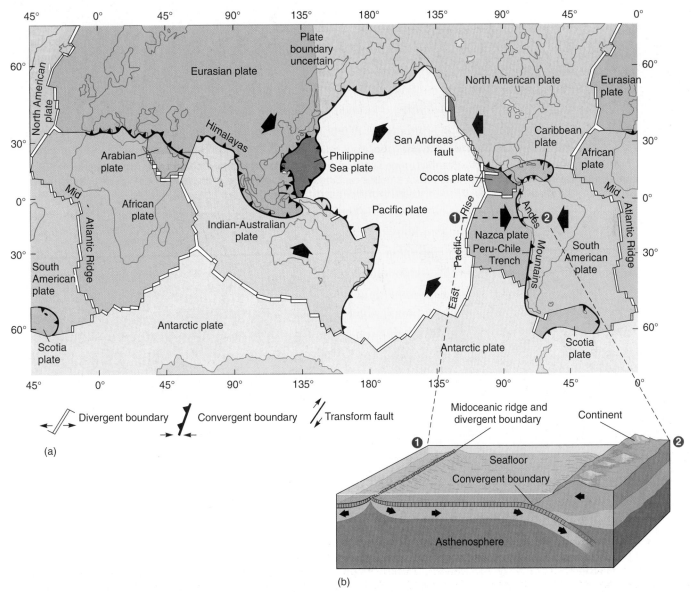

FIGURE 3.6 (a) Principal lithospheric plates of the world. Arrows indicate the direction of plate motion. **(b) Plate motion away from a divergent boundary toward a convergent boundary.**

FIGURE 3.7 An accurate map of the North Atlantic Ocean seafloor created by the National Oceanic and Atmospheric Administration using gravity measurements taken from satellite readings. The configuration of the seafloor is evidence of the dynamic processes shaping continents and ocean basins. Darker ocean colors indicate greater depth. © David T. Sandwell, 1995. Scripps Institution of Oceanography.

circum–Pacific Belt

▲ Young volcano
• Earthquake epicenter

FIGURE 3.8 Locations of young volcanoes and the epicenters of earthquakes. Notice that they are concentrated at the margins of the lithospheric plates, as comparison with Figure 3.5 reveals. The most important concentration of earthquakes is in the circum-Pacific belt, which encircles the rim of the Pacific Ocean and is popularly known as the "ring of fire." Volcanoes can also grow in the middle of a plate. The volcanoes of Hawaii, for example, are located in the middle of the Pacific plate. Map plotted by the Environmental Data and Information Service of NOAA; Earthquakes from U.S. Coast and Geodetic Survey.

section on diastrophism). Every year there are hundreds and sometimes thousands of casualties resulting from inadequate preparation for earthquakes. In some highly populated areas, the chances that damaging earthquakes will occur are very great. The distribution of earthquakes shown in Figure 3.8 reveals the potential dangers to densely settled areas of Japan, the Philippines, parts of Southeast Asia, and the western rim of the Americas.

Convergent movement of the lithospheric plates results in the formation of deep-sea trenches and continental-scale mountain ranges, as well as in the occurrence of earthquakes. The continental crust is made up of lighter rocks than is the oceanic crust. Where plates with different types of crust at their edges converge, there is a tendency for the denser but thinner oceanic crust to be forced down into the asthenosphere. Deep trenches form below the ocean at these convergent boundaries. This type of collision is termed **subduction** (Figure 3.9). The subduction zones of the world are shown in Figure 3.6a.

Most of the Pacific Ocean is underlain by a plate that, like the others, is constantly pushing and being pushed. The continental crust on adjacent plates is being forced to rise and fracture, making an active volcano zone of the Pacific Ocean rim (sometimes called the "ring of fire"). The tremendous explosion that rocked Mount St. Helens in the state of Washington in 1980 is an example of continuing volcanic activity along the Pacific rim. A number of damaging earthquakes have occurred along the San Andreas fault in recent years. Their epicenter (the point on the earth's surface directly above the focus of an earthquake) was on the fault. The most recent strong earthquake, in December 2003, did considerable damage to the city of Paso Robles, California.

Plate intersections are not the only locations susceptible to readjustments in the lithosphere. As lithospheric plates have moved, the earth's crust has been cracked or broken in virtually thousands of places. Some breaks are weakened to the point that they become *hot spots,* areas of volcanic eruption due to a rising plume of molten material. The molten material may explode out of a volcano or ooze out of cracks. Later in this chapter, when we discuss the earth-building forces, we will return to the discussion of volcanic activity.

TECTONIC FORCES

The earth's crust is altered by the constant forces resulting from plate movement. *Tectonic* (generated from within the earth) forces shaping and reshaping the earth's crust are of two types, either diastrophic or volcanic. **Diastrophism** is the great pressure acting on the plates that deforms them by folding, twisting, warping, breaking, or compressing rock. **Volcanism** is the force that transports heated material to or toward the surface of the earth. When particular places on the continents are subject to diastrophism or volcanism, the changes that take place can be as simple as the bending and cracking of rock or as dramatic as lava exploding from the crater and sides of Mount St. Helens.

Diastrophism

In the process of plate tectonics, pressures build in various parts of the earth's crust, and slowly, usually over thousands of years, the crust is transformed (see "Mount Everest: The Jewel in the Crown," p. 58). By studying rock formations, geologists are able to trace the history of the development of a region. Over geologic time, most continental areas have been subjected to both tectonic and gradational activity—building up and tearing down. They usually have a complex history of broad warping, folding, faulting, and leveling. Some flat plains in existence today may hide a history of great mountain development in the past.

Broad Warping

Great tectonic forces resulting from the movement of continents may bow an entire continent. Also, the changing weight of a large region may result in the **warping** of the surface. For example, the down-warping of the eastern United States is evident in the many irregularly shaped stream estuaries. As the coastal area warped downward, the sea advanced, forming estuaries and underwater canyons.

Folding

When the compressional pressure caused by plate movements is great, layers of rock are forced to buckle. The result may be a warping or bending effect, and a ridge or series of parallel **folds** may develop. Figure 3.10 shows a variety of structures

FIGURE 3.9 The process of subduction. When lithospheric plates collide, the denser oceanic crust is usually forced beneath the lighter continental material. See Figure 3.6a for the subduction zones of the world.

FIGURE 3.10 Stylized forms of folding. Degrees of folding vary from slight undulations of strata with little departure from the horizontal to highly compressed or overturned beds.

Mount Everest: The Jewel in the Crown

The fastest growing mountain range on Earth happens also to contain the world's tallest set of mountains. Nearly in the center of the Himalayas stands the world's highest peak, Mount Everest. Currently, Mount Everest is measured as standing 8844 meters (29,010 ft) above sea level. Recent measurements, however, indicate that Mount Everest and many of the other peaks, such as K-2, are growing at about 1 centimeter (1/2 in.) a year.

As the mountains build ever higher, their great weight softens underlying materials, causing the mountains to settle. In other words, there are two forces at work. The force building the mountains is that of the Indian plate moving northward, crashing into the Eurasian plate. The Himalayas, at the edge of the Eurasian plate, react to the great force by pushing higher and higher. But apparently a second force that works against the first keeps mountains on Earth from rising to heights of 15,000 to 18,000 meters (roughly 50,000 to 60,000 ft). One may think of these great mountains as being in a kind of equilibrium—the bigger they get, the heavier they get, and the more likely they are to sag.

The battle between the two plates began about 45 million years ago. Usually, one plate is forced under the more stationary plate (subduction). In this case, however, the rocks of the two plates are similar in weight and density. Thus, subduction has not taken place, and what normally would have been a modest crinkle on the earth's surface turned into the tallest, most rugged mountain range on Earth. Particularly interesting is one view of the Himalayas. The Indian plate contains the relatively low-elevation Indian subcontinent and, as a result, the view of the Himalayas from the plains of northern India is one of the great sights on Earth. No wonder Mount Everest is the jewel in the mountain climber's crown. Edmund Hillary and Tenzing Norgay were the first to reach the summit, in 1953. Since then, more than 1500 climbers have reached the top, most of them since 1990; 176 have died attempting to scale Mount Everest.

© Corbis RF.

resulting from folding. The folds can be thrust upward many thousands of feet and laterally for many miles. The Ridge and Valley region of the eastern United States is, at present, low parallel mountains—300 to 900 meters (1000 to 3000 ft) above sea level—but the rock evidence suggests that the tops of the present mountains were once the valleys between 9100-meter (30,000-ft) crests (Figure 3.11).

Faulting

A fault is a break or fracture in rock along which movement has taken place. The stress causing a fault results in displacement of the earth's crust along the fracture zone. Figure 3.12 diagramatically shows examples of fault types. There may be uplift on one side of the fault or downthrust on the other. In some cases, a steep slope known as a fault *escarpment,* which may be several hundred feet high and several hundred miles long, is formed. The stress can push one side up and over the other side, or a separation away from the fault may cause the sinking of land, creating a *rift valley* (Figure 3.13).

Many fractures are merely cracks (called *joints*) with little noticeable movement along them. In other cases, however, mountains such as the Sierra Nevadas of California have risen

FIGURE 3.11 **(a) The Ridge and Valley region of Pennsylvania,** now eroded to hill lands, is the relic of 9100-meter (30,000-ft) folds that were reduced to form *synclinal* (downarched) hills and *anticlinal* (uparched) valleys. The rock in the original troughs, having been compressed, was less susceptible to erosion. **(b) A syncline in Maryland on the border of Pennsylvania, exposed by a road cut.**

(b) © Mark C. Burnett/Photo Researchers.

FIGURE 3.12 **Faults,** in their great variation, are common features of mountain belts where deformation is great. The different forms of faulting are categorized by the direction of movement along the plane of fracture. The features shown here would not occur in a single setting.

as the result of faulting. Sometimes, the movement has been horizontal along the surface rather than upward or downward. The San Andreas transform fault, shown in Figures 3.14 and 3.15, is such a case.

Whenever movement occurs along a fault, or at another point of weakness, an earthquake results. The greater the movement, the greater the magnitude of the earthquake (see "Scaling Earthquakes," p. 63). Stress builds in rock as tectonic

forces are applied and, when a critical point is finally reached, an earthquake occurs and tension is reduced.

The earthquake that occurred in Alaska on Good Friday in 1964 was one of the strongest measured, with a magnitude of 9.2 on the Richter scale. Although the stress point of that earthquake was below ground 121 kilometers (75 mi) away from Anchorage, vibrations called *seismic waves* caused earth movement in the weak clays underneath the city. Sections

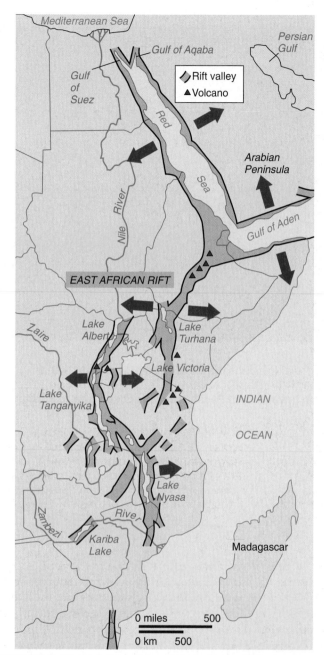

FIGURE 3.13 The rift valleys of East Africa. Great fractures in the earth's crust resulted in the creation, through subsidence, of an extensive rift valley system (see Figure 3.12) in East Africa. The parallel faults, some reaching more than 610 meters (2000 ft) below sea level, are bordered by steep walls of the adjacent plateau, which rises to 1500 meters (5000 ft) above sea level and from which the structure dropped.

of Anchorage slid downhill, and part of the business district dropped 3 meters (10 ft).

If an earthquake, a volcanic eruption, or an underwater landslide occurs below an ocean, jolting the waters above, the movement can generate sea waves called **tsunami** (from the Japanese *tsu,* for "harbor," and *nami,* for "wave,") (see "Tsunami," p. 65). Traveling at great speed in the open ocean, the waves may be hardly noticeable, resembling a fast-moving

tide—the reason they often are mistakenly referred to as "tidal waves" in spite of the fact that they are unrelated to tides. As the waves near shore and enter shallower water, however, friction with the ocean floor causes the waves to slow down, producing a buildup of water that can reach 15 meters (50 ft) or more above sea level. The water sweeps inland with massive force once it hits the shore, particularly when the narrowed topography of harbors and inlets focuses the waves into smaller spaces.

Earthquakes occur daily in hundreds of places throughout the world. Most are slight and only noticeable on *seismographs,* instruments that record seismic waves. But from time to time, large-scale earthquakes occur, such as those in Iran in 2003 (35,000 deaths) and China in 1976 (242,000 deaths). Most earthquakes take place on the Pacific rim (see Figure 3.8), where stress from the converging lithospheric plates is greatest. The Aleutian Islands of Alaska, Japan, Central America, and Indonesia experience a number of moderately severe earthquakes each year. The Haitian earthquake did massive amounts of damage (Figure 3.16; also see p. 2 in Chapter 1). In recent years, major earthquakes and volcanic activity have also occurred in non-Pacific areas, such as Turkey, Iran, and Algeria.

The huge earthquake that struck Kashmir on October 8, 2005, was a reminder that the Himalayas are along the boundary of three tectonic plates, making countries all the way from Afghanistan and Pakistan in the west to Myanmar in the east subject to quakes. For further information on earthquakes and other earth processes go to usgs.gov.

Volcanism

The second tectonic force is volcanism. The most likely places through which molten materials can move toward the surface are at or near the intersections of plates. However, other zones, such as hot spots, are also subject to volcanic activity (Figure 3.17). The volcanoes of Hawaii, for example, formed above a relatively stationary hot spot in the earth's interior.

If sufficient internal pressure forces the magma upward, weaknesses in the crust, or faults, enable molten materials to reach the surface. The material ejected onto the earth's surface may arrive as a series of explosions, forming a steep-sided cone composed of alternate layers of solidified lava and ash and cinders, termed a *strato* or *composite volcano* (Figure 3.18a). The eruption may also be without explosions, forming a gently sloping *shield volcano* (Figure 3.18b).

The major volcanic belt of the world coincides with the major earthquake and fault zones. This belt occurs at the convergence of plates. A second zone of volcanic activity is at diverging plate boundaries, such as in the center of the Atlantic Ocean.

Molten material can either flow smoothly out of a crater or be shot into the air with explosive force. Some relatively quiet volcanoes have long, gentle slopes indicative of smooth flow, whereas explosive volcanoes have steep sides. Steam and gases are constantly escaping from the nearly 300 active volcanoes in the world today.

FIGURE 3.14 **The San Andreas fault system in California, with the epicenters of magnitude 6.0 and greater earthquakes of the 20th century.** *Source: Map updated from* "The San Andreas Fault System, California," *ed. By Robert E. Wallace, U.S. Geological Survey Professional Paper 1515, 1990.*

When pressure builds, a crater can become a boiling cauldron with steam, gas, lava, and ash billowing out (Figure 3.19). In the case of Mount St. Helens in 1980, a large bulge had formed on the north slope of the mountain. An earthquake occurred and an explosion followed, shooting debris into the air, completely devastating an area of about 400 square kilometers (150 sq mi), causing about 1 centimeter (0.4 in.) of ash to rain down on eastern Washington and parts of Idaho and Montana and reducing the elevation of the mountain by more than 300 meters (1000 ft).

In many cases, the pressure beneath the crust is not intense enough to allow magma to reach the surface. In these instances, magma solidifies into a variety of underground formations of igneous rock that on occasion affect surface landform features. However, gradational forces may erode overlying rock, so that igneous rock, which is usually hard and resists erosion, becomes a surface feature. The Palisades, a rocky ridge facing New York City from the west, and Stone Mountain, near Atlanta, Georgia, are this type of landform.

On other occasions, a rock formation below the earth's surface may allow the growth of a mass of magma but denies exit to the surface because of dense overlying rock. Through the pressure it exerts, however, the magmatic intrusion may still buckle, bubble, or break the surface rocks. In addition, domes of considerable size may develop, such as the Black Hills of South Dakota. A by-product of volcanic eruptions is the large amount of ash that spews into the atmosphere, sometimes affecting weather and climate patterns thousands of miles away.

Evidence from the past shows that lava has sometimes flowed through fissures or fractures without forming volcanoes. These oozing lava flows have covered ocean floors. On continents, the Deccan Plateau of India and the Columbia Plateau of the Pacific Northwest in the United States are examples of this type of process (Figure 3.20).

GRADATIONAL PROCESSES

Gradational processes are responsible for the reduction of land surface. If a land surface where a mountain once stood is now a low, flat plain, gradational processes have been at work. The worn, scraped, or blown away material is deposited in new

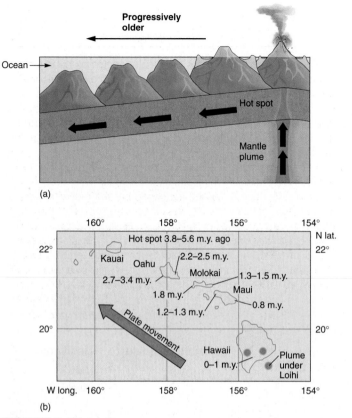

(a)

(b)

FIGURE 3.17 (a) Plumes, narrow columns of hot mantle rock, can form "hot spots" of volcanism on the earth's surface. Some plumes rise beneath the centers of oceanic plates rather than at their intersections. A plume under Hawaii rises in the middle of the Pacific plate. As the plate moved over the plume, a chain of volcanoes formed. Each was carried away from the hot spot as the Pacific plate moved northwestward. **(b) Ages of volcanic rock in the Hawaiian islands.** Note that the volcanoes become progressively older to the northwest. M.Y. means million years. The island of Hawaii contains two active volcanoes, shown by red dots.

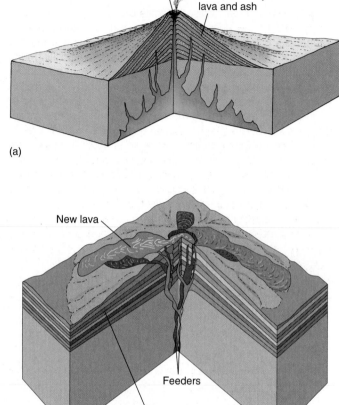

(a)

(b)

FIGURE 3.18 (a) Sudden decompression of gases contained within lavas results in explosions of rock material to form ashes and cinders. Composite volcanoes, such as the one diagrammed, are composed of alternate layers of solidified lava and of ash and cinders. **(b) Cutaway view of a shield volcano.** Composed of solidified lava flows, shield volcanoes are broad and gently sloping.

that occurs is called *hydrolysis.* When carbon dioxide gas from the atmosphere dissolves in water, a weak carbonic acid forms. The action of the acid, called *carbonation,* is particularly evident on limestone because the calcium bicarbonate salt created in the process readily dissolves and is removed by groundwater and surface water.

Weathering, either mechanical or chemical, does not itself create distinctive landforms. Nevertheless, it prepares rock particles for erosion and for the creation of soil. After the weathering process decomposes rock, the force of gravity and the erosional agents of running water, wind, and moving ice are able to carry the weathered material to new locations.

Mechanical and chemical weathering create *soil,* the thin layer of fine material containing organic matter, air, water, and weathered rock materials that rests on the solid rock below it. The type of soil formed is a function of the

climate of the region in which it occurs and of the kind of bedrock below it. Temperature and rainfall act on minerals, in conjunction with the decaying of overriding vegetation, to form soils. The topic of soils is discussed in more detail in Chapter 4.

Mass Movement

The force of gravity—that is, the attraction of the earth for bodies at or near its surface—is constantly pulling on all materials. The downslope movement of material due to gravity is called *mass wasting* or **mass movement.** Because it is more descriptive, this book uses the latter term. Small particles or huge boulders, if not held back by solid rock or other stable material, will fall down slopes. Spectacular acts of mass movement include avalanches and landslides. More widespread, but less noticeable, are mass movements such as soil-creep and the

Tsunami

The Indian Ocean tsunami of December 26, 2004, killed approximately 283,000 people and left some 1.5 million homeless. The effects were felt mainly along the coasts of Indonesia—the island of Sumatra, in particular—Thailand, Sri Lanka, India, and Somalia. The images of the city of Banda Aceh, at the north end of Sumatra, show the area several months before the tsunami struck and two days afterward.

Tsunami are generated by an underwater seismic disturbance: a submarine earthquake, eruption, or landslide. Water rushes in to fill the depression caused by the falling away of the ocean floor, then spreads out as swells in all directions. The initial waves travel very fast, at about the speed of a jet plane (640 kilometers or 440 miles per hour), but are not very high. As the waves approach land and the water becomes shallower, their speed decreases to about 48 kilometers (30 mi) per hour, but their height increases. The tsunami that struck Hilo, Hawaii, following the 1946 earthquake off the coast of Alaska were estimated to be 14 to 30 meters (45 to 100 ft) high. The water comes ashore with terrific force. One cubic yard of water weighs nearly a ton. Trees, automobiles, and pieces of roadway or buildings become lethal projectiles as the rushing water pushes inland, inundating low-lying areas along the shore.

The Indian Ocean tsunami resulted from a rare 9.2 magnitude earthquake (on the Richter scale) off the northwest coast of Sumatra. The quake occurred along a 1300-kilometer (800-mi) boundary between the Indian-Australian tectonic plate and the Eurasian plate, pushing the former some 20 meters (66 ft) beneath the latter.

In an attempt to minimize loss of life in Pacific coastal communities, the U.S. Coast and Geodetic Survey in 1948 established a tsunami early warning system based in Hawaii. Any major seismic disturbance in the Pacific region that is capable of generating tsunami is reported to the Tsunami Warning Center in Honolulu. If tsunami are detected, the center relays information about their source, speed, and estimated time of arrival to low-lying coastal communities in danger. Unfortunately, a similar warning system has not yet been established to detect tsunami in the Indian Ocean region.

2. Initial waves travel very fast, but are only a few feet in height.

3. Waves travel through shallower depths as they approach the coast.

4. Waves decrease in speed and increase in height.

5. Tsunami waves hit shores, depositing water and debris.

Sea level

1. Seismic event or displacement sends shock waves outward.

(a)

(b)

Satellite images of Banda Aceh on Sumatra **(a)** on June 23, 2004, and **(b)** two days after the tsunami of December 25. © *Digital Globe.*

(a)

(b)

(c)

FIGURE 3.19 (a) Mount St. Helens, Washington, before it erupted on May 18, 1980. (b) The eruption sent a cloud of steam and hot ash out of the cone 15 kilometers (9 mi) into the atmosphere, and a landslide carried ash and coarser debris down the slopes of the mountain. **(c)** The explosion blew away the top and much of one side of the volcano, lowering its summit by nearly 400 meters (1300 ft). *(a–c) U.S. Geological Survey.*

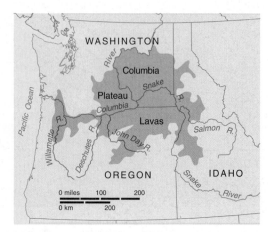

FIGURE 3.20 Fluid lavas created the Columbia Plateau, covering an area of 130,000 square kilometers (50,000 sq mi). Some individual flows were more than 100 meters (300 ft) thick and spread up to 60 kilometers (40 mi) from their original fissures. © *McGraw-Hill Companies, Inc.*

flow of mud down hillsides (Figure 3.21). In general, all non-rigid formations, such as water, ice, and wind, move downslope under the influence of gravity.

Especially in dry areas, a common but very dramatic landform created by the accumulation of rock particles at the base of hills and mountains is *talus*, pictured in Figure 3.21a. As pebbles, particles of rock, or even larger stones break away from exposed bedrock on a mountainside because of weathering, the masses fall and accumulate, producing large, conelike landforms. The larger rocks travel farther than the fine-grained sand particles, which remain near the top of the slope.

Erosional Agents and Deposition

Erosional agents, such as wind, water, and glaciers, carve already existing landforms into new shapes. Fast-moving agents carry debris, and slow-moving agents drop it. The material that has been worn, scraped, or blown away is deposited in new places, and new landforms are created. Each erosional agent is associated with a distinctive set of landforms.

Running Water

Running water is a powerful erosional agent. Water, whether flowing across land surfaces or in stream channels, plays an enormous role in wearing down and building up landforms.

Running water's ability to erode depends upon several factors: (1) the amount of precipitation; (2) the length and steepness of the slope; and (3) the kind of rock and vegetative cover. Steeper slopes and faster-flowing water results, of course, in more rapid erosion. Vegetative cover sometimes slows the flow of water. When this vegetation is reduced, perhaps because of farming or livestock grazing, erosion can be severe, as shown in Figure 3.22.

Even the impact of precipitation—heavy rain or hail—can cause erosion. After hard rain dislodges soil, the force of the rain causes the surface to become more compact; therefore, further precipitation fails to penetrate the soil. The result is that more water, prevented from seeping into the ground, becomes available for surface erosion. Soil and rock particles in the water are carried to streams, leaving behind gullies and small stream channels.

(a)

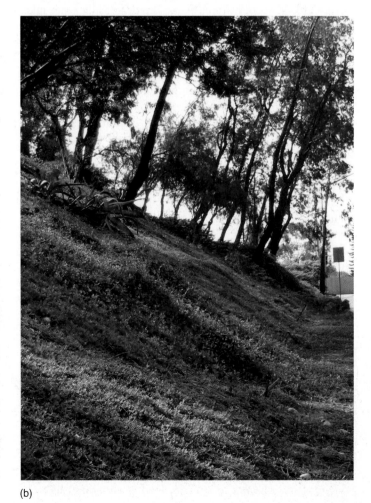

(b)

FIGURE 3.21 (a) Rockfall from this butte has created talus, an accumulation of broken rock at the base of a cliff. **(b)** Creeping soil has caused trees to tilt. *(a) © Robert N. Wallen; (b) Courtesy of Victoria Getis.*

FIGURE 3.22 **Gullying** can result from heavy rain and poor farming techniques, including overgrazing by livestock or many years of continuous row crops. Surface runoff removes topsoil easily when vegetation is too thin to protect it. *USDA-Natural Resources Conservation Service.*

FIGURE 3.23 **The delta of the Ganges River.** Notice the ongoing deposition of silt. © *Getty RF.*

Both the force of water and the particles contained in the stream are agents of erosion. Abrasion, or wearing away, takes place when particles strike against stream channel walls and along the streambed. Because of the force of the current, large particles, such as gravel, slide along the streambed, grinding rock on the way.

Floods and rapidly moving water are responsible for dramatic changes in channel size and configuration, sometimes forming new channels. In cities where paved surfaces cover soil that would otherwise have absorbed or held water, runoff is accentuated so that nearby rivers and streams rapidly increase in size and velocity after heavy rains. Oftentimes, flash floods and severe erosion result.

Small particles, such as clay and silt, are suspended in water and constitute—together with material dissolved in the water or dragged along the bottom—the *load* of a stream. Rapidly moving floodwaters carry huge loads. As high water or floodwater recedes, and stream velocity decreases, sediment contained within the stream no longer remains suspended, and particles begin to settle. Heavy, coarse materials drop the quickest; finer particles are carried longer and transported farther. The decline in velocity and the resulting deposition are especially pronounced and abrupt when streams meet slowly moving water in bays, oceans, and lakes. Silt and sand accumulate at the intersections, creating *deltas,* as pictured in Figure 3.23.

A great river, such as the Chang Jiang (Yangtze) in China, has a large, growing delta, but less prominent deltas exist at the mouths of many streams. Until the recent completion of the Aswan Dam, the huge delta of the Nile River had been growing. Now much of the silt is being dropped in Lake Nasser behind the dam.

In plains adjacent to streams, land is sometimes built up by the deposition of *stream load.* If the deposited material is rich, it may be a welcome and necessary part of farming activities, such as that historically known in Egypt along the Nile.

Should the deposition be composed of sterile sands and boulders, however, formerly fertile bottomland may be destroyed. By drowning crops or inundating inhabited areas, the floods themselves, of course, may cause great human and financial loss. More than 900,000 lives were lost in the floods of the Huang He (Yellow River) of China in 1887.

Stream Landscapes

A landscape is in a particular state of balance between the uplift of land and its erosion. Rapid uplift is not followed by nicely ordered stages of erosion. Recall that uplift and erosion take place simultaneously. At a given location, one force may be greater than the other at a given time, but as yet there is no way to predict accurately the "next" stage of landscape evolution.

Perhaps the most important factor differentiating the effect of streams on landforms is whether the recent climate (for example, the past several million years) has tended to be humid or arid.

Stream Landscapes in Humid Areas Perhaps weak surface material or a depression in rock allows the development of a stream channel. In its downhill run in mountainous regions, a stream may flow over precipices, forming *falls* in the process. The steep downhill gradient allows streams to flow rapidly, cutting narrow, V-shaped channels in the rock (Figure 3.24a). Under these conditions, the erosional process is greatly accelerated. Over time, the stream may have worn away sufficient rock for the falls to become rapids, and the stream channel becomes incised below the height of the surrounding landforms. This is evident in the upper reaches of the Delaware, Connecticut, and Tennessee rivers.

In humid areas, the effect of stream erosion is to round landforms. Streams flowing down moderate gradients tend to carve valleys that are wider than those in mountainous areas. Surrounding hills become rounded, and valleys eventually become **floodplains** as they broaden and flatten. Streams work to widen the floodplain. Their courses meander, constantly

FIGURE 3.25 Aerial view of damage caused by Hurricane Katrina the day after the hurricane hit, August 30, 2005. *FEMA—Federal Emergency Management Agency.*

carving out new river channels. The channels left behind as new ones are cut become *oxbow* lakes, hundreds of which are found in the Mississippi River floodplain. An oxbow lake is crescent-shaped and occupies the abandoned channel of a stream meander (Figure 3.24b).

In nearly flat floodplains, the highest elevations may be the banks of rivers, where *natural levees* are formed by the deposition of silt at river edges during floods. Floods that breach levees are particularly disastrous because floodwaters fill the floodplain as they equalize its elevation with that of the swollen river. The U.S. Army Corps of Engineers has augmented the natural levees in particularly susceptible areas, such as the banks of the lower Mississippi River, but some of these barriers failed during Hurricane Katrina in August 2005 (Figure 3.25).

Stream Landscapes in Arid Areas A distinction must be made between the results of stream erosion in humid regions and those in arid areas. The lack of vegetation in arid regions greatly increases the erosional force of running water. Water originating in mountainous areas sometimes never reaches the sea if the channel runs through a desert. In fact, stream channels may be empty except during rainy periods, when water rushes down hillsides to collect and form temporary lakes called *playas*. In the process, **alluvium** (sand and mud) builds up in the lakes and at lower elevations, and *alluvial fans* are formed along hillsides (Figure 3.26). The fan is produced by the deposition of silt, sand, and gravel outward as the stream reaches lowlands at the base of the slope it traverses. If the process has been particularly long-standing, alluvial deposits may bury the eroded mountain masses. In desert regions in Nevada, Arizona, and California, it is not unusual to observe partially buried mountains poking through eroded material.

Because streams in arid areas have only a temporary existence, their erosional power is less consistent than that of the freely flowing streams of humid areas. In some instances, they barely mark the landscape; in other cases, swiftly moving water may carve deep, straight-sided *arroyos*. Water may rush onto an

FIGURE 3.24 (a) V-shaped valley of a rapidly downcutting stream, the Yellowstone River in Wyoming. **(b) An oxbow-shaped lake** adjoining a meandering stream in Wyoming. *(a) © Robert N. Wallen; (b) U.S. Geological Survey.*

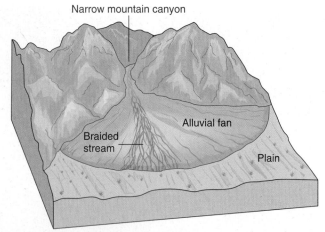

FIGURE 3.26 **Alluvial fans** are built where the velocity of streams is reduced as they flow out upon the more level land at the base of the mountain slope. The abrupt change in slope and velocity greatly reduces the stream's capacity to carry its load of coarse material. Deposition occurs, choking the stream channel and diverting the flow of water. With the canyon mouth fixing the head of the alluvial fan, the stream sweeps back and forth, building and extending a broad area of deposition. *Redrawn from Charles C. Plummer and David McGeary,* Physical Geology, *8th ed.*

FIGURE 3.27 **Canyonlands National Park, Utah.** The resistant caprock of the mesa protects softer, underlying strata from downward erosion. Where the caprock is removed, lateral erosion lowers the surface, leaving the mesa as an extensive and pronounced relic of the former higher-lying landscape. © *Corbis RF.*

alluvial plain in a complicated pattern resembling a multistrand braid, leaving in its wake an alluvial fan. The channels resulting from this rush of water are called *washes.* The erosional power of unrestricted running water in arid regions is dramatically illustrated by the steep-walled configuration of *buttes* and *mesas* (large buttes), such as those in Utah shown in Figure 3.27.

Groundwater

Some of the water supplied by rain and snow sinks underground into pores and cracks in rocks and soil, not in the form of an underground pond or lake but simply as subsurface material.

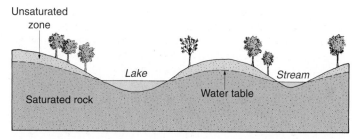

FIGURE 3.28 **The groundwater table** generally follows surface contours but in subdued fashion. Water flows slowly through the saturated rock, emerging at earth depressions that are lower than the level of the water table. During a drought, the table is lowered and the stream channel becomes dry.

When underground water accumulates, a zone of saturation called an *aquifer* forms, through which water can move readily. As indicated in Figure 3.28, the upper level of this zone is the **water table;** below it, the soils and rocks are saturated with water. A well must be drilled into an aquifer to ensure a supply of water. Groundwater moves constantly but very slowly (usually only centimeters a day). Most remains underground, seeking the lowest level. When the surface of the land dips below the water table, however, ponds, lakes, and marshes form. Some water finds its way to the surface by capillary action in the ground or in vegetation. When the ground surface extends below the level of the water table, the most common feature to develop is a stream.

Groundwater, particularly when combined with carbon dioxide, dissolves soluble materials by a chemical process called *solution.* Although groundwater tends to decompose many types of rocks, its effect on limestone is most spectacular. Many of the great caves of the world have been created by the underground movement of water through limestone regions. Water sinking through the overlying rock leaves carbonate deposits as it drips into empty spaces. The deposits hang from cave roofs (*stalactites*) and build upward from cave floors (*stalagmites*). In some areas, the uneven effect of groundwater erosion on limestone leaves a landscape pockmarked by a series of *sinkholes,* surface depressions in an area of collapsing caverns.

Karst topography refers to a large limestone region marked by sinkholes, caverns, and underground streams, as shown in Figure 3.29. East central Florida, a karst area, has suffered considerable damage from the creation and widening of sinkholes. This type of topography gets its name from a region on the Adriatic Sea at the Italy-Slovenia border. The Mammoth Cave region of Kentucky, another karst area, has many kilometers of interconnected limestone caves.

Glaciers

Another agent causing erosion and deposition to occur is glaciers. Although they are much less extensive today, glaciers covered a large part of the earth's land area as recently as 10,000 to 15,000 years ago. Many landforms were created by the erosional or depositional effects of glaciers.

FIGURE 3.29 **Limestone erodes easily** in the presence of water. **(a) *Karst topography,*** such as that shown here, occurs in humid areas where limestone in flat beds is at the surface. **(b)** This satellite photo of east central Florida shows the many round lakes formed in the sinkholes of a karst landscape. *(b) NASA.*

(a)

(b)

Glaciers form only in very cold places with short or nonexistent summers, where annual snowfall exceeds annual snowmelt and evaporation. The weight of the snow causes it to compact at the base and form ice. When the snowfall reaches a thickness of about 100 meters (328 ft), ice at the bottom becomes like thick toothpaste and begins to move slowly. A **glacier,** then, is a large body of ice moving slowly down a slope or spreading outward on a land surface (Figure 3.30). Some glaciers appear to be stationary simply because the melting and evaporation at the glacier's edge equal the speed of the ice advance. Glaciers can, however, move as much as a meter per day.

Most theories of glacial formation concern earth climatic cooling. Perhaps a combination of the following theories explains the evolution of glaciers. The first theory attributes cooling to periods when there may have been excessive amounts of volcanic dust in the atmosphere. The argument is that the dust, by reducing the amount of solar energy reaching the earth, effectively lowered temperatures at the surface. A second theory attributes the ice ages to known changes in the shape, tilt, and seasonal positions of the earth's orbit around the sun over the last half-million years. Such changes alter the

amount of solar radiation received by the earth and its distribution over the earth. A recent theory suggests that, when large continental plates drift over polar regions, temperatures on Earth become more extreme and, as a result, induce the development of glaciers. This theory, of course, cannot explain the most recent ice ages.

Today, continental-size glaciers exist on Antarctica, Greenland, and Baffin Island in Canada, but mountain glaciers are found in many parts of the world. About 10% of the earth's land area is under ice. During the most recent advance of ice, the continental ice of Greenland was part of an enormous glacier that covered nearly all of Canada (Figure 3.31) and the northernmost portions of the United States and Eurasia. The giant glacier reached thicknesses of 3000 meters (10,000 ft) (the depth in Greenland today), enveloping entire mountain systems. Another feature of the last ice age was the development of **permafrost,** a permanently frozen layer of ground that can be as much as 1500 meters (4900 ft) deep. Because the permafrost layer prevents the downward percolation of moisture, the surface soil may become saturated with water during the brief summer season, when only a thin surface thaws.

FIGURE 3.30 **Alpine glacial landforms.** Frost shattering and ice movement carve *cirques,* the irregular bottoms of which may contain lakes (*tarns*) after glacial melt. Where cirque walls adjoin from opposite sides, knifelike ridges called *arêtes* are formed, interrupted by overeroded passes, or *cols.* The intersection of three or more creates a pointed peak, or *horn.* Rock debris falling from cirque walls is carried along by the moving ice. *Lateral moraines* form between the ice and the valley walls; *medial moraines* mark the union of such debris where two valley glaciers join. *Recessional moraines* form where the end of the ice remains stationary long enough for an accumulation of sediment to form, while a *terminal moraine* marks the glacier's farthest advance. Small, conical hills of sediment are called *kames.*

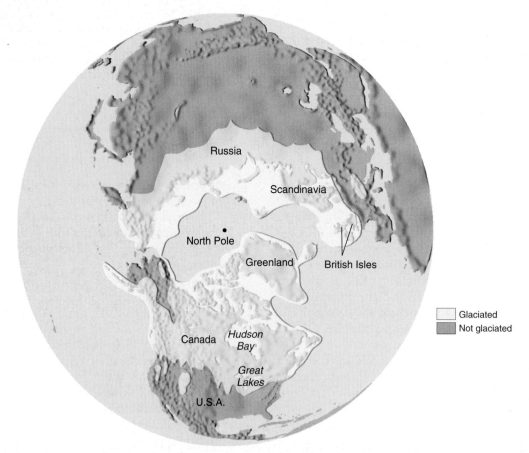

FIGURE 3.31 **Maximum extent of continental glaciation in the Northern Hemisphere (about 15,000 years ago).** Because sea level was lower than at present, due to the large volume of moisture trapped as ice on the land, glaciation extended beyond present continental shorelines. Separate centers of snow accumulation and ice formation developed. Large lakes were created between the western mountains of North America and the advancing ice front. To the south, huge rivers carried away glacial meltwaters.

The weight of glaciers breaks up underlying rock and prepares it for transportation by the moving mass of ice. Consequently, glaciers change landforms by erosion. Glaciers scour the land as they move, leaving surface scratches, or striations, on rocks that remain. Much of eastern Canada has been scoured by glaciers that left little soil but many ice-gouged lakes and streams. The erosional forms created by glacial scourings have a variety of names. A *glacial trough* is a deep, U-shaped valley visible only after the glacier has receded. If the valley is below sea level today, as in Norway or British Columbia, *fiords*, or arms of the sea, are formed. Some of the landforms created by scouring are shown in Figure 3.30. Figure 3.32 shows horns, *cirques*, and arêtes, sharp ridges that separate adjacent glacially carved valleys. Cirques are formed by ice erosion at the head of a glacial valley.

Glaciers create landforms when they deposit the debris they have transported. These deposits, called *till*, consist of rocks, pebbles, and silt. As the great tongues of ice move forward, debris accumulates in parts of the glacier. The ice that scours valley walls and the ice at the tip of the advancing tongue are particularly filled with debris. As a glacier melts, it leaves behind hills of till of different sizes and shapes, such as moraines, eskers, and drumlins (Figure 3.33).

Many other landforms have been formed by glaciers. The most important is the *outwash plain*, a gently sloping area in front of a melting glacier. The melting along a broad front sends thousands of small streams running out from the glacier in braided fashion, streams that deposit neatly stratified drift made up of sand and gravel. Outwash plains, which are essentially great alluvial fans, cover a wide area and provide new parent-material for soil formation. Most of the midwestern part of the United States owes some of its soil fertility to the effects of wind on glacial deposition (see Figure 3.38).

Before the end of the most recent ice age, at least three previous major advances occurred during the 1.5 million years of the Pleistocene period. Firm evidence is not available on whether we have emerged from the cycle of ice advance

FIGURE 3.32 Horns, cirques, and arêtes created by glaciation, San Juan Mountains, Colorado. © *McGraw-Hill Companies, Inc.*

FIGURE 3.33 Depositional features formed by ice sheets. The debris carried by continental glaciers and left behind as they retreat creates various landforms. Moraines of *till,* unsorted glacial drift, form at the retreating edge. Streams carry silt to form *outwash plains.* *Kames* are small, conical hills formed of outwash deposits; *drumlins* are elongated hills made of till and oriented in the direction of ice movement; and *eskers* are long ridges of sediment deposited by glacial meltwater. Enclosed depressions caused by the melting of a stagnant block of ice that was surrounded and buried by sediment are called *kettles.*

(a)

(b)

FIGURE 3.34 Formation of waves and breakers. (a) As the offshore swell approaches the gently sloping beach bottom, sharp-crested waves form, build up to a steep wall of water, and break forward in plunging surf. **(b)** Evenly spaced breakers form as successive waves touch bottom along a regularly sloping shore. *(b) © Punchstock RF.*

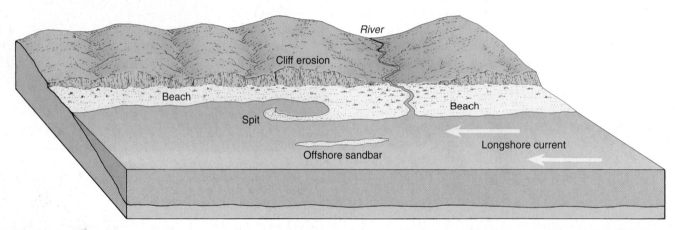

FIGURE 3.35 The cliffs behind the shore are eroded by waves during storms and high water. Sediment from the cliff and river forms the beach deposit; the longshore current moves some sediment downcurrent to form a *spit. Offshore sandbars* are created from material removed from the beach and deposited by retreating waves. Generally, not all the features shown here would occur in a single setting.

and retreat. Factors concerning the earth's changing temperature, which are discussed in Chapter 4, must be considered before assessing the likelihood of a new ice advance. For the first half of the 20th century, the world's glaciers were melting faster than they were building up. Current trends are not clear, although there is fear that the greenhouse effect (discussed in Chapter 4) is warming the earth and will cause the seas to rise.

Waves, Currents, and Coastal Landforms

Whereas glacial action is intermittent in earth history, the breaking of ocean waves on continental coasts and islands is unceasing and causes considerable change in coastal landforms. As waves reach shallow water close to shore, they are forced by friction along the seafloor to heighten until a breaker is formed, as shown in Figure 3.34. The uprush of water not only carries sand for deposition but also erodes the landforms at the coast, while the backwash carries the eroded material away. This type of action results in different kinds of landforms, depending on conditions.

If land at the coast is well above sea level, the wave action causes cliffs to form. Cliffs then erode at a rate dependent on the rock's resistance to the constant assault of salt water. During storms, a great deal of power is released by the forward thrust of waves, and much erosion takes place. Landslides are a hazard during coastal storms, and they occur particularly in areas where weak sedimentary rock or till exists.

Beaches are formed by the deposition of sand grains contained in the water. The sand originates from the vast amount of coastal erosion and streams (Figure 3.35). *Longshore currents,* which move roughly parallel to the shore, transport the sand, forming beaches and *spits.* A more sheltered area increases the chances of a beach being built.

The backwash of waves, however, takes sand away from beaches if no longshore current exists. As a result, *sandbars* can develop a short distance away from the shoreline. If sandbars become extensive, they can eventually close off the shore, creating a new coastal configuration that encloses *lagoons* or *inlets. Salt marshes* very often develop in and around these areas. For example, the Outer Banks of North Carolina, composed of long ribbons of sand, are constantly shifting as a result of currents and storms.

Coral reefs, made not from sand but from coral organisms growing in shallow tropical water, are formed by the secretion of calcium carbonate in the presence of warm water and sunlight. Reefs, consisting of millions of colorful coral skeletons, develop short distances offshore. Off the coast of northeastern Australia lies the most famous coral reef, the Great Barrier Reef. *Atolls,* found in the South Pacific, are reefs formed in shallow water around a volcano that has since been covered or nearly covered by water (Figure 3.36).

Wind

In humid areas, vegetation cover confines the effect of wind mainly to sandy beach areas, but in dry climates, wind is a powerful agent of erosion and deposition. Limited vegetation in dry areas leaves exposed particles of sand, clay, and silt subject to movement by wind. Thus, many of the sculptured features found in dry areas result from mechanical weathering, that is, from the abrasive action of sand and dust particles as they are blown against rock surfaces. Sand and dust storms occurring in a drought-stricken farm area may make it unusable for agriculture. Inhabitants of Oklahoma, Texas, and Colorado suffered greatly in the 1930s when their farmlands became the "Dust Bowl" of the United States.

Several types of landforms are produced by wind-driven sand. Figure 3.37 depicts one of these. Although sandy deserts are much less common than gravelly deserts, also called *desert pavement,* their characteristic landforms are better known. Most of the Sahara, the Gobi, and the western U.S. deserts are covered with rocks, pebbles, and gravel, not sand. Each also

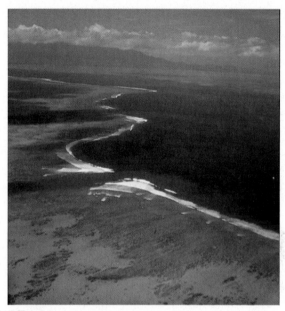

FIGURE 3.36 Aerial view of coral reefs in the Fiji Islands. *Photo by Diane R. Nelson.*

FIGURE 3.37 The prevailing wind from the left has given these transverse dunes a characteristic gentle windward slope and a steep, irregular leeward slope. *Courtesy of James A. Bier.*

GEOGRAPHY & *Public Policy*

Beaches on the Brink

Headlines such as "Beaches on the Brink," "Storm-Lashed Cape Is a Fragile Environment," "Fighting the Development Tide," and "State Looks for Money to Restore the Shore" signal a growing concern with the condition of coastlines. In addition, they raise the central question of how we can utilize coastlines without, at the same time, destroying them.

Because many of the world's people live or vacation on coasts, and because such areas are often densely populated, coastal processes have a considerable impact on humans. Nature's forces are continually shaping and reshaping the coasts; they are dynamic environments, always in a state of flux. Some processes are dramatic and induce rapid change: tropical cyclones (hurricanes and typhoons), tsunami, and floods can wreak havoc, take thousands of lives, and cause millions of dollars in damage in a matter of hours. A less hazardous process is beach erosion, although it tends to magnify the effects of storms.

Some beach erosion is caused by natural processes, both marine and land. Waves carry huge loads of suspended sand, and longshore currents constantly move sand along the shoreline. The weathering and erosion of sea cliffs produce sediment, and rivers carry silt from mountains to beaches.

Human activities affect both erosion and deposition, however. Dams, for example, decrease the flow of sand to the water's edge by trapping sediment upstream. We fill marshes, construct dikes, and bulldoze dunes or remove their natural stabilizing vegetation. We hasten erosion when we build roads, houses, and other structures on cliffs and dunes or when we plant trees and lawns on top of them.

Especially vulnerable to erosion are barrier islands, narrow strips of sand parallel to the mainland. Under natural conditions, they are not stable places; their ends typically migrate, and during storms, waves can wash right over them. Some barrier islands are highly developed and densely populated, including Atlantic City and Miami Beach.

Once hotels and condominiums, railroads, and highways have been built along the waterfront, people attempt to protect their investments by preventing beaches from eroding. Breakwaters, offshore structures built to absorb the force of large, breaking waves and to provide quiet water near shore, are designed to trap sand and thus retard erosion, but they are not always successful. Although some are locally beneficial by forming new areas of deposition, they almost invariably accelerate erosion in adjacent areas. The efforts of one community are often negated by those of nearby towns and cities, underscoring the need for agencies to coordinate efforts and develop comprehensive land use plans for an extensive length of shoreline.

An alternative to erecting artificial structures is beach replenishment: adding sand to beaches to replace that lost by erosion. This provides recreational opportunities; at the same time, it buffers property from damage by storms. Sand may be dredged from harbors or pumped from offshore sandbars. The disadvantages of this technique are that dredging disrupts marine organisms, sand of the right texture may be hard to obtain, and replenished beaches can be short-lived. For example, more than $5 million was spent replenishing the beach at Ocean City, New Jersey, in 1982. The beach disappeared within 3 months, after a series of northeasters hit the area. Similarly, a massive dredging project that cost more than $17 million replenished 8 kilometers (5 mi) of beaches along the San Diego coast in 2000. Within

has a small portion (and the Saudi Arabian Desert has a large area) covered with sand blown by wind into a series of waves, or *dunes*. Unless vegetation stabilizes them, the dunes move as sand is blown from their windward faces onto and over their crests. One of the most distinctive sand desert dunes is the crescent-shaped *barchan*. Along seacoasts and inland lakeshores, in both wet and dry climates, wind can create sand ridges that reach a height of 90 meters (300 ft). Sometimes, coastal communities and farmlands are threatened or destroyed by moving sand (see "Beaches on the Brink").

Another kind of wind-deposited material, silty in texture, is called **loess.** Encountered usually in midlatitude westerly wind belts, it covers extensive areas in the United States (Figure 3.38), central Europe, central Asia, and Argentina. It has its greatest development in northern China, where loess covers hundreds of thousands of square miles, often to depths of more than 30 meters (100 ft). The windborne origin of loess is confirmed by its typical occurrence downwind from extensive desert areas, though major deposits are assumed to have resulted from wind erosion of nonvegetated sediment deposited by meltwater from retreating glaciers. Because rich soils usually form from loess deposits, if climatic circumstances are appropriate, these areas are among the most productive agricultural lands in the world.

LANDFORM REGIONS

Every piece of land not covered by buildings and other structures contains clues as to how it has changed over time. Geomorphologists interpret these clues, studying such things as earth materials and soils, the availability of water,

Storm surge damage in coastal South Carolina resulting from Hurricane Hugo on September 22, 1989. *NOAA/National Weather Service.*

Considering the Issues

1. From 1994 to the present, the Army Corps of Engineers has spent millions of dollars annually to pump sand from the ocean bottom onto eroded beaches in New Jersey. This ongoing project is based on the assumption that additional replenishment will be required every 5 or 6 years as beaches erode. Currently, the federal government pays 65% of the cost, the state government 25%, and local governments 10%. New Jersey Senator Frank Lautenberg contends that beach replenishment is critical for the region's future. "People's lives and property are at stake. Jersey's beaches bring crucial tourist dollars to the state." But James Tripp of the Environmental Defense Fund argues that beach rebuilding is simply throwing taxpayers' money into the ocean. "Pumping all the sand in the world is not going to save the day." Do you think the beach replenishment project is a wise use of taxpayers' money? Does the federal government have an obligation to protect or rebuild storm-damaged beaches? Why or why not?

2. Coastal erosion is not a problem for beaches, only for people who want to use them. Do you believe that we should learn to live with erosion, not building in the coastal zone unless we are prepared to consider our structures temporary and expendable? Should communities adopt zoning plans that prohibit building on undeveloped lands within, say, 50 meters (164 ft) of the shore?

3. Should the federal government curtail programs that provide inexpensive storm insurance for oceanfront houses and businesses, as well as speedy grants and loans for storm repairs not covered by insurance? Should people be allowed to rebuild storm-damaged buildings even if they are vulnerable to future damage? Why or why not?

4. Coastal erosion will become more serious if the current rise in sea level—about 2.5 centimeters (1 in.) every 12 years—continues or even increases as global warming causes seawater to expand or the polar ice caps to melt. Many of the world's major cities would be threatened by this rise in sea level. What are some of those cities? How might they protect themselves?

months, after the largest waves of the year pounded the coast, more than half of the sand was gone.

The expense of maintaining coastal zones raises two basic questions: Who benefits? Who should pay? Some people contend that the interests of those who own coastal property are not compatible with the public interest, and it is unwise to expend large amounts of public funds to protect the property of only a few. People argue that shorefront businesses and homeowners are the chief beneficiaries of shore protection measures, that they often deny the public access to the beaches in front of their property, and therefore they should pay for the majority of the cost of maintaining the shoreline. At present, however, this is rarely the case; costs are typically shared by communities, states, and the federal government. Indeed, 51 federal programs subsidize coastal development and redevelopment. The largest is the National Flood Insurance Program, which offers low-cost insurance to homeowners in flood-prone areas. People have used the protection of that insurance to build anywhere, even in high-risk coastal areas.

drainage patterns, evidences of erosion, and glacial history. The scale of analysis may be as small as a stream or as large as a *landform region,* a large section of the earth's surface where a great deal of homogeneity occurs among the types of landforms that characterize it. A description of one landform region appears in "Landforms as Regions" in Chapter 13, pp. 437–438.

A foldout map inside the back cover of this book shows, in a general way, the kinds of landform regions found in different parts of the world. Note how the *mountain* belts generally coincide with convergent plate boundaries not found beneath the sea (see Figure 3.6) and with the earthquake-prone areas (see Figure 3.8). Vast *plains* exist in North and South America, Europe, Asia, and Australia. Many of these regions were created under former seas and appeared as land when seas contracted. These, and the smaller plains areas, are the drainage basins for some of the great rivers of the world, such as the Mississippi-Missouri, Amazon, Volga, Nile, Ganges, and Tigris-Euphrates. The valleys carved by these rivers and the silt deposited by them are among the most agriculturally productive areas in the world. The *plateau* regions are many and varied. The African plateau region is the largest. Much of the African landscape is characterized by low mountains and hills whose base is about 700 meters (2300 ft) above sea level. Generally quiet from the standpoint of tectonic activity, Africa is largely made up of geologically ancient continental blocks that have been in an advanced stage of erosion for millions of years.

FIGURE 3.38 Location of windblown silt deposits, including loess, in the United States. The thicker layers, found in the upper Mississippi Valley area, are associated with the wind movement of glacial debris. Farther west, in the Great Plains, wind-deposited materials are sandy in texture, not loessial. *Adapted from* Geology of Soils *by Charles B. Hunt, copyright 1972 W. H. Freeman and Company. Reprinted by permission of the author.*

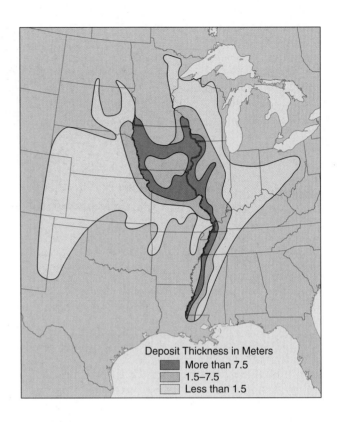

Deposit Thickness in Meters
More than 7.5
1.5–7.5
Less than 1.5

Humans affect and are affected by the landscape, land-forms, moving continents, and earthquakes; however, except at times of natural disaster, these elements of the physical world are, for most of us, quiet, accepted background. More immediate in affecting our lives and fortunes are the great patterns of climate. Climate helps define the limits of the economically possible with present levels of technology, the daily changes of weather that affect the success of picnics and crop yield alike, and the patterns of vegetation and soils. We turn our attention to these elements of the natural environment in Chapter 4.

Summary of Key Concepts

- Rocks, the materials that constitute the earth's surface, are classified as igneous, sedimentary, and metamorphic.

- In the most recent 200 million of the earth's 4.5 billion years, continental plates drifted on the asthenosphere to their present positions.

- At or near plate intersections, tectonic activity is particularly in evidence in two forms. Diastrophism, such as faulting, results in earthquakes and, on occasion, tsunami. Volcanism moves molten materials toward the earth's surface.

- The building up of the earth's surface is balanced by three gradational processes—weathering, mass movement, and erosion. Weathering, both mechanical and chemical, prepares materials for transport by disintegrating rocks and is instrumental in the development of soils. Talus slopes and soil-creep are examples of the effect of mass movement. The erosional agents of running water, groundwater, glaciers, waves and currents, and wind move materials to new locations.

- Examples of landforms created by the collection of eroded materials are alluvial fans, deltas, natural levees, moraines, and sand dunes.

Key Words

alluvium 69
asthenosphere 54
chemical weathering 63
continental drift 53
diastrophism 57
erosional agents 67
faults 55
floodplain 68
fold 57
glacier 71

gradational processes 61
igneous rock 51
karst topography 70
lithosphere 54
loess 76
mass movement 64
mechanical weathering 63
metamorphic rock 52
mineral 51
permafrost 71

plate tectonics 53
sedimentary rock 51
subduction 57
tsunami 60
volcanism 57
warping 57
water table 70
weathering 62

Thinking Geographically

1. How can rocks be classified? List three classes of rocks according to their origin. In what ways can they be distinguished from one another?

2. What evidence makes the theory of plausible?

3. What is *subduction?* What are its effects?

4. Explain what is meant by *gradation* and *volcanism.*

5. What is meant by *folding, joint,* and *faulting?*

6. Draw a diagram indicating the varieties of ways *faults* occur.

7. With what earth movements are earthquakes associated? What are *tsunami* and how do they develop?

8. What is the distinction between *mechanical* and *chemical weathering?* Is weathering responsible for landform creation? In what ways do glaciers engage in mechanical weathering?

9. Explain the origin of the various landforms one usually finds in desert environments.

10. How do *glaciers* form? What landscape characteristics are associated with glacial erosion? With glacial deposition?

11. How are alluvial fans, deltas, natural levees, and moraines formed?

12. How is groundwater erosion differentiated from surface water erosion?

13. How are the processes that bring about change due to waves and currents related to the processes that bring about change by the force of wind?

14. What processes account for the landform features of the area in which you live?

Flooding in New Orleans following the passage of Hurricane Katrina in August 2005. *NOAA.*

On August 29, 2005, the "Big Easy," New Orleans, a city built mostly at and below sea level near the delta of the Mississippi River, lay in the path of Hurricane Katrina. Because most residents had obeyed prehurricane evacuation orders, the city was largely deserted. It was mostly the poor and immobile who were left behind as the storm hit. Winds of about 200 kilometers per hour (125 mph) pounded the city, downing trees and power lines, and wind-driven high water poured ashore.

At first it looked as though New Orleans had escaped with no more damage than might have been expected, but the worst was yet to come. In several places the sea walls and levees that held back the Mississippi River and Lake Pontchartrain collapsed. The breaches proved catastrophic; for 2 days after the storm had passed, waters continued to rise and pour into the city. About 80% of New Orleans was flooded with anywhere from 1 to 3 meters (3 to 10 ft) of water (Figure 4.1). Approximately 1700 people are believed to have died in New Orleans and in other towns of Louisiana, Mississippi, and Alabama before the storm's fury dissipated over Tennessee.

When it was over, New Orleans was devastated. Katrina had proved to be one of the worst natural disasters in the history of the United States. All of the systems that make a city function had failed, including the water and sewer systems, the electric grid, the transportation network, and the telephone system. To add insult to injury, 3 weeks later Hurricane Rita attacked the Gulf Coast. Although Rita struck farther to the west, New Orleans suffered from renewed flooding. More than a month after the two hurricanes, most residents had not yet been allowed to return, because power was still out in large sections of the city and water for drinking had not yet been restored.

It would take billions of dollars to rebuild New Orleans. There were many tasks that had to be done before rebuilding could even begin: removal of debris, draining of floodwater, repair of levees and sea walls, cleanup of toxic materials, and restoration of electricity and the sewage system.

Whether storms such as Hurricane Katrina occur in Asia or North America, they do great damage, affecting the lives of everyone in their paths. Tropical storms are one extreme type of weather phenomenon. Most people are "weather watchers"—they watch television forecasts with great interest and plan their lives around weather events. In this chapter, we review the subsection of physical geography concerned with weather and climate. It deals with normal, patterned phenomena from which such extreme weather events as Hurricane Katrina occasionally emerge.

A weather forecaster describes current conditions for a limited region, such as a metropolitan area, and predicts future weather conditions. If the elements that make up the **weather,** such as temperature, wind, and precipitation, are recorded at specified moments in time, such as every hour, an inventory of weather conditions can be developed. By finding trends in data that have been gathered over an extended period of time, we can speak about typical conditions. These characteristic circumstances describe the **climate** of a region. Weather is a moment's view of the lower atmosphere, whereas climate is a description of typical weather conditions in an area or at a place over a period of time. Geographers analyze the differences in weather and climate from place to place in order to understand how climatic elements affect human occupance of the earth.

In geography, we are particularly interested in the physical environment that surrounds us. That is why the **troposphere,** the lowest layer of the earth's atmosphere, attracts our attention. This layer, extending about 10 kilometers (6 mi) above the ground, contains virtually all of the air, clouds, and precipitation of the earth (Figure 4.2).

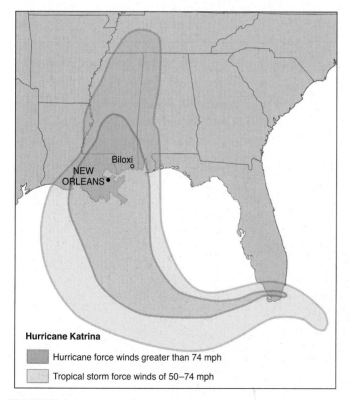

Hurricane Katrina

[legend] Hurricane force winds greater than 74 mph

[legend] Tropical storm force winds of 50–74 mph

FIGURE 4.1 Path of Hurricane Katrina in August 2005.

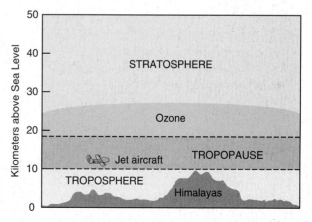

FIGURE 4.2 Virtually all of the air, clouds, and precipitation of the earth are contained in the troposphere.

In this chapter, we try to answer the questions usually raised regarding characteristics of the lower atmosphere. By discussing these answers from the viewpoint of averages or average variations, we attempt to give a view of the earth's climatic differences, a view held to be very important for understanding the way people use the land. Climate is a key to understanding, in a broad way, the distribution of world population. People have great difficulty living in areas that are, on average, very cold, very hot, very dry, or very wet. They are also negatively affected by huge storms or flooding. In this chapter, we first discuss the elements that constitute weather conditions and then describe the various climates of the earth.

AIR TEMPERATURE

Perhaps the most fundamental question about weather is "Why do temperatures vary from place to place?" The answer to this question requires the discussion of a number of concepts to help focus on the way heat accumulates on the earth's surface.

Energy from the sun, called *solar energy*, is transformed into heat, primarily at the earth's surface and secondarily in the atmosphere. Not every part of the earth or its overlying atmosphere receives the same amount of solar energy. At any given place, the amount of incoming solar radiation, or **insolation**, available depends on the intensity and duration of radiation from the sun. These are determined by both the angle at which the sun's rays strike the earth and the number of daylight hours. These two fundamental factors, plus the following five modifying variables, determine the temperature at any given location:

1. the amount of water vapor in the air
2. the degree of cloud cover (or cover in general)
3. the nature of the surface of the earth (land or water)
4. the elevation above sea level
5. the degree and direction of air movement

Let us look at these factors briefly.

Earth Inclination

The axis of the earth—that is, the imaginary line connecting the North Pole to the South Pole—always remains in the same position. It is tilted about 23.5° away from the perpendicular (Figure 4.3). Every 24 hours, the earth rotates once on that axis, as shown in Figure 4.4. While rotating, the earth is slowly revolving around the sun in a nearly circular annual orbit (Figure 4.5). If the earth were not tilted from the perpendicular, the solar energy received *at a given latitude* would not vary during the course of the year. The rays of the sun would directly strike the equator, and as distance away from the equator became greater, rays would strike the earth at ever-decreasing angles, therefore diminishing the intensity of the energy and giving climates a latitudinal standardization (Figures 4.6 and 4.7).

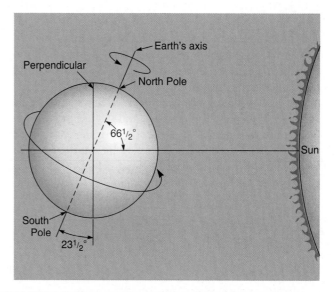

FIGURE 4.3 The earth's position relative to the sun.
The earth is in its summer position in the Northern Hemisphere (winter in the Southern Hemisphere).

FIGURE 4.4 The process of the 24-hour rotation of the earth on its axis.

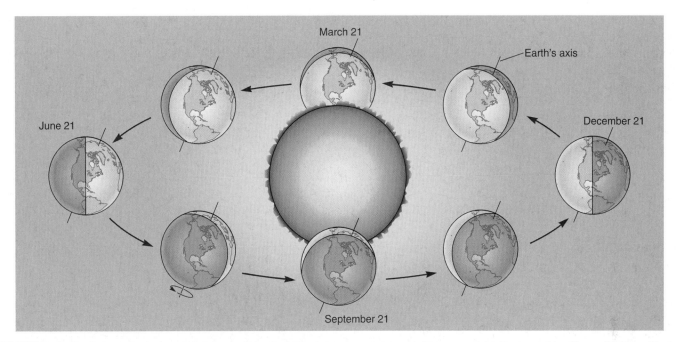

FIGURE 4.5 **The process of the yearly revolution of the earth around the sun.** The sun, which is about 93 million miles from Earth, is not drawn to scale; it is much larger relative to the size of the earth.

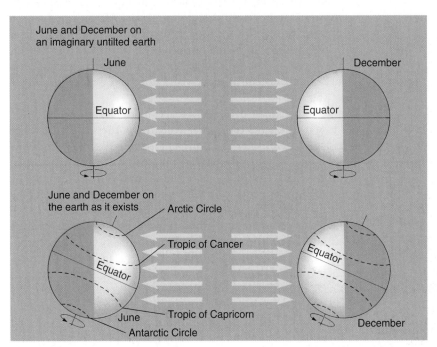

FIGURE 4.6 Notice on the bottom two diagrams that, as the earth revolves, the north polar area in June is bathed in sunshine for 24 hours, while the south polar area is dark. The most intense of the sun's rays are felt north of the equator in June and south of the equator in December. None of this is true in the untilted examples shown on the upper two diagrams.

Because of the inclination, however, the location of highest incidence of incoming solar energy varies during the course of the year. When the Northern Hemisphere is tilted directly toward the sun, the vertical rays of the sun are felt as far north as 23.5°N latitude (Tropic of Cancer). This position of the earth occurs about June 21, the summer *solstice* for the Northern

Hemisphere and the winter solstice for the Southern Hemisphere. About December 21, when the vertical rays of the sun strike near 23.5°S latitude (Tropic of Capricorn), it is the beginning of summer in the Southern Hemisphere and the onset of winter in the Northern Hemisphere. During the rest of the year, the position of the earth relative to the sun results in direct rays migrating from about 23.5°N to 23.5°S and back again. On about March 21 and September 21 (the spring and autumn *equinoxes*), the vertical rays of the sun strike the equator.

The tilt of the earth also means that the length of days and nights varies during the year. One-half of the earth is always illuminated by the sun, but only at the equator is it light for 12 hours each day of the year. As distance away from the equator becomes greater, the hours of daylight or darkness increase, depending on whether the direct rays of the sun are north or south of the equator. In the summer, daylight increases to the maximum of 24 hours from the Arctic Circle (66.5°N) to the North Pole, and during the same period, nighttime finally reaches 24 hours in length from the Antarctic Circle (66.5°S) to the South Pole.

Because of the 24-hour daylight, it would seem that much solar energy should be available in the summer polar region. The angle of the sun is so narrow (the sun is low in the sky), however, that solar energy is spread over a wide surface. By contrast, the combination of relatively long days and sun angles close to 90° makes an enormous amount of energy available to areas in the neighborhood of 15° to 30° north and south latitude during each hemisphere's summer.

(a)

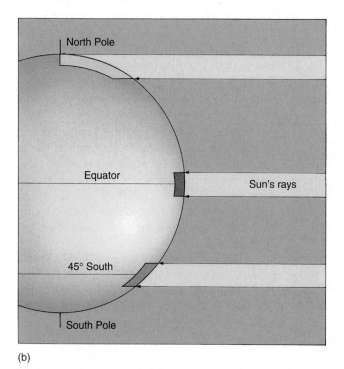

(b)

FIGURE 4.7 (a) Imaginary rays from the sun at spring and autumn equinoxes and summer and winter solstices.
(b) Three equal, imaginary rays from the sun are shown striking the earth at different latitudes at the time of the equinox. As distance away from the equator increases, the rays become more diffused, showing how the sun's intensity is diluted in the high latitudes.

Reflection and Reradiation

Much of the potentially receivable solar radiation is, in fact, sent back to outer space or diffused in the troposphere in a process known as **reflection.** Clouds, which are dense concentrations of suspended, tiny water or ice particles, reflect a great deal of energy. Light-colored surfaces, especially snow cover, also reflect large amounts of solar energy.

Energy is lost through reradiation as well as reflection. In the **reradiation** process, the earth's surface acts as a communicator of energy. As indicated in Figure 4.8, the energy that is absorbed into the land and water is returned to the atmosphere in the form of terrestrial radiation. On a clear night, when no clouds can block or diffuse movement, temperatures continually decrease, as the earth reradiates as heat the energy it has received and stored during the course of the day.

Some kinds of earth surface material, especially water, store solar energy more effectively than others. Because water is transparent, solar rays can penetrate a great distance below its surface. If water currents are present, heat is distributed even more effectively. On the other hand, land surfaces are opaque, so all of the energy received from the sun is concentrated at the surface. Land, having more heat available at the surface, reradiates its energy faster than water. Air is heated by the process of reradiation from the earth and not directly by energy from the sun passing through it. Thus, because land heats and cools more rapidly than water, hot and cold temperature extremes recorded on Earth occur on land and not the sea.

Temperatures are moderated by the presence of large bodies of water near land areas. Note in Figure 4.9 that coastal areas have lower summer temperatures and higher winter temperatures than those places at the same distance from the equator, excluding seacoasts. Land areas affected by the moderating influences of water are considered *marine* environments; those areas not affected by nearby water are *continental* environments.

Temperatures vary in a cyclical way each day. In the course of a day, as incoming solar energy exceeds energy lost through reflection and reradiation, temperatures begin to rise. The ground stores some heat, and temperatures continue to rise until the angle of the sun becomes so narrow that energy received no longer exceeds that lost by the reflection and reradiation processes. Not all of the heat loss occurs during the night, but long nights appreciably deplete stored energy.

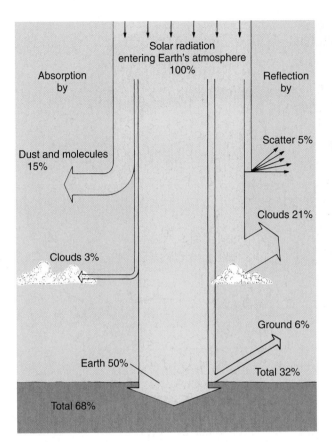

FIGURE 4.8 Consider the incoming solar radiation as 100%. The portion that is absorbed into the earth (50%) is eventually released to the atmosphere and then reradiated into space.

Lapse Rate

We may think that, as we move vertically away from the earth toward the sun, temperatures increase. However, this is not true within the troposphere. The earth absorbs and reradiates heat; therefore, temperatures are usually warmest at the earth's surface and lower as elevation increases. Note on Figure 4.10 that this temperature **lapse rate** (the rate of temperature change with altitude in the troposphere) averages about 6.4°C per 1000 meters (3.5°F per 1000 ft). For example, the difference in elevation between Denver and Pikes Peak is about 2700 meters (9000 ft), which normally results in a 17°C (32°F) difference in temperature. Jet planes flying at an altitude of 9100 meters (30,000 ft) are moving through air that is about 56°C (100°F) colder than ground temperatures.

The normal lapse rate does not always hold, however. Rapid reradiation sometimes causes temperatures to be higher above the earth's surface than at the surface itself. This particular condition, in which air at lower altitudes is cooler than air aloft, is called a **temperature inversion.** An inversion is important because of its effect on air movement. Warm air at the surface, which normally rises, may be blocked by the even warmer air of a temperature inversion (Figure 4.11). Thus, surface air is trapped; if it is filled with automobile exhaust

emissions or smoke, a serious smog condition may develop (see "The Donora Tragedy"). Because of the configuration of nearby mountains, Los Angeles often experiences temperature inversions, causing sunlight to be reduced to a dull haze (Figure 4.12).

The effect of air movement on temperature is made clear in the following section, "Air Pressure and Winds."

AIR PRESSURE AND WINDS

The second fundamental question about weather and climate concerns **air pressure:** How do differences in air pressure from place to place affect weather conditions? The answer to this question first requires that we explain why differences in air pressure occur.

Air is a gaseous substance whose weight affects air pressure. If it were possible to carve out 16.39 cubic centimeters (1 cu in.) of air at the earth's surface and weigh it, along with all the other cubic centimeters of air above it, under normal conditions the total weight would equal approximately 6.67 kilograms (14.7 lbs) of air as measured at sea level. Actually, this is not very heavy when you consider the dimensions of the column of air: 2.54 centimeters by 2.54 centimeters (1 in. by 1 in.) by about 9.7 kilometers (6 mi), or about 6.2 cubic meters (220 cu ft). The weight of air 4.8 kilometers (3 mi) above the earth's surface, however, is considerably less than 6.67 kilograms (14.7 lbs) because there is correspondingly less air above it. Thus, it is clear that air is heavier and air pressure is higher closer to the earth's surface.

It is a physical law that, for equal amounts of cold and hot air, the cold air is denser. This law exemplifies why hot-air balloons, filled with lighter air, can rise into the atmosphere. A cold morning is characterized by relatively heavy air, but as afternoon temperatures rise, air becomes lighter.

Barometers of various types are used to record changes in air pressure. Barometric readings in inches of mercury or millibars are a normal part, along with recorded temperatures, of every weather report. Air pressure at a given location changes as surfaces heat or cool. Barometers record a drop in atmospheric pressure when air heats and a rise in pressure when air cools.

In order to visualize the effect of air movements on weather, it is useful to think of air as a liquid made up of two fluids with different densities (representing light air and heavy air)—for example, water and gasoline. If the fluids are put into a tank at the same time, the lighter liquid will move to the top and the heavier air will move to the bottom, representing the vertical motion of air. The heavier liquid spreads out horizontally along the bottom of the tank, becoming the same thickness everywhere. This flow represents the horizontal movement of the air or wind on the earth's surface. Air attempts to achieve an equilibrium by evening out pressure imbalances that result from the heating and cooling processes. Air races from heavy (cold) air locations to light (warm) air locations. Thus, the greater the differences in air pressure between places, the greater the wind.

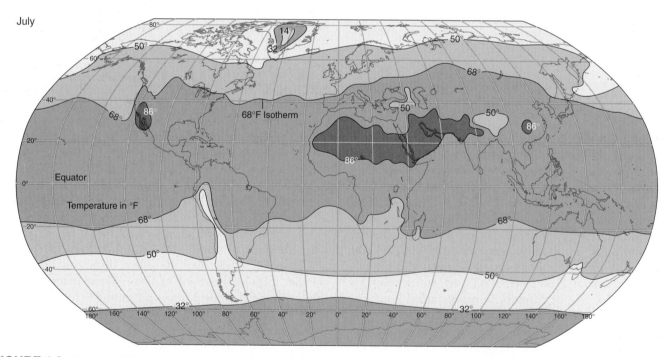

FIGURE 4.9 At a given latitude, water areas are warmer than land areas in winter and cooler in summer. *Isotherms* are lines of equal temperature.

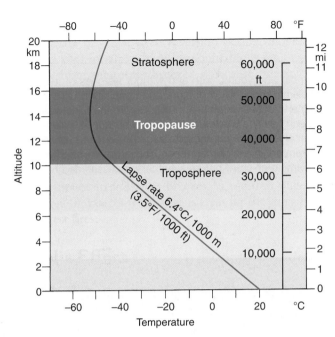

FIGURE 4.10 The temperature lapse rate under typical conditions. The *tropopause* is a transition zone between the troposphere and the stratosphere. It marks the level at which temperature ceases to fall with altitude.

(a)

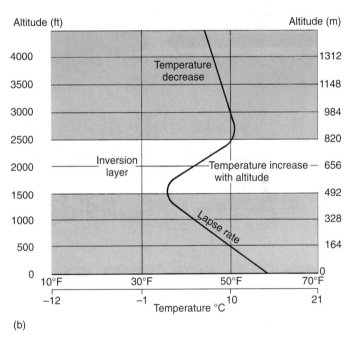

(b)

FIGURE 4.11 Temperature inversion. (a) A layer of warm, subsiding air acts as a cap, temporarily trapping cooler air close to the ground. **(b)** Note that air temperature decreases with distance from the ground until the warm inversion layer is reached, at which point the temperature increases.

Pressure Gradient Force

Because of differences in the nature of the earth's surface—water, snow cover, dark green forests, cities, and so on—and the other factors that affect energy receipt and retention, zones of high and low air pressure develop. Sometimes, these high- and low-pressure zones cover entire continents, but usually they are considerably smaller—several hundred miles wide—and within these regions, small differences are noted over short distances. When pressure differences exist between areas, a **pressure gradient force** causes air to blow from an area of high pressure toward an area of low pressure.

In order to balance pressure differences that have developed, air from the heavier high-pressure zones flows to low-pressure zones. Heavy air stays close to the earth's surface as it moves, producing winds, and forces the upward movement of warm air. The velocity, or speed, of the wind is in direct proportion to pressure differences. Winds are caused by pressure differences that induce airflow from zones of high pressure to zones of low pressure. If distances between high- and low-pressure zones are short, pressure gradients are steep and wind velocities are great. More gentle air movements occur when zones of different pressure are far apart and the degree of difference is not great.

The Convection System

A room's temperature is lower near the floor than the ceiling because warm air rises and cool air descends. The circulatory motion of descending cool air and ascending warm air is known as **convection** (Figure 4.13). A convectional wind system results when surface-heated warm air rises and is replaced by cool air from above.

The Coriolis effect and the pressure gradient force produce spirals rather than simple, straight-line patterns of wind, as indicated in Figure 4.15. The spiral of wind is the basic form of the many storms that are so important to the earth's air-circulation system. These storm patterns are discussed later in this chapter.

The Frictional Effect

Wind movement is slowed by the frictional drag of the earth's surface. The effect is strongest at the surface and declines until it becomes ineffective at about 1500 meters (about 1 mi) above the surface. Not only is wind speed decreased, but wind direction is changed as well. Instead of following a course exactly dictated by the pressure gradient force or by the Coriolis effect, the **frictional effect** causes wind to follow an intermediate path.

The Global Air-Circulation Pattern

Equatorial areas of the earth are zones of low pressure. Intense solar heating in these areas is responsible for a convectional effect. Note in Figure 4.16 how the warm air rises and tends to move away from the *equatorial low* pressure in both northerly and southerly directions. As equatorial air rises, it cools and eventually becomes dense. The lighter air near the surface cannot support the cool, heavy air. The heavy air falls, forming surface zones of high pressure. These areas of *subtropical high* pressure are located at about 30°N and 30°S of the equator.

When this cooled air reaches the earth's surface, it, too, moves in both northerly and southerly directions. The Coriolis effect, however, modifies wind direction and creates, in the Northern Hemisphere, belts of winds called the *northeast*

trades in the tropics and the *westerlies* (really the southwesterlies) in the midlatitudes. The names refer to the direction from which the winds come. Most of the United States lies within the belt of westerlies; that is, the air usually moves across the country from southwest to northeast. A series of ascending air cells also exists over the oceans to the north of the westerlies, called the *subpolar low*. These areas tend to be cool and rainy. The *polar easterlies* connect the subpolar low areas to the *polar high*. The general global air-circulation pattern is modified by local wind conditions.

It should be clear that these belts move in unison as the vertical rays of the sun change position. For example, equatorial low conditions are evident in the area just north of the equator during the Northern Hemisphere summer and just south of the equator during the Southern Hemisphere summer. Air circulation will be discussed in more detail in the section "Types of Precipitation."

The strongest flows of upper air winds, 9 to 12 kilometers (30,000 to 40,000 ft), are the **jet streams.** These air streams, moving at 160 to 320 kilometers per hour (100 to 200 mph), from west to east in both the Northern and Southern Hemispheres, circle the earth in an undulating pattern, first north then south as they move westward. There are three to six undulations at any one time in the Northern Hemisphere, but the waves are not always continuous. These undulations, or waves, control the flow of air masses on the earth's surface. More stable undulations are likely to create similar day-to-day weather conditions. These waves tend to separate cold polar air from warm tropical air. When a wave dips far to the south in the Northern Hemisphere, cold air is taken equatorward and warm air moves poleward, bringing severe weather changes to the midlatitudes. The jet stream is more pronounced in the winter than in the summer.

Nowhere does the manner in which the seasonal shift takes place have such a profound effect on humanity as in the densely populated areas of southern and eastern Asia. The wind, which comes from the southwest during summer in India, reaches the landmass after picking up a great deal of moisture over the warm Indian Ocean. As it crosses the coast mountains and foothills of the Himalayas, the monsoon rains begin. A **monsoon** wind is one that changes direction seasonally. The summer monsoon wind brings heavy showers over most of South Asia.

In the southern and eastern parts of Asia, the farm economy, and particularly the rice crop, is totally dependent on summer monsoon rainwater. If, for any of several possible reasons, the wind shift is late or the rainfall is significantly more or less than optimum, crop failure may result. The undue prolongation of the summer monsoon rains in 1978 caused disastrous flooding, crop failure, and the loss of lives in eastern India and Southeast Asia.

The transition to dry northerly monsoon winter winds occurs gradually across the region, first becoming noticeable in the north in September. By January, most of the subcontinent is dry. Then, beginning in March in southern areas, the yearly cycle repeats itself.

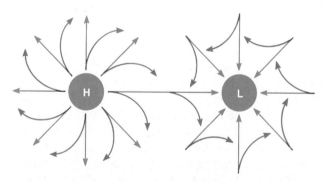

FIGURE 4.15 The effect of the Coriolis effect on flowing air in the Northern Hemisphere. The straight arrows indicate the paths that winds would follow flowing out of an area of high (H) pressure or into one of low (L) pressure, were they to follow the paths dictated by pressure differentials. The curved arrows represent the apparent deflecting effect of the Coriolis effect. Wind direction—indicated on the diagram by curved arrows—is always given by the direction *from* which the wind is coming.

FIGURE 4.16 **(a) The planetary wind and pressure belts as they would develop on an earth of homogeneous surface.** The high- and low-pressure belts represent surface pressure conditions; the wind belts are prevailing surface wind movements responding to pressure gradients and the Coriolis effect. Contrasts between land and water areas on the earth's surface, particularly evident in the Northern Hemisphere, create complex distortions of this simplified pattern. **(b) The general pattern of winds at increasing altitudes above the earth's surface.** When air descends, high pressure results; when air ascends, as at the equator, low pressure results.

OCEAN CURRENTS

Surface ocean currents correspond roughly to global wind direction patterns because the winds of the world set ocean currents in motion. In addition, just as differences in air pressure cause wind movements, so do differences in the density of water cause water movement. When water evaporates, residues of salt and other minerals that will not evaporate are left behind, making water denser. High-density water exists in areas of high pressure, where descending dry air readily picks up moisture. In areas of low pressure, where rainfall is plentiful, ocean water is low in density. Wind direction (including the Coriolis effect) and the differences in density cause water to move in wide paths from one part of the ocean to another (Figure 4.17).

There is an important difference between surface air movements and surface water movements. Landmasses are barriers to water movement, deflecting currents and sometimes forcing them to move in a direction opposite to the main current. Air, on the other hand, moves freely over both land and water.

The shape of an ocean basin also has an important effect on ocean current patterns. For example, the north Pacific current, which moves from west to east, strikes the western coast of Canada and the United States. The current is then forced to move both north and south, although the major movement is the cold ocean current that moves south along the California coast. In the Atlantic Ocean, however, as Figure 4.17 indicates, the current is deflected in a northeasterly direction by the shape of the coast (Nova Scotia and Newfoundland jut far into the Atlantic). It then moves freely across the ocean,

FIGURE 4.17 The principal surface ocean currents of the world. Notice how the warm waters of the Gulf of Mexico, the Caribbean, and the tropical Atlantic Ocean drift to northern Europe.

past the British Isles and Norway, finally reaching the extreme northwest coast of Russia. This massive movement of warm water to northerly lands, called the **North Atlantic drift,** has enormous significance to inhabitants of those areas. Without it, northern Europe would be much colder.

Ocean currents affect not only the temperature but also the precipitation on land areas adjacent to the ocean. A cold ocean current near land causes the air just above the water to be cold while the air above is warm. There is very little opportunity for convection, thus denying moisture to nearby land. Coastal deserts of the world usually border cold ocean currents. On the other hand, warm ocean currents—such as those off the coast of India—take moisture to the adjacent land area, especially when prevailing winds are landward (see "El Niño," p. 93).

The earlier question about ways in which differences in air pressure affect weather conditions is now answered, in terms of warm and cool air movement over various surfaces at different times of the year and different times of the day. A more complete answer regarding the causes of different types of weather conditions, however, requires an explanation of the susceptibility of places to receive precipitation, because rainfall and wind patterns are highly related.

MOISTURE IN THE ATMOSPHERE

Air contains water vapor (what we feel as humidity), which is the source of all precipitation. **Precipitation** is any form of water particles—rain, sleet, snow, or hail—that falls from the atmosphere and reaches the earth's surface. Ascending air can

FIGURE 4.18 The water-carrying capacity of air and relative humidity. The actual water in the air (water vapor) divided by the water-carrying capacity (×100) equals the relative humidity. The solid line represents the maximum water-carrying capacity of air at different temperatures.

expand easily because less pressure is on it. When heat from the lower air spreads through a larger volume in the troposphere, the mass of air becomes cooler. Cool air is less able to hold water vapor than warm air (Figure 4.18).

El Niño

El Niño is a term coined years ago by fishermen who noticed that the normally cool waters off the coasts of Ecuador and Peru were considerably warmer every 3 or 4 years around Christmastime, hence the name El Niño, Spanish for "the child," referring to the infant Jesus. The fish catch was significantly reduced during these periods. If fishermen had been able to identify the scientific associations that present-day oceanographers and climatologists make, they would have recognized a host of other effects that follow from El Niño.

During the winter of 1997–1998, an unusually severe El Niño caused enormous damage and hundreds of deaths. The West Coast of the United States, especially California, was inundated with rainfall amounts double, triple, and even quadruple normal. For the November to March winter period, San Francisco received 102.24 centimeters (40.25 in.) of rain—normal is 41.63 centimeters (16.39 in.). The 38 centimeters (15 in.) in February 1998 was the most for that month in the 150 years of record keeping in San Francisco. The resort city of Acapulco, Mexico, was badly battered by torrential rains and high, wind-blown tides. Parts of South America, especially Ecuador, Peru, and Chile, were ravaged by floods and mud slides, while droughts and fires scorched eastern South America, Australia, and parts of Asia, especially Indonesia. A stronger than usual southern branch of the jet stream generated by El Niño spawned dozens of tornadoes, which killed more than 100 people in Alabama, Georgia, and Florida.

The top diagram shows normal circumstances in the southern Pacific Ocean. Trade winds blow warm surface water westward and allow cold water to come to the surface along the South American coast. The bottom diagram shows that, during El Niño, winds from near Australia blow warm water eastward to the coast of South America.

Air is said to be *supersaturated* when it contains so much water vapor that the vapor condenses (changes from a gas to a liquid) and forms droplets if fine particles, called *condensation nuclei*, are present. These particles, mostly dust, pollen, smoke, and salt crystals, nearly always exist. At first, the tiny water droplets are usually too light to fall. As many droplets coalesce into larger drops, and become too heavy to remain suspended in air, they fall as rain. When temperatures below the freezing point cause water vapor to form ice crystals instead of water droplets, snow is created (Figure 4.19).

Large numbers of rain droplets or ice crystals form clouds, which are supported by slight upward movements of air. The form and altitude of clouds depend on the amount of water vapor in the air, the temperature, and wind movement. Descending air in high-pressure zones usually yields cloudless skies. Whenever warm, moist air rises, clouds form. The most dramatic cloud formation is probably the *cumulonimbus,* pictured in Figure 4.20. This is the anvil-head cloud that often accompanies heavy rain. Low, gray *stratus* clouds appear more often in cooler seasons than in warmer months. The very high, wispy *cirrus* clouds that appear in all seasons are made entirely of ice crystals. *Cumulus* clouds are often called fair-weather clouds.

Relative humidity is a percentage measure of the moisture content of the air, expressed as the amount of water vapor present relative to the maximum that can exist at the current temperature. As air gets warmer, the amount of water vapor it can contain increases. If the relative humidity is 100%, the air is completely saturated with water vapor. A relative humidity value of 60% on a hot day means the air is extremely humid and very uncomfortable. A 60% reading on a cold day, however, indicates that, although the air contains relatively large amounts of water vapor, it holds, in absolute terms, much less vapor than on a hot, muggy day. This example demonstrates that relative humidity is meaningful only if we keep air temperature in mind.

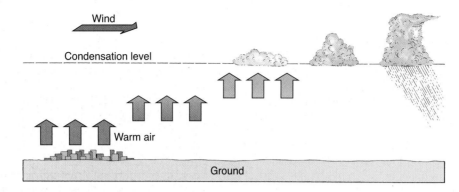

FIGURE 4.19 As warm air rises, it cools. As it cools, its water vapor condenses and clouds form. If the air becomes supersaturated, precipitation occurs.

FIGURE 4.20 Cloud types: (a) cumulonimbus, (b) stratus, (c) cirrus, (d) fair-weather cumulus. *(a) Corbis RF; (b) Courtesy of Jim W. Lee, National Weather Service; (c) NOAA; (d) Roger Scott.*

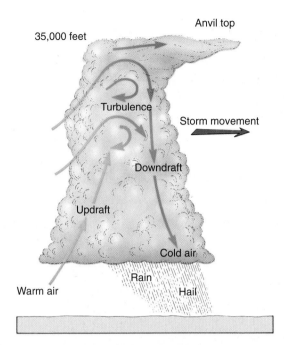

FIGURE 4.21 **Convectional precipitation.** When warm air laden with moisture rises, a cumulonimbus cloud may develop and convectional precipitation may occur. The falling particles within the system create a downdraft of cold upper-altitude air.

Dew on the ground in the morning means that nighttime temperatures dropped to the level at which condensation took place (see Figure 4.18). The critical temperature for condensation is called the **dew point.** Foggy or cloudy conditions on the earth's surface imply that the dew point has been reached and that relative humidity is valued at 100%.

Types of Precipitation

When large masses of air rise, precipitation may take place in one of three types: (1) convectional, (2) orographic, or (3) cyclonic, or frontal.

The first type, **convectional precipitation,** results from rising, heated, moisture-laden air. As air rises, it cools. When its dew point is reached, condensation and precipitation occur, as Figure 4.21 shows. This process is typical of summer storms or showers in tropical and continental climates. Usually, the ground is heated during the morning and early afternoon. Warm air that accumulates begins to rise, forming first cumulus clouds and then cumulonimbus clouds. Finally, lightning, thunder, and heavy rainfall occur, which may affect each part of the ground for only a brief period when the storm is moving. It is common for these convectional storms to occur in late afternoon or early evening.

If quickly rising air currents rapidly circulate air within a cloud, ice crystals may form near the top of the cloud. When these ice crystals are large enough to fall, a new updraft containing water can force them back up, enlarging the pieces of ice. This process may occur repeatedly until the updrafts can no longer sustain the ice pieces as they fall to the ground in the form of hail.

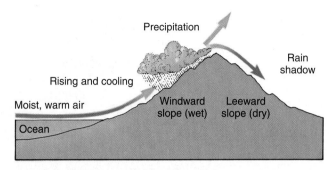

FIGURE 4.22 **Orographic precipitation.** Surface winds may be raised to higher elevations by hills or mountains lying in their paths. If such orographically lifted air is sufficiently cooled, precipitation occurs. Descending air on the leeward side of the upland barrier becomes warmer, its capacity to retain moisture is increased, and water absorption rather than release takes place.

Orographic precipitation, the second type and depicted in Figure 4.22, occurs as warm air is forced to rise because hills or mountains block moisture-laden winds. This type of precipitation is typical in areas where mountains and hills are downwind from oceans or large lakes. Saturated air from over the water blows onshore, rising as the land rises. Again, the processes of cooling, condensation, and precipitation take place. The *windward* side—the side exposed to the prevailing wind—of the hills and mountains receives a great deal of precipitation. The opposite side, called the *leeward* side or rain shadow, and the adjoining regions downwind are very often dry. The air that passes over the mountains or hills descends and warms. As we have seen, descending air does not produce precipitation, and warming air absorbs moisture from surfaces it passes over. A graphic depiction of the great differences in rainfall over very short distances is shown on the map of the state of Washington in Figure 4.23.

Cyclonic, or **frontal, precipitation,** the third type, is common to the midlatitudes, where cool and warm air masses meet. Although it is less frequent there, this type of precipitation also occurs in the tropics as the originator of hurricanes and typhoons. In order to understand cyclonic, or frontal, precipitation, first visualize the nature of air masses and the way cyclones develop.

Air masses are large bodies of air with similar temperature and humidity characteristics throughout; they form over a **source region.** Source regions include large areas of uniform surface and relatively consistent temperatures, such as the cold land areas of northern Canada, the north central part of Russia, and the warm tropical water areas in oceans close to the equator. Source regions for North America are shown in Figure 4.24. During a period of a few days or a week, an air mass may form in a source region. For example, in the fall in northern Canada, when snow has already covered the vast subarctic landscape, cold, dense, dry air develops over the frozen land surface.

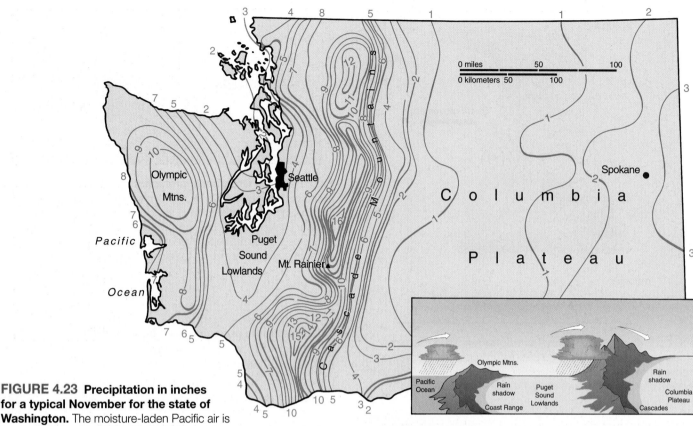

FIGURE 4.23 Precipitation in inches for a typical November for the state of Washington. The moisture-laden Pacific air is first forced up over the 1500- to 2100-meters (5000- to 7000-ft) Olympic Mountains; then it descends into the Puget Sound lowlands; then it goes up over the 2700- to 4300-meters (9000- to 14,000-ft) Cascade Mountains and finally down into the Columbia Plateau of eastern Washington. *Inset: From Robert N. Wallen, Introduction to Physical Geography. Copyright © 1993. McGraw-Hill Company, Inc., Dubuque, Iowa. All Rights Reserved. Reprinted by permission.*

This continental polar air mass begins to move toward the lighter, warmer air to the south. The leading edge of a tongue of air is called a **front.** The front, in this case, separates the cold, dry air from whatever other air is in its path. If a warm, moist air mass is in front of a polar air mass, denser, cold air hugs the ground and forces lighter air above it upward. The rising moist air condenses, and frontal precipitation occurs. On the other hand, the movement of rising warm air over cold air pushes the cold air back, again causing precipitation. In the first case, when cold air moves toward warm air, cumulonimbus clouds form and precipitation is brief and heavy. As the front passes, temperatures drop appreciably, the sky clears, and air becomes noticeably drier. In the second case, when warm air moves over cold air, steel-gray nimbostratus (*nimbo* means "rain") clouds form and precipitation is steady and long-lasting. As the front passes, warm, muggy air becomes characteristic of the area. Figure 4.25 summarizes the movement of fronts. Further discussion of air masses as regional entities can be found in Chapter 13.

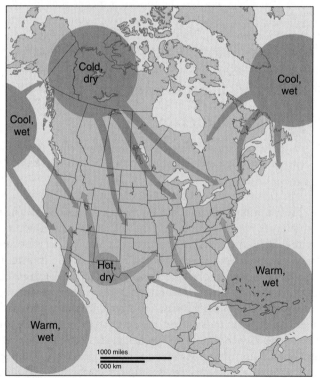

FIGURE 4.24 Source regions for air masses in North America. The United States and Canada, lying between major contrasting air-mass source regions, are subject to numerous storms and changes in weather. See also Figure 13.6. *From T. McKnight, Physical Geography: A Landscape Appreciation, 4th ed. Copyright © 1993. Adapted by permission of Prentice Hall, Englewood Cliffs, New Jersey.*

FIGURE 4.25 In this diagram, a cold front in the Northern Hemisphere has recently passed over city A and is heading in the direction of B. The meeting lines of unlike air masses are called *fronts.* The warm front is moving away from B and toward city C. The wind direction is shown by arrows and the air pressure by isobars, lines of equal atmospheric pressure. The isobars indicate that the lowest pressure is found at the intersection of the warm and cold fronts.

FIGURE 4.26 When warm and cold air come into contact along a low-pressure trough in the Northern Hemisphere midlatitudes, the possibility of cyclonic storm formation occurs. **(a)** A wave begins to form along the polar front. **(b)** Cold air begins to turn in a southerly direction, while warm air moves north. **(c)** Cold air, generally moving faster than warm air, begins to overtake the warm air, forcing it to rise and, in the process, the storm deepens. **(d)** Eventually, two sections of cold air join. The cyclonic storm dissipates as the cold front is reestablished.

Storms

Two air masses coming into contact (a front) creates the possibility of storms developing. If the contrasts in temperature and humidity are sufficiently great, or if wind directions of the two touching masses are opposite, a wave might develop in the front, as shown in Figure 4.26. Once established, the waves may enlarge. On one side of the front, cooler air moves along the surface, while on the other side, warm air moves up and over the cold air. The rising warm air creates a low-pressure center. Considerable precipitation is accompanied, in the Northern Hemisphere, by counterclockwise winds around the low-pressure area. A large system of air circulation centered on a region of low atmospheric pressure is called a midlatitude **cyclone,** which can develop into a storm.

An intense tropical cyclone, or **hurricane,** begins in a low-pressure zone over warm waters, usually in the Northern Hemisphere. In the developing hurricane, the warm, moist air at the surface rises, which helps suck up air from the surface. As a result, tall cumulonimbus clouds form. The energy released by these towering cloud formations warms the center of the growing storm. A feature of a hurricane is the calm, clear central core, called the *eye* (Figure 4.27a). The name given a hurricane in the western Pacific is **typhoon.**

Figure 4.27b shows the usual paths of hurricanes in the world. The winds of these storms move in a counterclockwise direction, converging near the center and rising in several concentric belts. Great damage is caused by the high winds (greater than 119 kilometers per hour [74 mph]) and the surge of ocean water into coastal lowlands. At the hurricane's center, the eye, air descends and results in gentle breezes and relatively clear skies. Over land, these storms lose their warm-water energy source and subside quickly. If they move farther into colder northern waters, they are pushed or blocked by other air masses and lose their energy source and abate. Table 4.1 describes increasingly devastating hurricanes.

(a)

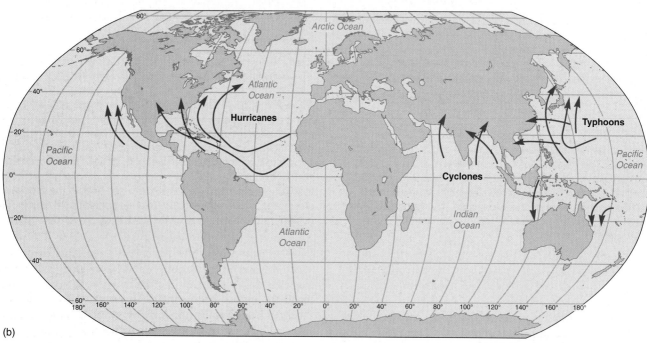

(b)

FIGURE 4.27 (a) Characteristics of a mature hurricane. Spiral bands of cumulonimbus clouds spawn heavy rainfall. Air ascends in the clouds near the center of the storm. The descending, warming air at the center creates an *eye,* a small area of calm on the surface. Intense convectional circulation creates strong winds away from the eye. **(b) General hurricane paths.** *(a) and (b) From Michael Bradshaw and Ruth Weaver,* Physical Geography: An Introduction to Earth Environment, *pp. 177, 179. Reprinted by permission of The McGraw-Hill Companies, Inc.*

The *New York Times* reported on February 26, 2010, that "a dangerous winter storm . . . walloped the Northeast overnight, leaving hundreds of thousands of winter-weary residents without power." The storm was one of several blizzards that attacked the East Coast in February 2010. A **blizzard** is the occurrence of heavy snow and high winds. Each of the February blizzards was created when a clash of air masses in the Rocky Mountains caused the jet stream to veer northeast along the East Coast. At the same time, a large low-pressure system along the Gulf of Mexico moved north, drawing an

additional stream of moist air from the Atlantic Ocean. In the meantime, a high-pressure system moved south with arctic air from Canada. These movements converged on the northeast United States. The results were strong winds and nearly a meter (3.3 ft) of crippling snow that brought cities such as Washington, D.C.; Baltimore; Philadelphia; New York; and Boston to a standstill (Figure 4.28a).

The most violent of all storms is the **tornado.** It is also the smallest storm (Figure 4.28b), typically measuring less than 30 meters (100 ft) in diameter. Tornadoes are spawned in the huge

TABLE 4.1

The Saffir-Simpson Hurricane Scale

Category	Barometric Pressure (Inches)	Wind (mph)	Damage
1	Over 28.94	74–95	Damage mainly to trees, shrubbery, unanchored mobile homes; storm surge damage for all categories. Storm surge generally 1.2 to 1.5 meters (4 to 5 ft) above normal.
2	28.50–28.94	96–110	Some trees blown down; major damage to exposed mobile homes; some damage to roofs. Storm surge: 1.8 to 2.4 meters (6 to 8 ft).
3	27.91–28.49	111–130	Trees stripped of foliage, large trees blown down; mobile homes destroyed; some structural damage to small buildings. Storm surge: 2.7 to 3.7 meters (9 to 12 ft).
4	27.17–27.90	131–155	All signs blown down; extensive damage to windows, doors, and roofs; flooding inland as far as 10 kilometers (6 mi); major damage to lower floors of structures near shore. Storm surge: 4.0 to 5.5 meters (13 to 18 ft).
5	Less than 27.17	Over 155	Severe damage to windows, doors, and roofs; small buildings overturned and blown away; major damage to structures less than 4.6 meters (15 ft) above sea level within 458 meters (500 yds) of shore. Storm surge: greater than 5.5 meters (18 ft) above normal.

cumulonimbus clouds that sometimes travel in advance of a cold front along a squall line. During the spring or fall, when adjacent air masses differ the most, the central United States is prone to many of these funnel-shaped killer clouds. Although winds can reach 500 kilometers per hour (about 300 mph), these storms are small and usually travel on the ground for less than a mile, so only limited areas are affected, though they may be devastated (Figure 4.28c). A tornado over water is called a *waterspout.*

The *Enhanced Fujita (EF) scale* of tornado intensity links reported damage to wind speed. It ranges from EF0, a "weak" tornado with wind speeds up to 137 kilometers per hour (85 mph), to EF5, a "violent" one, with winds as great as 322 kilometers per hour (200 mph). Most (74%) tornadoes are either EF0 or EF1, whereas 25% are classified as EF2 or EF3, "strong" tornadoes capable of causing major structural damage. Only 1% are in the violent (EF4 and EF5) categories.

CLIMATE REGIONS

We have traced some of the causes of weather changes that occur as air from high-pressure zones flows toward low-pressure areas, fronts pass and waves develop, dew points are reached, and sea breezes arise. Some parts of the world experience these changes more rapidly and more often than do other parts.

Day-to-day weather conditions can be explained by the principles explained in this chapter. However, the effect of weather elements—temperature, precipitation, and air pressure and winds—cannot be understood unless a person is conscious of the earth's surface features. Weather forecasters in each location on Earth must deal with weather elements in the context of their local physical and built environments.

The complexities of daily weather conditions may be summarized by statements about climate. The climate of an area is a generalization based on daily and seasonal weather conditions. Are summers warm, on the average? Is heavy snow in the winter likely? Are winds normally from the southeast? Are climatic averages typical of daily weather conditions, or are the day-to-day or week-to-week variations so great that one should speak of average variations rather than just averages? These are the questions we must ask in order to form an intelligent description of the differences in conditions from place to place.

The two most important elements that differentiate weather conditions are temperature and precipitation. Although air pressure is also an important weather element, differences in air pressure are hardly noticeable without the use of a barometer. Thus, we may regard warm, moderate, cold, or very cold temperatures as characteristic of a place or region. In addition, high, moderate, and low precipitation are good indicators of the degree of humidity or aridity in a place or region.

Figure 4.30 (see pp. 102–103) depicts the various climates of the world and is based on the type of information presented in Figure 4.31. Called the Köppen system, it is the best known of a number of similar climate classification schemes. Developed in 1918, it is based on natural vegetation in addition to temperature and precipitation criteria.

Table 4.2 on page 104 shows the multilevel system developed by Köppen. There are six broad categories, designated as A, B, C, D, E, and H. The A climates are tropical, B are dry, C are mild climates in the midlatitudes, D climates of the midlatitudes have severely cold winters, E are polar, and H are highland climates.

The column on the right in Table 4.2 lists the kinds of soils and vegetation typical of different climates. Soil types and various forms of vegetation go hand in hand with temperature levels and the seasonal distribution of precipitation. For a discussion of the relationship of climate to soils and vegetation, see Appendix 2.

(a)

(b)

(c)

FIGURE 4.28 Storms. (a) Blizzards bring the transportation systems of cities to a halt. **(b)** In the United States, tornadoes occur most frequently in the central and south central parts of the country (especially in Oklahoma, Kansas, and the Texas Panhandle), where cold polar air very often meets warm, moist Gulf air. **(c)** The Oklahoma City tornado of May 3, 1999, was an EF5; it leveled neighborhoods such as this one. *(a) © Brand X/Veer RF; (b) © Corbis RF; (c) Jeff Mitchell/Reuters.*

The letters of the Köppen system in the section headings that follow refer to those in Figure 4.30 and Table 4.2.

Tropical Climates (A)

Tropical climates are generally associated with earth areas lying between the northernmost and southernmost lines of the sun's vertical rays—the *Tropic of Cancer* and the *Tropic of Capricorn.* The location of tropical climates is shown in Figure 4.29.

Tropical Rain Forest (Af)

The areas that straddle the equator are generally located within the equatorial low-pressure zone. These regions are called **tropical rain forest.** They are warm, wet climates in both the winter and summer (Figure 4.31a, b). Rainfall usually comes from daily convectional thunderstorms, and although most days are sunny and hot, by afternoon, cumulonimbus clouds form and convectional rain falls. The caption for Figure 4.31a explains how to interpret a *climagraph.*

Tropical rain forests are typically filled with natural vegetation, which is still present but declining rapidly because of intentional fires in large areas of the Amazon Basin of South America and the Zaire River Basin of Africa. Tall, dense forests of broadleaf trees and heavy vines predominate. Among the hundreds of species of trees found in tropical rain forests, both dark woods and light woods, as well as spongy softwoods, such as balsa, and hardwoods, such as teak and mahogany, exist (Figure 4.31b). Rain forests also extend away from the equator along coasts where prevailing winds supply a constant source of moisture to coastal uplands. In addition, the orographic effect provides sufficient precipitation for heavy vegetation to develop in these forests.

Savanna (Aw)

As the sun's vertical rays extend farther from the equator in the summer, the equatorial low-pressure zone follows the sun's path. Thus, areas to the north and south of the rain forest are wet in the summer months, although still hot, but are dry the remainder of the year because the moist equatorial low has been replaced by the dry air of subtropical highs. These areas are known as **savanna** lands because of the kind of natural vegetation that grows here.

The natural vegetation of savannas resembles a form of scrub forest; however, these areas are now recognized as a grassland with widely dispersed trees. The natural tendency toward a more forested cover has been reduced by the periodic clearing by burning that local agriculturalists and hunters engage in. Savannas sometimes seem to have been purposely designed because of their parklike appearance, as indicated in Figure 4.32. The East African region of Kenya and Tanzania contains well-known grasslands—Serengeti National Park, for example—and fire-resisting species of trees, where large animals, such as giraffes, lions, and elephants, roam. The *campos* and *llanos* of South America are other huge savanna areas.

Monsoon (Am)

A special case in Asia needs mentioning. When summer monsoon winds carry water-laden air to the mainland, a significant increase in rainfall occurs on the hills, mountains, and adjacent plains. Notice the pattern of precipitation in Figure 4.33. As a result, vegetation is dense, even though the winters are dry. Jungle growth and large forests are the natural vegetation. Much of this vegetation, however, has ceased to exist because people have been using the land mainly for rice and tea production for many generations.

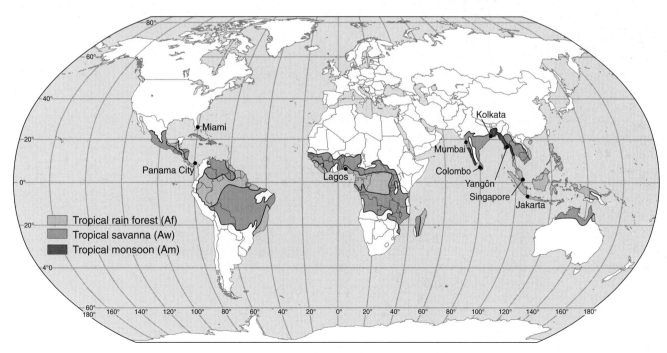

FIGURE 4.29 The location of tropical climates.

FIGURE 4.30 Climates of the world.

City: Singapore
Latitude: 1°20′N
Altitude: 11 meters (33 ft)
Yearly precipitation:
  256 centimeters (100.7 in.)

Climate designation: Af
Climate name: Tropical rain forest
Other cities with similar climates:
  Colombo, Panama City,
  Jakarta, Lagos

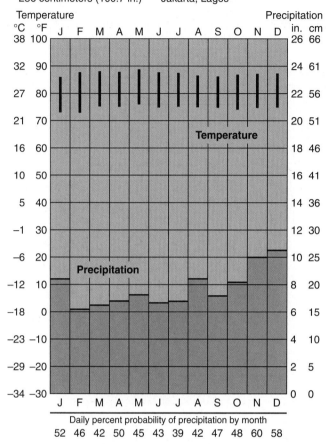

Daily percent probability of precipitation by month
52 46 42 50 45 43 39 42 47 48 60 58

(a)

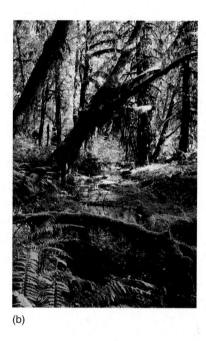

(b)

FIGURE 4.31 (a) This and succeeding climate charts (*climagraphs*) show average daily high and low temperatures for each month, the average precipitation for each month, and the probability of precipitation on any particular day in a designated month. For Singapore, the average daily high temperature in August is 30.5°C (87°F); the low is 24°C (75°F). The rainfall for the month, on average, is 21 centimeters (8.4 in.), and on a given day in August, there is a 42% chance of rainfall. **(b) Tropical rain forest.** The vegetation is characterized by tall, broadleaf, hardwood trees and vines. *(b) © Getty RF.*

FIGURE 4.32 The parklike landscape of grasses characteristic of the drier savanna. *© The McGraw-Hill Companies, Inc./Photo by Jill Wilson.*

Dryland Climates (B)

The location of these climates is shown in Figure 4.34. In the interior of continents where mountains block west winds, or in lands far from the reaches of moist tropical air, extensive regions of desert and *semidesert* conditions appear.

Hot Deserts (BWh)

On the poleward side of the savannas, grasses begin to shorten, and desert shrubs become evident. This is where we approach the belt of subtropical high pressure that brings considerable sunshine, hot summer weather, and very little precipitation. Note the minute amount of rainfall shown in Figure 4.35a. The precipitation that does fall is convectional but sporadic. As conditions become drier, fewer and fewer drought-resistant shrubs appear and, in some areas, only gravelly and sandy deserts exist, as suggested in Figure 4.35b.

The great, hot deserts of the world, such as the Sahara, the Arabian, the Australian, and the Kalahari, are all the products of high-pressure zones. Often, the driest parts of these deserts are along the western coasts, where cold ocean currents are found. Earlier, mention was made of the relationship between cold ocean currents and deserts.

Midlatitude Deserts and Semideserts (BWk, BS)

Figure 4.36a illustrates typical temperature and precipitation patterns in these midlatitude drylands. Occasionally, a summer convectional storm or a frontal system with some moisture occurs. The extreme dry areas are known as cold deserts. The moderately dry lands are called **steppes**. The natural vegetation is grass, although desert shrubs, pictured in Figure 4.36b, are found in drier portions of the steppes. Rain is not plentiful,

City: Yangôn, Myanmar
Latitude: 16°46′N
Altitude: 5.5 meters (18 ft)
Yearly precipitation:
  252 centimeters (99.2 in.)

Climate designation: Am
Climate name: Monsoon
Other cities with similar climates:
  Mumbai, Calcutta

FIGURE 4.33 Climagraph for Yangôn, Myanmar.

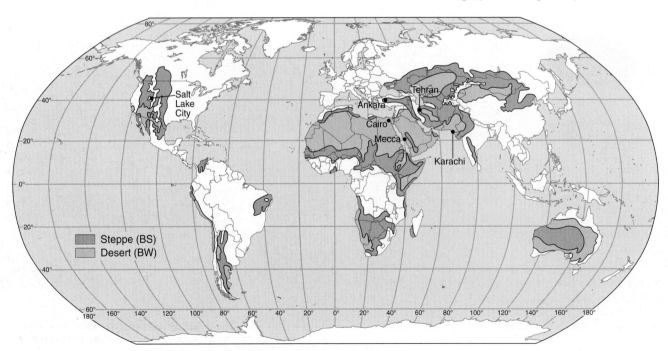

FIGURE 4.34 The location of steppe and desert climates.

City: Cairo, Egypt
Latitude: 29°52′N
Altitude: 116 meters (381 ft)
Yearly precipitation: 2 centimeters
(0.7 in.)

Climate designation: BWh
Climate name: Hot desert
Other cities with similar climates:
Mecca, Karachi

Temperature

Precipitation

°C °F   J F M A M J J A S O N D   in. cm
38 100
32 90
27 80
21 70   **Temperature**
16 60
10 50
 5 40
−1 30
−6 20
−12 10
−18 0
−23 −10
−29 −20   **Precipitation**
−34 −30

     J F M A M J J A S O N D
     Daily percent probability of precipitation by month
     3 3 3 0 0 0 0 0 0 0 3 3

26 66
24 61
22 56
20 51
18 46
16 41
14 36
12 30
10 25
 8 20
 6 15
 4 10
 2 5
 0 0

(a)

City: Tehran, Iran
Latitude: 35°41′N
Altitude: 1220 meters (4002 ft)
Yearly precipitation:
26 centimeters (10.1 in.)

Climate designation: BS
Climate name: Midlatitude dryland
Other cities with similar climates:
Salt Lake City, Ankara

Temperature

Precipitation

°C °F   J F M A M J J A S O N D   in. cm
38 100
32 90
27 80
21 70
16 60   **Temperature**
10 50
 5 40
−1 30
−6 20
−12 10
−18 0
−23 −10   **Precipitation**
−29 −20
−34 −30

     J F M A M J J A S O N D
     Daily percent probability of precipitation by month
     13 14 16 10 6 3 3 0 0 3 10 13

26 66
24 61
22 56
20 51
18 46
16 41
14 36
12 30
10 25
 8 20
 6 15
 4 10
 2 5
 0 0

(a)

(b)

FIGURE 4.35 (a) Climagraph for Cairo, Egypt. (b) Mohave Desert, California. Devoid of stabilizing vegetation, desert sands are constantly rearranged in complex dune formations.

(b) © Dr. Parvinder Sethi.

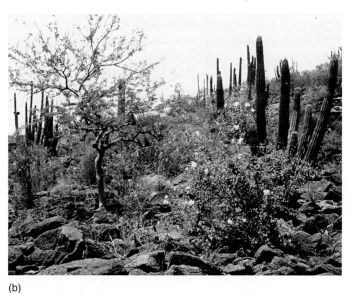

(b)

FIGURE 4.36 (a) Climagraph for Tehran, Iran. (b) Desert shrubs in the midlatitude drylands of northern Mexico.

(b) © Steven P. Lynch.

but soils are rich because the grasses return nutrients to the soil. The soils are dark brown to black and are among the most naturally fertile soils in the world. The steppes are also known for their hot, dry summers and biting winter winds, which sometimes bring blizzards.

Humid Midlatitude Climates (C)

Figure 4.37 shows the location of several climate types that are all humid—that is, not having desert conditions in the winter, summer, or both. In addition, winter temperatures well below those of the tropical climates are characteristic of the humid midlatitudes. These climate types would be neatly defined, paralleling the lines of latitude, were it not for mountain ranges, warm or cold ocean currents, and, particularly, land-water configurations. These factors cause the greatest variations in the middle latitudes.

Mediterranean Climate (Cs)

Midlatitude winds generally blow from the west in both the Northern and Southern Hemispheres, and a significant amount of the precipitation is produced from frontal systems. Thus, it is important to know if the water is cold or warm near land areas. Several climatic zones are noticeable in the middle latitudes, all marked by warm summer temperatures except those in areas cooled by westerly winds from the ocean.

To the poleward side of the hot deserts, a transition zone occurs between the subtropical high and the moist westerlies zones. Here, cyclonic storms bring rainfall only in the winter, when the westerlies shift toward the equator. Summers are dry and hot as the subtropical highs shift slightly poleward

(Figure 4.38a). Winters are not cold. The Mediterranean climate, is generally found on the western coasts of continents in the middle latitudes. Southern California, the Mediterranean area itself, western Australia, the tip of South Africa, and central Chile in South America are characterized by this type of climate. In these areas, shrubs and small deciduous trees, such as the scrub oak, grow (Figure 4.38b).

Humid Subtropical Climate (Cfa)

On the eastern coasts of continents, the transition is from the equatorial climate to the humid subtropical climate. Convectional summer showers and winter cyclonic storms are the sources of precipitation. As illustrated in Figure 4.39, this climate is characterized by hot, moist summers and moderate, moist winters. In the fall, on occasion, hurricanes that develop in tropical waters strike the coastal areas.

The generally even distribution of rainfall allows for the presence of deciduous forests containing hardwood trees, such as oak and maple, whose leaves turn orange and red before falling in autumn. In addition, conifers become mixed with deciduous trees as a second-growth forest. Southern Brazil, the southeastern United States, and southern China all have a humid subtropical climate.

Marine West Coast Climate (Cfb)

Closer to the poles, but still within the westerly wind belt, are areas of **marine west coast climate.** Here, cyclonic storms and orographic precipitation play a relatively large role. In the winter, more rainfall and cooler temperatures prevail than in the Mediterranean zones. Compare the patterns in Figures 4.38 and 4.40. In the transitional zone just poleward of the

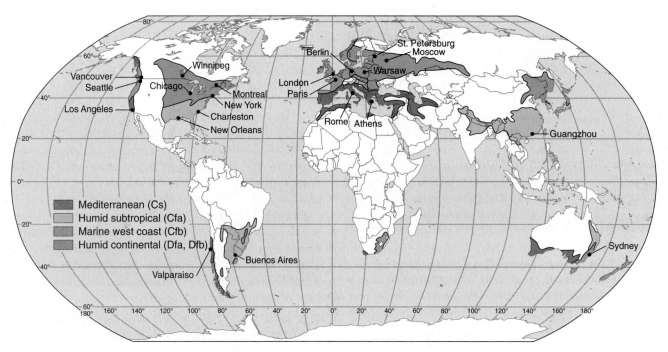

FIGURE 4.37 The location of humid midlatitude and continental climates.

City: Rome, Italy
Latitude: 41°48′N
Altitude: 115 meters (377 ft)
Yearly precipitation:
85 centimeters (33.3 in.)

Climate designation: Cs
Climate name: Mediterranean
Other cities with similar climates:
Athens, Los Angeles,
Valparaiso

Daily percent probability of precipitation by month

J	F	M	A	M	J	J	A	S	O	N	D
26	39	16	20	19	7	6	10	20	29	27	29

(a)

City: Sydney, Australia
Latitude: 33°58′S
Altitude: 9 meters (29 ft)
Yearly precipitation:
116 centimeters (46.5 in.)

Climate designation: Cfa
Climate name: Humid subtropical
Other cities with similar climates:
Guangzhou, Charleston,
New Orleans

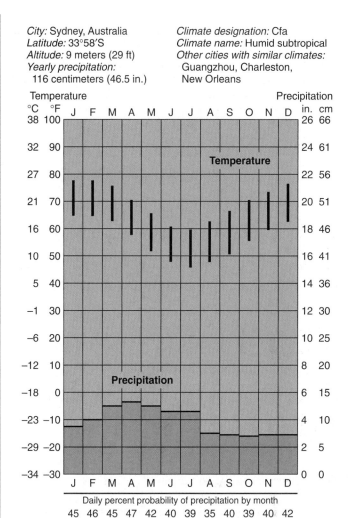

Daily percent probability of precipitation by month

J	F	M	A	M	J	J	A	S	O	N	D
45	46	45	47	42	40	39	35	40	39	40	42

FIGURE 4.39 Climagraph for Sydney, Australia. Because Sydney is in the Southern Hemisphere, the warmest days are in January and the coldest are in July.

(b)

FIGURE 4.38 (a) Climagraph for Rome, Italy. (b) Vegetation typical of an area with a Mediterranean climate (coastal California). Trees and brush are short and scattered. (b) © Digitalvision RF.

Mediterranean climate, little rainfall occurs during the summer. Closer to the poles, however, rainfall increases appreciably in the summer and even more so in the winter. Marine winds from the west moderate both summer and winter temperatures. Thus, summers are pleasantly cool, and winters, though cold, do not normally produce freezing temperatures.

This climate affects relatively small land areas in all but one region. Because northern Europe contains no great mountain belt to thwart the west-to-east flow of moist air, the marine west coast climate stretches well across the continent to Poland. In Poland, cyclonic storms originating in the Arctic regions are noticeable. Northern Europe's moderate climate also owes its existence to a relatively warm ocean current whose influence is felt for nearly 1600 kilometers (1000 mi), from Ireland to central Europe.

The orographic effect from mountains in areas such as the northwestern United States, western Canada, and southern Chile produces enormous amounts of precipitation, often in the form of snow on the windward side (see Figure 4.23). Vast coniferous forests—needle-leaf trees, such as pines, spruces,

City: Vancouver, Canada
Latitude: 49°17′N
Altitude: 14 meters (45 ft)
Yearly precipitation:
  105 centimeters (41.3 in.)

Climate designation: Cfb
Climate name: Marine west coast
Other cities with similar climates:
  Seattle, London,
  Paris

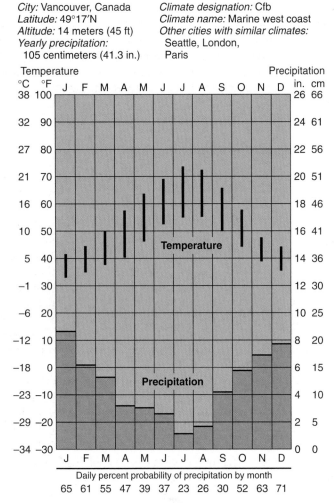

FIGURE 4.40 **Climagraph for Vancouver, Canada.**

City: Chicago, Illinois
Latitude: 41°52′N
Altitude: 181 meters (595 ft)
Yearly precipitation:
  85 centimeters (33.3 in.)

Climate designation: Dfa
Climate name: Humid continental
  (warm summer)
Other cities with similar climates:
  New York, Berlin,
  Warsaw

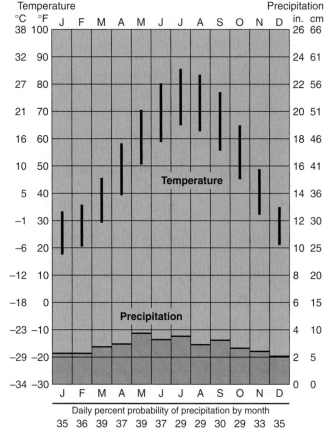

FIGURE 4.41 **Climagraph for Chicago, Illinois.**

and firs—cover the mountains' lower elevations. Because the mountains prevent moist air from continuing to the leeward side, midlatitude deserts are found to the east of these marine west coast areas.

Humid Continental Climates (D)

The poleward transition to the continental climates is accompanied by increasingly colder winters and shorter summers. In this direction as well, cyclonic storms become more responsible for rainfall than are convectional showers. The region can no longer be characterized as humid subtropical; rather, it is described as **humid continental** (Dfa, Dfb).

Air masses that originate close to the poles and drift toward the equator and other air masses that drift toward the poles from the tropics produce frontal precipitation. Whenever warmer air or marine air blocks cold continental air masses, or vice versa, frontal storms develop. Figure 4.41 shows the range and the dominance of winter temperatures within this climatic type.

The continental climate may be contrasted to marine west coast climates in that the former has prevailing winds from the land, the latter from the sea. Coniferous forests become more plentiful in the direction of the poles, until temperatures become so low that trees are denied an adequate growing season (Figure 4.42).

Three huge areas of the world are characterized by a humid continental climate: (1) the northern and central United States and southern Canada, (2) most of the European portion of Russia, and (3) northern China. Because there are no land areas at a comparable latitude in the Southern Hemisphere, this climate is not represented there. In fact, the only nonmountain cold climate in the Southern Hemisphere is the polar climate of Antarctica.

Subarctic Climates (Dfc, Dfd, Dwb)

Toward northern areas and into the interior parts of the North American and Eurasian landmasses, increasingly colder temperatures prevail (Figures 4.43 and 4.44a). Trees become stunted, and eventually only mosses and other cool-weather plants of the type shown in Figure 4.44b will grow.

Arctic Climates (E)

The word **tundra** (ET) is often used to describe the northern boundary zone beyond these treed subarctic regions. Because long, cold winters predominate, the ground is frozen most of the year. A few cool summer months, with an abundant supply of mosquitoes and flies, break up the monotony of extreme cold. Although very cold temperatures characterize the tundra, snowfall is not very abundant. Strong easterly winds blow snow, which, combined with ice fogs and little winter sunlight, contributes to a very bleak climate. Alaska, northern Canada, and northern Russia are covered with either the stunted trees of the subarctic climate or the bleak, treeless expanse of the tundra. Antarctica and Greenland, however, are icy deserts (EF).

Highland Climates (H)

We mentioned earlier (p. 85) that, under the normal lapse rate, temperatures decrease as altitude increases. As a result, highlands have lower temperatures than do lowlands at the same latitude. Highland climates are complex, however, because elevation and latitude are only two of the factors that determine their nature and the plant and animal life they can support. Some mountain slopes face the prevailing wind, while others are lee slopes. Some face the sun; others are shadowed and cool. Some are sunlit in the cool of the morning; others receive the hot afternoon sun. Mountain valleys have a different climate than do rugged peaks. Every mountain range, then, contains a mosaic of climates far too detailed to show on a map such as Figure 4.29.

These thumbnail sketches of climatic conditions throughout the world give us the basic patterns of large regions. On any given day, conditions may be quite different from those discussed or mapped in this chapter. However, the physical climatological processes, in general, are what concern us. We can deepen our understanding of climates by applying our knowledge of the elements of weather.

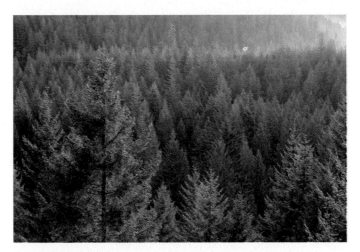

FIGURE 4.42 In the extensive region of east central Canada and the area around Moscow, Russia, the summers are long and warm enough to support a dense coniferous forest. Farther north, growth is less luxuriant. © *Getty RF.*

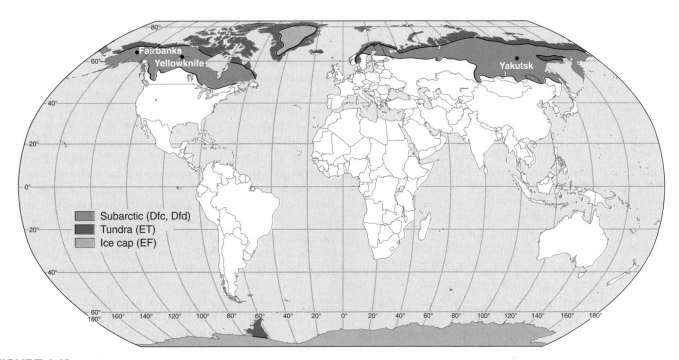

FIGURE 4.43 **The location of subarctic and Arctic climates.**

(b)

FIGURE 4.44 (a) Climagraph for Fairbanks, Alaska. (b) Tundra vegetation in Canada. *(b)* © *Getty RF.*

CLIMATIC CHANGE

We have stressed that climates are only averages of, perhaps, greatly varying day-to-day conditions. Figure 4.45 illustrates the global variation in yearly precipitation. Temperatures are less changeable than precipitation on a year-to-year basis, but they, too, vary. How can we account for these variations? Scientists in research stations all around the world are investigating this question. The data they use range from daily temperature and precipitation records to calculations concerning the position of the earth in relation to the sun. Because day-to-day records for most places date back only 50 to 100 years, scientists look for additional information about past climates in rock formations, the chemical composition of earth materials, ice cores, lake-floor sediments, tree rings, and other sources.

Long-Term Climatic Change

Significant variations in climate have occurred over geologic time. For example, approximately 65 million years ago, there was a sudden cooling of the earth's climate. This cooldown is thought to have caused the extinction of some 75% of all existing plant and animal species, including most dinosaurs. To take another example, cycles of ice sheet formation and breakup occurred at least five times during the last ice age, which lasted 100,000 years and ended only 11,000 years ago.

Climatologists have identified two major climatic periods just in the past 1000 years: a medieval warm period and a "little ice age." Between about A.D. 800 and 1200, during the medieval warm period, temperatures were as warm as or warmer than they are now. Settlement and farming expanded northward and to higher altitudes, the Vikings colonized Iceland and Greenland, and vineyards flourished in Britain. During the little ice age, which lasted from about A.D. 1300 to 1850, Arctic ice expanded, glaciers advanced, drier areas of the earth were desiccated, and crop failures and starvation were common.

Scientists have suggested several explanations for such long-term periodic changes in climate. Some of the climatic variations are thought to be due to three aspects of the earth's motion, all of which affect the amount of solar radiation reaching the planetary surface. First is the shape of the earth's orbit around the sun, which varies from nearly circular to more

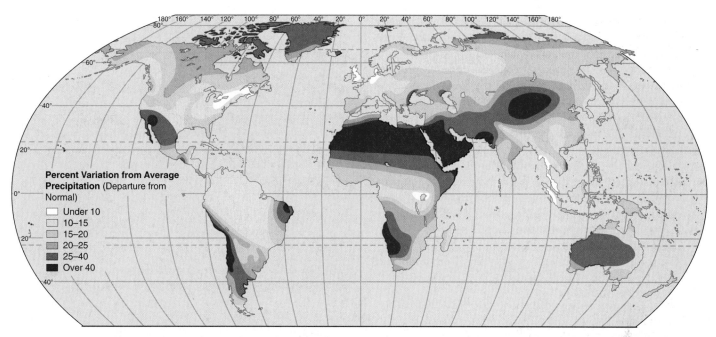

FIGURE 4.45 The world pattern of precipitation variability. Regions of low total precipitation tend to have high variability. In general, the drier the climate, the greater is the probability that there will be considerable differences in rainfall and/or snowfall from one year to the next.

elliptical over a period of about 100,000 years. When the orbit is nearly circular, the earth experiences relatively cold temperatures. When it is elliptical, as it is now, the earth is closer to the sun for several months, is exposed to more total solar radiation, and thus it has higher temperatures.

Another cycle corresponds to the tilt of the earth's axis relative to the orbital plane. The tilt varies from 21.5° to 24.5° every 41,000 years. The amount of solar radiation striking polar regions changes as the angle of tilt changes. A low tilt position—that is, a more perpendicular position of the earth—is accompanied by periods of colder climate. Cooler climates are thought to be critical in the formation of ice sheets.

Finally, like an unbalanced spinning top, the earth wobbles slightly as it rotates, changing the earth's orientation to the sun. The gyration of the rotation axis repeats every 23,000 years. When the tilt of the axis is greatest, the polar regions receive less solar radiation than they do at other times and become colder.

Short-Term Climatic Change

Climate can change more quickly and irregularly than the earth's cycles suggest. Great volcanic eruptions can alter climates for several years. They spew enormous amounts of ash, water vapor, sulfur dioxide, and other gases into the upper atmosphere. As these solid and liquid particles spread over much of the planet, they block some of the incoming solar radiation that normally would reach the earth's surface, producing a cooling effect. The famous "year without a summer"—1816—in New England, when snow fell in June and frost came in July, probably was caused by the eruption a year earlier of the Indonesian volcano Tambora. The explosion

ejected an estimated 200 million tons of gaseous aerosols and 50 cubic kilometers (30 cu mi) of dust and ash into the atmosphere. The reflective cooling effect lasted for years. A similar decline in temperatures occurred after the 1883 volcanic eruption of Krakatoa, also in Indonesia. A less extreme drop in temperatures in the early 1990s was attributed to the July 1991 eruption of Mount Pinatubo in the Philippines, which lowered average global temperatures by about 0.5°C (about 1°F).

Two other factors responsible for short-term climatic changes are alterations in patterns of oceanic circulation and sunspot activity. As described on page 93, for example, during an El Niño event, warm surface waters from the western Pacific Ocean move eastward, changing the climate along the western coasts of South and North America. Sunspots, relatively cool regions on the surface of the sun, vary in number and intensity over periods of years. They affect both the output of solar energy and the concentrations of ozone in the earth's upper atmosphere.

The Greenhouse Effect and Global Warming

All of the cycles and factors we have discussed are natural processes. In contrast, one of the most important questions has been whether human beings are contributing to climatic change through what is popularly termed the **greenhouse effect.** Put simply, the theory is that certain gases concentrate in the atmosphere, where they function as an insulating barrier, trapping infrared radiation that would otherwise be radiated back into the upper atmosphere and reradiating it earthward. In other words, like glass in a greenhouse, the gases admit incoming solar radiation but retard its reradiation back into space. You have experienced such a greenhouse effect if you have gotten into a car that has been in the sun; the car's interior is warmer than the outside air.

The earth has a *natural* greenhouse effect, provided mainly by water vapor that has evaporated from the ocean or evapotranspired from land. The water vapor remains a constant, but during the past 150 years or so, human activities have increased the amount of other greenhouse gases in the atmosphere, augmenting its heat-trapping ability. Most scientists fear that an *enhanced* greenhouse effect is responsible for a gradual increase in the earth's average surface temperature, with significant impacts on the earth's ecosystems, a process called **global warming.** *That* greenhouse effect is far less benign and nurturing than the name implies.

The Intergovernmental Panel on Climate Change (IPCC), made up of thousands of scientists from about 120 countries, reported in May 2007 that

> *Global atmospheric concentrations of carbon dioxide (CO$_2$), methane, and nitrous oxide have increased markedly as a result of human activities since 1750 and now far exceed pre-industrial values determined from ice cores spanning many thousands of years. The global increases in CO$_2$ concentration are due primarily to fossil fuel use and land use change, while those of methane and nitrous oxide are primarily due to agriculture.*

Carbon dioxide (CO$_2$) is the primary greenhouse gas whose amount has been increased by human activities. Although it occurs naturally, excessive quantities of it are released by burning fossil fuels. Beginning with the Industrial Revolution in the mid-1700s, large amounts of coal, petroleum, and natural gas have been burned to power industry, to heat and cool cities, and to drive vehicles. Their combustion has turned fuels into carbon dioxide and water vapor. At the same time, much of the world's forests have been destroyed by logging and to clear land for agriculture. Deforestation adds to the greenhouse effect in two ways: it means there are fewer trees to capture carbon dioxide and produce oxygen, and burning the wood sends CO$_2$ back into the atmosphere at an accelerated rate. The relative contribution of carbon dioxide to the potential for global warming is about 55%.

Other important greenhouse gases influenced by human activity are

1. methane, from natural gas and coal mining, agriculture and livestock, swamps, and landfills
2. nitrous oxides, from motor vehicles, industry, and nitrogen-containing fertilizers
3. chlorofluorocarbons, hydrofluorocarbons, and perfluorocarbons, widely used industrial chemicals

Although these gases may be present in small amounts, some of them trap heat much more effectively than does CO$_2$. Nitrous oxide, for example, has 360 times the capacity of CO$_2$ to trap heat, and even methane is 24 times more potent than CO$_2$ in absorbing heat close to the earth.

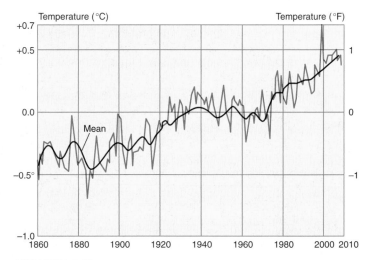

FIGURE 4.46 **Global temperature difference above and below the long-term average (set to 0), 1860–2005.**
Source: NOAA.

As the Industrial Revolution gained momentum in Europe and North America during the 19th century, the concentration of CO$_2$ in the atmosphere rose from its preindustrial level of about 274 parts per million (ppm) to 315 ppm in 1958; it rose since then to 379 ppm in 2005. The methane concentration in the lower atmosphere has *already* more than doubled from its preindustrial level and is currently increasing by just over 1% per year.

Scientists fear that the accelerated warming trend of the past 50 years has exceeded typical climate shifts and cite evidence such as the following:

- The 20th century was the warmest century of the past 600 years, and most of its warmest years were concentrated near its end. The world's average surface temperature rose about 0.6°C (a bit over 1°F) in the 20th century, and the 1990s were the hottest decade of the century (Figure 4.46).
- Winter temperatures in the Arctic have risen about 4°C (7°F) since the 1950s. The Arctic as a whole is losing its ice cap. Between 1978 and 2000, the coverage of Arctic sea ice in winter decreased by 6%, and the average thickness of Arctic ice declined by 42%, from 3.1 meters to 1.8 meters (10.2 to 5.9 ft). Similarly, the sea ice west of the Antarctic Peninsula has diminished more than 20% since 1970.
- On every continent, glaciers are thinning and retreating. For example, glaciers atop Mount Kilimanjaro and Mount Kenya in Africa shrank by 70% or more during the 20th century, and glaciers in the Swiss Alps are estimated to have lost half their volume since 1850. These patterns of glacial thinning and retreat are repeated in Alaska, Peru, Russia, India, China, Irian Jaya, New Zealand, and elsewhere. In some places (e.g., portions of Montana's Glacier National Park and the eastern Himalayas),

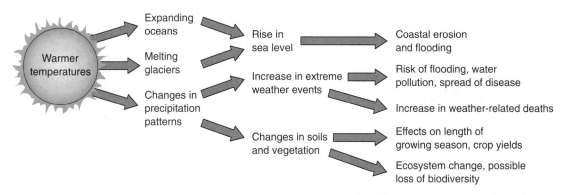

FIGURE 4.47 Potential effects of global warming. Global warming is projected to cause an increase in the frequency and severity of extreme weather events and weather-related disasters: heavy downpours, floods, hurricanes, heat waves, drought, and wildfires. Secondary effects of short-term extremes of weather would be shifts in plant and animal ranges; an increase in water pollution; and the spread of infectious diseases as warmer, wetter weather conditions widen the range of disease-carrying insects.

glaciers melted and disappeared altogether in the 20th century. Although glaciers have grown and retreated for thousands of years, the rate of melt has accelerated in the past few decades and now exceeds anything in recent centuries.

Whatever the attributable causes of global warming, most climatologists agree on certain of its general consequences, should it continue (Figure 4.47). Increases in sea temperatures would cause ocean waters to expand slightly (thermal expansion) and the polar ice caps to melt at least a bit. More serious consequences would result from the melting of the Greenland ice sheet and the rapid retreat or total melting of glaciers throughout the world. Although melting sea ice has no effect on sea levels, water melted from continental sources adds to ocean volumes. Inevitably, sea levels would rise, perhaps 1 meter (3.3 ft) in a hundred years, with devastating impacts, especially in the tropics and warm temperate regions, where many coastlines are heavily settled. As Figure 4.48 shows, the most vulnerable areas are along the north and west coasts of Africa, South and Southeast Asia, and low-lying coral atolls in the Pacific and Indian Oceans. In addition, higher temperatures bring on more extreme heat events, causing increased deaths among the elderly, infants, and the infirm.

Other problems would result from changes in precipitation patterns. The warming of lakes and oceans would speed evaporation, causing more active convection currents in the atmosphere. It is important to note that changes in precipitation would be regional, with some areas receiving more and others less precipitation than they do now. Polar and equatorial regions might get heavier rainfall, whereas the continental interiors of the midlatitudes could become drier and suffer at least periodic drought. More northerly agricultural regions, such as parts of Canada, Scandinavia, and Russia, might benefit from general temperature rises; the longer growing season would make them more productive. Changes in temperature and precipitation would affect soils and vegetation. The

composition of forests would change, as some areas would become less favorable for certain species of plants but more hospitable to others.

Many climatologists point out that climate prediction is not an exact science. Temperature differences are the engine driving the global circulation of winds and ocean currents and help create conditions inducing or inhibiting winter and summer precipitation and daily weather conditions. Exactly how those vital climate details would express themselves locally and regionally is not well understood.

Critics of the IPCC report claim that climate models don't adequately account for clouds and argue that global temperatures might stabilize or even decrease as the concentration of greenhouse gases increases. A hotter atmosphere, they say, would increase evaporation, sending up more water vapor, which could condense into clouds. The increased cloud cover might reflect so much sunlight that it would slow the rate at which the earth would be heated. Others contend that the increased evaporation would produce more rainfall. As it fell, the rain would cool the land and subsequently cool the air over the land.

Some scientists have gone so far as to suggest that global warming could, paradoxically, bring about the onset of another ice age. They reason that greenhouse-related temperature increases would likely warm upper latitudes sufficiently to permit heavy snowfall to commence in regions—such as northern Greenland—where snow now rarely falls. An increase in upper-latitude precipitation would yield a dramatic influx of fresh water and ice subject to melting in polar oceans. That influx would dilute the salt content of oceans; major ocean currents, such as the Gulf Stream (which provides northern Europe with a relatively warm climate), would slow and so would their warming effect on northern regions. An abrupt drop in polar temperatures can bring about significant changes in world climatic patterns. Recent evidence, it is claimed, indicates that polar regions did, in fact, grow slightly warmer before the onset of the previous glacial period, just as they are warming now.

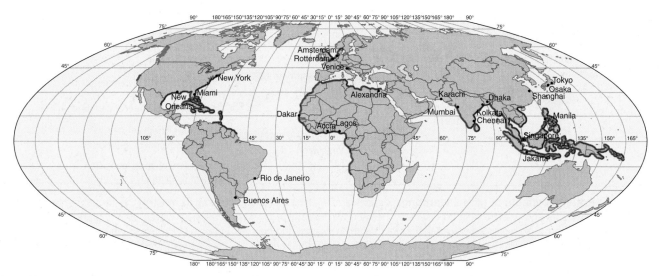

FIGURE 4.48 Coastal areas and major cities most affected by rise in sea level. The acceleration of global warming could produce significant changes in sea level and patterns of precipitation. Approximately one-sixth of the world's people live at or just a few meters above sea level, and hundreds of millions live in cities downstream from mountains where accelerated melting of glaciers or snow could contribute to severe flooding, especially if the river basins have been heavily deforested. Even a 1-meter (3-ft) rise in sea level would be enough to cover the Maldives and other low-lying island countries. The homes of between 50 and 100 million people would be inundated, a fifth of Egypt's arable land in the Nile delta would be flooded, and the impact on the people of Bangladesh who live on thousands of alluvial islands known as "chars" would be catastrophic.

Summary of Key Concepts

- Solar energy is the great generator of the main weather elements of temperature, moisture, and atmospheric pressure. Spatial variation in these elements is caused by two factors: the earth's broad physical characteristics, such as greater solar radiation at the equator than at the poles, and local physical characteristics, such as the effect of water bodies or mountains on local weather conditions.

- Climate regions help us simplify the complexities that arise from such special conditions as monsoon winds in Asia or cold ocean currents off the western coast of South America.

- Knowledge of climate tells us about the conditions within which one carries out life's daily tasks.

- Climate change results from both long-term and short-term natural processes.

- Human use of the earth affects the climate.

Although the following chapters focus mainly on the characteristics of human cultural landscapes, one should keep in mind that the physical landscape significantly affects human behavior.

Key Words

air mass 95	cyclonic (frontal) precipitation 95	hurricane 97
air pressure 85	dew point 95	insolation 82
blizzard 98	El Niño 93	jet stream 90
climate 81	frictional effect 90	land breeze 88
convection 87	front 96	lapse rate 85
convectional precipitation 95	global warming 114	marine west coast climate 108
Coriolis effect 89	greenhouse effect 113	monsoon 90
cyclone 97	humid continental climate 110	mountain breeze 89

North Atlantic drift 92
orographic precipitation 95
precipitation 92
pressure gradient force 87
reflection 84
relative humidity 93
reradiation 84

savanna 101
sea breeze 88
source region 95
steppe 106
temperature inversion 85
tornado 98
tropical rain forest 101

troposphere 81
tundra 111
typhoon 97
valley breeze 89
weather 81

Thinking Geographically

1. What is the difference between *weather* and *climate?*

2. What determines the amount of *insolation* received at a given point? Does all potentially receivable solar energy actually reach the earth? If not, why?

3. How is the atmosphere heated? What is the *lapse rate* and what does it indicate about the atmospheric heat source? Describe a *temperature inversion.*

4. What is the relationship between atmospheric pressure and surface temperature? What is a *pressure gradient* and of what concern is it in weather forecasting?

5. In what ways do land and water areas respond differently to equal insolation? How are these responses related to atmospheric temperatures and pressures?

6. Draw and label a diagram of the planetary wind and pressure system. Account for the occurrence and character of each wind and pressure belt. Why are the belts latitudinally ordered?

7. What is *relative humidity?* How is it affected by changes in air temperatures? What is the *dew point?*

8. What are the three types of large-scale *precipitation?* How does each occur?

9. What are *air masses?* What is a *front?* Describe the development of a cyclonic storm, showing how it relates to air masses and fronts.

10. What factors were chiefly responsible for today's weather?

11. Summarize the distinguishing temperature, moisture, vegetation, and soil characteristics of each type of climate.

12. What is the climate at Tokyo, London, São Paulo, and Bangkok?

13. What causes the greenhouse effect? What impact might it have on the environment?

What Is Energy?

People have built their advanced societies by using inanimate energy resources. **Energy**—the ability to do work—is either potential or kinetic. *Potential* energy is stored energy; when released, it is in a form that can be harnessed to do work. *Kinetic* energy is the energy of motion; all moving objects possess kinetic energy.

Assume that a reservoir contains a large amount of stored water. The water is a storehouse of potential energy. When the gates of the dam holding back the water are opened, water rushes out. Potential energy has become kinetic energy, which can be harnessed to do such work as driving a generator of electricity. No energy has been lost; it has simply been converted from one form to another.

Unfortunately, energy conversions are never complete. Not all of the potential energy of the water can be converted into electrical energy. Some potential energy is always converted to heat and dissipated to the surroundings. *Energy efficiency* is the measure of how well we can convert one form of energy into another without waste—that is, the ratio of energy that is produced to the amount of energy consumed in the production process.

solar energy stored in plants via photosynthesis. In fact, nearly all energy sources are really storehouses for energy originally derived from the sun. Among them are wood, water, the wind, and the fossil fuels. People have harnessed each of these energy sources, to a greater or lesser degree. Preagricultural societies depended chiefly on the energy stored in wild plants and animals for food, although people developed certain tools (such as spears) and customs to exploit the energy base. For example, they added to their own energy resources by using fire for heating, cooking, and clearing forest land.

Sedentary agricultural societies developed the technology to harness increasing amounts of energy. The domestication of plants and animals, the use of wind to power ships and windmills, and the use of water to turn waterwheels all expanded the energy base. For most of human history, wood was the predominant source of fuel, and even today at least half the world's people depend largely on fuelwood for cooking and heating.

However, it was the shift from renewable resources to those derived from nonrenewable minerals, chiefly fossil fuels, that sparked the Industrial Revolution, made possible the population increases discussed in Chapter 6, and gave population-supporting capacity to areas far in excess of what would be possible without inanimate energy sources. The enormous increase in individual and national wealth in industrialized countries has been built in large measure on an economic base of coal, oil, and natural gas. They are used to provide heat, to generate electricity, and to run engines.

Energy consumption goes hand in hand with industrial production and increases in per capita income. In general, the greater the level of energy consumption, the higher the gross national income per capita. As people grow richer, they want better homes, more cars, and all the other goods that characterize developed countries—which means a large increase in the global demand for energy and industrial raw materials. Two of the questions now being asked are whether the world has enough resources to meet the rising demand in the developing countries and what effects that demand will have on the supplies and prices of resources.

NONRENEWABLE ENERGY RESOURCES

Crude oil, natural gas, and coal have formed the basis of industrialization. Figure 5.5 shows past energy consumption patterns in the United States. Burning wood supplied most energy needs until about 1885, by which time coal had risen to prominence. The proportion of energy needs satisfied by burning coal peaked about 1910; from then on, oil and natural gas were increasingly substituted for coal. The graph shows the absolute dominance of the fossil fuels as energy sources during the last 100 years. In 2008, they accounted for about 90% of national energy consumption.

Crude Oil

Today, crude oil and its by-products account for almost 40% of the commercial energy (excluding wood and other traditional fuels) consumed in the world. Some world regions and industrial countries have a far higher dependency. Figure 5.6 shows the main producers and consumers of crude oil (also called petroleum).

FIGURE 5.5 Sources of energy in the United States, 1850–2008. The fossil fuels provided almost 90% of the energy supply in 2008.

After it is extracted from the ground, crude oil must be refined. The hydrocarbon compounds are separated and distilled into waxes and tars (for lubricants, asphalt, and many other products) and various fuels. Petroleum rose to importance because of its combustion characteristics and its adaptability as a concentrated energy source for powering moving vehicles. A barrel (42 U.S. gallons) of crude oil produces about 20 gallons of gasoline, 10 gallons of diesel fuel and home heating oil

(combined), 5 gallons of jet fuel, and other products. In the United States, transport fuels account for two-thirds of all oil consumption.

As Figure 5.7 shows, oil from a variety of production centers flows, primarily by water, to the industrially advanced countries. Note that the United States imports oil from a number of regions. The other major importers, Western Europe and Japan, import chiefly Middle Eastern oil.

The efficiency of pipelines, supertankers, and other modes of transport and the low cost of oil helped create a world dependence on that fuel, even though coal was still generally and cheaply available. The pattern is aptly illustrated by American reliance on foreign oil. For many years, U.S. oil production had remained at about the same level, 8 to 9 million barrels per day. Between 1970 and 1977, however, as domestic supplies became much more expensive to extract, consumption of oil from foreign sources increased dramatically, until almost half of the oil consumed nationally was imported. The dependence of the United States and other advanced industrial economies on imported oil gave the oil-exporting countries tremendous power, reflected in the soaring price of oil in the 1970s. During that decade, oil prices rose dramatically, largely as a result of the strong market position of the Organization of Petroleum Exporting Countries (OPEC).

Among the side effects of the oil "shocks" of 1973–1974 and 1979–1980 were worldwide recessions, large net trade deficits for oil importers, a reorientation of world capital flows, and a depreciation of the U.S. dollar against many other currencies. On the positive side, the soaring oil prices of the 1970s triggered oil exploration in non-OPEC countries, improvements in oil-drilling technology, and a search for alternative energy sources. Perhaps most important, for a number of years, they diminished total energy demand, partly because of the recession and partly because the high prices fostered conservation. Industrial countries have learned to use much less oil for each unit of output. In general, cars, planes, and other machines are more energy efficient than they were in the 1970s, as are industries and buildings constructed in recent years.

Since 1985, however, both global production and consumption of oil have increased steadily. And the United States, which satisfied 69% of its oil needs by domestic production in each year between 1982 and 1986, has since then relied increasingly on imports. By 2007, the United States depended on foreign sources for 66% of the oil it consumed annually (see "Fuel Economy and CAFE Standards," pp. 126–127).

It is particularly difficult to estimate the size of oil reserves. Not only are estimates constantly revised as oil is extracted and new reserves are located, but many governments tend to maintain some secrecy about the sizes of reserves, understating official national estimates. Nonetheless, it is clear that oil is a finite resource and that oil reserves are very unevenly distributed among the world's countries (Figure 5.8). Slightly more than 1200 billion barrels are classified as proved reserves, and another 900 billion are thought to exist in undiscovered reservoirs. If all

FIGURE 5.6 (a) Leading producers of oil. These seven countries produced 51% of the world's oil in 2008. Members of OPEC are marked with an asterisk. All told, OPEC countries accounted for 45% of oil production in 2008. **(b) Leading consumers of oil.** Only the six countries shown here each consumed 3% or more of the world's oil in 2008. *Source: Data from The BP Statistical Review of World Energy, June 2009.*

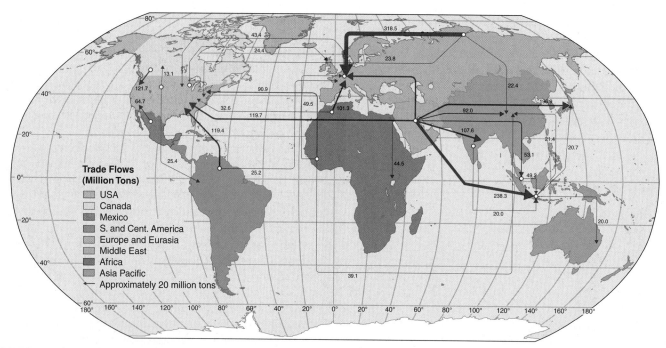

FIGURE 5.7 International crude oil flow by sea, 2008. Note the dominant position of the Middle East in terms of oil exports. The arrows indicate origin and destination, not specific routes. The line widths are proportional to the volume of movement. In 2008, the United States imported 66% of the oil it used. *Source: Data from* The BP Statistical Review of World Energy, *June 2009.*

the oil could be extracted from the known reserves, and if the current rate of production holds, the proved reserves would last only about 40 years. The ratio of production to reserves, however, gives some Middle Eastern countries more than a century of pumping at current rates before their oil fields run dry.

For more than 40 years, there have been predictions that the world would soon run out of oil. Pessimists still believe that global oil production could peak by 2015, whereas optimists think we will rely on oil for most if not all of this century. They argue that technological advances in exploration and production, such as deep-water drilling and enhanced recovery, will so significantly increase the amount of oil that can be recovered from beneath the ground that we needn't worry about gas pumps running dry.

Whereas it was once thought that offshore oil existed only in shallow waters, current thinking is that enormous amounts of oil lie thousands of feet below sea level off the Gulf of Mexico, Brazil, and West Africa. For several years now, a number of oil companies have pumped oil from the Gulf of Mexico at depths exceeding 1000 meters (3280 ft).

Even more promising is the possibility of recovering more oil from existing reservoirs. Currently, on average, only 30% to 35% of the oil in a reservoir is brought to the surface; most of the oil remains unrecovered. Oil industry optimists believe that enhanced recovery techniques (injecting water, gases, or chemicals into wells to force out more oil) will make 60% to 70% of the oil in a reservoir recoverable.

Finally, although most geologists agree that there are few huge oil fields left to be discovered, some of these have yet to be tapped in a major way. Industry analysts think significant

increases in production are likely to come from Russia and a number of the countries of the former Soviet Union (Kazakhstan, Tajikistan, Uzbekistan, Turkmenistan, Kyrgyzstan, and Azerbaijan). Kazakhstan, for example, is developing large new oil fields and constructing new pipelines out of the Caspian basin, and Russia has begun to develop huge offshore oil fields in its far east, near Sakhalin Island in the Sea of Okhotsk.

Coal

Coal was the fuel basis of the Industrial Revolution. From 1850 to 1910, the proportion of U.S. energy supplied by coal rose from 10% to almost 80%. Although the consumption of coal declined as the use of petroleum expanded, coal remained the single most important domestic energy source until 1950 (see Figure 5.5, p. 122).

Although coal is a nonrenewable resource, world supplies are so great that its resource life expectancy may be measured in centuries, not in the much shorter spans usually cited for oil and natural gas. The United States alone possesses nearly 240 billion tons of coal considered potentially mineable on an economic basis with existing technology. At current production levels, these demonstrated reserves would be sufficient to meet the domestic demand for coal for another 2.5 centuries.

Worldwide, the most extensive deposits are concentrated in the middle latitudes of the Northern Hemisphere, as shown in Figure 5.9. Two countries, China and the United States, have dominated world coal production in recent years, accounting for more than half the coal produced in the world. Since 1990, the use of coal worldwide has remained fairly steady, but distinct

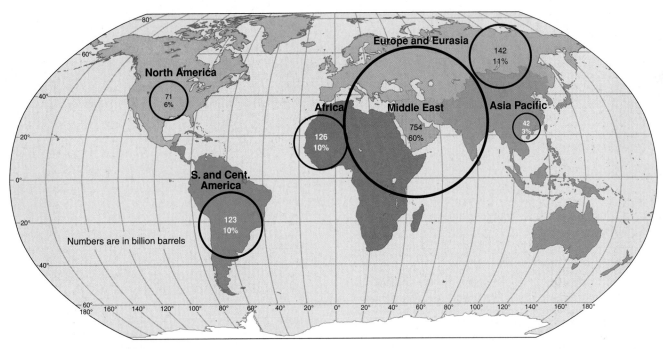

FIGURE 5.8 Regional shares of proved oil reserves, in billions of barrels, January 1, 2009. Oil supplies are finite, and some countries may deplete their reserves in the foreseeable future. The United States consumes about one-quarter of the world's oil supply but possesses only 2.4% of the world's reserves. Middle Eastern countries contain about three-fifths of the proved reserves (Saudi Arabia alone has 21% of the world's oil reserves). At the beginning of 2009, the world's proved oil reserves were estimated to be 1258 billion barrels, a figure that tends to rise over time with new methods of locating and extracting oil deposits and changes in price. In 2008, global consumption of oil was about 31 billion barrels per year. *Source: Data from* The BP Statistical Review of World Energy, *June 2009.*

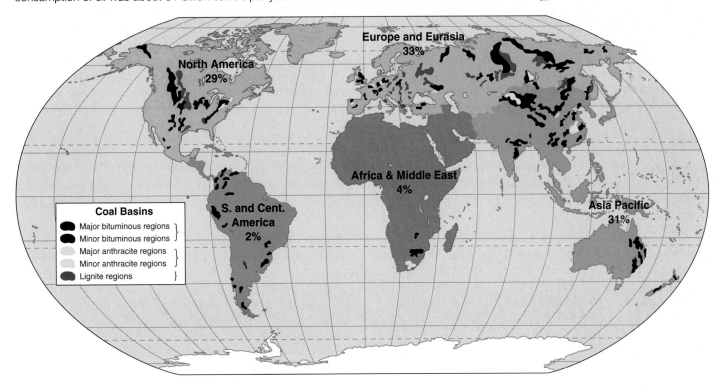

FIGURE 5.9 Regional shares of proved coal reserves, January 1, 2009. Major coal basins are concentrated in the Northern Hemisphere. Just five countries contain three-quarters of the world's coal reserves: the United States (29%), the Russian Federation (19%), China (14%), India (7%), and Australia (9%). Despite their large size, Africa and South America have very little coal. In 2008, China was the world's largest coal producer and consumer, followed by the United States. *Source: Reserve data from* The BP Statistical Review of World Energy, *June 2009.*

GEOGRAPHY & *Public Policy*

Fuel Economy and CAFE Standards

Some have likened the United States to a crude-oil junkie, dependent on daily fixes of petroleum. On average, every person in the United States uses almost 3 gallons of oil each day. Transportation accounts for 2 of those gallons. What are some of the implications of this dependence?

Consider the data in the following table.

Country	2008 Proved Reserves (Billion Barrels)	2008 Production (Billion Barrels)	2008 Consumption (Billion Barrels)
United States	31	2.4	7.1
Canada	29	1.2	0.8
Mexico	12	1.2	0.7

Notice the imbalance between yearly production and consumption for the United States. In contrast to its hemispheric neighbors, Canada and Mexico, the United States consumes far more oil than it produces. At current rates of consumption, and assuming no imports, the proved reserves would meet domestic demand for only 4 years. Americans continue to drive their cars, and their manufacturing plants continue to turn out a wide range of petroleum-based products, only because the country imports about 10 million barrels of oil a day. That is, the United States relies on foreign sources to meet about two-thirds of its crude-oil needs.

Slightly less than half of the oil used in the United States is burned as fuel in private automobiles, SUVs, and light trucks. When the price of oil tripled in the mid-1970s, Congress set fuel efficiency standards, and Americans began buying smaller cars, helping bring down the per capita consumption of gasoline. Between 1973 and 1987, the average fuel efficiency of new American automobiles increased from 13.1 miles per gallon (mpg) to 22.1 mpg. That increase alone cut gasoline consumption by 20 billion gallons per year, lowering oil imports by 1.3 million barrels of oil per day.

As the price of gasoline declined in the 1990s, however, Americans reverted to past practices, buying large, non-fuel-efficient vehicles, such as SUVs, minivans, and family-oriented pickup trucks with two rows of seats. They became so popular in the United States that they soon accounted for about half of all new passenger vehicles sold in the country. Big SUVs are gas guzzlers, and their popularity has driven down the average gas mileage (fuel-economy) ratings of vehicles driven in America. Despite advances in fuel-saving technology, the average vehicle is less efficient than it was in 1988.

The fuel efficiency of automobiles varies widely. The most efficient vehicles get more than 45 miles per gallon, while the least efficient average only 10. The high fuel consumption of large SUVs not only exacerbates U.S. dependence on foreign sources of oil but also has negative environmental impacts. If the average fuel efficiency of the vehicle fleet increased just 3 mpg, the United States would save 1 million barrels of oil per day, out of the roughly 10 million barrels it imports. Automobiles account for about 20% of the country's carbon dioxide emissions, and the more fuel a vehicle consumes, the greater its emissions. A car that gets 26 miles to the gallon has only half the emissions of one that averages 13 mpg. Every gallon of gasoline burned puts about 13 pounds of carbon dioxide into the atmosphere, contributing to the greenhouse effect and global warming. The nitrogen oxides and hydrocarbons emitted by vehicles contribute to acid rain and ozone smog (topics discussed in Chapter 12), respectively.

One way to address these environmental concerns and simultaneously reduce American dependence on imported oil would be

regional variations in its use are evident. Coal production has risen slightly in the United States but has fallen in Western Europe and the countries of the former Soviet Union, as governments have discontinued subsidies to the industry. The use of coal continues to grow in many Asian countries (India, Indonesia, South Korea, Vietnam, and Japan). China has doubled both its production and its consumption of coal since 2000, a result of its rapid economic growth. In the United States and other industrialized countries, coal is used chiefly for electric power generation and to make coke for steel production. In less-developed countries, coal is widely used for home heating and cooking, as well as to generate electricity and fuel factories.

Coal is not a resource of constant quality. It ranges from lignite (barely compacted from the original peat) through bituminous coal (soft coal) to anthracite (hard coal), each *rank* reflecting the degree to which organic material has been transformed. Anthracite has a fixed carbon content of about 90% and contains very little moisture. Conversely, lignite has the highest moisture content and the lowest amount of elemental carbon, and thus the lowest heat value. About half of the demonstrated reserve base in the United States is bituminous coal, concentrated primarily in the states east of the Mississippi River.

Besides rank, the *grade* of a coal, which is determined by its content of waste materials (particularly ash and sulfur), helps to determine its quality. Good-quality bituminous coals with the caloric content and the physical properties suitable for producing coke for the steel industry are decreasingly available readily and are increasing in cost. Anthracite, formerly a dominant fuel for home heating, is now much more expensive to mine and finds no ready industrial market. The Schuylkill

© Getty RF.

to increase energy efficiency. Current federal *Corporate Average Fuel Economy (CAFE) standards* require each automaker's fleet of new passenger cars to average 27.5 miles per gallon and its light truck fleet (pickups, SUVs, and minivans) 21.3 mpg. The less-stringent fuel-economy standard for light trucks originally was intended to avoid penalizing builders, farmers, and others who relied on pickup trucks for their work, but it opened the way for automakers to replace station wagons and sedans with vehicles that met the definition of a light truck: SUVs and minivans.

In 2007, Congress passed the Energy Independence and Security Act, the first overhaul of CAFE standards in decades. The act required automakers to boost fleetwide gas mileage to at least 35 mpg by the year 2020 and ordered the Department of Transportation to devise a timetable. Proponents of raising the CAFE standards significantly higher note that the technologies to boost automobile efficiency significantly without sacrificing safety already exist. They point out that Japanese standards mandate 30.3 mpg, and European regulations an even higher 33.0 mpg. Increased energy efficiency is the quickest and cheapest path to reduced fuel consumption and a cleaner and healthier world, they argue. Additionally, they contend that SUVs endanger other motorists because they limit visibility and because they cause more damage in a crash.

Automobile industry officials, however, point out that they offer a variety of vehicles, some more fuel efficient, some less, and that people are free to choose the model they like. Most Americans, they say, are more concerned about automotive safety, comfort, and performance than about fuel economy. Some buyers cite the safety of SUVs. As one SUV owner noted, "It's a very safe vehicle. I bought this thing because it was a big iron tanker that wouldn't bend. You get hit by something and don't feel it." Others value the space a minivan or an SUV offers: "When you have a boat to haul and a family to transport, you don't have a lot of choice; you need large capacity."

Considering the Issues

1. With which of the following statements do you agree? Disagree? Why?

   "Allowing the American free-market system to meet America's energy needs hasn't worked. The automobile industry cannot be trusted to regulate itself. Automakers won't improve the fuel economy of their fleets unless the government forces them to."

   "Government regulation isn't the way to go. Maybe $4-per-gallon gasoline will make people buy higher mileage vehicles."

   "Gas prices have to rise much higher to encourage people to buy vehicles with higher mileage. When adjusted for inflation, gasoline at $3 per gallon is still cheaper than it was in 1984."

   "We can't force people to buy more efficient vehicles. We have to balance environmental concerns with what customers want, and many of them favor bigger engines and vehicles more than fuel efficiency."

2. Do you think Congress should raise CAFE standards higher than it did in 2007? Domestic automakers have opposed raising the standards, claiming that would rob them of their profits and force them to lay off workers. What credence do you give their claims, given that in previous years automakers predicted that mandatory seat belts, catalytic converters, and emission controls would drive them out of business?

3. Should SUVs and minivans continue to be subject to less stringent regulations than other passenger cars? Why or why not?

4. Should automakers be allowed to pay penalties rather than comply with the CAFE standards?

---

anthracite deposits of eastern Pennsylvania are discussed as a special type of resource region in Chapter 13.

The value of a coal deposit is determined not only by its rank and grade but also by its accessibility, which depends on the thickness, depth, and continuity of the coal seam and its inclination to the surface. The two methods of extracting coal are surface mining and underground mining. In *surface mining* (also called *strip mining*), huge machines strip off the soil and rock above the vein of coal—the *overburden*—to get at the coal beneath. In general, surface mining is used if the overburden is less than 100 meters (328 ft) thick. If the overburden is thicker, coal is extracted using *underground mining* (also called *shaft mining*) where operators sink two or more shafts down to the coal deposit. Underground mining is not only expensive but is among the most hazardous occupations in the world.

In spite of their generally lower heating value, western U.S. coals are now attractive because of their low sulfur content. They do, however, require expensive transportation to markets or high-cost transmission lines if they are used to generate electricity for distant consumers (Figure 5.10).

The ecological, health, and safety problems associated with the mining and combustion of coal must also be figured into its cost. The mutilation of the original surface and the acid contamination of lakes and streams associated with the strip mining and burning of coal are partially controlled by environmental protection laws, but these measures add to the costs. Eastern U.S. coals have a relatively high sulfur content, and costly techniques for the removal of sulfur and other wastes from stack gases are now required by most industrial countries, including the United States.

FIGURE 5.10 Long-distance transportation adds significantly to the cost of low-sulfur western U.S. coals because they are remote from eastern U.S. markets. To minimize these costs, unit trains carrying only coal engage in a continuous shuttle movement between western strip mines and eastern utility companies. © *Craig Nelson/Index Stock Imagery/Photolibrary.*

The cost of moving coal influences its patterns of production and consumption. Coal is bulky and is not as easily transported as nonsolid fuels. As a rule, coal is usually consumed in the general vicinity of the mines. Indeed, the high cost of transporting coal induced the development of major heavy industrial centers directly on coal fields—for example, Pittsburgh, the Ruhr, the English Midlands, and the Donets district of Ukraine.

Natural Gas

Coal is the most abundant fossil fuel, but natural gas has been called the nearly perfect energy source. It is a highly efficient, versatile fuel that requires little processing and is environmentally benign. Of the fossil fuels, natural gas (which is mainly methane) has the least impact on the environment. It burns cleanly. The chemical products of burned methane are carbon dioxide and water vapor, which are not pollutants, although they are greenhouse gases.

As Figure 5.5 indicates, the 20th century saw an appreciable growth in the proportion of U.S. energy supplied by gas. In 1900, it accounted for about 3% of the national energy supply. By 1980, the figure had risen to 30%, but then it declined to 25% by 2009. The trend in the rest of the world has been in the opposite direction. Global production and consumption increased significantly after the oil shock of 1973–1974 and by 2007 had nearly doubled, accounting for almost 25% of global energy consumption.

Most gas is used directly for industrial and residential heating. In fact, gas has overtaken both coal and oil as a house-heating fuel, and more than half of the homes in the United States are now heated by gas. A portion is also used in electricity-generating plants, and some is chemically processed into products as diverse as motor fuels, plastics, synthetic fibers, and insecticides.

Very large natural gas fields were discovered in Texas and Louisiana as early as 1916. Later, additional large deposits were found in the Kansas–Oklahoma–New Mexico region. At that time, the south-central United States was too sparsely settled to make use of the gas, and in any case, it was oil, not gas, that was being sought. Many wells that produced only gas were capped. Gas found in conjunction with oil was vented or burned at the wellhead as an unwanted by-product of the oil industry. The situation changed only in the 1930s, when pipelines were built to link the southern gas wells with customers in Chicago, Minneapolis, and other northern cities. Like oil, natural gas flows easily and cheaply by pipeline. In the United States, the pipeline system is more than 1.6 million kilometers (1 million mi) long.

Unlike oil, however, gas does not move as freely in international trade (Figure 5.11). Transoceanic shipment involves costly equipment for liquefying the gas by cooling it to $-126°C$ ($-260°F$), for double-hulled tankers that can contain the liquid under appropriate temperature conditions, and for reheating facilities at the destination port, where it is injected into the local pipeline system. **Liquefied natural gas (LNG)** is extremely hazardous because the mixture of methane and air is explosive. The United States imports some LNG, chiefly from Trinidad and Tobago. By 2009, eight terminals for receiving LNG were open in the United States, and 40 more had been proposed. Because an accident or a terrorist strike on an LNG tanker carrying millions of gallons of highly flammable fuel would generate an enormous fireball, onshore facilities are risky. Offshore facilities, from which the gas is piped underwater to the port, are less hazardous but pose environmental dangers to marine ecosystems.

Like other fossil fuels, natural gas is nonrenewable; its supply is finite. Estimates of reserves are difficult to make because they depend on what customers are willing to spend for the fuel, and estimates have risen as the price of gas has increased. Further complicating the estimate of supplies is uncertainty about potential gas resources in unusual types of geologic formations. These include tight sandstone formations, deep (below 6000 meters, or 20,000 ft) geologic basins, and shale and coal beds.

Worldwide, just two regions contain two-thirds of the proved gas reserves: Russia (23%) and the Middle East (41%) (Figure 5.12). The remaining 36% is divided roughly equally among North America, Western Europe, Africa, Asia, and Latin America, each of which has from 4% to 8% of the total. The gas in the proved reserves would last about 65 more years at current production rates, but developing countries, particularly in South and Southeast Asia, may well have undiscovered deposits that could add significantly to the life expectancy of world reserves if they were developed.

In the United States, the Texas-Louisiana and Kansas–Oklahoma–New Mexico regions account for about 90% of the domestic natural gas output, but there are thought to be gas

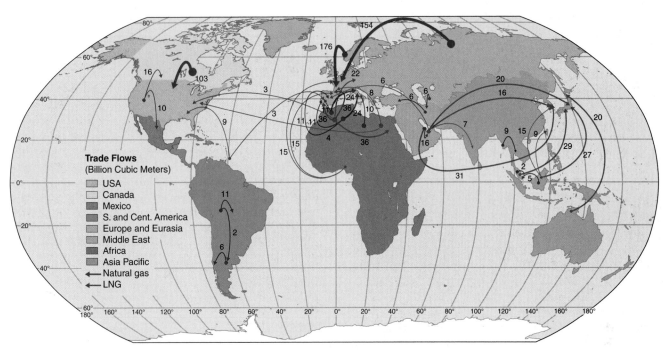

FIGURE 5.11 Major worldwide trade flows of natural gas, 2008. Russia exported gas to more than 20 other European countries, accounting for nearly 30% of the worldwide trade flows. The Netherlands and Norway accounted for another 25%. Most natural gas flows by pipeline, but diminishing supplies of natural gas in many developed countries, the discovery of large reserves of natural gas in remote regions, and a reduction in the costs associated with trade in liquefied natural gas (LNG) are combining to make LNG more attractive. In 2008, only five countries—Japan, South Korea, France, Spain, and Taiwan—imported significant amounts of LNG, accounting for 80% of the world trade in the fuel, but that pattern may shift during the next decade. *Source: Data from* The BP Statistical Review of World Energy, *June 2009.*

deposits beneath almost all states. In addition, many offshore areas are known to contain gas. Potential Alaskan reserves are estimated to be at least twice as large as today's proved reserves in the rest of the country, containing enough gas to heat all of the houses in the country for a decade. If the technology necessary to produce gas from unconventional sources is developed, gas reserves may be sufficient for another century. Of course, these less-accessible supplies will be more costly to develop, and hence more expensive.

Oil Shale and Tar Sands

A similar situation affects the prospects of the extraction of oil from unconventional fossil fuels: oil shale and tar sands. Both are stored in unconventional places, within rock and sand.

Neither shale nor oil, **oil shale** is fine-grained sedimentary rock rich in organic material called *kerogen*. A tremendous potential reserve of hydrocarbon energy, the rocks are calcium and magnesium carbonates more similar to limestone than to shale, and the hydrocarbon, kerogen, is not oil but a waxy, tar-like substance that adheres to the grains of carbonate material. The crushed rock is heated to a temperature high enough (more than 480°C, or 900°F) to decompose the kerogen, releasing a liquid oil product, *shale oil.*

World reserves of oil shale are enormous. Known deposits estimated to contain at least 800 billion barrels of recoverable shale oil are found in the United States, Brazil, Russia, China,

and Australia (Figure 5.13). The richest deposits in the United States are in the Green River formation, which lies beneath Colorado, Utah, and Wyoming. They contain enough oil to supply the needs of the United States for another century, and in the 1970s were thought to be the answer to national energy self-sufficiency. Several billion dollars were invested in oil shale research and development operations in the Piceance Basin near Grand Junction, Colorado, but as oil prices fell in the 1980s, interest in the projects waned. The last plant, that at Parachute Creek, Colorado, was abandoned in 1992.

Another source of petroleum liquids is **tar sand.** Also called oil sands, tar sands are a mixture of sand, clay, and silt (85%), water (5%), and *bitumen* (10%), a very thick, tar-like, high-carbon petroleum. The crude bitumen is too thick to flow out of the rock, so the tar sand must be mined, crushed, and heated to extract the petroleum. Global tar-sand resources are thought to be many times larger than conventional oil resources, containing more than 2 trillion barrels of oil, much of it in the province of Alberta, Canada (Figure 5.14). Four major deposits in Alberta are estimated to contain as much as 1 trillion barrels of bitumen. The largest deposit, the Athabasca, supplies about 10% of Canada's annual oil demand. Tar-sand deposits are also found in Venezuela, Trinidad, Russia, and Utah.

Producing oil from either oil shale or tar sands requires high capital outlays and carries substantial environmental costs. It requires a great deal of energy and fresh water, disturbs large areas of land, and produces enormous amounts of

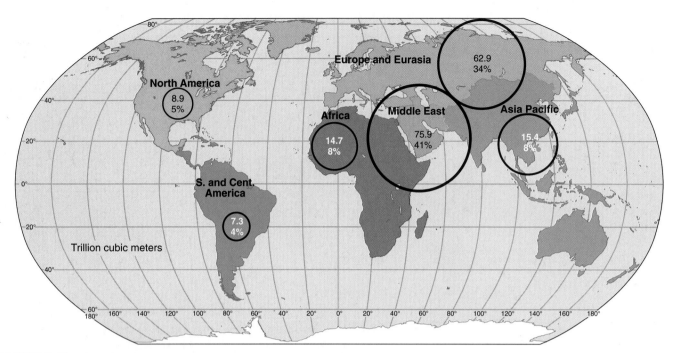

FIGURE 5.12 Proved natural gas reserves, January 1, 2009. Russia contains the largest natural gas reserves of any single country, about 23% of the world total (more than 6 times the size of U.S. reserves). Major reserves also exist in the countries of the Middle East, particularly Iran and Qatar. *Source: Data from* The BP Statistical Review of World Energy, *June 2009.*

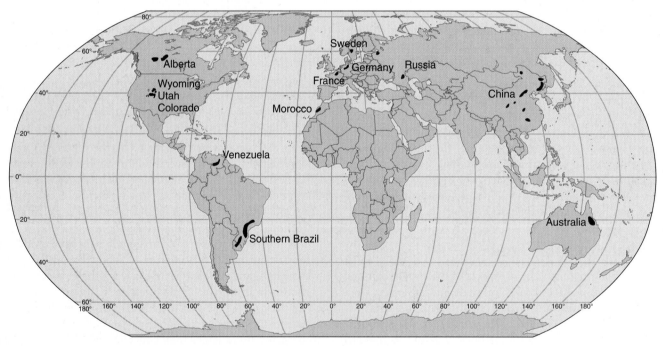

FIGURE 5.13 Oil shale deposits. The United States contains about two-thirds of the world's known supply of oil shale, with the richest deposits located in the Green River formation. Oil shale is unlikely to become an important resource until ways are found to process it economically and to solve the waste-disposal and land-reclamation problems its mining poses.

waste. The production also creates greenhouse gases and pollutes air, water, and surrounding soil.

Nevertheless, because they exist in vast amounts, oil shale and tar sands could be plentiful sources of gaseous and liquid fuels. Unlike nuclear energy or most renewable energy sources (such as solar or hydroelectric power), they could provide the gasoline, jet, and other fuels on which industrialized societies depend. The lowering of oil and gas prices in the 1980s and a decline in government support put a temporary halt to efforts to make alternative fuels economically competitive with oil. As reserves of oil and natural gas become depleted, however, at some point their prices are bound to rise. When that occurs, countries

(a)

(b)

FIGURE 5.14 **(a) Tar-sand deposits in Alberta, Canada.**
(b) Production of synthetic oil from the tar sands involves four
steps: (1) the removal of overburden; (2) mining and transportation
to extraction units; (3) the addition of steam and hot water
to separate the bitumen from the tailings residue; and (4) the
refinement of the bitumen into coke and distillates. It takes about
2 tons of sand to yield a single barrel of oil. *(b) © Wally Bauman/ALAMY.*

are likely to turn to these more unconventional sources of fuel.
In the meantime, technologies employing nuclear energy as a
source of nonfuel power are already developed.

Nuclear Energy

Proponents consider nuclear power a major long-term solution
to energy shortages. Assuming that the technical problems
can be solved, they contend that nuclear fuels could provide
a virtually inexhaustible source of energy. Other commentators, pointing to the dangers inherent in any system dependent
on the use of radioactive fuels, argue that nuclear power poses
technological, political, social, and environmental problems for
which society has no solutions. Basically, energy can be created
from the atom in two ways: nuclear fission and nuclear fusion.

Nuclear Fission

The conventional form of **nuclear fission** for power production involves the controlled "splitting" of an atomic nucleus
of uranium-235, the only naturally occurring fissile isotope.
When U-235 atoms are split, about one-thousandth of the
original mass is converted to heat. The released heat is transferred through a heat exchanger to create steam, which drives
turbines to generate electricity.

A single pound of U-235 contains the energy equivalent of nearly 5500 barrels of oil. More than 440 commercial
nuclear reactors around the world tap that energy, generating
about 16% of the world's electricity (Figure 5.15). About one-
fourth of those plants are in the United States.

Some countries are much more dependent than others on
nuclear power. Nuclear power provides more than 75% of the
electricity in France and Lithuania, and about 50% in Belgium
and Sweden, but it accounts for only 20% or less of the electric power generated in both the United States and Canada.
Several countries have rejected the nuclear option altogether.
Denmark, Italy, Greece, Australia, and New Zealand are
among the countries that decided to remain "nuclear-free" and
never built nuclear power plants. A few countries, including
Germany, Sweden, and the Philippines, plan to phase out and
dismantle their reactors.

Many countries, however, have seen a recent revival of
interest in nuclear power, stemming in part from the belief that
nuclear energy is the best way to reduce carbon emissions and
slow the rate of climate change. Worldwide, 27 reactors are
under construction in 13 countries, with another hundred or
so planned or proposed. With the world's third-largest nuclear
power industry (after the United States and France), Japan
relies on its 55 nuclear power plants to generate almost one-
third of its electricity, and government plans call for building
11 new plants. In China, a soaring demand for electricity and
a desire to reduce reliance on imported oil and natural gas and
heavily polluting coal-fired power plants have prompted the
government to continue building new reactors. Other countries building new capacity are Finland, India, South Korea,
Taiwan, and Russia.

Expansion of the nuclear power industry in the United
States is less certain. For a variety of reasons, no new plants
have been ordered since 1979 (Figure 5.16). The high costs of
constructing, licensing, and operating the plants made nuclear

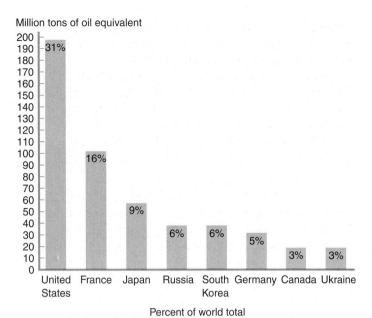

Million tons of oil equivalent

FIGURE 5.15 **Leading producers and consumers of nuclear energy, 2008.** These eight countries produce and use about four-fifths of the world's nuclear energy. The percent of world total nuclear energy consumption is indicated for each country. Few nuclear power plants exist in developing countries. *Source: Data from The BP Statistical Review of World Energy, June 2009.*

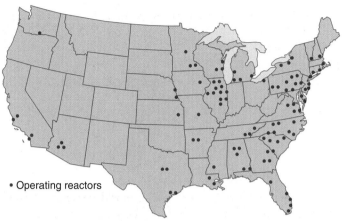

• Operating reactors

FIGURE 5.16 **Operating nuclear power plants in the United States, 2009.** The 104 plants produce about 20% of the country's electricity. In the next few years, a number of power companies are expected to file applications for new nuclear reactors at 19 power plants around the country. *Source: Data from U.S. Nuclear Regulatory Commission.*

power more expensive than energy derived from other sources. The partial reactor meltdown in Three Mile Island, Pennsylvania, in 1979 and the catastrophe at the Chernobyl plant in Ukraine in 1986 heightened concerns about safety. The lack of safe storage sites for radioactive reactor waste has also eroded public support for nuclear energy. Finally, particularly after September 11, 2001, many view nuclear plants as tempting targets for terrorist attacks.

Despite these concerns, nuclear power may be on the verge of a comeback in the United States. Many of the older reactors will be closed in the coming years as their steam generators corrode and steel pressure vessels become too brittle to operate safely. Several companies either have applied to the Nuclear Regulatory Commission for approval to replace their reactors or have indicated their intent to do so. The energy bill approved by Congress in 2005 included billions of dollars in incentives—including tax credits, subsidies, loan guarantees, and federal insurance—to encourage production of nuclear energy.

Nuclear Fusion

Unlike a fission reaction, which splits an atom, a **nuclear fusion** reaction forces forms of hydrogen known as deuterium and tritium to combine to form helium, releasing tremendous amounts of energy. Fusion is the process that makes the sun and other stars burn; it is also the basis of the hydrogen bomb, which uses a brief, uncontrolled thermonuclear fusion reaction.

More difficult to achieve than fission, nuclear fusion requires heating the atoms to extremely high temperatures, until their nuclei collide and fuse. One of the technological problems facing fusion researchers is finding material for the containment vessel that is resistant to radiation and temperatures 100 million°C or higher. A seven-member consortium of the United States, European Union, India, Russia, China, South Korea, and Japan is collaborating on construction of the world's first large-scale nuclear fusion reactor in France. The International Thermonuclear Experimental Reactor (ITER) is intended to be a demonstration plant to prove that fusion can be harnessed as an economically viable source of energy. It will take at least a decade to build the plant.

If the developmental problems associated with nuclear fusion are solved, Earth's electricity requirements would presumably be satisfied for millions of years. One cubic kilometer of ocean water, the source of deuterium atoms, contains as much potential energy as the world's entire known oil reserves. Advocates of fusion cite other advantages. The radioactive processes are short-lived, and the waste products are benign. Unlike fission reactors, fusion reactors do not use uranium-235, a raw material that is in short supply; and unlike conventional power plants, they would not emit the pollutants carbon dioxide, sulfur dioxide, and nitric oxide.

Skeptics point out that, despite 50 years of research, scientists have not solved the problem of controlling fusion so that its released energy can be used. They argue that the costs of a fusion plant will be enormous and that electricity can be supplied more cheaply by conventional means. Finally, they say, fusion energy could be accompanied by health and environmental problems we have not conceived of yet.

RENEWABLE ENERGY RESOURCES

The problems posed by the use of nuclear energy, the threatened depletion of some finite fossil fuels, and the desire to be less dependent on foreign sources of energy have increased interest in industrialized countries in the *renewable* resources. One of the advantages of such resources is their ubiquity. Most places on Earth have an abundance of sunlight, rich plant growth, strong wind, or heavy rainfall. Another advantage is ease of use. It doesn't take advanced technology to utilize many of the renewable resources, one reason for their widespread use in developing countries. The most common renewable source of energy is plant matter.

Biomass Fuels

More than half of the people in the world depend on wood and other forms of biomass for their daily energy requirements. **Biomass fuel** is any organic material produced by plants, animals, or microorganisms that can be burned directly as a heat source or converted into a liquid or gas. In addition to wood, biomass fuels include leaves, crop residues, peat, manure, and other plant and animal material. In Ethiopia and Bangladesh, biomass supplies 90% or more of the total energy consumed; in India and Pakistan, the figure is about 40%. In contrast, energy from the conversion of wood, grasses, and other organic matter is insignificant in the developed world.

There are two major sources of biomass: (1) trees, grain and sugar crops, and oil-bearing plants such as sunflowers, and (2) wastes, including crop residues, animal wastes, garbage, and human sewage. Biomass can be transformed into fuel in many ways, including direct combustion, gasification, and anaerobic digestion. Further, conversion processes can be designed to produce, in addition to electricity, solid (wood and charcoal), liquid (oils and alcohols), and gaseous (methane and hydrogen) fuels that can be easily stored and transported.

Wood

The great majority of the energy that is produced from biomass comes from *wood*. In 1850, the United States obtained about 90% of its energy needs from wood. Although wood now contributes only 3% to the energy mix of the country as a whole, the percentage varies by region, with wood fuel providing about 15% of the energy used in Maine and Vermont. In developing countries, wood is a key source of energy, used for space heating, cooking, water heating, and lighting. This dependence on wood is leading in places to severe depletion of forests, a subject discussed later in this chapter (see "Forest Resources," pp. 149–154).

A second biomass contribution to energy systems is *alcohol*, which can be produced from a variety of plants. After the oil shortages of the 1970s, Brazil, which is poorly endowed with fossil fuels, embarked on an effort to develop its indigenous energy supplies in order to reduce the country's dependence on imported oil. All gasoline sold in Brazil contains 25% grain alcohol (*ethanol*) made from sugarcane, a mixture on which conventional automobile engines can run without modifications. In 2003, "flex-fuel" cars made their debut in Brazil. The modified engines of these cars are designed to run on pure gasoline, alcohol, or any combination of the two. Buyers are attracted by the low price of alcohol and the fact that virtually all of the country's service stations sell the fuel. By 2010, 90% of the new cars sold in Brazil had flex-fuel engines.

Ethanol currently accounts for only 3% of America's gasoline use, but the desire to reduce dependence on imported oil has sparked interest in doubling ethanol production by 2012 and tripling it by 2017. In the United States, 95% of all ethanol is derived from corn, a fuel with significant disadvantages when compared with sugarcane.

- Sugarcane can be grown on marginal soils in a tropical climate. As grown in the United States, corn requires good land and heavy applications of nitrogen fertilizer, herbicides, and pesticides, which pollute water supplies.
- Corn takes a lot of land to grow. To replace an additional 5% of U.S. gasoline consumption, roughly 117 million acres (the size of Wisconsin and Nebraska combined) would have to be planted in corn.
- Because sugarcane is more energy efficient, Brazil produces far more ethanol per hectare than the United States does with corn.
- The energy balance, or fossil-fuel energy used to make the fuel (input) compared with the energy in the fuel (output), tilts heavily in favor of sugarcane. Cane yields 8 units of ethanol for every 1 unit of fossil fuel; for corn, the energy ratio is just 1.3 units of ethanol for every unit of fossil fuel.
- Cane is cheaper to process because it's already sugar and doesn't need converting before distillation. Corn, however, is ground up and combined with water and enzymes that convert the starch into sugars, which turn into alcohol during fermentation. Distillation separates the alcohol from the water.
- Rising prices for corn will encourage farmers to plant millions of acres of farmland now set aside for soil and wildlife conservation.
- Ethanol distilleries currently consume about one-fifth of the U.S. corn crop. Converting more corn to fuel will drive up the prices of livestock feed, meat, cereals, and other goods. A way to generate biofuels without competing with food crops is by using waste.

Waste

Waste, including crop residues and animal and human refuse, represents the second broad category of organic fuels. Particularly in rural areas, energy can be obtained by fermenting such wastes to produce methane gas (also called *biogas*) in a process known as *anaerobic digestion* (Figure 5.17). A number of countries, including India, South Korea, and Thailand, have national biogas programs, but the largest effort to generate substantial quantities of methane gas for rural households has been undertaken in China. There, backyard fermentation tanks (biodigesters) supply as many as 35 million people with fuel for cooking, lighting, and heating. The technology has been kept intentionally simple. A stone fermentation tank

FIGURE 5.17 A biogas generator in Nepal. Animal and vegetable wastes are significant sources of fuel in countries such as Nepal, Pakistan, India, and China. Wastes inserted into the tank in the foreground are mixed with water and decaying organic material. As the wastes decompose, gases are emitted. The unit in the background is the gas-collection chamber. Tubes lead from it to family kitchens. © Sean Sprague/Panos Pictures.

is fed with wastes, which can include straw and other crop residues in addition to manure. These are left to ferment under pressure, producing methane gas that is later drawn through a hose into the farm kitchen. After the gas is spent, the remaining waste is pumped out and used in the fields for fertilizer.

Hydropower

Biomass, particularly wood, is the most commonly used source of renewable energy. The second most common is **hydropower,** which exploits the energy present in falling or flowing water. Hydropower is generated when water falls or flows from one level to another, either naturally or over a dam. The falling water can then be used to turn waterwheels, as it was in ancient Egypt, or modern turbine blades, powering a generator to produce electricity. Hydropower is a clean source of energy. The water is neither polluted nor consumed during power generation, although in arid areas some water in the reservoir may be lost to evaporation. Generally speaking, as long as a stream continues to flow, hydropower is renewable.

Tied as it is to a source of water, hydroelectric power production is location-specific with regard to generation. Although most countries generate some hydropower, just five countries account for more than half the total world hydroelectric production: Canada, the United States, Brazil, China, and Russia. In the United States, hydropower is generated at more than 1900 sites in 47 states. Still, just 6 states generate about two-thirds of the country's hydropower (Figure 5.18), and more than 75% of the country's developed capacity is concentrated in just three areas: the northwest (Washington,

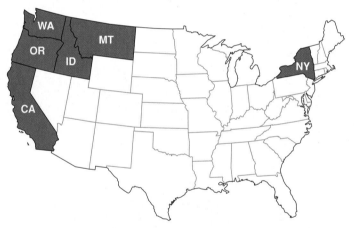

FIGURE 5.18 Leading hydropower-producing states, 2007. Washington, the location of the country's largest hydroelectric facility—the Grand Coulee Dam—generates 32% of the total U.S. hydropower. The United States has developed about half of its hydroelectric capacity. Source of data: Energy Information Administration, Renewable Energy Trends in Consumption and Electricity, April 2009.

Oregon, Idaho, and California), the multistate Tennessee River valley area of the southeast, and the northeast. That pattern is a result of both the location of the resource base and the role that agencies such as the Tennessee Valley Authority (TVA) have played in hydropower development.

Transmitting hydroelectricity over long distances is costly, so it is generally consumed in the region where it is produced. This fact helps account for variations in the pattern of consumption and for the energy mix used in specific regions. Thus, although hydropower provides the United States as a whole with about 7% of its electricity, it supplies all of Idaho's needs and about 90% of the electricity used in Oregon and Washington.

Consumption patterns around the world are shown in Figure 5.19. Hydropower's contribution to a country's energy supplies varies greatly. Several countries—New Zealand, Switzerland, and Brazil—obtain more than three-quarters of their electricity from hydropower. Hydroelectric power plants provide virtually all of the electricity in Paraguay and Norway. It is estimated that people use only 10% of the world's potential hydropower supply. Water resources that haven't yet been exploited for hydropower are still abundant in Central and South America, Africa, India, and China.

In addition to supplying electrical power, dams provide flood protection and irrigation water. Despite these and other advantages, the exploitation of hydropower has significant environmental and social costs (see "Dammed Trouble," pp. 136–137). Flooding valleys for water storage submerges forests, farmlands, and villages, sometimes resulting in the displacement of tens of thousands or even millions of people. The reservoirs flood natural wetlands and river habitats, alter stream-flow patterns, and trap silt that otherwise would flow downstream to be deposited on agricultural lands, leading to long-term declines in soil fertility. The disruption of downstream ecosystems that evolved to take advantage of a river's sporadic flood pattern typically reduces the diversity of aquatic species.

Solar Energy

Each year, the earth intercepts solar energy that is equivalent to many thousands of times the energy people currently use. Inexhaustible and nonpolluting, **solar energy** is the ultimate origin of most forms of utilized energy: fossil fuels and plant life, waterpower and wind power. It is, however, the direct capture of solar energy that is seen by many as the best hope of satisfying a proportion of future energy needs with minimal environmental damage and maximum conservation of earth resources. The chief drawback to solar power is its diffuse and intermittent nature. Being diffuse, it must be collected over a large area to make it practical to use, and because it is intermittent, it requires some means of storage.

The technology for using solar energy for domestic uses such as hot-water heating and space heating is well known. In the United States, both passive and active solar-heating technologies have secured a permanent foothold in the marketplace. More than half a million homes use solar radiation for water and space heating. Japan is reported to have some 4 million solar hot-water systems, and in China and Israel, more than half of all homes heat water with solar energy. The use of solar panels for individual homes is best in climates that are warm and sunny, with not too much cloud cover and not too many hours of darkness in winter, when the demand for energy is at its highest.

A second type of solar-energy use involves converting concentrated solar energy into thermal energy to generate electricity. Research efforts are focusing on a variety of thermal-electric systems, including power towers, parabolic troughs, and solar ponds. Most involve the concentration of the sun's rays onto a collecting system. In a parabolic trough system, long troughs of curved mirrors guided by computers follow the sun, focusing solar energy onto a steel tube filled with synthetic oil (Figure 5.20). Heated to 390°C (735°F), the oil in turn heats water to produce steam to power generators. Several plants of this type are operating in the Mojave Desert, producing enough electricity for the residential needs of 270,000 people.

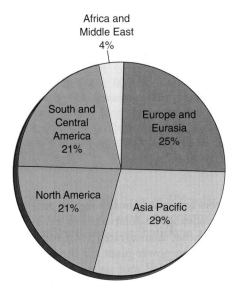

FIGURE 5.19 **Consumption of hydropower by region, 2008.** The percent of world hydropower consumption is indicated for each region. Hydropower's contribution to the electricity supply is not limited to industrialized countries. In South America, for example, hydropower provides about 70% of the electricity; the figure for the developing world as a whole is 44%. *Source: Data from The BP Statistical Review of World Energy, June 2009.*

FIGURE 5.20 **Parabolic trough reflectors at a solar thermal energy plant in the Mojave Desert near Daggett, California.** The facility uses sunlight to produce steam to generate electricity. Guided by computers, the parabolic reflectors follow the sun, focusing solar energy onto a steel tube filled with heat transfer fluid. *© The McGraw-Hill Companies, Inc./Photo by Dong Sherman.*

Geothermal fields are usually associated with areas where magmas are relatively near the earth's surface—that is, in areas of recent volcanic activity above the subduction zones. Thus, Iceland, Mexico, the United States, the Philippines, Japan, and New Zealand are among the 21 countries that produce geothermal energy (Figure 5.21). In Iceland, half of the geothermal energy is used to produce electricity; half is used for heating. Almost all the houses and commercial buildings in Reykjavik, the capital of Iceland, are heated by geothermal steam.

Although relatively few places have geothermal steam that can be exploited to generate electricity, geothermal energy can also be used directly for heating and cooling. *Geothermal heat pumps* (also known as ground-source heat pumps) take advantage of the constant temperature found in soil below the frost line to heat or cool air pumped through a building. Loops of piping are buried in the ground; an electric compressor circulates refrigerant through them and then cools or heats the air, which is distributed throughout a building. Energy-efficient and environmentally clean, geothermal heating systems have grown in popularity in the United States in recent years, particularly for new construction.

Wind Power

Although wind power was used for centuries to pump water, grind grain, and drive machinery, its contribution to the energy supply in the United States virtually disappeared more than a century ago, when windmills were replaced first by steam and later by the fossil fuels. Windmills offer many advantages as sources of electrical power. They can turn turbines directly, do not use any fuel, and can be built and erected rather quickly. They need only strong, steady winds to operate, and these exist at many sites. Furthermore, wind turbine generators do not pollute the air or water and do not deplete scarce natural resources. Technological advances in design have lowered the cost of using wind turbines to generate electricity, so they are becoming increasingly competitive with conventional power plants. Wind power now costs from 3 to 6 cents per kilowatt-hour, about the same as power plants fired by fossil fuels.

In the 1980s, California dominated the worldwide development of wind energy, spurred by the gasoline shortages of previous years, federal and state tax incentives, and favorable long-term utility contracts. By 1987, some 15,000 turbines had been installed in three parts of the state, representing 90% of the world's wind capacity (Figure 5.22). That percentage declined steadily during the 1990s as other states and a number of European countries began to invest in **wind farms,** clusters of wind-powered turbines producing commercial electricity.

In the 1990s, a commitment to reducing dependence on fossil fuels and developing renewable resources stimulated the growth of wind-power installations in several European countries, particularly Germany, Spain, and Denmark. In terms of megawatts of installed capacity, Germany and the United States are the world's leading producers of wind-powered energy, followed by Spain. Denmark, however, has the highest per capita output of wind energy in the world. With the exception of India, Asian countries have been somewhat slower to build wind farms, but sizeable projects are under construction in China and Japan.

Offshore wind turbine installations are expected to play a growing role in the coming years, particularly in northern Europe. The world's biggest offshore windmill park is at the entrance to Copenhagen's harbor. It and other installations provide about 20% of the country's electricity. The Netherlands and Sweden also have offshore windmill parks, and planned or under construction are parks off the coasts of Britain, Ireland, Belgium, Germany, and Spain.

The chief disadvantage of wind power is that it is unreliable and intermittent; because its energy cannot be easily stored, it requires a backup system. Additionally, in some countries wind power is most plentiful in remote areas, far from the existing power grid, and costly new transmission lines would have to be installed to bring it to consumers. Detractors point out that it takes thousands of wind turbines to produce the same amount of electricity as a single nuclear power plant. Environmental concerns include the aesthetic impact of wind farms (they are very visible, often covering entire hillsides and dominating the landscape) and the hazard they pose to migrating birds.

NONFUEL MINERAL RESOURCES

The mineral resources already discussed provide the energy that enables people to do their work. Equally important to our economic well-being are the *nonfuel* minerals, for they can be processed into steel, aluminum, and other metals and into glass, cement, and other products. Our buildings, tools, and weapons are chiefly mineral in origin.

Virtually all the resources we deem essential, including metals, nonmetallic minerals, rocks, and the fuels, are contained in the earth's crust, the thin outer skin of the planet. Of the 92 natural elements, just 8 account for more than 98% of the mass of the earth's crust (Figure 5.23). They can be thought of as geologically abundant, and all others as geologically scarce. In most places, minerals exist in concentrations too low to make their exploitation profitable. If the concentration is high enough to make mining feasible, the mineral deposit is called an **ore.** Thus what is or is not an ore depends on demand, price, and technology and changes over time.

Exploitation of a mineral resource typically involves six steps:

1. *exploration* (finding concentrated deposits of the material)
2. *extraction* (removing it from the earth)
3. *concentration* (separating the desired material from the ore)
4. *smelting* and/or *refining* (breaking down the mineral to the desired pure material)
5. *transporting* it to where it will be used
6. *manufacturing* the ore into a finished product

Each step requires inputs of energy and materials.

(a)

(b)

FIGURE 5.21 (a) Geothermal power plants worldwide. Most areas where geothermal energy is tapped are along or near plate boundaries. Because the number of sites suitable for geothermal power generation is limited, and most are far from large cities where the demand for power is great, geothermal power is likely to remain a minor contributor to world energy production. **(b) One of the 21 geothermal power plants at The Geysers, an area of about 78 square kilometers (30 sq mi) in northern California.** Magma radiates heat through the rock above it, heating water in underground reservoirs. Drilled wells tap the steam and bring it to the surface, where it is piped to the power plant. As the photograph suggests, one drawback of geothermal plants is that they release gases into the atmosphere, although scrubbers like those used on coal stacks can reduce gaseous emissions to an acceptable level.

(a) Carla Montgomery, Environmental Geology, *6/e, Figure 14.22, p. 353. McGraw-Hill: Boston, 2003; (b) Photo by M. Smith/USGS.*

(a)

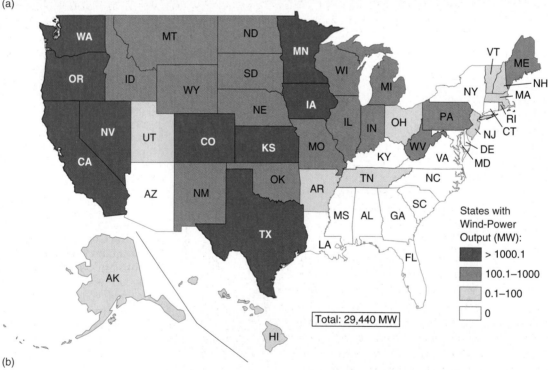

(b)

FIGURE 5.22 (a) A wind farm in the San Gorgonio Pass, near Palm Springs, California. The wind turbine generators harness wind power to produce electricity. **(b) Wind-generating capacity by state, in megawatt output, June 2009.** Although only a small portion of the country's wind potential has been tapped, new wind-power projects are underway in a number of states. Wind turbine technology advanced dramatically during the 1990s; modern turbines are significantly more powerful and reliable than earlier ones. In recent years, wind energy has been the fastest-growing source of electrical generation in both the United States and the world as a whole. *(a) © Roger Scott; (b) Source of data: American Wind Energy Association.*

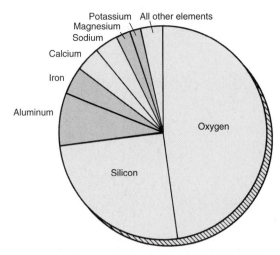

FIGURE 5.23 **The relative abundance, by weight, of elements in the earth's crust.** Only four of the economically important elements—those shown in purple—are geologically abundant, accounting for more than 1% of the total weight of the earth's crust. Fortunately, these and other commercially valuable minerals have been concentrated in specific areas within the crust. Were they uniformly disseminated throughout the crust, their exploitation would not be feasible.

TABLE 5.1
Projected Lifetimes of Reserves of Selected Minerals

Mineral	YEARS REMAINING OF PROVED RESERVES	
	World	**United States**
Silver	13	22
Lead	21	18
Zinc	16	18
Copper	35	27
Tin	17	0
Nickel	43	0
Phosphate	90	39
Manganese	36	0
Bauxite	132	0
Potash	231	75

Source: Mineral Commodity Summaries 2008, U.S. Geological Survey.
Note: These figures reflect the approximate number of years the proved reserves of selected minerals will last, based on current rates of production and consumption. Such figures are only suggestive, because reserve totals and consumption rates fluctuate over time. A decline in the costs of exploitation, increase in value of the material, and/or new discoveries of deposits will extend the lifetimes shown here.

Five factors help determine the practicality and profitability of mining a specific deposit of a mineral: its value, the quantity available, the richness of the ore in a particular deposit, the distance to market, and land-acquisition and royalty costs. Even if these conditions are favorable, mines may not be developed or even remain operating if supplies from competing sources are available more cheaply. In the 1980s, more than 25 million tons of iron ore-producing capacity was permanently shut down in the United States and Canada. Similar declines occurred in North American copper, nickel, zinc, lead, and molybdenum mining as market prices fell below domestic production costs. Beginning in the early 1990s, as a result of both resource depletion and low-cost imports, the United States became a net importer of nonfuel minerals for the first time. Although increases in mineral prices may lead to the opening or reopening of mines that have been deemed unprofitable, the developed industrial countries with market economies find themselves at a competitive disadvantage against developing country producers with lower-cost labor and state-owned mines with abundant reserves.

Natural processes produce minerals so slowly that they fall into the category of nonrenewable resources, existing in finite deposits. The supplies of some, however, are so abundant that a ready supply will exist far into the future. These include coal, sand and gravel, and potash. The supply of others, such as tin and mercury, is small and getting smaller as industrial societies place ever-greater demands on them. Table 5.1 gives one estimate of "years remaining" for some important metals. It should be taken as suggestive rather than definitive, because mineral reserves are difficult to estimate. As we noted in the case of fossil fuels, such estimates are based on economic and technological conditions, and we cannot predict either future prices for minerals or improvements in technology. The depletion of the currently identified, usable reserves of a valuable mineral will drive up the price of the mineral, which will make it profitable to mine some of what are now classified as subeconomic deposits (see Figure 5.4). Those deposits would then be reclassified as proved reserves. The discovery of new deposits and/or improvements in mineral-processing technology would also increase the reserve figure and thus its projected lifetime.

Although human societies began to use metals as early as 3500 B.C., world demand remained small until the Industrial Revolution. It was not until after World War II that increasing shortages and rising prices (and in the United States, increasing dependence on foreign sources) began to impress themselves on the general consciousness. Worldwide technological development has established ways of life in which minerals are the essential constituent. That industrialization has proceeded so rapidly and so cheaply is the direct result of the earlier ready availability of rich and accessible deposits of the requisite materials. Economies grew fat by skimming the cream. The question, yet unanswered, is whether the remaining supplies of scarce minerals will limit the expansion of industrialized and developing economies or whether, and how, people will find a way to cope with shortages.

The Distribution of Nonfuel Minerals

Because the distribution of mineral resources is the result of long-term geologic processes that concentrated certain elements into commercially exploitable deposits, it follows

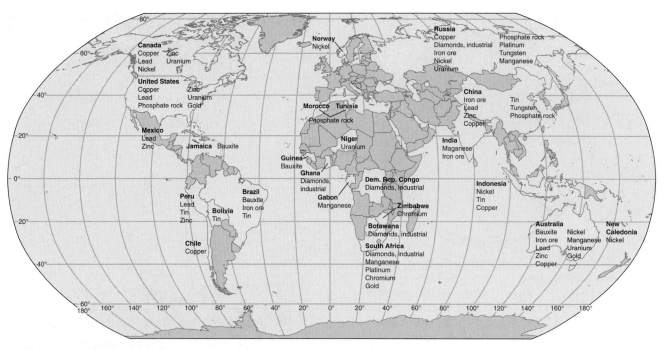

FIGURE 5.24 Leading producers of selected minerals. The countries shown are not necessarily those with the largest deposits. India, for example, contains reserves of bauxite, Brazil of uranium, and South Africa of phosphates, but none is yet a major producer of those materials. *Data from World Resources Institute.*

that, the larger the country, the more likely it is to contain such deposits. And in fact, Russia, China, Canada, the United States, Brazil, and Australia possess abundant and diverse mineral resources. As Figure 5.24 indicates, these are the leading mining countries. They contain roughly half of the nonfuel mineral resources and produce the bulk of the metals (e.g., iron, manganese, and nickel) and nonmetals (e.g., potash and sulfur).

Many types of nonfuel minerals are concentrated in a small number of countries, and some scarce elements occur in just a few regions of the world. Thus, extensive deposits of cobalt and diamonds are largely confined to Russia and central-southern Africa. South Africa has nearly half of the world's gold ore and more than three-quarters of the chromium and platinum-group metals. Some countries contain only one or two exploitable minerals—Morocco has phosphates, for example, and New Caledonia, nickel. Several countries with large populations are at a disadvantage with respect to mineral reserves. They include industrialized countries such as France and Japan, which are able to import the resources, as well as developing countries such as Nigeria and Bangladesh, which are less able to afford imports.

It is important to note that no country contains all of the economically important mineral resources. Some, such as the United States, which were bountifully supplied by nature, have spent much of their assets and now depend on foreign sources. Although the United States was virtually self-sufficient in mineral supplies in the 1940s and 1950s, it is not today. Because of its history of use of domestic reserves and its continually expanding economy, the United States now depends on other countries for more than 50% of its supply of a number of essential minerals, some of which are shown in Table 5.2.

The increasing costs and declining availability of metals encourage the search for substitutes. The fact that industrial chemists and metallurgists have been so successful in the search for new materials that substitute for the traditional resources has tended to allay fears of possible resource depletion. But it must be understood that no adequate replacements have been found for some minerals, such as cobalt and chromium. Many other substitutes are synthetics, often employing increasingly scarce and costly hydrocarbons in their production. Many, in their use or disposal, constitute environmental hazards, and all have their own high and increasing price tags.

Copper: A Case Study

Table 5.1 indicates that the world reserves of copper will last only another generation or so, based on current rates of production and consumption and assuming that no new extractable reserves appear. Copper is a relatively scarce mineral, and its importance to industrialized societies is evidenced by the fact that more copper is mined annually than any other non-ferrous metal except aluminum.

Three properties make copper desirable: it conducts both heat and electricity extremely well, it is malleable and thus can be hammered or drawn into thin films or wires, and it resists corrosion. Copper is a major industrial metal with many applications. It is used in building construction, industrial and farm machinery, power transmission and generation,

TABLE 5.2
U.S. Reliance on Foreign Supplies of Selected Nonfuel Minerals, 2008

Mineral	% Imported	Major Sources	Major Uses
Bauxite and alumina	100%	Australia, Jamaica, Guinea	Aluminum production
Manganese	100	S. Africa, Gabon, China	Steelmaking, batteries, agricultural chemicals
Mica	100	India, Belgium, China	Electronic and electrical equipment
Quartz crystal	100	China, Japan, Russia	Electronics, optical applications
Strontium	100	Mexico, Germany	TV picture tubes, ferrite magnets, pyrotechnics
Yttrium	100	China, Japan, France	Light emitting diodes (LEDs) in TV sets, lights
Tantalum	100	Australia, Canada, China	Capacitors, superalloys, cemented carbide tools
Platinum	91	S. Africa, United Kingdom, Germany	Catalysts in the automotive and chemical industries
Cobalt	81	Norway, Russia, China	Superalloys for jet engines, cutting tools, magnets, chemicals
Potash	81	Canada, Belarus, Russia	Fertilizers, chemicals
Barite	79	China, India	Oil and gas well drilling fluids, chemicals
Zinc	73	Canada, Mexico, Peru	Galvanizing, zinc-base alloys, brass and bronze
Tungsten	61	China, Canada, Germany	Electronic and electrical components, tool steel
Silver	60	Mexico, Canada, Peru	Photographic materials, electrical products, catalysts
Chromium	54	S. Africa, Kazakhstan, Zimbabwe	Steel chemicals, refractories

Source: U.S. Geological Survey.

telecommunications, electrical wire and equipment, electronic products, transportation, plumbing fittings and pipes, coinage, and consumer and general products (e.g., cookware, musical instruments, and statues). A significant proportion of copper is also used as alloys in bronze, brass, and other metals.

Like most minerals, copper is unevenly distributed in the earth's crust. The largest copper deposits are found at convergent tectonic margins in western North America, western South America, and Australia. Copper deposits in sedimentary basins include those extending across northern Europe, from England to Poland, and the copper-belt of central Africa (Zambia and Democratic Republic of Congo). Chile leads the world in copper production (about 36% of the total), followed by the United States, Indonesia, and Peru. Because the United States consumes more copper than it produces, it imports significant amounts to meet its demand for the metal.

Globally, the production of copper increased fairly steadily from 9.5 million metric tons in 1984 to a little over 17 in 2007. Nevertheless, the demand for the metal outstrips the supply, due both to its increased use in motors and electronic equipment and to rising consumption of the metal in Russia, India, and China. The quintupling of the price of copper from $0.60 per pound in 1999 to $3.30/lb in 2010 reflects the demand.

The scarcity of copper supplies has had several effects that suggest how societies will cope with shortages of other raw materials. First, in the United States, the grade of mined ores has decreased steadily. Those with the highest percentage of copper (2% and above) were mined early (Figure 5.25).

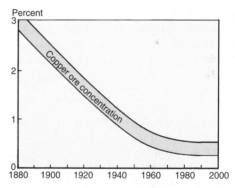

FIGURE 5.25 Concentration of copper needed in order to be mined economically. In 1880, 3% copper ore rock was necessary, but today, rock with 0.4% or less copper is mined. As the supply of a metal decreases and its price increases, the concentration needed for economic recovery goes down.
Source: Data from the U.S. Bureau of Mines, U.S. Department of the Interior.

Now, ore of 0.4% grade is the average. Thus, 1000 tons of rock must be mined and processed to yield 4 tons of copper—or, in more practical terms, 3 tons of rock are necessary to equip one automobile with the copper used in its radiator and its various electrical components. The remaining 2.985 tons is waste, generated at the mine, the concentrator, and the smelter.

Second, the recovery of copper by recycling has increased. Virtually all products made from copper can be recycled. Unlike some minerals, copper lends itself to recycling because much of it is used in pure form in sizeable pieces. It is less expensive to remanufacture recycled, or "secondary," copper into new products than to produce it by mining and refining new ore. Recycling contributes significantly to the copper supply in the United States.

Increasing demand for copper has led to the search for additional deposits. Two companies are actively exploring the feasibility of extracting copper, gold, silver, and other metals from underneath the South Pacific Ocean, where the minerals are concentrated in mounds at midoceanic ridges and the crests of undersea volcanoes. Nearly 2 kilometers (about 1 mi) below sea level, the high-grade sulfide deposits are thought to contain 12% copper. Critics of deep seabed mining argue that it has the potential to be environmentally destructive, with adverse effects on marine life, while its advocates contend that it is less disruptive than land-based mining.

Finally, price rises have spurred the search for substitutes. In many of its applications, copper is being replaced by other, less expensive materials. Aluminum is replacing copper in some electrical applications and in heat exchangers. Plastics are supplanting copper in plumbing pipes and building materials. Glass fibers are employed in many telephone transmission lines, and steel can be used in shell casings and coinage.

LAND RESOURCES

The mineral resources we have just discussed are nonrenewable. We turn our attention now to land resources that are potentially renewable, examining the distribution and status of three of those resources: soils, wetlands, and forests. Because they support or are living things, they are sometimes called *biological resources.*

Soils

By design or by accident, people have brought about many changes in the physical, chemical, and biochemical nature of the soil and altered its structure, fertility, and drainage characteristics. The exact nature of the changes in any area depends on past practices as well as on the original nature of the land.

Over much of the earth's surface, the thin layer of topsoil upon which life depends is only a few inches deep, usually less than 30 centimeters (1 ft). Below it, the lithosphere is a complex mixture of rock particles, inorganic mineral matter, organic material, living organisms, air, and water. Under natural conditions, soil is constantly being formed by the physical and chemical decomposition of rock material and by the decay of organic matter. It is simultaneously being eroded, for **soil erosion**—the removal of soil particles, usually by wind or running water—is as natural a process as soil formation, and it occurs even when land is totally covered by forests or grass. Under most natural conditions, however, the rate of soil formation equals or exceeds the rate of soil erosion, so that soil depth and fertility tend to increase with time.

FIGURE 5.26 The tropical rain forest was cleared on this tract in Amazonia, Brazil, to make room for a tin-mining operation. Exposed soils quickly deteriorate in structure and fertility and are easily eroded. © *Getty RF.*

When land is cleared and planted to crops, or when the vegetative cover is broken by overgrazing or other disturbances, the process of erosion accelerates. When its rate exceeds that of soil formation, the topsoil becomes thinner and eventually disappears, leaving behind only sterile subsoil or barren rock. At that point, the renewable soil resource has been converted through human impact into a nonrenewable and dissipated asset. Carried to the extreme of bare rock hillsides or wind-denuded plains, erosion spells the total end of agricultural use of the land.

Such massive destruction of the soil resource could endanger the survival of the civilization it has supported. For the most part, however, farmers devise ingenious ways to preserve and even improve the soil resource upon which their lives and livelihoods depend. Farming skills have not declined in recent years, but pressures upon farmlands have increased with population growth. Farming has been forced higher up onto steeper slopes, more forest land has been converted to cultivation, grazing and crops have been pushed farther and more intensively into semiarid areas, and existing fields have had to be worked more intensively and less carefully. Many traditional agricultural systems and areas that were ecologically stable and secure as recently as 1950, when world population stood at 2.5 billion people, are disintegrating under the pressures of more than 6 billion people.

The pressure of growing population numbers is having an especially destructive effect on tropical rain forests. Expanded demand for fuel and commercial wood and a midlatitude market for beef that can be satisfied profitably by replacing tropical forest with cleared grazing land are responsible for some of the loss, but the major cause of *deforestation* is clearing the land for crops. Extending across parts of Asia, Africa, and Latin America, the tropical rain forests are the most biologically diverse places on Earth, but vast expanses are being destroyed every year. About 45% of their original expanse has already been cleared or degraded.

Deforestation is discussed in more detail on pages 149–154, but it is important to note here that accelerated soil erosion quickly removes tropical forest soils from deforested areas. Lands cleared for agriculture almost immediately become unsuitable for that use, partially because of soil loss (Figure 5.26).

The tropical rain forests can succumb to deliberate, massive human assaults and be irretrievably lost. With much less effort, and with no intent to destroy or alter the environment, humans are similarly affecting the arid and semiarid regions of the world. The process is called **desertification,** the expansion or intensification of areas of degraded or destroyed soil and vegetation cover; it usually occurs in arid and semi-arid environments. Climatic change—unpredictable cycles of rainfall and drought—is often a contributing cause, but desertification accelerates because of human activity, mainly overgrazing, deforestation for fuelwood, clearing of original vegetation for cultivation, and burning. Desertification implies a continuum of ecological alteration from slight to extreme (Figure 5.27).

Whatever its degree of development, when the process results from human rather than climatic change, it begins in the same fashion: the disruption or removal of the native cover of grasses and shrubs through farming or overgrazing (Figure 5.28). If the disruption is severe enough, the original vegetation cannot reestablish itself, and the exposed soil is made susceptible to erosion during the brief, heavy rains

that dominate precipitation patterns in semiarid regions. Water runs off the land surface instead of seeping in, carrying soil particles with it. When the water is lost through surface flow rather than seepage downward, the water table is lowered. Eventually, even deep-rooted bushes are unable to reach groundwater, and all natural vegetation is lost. The process is accentuated when too many grazing animals pack the earth down with their hooves, blocking the passage of air and water through the soil. When both plant cover and soil moisture are lost, desertification has occurred.

It happens with increasing frequency in many areas of the earth as pressures upon the land continue. Africa is most at risk; the United Nations has estimated that 40% of that continent's nondesert land is in danger of human-induced desertification. But nearly a third of Asia and a fifth of Latin America's land are similarly endangered. In countries where desertification is particularly extensive and severe (Algeria, Ethiopia, Iraq, Jordan, Lebanon, Mali, and Niger), per capita food production declined by some 40% between 1950 and the early 2000s. The resulting threat of starvation spurs populations of the affected areas to increase their farming and livestock pressures on the denuded land, further contributing to their desertification.

Desertification is but one expression of land deterioration leading to accelerated soil erosion. The evidence of that deterioration is found in all parts of the world. In Guatemala, for example, some 40% of the productive capacity of the land

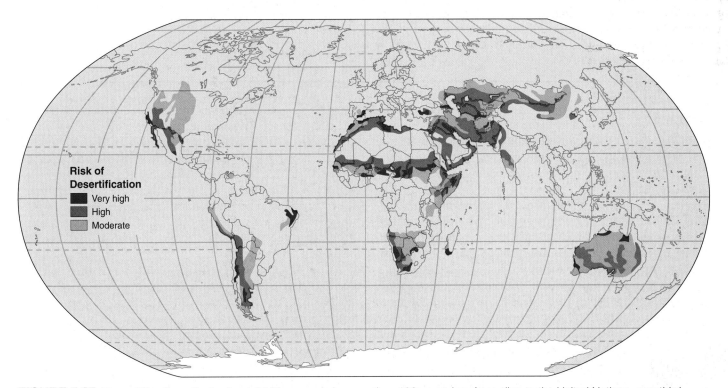

Risk of Desertification
- Very high
- High
- Moderate

FIGURE 5.27 Desertification affects about 1 billion people in more than 100 countries. According to the United Nations, one-third of the world's land surface is at risk of becoming desert wasteland. Most at risk are dry regions on the edges of deserts. Many factors contribute to the desertification of dry areas: climate shifts, population growth, overexploitation of water supplies, diversion of rivers for irrigation, destructive farming practices that expose topsoil to wind and water erosion, overgrazing of grasslands by livestock, and cutting of trees and shrubs for firewood. *Source: John Allen,* Student Atlas of World Geography, *5/e, Map 81, p. 97.*

FIGURE 5.28 Windblown dust is engulfing the scrub forest in this drought-stricken area of Mali, near Timbuktu. The district is part of the Sahel region of Africa, where desertification has been accelerated by both the climate and human pressures on the land. The cultivation of marginal land, overgrazing by livestock, and recurring droughts have led to the destruction of native vegetation, erosion, and land degradation. © *Wolfgang Kaehler.*

has been lost through erosion, and several areas of the country have been abandoned because agriculture has become economically impracticable. The figure is 50% in El Salvador, and Haiti has no high-value soil left at all. In Turkey, about half of the land is severely or very severely eroded. A full one-quarter of India's total land area has been significantly eroded.

In recent years, soil erosion in the United States has been at an all-time high (Figure 5.29) (see "Maintaining Soil Productivity p. 148"). Wind and water are blowing and washing soil off croplands in Iowa and Missouri, pasturelands in the Great Plains, and ranches in Texas. America's croplands lose almost 2 billion tons of soil per year to erosion, an average annual loss of more than 4 tons per acre. In some areas, the average is 15 to 20 tons per acre. Of the roughly 167 million hectares (413 million acres) of land that are intensively cropped in the United States, more than one-third are losing topsoil faster than it can be replaced naturally (it can take up to a century to replace an inch of topsoil). In parts of Iowa and Illinois where the topsoil was once a foot deep, less than half of it remains.

Like most processes, soil erosion has secondary effects. As the soil quality and quantity decline, croplands become less productive and yields drop. Streams and reservoirs experience accelerated siltation. In countries where the topsoil is heavily laden with agricultural chemicals, erosion-borne silt pollutes water supplies. The danger of floods increases as bottomlands fill with silt, and the costs of maintaining navigation channels grow.

Accelerated erosion is a primary cause of agricultural soil deterioration, but in arid and semiarid areas, salt accumulation can be a contributing factor. **Salinization** is the concentration of salts in the topsoil as a result of the evaporation of surface water. It occurs in poorly drained soils in dry climates, where evaporation exceeds precipitation. As water evaporates, some of the salts are left behind to form a white crust on the surface of the soil (Figure 5.30).

Like erosion, salinization is a natural process that has been accelerated by human activities. Poorly drained irrigation systems are the primary culprit, because irrigation water tends to move slowly and thus to evaporate rapidly. All irrigation water contains dissolved salts, which are left behind on the surface when water evaporates. Mild or moderate salinity makes soil less productive and lowers crop yields; extreme salinity ultimately can render the land unsuitable for agriculture.

Thousands of once fertile acres have been abandoned in Iran and Iraq; over 25% of the irrigated areas of India, Pakistan, Syria, and Egypt are affected by salinization. Approximately

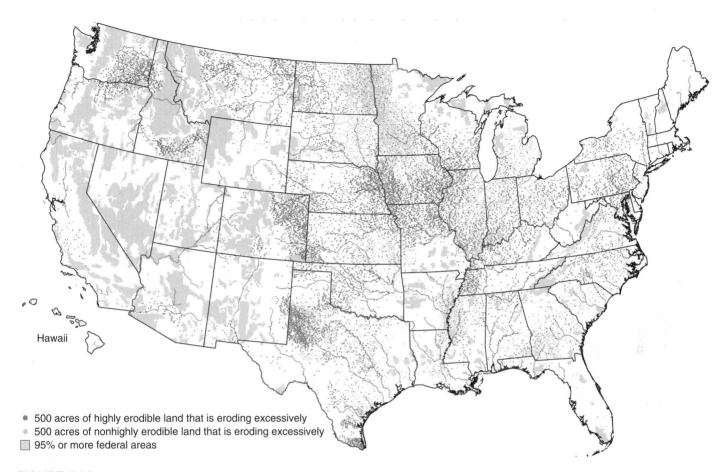

- ● 500 acres of highly erodible land that is eroding excessively
- ● 500 acres of nonhighly erodible land that is eroding excessively
- ▢ 95% or more federal areas

FIGURE 5.29 Excessive erosion on cropland. This dot-density map shows areas where excessive erosion from wind and water is occurring on cropland. Excessive erosion is defined as erosion greater than the rate that will permit crop productivity to be sustained economically and indefinitely. Data were not collected on federal land, areas shaded gray in the map. *Source: U.S. Department of Agriculture.*

FIGURE 5.30 Salinization has left a white crust of salt on the surface of this soil in Colorado. The problem is most severe in hot, dry areas where irrigation is practiced. *USDA Natural Resources Conservation Service, photo by Tim McCabe.*

1.6 million hectares (4 million acres) of cultivated soils in the Canadian provinces of Saskatchewan and Alberta are classified as overly saline. Areas of serious salinization also appear in the U.S. Southwest, particularly in the Colorado River drainage basin and in the Central Valley of California. Ironically, the irrigation water that transformed that arid, 430-kilometer-long (270-mi-long) valley into one of the country's most productive farming regions now threatens to make portions of it worthless again.

Wetlands

Vegetated land surfaces that are periodically or permanently covered by or saturated with standing water are called **wetlands.** Transitional zones between land and water, wetlands take a variety of forms, including grassy marshes, wooded swamps, tidal flats, and estuaries, and are found on all continents. Some are permanently wet; others have standing water for only part of the year. In North America, wetlands range in size from the small prairie potholes of the Midwest and Alberta, Canada, to areas as large as Florida's Everglades. Among the best known wetlands of the United States are the Okefenokee Swamp in Georgia and the bayous of Louisiana and Mississippi. Alaska has large expanses of wetlands, mostly peatlands.

The two major categories of wetlands are *inland* and *coastal.* In the United States, most wetlands are freshwater inland wetlands. They include bogs, marshes, swamps, and floodplains

Maintaining Soil Productivity

In much of the world, increasing population numbers are largely responsible for accelerated soil erosion. In the United States, economic conditions rather than population pressures have often contributed to excessive rates of erosion. Federal tax laws and the high farmland values of the 1970s encouraged farmers to plow virgin grasslands and to tear down windbreaks to increase their cultivable land and yields. The secretary of agriculture exhorted farmers to plant all of their land, "from fencerow to fencerow," to produce more grain for export. Land was converted from cattle grazing to corn and soybean production as livestock prices declined.

When prices of both land and agricultural products declined in the 1980s, farmers felt impelled to produce as much as they could in order to meet their debts and make any profit at all. To maintain or increase their productivity, many farmers neglected conservation practices, plowing under marginal lands and using fields for the same crops every year.

Conservation techniques were not forgotten, of course. They are practiced by many and persistently advocated by farm organizations and soil conservation groups. Techniques to reduce erosion by holding the soils in place are well known. They include contour plowing, terracing, strip-cropping and crop rotation, erecting windbreaks and constructing water diversion channels, and practicing no-till or reduced tillage farming (the practice of sowing seeds without turning over the soil, thus allowing plants to grow amid the stubble of the previous year's crop).

Another method of reducing erosion and reclaiming land that is badly damaged is to pay farmers to stop producing crops on highly erodible farmland. After the mid-1980s, federal farm programs attempted to reverse some of the damage resulting from past economic pressures and farming practices. One objective has been to retire for conservation purposes some 18.6 million hectares (46 million acres) of croplands that were eroding faster than three times the natural rate of soil formation. The Conservation Reserve Program of 1985 pays farmers to take highly erodible land out of production; in return, farmers agree to plant the land in trees or a grass or legume cover and then retire it from further use for 10 years.

In 1996, however, Congress passed the Federal Agriculture Improvement and Reform Act, which contained as its cornerstone a program known as "Freedom to Farm." The premise of the program is that the market and not the federal government should determine which crops are planted. Almost immediately, farmers began expanding their acreage, planting crops with a high market value on land that had been set aside. It remains to be seen how much land that was previously protected by conservation measures will be cultivated using more destructive farming methods.

Only by reducing the economic pressures that lead to abuse of farmlands and by continuing to practice known soil conservation techniques can the country maintain the long-term productivity of soil, the resource base upon which all depend.

Contour plowing and strip-cropping. © Jerry Irwin/Photo Researchers.

No-till farming. © Gene Alexander/Soil Conservation Service/USDA.

adjacent to rivers. Either fresh or salt water covers coastal wetlands, which are crucial to marine ecosystems. The part of the sea lying above the continental shelf is the most productive of all ocean waters, supporting the major commercial marine fisheries. Because it is not very deep, this *neritic zone* is penetrated and warmed by sunlight. It also receives the nutrients flowing into oceans from streams and rivers, so that vegetation and a great variety of aquatic life can flourish. However, the neritic zone depends to a considerable extent on the continued functioning of the **estuarine zone,** the relatively narrow area of

wetlands along coastlines where salt water and fresh water meet and mix (Figure 5.31).

Extremely valuable ecological systems, wetlands perform a number of vital functions. Trapping and filtering the silt, pollutants, and nutrients that rivers bring downstream, wetlands improve water quality and help replenish underground aquifers. Among the most diverse and productive of all ecosystems, wetlands provide habitat and food for a wide variety of plants and animals. Indeed, wetlands are essential to the survival of many species of fish and shellfish by serving as their spawning

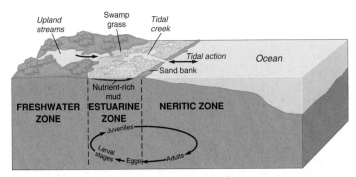

FIGURE 5.31 The estuarine zone. The outflow of fresh water from streams and the action of tides and wind mix deep ocean waters with surface waters in estuaries, contributing to their biological productivity. The saline content of estuaries is lower than that of the open sea. Many fish and shellfish require water of low salinity at some point in their life cycles.

grounds. Wetlands are also major breeding, feeding, nesting, and wintering grounds for many types of birds (Figure 5.32). Not only are these areas extraordinarily productive themselves, but they also contribute to the productivity of the neritic zone, where fish feed on the life that flows from wetlands into the sea.

Importantly, wetlands absorb floodwaters and help stabilize shorelines by providing barriers to coastal erosion. One reason Hurricane Katrina did so much damage to New Orleans was that much of the wetlands that used to buffer the city from storms were gone—due to the draining of swamps and marshes to create new land for houses and businesses and to U.S. Army Corps of Engineers (USCOE) projects that reshaped the Mississippi River and built canals and locks to make shipping easier.

People have not always recognized or appreciated the value of wetlands, tending to view them as swampy, smelly areas that provide breeding grounds for mosquitoes and impeded settlement—wastelands that should be reclaimed for productive uses such as agriculture and commercial development. Indeed, in the United States, Congress in the mid-1800s passed the Swamp Land Acts, which made it national policy to drain and fill wetlands. Scientists estimate that half the wetlands of the world have been destroyed. Australia and New Zealand are thought to have lost abut 90% of their original wetlands, and Europe at least 60%. Since the 1780s, the contiguous United States has lost more than half of its wetlands, going from some 87 million hectares (215 million acres) to 42 million hectares (105 million acres).

Wetlands have been drained, dredged, filled and built upon, converted to cropland, and used as garbage dumps. They are polluted by chemicals, excess nutrients, and other waterborne wastes. Natural shorelines have been bulldozed, and artificial levees and breakwaters interfere with the flooding that nurtures wetlands with fresh infusions of sediment and water. Habitat alteration or destruction inevitably disrupts the intricate ecosystems of the wetlands.

Growing awareness of the importance of wetlands and of how much wetland acreage has been damaged or destroyed has led in the United States and elsewhere to efforts to preserve and protect them. In the United States, the Clean Water Act of 1972 and subsequent amendments gave wetlands a measure of federal protection. The act prohibits the filling of wetlands without a permit issued by the USCOE, a provision critics have likened to putting a fox in charge of the hen house, because the corps has long emphasized dredging, stream straightening, and dike building. Officially, the government since 1989 has had a "no net loss" policy. If a development project destroys wetlands, that loss must be offset by restoring or creating a comparable amount of wetlands elsewhere.

Federal protection does not mean a wetland cannot be developed, however, and the USCOE has issued thousands of permits letting homeowners and developers fill in hundreds of thousands of acres of wetlands. Prosecutions for degrading or filling wetlands, or for failing to offset their loss, have been extremely rare. As a result, although the rate of wetland loss has slowed in recent years, many of the wetlands that remain are in danger of degradation or loss.

Forest Resources

Wetlands are only one of the renewable resources in danger of irreparable damage by human action. In many parts of the world, forests are similarly endangered.

After the retreat of continental glaciers some 12,000 years ago, and before the rise of agriculture, the world's forests and woodlands probably covered some 45% of the earth's land area

FIGURE 5.32 A salt marsh in Louisiana. Tidal marshlands have been subjected to dredging and filling for residential and industrial development. The loss of such areas reduces the essential habitat of waterfowl, fish, crustaceans, and mollusks. Many waterfowl breed and feed in coastal marshes and use them for rest during long migrations. © *Franke Keating/Photo Researchers.*

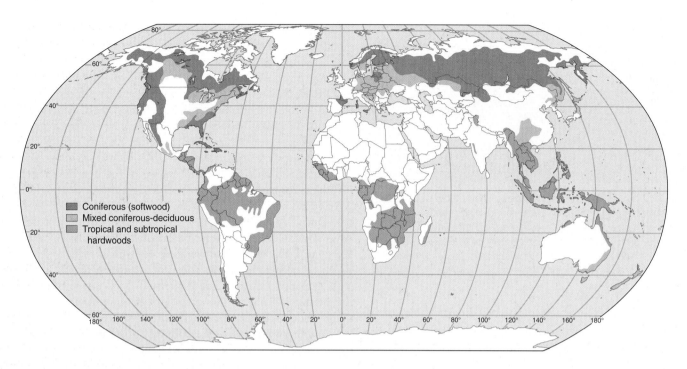

FIGURE 5.33 Major commercial forest regions. Much of the original forest, particularly in midlatitude regions, has been cut over. Many treed landscapes that remain do not contain commercial stands. Significant portions of the northern forests are not readily accessible and at current prices cannot be considered commercial.

exclusive of Antarctica. They were a sheltered and productive environment for earlier societies that subsisted on gathered fruits, nuts, berries, leaves, roots, and fibers collected from trees and woody plants. Few such cultures remain, though the gathering of forest products is still an important supplemental activity, particularly among subsistence agricultural societies.

Even after millennia of land clearance for agriculture and, more recently, commercial lumbering, cattle ranching, and fuelwood gathering, forests still cover about one-third of the world's land area. As an industrial raw material source, however, forests are more restricted in area. Although forests of some type reach discontinuously from the equator northward to beyond the Arctic Circle and southward to the tips of the southern continents, *commercial forests* are restricted to two very large global belts (Figure 5.33). One, nearly continuous, occupies the upper-middle latitudes of the Northern Hemisphere. The second straddles the equatorial zones of South and Central America, Central Africa, and Southeast Asia. These forest belts differ in the types of trees they contain and in the type of market or use they serve.

The *northern coniferous*, or softwood, forest is the largest and most continuous stand, circling the globe below the polar regions. Its pine, spruce, fir, and other types of conifers are used for construction lumber and to produce pulp for paper, rayon, and other cellulose products. To its south are the *temperate hardwood* forests, containing deciduous species such as oak, hickory, maple, and birch. These and the trees of the mixed forest lying between the hardwood and softwood belts have been greatly reduced in areal extent by centuries of agricultural and urban settlement and development, though they still are commercially important for hardwood applications: furniture, veneers, railroad ties, and so on.

FIGURE 5.34 Logging trucks in Indonesia. © *Corbis RF.*

The *tropical lowland hardwood* forests are exploited primarily for fuelwood and charcoal, on which the populations of developing countries are heavily dependent. About 90% of world fuelwood production comes from the forests of Africa, Asia, Oceania, and Latin America. An increasing quantity of special-quality woods from the tropical forests is cut for export as lumber, however. Southeast Asian countries such as Myanmar and Indonesia now account for much of the world's hardwood log exports (Figure 5.34).

The adage about not being able to see the forest for the trees is applicable to those who view forests only for the commercial value of the trees they contain. Forests are more than trees, and timbering is only one purpose that forests serve.

(a)

(b)

FIGURE 5.35 **(a) Clear cutting in the Willamette National Forest, in the Cascade Mountain Range of western Oregon.** Cutting every tree, regardless of species or size, drives out wildlife, damages watersheds, disrupts natural regeneration, and removes protective ground cover, exposing slopes to erosion. **(b) Selective cutting in eastern Canada.** Older, mature specimens are removed at first cutting. Younger trees are left for later harvesting. *(a) © BigStock Photo; (b) © R. Moller/Valan Photos.*

the forest will be managed differently than if it is designed for public recreation or the protection of watersheds. Even if the use to be emphasized is timber production, different management approaches may be taken. Logging techniques for the production of plywood or wood chips, for example, differ from those used for the production of high-quality lumber.

Commercial forests can be considered a renewable resource only if sustained-yield techniques are practiced—that is, if harvesting is balanced by new growth (see the term *maximum sustainable yield* in Chapter 10). Timber companies employ a number of methods of tree harvesting and regeneration. Two quite different practices, clear cutting and selective cutting, illustrate the diversity of such approaches (Figure 5.35).

Clear cutting is one of the most controversial logging practices. As the name implies, all the trees are removed from a given area at one time. The site is then left to regenerate naturally or is replanted, often with fast-growing seedlings of a single species. Excessive clear cutting, particularly on steep slopes, destroys wildlife habitats, accelerates soil erosion and water pollution, replaces a mixed forest with a wood plantation of no great genetic diversity, and reduces or destroys the recreational value of the area.

Selective cutting is practiced in mixed-forest stands containing trees of varying ages, sizes, and species. Medium and large trees are cut either singly or in small groups, encouraging the growth of younger trees that will be harvested later. Over time, the forest will regenerate itself. From the point of view of the harvester, selective cutting is not as efficient or economical as clear cutting. Moreover, the practice is often followed very loosely, and the construction of logging roads can still cause extensive damage to the forest.

U.S. National Forests

Roughly one-third of the United States is forested, the same proportion for the world as a whole. Only some 40% of those forests provide the annual harvest of commercial timber. The remaining forests do not contain economically valuable species; are in small, fragmented holdings; are inaccessible; or are in protected areas. Of that 40% of commercial forest land, almost half is in 155 national forests owned by the public and managed by the U.S. Forest Service (Figure 5.36). Logging by private companies is permitted; timber companies pay for the right to cut designated amounts of timber. Currently, the Forest Service is at the center of debates over how the forests should be managed. Among the issues are methods of harvesting, the cutting of very old tree stands, road building, and rates of reforestation.

Chief among the other purposes are soil and watershed conservation, the provision of a habitat for wildlife, and recreation. Forests also play a vital role in the global recycling of water, carbon, and oxygen.

Because forests serve a variety of purposes, the kind of management techniques employed in any one area depend on the particular use(s) to be emphasized. Thus, if the goal is to maintain a diversity of native plant species in order to provide a maximum number of ecological niches for wildlife,

FIGURE 5.38 Tropical rain forests exist in tropical latitude regions with high temperatures and high levels of humidity year-round. The Amazon River Basin has the world's largest continuous area of rain forests. Three countries contain more than half of the tropical rain forests: Brazil, the Democratic Republic of Congo, and Indonesia. Large tracts are being cleared to make way for farming, cattle ranching, commercial logging, and development projects.

been cleared annually in recent years, or slightly less than 1% per year of the remaining forests. Satellite imagery of the Brazilian forests in the Amazon yields a similar figure. In Brazil, this means that, on average, an area roughly the size of Connecticut is deforested each year.

Deforestation in Brazil has become the focus of international attention because it has both the largest area of tropical rain forests *and* one of the highest rates of clearing. No country better illustrates the fact that deforestation is a complicated issue that pits the governments of developing countries against those of industrialized countries, international development organizations against environmental groups, and multinational corporations against advocates of human rights. To critics of its policy of deliberately developing the Amazon Basin, Brazilians respond that it is justified because it relieves high population densities in its crowded northeast; gives farmers and ranchers land on which to build a livelihood; permits the country to tap unexploited natural resources; and helps Brazil repay its huge foreign debt. Pointing out that most of the forests in Western Europe and the United States were cleared decades if not centuries ago, and that subsequent resource exploitation led to wealth and prosperity, Brazilians ask why they shouldn't be able to use their natural resources in what they deem to be their own best interest.

There are good reasons, however, that North Americans should care what happens to the tropical rain forests. Their destruction raises three principal global concerns and a host of local ones. First, all forests play a major role in maintaining the oxygen and carbon balance of the earth. People and their industries consume oxygen; vegetation both extracts the carbon from atmospheric carbon dioxide and releases oxygen back into the atmosphere. Indeed, the forests of the Amazon have been called the "lungs of the world" for their major contribution to the oxygen breathed by humankind. When the tropical forest is cleared, its role both as a carbon "sink" and as an oxygen-replenisher is lost.

A second global concern is the contribution of forest clearing to air pollution and climate change. Deforestation by burning releases vast quantities of carbon dioxide into the atmosphere. Brazilian scientists estimate that the thousands of fires that are set to clear the Amazon forest account for one-tenth of the global production of carbon dioxide, contributing to the warming of the atmosphere (Figure 5.39). In addition,

the fires generate gases (nitrogen oxides and methane) that create acid rain and contribute to the depletion of the ozone layer, topics discussed in Chapter 12.

Finally, the eradication of tropical forests is already leading to the loss of a major part of the biological diversity of the planet. The forests are one component in an intricate ecosystem that has developed over millions of years. The trees, vines, flowering plants, animals, and insects depend on one another for survival. The destruction of the habitat by clearance annually causes the extinction of thousands of plant and animal species that exist nowhere else. Although the tropical rain forests now occupy less than 10% of the earth's land surface, they are thought to contain anywhere from 50% to 70% of all the species of plants, animals, and microorganisms in the world. Many of the plants have become important world staple food crops, among them rice, corn, cassava, squash, banana, pineapple, and sugarcane. Unknown additional potential food species remain as yet unexploited. In addition, the tropical forests yield an abundance of industrial products (oils, gums, latexes, and turpentines) and are the world's main storehouse of medicinal plants (see "Tropical Forests and Medical Resources").

Deforestation also incurs heavy environmental, economic, and social costs on a more local basis. All forests anchor topsoil and absorb excess moisture. In a vicious cycle, forest clearance accelerates soil erosion and siltation of streams and irrigation channels, leaving the area vulnerable to flooding and drought, leading in turn to future shortages of food and fuelwood. Within a matter of years, land that has been cleared for agriculture can become unsuitable for that use. In the Himalayan watershed, in the Ethiopian highlands, and in numerous other places, deforestation, erosion, and rainfall runoff have aggravated floods that have killed tens of thousands of people and left millions of others homeless.

RESOURCE MANAGEMENT

The destruction of the rain forests is a tragedy that yields no long-term benefits. The world is approaching the end of a period in which resources were cheap, readily available, and lavishly used. Over the centuries, the earth has been viewed as an almost inexhaustible storehouse of resources for humans to

1975   1989   2001

FIGURE 5.39 Deforestation in the Amazon Basin between 1975 and 2001. These satellite images of a portion of the state of Rondônia, Brazil, near the city of Ariquemes reveal the effect of the systematic destruction of the tropical rain forests. In 1975, the area was virtually untouched. Typically, clearing of the forest vegetation began along roads and then fanned out to create the "fishbone" pattern evident in the 1989 image. By 2001, the extent of deforestation had more than doubled. The fastest and cheapest way to clear areas for farms and ranches is to burn them. About the size of Oregon, Rondônia is the Brazilian state with the largest percentage of its forest cover destroyed by fire, although the states of Mato Grosso and Pará also show significant deforestation. Likened by some to an environmental holocaust, the fires generate hundreds of millions of tons of gases that contribute to global warming and depletion of the earth's protective ozone layer. *Source: Courtesy United Nations Environment Programme.*

exploit and, simultaneously, as a vast repository for the waste products of society. Now there is a growing realization that resources can be depleted, even renewable ones, such as forests; that many have life spans measured only in decades; and that the air and water—also resources—cannot absorb massive amounts of pollutants yet retain their life-supporting abilities.

That realization was reflected in June 1992, at the Earth Summit in Rio de Janeiro, when the world's governments agreed to form the UN Commission on Sustainable Development. Since that time, more than 70 countries, including the United States, have launched efforts to chart a path toward **sustainable development,** which is generally defined as development that satisfies current needs without jeopardizing the ability of future generations to meet their own needs. The principles of sustainability are straightforward. The sustainable use of renewable resources means using them at rates within their capacity for regeneration. Over the long term,

- soil erosion cannot exceed soil formation
- forest destruction cannot exceed forest regeneration
- species extinction cannot exceed species evolution
- fish catches cannot exceed the regenerative capacity of fisheries
- pollutants cannot exceed the capacity of the system to absorb them

A society can violate the principles of sustainability in the short run but not in the long run and still endure.

Defining *sustainable development* is easy, but achieving it will be difficult. The implementation of sustainable development policies will require, among other things, educating the public about the need for such policies; forging agreement on policy initiatives among government leaders, the business community, and environmentalists; providing financial incentives to resource users to practice sustainable development; and ensuring consistency in governmental implementation of agreements. Developed countries are in the best position to promote sustainable development, because they are wealthy enough to invest in the necessary research and technology. At the same time, they will have to recognize that developing countries (1) see the consumption (some would say overconsumption) of material resources by developed countries as in large measure responsible for the dwindling supplies of many of those resources, and (2) do not want to be told they cannot follow the path toward economic development and prosperity that other countries already have taken.

Moving toward the wise management of resources is not impossible, however. It entails three strategies: conservation, reuse, and substitution. By **conservation** we mean the careful use of resources so that future generations can obtain as many benefits from them as we now enjoy. It includes decreasing our consumption of resources, avoiding their wasteful use, and preserving their quality. Thus, soils can be conserved and their fertility maintained by contour plowing, crop rotation, and a variety of other practices. Properly managed, forests can be preserved even as their resources are tapped.

Opportunities to reduce the consumption of energy resources are many and varied. Nearly everything can be made more energy efficient. Motor vehicles use a significant portion of the world's oil output. Doubling their fuel efficiency by reducing vehicle weight and using more-efficient engines and tires would save at least 20% of the world's total annual oil output. Industries have an enormous potential for saving

Tropical Forests and Medical Resources

Tropical forests are biological cornucopias, possessing a stunning array of plant and animal life. Costa Rica, about the size of South Carolina, contains as many bird species as all of North America, more species of insects, and nearly half the number of plant species. Scientists have identified 1300 butterfly species in Peru's rain forest. One stand of rain forest in Kalimantan (formerly Borneo) contains more than 700 species of tree, as many as exist in North America. Seventy-two species of ant inhabit a single tree species in Peru, dependent on it for food and shelter and providing, in return, protection from other insects.

The tropical forests yield an abundance of chemical products used to manufacture alkaloids, steroids, anesthetics, and other medicinal agents. Indeed, half of all modern drugs, including strychnine, quinine, curare, and ipecac, come from the tropical forests. A single flower, the Madagascar periwinkle, produces two drugs used to treat leukemia and Hodgkin's disease.

As significant as these and other modern drugs derived from tropical plants are, scientists believe that the medical potential of the tropical forests remains virtually untapped. They fear that deforestation will eradicate medicinal plants and traditional formulas before their uses become known, depriving humans of untold potential benefits that may never be realized. Tribal peoples make free use of plants of the rain forest for such purposes as treating stings and snakebites, relieving burns and skin fungi, reducing fevers, and curing earaches, yet botanists have only recently begun to identify tropical plants and study traditional herbal medicines to discover which of them might contain medically important compounds.

---

energy by using more-efficient equipment and processes. The Japanese steel industry, for example, uses one-third less energy to produce a ton of steel than does that industry in most other countries. Energy used for heating, cooling, and lighting homes and office buildings could be reduced by half if they were properly constructed and furnished. Compact fluorescent lightbulbs, for example, use only 20% of the energy of incandescent bulbs and last eight times longer.

The *reuse* of materials also reduces the consumption of resources. Instead of being buried in landfills, waste can be burned or decomposed and fermented to provide energy. Recycling of steel, aluminum, copper, glass, and other materials can be greatly increased, not only to recover the materials themselves but also to recoup the energy invested in their production (Figure 5.40). It takes only 5% as much electricity to make aluminum from scrap as from raw materials. In other words, manufacturers can make 20 cans out of recycled material with the same energy it takes to make a single can out of new material. See "Source Reduction and Recycling" in Chapter 12 (pp. 425–426) for a further discussion of this topic.

The *substitution* of other energy sources for gas and oil can be more actively pursued. If the technology to exploit them economically can be developed, coal and oil shale could supply fuel needs well into the future. In addition, the renewable energy resources, such as biomass, solar, and geothermal power, are virtually infinite in their amount and variety. Although no single renewable source is likely to be as important as oil or

FIGURE 5.40 Compressed cans ready for recycling.
Americans buy about 100 billion aluminum cans a year, only 40% to 45% of which are recycled. The rest end up in landfills and will still be there a century from now. Recycling reduces the amount of land that must be strip-mined for bauxite to produce aluminum, the air pollution from refineries, and water pollution from waste piles.
© *Punchstock RF.*

gas, collectively they could make a significant contribution to energy needs. Finally, the substitution of other materials for nonfuel minerals in short supply can extend the lifetimes of their reserves. Non-metals such as ceramics or fiber products can substitute for metals in some applications.

Summary of Key Concepts

- Natural resources can be classified as renewable, those that can be regenerated in nature as fast as or faster than societies exploit them, and nonrenewable, those that are generated so slowly that they are thought of as existing in finite amounts. The proved reserves of a resource are the amounts that have been identified and that can be extracted profitably.

- Industrially advanced countries depend heavily on resources derived from nonrenewable minerals, chiefly the fossil fuels crude oil, natural gas, and coal, all of which are unevenly distributed. Some countries receive more than half of their electricity from nuclear power plants, while others have none.

- Renewable natural resources are more widely and evenly distributed than the nonrenewable ones. Wood and other forms of biomass are the primary source of energy for more than half of the world's people, and hydropower is a major source of electricity in many countries. Other renewable resources, including solar power, geothermal energy, and wind power, make a more localized and limited contribution to energy needs.

- The nonfuel mineral resources from which people fashion metals, glass, stone, and other products are nonrenewable. Some exist in vast amounts, others in relatively small quantities; some are widely distributed, others concentrated in just a few locations.

- Human activities have had and continue to have a severe impact on wetlands and forests, both of which play vital ecological roles.

- The growing demand for resources, induced by population increases and economic development, strains the earth's supply of raw materials. The wise and careful management of natural resources of all types involves conservation, reuse, and substitution.

Key Words

biomass fuel 133	nuclear fission 131	resource 119
conservation 155	nuclear fusion 132	salinization 146
desertification 145	oil shale 129	soil erosion 144
energy 122	ore 138	solar energy 135
estuarine zone 148	perpetual resource 120	sustainable development 155
geothermal energy 137	photovoltaic (PV) cell 136	tar sand 129
hydropower 134	potentially renewable resource 120	wetland 147
liquefied natural gas (LNG) 128	proved (usable) reserves 121	wind farm 138
nonrenewable resources 120	renewable resource 120	

Thinking Geographically

1. What is the basic distinction between a *renewable* and a *nonrenewable* resource? Why do estimates of *proved reserves* vary over time?

2. Why are energy resources called the "master" natural resources? What is the relationship between energy consumption and industrial production? Briefly describe historical energy consumption patterns in the United States.

3. Why has oil become the dominant form of commercial energy? Which countries are the main producers of crude oil? Why is it difficult to predict how long proved reserves of oil are likely to last?

4. In 1974, when the United States imported 35% of the oil it consumed, President Richard M. Nixon in his State of the Union Address said, "Let this be our national goal. . . . The United States will not be dependent on any other country for the energy we need to provide our jobs, to heat our homes, and to keep our transportation moving." The aim of his Project Independence was to be independent of foreign energy sources by 1980. How do you account for the fact that, more than 35 years later, the United States imports more than 60% of the oil it consumes?

5. Why has the proportion of U.S. energy supplied by coal increased since 1961? What ecological and social problems are associated with the use of coal?

6. What are the different methods of generating nuclear energy? Why is there public opposition to nuclear power?

7. Which are the most widely used ways of using renewable resources to generate energy? What are the advantages of using such resources? The disadvantages?

8. What, in general, are the leading mining countries? What role do developing countries play in the production of critical raw materials? How have producing countries reacted to the threatened scarcity of copper?

9. Since soil erosion is a natural process, why is it of concern? What are some commonly used methods of reducing erosion? Under what conditions and in what types of areas do desertification and salinization occur?

10. What are some types of wetlands? Why are they important, and why have so many disappeared?

11. What vital ecological functions do forests perform? Where are the tropical rain forests located, and what concerns are raised by their destruction?

12. Discuss three ways of reducing demands on resources.

The Culture-Environment Tradition

The Crow country. The Great Spirit put it exactly in the right place; while you are in it, you fare well; whenever you get out of it, whichever way you travel, you fare worse. . . . The Crow country is in exactly the right place. It has snowy mountains and sunny plains; all kinds of climates and good things for every season. When the summer heats scorch the prairies, you can draw up under the mountains, where the air is sweet and cool. . . . In the autumn when your horses are fat and strong from the mountain pastures, you can go down on the plains and hunt the buffalo or trap beaver on the streams. And when winter comes on, you can take shelter in the woody bottoms along the rivers.

The Crow country is exactly in the right place. Everything good is found there. There is no country like the Crow country.

Such was the opinion of Arapoosh, chief of the Crows, speaking of the Big Horn basin country of Wyoming in the early 19th century. In contrast, in the 1860s, Captain Raynolds reported to the Secretary of War that the basin was "repelling in all its characteristics, surrounded on all sides by mountain ridges [and offering] but few agricultural advantages."

In the three chapters of Part One, our primary concern was with the physical landscape. Although the physical environment may be described by process and data, it takes on human meaning only through the filter of culture. Arapoosh and Raynolds viewed the same landscape, but from the standpoints of their separate cultures and conditioning. Culture is like looking through tinted glass, affecting and distorting our view of the earth. Culture conditions the way people think about the land, the way they use and alter the land, and the way they interact with one another on the land.

Such conditioning is the focus of the culture-environment tradition of geography—a tradition concerned with the landscape, but not in the physical science sense of Part One of this book. In Part Two, humans are the focus. Of course, the physical environment is always in our minds as we develop the notion of cultural difference and reality. Our landscapes, however, take on an added dimension and become cultural rather than purely physical.

The four chapters in this part of our study, therefore, concentrate on the "people" portion of geography's environment-culture-people relationship. In Chapter 6, "Population Geography," we start with the basics of human populations in their numbers, compositions, distributions, and growth trends and the pressures they exert on the resources of the lands they occupy. These quantitative and distributional aspects of peoples are important current concerns, as attested to by the frequent popular reference to a "population explosion," public debate about legal and undocumented immigration, and speculation about population growth and food availability. More fundamentally, of course, numbers and locations of people are the essential background to all other aspects of human geography.

People are, however, more than numbers in a global counting parlor. They are individuals who think, react, and behave in response to the physical and social environments they occupy. In turn, those thoughts, actions, and responses are strongly conditioned by the standards and structures of the cultures to which the individuals belong. The world is a mosaic of culture groups and human landscapes that invite geographic study. Chapter 7, "Cultural Geography," introduces that study by examining the components and subsystems of culture, the ways in which culture changes, and the key variables in

defining a culture and in producing variations in culture from place to place.

The world patterns of those variations are not permanent. They represent merely the current consequences of past movements of people, export and adaptation of ideas and technologies, and histories of conquest and settlement. They represent the results of the past and present interaction of people and their cultures with their environment. Regularities of human spatial behavior and the factors that account for the manner in which people use the earth are the subject of Chapter 8, "Spatial Interaction." The individual and group behaviors of humans create the cultural landscape in all its variations, including those of production, resource utilization, and urban settlement, which will be the topics of Part Three of this book.

A controlling setting for those later cultural considerations is explored in Chapter 9, "Political Geography." Political systems and processes strongly influence the form and distribution of many elements of culture. Economic and transportation systems coincide with national boundaries. Political regulations, whether detailed zoning codes or broad environmental protection laws, have a marked effect on the economic and urban landscape. In some countries, even such apparently nonpolitical matters as religion, literature, music, and the fine arts may be conditioned by governmental support for certain forms of expression and the rejection and prohibition of others. Certainly, governmental direction and political ideology are essential elements in the establishment and maintenance of the economic systems that determine resource exploitation and livelihood patterns of people across the world, systems subject to change as governments fall or as supranational political associations—the European Union, for example—impose new patterns of behavior on established national cultures.

Our theme in Part Two, therefore, is people and the cultural landscapes they create or envision. Let us begin with people themselves before we move on to consider their cultures and behaviors.

Opposite page: This Orthodox Jewish man is praying facing the Western Wall (Wailing Wall) in Jerusalem. The Western Wall is a remnant retaining wall from Herod's 1st Century BCE restoration of the Second Temple and the most sacred site on Earth for Jews. © 1998 Copyright IMS Communications Ltd./Capstone Design. All Rights Reserved.

CHAPTER SIX

Population Geography

CHAPTER OUTLINE

Al Qahirah (Cairo), Egypt, the largest city in Africa, has been nicknamed the "city of a thousand minarets." In 2005, the United Nations estimated its population at 11.1 million, making it the 16th largest city in the world. The slender tower in the background of this bustling shopping street is a distinctive feature of Islamic architecture used in the call to prayer. © *Kate Sidlo.*

"Zero, possibly even negative [population growth" was the 1972 slogan proposed by the prime minister of Singapore, an island country in Southeast Asia. His nation's population, which stood at a million at the end of World War II (1945), had doubled by the mid-1960s. To avoid the overpopulation he foresaw, the government decreed, "Boy or girl, two is enough," and refused maternity leaves and access to health insurance for third or subsequent births. Abortion and sterilization were legalized, and children born fourth or later in a family were to be discriminated against in school admissions policy. In response, by the mid-1980s, birth rates had fallen below the level necessary to replace the population, and abortions were terminating more than one-third of all pregnancies.

"At least two. Better three. Four if you can afford it" was the national slogan proposed by the same prime minister in 1986, reflecting fears that the stringencies of the earlier campaign had gone too far. From concern that overpopulation would doom the country to perpetual Third World poverty, Prime Minister Lee Kuan Yew was moved to worry that population limitation would deprive it of the growth potential and national strength implicit in a youthful, educated workforce adequate to replace and support the present aging population. His 1990 national budget provided for sizeable, long-term tax rebates for second children born to mothers under 28. Not certain that financial inducements alone would suffice to increase the population, the Singapore government annually renewed its offer to take 100,000 Hong Kong Chinese who might choose to leave when China took over that territory in 1997. The policy reversal in Singapore reflects an inflexible population reality: the structure of the present controls the content of the future. The size, characteristics, growth trends, and migrations of today's populations help shape the well-being of peoples yet unborn but whose numbers and distributions are now being determined. The numbers, age, and sex distribution of people; the patterns and trends in their fertility and mortality; and their density of settlement and rate of growth all affect and are affected by the social, political, and economic organization of a society. Through population data we begin to understand how the people in a given area live, how they may interact with one another, how they use the land, what pressure on resources exists, and what the future may bring.

Population geography provides the background tools and understandings of those interests. It focuses on the number, composition, and distribution of human beings in relation to variations in the conditions of earth space. It differs from **demography,** the statistical study of human population, in its concern with *spatial* analysis—the relationship of numbers to area. Regional circumstances of resource base, type of economic development, standard of living, food supply, and conditions of health and well-being are basic to geography's population concerns. They are, as well, fundamental expressions of the human-environment relationships that are the substance of all human geographic inquiry.

POPULATION GROWTH

Sometime in 2011, a human birth will raise Earth's population to 7 billion people. In 1999, the count was 6 billion. As of mid-2010, the world population was growing by an average of 74 million people annually, or some 202,000 per day. While the increases are substantial, they have been declining over the years. During the early 1990s, the U.S. Census Bureau and the United Nations Population Division regularly reported yearly growth at 85 to 90 million. Even with the slower pace of recorded increase, in 2006 the United Nations projected that the world would likely contain about 9.2 billion inhabitants in 2050. Even then, it would continue to add a few million annually and grow to perhaps 9.4 or 9.5 billion by the year 2100.

Impressed by dramatic birth rate reductions reported by 2007 for many developing and populous countries—India, importantly—many demographers lowered their estimates to predict end-of-century world totals peaking at between 8 and 9 billion, followed by numerical decline, not stability or slow increase. All do agree, however, that essentially all or any future growth will occur in countries now considered "developing" (Figure 6.1), with especially rapid growth in the 50 least-developed states. The majority of the world's most populous countries are developing countries, and that trend will have become more pronounced by 2050 (Table 6.1). We will return to these projections later in this chapter and to the difficulties and disagreements inherent in making them.

Just what is implied by numbers in the millions and billions? With what can we compare the 2010 population of Estonia in Europe (about 1.3 million) or of China (about 1.3 billion)? Unless we have some grasp of their scale and meaning, our understanding of the data and data manipulations of the population geographer can at best be superficial. It is difficult to appreciate a number as vast as 1 million or 1 billion and the great distinction between them. Two examples offered by the Population Reference Bureau may help in visualizing their immensity and implications:

- A 2.5-centimeter (1-in.) stack of U.S. paper currency contains 233 bills. If you had a *million* dollars in thousand-dollar bills, the stack would be 11 centimeters (4.3 in.) high. If you had a *billion* dollars in thousand-dollar bills, your pile of money would reach 109 meters (358 ft)—about the length of a football field.

- You had lived a *million* seconds when you were 11.6 days old. You won't be a *billion* seconds old until you are 31.7 years of age.

The implications of the present numbers and the potential increases in population are of vital current social, political, and ecological concern. Population numbers were much smaller some 12,000 years ago, when continental glaciers began their retreat, people spread to formerly unoccupied portions of the globe, and human experimentation with food sources initiated the Agricultural Revolution. The 5 or 10 million people who then constituted all of humanity obviously had considerable potential to expand their numbers. In retrospect, we see

(a)

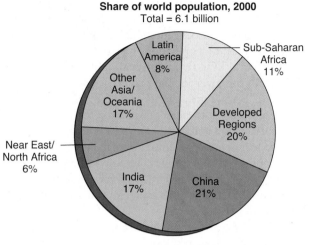

Share of world population, 2000
Total = 6.1 billion

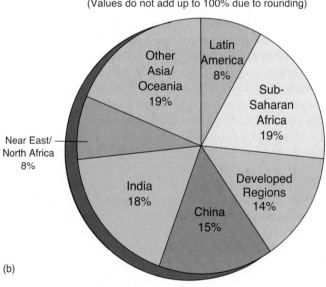

Estimated share of world population, 2050
Total = 9.2 billion
(Values do not add up to 100% due to rounding)

(b)

FIGURE 6.1 World population numbers and projections.
(a) After two centuries of slow growth, world population began explosive expansion after World War II (1939–1945). United Nations demographers project a global population of 9.2 billion in 2050. Declining growth rates in much of the developing world have lowered earlier year 2100 estimates of global population from 10 billion to no more than 9.4 to 9.5 billion; some demographers argue for further reducing it to between 8 and 9 billion. Numbers in more-developed regions at the middle of the century will be the same or lower than at its start, thanks to population stability or decline below early 2000 levels in 51 countries and areas. However, higher fertility rates and immigration are projected to increase the U.S. population by more than 50% between 2000 and 2050, and large-volume immigration into Europe could alter its population decline projections. In contrast, the populations of the less-developed regions may increase by more than 60% between 2000 and 2050. **(b)** Although only a little more than 80% of world population was found in regions considered "less-developed" in 2000, more than 9 out of 10 of a larger total will be located there in 2050. *Sources: (a) Estimates from Population Reference Bureau and United Nations Population Fund; (b) Based on United Nations and U.S. Bureau of the Census data and projections.*

that the natural resource base of the earth had a population-supporting capacity far in excess of the pressures exerted on it by early hunting and gathering groups.

Some observers maintain that, despite present numbers or even those we can reasonably anticipate for the future, the adaptive and exploitative ingenuity of humans is in no danger of being taxed. Others, however, frightened by the resource demands of a growing world population that had already expanded four-fold—from 1.6 billion to 6.1 billion—in the century from 1900 to 2000, compare Earth to a self-contained spaceship and declare with chilling conviction that a finite vessel cannot bear an ever-increasing number of passengers. They point to recurring problems of malnutrition and starvation (though these are realistically more a matter of failures of distribution than of inability to produce enough foodstuffs worldwide). They cite dangerous conditions of air and water pollution, the loss of forest and farmland, the apparent nearing exhaustion of many minerals and fossil fuels, and other

evidences of strains on world resources as foretelling the discernible outer limits of population growth.

On a worldwide basis, populations grow only one way: the number of births in a given period exceeds the number of deaths. Current estimates of slowing world population growth and eventual stability or decline clearly indicate that humans, by their individual and collective decisions, may effectively limit growth and control global population numbers. The implications of these observations will become clearer after we define some terms important in the study of world population and explore their significance.

SOME POPULATION DEFINITIONS

Demographers use a wide range of measures of population composition and trends, though all their calculations start with a count of events: of individuals in the population, births, deaths, marriages, and so on. To those basic counts,

TABLE 6.1
World's Most Populous Countries in 2009 and 2050

2009		2050	
Country	**Population (Millions)**	**Country**	**Population (Millions)**
China	1331	India	1748
India	1171	China	1437
United States	307	United States	439
Indonesia	243	Indonesia	343
Brazil	191	Pakistan	335
Pakistan	181	Nigeria	285
Bangladesh	162	Bangladesh	222
Nigeria	153	Brazil	215
Russia	142	Congo, Dem. Rep.	189
Japan	128	Philippines	150

Source: Population Reference Bureau.

demographers add refinements that make the figures more meaningful and useful in population analysis. Among them are *rates* and *cohort* measures.

Rates simply record the frequency of the occurrence of an event during a given time frame for a designated population—for example, the marriage rate as the number of marriages performed per 1000 population in the United States last year. **Cohort** measures refer data to a population group unified by a specified common characteristic—the age cohort of 1–5 years, perhaps, or the college class of 2012 (Figure 6.2). Basic numbers and rates useful in the analysis of world population and population trends have been reprinted in this book with the permission of the Population Reference Bureau as Appendix 3. Examination of them will help illustrate the discussion that follows.

Birth Rates

The **crude birth rate (CBR)**, often referred to simply as the *birth rate*, is the annual number of live births per 1000 population. It is "crude" because it relates births to total population without regard to the age or sex composition of that population. A country with a population of 2 million and with 40,000 births a year has a crude birth rate of 20 per 1000.

$$\frac{40{,}000}{2{,}000{,}000} = 20 \text{ per } 1000$$

The birth rate of a country is strongly influenced by the age and sex structure of its population, by the customs and family size expectations of its inhabitants, and by its adopted population policies. Because these conditions vary widely, recorded national birth rates vary—early in the 21st century, from a high of 50 or more in some West African states to lows of 9 or 10 per 1000 in 20 or more European countries. Although birth rates of 30 or above per 1000 are considered *high*, almost one-fifth of the

world's people (down from one-half in 1990) live in countries with rates that high or higher (Figure 6.3). In these countries—chiefly in Africa, western and southern Asia, and Latin America—the population is predominantly agricultural and rural, and a high proportion of the female population is young. In many of them, birth rates may be significantly higher than official records indicate. Available data suggest that, every year, about 50 million births go unregistered and therefore uncounted.

Birth rates of less than 18 per 1000 are reckoned *low* and are characteristic of industrialized, urbanized countries. All European countries, including Russia, Anglo America, Japan, Australia, and New Zealand, have low rates, as do an increasing number of developing states. Some of these, such as China, have adopted effective family planning programs (see "China's Way—and Others," page 165). In others,

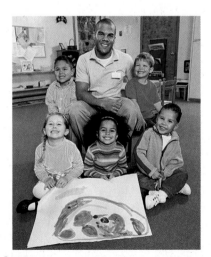

FIGURE 6.2 Whatever their differences may be by race, sex, or ethnicity, these children around their nursery school teacher will forever be clustered demographically into a single *birth cohort*. © Getty RF.

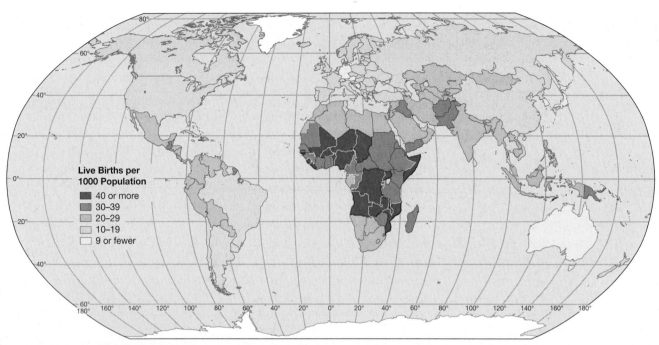

FIGURE 6.3 Crude birth rates, 2009. The map suggests a degree of precision that is misleading in the absence of reliable, universal registration of births. The pattern shown serves, however, as a generally useful summary of comparative reproduction patterns if class divisions are not taken too literally. Reported or estimated population data vary annually, so this and other population maps may not agree in all details with the figures recorded in Appendix 3. *Source: Data from Population Reference Bureau.*

changed cultural norms have reduced desired family size. *Transitional* birth rates (between 18 and 30 per 1000) characterize some, mainly smaller developing and newly industrializing countries, although giant India entered that group in 1994.

As the recent population histories of Singapore and China indicate, birth rates are subject to change. The decline to current low birth rates of European countries and of some of the areas that they colonized is usually ascribed to industrialization, urbanization, and in recent years maturing populations. While restrictive family planning policies in China rapidly reduced the birth rate from over 33 per 1000 in 1970 to 18 per 1000 in 1986, industrializing Japan experienced a comparable 15-point decline in the decade 1948–1958 with little governmental intervention. Indeed, the stage of economic development appears closely related to variations in birth rates among countries, although rigorous testing of this relationship proves it to be imperfect (Figure 6.3). As a group, the more-developed states of the world showed a crude birth rate of 12 per 1000 in 2009; less-developed countries (excluding China) registered 26 per 1000 (down from 35 in 1990).

Religious and political beliefs can also affect birth rates. The convictions of many Roman Catholics and Muslims that their religion forbids the use of artificial birth control techniques often lead to high birth rates among believers. However, predominantly Catholic Italy has one of the world's lowest birth rates. Islam itself does not prohibit contraception. Similarly, some European governments—concerned about birth rates too low to sustain present population levels—subsidize births in an attempt to raise those rates. Regional variations in projected percentage contributions to world population growth are summarized in Figure 6.4.

Fertility Rates

Crude birth rates may display such regional variability because of differences in age and sex composition or disparities in births among the reproductive-age, rather than total, population. The rate is "crude" because its denominator contains persons who have no chance at all of giving birth—males, young girls, and elderly women. The **total fertility rate (TFR),** which is the average number of children a woman will have over the course of her childbearing years, is a more-refined and thus more satisfactory statement than the crude birth rate.

The TFR (Figure 6.5) is calculated by assuming that, over her childbearing years, a woman bore children at the current year's rate for women that age. Thus, a TFR of 3 means that the average woman in a population would be expected to have three offspring in her lifetime. The fertility rate minimizes the effects of fluctuation in the population structure and summarizes the demonstrated and expected reproductive behavior of women. Thus, for regional comparative and predictive purposes, it is a more useful and more reliable figure than the crude birth rate.

A useful concept here is *replacement level fertility*—the level of fertility at which each successive generation of women produces exactly enough children to ensure that the same number of women survive in that generation to have offspring themselves. Although a TFR of 2.0 would seem sufficient exactly to

China's Way—and Others

An ever-larger population is "a good thing," Chairman Mao announced in 1965, when China's birth rate was 37 per 1000 and its population totaled 540 million. At Mao's death in 1976, numbers reached 852 million, although the birth rate then had dropped to 25. During the 1970s, when it became evident that population growth was consuming more than half the annual increase in the country's gross domestic product, China introduced a well-publicized campaign advocating the "two-child family" and providing services, including abortions, supporting that program. In response, China's birth rate dropped to 19.5 per 1000 by the late 1970s.

"One couple, one child" became the slogan of a new and more vigorous population control drive launched in 1979, backed by both incentives and penalties to assure its success in China's tightly controlled society. Late marriages were encouraged; free contraceptives, cash awards, abortions, and sterilizations were provided to families limited to a single child. Penalties, including steep fines, were levied for second births. At the campaign's height in 1983, the government ordered the sterilization of either husband or wife for couples with more than one child. Infanticide—particularly the exposure or murder of female babies—was a reported means of both conforming to a one-child limit and increasing the chances that the one child would be male.

By 1986, China's officially reported crude birth rate had fallen to 18 per 1000, far below the 37 per 1000 then registered among the rest of the world's less-developed countries. The one-child policy was effectively dropped in 1984 to permit two-child limits in rural areas, where 63% of the Chinese population still resides, but in 2002 it was reinstated as nationwide law following the documentation of extensive underreporting of rural births. In contrast, newly prosperous urbanites have voluntarily reduced their fertility to well below replacement levels, with childless couples increasingly common.

Nationally, past and current population controls have been so successful that, by 2000, China's population was 300 million less than it otherwise would have been. By 2001, serious concerns were being expressed by demographers and government officials that population decrease, not increase, is the problem next to be confronted. Projections suggest that, by 2042, because of lowered fertility rates, China's population numbers will actually start falling. The country is already beginning to face a pressing social problem: a declining proportion of working-age persons and an absence of an adequate welfare network to care for a rapidly growing number of senior citizens.

Concerned with their own increasing numbers, many developing countries have introduced their own less-extreme programs of family planning, stressing access to contraception and sterilization. International agencies have encouraged these programs, buoyed by such presumed success as the 21% fall in fertility rates in Bangladesh from 1970 to 1990 as the proportion of married women of reproductive age using contraceptives rose from 3% to 40% under intensive family planning encouragement and frequent adviser visits. The costs per birth averted, however, were reckoned at more than the country's $160 per capita gross domestic product.

Research suggests that fertility falls because women decide they want smaller families, not because they have unmet needs for contraceptive advice and devices. Nineteenth-century northern Europeans without the aid of science, it is observed, had lower fertility rates than their counterparts today in middle-income countries. With some convincing evidence, improved women's education has been proposed as a surer way to reduce births than either encouraged contraception or China's coercive efforts. Studies from individual countries indicate that 1 year of female schooling can reduce the fertility rate by between 5% and 10%. However, the fertility rate of uneducated Thai women is only two-thirds that of Ugandan women with secondary education. Obviously, the demand for babies is not absolutely related to educational levels.

Instead, that demand seems closely tied to the use value poor families place on children in some parts of the developing world. Where those families share in such communal resources as firewood, animal fodder, grazing land, and fish, the more of those collective resources that can be converted to private family property and use, the better off is the family. Indeed, the more communal resources that are available for "capture," the greater are the incentives for a household to have more children to appropriate them. Some population economists conclude that only when population numbers increase to the point of total conversion of communal resources to private property—and children have to be supported and educated, rather than employed—will poor families in developing countries want fewer children. If so, coercion, contraception, and education may be less effective as checks on births than the economic consequence of population increase itself.

© The McGraw-Hill Companies, Inc. / Photo by Alasdair Drysdale.

replace present population (one baby to replace each parent), in reality, replacement fertility levels must be slightly higher to compensate for the higher percentage of boys that are born and for mortalities among women before they complete their childbearing years. In developed countries, replacement levels of fertility are assumed to be 2.1. However, the higher the level of mortality in a population, the higher the replacement level of fertility will be. For Mozambique early in the 21st century, for example, the replacement level fertility was 3.4 children per woman.

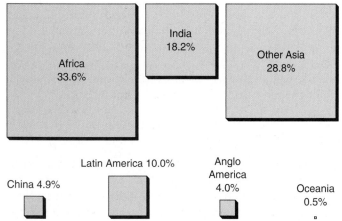

FIGURE 6.4 Projected percentage contributions to world population growth by region, 2000–2050. Birth rate changes recorded by differently sized regional populations with differing age structures are altering the world pattern of population increase. Africa, containing 13% of world population in 2000, will probably account for more than one-third of total world increase between 2000 and 2050. Between 1965 and 1975, China's contribution to world growth was 2.5 times that of Africa; between 2000 and 2050, Africa's numerical growth will be more than 8 times that of China. India, which reached the 1 billion level in 2000, is projected to grow by more than 50% over the first half of the 21st century and have by far the world's largest population. In contrast to the growth within the world regions shown, Europe's population is expected to decrease by 90 million over the same half-century period, according to the UN 2002 projections. *Source: Projections based on World Bank and United Nations figures.*

On a worldwide basis, the TFR in 2009 was 2.6; 20 years earlier, it was 3.6. The more-developed countries recorded a 1.7 TFR in 2009, down from a near-replacement 2.0 in 1987. That decrease has been dwarfed in amount and significance by the rapid changes in reproductive behavior in much of the developing world. Since 1960, the average TFR in the less-developed world fell by half from the traditional 6 or more to 2.7 in 2009. That dramatic decline reflects the fact that women and men in developing countries are marrying later and having fewer children, following the pattern set earlier in the developed world. There has been, as well, a great increase in family planning and contraceptive use. In 2001, according to a UN world fertility report, 92% of all national governments supported family planning and distributed contraceptives, either directly or indirectly.

The recent fertility declines in developing states have been more rapid and widespread than anyone expected. The TFRs for so many of them have dropped so dramatically since the early 1960s (Figure 6.6) that earlier, widely believed world population projections anticipating 10.5 billion or more at the end of this century are now generally discounted and rejected. Indeed, worldwide in 2009, 81 countries and territories containing nearly 50% of global population had fertility rates of 2.1 or less, with more poised to join their ranks. China's decrease from a TFR of 5.9 births per woman in the period 1960–1965 to (officially) about 1.8 in 2000 (an estimated 1.6 in 2009) and comparable drops in TFRs of Bangladesh, Brazil, Mozambique, and other states demonstrate that

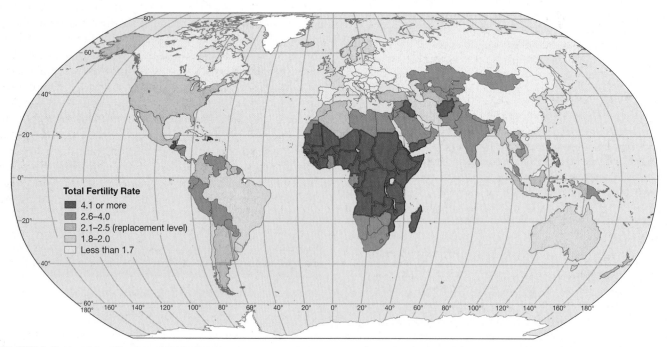

FIGURE 6.5 Total fertility rate (TFR) 2009 indicates the average number of children that would be born to each woman if, during her childbearing years, she bore children at the same rate as women of those ages actually did in a given year. Because the TFR is age-adjusted, two countries with identical birth rates may have quite different fertility rates and therefore different prospects for growth. Depending on mortality conditions, a TFR of 2.1 to 2.5 children per woman is considered the "replacement level," at which a population will eventually stop growing. *Source: 2009 data from Population Reference Bureau.*

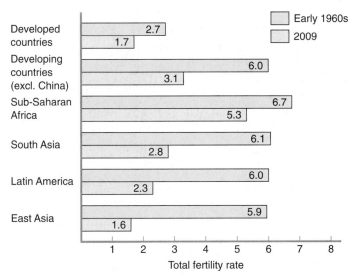

FIGURE 6.6 Differential fertility rate declines, 1960s to 2009. Fertility declined most rapidly in Latin America and East Asia and much more slowly in sub-Saharan Africa. Europe is far below replacement, with a 2007 TFR of 1.5; the United States, however, with a TFR of 2.1, is just at the replacement point. *Sources: Population Reference Bureau, 2009 and United Nations Population Fund.*

fertility reflects cultural values, not biological imperatives. If those values now favor fewer children than formerly, population projections based on earlier, higher TFR rates must be adjusted.

In fact, demographers have long assumed that recently observed developing country—and therefore global—fertility rate declines to the replacement level would continue and, in the long run, lead to stable population numbers. However, nothing in logic or history requires population stability at any level. Rather than assume, as in the past, a fertility decline to a constant continuing rate of 2.1, the 2008 United Nations world population projection predicts a long-term (2050) fertility rate of 2.02—*below* the replacement level. Should the UN's new assessment of fertility prove correct, world population will not just stop growing, as its past projections envisioned; it will inevitably decline (see "A Population Implosion?"). Of course, should cultural values change to again favor children, growth would resume. Different TFR estimates imply conflicting population projections and vastly different regional and world population concerns.

Individual country projections based on current fertility rates may be inaccurate due to migration. Massive international population movements are occurring in response to political instabilities and, particularly, to differentials in perceived economic opportunities. For example, the European Union in recent years has had a negative rate of natural increase, yet since 2000 it has experienced essentially a constant population solely because of immigrant influx from Eastern Europe, Asia, and Africa.

World regional and national fertility rates reported in Appendix 3 and other sources are summaries that conceal significant variations between population groups. The Caribbean

region, for example, showed a total fertility rate of 2.5 in 2009, but the TFRs of individual states ranged from a low of 16 in Cuba to a high of 4.0 in Haiti. The United States 2007 national average fertility rate of 2.1 did not reveal that the TFR for Hispanics was about 2.8, about 2.1 for African Americans, and only 1.8 for non-Hispanic whites.

Death Rates

The **crude death rate (CDR),** also called the **mortality rate,** is calculated in the same way as the crude birth rate: the annual number of events per 1000 population. In the past, a valid generalization was that the death rate, like the birth rate, varied with national levels of development. Characteristically, the highest rates (over 20 per 1000) were found in the less-developed countries of Africa, Asia, and Latin America; the lowest rates (less than 10) were associated with the developed states of Europe and Anglo America. That correlation became decreasingly valid as dramatic reductions in death rates occurred in developing countries in the years following World War II. Infant mortality rates and life expectancies improved as antibiotics, vaccinations, and pesticides to treat diseases and control disease carriers were made available in almost all parts of the world and as increased attention was paid to funding improvements in urban and rural sanitary facilities and safe water supplies.

Distinctions between more-developed and less-developed countries in mortality (Figure 6.7) have been so reduced that, by 1994, death rates for less-developed countries as a group actually dropped below those for more-developed states and have remained lower since. Notably, that reduction did not extend to infant or maternal mortality rates (see "The Risks of Motherhood"). Like crude birth rates, death rates are meaningful for comparative purposes only when we study identically structured populations. Countries with a high proportion of elderly people, such as Denmark and Sweden, would be expected to have higher death rates than those with a high proportion of young people, such as Iceland, assuming equality in other national conditions affecting health and longevity. The pronounced youthfulness of populations in developing countries, as much as improvements in sanitary and health conditions, is an important factor in the recently reduced mortality rates of those areas.

To overcome that lack of comparability, death rates can be calculated for specific age groups. The *infant mortality rate,* for example, is the ratio of deaths of infants age 1 year or under per 1000 live births:

$$\frac{\text{deaths age 1 year of less}}{1000 \text{ live births}}$$

Infant mortality rates are significant because it is at these ages that the greatest declines in mortality have occurred, largely as a result of better health services. The drop in infant mortality accounts for a large part of the decline in the general death rate in the last few decades, because mortality during the first year of life is usually greater than in any other year.

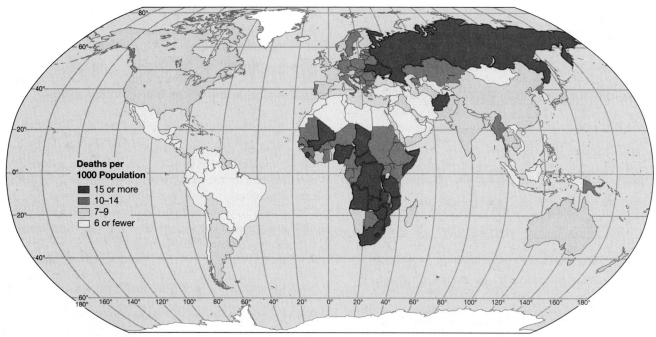

FIGURE 6.7 Crude death rates show less worldwide variability than do the birth rates displayed in Figure 6.3. The widespread availability of at least minimal health protection measures and a generally youthful population in the developing countries yield death rates frequently lower than those recorded in "old age" Europe. *Source: 2009 data from Population Reference Bureau.*

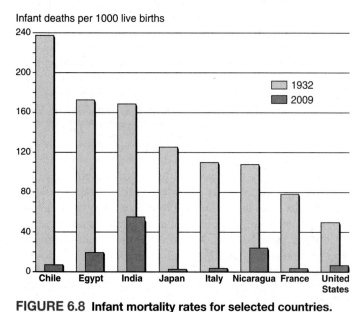

FIGURE 6.8 Infant mortality rates for selected countries. Dramatic declines in the rate have occurred in all countries, a result of international programs of health care delivery aimed at infants and children in developing states. Nevertheless, the decreases have been proportionately greatest in the urbanized, industrialized countries, where sanitation, safe water, and quality health care are widely available. *Source: Data from U.S. Bureau of the Census and Population Reference Bureau.*

Two centuries ago, it was not uncommon for 200 to 300 infants per 1000 to die in their first year. Even today, despite significant declines in those rates over the last 60 years in many countries (Figure 6.8), striking world regional and national variations remain. For all of Africa, infant mortality rates are about 75 per 1000, and individual African states (for example, Angola, Liberia, Niger, and Sierra Leone) showed rates above 150 early in this century. Nor are rates uniform within single countries. The former Soviet Union reported a national infant mortality rate of 23 (1991), but it registered above 110 in parts of its Central Asian region. In contrast, infant mortality rates in Anglo America and western and northern Europe are more uniformly in the 2 to 7 range.

Modern medicine and sanitation have increased life expectancy and altered age-old relationships between birth and death rates. In the early 1950s, only 5 countries, all in northern Europe, had life expectancies at birth of more than 70 years. By 2009, some 80 countries outside Europe and North America—although none in sub-Saharan Africa—were on that list. The availability and employment of modern methods of health and sanitation have varied regionally, and the least-developed countries have least benefited from them. In such underdeveloped and impoverished areas as much of sub-Saharan Africa, the chief causes of death other than HIV/AIDS are those no longer of immediate concern in more-developed lands: diseases such as malaria; intestinal infections; typhoid; cholera; and, especially among infants and children, malnutrition and dehydration from diarrhea.

HIV/AIDS is the tragic and, among developing regions particularly, widespread exception to observed global improvements in life expectancies and reductions in adult death rates and infant and childhood mortalities. AIDS has become the fourth most common cause of death worldwide and is forecast to surpass the Black Death of the 14th century—which caused an estimated 25 million deaths in Europe and 13 million in China—as history's worst-ever epidemic. According to

A Population Implosion?

For much of the last half of the 20th century, demographers and economists focused on a "population explosion" and its implied threat of a world with too many people and too few resources of food and minerals to sustain them. For some observers, by the end of that century, those fears were being replaced by a new prediction of a world with too few rather than too many people.

That possibility was suggested by two related trends. The first had become apparent by 1970, when it was noted that the total fertility rates (TFRs) of 19 countries, almost all of them in Europe, had fallen below the **replacement level**—the level of fertility at which populations replace themselves—of 2.1. Simultaneously, Europe's population pyramid began to become noticeably distorted, with a smaller proportion of young and a growing share of middle-age and retirement-age inhabitants. By 1970, the decrease in native working-age cohorts had already encouraged the influx of non-European "guest workers" whose labor was needed to maintain economic growth and to sustain the generous security provisions guaranteed to what was becoming the oldest population of any continent.

Many countries of Western and Eastern Europe sought to reverse their birth rate declines by adopting pronatalist policies. The communist states of the East rewarded pregnancies and births with generous family allowances, free medical and hospital care, extended maternity leaves, and child care. France, Italy, the Scandinavian countries, and others gave similar bonuses or awards for first, second, and later births. Despite those inducements, however, reproduction rates continued to fall. By 2003, every one of the 43 European countries and territories had fertility rates below replacement levels in widespread response to a host of cultural and personal lifestyle decisions. Those decisions were influenced by the increased educational levels of women, with longer years of schooling and deferred marriage ages; opportunities for women to experience challenging professional or employment careers; the increasing cost of rearing multiple children; and the attractiveness of enjoying, without restrictive family obligations, the increasing number of recreational opportunities growing prosperity afforded. The effect on national growth prospects has been striking. For example, the populations of Spain and Italy are projected to shrink by a quarter between 2000 and 2050 (and that of Ukraine by 43% between 2005 and 2050). Europe as a whole is forecast to shrink by 70 million people by mid-century. "In demographic terms," France's prime minister remarked, "Europe is vanishing."

Europe's experience soon was echoed in other societies of advanced economic development on all continents. By 1995, the United States, Canada, Australia, New Zealand, Japan, Taiwan, South Korea, Singapore, and other older and newly industrializing countries (NICs) had registered fertility rates below the replacement level. As they have for Europe, simple projections foretold their aging and declining population. Japan's numbers, for example, began to decline in 2006, when 21% of its population was age 65 or older. Taiwan forecasts negative growth by 2035. Even China's population will be declining by the early 2030s, and the UN projects that by 2050 populations will be lower in 50 countries than they were in 2006.

The second indication that world population numbers should stabilize and even decline during the lifetimes of today's college cohort is a simple extension of the first: TFRs are being reduced to or below the replacement levels in countries at all stages of economic development in all parts of the world. While only 18% of total world population in 1975 lived in countries with a fertility rate below replacement level, nearly 45% did so by the end of the century. By 2015, demographers estimate, half the world's countries and about two-thirds of its population will show TFRs below 2.1 children per woman. Exceptions to the trend are and still will be found in Africa, especially sub-Saharan Africa, and in some areas of South, Central, and West Asia; however, even in those regions, fertility rates have been decreasing in recent years. "Powerful globalizing forces [are] at work pushing toward fertility reduction everywhere" was a 1997 observation from the French National Institute of Demographic Studies.

That conclusion is plausibly supported by assumptions of the United Nations 2008 forecast of a decline of long-term fertility rates in less-developed regions to 2.05. The same UN assessment envisions that those countries will reach those below-replacement fertilities by or before 2050. Should those assumptions prove valid, global depopulation could commence before mid-century. Between 2040 and 2050, one projection indicates, world population will fall by about 85 million (roughly the amount of its annual growth during much of the 1990s) and will shrink further by about 25% with each successive generation.

If the UN scenario is realized in whole or in part, a much different worldwide demographic and economic future is promised than that prophesied recently by "population explosion" forecasts. Declining rather than increasing pressure on world food and mineral resources will be in our future, along with shrinking rather than expanding world, regional, and national economies. Even the achievement of **zero population growth (ZPG),** a condition for individual countries when births plus immigration equal deaths plus emigration, has social and economic consequences not always perceived by its advocates. These inevitably include an increasing proportion of older citizens, fewer young people, a rise in the median age of the population, and a growing old-age dependency ratio with ever-increasing pension and social services costs borne by a shrinking labor force.

---

a report by UNAIDS, AIDS is expected to kill 68 million people between 2000 and 2020 in the 45 most affected countries; about 55 million of those deaths will occur in sub-Saharan Africa. The United Nations estimated approximately 30 to 36 million people were HIV positive in 2007. Some 90% of those infected lived in developing countries and 65% in sub-Saharan Africa, where women account for 60% of all cases. In that hardest-hit region, as much as one-fourth of the adult population in some countries is HIV positive, and average life expectancy has been cut drastically. In South Africa, the life

The Risks of Motherhood

The worldwide leveling of crude death rates does not apply to pregnancy-related deaths. In fact, the maternal mortality ratio—maternal deaths per 100,000 live births—is the single greatest health disparity between developed and developing countries. According to the World Health Organization, approximately 536,000 women die each year from causes related to pregnancy or childbirth; more than 99% of them live in less-developed states where, as a group, the maternal mortality ratio is some 50 times greater than in the more-developed countries. Complications of pregnancy, childbirth, and abortions are the leading slayers of women of reproductive age throughout the developing world, although the incidence of maternal mortality is by no means uniform, as the chart indicates.

According to 2005 data, in Africa the adult lifetime risk of maternal death (defined as the probability of dying from a maternal cause during a woman's reproductive life span) is 1 in 26, compared with 1 in 290 in Latin America and the Caribbean and 1 in 5700 in Europe. Country-level differences are even more striking: in Niger, for example, the lifetime risk is 1 in 7, compared with 1 in almost 48,000 in Ireland.

The developing countries as a group in 2005 had a maternal mortality ratio of 450, and 10% of all deaths were due to perinatal and maternal causes; least-developed states registered a ratio of 870. In 2005, Africa and Asia recorded the largest number of maternal deaths (51.5% and 45% of the world total, respectively), but sub-Saharan African women, burdened with just over one-half of total world maternal mortality, were at greatest statistical risk. There, maternal death ratios in 2005 reached above 1400 in Angola, Chad, Niger, and Somalia and to more than 2100 in Sierra Leone; 1 in 16 women in sub-Saharan Africa dies of maternal causes. In contrast, the maternal mortality ratio in developed countries as a group (excluding the commonwealth of independent states—the former Soviet Union minus Estonia, Latvia, and Lithuania) is 9, and in some—Denmark, Ireland, and Sweden, for example—it is as low as 1 to 3 (it was 7 in Canada and 11 in the United States in 2005).

The vast majority of maternal deaths in the developing world are preventable. Most result from causes rooted in the social, cultural, and economic barriers confronting females in their home environment throughout their lifetimes: malnutrition, anemia, lack of access to timely basic maternal health care, physical immaturity due to stunted growth, and unavailability of adequate prenatal care or trained medical assistance at birth. Part of the problem is that women are considered expendable in societies where their status is low, although the correlation between women's status and maternal mortality is not exact. In those cultures, little attention is given to women's health or their nutrition, and pregnancy, although a major cause of death, is simply considered a normal condition warranting no special consideration or management. To alter that perception and increase awareness of the affordable measures available to reduce maternal mortality worldwide, 1998 was designated "The Year of Safe Motherhood" by a United Nations interagency group.

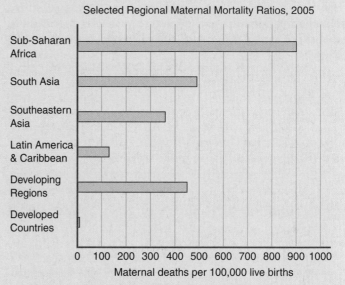

Selected Regional Maternal Mortality Ratios, 2005

Maternal deaths per 100,000 live births

Source: Graph data from Maternal Mortality in 2005. Geneva, Switzerland: WHO Press, 2007.

---

expectancy of a baby born in the early 21st century should have been 66 years; AIDS cut that down to 47. In Botswana, it is 34 years instead of 70; in Zimbabwe, the decline has been from 69 years to 37. Overall, AIDS has killed some 17 million Africans since the 1950s, when HIV (originally a disease of monkeys) appears to have established itself in Africa as a virulent human epidemic strain. Along with the deep cuts in sub-Saharan life expectancies, total population by 2015 is now projected to be 60 million less than it would have been in the absence of the disease.

Economically, AIDS cut an estimated 12% off national incomes in sub-Saharan countries, as of 2008. Southern Africa's economies are based on farming, and women do much of the farming as well as run households. Because AIDS kills more women than men, sub-Saharan food insecurity is rising and food shortages result because many young adults are too feeble to farm. Thus, malnutrition, starvation, and susceptibility to other diseases are AIDS costs added to impersonal national income reductions.

Nonetheless, because of their high fertility rates, populations in all sub-Saharan countries except South Africa are still expected to grow significantly between 2000 and 2050, adding nearly 1 billion to the continent's total. Indeed, despite high mortality rates due to HIV/AIDS, according to UN projections the population of the world's 50 least-developed countries as a group will almost triple between 2000 and 2050, the consequence of their high fertility levels. However, warnings of the rapid spread of the AIDS epidemic in Russia, Ukraine, and South and East Asia—particularly China and India—raise new global demographic concerns even as more hopeful reports of declining infection and mortality rates in some African and Southeast Asian countries are appearing.

Population Pyramids

Another means of comparing populations is through a **population pyramid,** a graphic device that represents a population's age and sex composition. The term *pyramid* describes the diagram's shape for many countries in the 1800s, when the display was created: a broad base of younger age groups and a progressive narrowing toward the apex as older populations were thinned by death. Now, many different shapes are formed, each reflecting a different population history (Figure 6.9), and "population profile" may be a more appropriate label. By grouping several generations of people, the pyramids, or profiles, highlight the impact of "baby booms," population-reducing wars, birth rate reductions, and external migrations.

A rapidly growing country, such as Uganda, has most people in the lowest age cohorts; the percentage in older age groups declines successively, yielding a pyramid with markedly sloping sides. Typically, female life expectancy is reduced in older cohorts of less-developed countries, so that for Uganda the proportion of females in older age groups is lower than in, for example, Sweden. Female life expectancy and mortality rates may also be affected by cultural rather than economic developmental causes (see "Millions of Women Are Missing"). In Sweden, a wealthy country with a very slow rate of growth, the population is nearly equally divided among the age groups, giving a "pyramid" with almost vertical sides. Among older

cohorts, as Austria shows, there may be an imbalance between men and women because of the greater life expectancy of the latter. The impacts of war, as Russia's 1992 pyramid vividly demonstrated, were evident in that country's depleted age cohorts and male-female disparities. The sharp contrasts between the composite pyramids of sub-Saharan Africa and Western Europe summarize the differing population concerns of the developing and developed regions of the world; the projection for Botswana suggests the degree to which accepted pyramid shapes can quickly change (Figure 6.10).

The population profile provides a quickly visualized demographic picture of immediate practical and predictive value. For example, the percentage of a country's population in each age group strongly influences demand for goods and services within that national economy. A country with a high proportion of young has a high demand for educational facilities and certain types of health delivery services. In addition, of course, a large portion of the population is too young to be employed (Figures 6.10 and 6.11). On the other hand, a population with a high percentage of elderly people also requires medical goods and services specific to that age group, and these people must be supported by a smaller proportion of workers. As the profile of a national population changes, differing demands are placed on a country's social and economic systems (Figure 6.12). A **dependency ratio** is a simple measure of the number of economic dependents, old or young, that each 100 people in the productive years (usually, ages 15–64) must support. Population pyramids give quick visual evidence of that ratio.

They also foretell future problems resulting from present population policies or practices. The strict family-size rules and widespread preferences for sons in China, for example, skews the pyramid in favor of males. On current evidence,

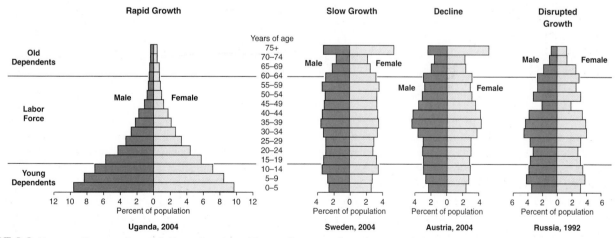

FIGURE 6.9 Four patterns of population structure. These diagrams show that population "pyramids" assume many shapes. The age distribution of national populations reflects the past, records the present, and foretells the future. In countries such as Uganda, social costs related to the young are important and economic expansion is vital to provide employment for new entrants into the labor force. Their 2004 pyramids suggest Sweden will slowly grow only by 6% between 2025 and 2050 and Austria will decline by 2.5% over the same period. For comparison, in 2004 the United States was projected to increase by 20% over that quarter-century. Austria's negative growth means a future with fewer workers to support a growing demand for social services for the elderly. The 1992 pyramid for Russia reported the sharp decline in births during World War II as a "pinching" of the 45–49 cohort and showed in the large deficits of men above age 65 the heavy male mortality of both World Wars and late-Soviet period sharp reductions in Russian male longevity. *Sources: U.S. Bureau of the Census, International Data Base; and for Russia: Carl Haub, "Population Change in the Former Soviet Republics," Population Bulletin 49, no. 4 (1994).*

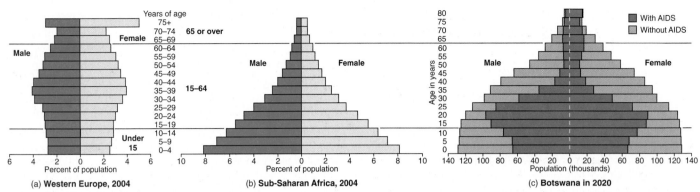

FIGURE 6.10 Summary population pyramids. The 2004 pyramids for **(a)** Western Europe and **(b)** sub-Saharan Africa show the sharp contrasts in the age structure of older developed regions with their characteristic lowered birth and total fertility rates and that of the much more-youthful developing sub-Saharan states. Even in 2004, about 44% of the sub-Saharan population was below age 15. That percentage, however, was smaller than it had been just 5 years earlier and hinted at more dramatic declines possible in years to come. Part of the projected decline will come as a result of economic development and changing family size decisions, but **(c)** for some countries, and perhaps for the region as a whole, tremendous pyramid distortions will result from the demographic impact of AIDS. By 2020, the otherwise expected "normal" pyramid of Botswana may well be distorted into a "population chimney," in which there are more adults in their sixties and seventies than adults in their forties and fifties. *Sources: (a) and (b) U.S. Bureau of the Census, International Data Base; (c) U.S. Bureau of the Census, World Population Profile: 2000.*

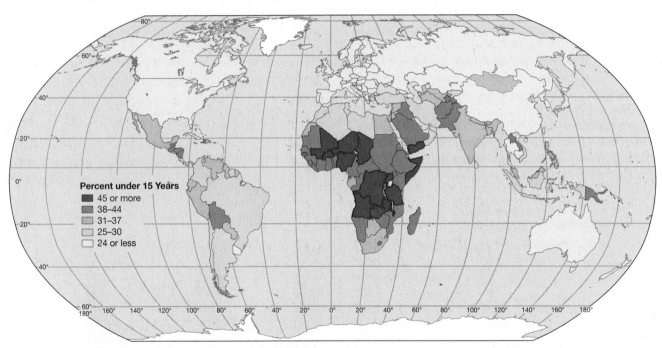

FIGURE 6.11 Percentage of population under 15 years of age. A high proportion of a country's population under 15 increases the dependency ratio of that state and promises future population growth as the youthful cohorts enter childbearing years. *Source: 2009 data from Population Reference Bureau.*

about 1 million excess males a year will enter an imbalanced marriage market in China. Even now, the Chinese population pyramid shows that never-married men ages 20–44 outnumber their female counterparts by nearly 2 to 1. The 40 million bachelors China is likely to have in 2020, unconnected to society by wives and children, may pose threats to social order and, perhaps, national stability not foreseen or planned when family control programs were put in place but clearly suggested when made evident by population pyramid distortions.

Natural Increase and Doubling Times

Knowledge of a country's sex and age distributions also enables demographers to forecast its future population levels, though the reliability of projections decreases with increasing length of forecast (Figure 6.13). Thus, a country with a high proportion of young people will experience a high rate of natural increase unless there is a very high mortality rate among infants and juveniles or fertility and birth rates change materially.

Millions of Women Are Missing

Worldwide, according to one UN estimate, as many as 200 million women are demographically missing, victims of nothing more than their sex. Their absence is the result of sex-selective abortion and female infanticide in countries where boys are favored; deprivation of food and medical attention disproportionately given to brothers, fathers, husbands, and sons; "honor killings" in Muslim communities, dowry deaths in India, and other forms of domestic violence. If the UN estimate is correct, between 1.5 and 3 million women and girls are lost to gender-based discrimination and violence each year in a regionally variable pattern. The majority of that loss appears to be due to birth disparities.

In China, India, Pakistan, New Guinea, and many other developing countries, a traditional preference for boys has meant neglect and death for girls, millions of whom are killed at birth, deprived of adequate food, or denied the medical attention provided to sons favored as old-age and wealth-gathering insurance for parents. In both China and India, ultrasound and amniocentesis tests are employed, often against government directives, to determine the sex of a fetus, so that it can be aborted if it is a female.

The evidence for the missing women starts with one fact: about 106 males are conceived and born for every 100 females. Normally, girls are hardier and more resistant to disease than boys, and in populations where the sexes are treated equally in matters of nutrition and health care, there are about 105 to 106 females for every 100 males. However, the 2001 census of India found just 93.2 females for every 100 males, whereas in China (according to its latest census) nearly 10% of all girls of the 1990s birth cohorts are "missing," and in 2000 there were 120 boys under age 5 for every 100 girls. China's 2000 census recorded a national average disparity in births of 117 boys for every 100 girls—a deepening imbalance from the 1990 census ratio of

111 newborn boys to 100 newborn girls. Even higher year 2000 differentials were registered in Hainan and Guangdong provinces in southeastern China, with newborn ratios of between 130 and 140 males to 100 females.

Ratio deviations are most striking for second and subsequent births. In China, South Korea, Taiwan, and Hong Kong, for example, the most recent figures for first-child sex ratios are near normal but rise to 121 boys per 100 girls for a second Chinese child and to 185 per 100 for a third Korean child. On that evidence, the problem of missing females is getting worse. Conservative calculations suggest there are more than 60 million females missing in China alone, almost 5% of the national population and more than are unaccounted for in any other country.

The problem is seen elsewhere. In much of South and West Asia and North Africa, there are only some 94 females for every 100 males, a shortfall of about 12% of normal (Western) expectations. A 2000 United Nations report on South Asia declared that abortions of female fetuses along with infanticide and the food favoritism shown boys meant that 79 million lost females were attributable to discrimination in South Asia, including some 40 million in India alone. In total, the UN reports, if Asia's overall sex ratio had been the same as elsewhere in the world, in 2005 the continent's population would have included almost 163 million more women and girls.

But not all poor countries show the same disparities. In sub-Saharan Africa, where poverty and disease are perhaps more prevalent than on any other continent, but there is no tradition of deadly violence against women, there are 102 females for every 100 males and, in Latin America and the Caribbean, there are equal numbers of males and females. Cultural norms and practices, not poverty or underdevelopment, seem to determine the fate and swell the numbers of the world's millions of missing women.

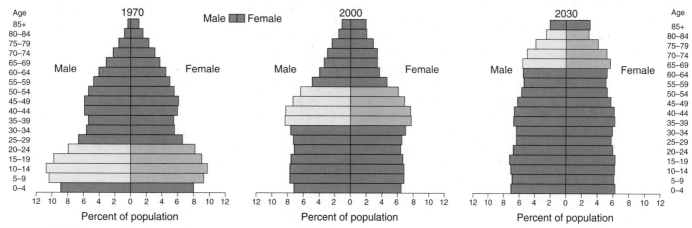

FIGURE 6.12 **The progression of the "boomers"**—the baby boom cohort born between 1946 and 1964—through the U.S. population pyramid has been associated with changing American lifestyles and expenditure patterns. In 1970, national priorities focused on childhood and young adult interests and the needs, education, and support of younger age groups. At the start of the 21st century, boomers formed the largest share of the working-age adult population and their wants and spending patterns shaped the national culture and economy. By 2030, the pyramid foretells, their desires and support needs—now for retirement facilities and old-age care—will again be central concerns. *Source: Redrawn from Christine L. Himes, "Elderly Americans."* Population Bulletin 56, no. 4 *(Dec. 2001), Fig. 1.*

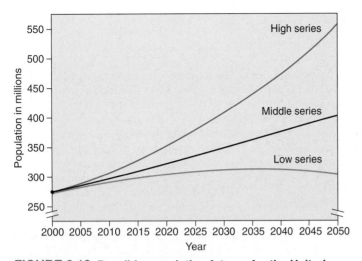

FIGURE 6.13 Possible population futures for the United States. As these population projections to 2050 illustrate, expected future numbers vary greatly because the fertility, birth and death rate, and immigration flow assumptions they are based on are different. Depending on those assumptions, 2000 Census Bureau projections of U.S. population in 2050 ranged from 313.5 million (low series) to 552.7 million (high series). The middle series estimate of 403.6 million is the one most often cited. The folly of basing planning decisions on very long-range projections is made clear by the Bureau's extension of its trends for a full century. By 2100, it calculated, U.S. population could range from a low series 282.7 million to a high series 1.18 billion. *Source: U.S. Bureau of the Census.*

The **rate of natural increase** of a population is derived by subtracting the crude death rate from the crude birth rate. *Natural* means that increases or decreases due to migration are not included. If a country had a birth rate of 22 per 1000 and a death rate of 12 per 1000 for a given year, the rate of natural increase would be 10 per 1000. This rate is usually expressed as a percentage—that is, as a rate per 100 rather than per 1000. In the example given, the annual increase would be 1%.

The rate of natural increase can be related to the time it takes for a population to double if the current growth rate remains constant—that is, the **doubling time.** Table 6.2 shows that it would take 70 years for a population with a rate of increase of 1% (approximately the rate of natural growth of Thailand or Argentina at the start of the 21st century) to double. A 2% rate of increase—recorded in 2009 by Libya, Sierra Leone, and Venezuela—means that the population would double in only 35 years. (Population doubling time can be roughly determined by applying the Rule of 72, which simply involves dividing 72 by the growth rate.) How could adding only 20 people per 1000 cause a population to grow so quickly? The principle is the same as that used to compound interest in a bank. Until recently, for the world as a whole, the rates of increase have risen over the span of human history. Therefore, the doubling time has steadily decreased (Table 6.3). Growth rates vary regionally, and in countries with high rates of increase (Figure 6.14), the doubling time is less than the 60 years projected for the world as a whole at 2009 growth rates. Should world fertility rates

TABLE 6.2
Doubling Time in Years at Different Rates of Increase

Annual Percentage Increase	Doubling Time (years)
0.5	140
1.0	70
2.0	35
3.0	24
4.0	17
5.0	14
10.0	7

TABLE 6.3
Population Growth and Approximate Doubling Times since A.D. 1

Year	Estimated Population	Doubling Time (years)
1	250 million	
1650	500 million	1650
1804	1 billion	154
1927	2 billion	123
1974	4 billion	47
World population may reach:		
2030	8 billion	56[a]

Source: United Nations.
[a]The final estimate of doubling reflects assumptions of decreasing and stabilizing fertility rates. No current projections contemplate a further doubling to 16 billion people.

decline (as they have in recent years), theoretical population doubling time would correspondingly increase, as it has since 1990.

Here, then, lies the answer to the question posed earlier. Even small annual additions accumulate to large total increments because we are dealing with geometric, or exponential (1, 2, 4, 8), rather than arithmetic (1, 2, 3, 4), growth. The ever-increasing world base population has reached such a size that each additional doubling would, if actually achieved, result in an astronomical increase in the total. A simple mental exercise suggests the inevitable consequences of such doubling, or **J-curve,** growth. Take a very large sheet of the thinnest paper you can find and fold it in half. Fold it in half again. After 7 or 8 folds, the sheet will have become as thick as a book—too thick for further folding by hand. If you could make 20 folds, the stack would be nearly as high as a football field is long. From then on, the results of further

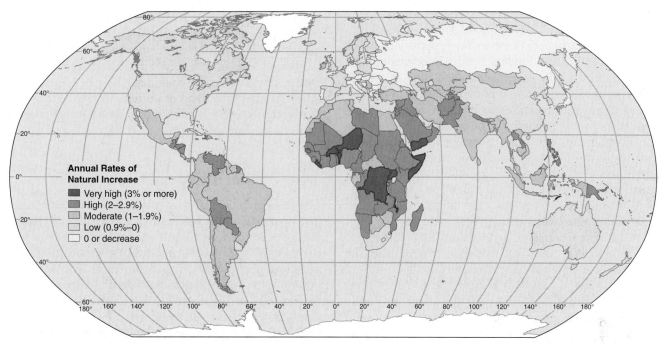

FIGURE 6.14 Annual rates of natural increase. The world's 2009 rate of natural increase (1.2%) would mean a doubling of population in 60 years. Because demographers now anticipate world population—above 6.8 billion in 2009—will stabilize at around 9.5 billion (in about A.D. 2100) and perhaps actually decline after that, the "doubling" implication and time frame of current rates of natural increase reflect mathematical, not realistic, projections. Many individual continents and countries, of course, deviate widely from the global average rate of growth and have vastly different potential doubling times. Africa as a whole has the highest rates of increase, followed by Central America and western Asia. Europe as a whole (including Russia) had negative growth early in the 21st century, with some individual countries showing increases so small that their doubling times would be measured in millennia. *Source: 2009 data from Population Reference Bureau.*

doubling would be astounding. At 40 folds, the stack would be well on the way to the moon, and at 70 it would reach twice as far as the distance to the nearest star. After 1950, rounding the bend on the J-curve, which Figure 6.15 suggests world population did around 1900, fostered dire predictions of inevitable, unsupportable pressures on the planet's population support capabilities.

Today, it is apparent that few developed countries, particularly in Europe, were likely in the foreseeable future or ever to double their population size if their growth were projected—as is usually done—solely on current rates of natural increase. But individual country growth is also dependent on patterns of immigration and emigration and of changes in life expectancy. That is, a country's "natural" population growth based solely on births and deaths may yield significantly lower population projections and longer doubling times than does the same country's "overall" growth, taking migration into account. The contrast may be striking. The United States in 2009 had a 0.6% rate of natural increase and a doubling time of 120 years; however, with migration, it had an *overall* growth rate of 0.9% with a doubling time of 80 years.

With immigration largely absent, declining fertility rates in most of the developing world and the incidence of AIDS in sub-Saharan Africa and parts of populous Asia cast doubt on the utility or applicability of long-term doubling time projections, even for present high growth rate countries. Although the United Nations estimates that the population of the 50 least-developed

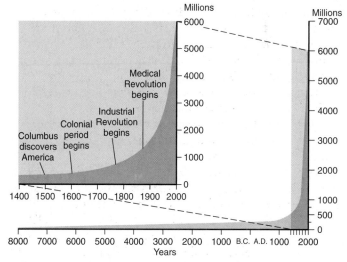

FIGURE 6.15 World population growth, 8000 B.C. to A.D. 2000. Notice that the bend in the J-curve begins in about the mid-1700s when industrialization started to provide new means to support the population growth made possible by revolutionary changes in agriculture and food supply. Improvements in medical science, sanitation, and nutrition reduced death rates near the opening of the 20th century in the industrializing countries.

countries may almost triple between 2000 and 2050, we should understand that doubling time assumptions are inherently misleading and actual population increases are limited.

THE DEMOGRAPHIC TRANSITION

The theoretical consequence of exponential population growth cannot be realized. Some form of braking mechanism must operate to control totally unregulated population growth. If voluntary population limitation is not undertaken, involuntary controls of an unpleasant nature may be set in motion.

One attempt to summarize a historically observed voluntary limitation of population growth—and relating that control to economic development—is the **demographic transition** model. It traces the changing levels of human fertility and mortality presumably associated with industrialization and urbanization. Over time, the model assumes, high birth and death rates will gradually be replaced by low rates (Figure 6.16). The *first stage* of that replacement process—and of the demographic transition model—is characterized by high birth rates and high but fluctuating death rates.

As long as births only slightly exceed deaths, even when the rates of both are high, the population will grow only slowly. This was the case for most of human history until about A.D. 1750. Demographers think that it took from approximately A.D. 1 to A.D. 1650 for the population to increase from 250 million to 500 million, a doubling time of more than a millennium and a half.

Growth was not steady, of course. There were periods of regional expansion, which were usually offset by sometimes catastrophic decline. Wars, famine, and other disasters took heavy tolls. For example, the bubonic plague (the Black Death), which swept across Europe in the 14th century, is estimated to have killed between one-third and one-half of the population of that continent, and epidemic diseases Europeans brought to the Western Hemisphere are believed to have reduced New World native populations by 95% within a century or two of first contact. The first stage of the demographic transition model is no longer found in any country. At the end of the 20th century, few countries—even in poorer regions of sub-Saharan Africa—had death rates as high as 20 per 1000. However, in several African states, birth rates approached or were above 50 per 1000.

The Western Experience

The demographic transition model was developed to explain the population history of Western Europe, parts of which began to experience declining death rates through the conversion of epidemic diseases to endemic forms even before the Industrial Revolution, which began about 1750. The *second stage* of the transition model, however, is usually associated with the modernizing consequences of the industrialization of Europe. Its effects—declining death rates accompanied by continuing high birth rates—were gradually dispersed worldwide, even without universal conversion to an industrial economy.

Rapidly rising population during the second demographic stage results from dramatic increases in life expectancy. That, in turn, reflects falling death rates due to advances in medical and sanitation practices, improved foodstuff storage and distribution, a rising per capita income, and the urbanization that provides the environment in which sanitary, medical, and food distributional improvements are concentrated (Figure 6.17). Birth rates do not fall as soon as death rates; ingrained cultural patterns change more slowly than technologies. In many agrarian societies, large families are considered advantageous. Children contribute to the family by starting to work at an early age and by supporting their parents in old age.

Many countries in southern Asia and Latin America display the characteristics of the second stage in the population model. Yemen, with a birth rate of 38 and a death rate of 8, and Guatemala, with respective rates of 34 and 6 (2009 estimates), are typical. The annual rates of increase of Yemen, for example, is 30 per 1000, or 3%, giving it a doubling time of about 24 years. Such rates, of course, do not mean that the full impact of the Industrial Revolution has been worldwide; they do mean that the underdeveloped societies have been beneficiaries of the life preservation techniques associated with it.

The *third stage* follows when birth rates decline as people begin to control family size. The advantages of having many children in an agrarian society are not as evident in urbanized, industrialized cultures. In fact, such cultures may view children as economic liabilities rather than assets. When the birth rate falls and the death rate remains low, the population size begins to level off. Many countries are now registering the low death rates and transitional birth rates of the third stage.

The classic demographic transition model ends with the *fourth* stage, characterized by very low birth and death rates. This stage yields at best only very slight percentage increases in population, and doubling times stretch to a thousand years

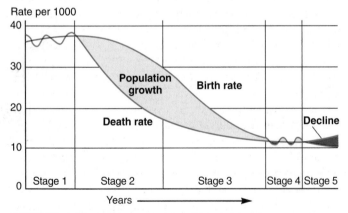

FIGURE 6.16 Stages in the demographic transition. During the first stage, birth and death rates are both high, and population grows slowly. When the death rate drops and the birth rate remains high, there is a rapid increase in numbers. During the third stage, birth rates decline and population growth is less rapid. The fourth stage is marked by low birth and death rates and, consequently, by a low rate of natural increase or even by decrease if death rates exceed those of births. The negative growth rates of many European countries and the falling birth rates in other regions suggest that a fifth stage, one of population decline, is regionally—and ultimately worldwide—a logical extension of the transition model.

FIGURE 6.17 **Liverpool, England in the late 19th century.** A modernizing Europe experienced improved living conditions and declining death rates during that century of progress. © *Topham/Image Works.*

or more. A significant and irreversible aging of the world's population is a direct and profound consequence of the worldwide transition from high to low levels of fertility and mortality associated with the fourth stage of the model (see p. 192). In a few countries, death rates have begun to equal or exceed birth rates and populations are actually declining.

So far, this extension of the fourth stage into a *fifth* of population decrease has been largely confined to the rich, industrialized world—notably, Europe and Japan—but increasingly promises to affect much of the rest of the world as well. The dramatic decline in fertility recorded in almost all countries since the 1980s means that, by 2010, a majority of the world's population resided in areas where the only significant population growth will result from demographic momentum (see p. 192), not from second-stage expansion.

The original transition model was devised to describe the experience of northwest European countries as they went from rural-agrarian societies to urban-industrial ones. It may not fully reflect the prospects of contemporary developing countries. In Europe, church and municipal records, some dating from the 16th century, show that people tended to marry late or not at all. In England before the Industrial Revolution, as many as half of all women in the 15 to 50 age cohort were unmarried. Infant mortality was high; life expectancy was low. With the coming of industrialization in the 18th and 19th centuries, immediate factory wages instead of long apprenticeship programs permitted earlier marriage and more children. Since improvements in sanitation and health came only slowly, death rates remained high. Around 1800, 25% of Swedish infants died before their first birthday. Population growth rates remained below 1% per year in France throughout the 19th century.

Beginning about 1860, first death rates and then birth rates began their significant, though gradual decline. This "mortality revolution" came first, as an *epidemiologic transition* echoed the demographic transition with which it is associated. Many formerly fatal epidemic diseases—already locally in decline a century earlier—became endemic—that is, essentially continual within a population—and mortality patterns showed a shift from communicable to noncommunicable diseases. As people developed partial immunities, mortalities associated with them declined. Improvements in animal husbandry, crop rotation and other agricultural practices, and new foodstuffs (the potato was an early example) from overseas colonies raised the level of health of the European population in general.

At the same time, sewage systems and sanitary water supplies became common in larger cities, and general levels of hygiene improved everywhere (Figure 6.18). Deaths due to infectious, parasitic, and respiratory diseases and to malnutrition declined, while those related to chronic illnesses associated with a maturing and aging population increased. Western Europe passed from a first-stage "Age of Pestilence and Famine" to a presumed ultimate "Age of Degenerative and Human-Origin Diseases." However, recent increases in antibiotic-resistant diseases, the pesticide resistance of disease-carrying insects, and such new scourges of both the less-developed and the more-developed countries as AIDS cast doubt on the finality of that "ultimate" stage (see "Our Delicate State of Health"). Nevertheless, even the resurgence of old scourges and the emergence of new ones, such as malaria, tuberculosis, and AIDS, are unlikely to have decisive demographic consequences on the global scale.

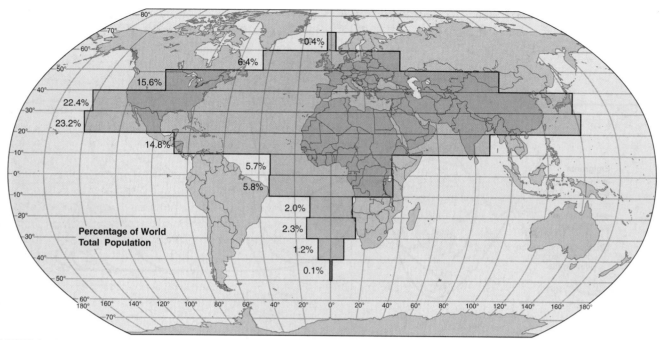

FIGURE 6.22 The population dominance of the Northern Hemisphere is strikingly evident from this bar chart. Only one out of nine people lives south of the Equator—not because the Southern Hemisphere is underpopulated but because it is mainly water.

any latitude, and some tropical lowlands and river valleys that are marshy, forested, and disease-infested are also unevenly settled.

Within the sections of the world generally conducive to settlement, four areas contain great clusters of population: East Asia, South Asia, Europe, and northeastern United States/southeastern Canada. The *East Asia* zone, which includes Japan, China, Taiwan, and South Korea, is the largest cluster in both area and numbers. The four countries forming it contain nearly 25% of all people on Earth; China alone accounts for one in five of the world's inhabitants. The *South Asia* cluster is composed primarily of countries associated with the Indian subcontinent—Bangladesh, India, Pakistan, and the island state of Sri Lanka—although some might add to it the Southeast Asian countries of Cambodia, Myanmar, and Thailand. The four core countries contain another 22% of the world's inhabitants. Thus, the South and the East Asian concentrations are home to nearly one-half the world's people.

Europe—southern, western, and eastern through Ukraine and much of European Russia—is the third extensive population concentration, with another 12% of the world's inhabitants. Much smaller in extent and total numbers is the cluster in *northeastern United States/southeastern Canada*. Other smaller but pronounced concentrations are found around the globe: on the island of Java in Indonesia, along the Nile River in Egypt, and in discontinuous pockets in Africa and Latin America.

The **ecumene** comprises the permanently inhabited areas of the earth's surface. The ancient Greeks used the word, derived from their verb for "to inhabit," to describe their known world between what they believed to be the unpopulated, searing southern equatorial lands and the permanently

frozen northern polar reaches of the earth. Clearly, natural conditions are less restrictive than Greek geographers believed. Both ancient and modern technologies have rendered habitable the areas that natural conditions make forbidding. Irrigation, terracing, diking, and draining are among the methods devised to extend the ecumene locally (Figure 6.23).

At the world scale, the ancient observation of habitability appears remarkably astute. The earth's **nonecumene,** or *anecumene*, the uninhabited or very sparsely occupied zone, does include the permanent ice caps of the Far North and Antarctica and large segments of the tundra and coniferous forest of northern Asia and North America. But the nonecumene is

FIGURE 6.23 Terracing of hillsides is one device to extend a naturally limited productive area. The technique is used effectively on the island of Bali, Indonesia. © *Getty RF.*

not continuous, as the ancients supposed. It is discontinuously encountered in all portions of the globe and includes parts of the tropical rain forests of equatorial zones, midlatitude deserts of both the Northern and Southern Hemispheres, and high mountain areas.

Even parts of these unoccupied or sparsely occupied districts have localized, dense settlement nodes, or zones, based on irrigation agriculture, mining and industrial activities, and the like. Perhaps the most striking case of settlement in an environment elsewhere considered part of the nonecumene world is that of the dense population in the Andes Mountains of South America and the plateau of Mexico. There, Native Americans found temperate conditions away from the dry coastal regions and the hot, wet Amazon Basin. The fertile high basins have served a large population for more than a thousand years.

Even with these locally important exceptions, the non-ecumene portion of the earth is extensive; 35% to 40% of all the world's land surface is inhospitable and without significant settlement. Admittedly, this is a smaller proportion of the earth than would have qualified as uninhabitable in ancient times or even during the 19th century. Since the end of the Ice Age some 12,000 years ago, humans have steadily expanded their areas of settlement.

POPULATION DENSITY

The margins of habitation could only be extended as humans learned to support themselves from the resources of new settlement areas. The numbers that could be sustained in old or new habitation zones were and are related to the resource potential of those areas and the cultural levels and technologies possessed by the occupying populations. A **population density** is the relationship between the number of inhabitants and the area they occupy.

Density figures are useful, if sometimes misleading, representations of regional variations of human distribution. The **crude density,** or **arithmetic density,** of population is the most-common and least-satisfying expression of that variation. It is the calculation of the number of people per unit area of land, usually within the boundaries of a political entity. It is an easily reckoned figure; all that is required is information on total population and total land area, both commonly available for national or other political units. The figure can, however, be misleading and may obscure more of reality than it reveals. The calculation is an average that blankets a country's largely undevelopable or sparsely populated regions, along with its intensively settled and developed districts. A national average density figure reveals nothing about either class of territory. In general, the larger the political unit for which crude density is calculated, the less useful is the figure.

Various modifications may be made to refine density as a meaningful abstraction of distribution. Its descriptive precision is improved if the area in question can be subdivided into comparable regions or units. Thus, it is more revealing to know

that, in 2005, New Jersey had a density of 454 and Wyoming of 2 persons per square kilometer (1175 and 5.2 per sq mi) of land area than to know only that the figure for the conterminous United States (48 states) was 38.5 per square kilometer (99.6 per sq mi). If Hawaii and large, sparsely populated Alaska are added, the U.S. density figure drops to 32.4 per square kilometer (83.8 per sq mi). The calculation may also be modified to provide density distinctions between classes of population—rural versus urban, for example. Rural densities in the United States rarely exceed 115 per square kilometer (300 per sq mi), while portions of major cities can have many thousands of people in an equivalent space.

Another revealing refinement of crude density relates population not simply to total national territory but to the area of a country that is or may be cultivated—that is, to *arable* land. When total population is divided by arable land area alone, the resulting figure is the **physiological density,** which is, in a sense, an expression of population pressure exerted on agricultural land. Countries differ in physiological density and the contrasts between the crude and physiological densities of countries point up actual settlement pressures that are not revealed by crude densities alone. The calculation of physiological density, however, depends on uncertain definitions of arable and cultivated land, assumes that all arable land is equally productive and comparably used, and includes only one part of a country's resource base.

Agricultural density is another useful variant. It simply excludes city populations from the physiological density calculation and reports the number of rural residents per unit of agriculturally productive land. It is, therefore, an estimate of the pressure of people on the rural areas of a country. See Table 6.4.

Overpopulation

It is an easy and common step from concepts of population density to assumptions about overpopulation or overcrowding. It is wise to remember that **overpopulation** is a value judgment reflecting an observation or a conviction that an environment or a territory is unable to support its present population. (The related but opposite concept of *underpopulation* is the circumstance of too few people to sufficiently develop the resources of a country or region to improve the level of living of its inhabitants.)

Overpopulation is not the necessary and inevitable consequence of high density of population. Tiny Monaco, a principality in southern Europe about half the size of New York's Central Park, has a crude density of 17,000 people per square kilometer (44,000 people per sq mi). Mongolia, a sizeable state of 1,565,000 square kilometers (604,000 sq mi) between China and Siberian Russia, has 1.6 persons per square kilometer (4.1 per sq mi); Iran, only slightly larger, has 42 per square kilometer (110 per sq mi). Macao, a former island possession of Portugal off the coast of China, has some 24,000 persons per square kilometer (62,000 per sq mi); the Falkland Islands

TABLE 6.4

Comparative Densities for Selected Countries

Country	CRUDE DENSITY		PHYSIOLOGICAL DENSITY[a]		AGRICULTURAL DENSITY[b]	
	sq mi	km²	sq mi	km²	sq mi	km²
Argentina	36	14	366	141	40	16
Australia	7	3	111	43	10	4
Bangladesh	2681	1035	4851	1873	3735	1442
Canada	8	3	187	72	35	14
China	357	138	3303	1276	1340	517
Egypt	189	73	6639	2563	3613	1395
India	891	344	1836	709	1321	510
Iran	111	43	1145	442	378	146
Japan	876	338	7586	2929	1593	615
Nigeria	404	156	1226	473	687	625
United Kingdom	650	251	2758	1064	249	96
United States	80	31	449	173	94	36

Sources: UN Department of Economic and Social Affairs, *Environmental Indicators*, and Population Reference Bureau, *World Population Data Sheet 2007*.
[a]Total population divided by area of arable land.
[b]Rural population divided by area of arable land.
Rounding may produce apparent conversion discrepancies.

off the Atlantic coast of Argentina count at most 1 person for every 5 square kilometers (2 sq mi) of territory. No conclusions about conditions of life, levels of income, the adequacy of food, or the prospects for prosperity can be drawn from these density comparisons.

Overcrowding is a reflection not of numbers per unit area but of the **carrying capacity** of land—the number of people an area can support on a sustained basis, given the prevailing technology. A region devoted to energy-intensive commercial agriculture that makes heavy use of irrigation, fertilizers, and biocides can support more people at a higher level of living than one engaged in the shifting cultivation agriculture described in Chapter 10. An industrial society that takes advantage of resources such as coal and iron ore and has access to imported food will not feel population pressure at the same density levels as a country with rudimentary technology.

Since carrying capacity is related to the level of economic development, maps such as Figure 6.21, displaying present patterns of population distribution and density, do not suggest a correlation with conditions of life. Many industrialized, urbanized countries have lower densities and higher levels of living than do less-developed ones. Densities in the United States, where there is a great deal of unused and unsettled land, are considerably lower than those in Bangladesh—where essentially all land is arable and which, with (in 2007) some 1035 people per square kilometer (2681 per sq mi), is the most densely populated nonisland state in the world. At the same time, many African countries have low population densities

and low levels of living, whereas Japan combines both high densities and wealth.

Overpopulation can be equated with levels of living or conditions of life that reflect a continuing imbalance between numbers of people and carrying capacity of the land. One measure of that imbalance might be the unavailability of food supplies sufficient in caloric content to meet individual daily energy requirements or so balanced as to satisfy normal nutritional needs. Unfortunately, dietary insufficiencies—with long-term adverse implications for life expectancy, physical vigor, and mental development—are most likely to be encountered in the developing countries, where much of the population is in the younger age cohorts (see Figure 6.11).

If those developing countries simultaneously have rapidly increasing population numbers dependent on domestically produced foodstuffs, the prospects must be for continuing undernourishment and overpopulation. Much of sub-Saharan Africa finds itself in this circumstance. Its per capita food production decreased during the 1990s, with continuing decline predicted over the following quarter-century as the population-food gap widens (Figure 6.24). The countries of North Africa are similarly strained. Egypt already must import well over half the food it consumes. Africa is not alone. The international Food and Agriculture Organization (FAO) estimates that, early in the 21st century, at least 65 countries with over 30% of the population of the developing world are unable to feed their inhabitants adequately from their own national territories at the low level of agricultural technology and inputs employed. Even rapidly industrializing

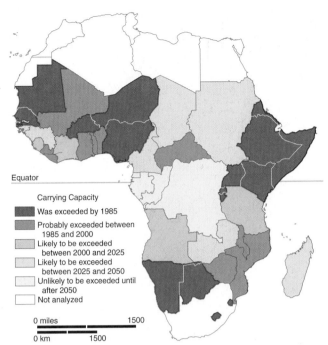

FIGURE 6.24 Carrying capacity and potentials in sub-Saharan Africa. The map assumes that (1) all cultivated land is used for growing food; (2) food imports are insignificant; and (3) agriculture is conducted by low-technology methods. *Source: World Bank; United Nations Development Programme; Food and Agriculture Organization (FAO); and Bread for the World Institute.*

China, an exporter of grain until 1994, in most years now is a net grain importer.

In the contemporary world, an insufficiency of domestic agricultural production to meet national caloric requirements cannot be considered a measure of overcrowding or poverty. Only a few countries are agriculturally self-sufficient. Japan, a leader among the advanced states, is the world's biggest food importer and, from its own production, supplies only 40% of the calories its population consumes. Its physiological density is high, as Table 6.4 indicated, but it obviously does not rely on an arable land resource for its present development. Largely lacking in either agricultural or industrial resources, nonetheless it ranks well on all indicators of national well-being and prosperity. For countries such as Japan, South Korea, Malaysia, and Taiwan—all of which currently import more than 70% of the grain they consume—a sudden cessation of the international trade that permits the exchange of industrial products for imported food and raw materials would be disastrous. Domestic food production could not maintain the dietary levels now enjoyed by their populations and they, more starkly than many underdeveloped countries, would be "overpopulated."

Urbanization

Pressures on the land resource of countries are increased not just by their growing populations but also by the reduction of arable land caused by such growth. More and more of the world population increase must be accommodated not in rural areas but in cities that hold the promise of jobs and access to health, welfare, and other public services. As a result, the *urbanization* (transformation from rural to urban status according to individual countries' definition of *urban*) of population in developing states is increasing dramatically. Since the 1950s, cities have grown faster than rural areas in nearly all developing countries. Indeed, because of the now rapid flow of migrants from countrysides to cities, population growth in the rural areas of the developing world has essentially stopped. Although Latin America, for example, has experienced substantial overall population increase, the size of its rural population is actually declining, according to definitions of *urban* applied in most of its countries.

On UN projections, essentially all world population increase between 2000 and 2030 will be in urban areas and almost entirely within the developing regions and countries, continuing a pattern established by 1950 (Figure 6.25). In those areas collectively, cities are growing by over 3% a year, and the poorest regions are experiencing the fastest growth. By 2020, the UN anticipates, a majority of the population of less-developed countries will live in urban areas. In East, West, and Central Africa, for example, cities are expanding by 5% a year, a pace that can double their population every 14 years. Global urban population, just 750 million in 1950, grew to more than 3.3 billion by 2007 and is projected to rise to 6.4 billion by 2050. The uneven results of past urbanization are summarized in Figure 6.26.

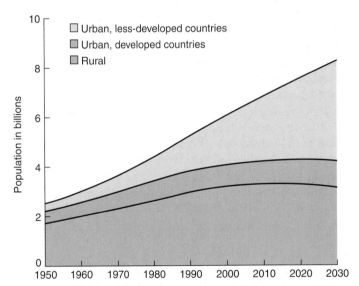

FIGURE 6.25 Past and projected urban and rural population growth, 1950 to 2030. According to UN projections, some 65% of the world's total population may be urbanized by 2030. No universal definition of *urban* exists; the Population Reference Bureau, however, notes that, "typically, the population living in towns of 2000 or more . . . is classified as 'urban.'" *Redrawn from* Population Bulletin vol. 53, no. 1, *Figure 3, page 12 (Population Reference Bureau, 1998).*

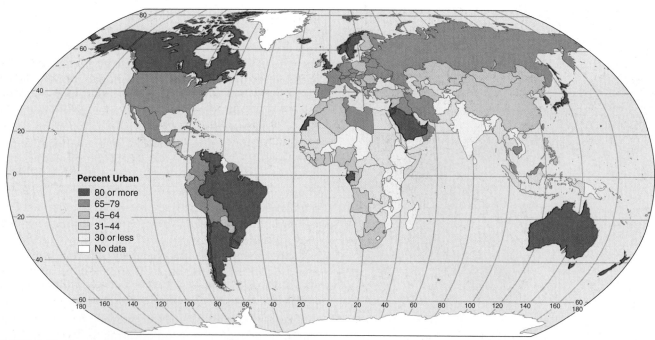

FIGURE 6.26 **Percentage of national population that is classified as urban, 2009.** Urbanization has been particularly rapid in the developing continents. In 1950, only 17% of Asians and 15% of Africans were urban; by 2009, nearly 40% of Africans and more than 40% of Asians were city dwellers. *Source: Data from Population Reference Bureau.*

The sheer growth of cities in people and territory has increased pressures on arable land and adjusted upward both crude and physiological densities. Urbanization consumes millions of hectares of cropland each year. In Egypt, for example, urban expansion and new development between 1965 and 1985 took out of production as much fertile soil as the massive Aswan Dam on the Nile River made newly available through irrigation with the water it impounded. During much of the 1990s, China lost close to 1 million hectares (2.5 million acres) of farmland each year to urbanization, road construction, and industrialization. The pace of such loss continued into this century, for the rural-to-urban population shift in China now is the largest mass migration in world history. By themselves, some of the developing world cities, many of them surrounded by concentrations of people living in uncontrolled settlements, slums, and shantytowns (Figure 6.27), are among the most densely populated areas in the world. They face massive problems in trying to provide housing, jobs, education, and adequate health and social services for their residents. These and other matters of urban geography are the topics of Chapter 11.

POPULATION DATA AND PROJECTIONS

Population geographers, demographers, planners, governmental officials, and a host of others rely on detailed population data to make their assessments of present national and world population patterns and to estimate future conditions. Birth rates and death rates, rates of fertility and of natural increase, age and sex composition of the population, and other items are all necessary ingredients for their work.

Population Data

The data that students of population use come primarily from the United Nations Statistical Office, the World Bank, the Population Reference Bureau, and ultimately national censuses and sample surveys. Unfortunately, the data as reported may be more misleading than informative. For much of the developing world, a national census is a massive undertaking. Isolation and poor transportation, insufficiency of funds and trained census personnel, high rates of illiteracy limiting the type of questions that can be asked, and populations suspicious of government data collectors restrict the frequency, coverage, and accuracy of population reports.

However derived, detailed data are published by the major reporting agencies for all national units, even when those figures are poorly based on fact or are essentially fictitious. For example, for years, data on the total population, birth and death rates, and other vital statistics for Somalia were regularly reported and annually revised. The fact was, however, that Somalia had never had a census and had no system for recording births. Seemingly precise data were regularly reported as well for Ethiopia. When that country had its first-ever census in 1985, at least one data source had to drop its estimate of the country's birth rate by 15% and increase its figure for Ethiopia's total population by more than 20%. And a disputed 1991 census of Nigeria officially reported a population of 88.5 million, far below the then generally accepted and widely cited estimates of between 110 and 120 million Nigerians. The 2006 census in Nigeria was surrounded by protests, boycotts, and fraud charges, despite a lack of questions about religious and ethnic identity, which are controversial in a country with over 250 ethnic groups and a population nearly evenly divided

FIGURE 6.27 Millions of people of the developing world live in shantytowns on the fringes of large cities, without benefit of running water, electricity, sewage systems, or other public services. The UN reports that up to 40% of all urban dwellers worldwide live in such squatter settlements and slums. The hillside slum pictured here is one of the many *favelas* that are home for up to one-third of greater Rio de Janeiro's 11 million residents. © *The McGraw-Hill Companies, Inc./Barry Barker, photographer.*

Population Projections

For all their inadequacies and imprecisions, current data reported for country units form the basis of **population projections,** estimates of future population size, age, and sex composition. Projections are not forecasts, and demographers are not the social science equivalent of meteorologists. Weather forecasters work with a myriad of accurate observations applied against a known, tested model of the atmosphere. Demographers, in contrast, work with sparse, imprecise, out-of-date, and missing data applied to human actions that will be unpredictably responsive to stimuli not yet evident.

Population projections, therefore, are based on assumptions for the future applied to current data, which themselves are frequently suspect. Since projections are not predictions, they can never be wrong. They are simply the inevitable result of calculations about fertility, mortality, and migration rates applied to each age cohort of a population now living, as well as the making of birth rate, survival, and migration assumptions about cohorts yet unborn. Of course, the perfectly valid *projections* of future population size and structure resulting from those calculations may be dead wrong as *predictions.*

Because those projections are invariably treated as scientific expectations by a public that ignores their underlying qualifying assumptions, agencies (such as the UN) that estimate the population of—say, Africa in the year 2025—do so by not one but three or more projections: high, medium, and low, for example. For areas as large as Africa, a medium projection is assumed to benefit from compensating errors and

between Muslims and Christians. Fortunately, census coverage on a world basis is improving. Almost every country has now had at least one census of its population and most have been subjected to periodic sample surveys (Figure 6.28). However, only about 10% of the developing world's population live in countries with anything approaching complete systems for registering births and deaths. Estimates are that 40% or less of live births in Indonesia, Pakistan, India, and the Philippines are officially recorded; sub-Saharan Africa has the highest percentage of unregistered births (71%), according to UNICEF. Throughout Asia, apparently deaths are even less completely reported than birth. And whatever the deficiencies of Asian states, African statistics are still less complete and reliable. It is on just these basic birth and death data that projections about population growth and composition are founded.

FIGURE 6.28 Nearly all countries in the world conduct regular censuses, although some are of doubtful completeness or accuracy. This photo shows Indian census-takers collecting data in a rural community. To count the world's second largest population for the 2011 Indian census, each person over the age of fifteen was photographed and fingerprinted. Like many countries, the Indian census collects additional data beyond population counts such as economic activity, literacy, education levels, housing conditions, and the availability of drinking water and electricity. © *AFP/Getty.*

statistically predictable behaviors of very large populations. For individual African countries and smaller populations, the medium projection may be much less satisfying. The usual tendency in projections is to assume that something like current conditions will be applicable in the future. Obviously, the more distant the future, the less likely is that assumption to remain true. The resulting observation should be that, the further into the future the population structure of small areas is projected, the greater is the implicit and inevitable error (see Figure 6.13).

POPULATION CONTROLS

All population projections include an assumption that at some point in time population growth will cease and plateau at the replacement level. Without that assumption, future numbers become unthinkably large. For the world at unchecked present growth rates, there would be 1 trillion people three centuries from now, 4 trillion four centuries in the future, and so on. Although there is reasonable debate about whether the world is now overpopulated and about what either its optimum or maximum sustainable population should be, totals in the trillions are beyond any reasonable expectation.

Population pressures do not come from the amount of space humans occupy. It has been calculated, for example, that the entire human race could easily be accommodated within the boundaries of the state of Delaware. The problems stem from the food, energy, and other resources necessary to support the population and from the impact on the environment of the increasing demands and the technologies required to meet them. Rates of growth currently prevailing in many countries make it nearly impossible for them to achieve the kind of social and economic development they would like.

Clearly, at some point, population will have to stop increasing as fast as it has been. That is, either the self-induced limitations on expansion implicit in the demographic transition will be adopted or an equilibrium between population and resources will be established in a more dramatic fashion. Recognition of this eventuality is not new. "Pestilence, and famine, and wars, and earthquakes have to be regarded as a remedy for nations, as the means of pruning the luxuriance of the human race" was the opinion of the theologian Tertullian during the 2d century A.D.

Thomas Robert **Malthus** (1766–1834), an English economist and demographer, put the problem succinctly in a treatise published in 1798: all biological populations have a potential for increase that exceeds the actual rate of increase, and the resources for the support of increase are limited. In later publications, Malthus amplified his thesis by noting the following:

1. Population is inevitably limited by the means of subsistence.
2. Populations invariably increase with increase in the means of subsistence unless prevented by powerful checks.
3. The checks that inhibit the reproductive capacity of populations and keep it in balance with means of subsistence are either "private" (moral restraint, celibacy, and chastity) or "destructive" (war, poverty, pestilence, and famine).

The deadly consequences of Malthus's dictum that unchecked population increases geometrically, while food production can increase only arithmetically,[2] have been reported throughout human history, as they are today. Starvation, the ultimate expression of resource depletion, is no stranger to the past or present. By conservative estimate, during the 2 minutes it takes you to read this page, more than 40 people worldwide will die of causes related to hunger and malnutrition (11 million per year); half will be children under 5. They will, of course, be more than replaced numerically by new births during the same 2 minutes. Losses are nearly always recouped. All battlefield deaths, perhaps 70 million, in all of humankind's wars over the past 300 years equal less than a 1-year replacement period at present rates of natural increase.

However, inevitably—following the logic of Malthus, the apparent evidence of history, and observations of animal populations—equilibrium must be achieved between numbers and support resources. When overpopulation of any species occurs, a population dieback is inevitable. The madly ascending leg of the J-curve is bent to the horizontal, and the J-curve is converted to an **S-curve.** It has happened before in human history, as Figure 6.29 summarizes. The top of the S-curve represents a population size consistent with and supportable by the exploitable resource base. When the population is equivalent to the carrying capacity of the occupied area, it is said to have reached a **homeostatic plateau.**

In animals, overcrowding and environmental stress apparently release an automatic physiological suppressant of fertility. Although famine and chronic malnutrition may reduce fertility in humans, population limitation usually must be either forced or self-imposed. The demographic transition to low birth rates matching reduced death rates is cited as evidence that Malthus's first assumption was wrong: human populations do not inevitably grow geometrically. Fertility behavior, it was observed, is conditioned by social determinants, not solely by biological or resource imperatives.

Although Malthus's ideas had been discarded as deficient by the end of the 19th century in light of the European population experience, the concerns he expressed were revived during the 1950s. Observations of population growth in underdeveloped countries and the strain that growth placed on their resources inspired the viewpoint that improvements in living standards could be achieved only by raising investment per worker. Rapid population growth was seen as a serious diversion of scarce resources away from capital investment and into unending social welfare programs. In order to lift living standards, the existing national efforts to lower mortality rates had to be balanced by governmental programs to reduce birth rates. **Neo-Malthusianism,** as this viewpoint became known, has been the underpinning of national and international programs of population limitation primarily through birth control and family planning (Figure 6.30).

---

[2] "Within a hundred years or so, the population can increase from fivefold to twentyfold, while the means of subsistence . . . can increase only from three to five times" was the observation of Hung Liangchi of China, a spatially distant early 19th-century contemporary of Malthus.

FIGURE 6.29 The steadily higher *homeostatic plateaus* (states of equilibrium) achieved by humans are evidence of their ability to increase the carrying capacity of the land through technological advance. Each new plateau represents the conversion of the J-curve into an S-curve. "Medical Revolution" implies the range of modern sanitary and public health technologies and disease preventative and curative advances that materially reduced morbidity and mortality rates.

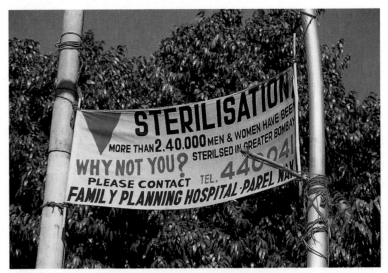

FIGURE 6.30 A Mumbai, India, sign promoting the government's continuing program to reduce the country's high fertility rate. Female sterilization is the world's most popular form of birth prevention, and in India, Brazil, and China a reported one-third or more of all married women have been sterilized. The comparable worldwide married male sterilization rate, in contrast, is 4%. © *Carl Purcell.*

Neo-Malthusianism has had a mixed reception. In general, Asian countries, led by China and India, have—though with differing successes—adopted family planning programs and policies. In some instances, success has been declared complete. Singapore established its Population and Family Planning Board in 1965, when its fertility rate was 4.9 lifetime births per woman. By 1986, that rate had declined to 1.7, well below the 2.1 replacement level for developed countries, and the board was abolished as no longer necessary. Caribbean and South American countries, even the poorest and most agrarian, have also experienced declining fertility rates, though often these reductions have been achieved despite pronatalist views of governments influenced by the Roman Catholic Church.

Africa and the Middle East have generally been less responsive to the neo-Malthusian arguments because of ingrained cultural convictions among people, if not in all governmental circles, that large families—six or seven children—are desirable. Although total fertility rates have begun to decline in most sub-Saharan African states, they still remain above replacement levels nearly everywhere. Islamic fundamentalism opposed to birth restrictions also is a cultural factor in the Near East and North Africa. However, the Muslim theocracy of Iran has endorsed a range of contraceptive procedures and developed one of the world's more aggressive family planning programs.

Other barriers to fertility control exist. When first proposed by Western states, neo-Malthusian arguments that family planning is necessary for development were rejected by many less-developed countries. Reflecting both nationalistic and Marxist concepts, they maintained that remnant colonial-era social, economic, and class structures rather than population increase hinder development. Some governmental leaders think there is a correlation between population size and power and pursue pronatalist policies, as did Mao's China during the 1950s and early 1960s. And beginning in the 1980s, a number of American economists called *cornucopians* expressed the view that population growth is a stimulus, not a deterrent, to development and that human minds and skills are the world's ultimate resource base. Since the time of Malthus, they observe, world population has grown from 900 million to over 6.8 billion (2010) without the predicted dire consequences—proof that Malthus failed to recognize the importance of technology in raising the carrying capacity of the earth. Still higher population numbers, they suggest, are sustainable, perhaps even with improved standards of living for all.

A third view, modifying cornucopian optimism, admits that products of human ingenuity, such as the Green Revolution (see pages 324–326), have made possible increases in food production that have managed to keep pace with rapid population growth since 1970. But its advocates argue that scientific and technical ingenuity to enhance food production does not automatically appear; both complacency and inadequate research support have hindered continuing progress in recent years. And even if further advances are made, they observe, not all countries or regions have the social and political will or capacity to take advantage of them. Those that do not, third-view advocates warn, will fail to keep pace with the needs of their populace and will sink into varying degrees of poverty and environmental decay, creating national and regional—though not necessarily global—crises.

POPULATION PROSPECTS

Regardless of population philosophies, theories, or cultural norms, the fact remains that many or most developing countries are showing significantly declining population growth rates. Global fertility and birth rates appear to be falling to an extent not anticipated by pessimistic Malthusians and at a pace that suggests a peaking of world population numbers sooner—and at lower totals—than previously projected (see

"A Population Implosion?" p. 169). In all world regions, steady and continuous fertility declines have been recorded over the past years, reducing fertility from global levels of 5 children per woman in the early 1950s to 2.7 per woman in 2007.

Momentum

Reducing fertility levels even to the replacement level of about 2.1 births per woman does not mean an immediate end to population growth. Because of the age composition of many societies, numbers of births will continue to grow even as fertility rates per woman decline. The reason is to be found in **population (demographic) momentum,** and the key to that is the age structure of a country's population.

When a high proportion of the population is young, the product of past high fertility rates, larger and larger numbers enter the childbearing age each year; that is the case for major parts of the world early in the 21st century. The populations of developing countries are far younger than those of the established industrially developed regions (see Figure 6.11), with 30% (in Asia and Latin America) to over 40% (in Africa) below the age of 15. The consequences of the fertility of these young people are yet to be realized. A population with a greater number of young people tends to grow rapidly, regardless of the level of childbearing. The results will continue to be felt until the now youthful groups mature and work their way through the population pyramid.

Inevitably, while this is happening, even the most stringent national policies limiting growth cannot stop it entirely. A country with a large present population base will experience large numerical increases despite declining birth rates. Indeed, the higher fertility is to begin with and the sharper its drop to low levels, the greater will be the role of momentum even after rates drop below replacement. A simple comparison of South Korea and the United Kingdom may demonstrate the point. In 2002, the two countries had the same level of fertility, with women averaging about 1.6 children each. Between that year and 2025, the larger population of the UK (without considering immigration or the births associated with newcomers) was projected to decline by 2 million persons, whereas smaller, more youthful South Korea was expected to continue growing, adding 2 million people. Increasingly, population momentum will be responsible for nearly all of the world's population growth (Figure 6.31).

Aging

Eventually, of course, young populations grow older, and even the youthful developing countries are beginning to face the consequences of that reality. The problems of a rapidly aging population that already confront the industrialized economies are now being realized in the developing world as well. Before 2000, young people always outnumbered the elderly; with the start of this century, old people outnumber the young. Globally,

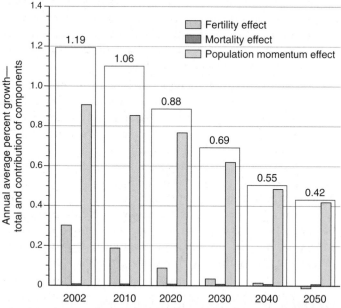

FIGURE 6.31 Effects of population momentum, 2002–2050. Worldwide declines in total fertility rates will not soon be reflected by equivalent declines in the growth of population. Because of past fertility levels, the numbers of women in their childbearing years are increasing both absolutely and relative to the rest of the population. As a result, fertility's contribution to global growth will steadily decline and population momentum will account for a growing share of projected world population increase. *Source: U. S. Bureau of the Census, 2004.*

FIGURE 6.32 These senior residents of a Moroccan nursing home are part of the rapidly aging population of many developing countries. Worldwide, the over-60 cohort will number some 22% of total population by 2050 and be larger than the number of children less than 15 years of age. But by 2020, a third of Singapore citizens will be 55 or older and China will have as large a share of its population over 60—about one in four—as will Europe. Already the numbers of old people in the world's poorer countries are beginning to dwarf those in the rich world. At the start of the 21st century, there were nearly twice as many persons over 60 in developing countries as in the advanced ones, but most are without the old-age assistance and welfare programs the developed countries have put in place. © *Nathan Benn/Corbis Images.*

there will be more than 1 billion persons 60 years of age or older by 2025 and nearly 1.9 billion by 2050, when the world will contain more people age 60 or above than children under the age of 15. That momentous reversal in relative proportions of young and old already occurred in 1998 in the more-developed regions.

The progression toward older populations is considered irreversible, the result of the now global demographic transition from high to low levels of fertility and mortality. The youthful majorities of the past are unlikely to occur again, for globally the population of older persons early in this century is growing by 2% per year—much faster than the population as a whole—and between 2025 and 2030, the 60+ growth rate will reach 2.8% per year. By 2050, the UN projects, one out of five persons worldwide will be 60 years old or older.

About 80% of the mid-century elderly folk will live in the less-developed world, for the growth rate of older people is three times as high in developing countries as in the developed ones. In the developing world, older persons are projected to make up 20% of the population by 2050, in contrast to the 8% over age 60 there in 2000. Because the pace of aging is much faster in the developing countries, they will have less time than the developed world did to adjust to the consequences of that aging. And those consequences will be experienced at lower levels of personal and national income and economic strength.

In both rich and poor countries, the working-age populations will face increasing burdens and obligations. The potential support ratio (PSR), the number of persons ages 15 to 64 years per one citizen age 65 or older, has steadily fallen. Between 1950 and 2000, it dropped from 12 to 9 workers for each older person; by mid-century, the PSR is projected to drop to 4. The implications for Social Security schemes and social support obligations are obvious and are made more serious because the older population itself is aging. By the middle of the century, one-fifth of older persons will be 80 years old or older and, on average, will require more support expenditures for health and long-term care than do younger seniors. The consequences of population aging appear most intractable for the world's poorest developing states that generally lack health, income, housing, and social service support systems adequate for the needs of their older citizens. Therefore, to the social and economic implications of their present population momentum, developing countries must add the aging consequences of past patterns and rates of growth (Figure 6.32).

Summary of Key Concepts

- Birth, death, fertility, migration, and growth rates are basic for understanding the numbers, composition, distribution, and spatial trends of population.

- Predictions of ever-increasing population numbers now appear faulty. Birth rates, already below replacement levels in most developed countries, are dropping as well in less-developed regions. Even so, essentially all future numerical increases will occur in areas currently considered underdeveloped where total fertility rates still remain significantly above the replacement level.

- Death rates everywhere have declined steeply as the availability of preventative and curative health care has spread to all parts of the world. Reductions in birth and death rates result in a *demographic transition* from high to low levels of both and a corresponding stabilization or reduction in numbers regionally and globally. Areal numbers are also determined by a *demographic equation*, which includes the effects of population relocations and migrations.

- People are unevenly distributed globally, latitudinally, and areally. The Northern Hemisphere, mid-latitudes, lowlands, and coastal locations house two-thirds of the world's people on less than 10% of its land. East Asia, South Asia, Europe, and eastern North America together contain two-thirds of the total. Urban areas everywhere are growing and now hold more than half of total world population.

- Various measures of density have been devised, but differences in population numbers and densities have no necessary correlation with observations about over- or underpopulation; these are concepts relative to means of support, not to absolute numbers.

- Population projections are based on assumptions about future conditions, which may not be realized. The larger the area and the more distant the future for which projections are made, the less accurate are they likely to be.

- All projections must take into account natural and cultural controls of population numbers, such as the carrying capacity of the environment and individual and group reproduction decisions. Future population levels will be significantly affected by the current age and sex structure summarized by a region's *population pyramid*. That structure influences the inevitable growth through the *population momentum* implicit in a youthful majority or the numerical decline suggested by regional and global aging of populations.

Human populations cannot be understood solely through statistical analysis. Societies are distinguished not just by the abstract data of their numbers, rates, and trends but also by the experiences, beliefs, understandings, and aspirations that collectively constitute the human spatial and behavioral variable called *culture*. It is to that fundamental human diversity that we next turn our attention.

Key Words

agricultural density 185	doubling time 174	population (demographic)
carrying capacity 186	ecumene 184	momentum 192
cohort 163	homeostatic plateau 190	population projection 189
crude birth rate (CBR) 163	J-curve 174	population pyramid 171
crude death rate (CDR)	Malthus 190	rate 163
(mortality rate) 167	neo-Malthusianism 190	rate of natural increase 174
crude density (arithmetic density) 185	nonecumene 184	replacement level 169
demographic equation 180	overpopulation 185	S-curve 190
demographic transition 176	physiological density 185	total fertility rate (TFR) 164
demography 161	population density 185	zero population growth (ZPG) 169
dependency ratio 171	population geography 161	

Thinking Geographically

1. How do the *crude birth rate* and the *fertility rate* differ? Which measure is the more accurate statement of the amount of reproduction occurring in a population?

2. How is the *crude death rate* calculated? What factors account for the worldwide decline in death rates since 1945?

3. How is a *population pyramid* constructed? What shape of "pyramid" reflects the structure of a rapidly growing country? Of a population with a slow rate of growth? What can we tell about future population numbers from those shapes?

4. What variations do we discern in the spatial pattern of the *rate of natural increase* and, consequently, of population growth? What rate of natural increase would double population in 35 years?

5. How are population numbers projected from present conditions? Are projections the same as predictions? If not, in what ways do they differ?

6. Describe the stages in the *demographic transition*. Where has the final stage of the transition been achieved? What appears to be the applicability of the demographic transition to other parts of the world?

7. Contrast *crude population density, physiological density,* and *agricultural density*. For what different purposes might each be useful? How is *carrying capacity* related to the concept of density?

8. What was Malthus's underlying assumption concerning the relationship between population growth and food supply? In what ways do the arguments of *neo-Malthusians* differ from the original doctrine? What governmental policies are implicit in neo-Malthusianism?

9. Why is *population momentum* a matter of interest in population projections? In which world areas are the implications of demographic momentum most serious in calculating population growth, stability, or decline?

CHAPTER SEVEN

Cultural Geography

CHAPTER OUTLINE

A portion of the elaborately sculpted façade of Singapore's Hindu temple of Sri Mariamman. © *Corbis RF.*

The Gauda's[1] son is 18 months old. Every morning, a boy employed by the Gauda carries the Gauda's son through the streets of Gopalpur. The Gauda's son is clean; his clothing is elegant. When he is carried along the street, the old women stop their ceaseless grinding and pounding of grain and gather around. If the child wants something to play with, he is given it. If he cries, there is consternation. If he plays with another boy, watchful adults make sure that the other boy does nothing to annoy the Gauda's son.

Shielded by servants, protected and comforted by virtually everyone in the village, the Gauda's son soon learns that tears and rage will produce anything he wants. At the same time, he begins to learn that the same superiority which gives him license to direct others and to demand their services places him in a state of danger. The green mangoes eaten by all of the other children in the village will give him a fever; coarse and chewy substances are likely to give him a stomachache. While other children clothe themselves in mud and dirt, he finds himself constantly being washed. As a Brahmin [a religious leader], he is taught to avoid all forms of pollution and to carry out complicated daily rituals of bathing, eating, sleeping, and all other normal processes of life.

In time, the Gauda's son will enter school. He will sit motionless for hours, memorizing long passages from Sanskrit holy books and long poems in English and Urdu. He will learn to perform the rituals that are the duty of every Brahmin. He will bathe daily in the cold water of the private family well, reciting prayers and following a strict procedure. The gods in his house are major deities who must be worshipped every day, at length and with great care.[2]

The Gauda and his family are not Americans, as references and allusions in the preceding paragraphs make plain. The careful reader would infer, correctly, that they are Indians—and if one were to read more of the book from which this excerpt is taken, it would become evident that the Gauda lives in a village in southern India. The class structure, the religion, the language, the food, and other strands of the fabric of life mentioned in the passage place the Gauda, his family, and his village in a specific time and place. They bind the people of the region together as sharers of a common culture and set them off from those of other areas with different cultural heritages. The approximately 7 billion people who were the subject of Chapter 6 are of a single human family, but it is a family differentiated into many branches, each characterized by a distinctive *culture.*

To some writers and commentators, *culture* means the arts (literature, painting, music, etc.). To a social scientist, **culture** is the specialized behavioral patterns, understandings, and adaptations that summarize the way of life of a group of people. In

this broader sense, culture is as much a part of the regional differentiation of the earth as are topography, climate, and other aspects of the physical environment. The visible and invisible evidences of culture—buildings and farming patterns, language and political organization—are elements in the spatial diversity that invites and is subject to geographic inquiry. Cultural differences in area result in human landscapes with variations as subtle as the differing "feel" of urban Paris, Moscow, and New York or as obvious as the sharp contrasts of rural Zimbabwe and a cash grain farm in America's Midwest (Figure 7.1).

Because such differences exist, cultural geography exists, and one branch of cultural geography addresses a whole range of "why?" and "what?" and "how?" questions. Why, since humankind constitutes a single species, are cultures so varied? What are the most pronounced ways in which cultures and culture regions are distinguished? What were the origins of the different culture regions we now observe? How, from whatever limited areas in which single culture traits and amalgams developed, were they diffused over a wider portion of the globe? Why do cultural contrasts between recognizably distinct groups persist even in such presumed "melting pot" societies as that of the United States or in the outwardly homogeneous, long-established countries of Europe? How is knowledge about cultural differences important to us today? These and similar questions are the concerns of the present chapter and, in part, of Chapters 8 and 9.

COMPONENTS OF CULTURE

Culture is transmitted within a society to succeeding generations by imitation, instruction, and example. It is learned, not biological, and has nothing to do with instinct or with genes. As members of a social group, individuals acquire integrated sets of behavioral patterns, environmental and social perceptions, and knowledge of existing technologies. Of necessity, we learn the culture in which we are born and reared. But we need not—indeed, cannot—learn its totality. Age, sex, status, and occupation dictate the aspects of the cultural whole in which we become fully indoctrinated.

A culture displays a social structure—a framework of roles and interrelationships of individuals and established groups. Despite overall generalized and identifying characteristics and even an outward appearance of uniformity, a culture is not homogeneous. The "American" culture, for example, contains innumerable complex, composite, and often competing subgroups: farmers and city dwellers; males and females; teenagers and retirees; liberals and conservatives; owners and employees; members of different religious, political, social, or other formal organizations; and the like. Each individual learns and is expected to adhere to the rules and conventions not only of the culture as a whole but also specific to the subgroups to which he or she belongs. And those subgroups may have their own recognized social structures.

Culture is a complexly interlocked web of behaviors and attitudes. Realistically, its full and diverse content cannot be appreciated, and in fact may be wholly misunderstood, if we concentrate our attention only on limited, obvious traits.

---

[1]Gauda = village headman.

[2]Excerpt from *Gopalpur: A South Indian Village,* by Alan R. Beals, copyright © by Holt, Rinehart and Winston, Inc., and renewed 1990 by Alan R. Beals, reprinted by permission of the publisher.

(a)

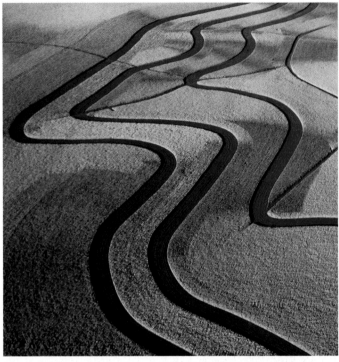

(b)

FIGURE 7.1 Cultural and economic contrasts are clearly evident between **(a)** a subsistence maize plot in Zimbabwe and **(b)** the extensive fields and mechanized farming of the U.S. Midwest. *(a) © Ian Murphy/Getty Images; (b) Tim McCabe, U.S. Dept. of Agriculture National Resource Conservation Service.*

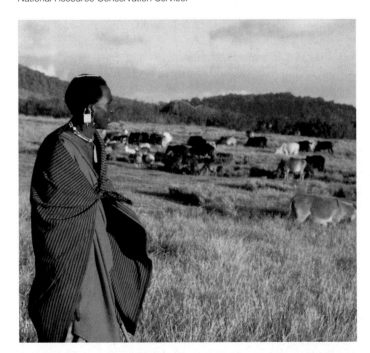

FIGURE 7.2 The formerly migratory Masai of eastern Africa are now largely sedentary, partially urbanized, and frequently owners of fenced farms. Cattle formed the traditional basis of Masai culture and were the evidence of wealth and social status. They provided as well the milk and blood important in the Masai diet. *© The McGraw-Hill Companies, Inc./Barry Baker, photographer.*

Distinctive eating utensils, the use of gestures, or the ritual of religious ceremony may summarize and characterize a culture for the casual observer. These are, however, individually insignificant parts of a much more complex structure that can be appreciated only when the whole is experienced.

Out of the richness and intricacy of human life we seek to isolate for special study those more fundamental cultural variables that give structure and spatial order to societies. We begin with culture traits, the smallest distinctive items of culture. **Culture traits** are units of learned behavior ranging from the language spoken to the tools used or to the games played. A trait may be an object (a fishhook, for example), a technique (weaving and knotting of a fish net), a belief (in the spirits resident in water bodies), or an attitude (a conviction that fish is superior to other animal flesh). Of course, the same trait—the Christian religion, perhaps, or the Spanish language—may be part of more than one culture. Traits are the most elementary expressions of culture, the building blocks of the complex behavioral patterns of distinctive groups of peoples.

Individual culture traits that are functionally interrelated constitute a **culture complex.** The existence of such complexes is universal. At one time, keeping cattle was a *culture trait* of the Masai of Kenya and Tanzania. Related traits included the measurement of personal wealth by the number of cattle owned; a diet containing the milk and blood of cattle; and disdain for labor unrelated to herding. The assemblage of these and other related traits yielded a *culture complex* descriptive of one aspect of Masai society (Figure 7.2). In exactly the same way, religious complexes, business behavior complexes, sports complexes, and others can easily be recognized in American or any other society.

A **culture system** is a broader generalization and refers to a collection of interacting culture traits and culture complexes that are shared by a group within a particular territory. Multiethnic societies, perhaps further subdivided by linguistic differences, varied food preferences, and a host of other internal differentiations, may nonetheless share enough joint characteristics to be recognizably distinctive cultural entities to themselves and others. Certainly, citizens of "melting pot" United States would identify themselves as *Americans,* together constituting a unique culture system on the world scene.

Culture traits, complexes, and systems have spatial extent. When they are plotted on maps, the regional character of the components of a culture is revealed. Geographers are interested in the spatial distribution of these individual elements, but their usual concern is with the **culture region,** a portion of the earth's surface occupied by people sharing recognizable and distinctive cultural characteristics. Examples include the political organizations societies devise, their religions, their form of economy, and even their clothing, eating utensils, and housing. There are as many such culture regions as there are separate culture traits and complexes of population groups.

Finally, a set of culture regions showing related culture complexes and landscapes may be grouped to form a **culture realm.** The term recognizes a large segment of the earth's surface having fundamental uniformity in its cultural characteristics and showing a significant difference in them from adjacent realms. Culture realms are, in a sense, culture regions at the broadest scale of generalization. In fact, the scale is so broad and the diversity within the recognized realms so great that the very concept of realm may mislead more than it informs.

Indeed, the current validity of distinctive culture realms such as those suggested in Figure 7.3 has been questioned in light of an assumed globalization of all aspects of human society and economy. The result of that globalization, some observers maintain, is a homogenization of cultures as economies are integrated and uniform consumer demands are satisfied by standardized commodities produced by international corporations. Others insist, however, that the world is far from homogenized and observe that globalization continues to be countered by powerful forces of regionalism, place identity, and ethnicity. One of the many possible divisions of human cultures into realms is offered in Figure 7.3. Culture realms, regions, systems, complexes, and traits are all elements in the spatial hierarchy of cultural geography. Direct and indirect reference to them will be encountered throughout this chapter.

INTERACTION OF PEOPLE AND ENVIRONMENT

Culture develops in a physical environment that, in its way, contributes to differences among people. In premodern subsistence societies, the acquisition of food, shelter, and clothing—all parts of culture—depends on the utilization of the natural resources at hand. The interrelations of people with the environment of a given area, their perceptions and use of it, and their impact on it are interwoven themes of geography. They are the special concerns of those geographers and anthropologists exploring **cultural ecology,** the study of the relationship between a culture group and the natural environment it occupies.

Cultural ecologists see evidence that subsistence pastoralists, hunter-gatherers, and gardeners adapted their productive activities—and, by extension, their social organizations and relationships—to the specific physical limitations of their different local habitats. Presumably, similar natural environmental conditions influenced the development of similar adaptive

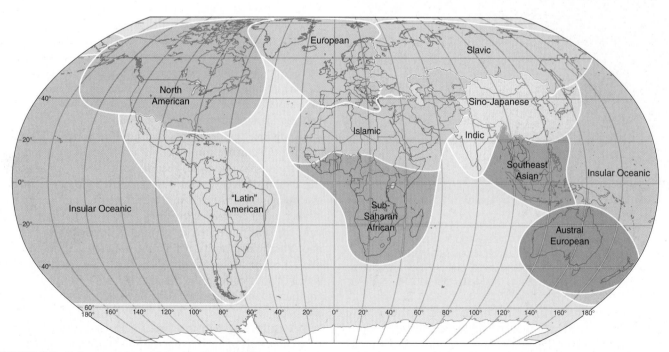

FIGURE 7.3 Culture realms of the modern world. Culture realms, regions, systems, complexes, and traits are all elements in the spatial hierarchy of cultural geography. This map proposes just one of many possible subdivisions of the world into multifactor culture regions.

responses and cultural outcomes in separate, unconnected locales. That initial influence, of course, does not predetermine the details of the subsequent culture.

Environments as Controls

Geographers have long dismissed as invalid and intellectually limiting the ideas of **environmental determinism.** Environmental determinism, which peaked in popularity in the late 19th and early 20th centuries, taught that the physical environment—in particular, the climate—determined which cultures would become the most advanced and economically developed. However, the cultural variations that occur around the world are not determined by a society's physical surroundings. Levels of technology, systems of social organization, and ideas about what is true and right have no obvious relationship to environmental circumstances.

The environment does place certain limitations on the human use of territory. However, such limitations must be seen not as absolute, enduring restrictions but as relative to technologies, cost considerations, national aspirations, and linkages with the larger world. Human choices in the use of landscapes are affected by group perception of the possibility and desirability of their settlement and exploitation. These are not circumstances inherent in the land.

Possibilism is the viewpoint that people, not environments, are the dynamic forces of cultural development. The needs, traditions, and technological level of a culture affect how that culture both assesses the possibilities of an area and shapes the choices that it makes regarding them. Each society uses natural resources in accordance with its culture. Changes in a group's technical abilities or objectives bring about changes in its perceptions of the usefulness of the land. Of course, there are some environmental limitations on use of area. For example, if resources for feeding, clothing, or housing ourselves within an area are lacking, or if we do not recognize them there, there is no inducement for people to occupy that territory. Environments that do contain such recognized resources provide the framework within which a culture operates.

Human Impacts

People are also able to modify their environment, and this is the other half of the human-environmental relationship of geographic concern. Geography, including cultural geography, examines both the reactions of people to the physical environment and their impact on that environment. By using it, we modify our environment—in part, through the material objects we place on the landscape: cities, farms, roads, and so on (Figure 7.4). The form these take is the product of the kind of culture group in which we live. The **cultural landscape,** the earth's surface as modified by human action, is the tangible, physical record of a given culture. House types, transportation networks, parks and cemeteries, and the size and distribution of settlements are among the indicators of the use that humans have made of the land.

As a rule, the more technologically advanced and complex the culture, the greater its impact on the environment, although preindustrial societies can and frequently do exert destructive pressures on the lands they occupy (see "Chaco Canyon Desolation," p. 201). In sprawling urban industrial societies, the cultural landscape has come to outweigh the natural physical environment in its impact on people's daily lives. It interposes itself between "nature" and humans. Residents of the cities of such societies—living and working in climate-controlled buildings, driving to enclosed shopping malls—can go through life with very little contact with or concern about the physical environment.

SUBSYSTEMS OF CULTURE

Understanding a culture fully is, perhaps, impossible for one who is not part of it. For analytic purposes, however, the traits and complexes of culture—its building blocks and expressions—can be grouped and examined as subsets of the whole. The anthropologist Leslie White suggested that a culture can be viewed as a three-part structure composed of subsystems that he termed *technological, sociological,* and *ideological.* In a separate but similar classification, three interrelated components of culture have been identified: *artifacts, sociofacts,* and *mentifacts.* Together, according to these interpretations, the subsystems—recognized by their separate components—constitute the structure of culture as a whole. But they are integrated; each reacts to the others and is affected by them in turn.

The **technological subsystem** is composed of the material objects and the techniques of their use by means of which people are able to live. Such objects are the tools and other instruments that enable us to feed, clothe, house, defend, transport, and amuse ourselves. The **sociological subsystem** of a culture is the sum of those expected and accepted patterns of interpersonal relations that find their outlet in economic, political, military, religious, kinship, and other associations. The **ideological subsystem** consists of the ideas, beliefs, and knowledge of a culture and of the ways in which they are expressed in speech or other forms of communication.

The Technological Subsystem

Examination of variations in culture and in the manner of human existence from place to place centers on a series of commonplace questions: How do the people in an area make a living? What resources and what tools—what artifacts—do they use to feed, clothe, and house themselves? Is a larger percentage of the population engaged in agriculture than in manufacturing? Do people travel to work in cars, on bicycles, or on foot? Do they shop for food or grow their own?

These questions concern the adaptive strategies used by different cultures in "making a living." In a broad sense, they address the technological subsystems at the disposal of those cultures—the instruments and tools people use in the daily cycle of existence. For most of human history, people lived by hunting and gathering, taking the bounty of nature with only

FIGURE 7.4 The physical and cultural landscapes in juxtaposition. Advanced societies are capable of so altering the circumstances of nature that the cultural landscapes become controlling environments. The city of Los Angeles, California, is a built environment constructed atop and often obscuring its physical surroundings. Consider how much this landscape has changed with human settlement. © *Getty RF.*

minimal dependence on weaponry, implements, and the controlled use of fire. Their adaptive skills were great, but their technological level was low. They had few specialized tools, could exploit only a limited range of potential resources, and had little or no control of nonhuman sources of energy. Their impact on the environment was small, but at the same time the "carrying capacity" of the land discussed in Chapter 6 was low everywhere, for technologies and artifacts were essentially the same among all groups.

The retreat of the last glaciers about 12,000 to 13,000 years ago marked the start of a period of unprecedented cultural development. It led from primitive hunting and gathering economies at the outset through the evolution of agriculture and animal husbandry to, ultimately, urbanization, industrialization, and the intricate complexity of the modern

technological subsystem. Since not all cultures passed through all stages at the same time, or even at all, *cultural divergence* between human groups became evident.

Cultural diversity among ancient societies reflected the proliferation of technologies that followed a more assured food supply and made possible a more intensive and extensive utilization of resources. Different groups in separate environmental circumstances developed specialized tools and behaviors to exploit resources they recognized. Beginning with the Industrial Revolution of the 18th century, however, a reverse trend—toward commonality of technology—began.

Today, advanced societies are nearly indistinguishable in the tools and techniques at their command. They have experienced *cultural convergence*—the sharing of technologies,

Chaco Canyon Desolation

It is not certain when they first came, but by A.D. 1000 the Anasazi people were building a flourishing civilization in what are now the states of Arizona and New Mexico. They were corn farmers thriving during the 300 years or so of the medieval warm period beginning about A.D. 900 in the American Southwest. In Chaco Canyon alone, they erected as many as 75 towns, all centered around pueblos, huge stone-and-adobe apartment buildings as tall as five stories and with as many as 800 rooms. These were the largest and tallest buildings of North America prior to the construction of iron-framed "cloud scrapers" in major cities at the end of the 19th century. An elaborate network of roads and irrigation canals connected and supported the pueblos. At about A.D. 1200, the settlements were abruptly abandoned. The Anasazi, advanced in their skills of agriculture and communal dwelling, were—according to some scholars—forced to move on by the ecological disaster their pressures had brought to a fragile environment.

They needed forests for fuel and for the hundreds of thousands of logs used as beams and bulwarks in their dwellings. The pinyon-juniper woodland of the canyon was quickly depleted. For larger timbers needed for construction, they first harvested stands of ponderosa pine found some 40 kilometers (25 mi) away. As early as A.D. 1030, these, too, were exhausted, and the community switched to spruce and Douglas fir from distant mountaintops surrounding the canyon. When they were gone by 1200, the Anasazi's fate was sealed—not only by the loss of forest but also by the irreversible ecological changes deforestation and agriculture had occasioned. With forest loss came erosion that destroyed the topsoil. The surface water channels that had been built for irrigation were deepened by accelerated erosion, converting them into enlarging arroyos, useless for agriculture.

The material roots of their culture destroyed, the Anasazi turned on themselves and warfare convulsed the region. Smaller groups sought refuge elsewhere, re-creating on a reduced scale their pueblo way of life, but now in nearly inaccessible, highly defensible mesa and cliff locations. The destruction they had wrought destroyed the Anasazi in turn.

© Jon Malinowski/Human Landscape Studio.

organizational structures, and even culture traits and artifacts that is so evident among widely separated societies in a modern world united by instantaneous communication and efficient transportation. Those differences in technological traditions that still exist between developed and underdeveloped societies reflect, in part, national and personal wealth, stage of economic advancement and complexity, and, importantly, the level and type of energy used (Figure 7.5).

In technologically advanced countries, many people are employed in manufacturing or allied service trades. Per capita incomes tend to be high, as do levels of education and nutrition, life expectancies, and medical services. These countries wield great economic and political power. In contrast, technologically less-advanced countries have a high percentage of people engaged in farming, with much of the agriculture at a subsistence level (Figure 7.6). The gross national incomes, or GNI (which measures the total domestic and foreign value added of all goods and services claimed by residents of a country during a year) of these countries are much lower than those of industrialized states. Per capita incomes (Figure 7.7), life expectancies, and literacy rates also tend to be low.

(a)

(b)

FIGURE 7.5 **(a)** This Rajasthan, India, farmer working with draft animals employs tools typical of the low technological levels of subsistence economies. **(b)** Cultures with advanced technological subsystems use complex machinery to harness inanimate energy for productive use. *(a) Getty RF; (b) Scott Bauer/USDA Agricultural Research Service.*

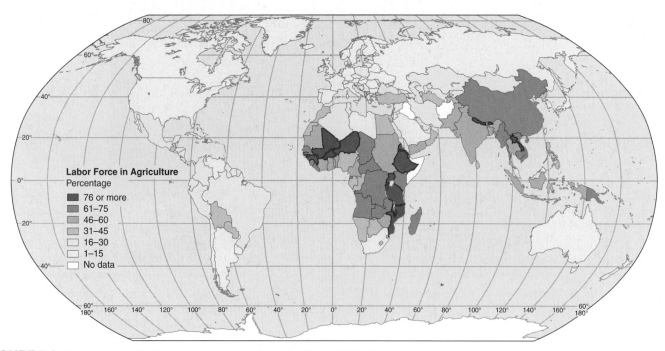

FIGURE 7.6 **Percentage of labor force engaged in agriculture, 2004.** For the world as a whole, agricultural workers make up less than half of the total labor force. Highly developed economies usually have very low proportions of their labor forces in the agricultural sector, but the contrast between advanced and underdeveloped countries in the agricultural labor force measure is diminishing. Rapid population growth in developing countries has resulted in increased rural landlessness and poverty, from which escape is sought by migration to cities. The resulting reduction in the agricultural labor force percentage is an expression of relocation of poverty and unemployment, not of economic advancement. *Sources: FAO 2006 and CIA* World Fact Book *2007.*

Labels such as *advanced–less-advanced, developed–underdeveloped,* and *industrial-nonindustrial* can be misinterpreted to mean "superior-inferior." This belief is totally improper because the terms relate solely to economic and technological circumstances and bear no qualitative relationship to such vital aspects of culture as music, art, religion, and personal relationships.

Properly understood, however, terms and measures of economic development can reveal important national and world regional contrasts in the technological subsystems of different

(a)

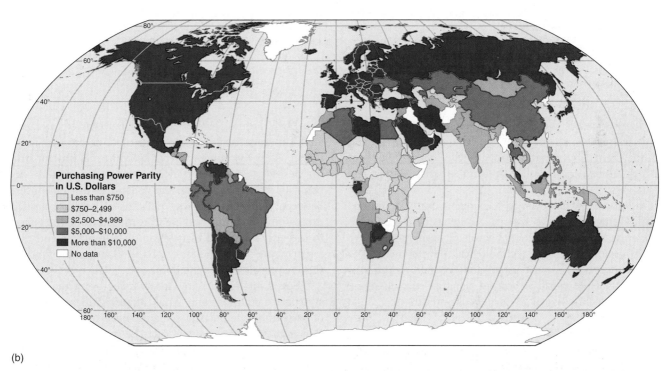

(b)

FIGURE 7.7 Two contrasting views of income. Both assume that total national income is evenly divided among all citizens, but each takes a different view of the meaning of the per capita income that division implies. **(a) Gross national income per capita, 2007.** GNI per capita expresses the individual's presumed income converted into U.S. dollars at official market exchange rates. Showing great contrasts between more- and less-advanced economies, it is a frequently employed summary of degree of technological development, though high incomes in sparsely populated, oil-rich countries may not have the same meaning in subsystem terms as do comparable per capita values in industrially advanced states. The map implies an unrealistic precision. For many states, when uncertain GNI is divided by unreliable population totals, the resulting GNI per capita is at best a rough approximation. A comparison of this map with Figure 7.6 presents an interesting study in regional contrasts. **(b) Purchasing power parity (PPP), 2007,** takes account of variations in price levels to measure the relative size of economies. It is based on the idea that identical baskets of traded goods should cost the same in all countries and thus attempts to measure the relative domestic purchasing power of local currencies. By this more realistic measure, the abject poverty suggested by per capita GNI is seen to be much reduced in many developing countries. *Source: Data from the World Bank, 2008.*

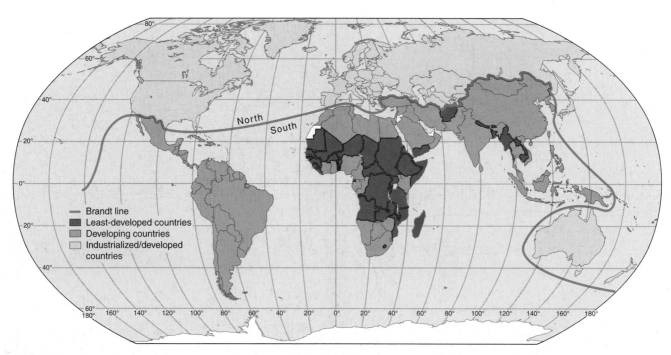

FIGURE 7.8 Comparative development levels. The "North–South" line of the 1980 *Brandt Report* suggested a simplified world contrast of development and underdevelopment based largely on degree of industrialization and per capita wealth recorded then. In 2004, the United Nations Economic and Social Council and the UN Conference on Trade and Development (UNCTAD) recognized 50 "least-developed countries." That recognition now reflects low ratings in three criteria: gross domestic income per capita, human resources as measured by a series of "quality of life" indicators, and level of economic diversification. The inclusive category of "developing countries" ignores recent significant economic and social gains in several Asian and Latin American states, raising them now to "industrialized/developed" status. Some "least-developed" states are small island countries not shown at this map scale. *Sources: UNCTAD and United Nations Development Programme.*

cultures and societies. Figure 7.8 suggests that technological status is relatively high in nearly all European countries and Japan, the United States, and Canada—the "North." Most of the less-developed countries are in Latin America, Africa, and southern Asia—the "Global South."[3]

It is important, however, to recognize that these implied national averages conceal internal contrasts. All countries include areas that are at different levels of development. We must also remember that technological development is a dynamic concept. It is most useful and accurate to think of the countries of the world as arrayed along an ever-changing continuum of technological levels and subsystems.

The Sociological Subsystem

Continuum and change also characterize the religious, political, formal and informal educational, and other institutions that constitute the sociological subsystem of culture. Together, these *sociofacts* define the social organizations of a culture. They regulate how the individual functions relative to the group, whether it be family, church, or state.

[3]The use of the terms *North* and *South* to describe relative developmental levels was introduced in *North–South: A Programme for Survival* (sometimes called the *Brandt Report*), published in 1980 by the Independent Commission on International Development Issues. The former Soviet Union was at that time included within the North; since its breakup in 1991, Georgia, Uzbekistan, and other former Soviet republics in Asia have been classified as less-developed by the United Nations.

There are no "givens" as far as patterns of interaction in any of these associations are concerned, except that most cultures possess a variety of formal and informal ways of structuring behavior. The importance to the society of the differing behavior sets varies among, and constitutes obvious differences between, cultures. Differing patterns of behavior are learned expressions of culture and are transmitted from one generation to the next by formal instruction or by example and expectation (Figure 7.9). The story of the Gauda's son that opened this chapter illustrates the point.

Social institutions are closely related to the technological system of a culture group. Thus, hunter-gatherers have one set of institutions; industrial societies have quite different ones. Preagricultural societies tended to be composed of small bands based on kinship ties, with little social differentiation or specialization of function in the band; the San (Bushmen) of arid southern Africa and isolated rain forest groups in Amazonia might serve as modern examples (Figure 7.10).

The revolution in food production occasioned by plant and animal domestication beginning around 10,000 years ago touched off a social transformation that included increases in population, urbanization, work specialization, and structural differentiation within the society. Politically, the rules and institutions by which people were governed changed with the formation of sedentary, agricultural societies. Loyalty was transferred from the kinship group to the state; resources

FIGURE 7.9 All societies prepare their children for membership in the culture group. In each of these settings, certain values, beliefs, skills, and proper ways of acting are being transmitted to young people. *(a) © Cary Wolinsky/Stock Boston; (b) © John Eastcott/Momatiuk/The Image Works; (c) © Yigol Pardo/Hillstrom Stock Photo; (d) © Stephanie Maze/Corbis Images.*

became possessions rather than the common property of all. Equally far-reaching changes occurred after the 18th-century Industrial Revolution, leading to the complex of human social organizations that we experience and are controlled by today in "developed" states and that increasingly affect all cultures everywhere.

Culture is a complexly intertwined whole. Each organizational form or institution affects, and is affected by, related culture traits and complexes in intricate and variable ways. Systems of land and property ownership and control, for example, are institutional expressions of the sociological subsystem. They are simultaneously explicitly central to the classification of economies and to the understanding of spatial and structural patterns of economic development, as Chapter 10 will examine. Again, for each country the adopted system of laws and justice is a cultural variable identified with the sociological

subsystem but extending its influence to all aspects of economic and social organization, including the political geographic systems discussed in Chapter 9.

The Ideological Subsystem

The third class of elements defining and identifying a culture is the ideological subsystem. This subsystem consists of ideas, beliefs, and knowledge, as well as the ways we express these things in our speech and other forms of communication. Mythologies, theologies, legend, literature, philosophy, folk wisdom, and commonsense knowledge make up this category. Passed on from generation to generation, these abstract belief systems, or *mentifacts,* tell us what we ought to believe, what we should value, and how we ought to act. Beliefs form the basis of the socialization process.

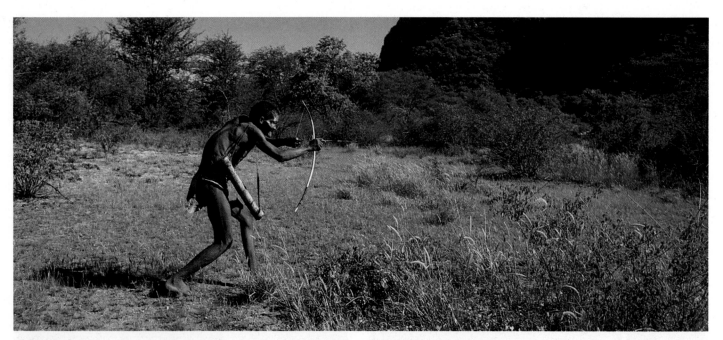

FIGURE 7.10 Hunter-gatherers practiced the most enduring lifestyle in human history, trading it for the more arduous life of farmers under the necessity to provide larger quantities of less-diversified foodstuffs for a growing population. Unlike their settled farmer rivals and successors, among hunter-gatherers age and sex differences, not caste or economic status, were and are the primary basis for interpersonal relations and the division of labor. This San (Bushman) hunter of Botswana is a member of one of the very few groups in Africa or the world still at least partially pursuing this ancient lifestyle. © *Aubrey Lang/Valan Photos.*

Often, we know—or think we know—what the beliefs of a group are from written sources. Sometimes, however, we must depend on the actions or objectives of a group to tell us what its true ideas and values are. "Actions speak louder than words" and "Do as I say, not as I do" are commonplace recognitions of the fact that actions and words do not always coincide. The values of a group cannot be deduced from the written record alone.

Nothing in a culture stands totally alone. Changes in the ideas that a society holds may affect the sociological and technological systems, just as, for example, changes in technology force changes in the social system. The abrupt alteration after World War I (1914–1918) of the ideological structure of Russia from a monarchical, agrarian, capitalist system to an industrialized, communist society involved sudden alteration in all facets of that country's culture system. The equally abrupt disintegration of Russian communism in the early 1990s was similarly disruptive of all its established economic, social, and administrative organizations. The interlocking nature of all aspects of a culture is termed **cultural integration.**

The recognition of three distinctive subsystems of culture, although helping us appreciate its structure and complexity, can at the same time obscure the many-sided nature of individual elements of culture. *Cultural integration* means that any cultural object or act may have a number of meanings. Clothing, for example, serves as an artifact of bodily protection appropriate to climatic conditions, available materials and techniques, or the activity in which the wearer is engaged. But garments also may be sociofacts, identifying an individual's role in the social structure of the community or culture, and mentifacts, evoking larger community value systems (Figure 7.11).

CULTURE CHANGE

The recurring theme of cultural geography is change. No culture is, or has been, characterized by a permanently fixed set of material objects, systems of organization, or even ideologies, although all of these may be long-enduring within a stable, isolated society. Such isolation and stability have always been rare. On the whole, although cultures are essentially conservative, they are always in a state of flux.

Many individual changes, of course, are so slight that they initially are almost unnoticed, though collectively they may substantially alter the affected culture. Think of how the culture of the United States differs today from what it was in 1940—not in essentials, perhaps, but in the innumerable electric, electronic, and transportational devices that have been introduced and in the recreational, social, and behavioral adjustments they and other technological changes have wrought. Among the latter have been shifts in employment patterns to include greater participation by women in the waged workforce and associated changes in attitudes toward the role of women in the society at large. Such cumulative changes occur because the culture traits of any group are not independent; they are clustered in a coherent and integrated pattern. Change on a small scale will have wide repercussions as associated traits also change to accommodate the adopted adjustment. Change, both major and minor, within cultures is induced by *innovation, spatial diffusion,* and *acculturation.*

(a)

(b)

(c)

FIGURE 7.11 **(a)** Houses are important *artifacts,* providing shelter for their occupants. These traditional houses on Nias Island off the west coast of Sumatra, Indonesia, reflect an ingenious cultural adaptation to a hot, humid tropical climate. The elevated floor keeps occupants dry in heavy downpours and allows cooling breezes to circulate. The steep roof sheds rain and shades the interior from the tropical sun. **(b)** Houses are also *sociofacts,* reflecting the family, kinship, and communal ideals of a culture. This landscape of detached, single-family houses and backyard swimming pools in Las Vegas, Nevada, reflects social relations in the United States, with an emphasis on individualism, privacy, and the nuclear family. **(c)** Houses are also *mentifacts,* reflecting a culture group's ideas about appropriate design, orientation, and building materials. The White House in Washington, D.C., reflects cultural ideals of beauty and symmetry drawn from classical Greek architecture and Palladian and Georgian houses in Europe. *(a) Wolfgang Kaehler; (b) USDA/ NRCS Natural Resource Conservation Service; (c) © Getty RF.*

Innovation

Innovation implies changes to a culture that result from ideas created within the social group itself and adopted by the culture. The novelty may be an invented improvement in material technology, such as the bow and arrow or the jet engine. It may involve the development of nonmaterial forms of social structure and interaction: feudalism or Christianity, for example.

Premodern and traditional societies characteristically are slower to innovate or accept change. In societies at equilibrium with their environment and with no unmet needs, change has no adaptive value and has no reason to occur. Indeed, all societies have an innate resistance to change, since innovation inevitably creates tensions between the new reality and other established socioeconomic conditions. Those tensions can be resolved only by adaptive changes elsewhere in the total system. The gap that may develop between, for example, a newly adopted technology and other, slower-paced social traits has been called *cultural lag.* Complaints about youthful fads and the glorification of times past are familiar examples of reluctance to accept or adjust to change.

Innovation (invention), frequently under stress, has marked the history of humankind. An expanded food base accompanied the pressures of growing populations at the end of the Ice Age. Domestication of plants and animals appears

to have occurred independently in several recognizable areas of "invention" of agriculture, shown in Figure 7.12. From them, presumably, came a rapid diffusion of food types, production techniques, and new modes of economic and social organization as the majority of humankind changed from hunting-gathering to sedentary farming at least 2000 years ago. All innovation has a radiating impact on the web of culture; the more basic the innovation, the more pervasive its consequences.

Few innovations in human history have been more basic than the Agricultural Revolution. It affected every aspect of society and created irreconcilable conflict between preagricultural hunter-gatherers and sedentary farming cultures. Where those two groups came into contact, farmers were the victors and hunter-gatherers the losers in competition for territorial control. The contest continued into modern times. During the past 500 years, European expansion totally dominated the hunting and gathering cultures it encountered in large parts of the world, such as North America and Australia (see "Is Geography Destiny?"). With agriculture and its sedentary way of life, culture altered at an accelerating pace, and change itself became a way of life. Humans learned the arts of spinning and weaving plant and animal fibers. They learned to use the potter's wheel, to fire clay, and to make utensils. They developed the techniques of brick making, mortaring, and building construction. They discovered the skills of mining, smelting, and casting

Is Geography Destiny?

In his 1997 Pulitzer Prize–winning book, *Guns, Germs and Steel: The Fates of Human Societies,* Jared Diamond argues, "History followed different courses for different peoples because of differences among peoples' environments, not because of biological differences among peoples themselves." The environmental differences that counted—and that led to world dominance by Eurasians—were the availability in Eurasia of an abundance of plants and animals suitable for domestication and a landmass whose east–west orientation enabled long-distance transfer of animals, food crops, and technologies. No other continent had either of those advantages.

Food production was the key. Although agriculture was independently developed in several world areas after the end of the Ice Age, the inhabitants of the Middle East were fortunate in having an abundance of plants suitable for domestication, including six of the eight most important food grasses, among them ancestral wheat. These plants adapted easily to cultivation, grew rapidly, had high nutritive value, and could support large populations. Eurasia also had an abundance of large animals that could be domesticated, including the cow, goat, pig, sheep, and horse, further spurring population growth. In addition, by living in close proximity to animals, Eurasians contracted the epidemic diseases that were to prove so devastating later to the inhabitants of other continents and simultaneously developed their own immunities to those maladies.

The food-producing technologies developed in such hearth regions as the Middle East were easily diffused along the immense east–west axis of Eurasia, where roughly similar climates suited to the same mix of crops and livestock were encountered from China to Spain. Eurasia's great size meant, as well, a great number of different peoples, each capable of developing new technologies that in turn could be diffused over long distances. Population growth, agricultural productivity, and inventive minds led to civilizations—central governments, cities, labor specializations, textiles, pottery, writing, mathematics, long-distance trade, metalworking, and eventually, the guns that conquering Eurasians carried to other continents.

No other world region enjoyed Eurasia's environmental and subsequent population and technological advantages. The few food crops developed in Africa or the Americas could not effectively diffuse across the climatic and ecological barriers in those north–south aligned continents. Because of accidents of nature or massive predation of large animals by early inhabitants, sub-Saharan Africa and Australia yielded no domesticated animals and the Americas had only the localized llama. Without the food bases and easy latitudinal movement of Eurasia, populations elsewhere remained smaller, more isolated, and collectively less inventive. When the voyages of discovery and colonization began in the 15th century, Eurasian advantages proved overwhelming. Decimated by diseases against which they had no resistance, and lacking the horses, armor, firearms, and organization of their conquerors, inhabitants of other continents found themselves quickly subdued and dominated—not, in Jared Diamond's opinion, because of innate inferiority but because of geographical disadvantages that limited or delayed their developmental prospects.

---

metals. Special local advantages in resources or products promoted the development of long-distance trading connections. On the foundation of such technical advancements a more complex, exploitative culture appeared, including a stratified society to replace the rough equality of hunting and gathering economies.

The source regions of such social and technical revolutions were initially spatially confined. The term **culture hearth** is used to describe those restricted areas of innovation from which key culture elements diffused to exert an influence on surrounding regions. The hearth may be viewed as the "cradle" of any culture group whose developed systems of livelihood and life created a distinctive cultural landscape. Most of the thousands of hearths that evolved across the world in all regions and natural settings remained at low levels of social and technical development. Only a few produced the trappings of *civilization,* which are usually assumed to include writing (or other forms of record keeping), metallurgy, long-distance trade connections, astronomy and mathematics, social stratification and labor specialization, formalized governmental systems, and a structured urban society. Several major culture hearths emerged, some as early as 7000 to 8000 years ago, following the initial revolution in food production. Prominent centers of early creativity were located in Egypt, Mesopotamia, the Indus Valley of the Indian subcontinent, northern China, southeastern Asia, and several locations in Africa, the Americas, and elsewhere (Figure 7.13).

In most modern societies, innovative change has become common, expected, and inevitable, though it may be rejected by some of their separate culture groups. The rate of invention, at least as measured by the number of patents granted, has steadily increased, and the period between idea conception and product availability has been decreasing. A general axiom is that, the more ideas available and the more minds able to exploit and combine them, the greater the rate of innovation. The spatial implication is that larger urban centers of advanced economies tend to be centers of innovation, not just because of their size but also because of the number of ideas interchanged. Indeed, ideas not only stimulate new ideas but also create circumstances in which new solutions must be developed to maintain the forward momentum of the society (Figure 7.14).

Diffusion

Spatial diffusion is the process by which a concept, a practice, an innovation, or a substance spreads from its point of origin to new territories. Diffusion can assume a variety of forms, but basically two processes are involved. Either people move to a

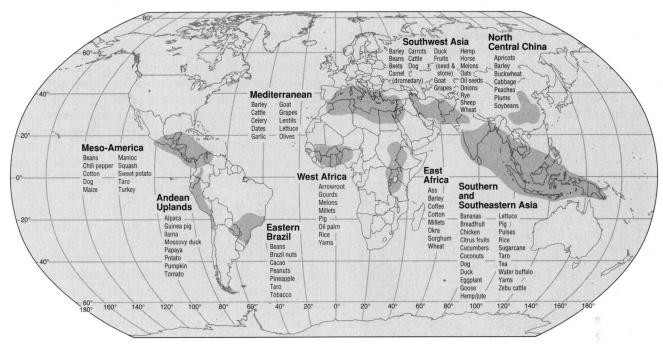

FIGURE 7.12 Chief centers of plant and animal domestication. The southern and southeastern Asia center was characterized by the domestication of plants, such as taro, that are propagated by the division and replanting of existing plants (vegetative reproduction). Reproduction by the planting of seeds (e.g., maize and wheat) was more characteristic of Meso-America and Southwest Asia. The African and Andean areas developed crops reproduced by both methods. The lists of crops and livestock associated with the separate origin areas are selective, not exhaustive.

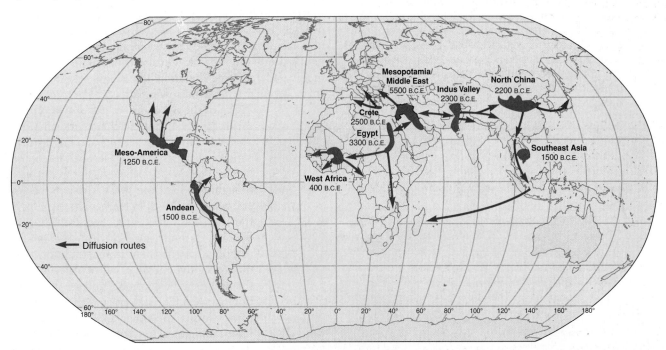

FIGURE 7.13 Early culture hearths of the Old World and the Americas. The B.C.E. (Before the Common Era) dates approximate times when the hearths developed complex social, intellectual, and technological bases and served as cultural diffusion centers.

new area and take their culture with them (as the immigrants to the American colonies did) or information about an innovation (such as barbed wire or hybrid corn) can spread throughout a culture. In either case, new ideas are transferred from their source region to new areas and to different culture groups. Spatial diffusion will be discussed in more detail in Chapter 8.

It is not always possible to determine whether the existence of a culture trait in two different areas is the result of diffusion or of independent (or *parallel*) innovation. Cultural similarities do not necessarily prove that spatial diffusion has occurred. The pyramids of Egypt and of Central America most likely were separately conceived and are not evidence, as some have proposed, of pre-Columbian voyages from the Mediterranean to the Americas. A Stone Age monument-building culture, after all, has only a limited number of shapes from which to choose.

Historical examples of independent, parallel invention are numerous: logarithms by Napier (1614) and Burgi (1620), calculus by Newton (1672) and Leibnitz (1675), and the telephone by Elisha Gray and Alexander Graham Bell (1876) are commonly cited examples. It appears beyond doubt that agriculture was independently invented not only both in the New

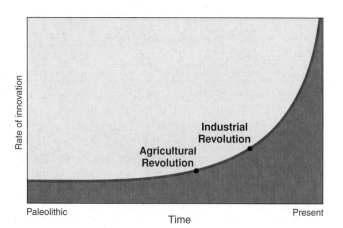

FIGURE 7.14 The trend of innovation through human history. Hunter-gatherers, dwelling in close relationship with their environment and their resource base, had little need for innovation and no necessity for cultural change. The Agricultural Revolution accelerated the diffusion of the ideas and techniques of domestication, urbanization, and trade. With the Industrial Revolution, dramatic increases in all aspects of socioeconomic innovation began to alter cultures throughout the world.

FIGURE 7.15 Motivated by religious conviction that the "good life" must be reduced to its simplest forms, the Amish community of east central Illinois shuns all modern luxuries of the majority, secular society around them. Children use horse and buggy, not school bus or automobile, on the daily trip to their rural school. *Courtesy of Jean Fellmann.*

World and in the Old but also in more than one culture hearth in each of the hemispheres.

All cultures are amalgams of innumerable innovations spread spatially from their points of origin and integrated into the structure of the receiving societies. It has been estimated that no more than 10% of the cultural items of any society are traceable to innovations created by its members and that the other 90% come to the society through diffusion (see "A Homemade Culture," p. 212).

Barriers to diffusion do exist, of course, as Chapter 8 explains. Generally, the closer and the more similar two cultural areas are to one another, the lower those barriers are and the greater is the likelihood of the adoption of an innovation, because diffusion is a selective process. Of course, the receiver culture may selectively adopt some goods or ideas from the donor society and reject others. The decision to adopt is governed by the receiving group's own culture. Political restrictions, religious taboos, and other social customs are cultural barriers to diffusion. The French Canadians, although geographically close to many centers of diffusion, such as Toronto, New York, and Boston, are only minimally influenced by them. Both their language and their culture complex govern French Canadian selective acceptance of Anglo influences. Traditional groups, perhaps controlled by firm religious conviction—such as the Hasidic Jewish community of New York City—may very largely reject culture traits and technologies of the larger society in whose midst they live (see "Folk and Popular Culture," p. 219, and Figure 7.15).

Adopting cultures do not usually accept intact items originating from the outside. Diffused ideas and artifacts commonly undergo some alteration of meaning or form that makes them acceptable to a borrowing group. The process of the fusion of the old and new, called **syncretism,** is a major feature of cultural change. It can be seen in alterations to religious ritual and dogma made by convert societies seeking acceptable conformity between old and new beliefs. For example, slaves brought voodoo from West Africa to the Americas, where it thrived in Haiti and Louisiana. Over the years it absorbed influences from French and Spanish Catholicism, American Indian spiritual practices, and even Masonic tradition. Despite those adaptive mixings, many believers consider themselves to be Catholics and see no contradiction between Christianity and their faith in protective spirits and other tenets of voodoo. On a more familiar level, syncretism is reflected in subtle or blatant alterations of imported cuisines to make them conform to the demands of America's fast-food franchises.

Acculturation

Acculturation is the process by which one culture group undergoes a major modification by adopting many of the characteristics of another, usually dominant culture group. In practice, acculturation may involve changes in the original cultural patterns of either or both of two groups involved in prolonged firsthand contact. Such contact and subsequent cultural alteration may occur in a conquered or colonized region. Very often, the subordinate or subject population is forced to acculturate or does so voluntarily, overwhelmed by the superiority in numbers or the technical level of the conqueror.

The tribal Europeans in areas of Roman conquest, native populations in the wake of Slavic occupation of Siberia, and Native Americans following European settlement of North America experienced this kind of acculturation. In a different fashion, it is evident in the changes in Japanese political organization and philosophy imposed by occupying Americans after World War II or in the Japanese adoption of some more recreational aspects of American life (Figure 7.16). In turn, American life was enriched by awareness of Japanese food, architecture, philosophy, and popular culture, demonstrating the two-way nature of acculturation.

On occasion, the invading group is assimilated into the conquered society, as the older, richer Chinese culture prevailed over that of the conquering tribes of invading Mongols during the 13th and 14th centuries. The relationship of a mother country to its colony may also result in permanent changes in the culture of the colonizer, even though little direct population contact is involved. The European spread of tobacco addiction (see "Documenting Diffusion," in Chapter 8), potatoes, maize, and turkeys reflected colonial contact with the Americas. In Great Britain, drinking tea and eating curry are national traditions, but both are imports, reflecting the colonial experience in India.

In the modern period, the population relocations and immigration impacts discussed in Chapter 6 (pp. 180–182) have resulted in unprecedented cultural mixings throughout the world. The traditional "melting pot" view—more formally, **amalgamation theory**—of immigrant integration into, for example, U.S. society suggests that the receiving society and the varied arriving newcomer groups eventually merge into a composite mainstream culture, incorporating the many traits of its collective components. More realistically, in order to be accepted, newcomer groups must learn the accustomed patterns of behavior and response and the dominating language of the workplace and government of the culture they have entered. Acculturation for them involves the adoption of the values, attitudes, ways of behavior, and speech of the receiving society, which itself undergoes change from absorption of the arriving group. In that process, the immigrant group loses much of its separate cultural identity to the extent that it accepts over time the culture of the larger host community.

FIGURE 7.16 Baseball, an import from America, is one of the most popular sports in Japan, attracting millions of spectators annually. Similarly, a generation ago most Americans considered soccer a foreign and exotic game of little or no interest. Today, soccer is one of the most popular youth sports in the United States. © *Geoffrey Hiller/eStock Photography/Leo de Wys.*

A Homemade Culture

Reflecting on an average morning in the life of a "100% American," Ralph Linton noted:

> Our solid American citizen awakens in a bed built on a pattern which originated in the Near East but which was modified in northern Europe before it was transmitted to America. He throws back covers made from cotton, domesticated in India, or linen, domesticated in the Near East, or wool from sheep, also domesticated in the Near East, or silk, the use of which was discovered in China. All of these materials have been spun and woven by processes invented in the Near East. . . . He takes off his pajamas, a garment invented in India, and washes with soap invented by the ancient Gauls. . . .
>
> Returning to the bedroom, . . . he puts on garments whose form originally derived from the skin clothing of the nomads of the Asiatic steppes [and] puts on shoes made from skins tanned by a process invented in ancient Egypt and cut to a pattern derived from the classical civilizations of the Mediterranean. . . . Before going out for breakfast he glances through the window, made of glass invented in Egypt, and if it is raining puts on overshoes made of rubber discovered by the Central American Indians and takes an umbrella invented in southeastern Asia. . . .

[At breakfast,] a whole new series of borrowed elements confronts him. His plate is made of a form of pottery invented in China. His knife is of steel, an alloy first made in southern India, his fork a medieval Italian invention, and his spoon a derivative of a Roman original. He begins breakfast with an orange, from the eastern Mediterranean, a cantaloupe from Persia, or perhaps a piece of African watermelon. With this he has coffee, an Abyssinian plant. . . . [H]e may have the egg of a species of bird domesticated in Indo-China, or thin strips of flesh of an animal domesticated in Eastern Asia which have been salted and smoked by a process developed in northern Europe.

When our friend has finished eating . . . he reads the news of the day, imprinted in characters invented by the ancient Semites upon a material invented in China by a process invented in Germany. As he absorbs the accounts of foreign troubles he will, if he is a good conservative citizen, thank a Hebrew deity in an Indo-European language that he is 100 percent American.

Ralph Linton, *The Study of Man,* © 1936, renewed 1964, pp. 326–327. Reprinted by permission of Prentice Hall, Inc., Englewood Cliffs, New Jersey.

Although acculturation usually involves a minority group adopting the patterns of the dominant population, the process can be reciprocal. That is, the dominant group may also adopt at least some patterns and practices identified with new minority groups as a broader, more diverse composite culture is created. Instead of the presumed ideal of the "melting pot," a "salad bowl" or "lumpy stew" cultural mixture results.

When the integration process is completed, **assimilation** has occurred. But assimilation does not necessarily mean that consciousness of original cultural identity is reduced or lost. *Competition theory,* in fact, suggests that, as cultural minorities begin to achieve success and enter into mainstream social and economic life, awareness of cultural differences may be heightened, transforming the strengthening immigrant group into a self-assertive minority, pursuing goals and interests that defend and protect its position within the larger society. Carried to extremes, militant minority self-assertion may result in the loss of the larger social and cultural integration the acculturation process seeks to assure—a circumstance of increasing concern in Western European and Anglo American destination countries.

CULTURAL DIVERSITY

We began our discussion of culture with its subsystems of technological, sociological, and ideological content. We have learned that the distinctive makeup of those subsystems—the combinations and interactions of traits and complexes characteristic of particular cultures—is subjected to, and is the product of, change through innovation, spatial diffusion, adoption, and acculturation. Those processes of cultural development and alteration have not, however, led to a homogenized world culture, even after thousands of years of cultural contact and exchange since the origins of agriculture.

As we earlier observed, it is true that, in an increasingly integrated world, access to the material trappings and technologies of modern life and economy is widely available to most peoples and societies. As a result, important cultural commonalities have developed. Nevertheless, all of our experience and observation indicate a world still divided, not unified, in culture. Our concern as geographers is to identify culture traits that have spatial expression and to indicate how that culture is significantly different from other culture complexes.

We may reject as superficial and meaningless generalizations derived from trivialities: the foods people eat for breakfast, for example, or the kinds of eating implements they use. This rejection is a reflection of the kinds of understanding and the level of generalization we seek. There is no single most appropriate way to designate or recognize a culture or to delimit a culture region. As geographers concerned with world systems, we are interested in those aspects of culture that vary over extensive regions of the world and differentiate societies in a broad, summary fashion.

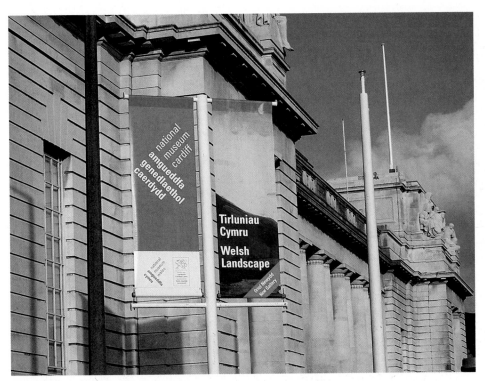

FIGURE 7.17 The survival of Welsh (Cymraeg), a Celtic language, within Great Britain demonstrates the importance of language to cultural identity. After more than a century of decline as English came to dominate education and public life, laws passed in the 1990s gave Welsh equal status with English in Wales. Instruction in Welsh is compulsory up to age 16 and most government publications and road signs in Wales are bilingual. The British government has been supportive of Wales, devolving power to the Wales Assembly Government. © Mark Bjelland.

possibilities of area, and it assures that the status of women is a cultural spatial variable of fundamental significance.

LANGUAGE

Forever changing and evolving, language in spoken or written form makes possible the cooperative efforts, the group understandings, and the shared behavioral patterns that distinguish culture groups. *Language,* defined simply as an organized system of speech by which people communicate with each other with mutual comprehension, is the most important medium by which culture is transmitted. Language enables parents to teach their children what the world they live in is like and what they must do to become functioning members of society. Some argue that the language of a society structures the perceptions of its speakers. By the words it contains and the concepts it can formulate, language is said to determine the attitudes, the understandings, and the responses of the society. Language, therefore, can be both a cause and a symbol of cultural differentiation (Figure 7.17).

Language, religion, ethnicity, and gender meet our criteria and are among the most prominent of the differentiating culture traits of societies and regions. Language and religion are basic components of culture, helping identify who and what we are as individuals and clearly placing us within larger communities of persons with similar characteristics. In our earlier terminology, they are mentifacts, components of the ideological subsystem of culture that help shape the belief system of a society and transmit it to succeeding generations.

Ethnicity is a cultural summary rather than a single trait. It is based on the firm understanding by members of a group that they are, in some fundamental ways, different from others who do not share their distinguishing composite characteristics, which may include language, religion, national origin, unique customs, or other identifiers. Like language and religion, ethnicity has spatial identification. Like them, too, it may serve as an element of diversity and division within culturally complex societies and states.

Language, religion, and ethnicity treat all members (or all adult members) of a society uniformly. However, among the most prominent strands in the fabric of culture are the social structures (sociofacts) and relationships that establish distinctions between males and females in the duties assigned and the rewards afforded to each. *Gender* is the reference term recognizing those socially created distinctions. It conditions the way people use space and assess economic and cultural

If that conclusion is true, one aspect of cultural heterogeneity may be easily understood. The approximately 7 billion people on Earth speak nearly 7000 different languages. Knowing that Africa as a whole contains nearly one-third of all living languages (though 85% of Africans speak one or more variants of 15 core languages) gives us a clearer appreciation of the political and social division in that continent. Europe alone has some 230 languages and dialects (Figure 7.18). Language is a hallmark of cultural diversity, and the present world distribution of major languages (Figure 7.19) records not only the migrations and conquests of our linguistic ancestors but also the continuing dynamic pattern of human movements, settlements, and colonizations of more recent centuries.

Languages differ greatly in their relative importance, if *importance* can be taken to mean the number of people using them. More than half of the world's inhabitants are native speakers of just eight of its thousands of tongues, and at least half regularly use or have competence in just four of them. Table 7.1, p. 214, lists those languages spoken by more than 60 million people, a list that includes nearly 90% of the world's population. At the other end of the scale are a number of rapidly declining languages whose speakers number in the hundreds or, at most, the few thousands. Indeed, the world today has far less linguistic diversity than it has had historically, and each year sees the loss of additional tongues, displaced through the spread of English and the other "big" languages. Scholars estimate that

TABLE 7.1
Languages Spoken by 60 Million or More People, 2007

Languages	Millions of Speakers (as primary or secondary language)	Approx. Percentage of World Population
Mandarin[a] (China)	1100	17
English	1000	16
Hindi/Urdu[b] (India, Pakistan)	750	12
Spanish	450	7
Russian/Belorussian	270	4
Arabic[c]	260	4
Bengali (Bangladesh, India)	250	4
Malay/Indonesian	205	3
Portuguese	195	3
Japanese	132	2
French	125	2
German	121	2
Thai/Lao	90	1
Punjabi	85	1
Wu (China)	85	1
Javanese	80	1
Turkish/Azeri/Turkmen (Turkey/Azerbaijan/ Turkmenistan)	80	1
Korean (Korea, China, Japan)	78	1
Marathi (India)	77	1
Vietnamese	75	1
Telugu (India)	75	1
Tamil (India, Sri Lanka)	74	1
Yue (Cantonese) (China)	70	1
Italian	68	1
Ukrainian	65	1

Sources: Based on data from *Ethnologue: Languages of the World*, 15th ed.; *Linguasphere 2000;* and other sources.

[a]The official dialect of Mandarin is spoken by perhaps 650 million; as many as 1500 other dialects, many mutually incomprehensible, are also designated as "Mandarin."

[b]Hindi and Urdu are basically the same language: Hindustani. Written in the Devangari script, it is called *Hindi*, the official language of India; in the Arabic script it is called *Urdu*, the official language of Pakistan.

[c]The figure given includes speakers of the many, often mutually unintelligible versions of colloquial Arabic. Classical or literary Arabic, the language of the Koran, is uniform and standardized but restricted to formal usage as a spoken tongue. Because of its religious association, Arabic is a second language for many inhabitants of Muslim countries with other native tongues.

about half the currently spoken languages are endangered—meaning that children no longer learn them and their youngest speakers are now middle-aged—and will disappear within the next century.

The diversity of languages is simplified when we recognize among them related families. A **language** (or *linguistic*) **family** is a group of languages thought to have a common origin in a single, earlier tongue. The Indo-European family of languages is among the most prominent of such groupings, embracing most of the languages of Europe and a large part of Asia, as well as the introduced—not the native—languages of the Americas (Figure 7.19). All told, languages in the Indo-European family are spoken by about half the world's peoples.

By recognizing similar words in most Indo-European languages, linguists deduce that these languages derived from a common ancestor tongue called *proto-Indo-European*, which was spoken by people living somewhere in Eastern Europe about 5000 years ago (though some conclude that central Turkey was the more likely site of origin). By at least 2500 B.C., their society had apparently fragmented; the homeland was left and segments of the parent culture migrated in different directions. Wherever this remarkable people settled, they appear to have dominated local populations and imposed their language on them.

Within a language family, we can distinguish *subfamilies*. The Romance languages (including French, Spanish, and Italian)—offsprings of Latin—and the Germanic languages (such as

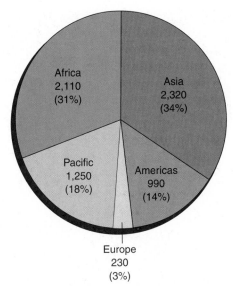

FIGURE 7.18 **World distribution of living languages, 2009.**
Of the perhaps 6900 languages still spoken today, one-third are found in Asia. Linguists' estimates of the number of languages ever spoken on Earth range from 31,000 to as many as 300,000 or more. Assuming the lower estimate or even one considerably smaller, dead languages far outnumber the living. One or two additional tongues, most spoken in the forests of Papua New Guinea or in Indonesia, are lost each week. In contrast, as a result of the vast mixing of peoples and cultures, more than 100 new languages have been created over the past four centuries. *Source: Estimates based on* Lewis, M. Paul (ed.), 2009. *Ethnologue: Languages of the World,* Sixteenth edition. Dallas, Tex.: SIL International.

English, German, and Dutch) are subfamilies, or branches, of Indo-European. The languages in a subfamily often show similarities in sounds, grammatical structure, and vocabulary, even though they are mutually unintelligible. English *daughter,* German *Tochter,* and Swedish *dotter* are Germanic examples.

Language Spread and Change

Language spread as a geographic event represents the increase or relocation through time in the area over which a language is spoken. The more than 300 Bantu languages found south of the "Bantu line" in sub-Saharan Africa, for example, are variants of a proto-Bantu carried by an expanding, culturally advanced people who displaced linguistically different preexisting populations (Figure 7.20, p. 218). More recently, the languages of European colonists similarly replaced native tongues in their areas of settlement in North and South America, Australasia, and Siberia. That is, languages may spread because their speakers occupy new territory.

Latin, however, replaced earlier Celtic languages in Western Europe not by force of numbers—Roman legionnaires, administrators, and settlers never represented a majority population—but by the gradual abandonment of their former tongues by native populations brought under the influence and control of the Roman Empire. Adoption rather than eviction of language appears the rule followed in the majority of historical and contemporary instances of language spread. That is, languages may spread because they acquire new speakers.

Either form of language spread—the dispersion of speakers or the acquisition of speakers—may, through segregation and isolation, give rise to separate, mutually incomprehensible tongues because the society speaking the parent protolanguage no longer remains unitary. Comparable changes occur normally and naturally within a single language in word meaning, pronunciation, vocabulary, and *syntax* (the way words are put together in phrases and sentences). Because they are gradual, such changes tend to go unremarked, yet cumulatively they can result in language change so great that, in the course of centuries, an essentially new language has been created. The English of 17th-century Shakespearean writings or the King James Bible (1611) sounds stilted to our ears, and 8th-century *Beowulf* is practically unintelligible.

Language evolution may be gradual and cumulative, with each generation deviating in small degree from the speech patterns and vocabulary of its parents, or it may be massive and abrupt—reflecting conquests, migrations, new trade contacts, and other disruptions of cultural isolation. English owes its form to the Celts, the original inhabitants of the British Isles, and to successive waves of invaders, including the Latin-speaking Romans and the Germanic Angles, Saxons, and Danes. The French-speaking Norman conquerors of the 11th century added about 10,000 new words to the evolving English tongue.

Discovery and colonization of new lands and continents in the 16th and 17th centuries greatly and necessarily expanded English as new foods, vegetation, animals, and artifacts were encountered and adopted along with their existing aboriginal American, Australian, Indian, or African names. The Indian languages of the Americas alone brought more than 200 relatively common daily words to English, 80 or more from the North American native tongues and the rest from Caribbean, Central, and South American languages. More than 2000 more specialized or localized words were also added. *Moose, raccoon, skunk, maize, squash, succotash, igloo, toboggan, hurricane, blizzard, hickory, pecan,* and a host of other names were taken directly into English; others were adopted secondhand from Spanish variants of South American native words: *cigar, potato, chocolate, tomato, tobacco, hammock.*

A worldwide diffusion of the language resulted as English colonists carried it to the Western Hemisphere and Australasia and as trade, conquest, and territorial claim took it to Africa and Asia. In that areal spread, English was further enriched by its contacts with other languages. By becoming the accepted language of commerce and science, it contributed in turn to the common vocabularies of other tongues. Within some 400 years, English has developed from a localized language of 7 million islanders off the European coast to a truly international language with some 400 million native speakers, perhaps 600 million who use it as a second, sometimes nationally official lauguage, and additional millions who have reasonable competence in English as a foreign language. English serves as an official language of some 60 countries (Figure 7.21), far exceeding in that role French (32), Arabic (25), or Spanish (21), the other leading current international languages. English has become the dominant language facilitating increased global interaction. It is used in many international scientific

FIGURE 7.19 *World language families.*
Language families are groups of individual tongues that have a common but remote ancestor. By suggesting that the area assigned to a language or language family uses that language exclusively, the map pattern conceals important linguistic detail. Many countries and regions have local languages spoken in territories too small to be recorded at this scale. The map also fails to report that the population in many regions is fluent in more than one language, or that a second language serves as the necessary vehicle of commerce, education, or government. Nor is important information given about the number of speakers of different languages; the fact that there are more speakers of English in India or Africa than in Australia is not even hinted at by a map at this scale.

Language Families

1 Indo-European
   a. Romance b. Germanic c. Slavic
   d. Baltic e. Celtic f. Albanian g. Greek
   h. Armenian k. Indo-Iranian
2 Uralic-Altaic
3 Sino-Tibetan
4 Japanese-Korean
5 Dravidian
6 Afro-Asiatic
7 Niger-Congo
8 Sudanic
9 Saharan
10 Khoisan
11 Paleo-Asiatic
12 Austro-Asiatic
13 Malayo-Polynesian
14 Australian
15 Amerindian
   Other
   16. Eskimo-Aleut 17. Papuan 18. Caucasian
   19. Basque 20. Vietnamese
16 Unpopulated

conferences, air traffic control, and international diplomacy. In the 1990s, English web pages dominated the Internet, although that dominance is declining as other major languages gain ground.

Standard and Variant Languages

People who speak a common language, such as English, are members of a *speech community*, but membership does not necessarily imply linguistic uniformity. A speech community usually possesses both a **standard language** comprising the accepted community norms of syntax, vocabulary, and pronunciation and a number of more or less distinctive **dialects,** the ordinary speech of areal, social, professional, or other subdivisions of the general population.

An official or unofficial standard language is the form carrying governmental, educational, or societal sanction. In Arab countries, for example, classical Arabic is the language of the mosque, of education, and of the newspapers and is standardized throughout the Arabic-speaking world. Colloquial Arabic is used at home, in the street, and at the market—and in its regional variants, it may be as widely different as are, for example, Portuguese and Italian. On the other hand, the United States, English-speaking Canada, Australia, and the United Kingdom all have only slightly different forms of standard English.

Just as no two individuals talk exactly the same, all but the smallest and most closely knit speech communities display recognizable speech variants called dialects. Vocabulary, pronunciation, rhythm, and the speed at which the language

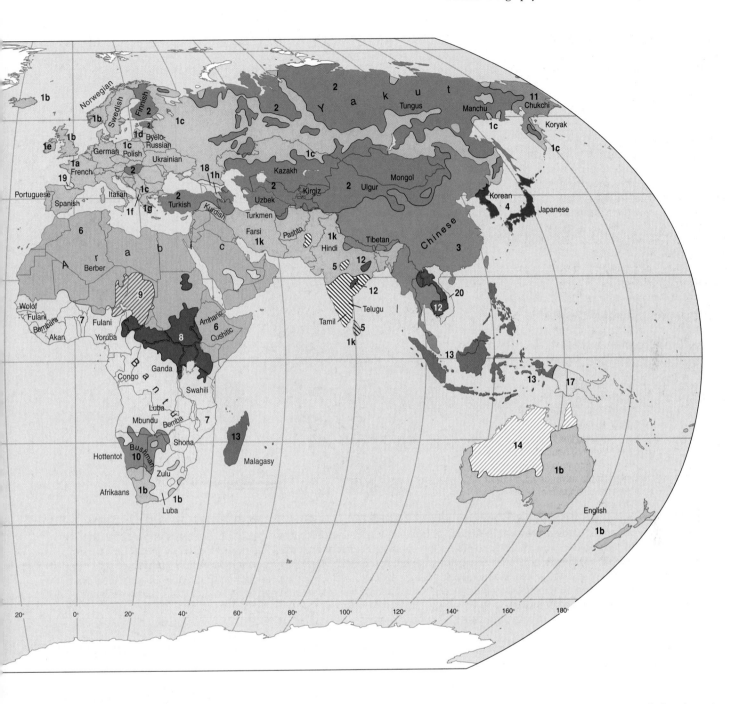

is spoken may clearly set groups of speakers apart from one another. Most dialects exhibit clear spatial patterns. Speech is a geographic variable. Each locale is likely to have its own, perhaps slight language differences from neighboring places. Such differences in pronunciation, vocabulary, word meanings, and other language characteristics help define the *linguistic geography*—the study of the character and spatial pattern of *geographic*, or *regional*, *dialects*—of a generalized speech community. Figure 7.22 records the variation in usage associated with just one phrase. In the United States, Southern English and New England speech are among the regional dialects that are most easily recognized by their distinctive accents. In some instances, there is so much variation among geographic dialects that some are almost foreign tongues to other speakers

of the same language. Effort is required for Americans to understand Australian English or that spoken in Liverpool, England, or in Glasgow, Scotland (see "World Englishes," p. 222). An interesting United States example is discussed in the regional study "Gullah as Language," in Chapter 13.

Local dialects and accents do not display predictable patterns of consistency or change. In the ethnically and regionally complex United States, for example, mixed conclusions concerning local speech patterns have been drawn by researchers examining the linguistic results of an increasingly transient population, immigration from other countries and cultures, and the pervasive and presumed leveling effects of the mass media. The distinct evidence of increasing contrasts among the speech patterns and accents of Chicago, New York,

FIGURE 7.20 Bantu advance, Khoisan retreat in Africa. Linguistic evidence suggests that proto-*Bantu* speakers originated in the region of the Cameroon-Nigeria border, spread eastward across the southern Sudan, then turned southward to Central Africa. From there they dispersed slowly eastward, westward, and, against slight resistance, southward. The earlier *Khoisan*-speaking occupants of sub-Saharan Africa were no match against the advancing metal-using Bantu agriculturalists. Pygmies, adopting a Bantu tongue, retreated deep into the forests. Bushmen and Hottentots retained their distinctive Khoisan "click" language but were forced out of forest and grasslands into the dry steppes and deserts of the southwest.

Birmingham, St. Louis, and other cities is countered by reports of decreasing local dialect pronunciations in such centers as Dallas and Atlanta, which have experienced major influxes of northerners.

Language is rarely a total barrier to communication between peoples. Bilingualism or multilingualism may permit skilled linguists to communicate in a jointly understood third language, but long-term contact between less-able populations may require the creation of a new language—a pidgin—learned by both parties. A **pidgin** is an amalgam of languages, usually a simplified form of one of them, such as English or French, with borrowings from another, perhaps non-European local language. In its original form, a pidgin is not the mother tongue of any of its speakers; it is a second language for everyone who uses it, one generally restricted to such specific functions as commerce, administration, and work supervision.

Pidgins are characterized by a highly simplified grammatical structure and a sharply reduced vocabulary adequate to express basic ideas but not complex concepts. If a pidgin becomes the first language of a group of speakers—who may have lost their former native tongue through disuse—a **creole** has evolved. Creoles invariably acquire a more complex grammatical structure and enhanced vocabulary.

Creole languages have proved to be useful integrative tools in linguistically diverse areas; several have become symbols of nationhood. Swahili, a pidgin formed from a number of Bantu dialects with major vocabulary additions from Arabic, originated in the coastal areas of East Africa and spread inland first by Arab ivory and slave caravans and later by trade during the period of English and German colonial rules. When Kenya and Tanzania gained independence, they made Swahili the national language of administration and education. Other examples of creolization are Afrikaans (a pidginized form of 17th-century Dutch used in the Republic of South Africa); Haitian Creole (the language of Haiti, derived from the pidginized French used in the slave

Folk and Popular Culture

Not all culture groups, even in "developed" societies, readily adopt or adjust to cultural change. In general understanding, *culture* is taken to mean "our way of life"—how we act (and why), what we eat and wear, how we amuse ourselves, what we believe, whom we admire. There are distinctions to be made, however, on the universality of the "way of life" that is accepted.

Folk groups exist in either spatial or self-imposed social isolation from the common culture of the larger societies of which they are presumably a part. **Folk culture** connotes the traditional and nonfaddish way of life characteristic of a homogeneous, cohesive, largely self-sufficient group that is essentially isolated from or resistant to outside influences. Tradition controls folk culture, and resistance to change is strong. The homemade and handmade dominate in tools, food, music, story, and ritual. *Folk life* is a cultural whole composed of both tangible and intangible elements. **Material culture** is the tangible part, made up of physical, visible things: everything from musical instruments to furniture, tools, and buildings. In folk societies, these things are products of the household or community itself, not of commercial mass production. Their intangible **nonmaterial culture** comprises the mentifacts and sociofacts expressed in oral tradition, folk song and folk story, and customary behavior; ways of speech, patterns of worship, outlooks and philosophies are passed to following generations by teachings and examples.

Within Anglo America, true folk groups are few and dwindling. Their earlier, larger numbers were based on the customs and beliefs brought to the New World by immigrant groups distinguished by their different languages, religious beliefs, and areas of origin. With time, many of their imported ethnic characteristics became transmuted into American "folk" features. For example, the traditional songs of western Virginia can be considered both nonmaterial folk expressions of the Upland South and evidence of an immigrant ethnic heritage derived from rural English forebears.

In that respect, each of us bears the evidence of ethnic origin and folk life. Each of us uses proverbs traditional to our family or culture; each is familiar with childhood nursery rhymes and fables. We rap wood for luck, have heard how to plant a garden by phases of the moon, and know what is the "right" way to celebrate a holiday or prepare a favorite dish. For most, however, such evidences of folk culture are minor elements in our life, and only a few groups—such as the Old Order Amish, with their rejection of electricity, the internal combustion engine, and other "worldly" accouterments in favor of buggy, hand tools, and traditional dress—remain in the United States as reminders of the folk cultural distinctions formerly widely recognizable. Canada, on the other hand, has retained a greater number of clearly recognizable ethnically unique folk and decorative arts traditions.

Popular culture stands in opposition—and as the replacement for—folk culture. *Popular* implies the general mass of people, not the small-group distinctiveness and individuality of folk culture. It suggests a process of constantly adopting, conforming to, and quickly abandoning ever-changing fads and common modes of behavior. In that process, locally distinctive lifestyles and material and nonmaterial folk culture traits are largely replaced and lost; uniformity is substituted for variety, and small-group identity is eroded. For most of us, it is a sought-after uniformity. In the 1750s, George Washington wrote to his British agent to request ". . . two pair of Work'd Ruffles . . . ; if work'd Ruffles shou'd be out of fashion send such as are not . . ." and "whatever goods you may send me . . . you will let them be fashionable." His desire, echoed today, was to fit in with the peer group and larger social milieu of which he was a part.

Popular culture may be seen as both a leveling and a liberating force. On the one hand, it obliterates those locally distinctive folk culture lifestyles that emerge when groups remain isolated and self-sufficient. At the same time, however, individuals are exposed to a broader range of available opportunities—in clothing, foods, tools, recreations, and lifestyles—than ever are available to them in a cultural environment controlled by the restrictive and limited choices imposed by custom and isolation. Broad areal uniformity—in the form of the repetitive content of national discount stores, duplicate retailers in identical shopping malls, or the same fast-food chains—may displace folk cultural localisms. While the diffusion of popular culture opens an immense and ever-changing range of possibilities, it undermines traditional folk practices, as well as social and religious values that are not always fully appreciated until they are lost.

trade); and Bazaar Malay (a pidginized form of the Malay language, a version of which is the official national language of Indonesia).

A **lingua franca** is an established language used habitually for communication by people whose native tongues are mutually incomprehensible. For them, it is a *second language,* one learned in addition to the native tongue. Lingua franca (literally, "Frankish tongue") was named from the French dialect adopted as a common language by the Crusaders at war in the Holy Land. Later, Latin became the lingua franca of the Mediterranean world until, finally, it was displaced by vernacular European tongues. Arabic followed Muslim conquest as the unifying language of that international religion after the 7th century. Mandarin Chinese and Hindi in India have traditionally had a lingua franca role in their linguistically diverse countries. The immense linguistic complexity of Africa has made regional lingua francas there necessary and inevitable—Swahili in East Africa, for example, and Hausa in parts of West Africa.

Language and Culture

Language embodies the culture complex of a people, reflecting both environment and technology. Arabic has 80 words related to camels, an animal on which a regional culture relied for food, transport, and labor, and Japanese contains more than 20 words

World Englishes

Non-native speakers of English far outnumber those for whom English is the first language. Most of the more than 1 billion people who speak and understand at least some English as a second language live in Asia; they are appropriating the language and remaking it in regionally distinctive fashions to suit their own cultures, linguistic backgrounds, and needs.

It is inevitable that widely spoken languages separated by distance, isolation, and cultural differences will fragment into dialects, which in turn evolve into new languages. Latin splintered into French, Spanish, Italian, and other Romance languages; the many national variants of spoken Arabic are effectively different tongues. English is similarly experiencing that sort of regional differentiation, shaped by the variant needs and inputs of its far-flung community of speakers and following the same path to mutual unintelligibility. Although standard English may be one of or the sole official language of their countries of birth, millions of people around the world claiming proficiency in English or English as their national language cannot understand each other. Even teachers of English from India, Malaya, Nigeria, or the Philippines, for example, may not be able to communicate in their supposedly common tongue—and find cockney English of London utterly alien.

The splintering of spoken English is a fact of linguistic life, and its offspring—called "World Englishes" by linguists—defy frequent attempts by various governments to remove localisms and encourage adherence to international standards. Singlish (Singapore English) and Taglish (a mixture of English and Tagalog, the dominant language of the Philippines) are commonly cited examples of the multiplying World Englishes but equally distinctive regional variants have emerged in India, Malaysia, Hong Kong, Nigeria, the Caribbean, and elsewhere. One linguist suggests that, beyond an "inner circle" of countries where English is the first and native language—e.g., Canada, Australia, the United States—lies an "outer circle" where English is a second language (Bangladesh, Ghana, India, Kenya, Pakistan, Zambia, and many others) and where the regionally distinctive World Englishes are most obviously developing. Even farther out is an "expanding circle" of such as China, Egypt, Korea, Nepal, and Saudi Arabia where English is a foreign language and distinctive local variants in common usage have not yet developed.

Although the constant modern world electronic and literary interaction between the variant regional Englishes make it likely that the common language will remain universally intelligible, it also seems probable that mutually incomprehensible forms of English will become entrenched as the language is taught, learned, and used in world areas far removed from contact with first-language users. "Our only revenge," said a French official deploring the declining role of French within the European Union, "is that the English language is being killed by all these foreigners speaking it so badly."

---

meaning "the long river," was recorded by Lewis and Clark as "Quisconsing," later to be further distorted into "Wisconsin." Milwaukee, Winnipeg, Potomac, Niagara, Adirondack, Chesapeake, Shenandoah, and Yukon; the names of 28 of the 50 United States; and the present identity of thousands of North American places and features, large and small, had their origin in Native American languages.

RELIGION

Enduring place-names are one measure of the importance of language as a powerful, unifying thread in the culture complex of people. But language is not alone in that role. In some ways, it yields to religion as a cultural rallying point. French Catholics slaughtered French Huguenots (Protestants) in the name of religion in the 16th century. English Roman Catholics were hounded from the country after the establishment of the Anglican church. Religious enmity between Muslims and Hindus forced the partition of the Indian subcontinent after the departure of the British in 1947. And recent years have witnessed continuing religious confrontations between, for example, Catholic and Protestant Christian groups in Northern Ireland; Muslim sects in Lebanon, Iran, and Iraq; Muslims and Jews in Palestine; Christians and Muslims in the Balkans, the Philippines, Nigeria, and Lebanon; and Buddhists and Hindus in Sri Lanka.

However, unlike language, which is an attribute of all people, religion varies in its cultural role—dominating in some societies, unimportant, rejected, or even repressed in others. All societies have value systems—common beliefs, understandings, expectations, and controls—that unite their members and set them off from other, different culture groups. Such a value system is termed a *religion* when it involves systems of formal or informal worship of and faith in the sacred and divine. In a more inclusive sense, religion may be viewed as a unified system of beliefs and practices that join all those who adhere to them into a single moral community.

Religion may intimately affect all facets of a culture. Religious belief is, by definition, an element of the ideological subsystem; formalized and organized religion is an institutional expression of the sociological subsystem. And religious beliefs strongly influence attitudes toward the tools and rewards of the technological subsystem.

Nonreligious value systems—humanism or Marxism, for example—can be just as binding on the societies that espouse them as are more traditional religious beliefs. Even societies that largely reject religion, however, are strongly influenced by traditional values and customs set by predecessor religions—in days of work and rest or in legal principles, for example.

Because religions are formalized views on questions of ultimate significance, each carries a distinct conception of the meaning and value of this life, and most contain strictures

FIGURE 7.24 Worshipers gathered during *hajj,* the pilgrimage to Mecca. The black structure is the Ka'ba, the symbol of Allah's (God's) oneness and of the unity of God and humans. Many rules concerning daily life are given in the Koran, the holy book of the Muslims. All Muslims are expected to observe the five pillars of the faith: (1) repeated saying of the basic creed; (2) prayers five times daily, facing Mecca; (3) a month of daytime fasting (Ramadan); (4) almsgiving; and (5) if possible, a pilgrimage to Mecca. © *Topham/*The Observer/*Image Works.*

about what must be done to achieve salvation (Figure 7.24). These beliefs become interwoven with the traditions of a culture. One cannot understand India without a knowledge of Hinduism, or Israel without an appreciation of Judaism.

Economic patterns may be intertwined with past or present religious beliefs. Traditional restrictions on food and drink may affect the kinds of animals that are raised or avoided, the crops that are grown, and the importance of those crops in the daily diet. Occupational assignment in the Hindu caste system is, in part, religiously supported. In many countries, there is a state religion; that is, religious and political structures are intertwined. Buddhism, for example, has been the state religion in Myanmar, Laos, and Thailand. By their official names, the Islamic Republic of Pakistan and the Islamic Republic of Iran proclaim their identity of church and government. Despite the country's overwhelming Muslim majority, Indonesia sought and formerly found domestic harmony by recognizing five official religions and a state ideology—*pancasila*—whose first tenet is belief in one god.

Classification and Distribution of Religions

Religions are cultural innovations. They may be unique to a single culture group, closely related to the faiths professed in nearby areas, or derived from or identical to belief systems spatially far removed. Although interconnections and derivations among religions can frequently be discerned—as Christianity and Islam can trace descent from Judaism—family groupings are not as useful in classifying religions as they are in studying languages. A distinction between *monotheism,* belief in a single deity, and *polytheism,* belief in many gods, is frequent but not particularly spatially relevant. It is more useful for the spatial interests of geographers to categorize religions as *universalizing, ethnic,* or *tribal (traditional).*

Christianity, Islam, and Buddhism are the major world **universalizing religions,** faiths that claim applicability to all humans and that seek to transmit their beliefs to all lands through missionary work and conversion. Membership in

GEOGRAPHY & *Public Policy*

An Official U.S. Language?

Within recent years in Lowell, Massachusetts, public school courses were offered in Spanish, Khmer, Lao, Portuguese, and Vietnamese, and all messages from schools to parents were translated into five languages. Polyglot New York City gave bilingual programs in Spanish, Chinese, Haitian Creole, Russian, Korean, Vietnamese, French, Greek, Arabic, and Bengali. In most states, it is possible to get a high school equivalency diploma without knowing English, because tests are offered in French and Spanish. In at least 39 states, driving tests are available in foreign languages; California provides 30 varieties, New York 23, and Michigan 20, including Arabic and Finnish. And as required by the 1965 federal Voting Rights Act, multilingual ballots are provided in some 300 electoral jurisdictions in 30 states.

These, and innumerable other evidences of governmentally sanctioned linguistic diversity, may come as a surprise to the many Americans who assume that English is the official language of the United States. It isn't; nowhere does the Constitution provide for an official language, and no federal law specifies one. The country was built by a great diversity of cultural and linguistic immigrants, who nonetheless shared an eagerness to enter mainstream American life. At the start of the 21st century, a reported 18% of all American residents spoke a language other than English in the home. In California public schools, one out of three students uses a non-English tongue within the family. The 21,000 students in Fairfax County, Virginia, schools speak more than 140 different languages, a linguistic diversity duplicated in many major city school systems.

Nationwide bilingual teaching began as an offshoot of the civil rights movement in the 1960s, was encouraged by a Supreme Court opinion authored by Justice William O. Douglas, and has been actively promoted by the U.S. Department of Education under the Bilingual Education Act of 1974 as an obligation of local school boards. Its purpose has been to teach subject matter to minority-language children in the language in which they think while introducing them to English, with the hope of achieving English proficiency in 2 or 3 years. Disappointment with the results led to a successful 1998 California anti-bilingual education initiative, Proposition 227, to abolish the program. Similar rejection elsewhere—Arizona in 2000 and Massachusetts in 2003, for example—has followed California's lead.

Opponents of the implications of governmentally encouraged multilingual education, bilingual ballots, and ethnic separatism argue that a common language is the unifying glue of the United States and all countries; without that glue, they fear, the process of "Americanization" and acculturation—the adoption by immigrants of the values, attitudes, behavior, and speech of the receiving society—will be undermined. Convinced that early immersion and quick proficiency in English are the only sure ways for minority newcomers to gain necessary access to jobs, higher education, and full integration into the economic and social life of the country, proponents of "English only" use in public education, voting, and state and local governmental agencies successfully passed Official English laws and constitutional amendments in 28 states.

---

universalizing religions is open to anyone who chooses to make a symbolic commitment, such as baptism in Christianity. No one is excluded because of nationality, ethnicity, or previous religious belief.

Ethnic religions have strong territorial and cultural group identification. One usually becomes a member of an ethnic religion by birth or by adoption of a complex lifestyle and cultural identity, not by a simple declaration of faith. These religions do not usually proselytize (attempt to convert nonbelievers), and their members form distinctive closed communities identified with a particular ethnic group, region, or political unit. An ethnic religion—for example, Judaism, Indian Hinduism, or Japanese Shinto—is an integral element of a specific culture. To be part of the religion is to be immersed in the totality of the culture.

Tribal (or *traditional*) **religions** are special forms of ethnic religions distinguished by their small size, their unique identity with localized culture groups not yet fully absorbed into modern society, and their close ties to nature. *Animism* is the

name given to their belief that life exists in all objects, from rocks and trees to lakes and mountains, or that such objects are the abode of the dead, of spirits, and of gods. *Shamanism* is a form of tribal religion that involves community acceptance of a *shaman* who, through special powers, can intercede with and interpret the spirit world.

The nature of the different classes of religions is reflected in their distributions over the world (Figure 7.25) and in their number of adherents. Universalizing religions tend to be expansionary, carrying their message to new peoples and areas. Ethnic religions, unless their adherents are dispersed, tend to be regionally confined or to expand only slowly and over long periods. Tribal religions tend to contract spatially as their adherents are incorporated increasingly into modern society and converted by proselytizing faiths.

As we expect in cultural geography, the map records only the latest stage of a constantly changing reality. While established religious institutions tend to be conservative and

© The McGraw-Hill Companies Inc./Mark Dierker, photographer.

Although the amendments were supported by sizeable majorities of the voting population, resistance to them—and to their political and cultural implications—was, in every instance, strong and persistent. Ethnic groups—particularly Hispanics, who are the largest of the linguistic groups affected—charged that they were evidence of blatant Anglocentric racism, discriminatory and repressive in all regards. Some educators argued persuasively that all evidence proved that, although immigrant children eventually acquire English proficiency in any event, they do so with less harm to their self-esteem and subject-matter acquisition when initially taught in their own language. Businesspeople with strong minority labor and customer ties and political leaders—many themselves members of ethnic communities or with sizeable minority constituencies—argued against "discriminatory" language restrictions.

And historians noted that it had all been tried unsuccessfully before. The anti-Chinese Workingmen's Party in 1870s California led the fight for English-only laws in that state. The influx of immigrants from central and southeastern Europe at the turn of the 20th century led Congress to make oral English a requirement for naturalization, and anti-German sentiment during and after World War I led some states to ban any use of German. The Supreme Court struck down those laws in 1923, ruling that the "protection of the Constitution extends to all, to those who speak other languages as well as to those born with English on their tongue." Following suit, some of the recent state language amendments have also been voided by state courts. In ruling its state's English-only law unconstitutional, Arizona's Supreme Court in 1998 noted it "chills First Amendment rights."

To counter those judicial restraints and the possibility of an eventual multilingual, multicultural United States in which English and, likely, Spanish would have coequal status and recognition, U.S. English—an organization dedicated to the belief that "English is, and ever must remain, the only official language of the people of the United States"—actively supports legislation that would make English the official language of the U.S. government. The proposed legislation would simply establish English as the official national language but would impose no duty on people to learn English and would not infringe upon any right to use other languages. Whether or not these modern attempts to designate an official U.S. language eventually succeed, they represent a divisive subject of public debate affecting all sectors of American society.

Considering the Issues

1. Do you think that multiple languages and ethnic separatism represent a threat to America's cultural unity that can be avoided only by viewing English as a necessary unifying force? Or do you think making English the official language might divide its citizens and damage its legacy of tolerance and diversity?

2. Do you believe that immigrant children would learn English faster if bilingual classes were reduced and immersion in English were more complete? Or do you think that a slower pace of English acquisition is acceptable if subject-matter comprehension and cultural self-esteem are enhanced?

3. Do you think Official English laws inflame prejudice against immigrants or provide all newcomers with a common standard of admission to the country's political and cultural mainstream?

resistant to change, religion as a culture trait is dynamic. Personal and collective beliefs may alter in response to developing individual and societal needs and challenges. Religions may be imposed by conquest, adopted by conversion, or defended and preserved in the face of surrounding hostility or indifference.

Nor does the map present a full picture even of current religious regionalization or affiliation. Few societies are homogeneous, and most modern ones contain a variety of faiths or, at least, variants of the dominant professed religion. Some of those variants in many religions are intolerant or antagonistic toward other faiths or toward the sects and members of their own faith deemed insufficiently committed or orthodox (see "Militant Fundamentalism," p. 229).

Frequently, members of a particular religion show areal concentration within a country. Thus, in urban Northern Ireland, Protestants and Catholics reside in separate areas whose boundaries are clearly understood and respected. The "Green Line" in Beirut, Lebanon, marked a guarded border between the Christian east and the Muslim west sides of the city, whereas, within the country as a whole, regional concentrations of adherents of different faiths and sects are clearly recognized (Figure 7.26). Religious diversity within countries may reflect the degree of toleration a majority culture affords minority religions. In dominantly (55% to 88%, depending on the definition) Muslim Indonesia, Christian Bataks, Hindu Balinese, and Muslim Javanese lived in peaceful coexistence for many years. By contrast, the fundamentalist Islamic regime in Iran has persecuted and executed those of the Baha'i faith.

One cannot assume that all people within a mapped religious region are adherents of the designated faith, nor can it be assumed that membership in a religious community means active participation in its belief system. *Secularism,* an indifference to or rejection of religion and religious belief, is an increasing part of many modern societies, particularly of the

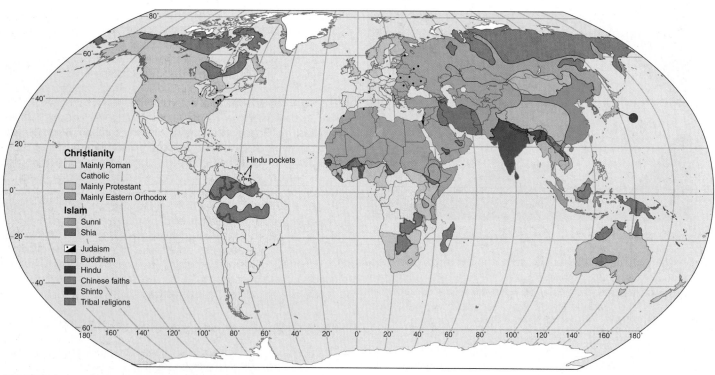

FIGURE 7.25 Principal world religions. The assignment of individual countries to a single religion category conceals a growing intermixture of faiths in countries that have experienced major immigration flows or religious change. In some instances, those influxes are altering the effective, if not the numerical, religious balance. In nominally Christian, Catholic France, for example, low church-going rates suggest that now more Muslims than practicing Catholics reside there and, considering birth rate differentials, that someday Islam may be the country's predominant religion as measured by the number of practicing adherents. Secularism—rejection of religious belief—is common in many countries but is not locationally indicated on this map. Areas of sub-Saharan Africa labeled Christian are intermixed with tribal religions they have displaced.

industrialized countries and those now or recently under communist regimes. In England, for example, the state Church of England claims 20% of the British as communicants, but only 2% of the population attends its Sunday services. Even in devoutly Roman Catholic South American states, low church attendance attests to the rise of at least informal secularism. In Colombia, only 18% of the people attend Sunday services; in Chile, the figure is 12%; in Mexico, 11%; and in Bolivia, 5%.

The Principal Religions

Each of the major religions has its own unique mix of cultural values and expressions, each has had its own pattern of innovation and spatial diffusion (Figure 7.27), and each has had its own impact on the cultural landscape. Together, they contribute importantly to the worldwide pattern of human diversity.

Judaism

We can begin our review of world faiths with *Judaism,* whose belief in a single God laid the foundation for both Christianity and Islam. Unlike its universalizing offspring, Judaism is closely identified with a single ethnic group and with a complex and restrictive set of beliefs and laws. It emerged some 3000 to 3500 years ago in the Near East, one of the ancient culture hearth regions (see Figure 7.13).

Judaism is a distinctively *ethnic* religion, the determining factors of which are descent from Israel (the patriarch Jacob), the Torah (law and scripture), and the traditions of the culture and the faith. Early military success gave the Jews a sense of territorial and political identity to supplement their religious self-awareness. Later conquests by nonbelievers led to their dispersion (*diaspora*) to much of the Mediterranean world and farther east into Asia by A.D. 500 (Figure 7.28).

During the 13th and 14th centuries, many Jews sought refuge in Poland and Russia from persecution in western and central Europe; during the later 19th and early 20th centuries, Jews were important elements of the European immigrant stream to the Western Hemisphere. The mass destruction of Jews in Europe before and during World War II—the Holocaust—drastically reduced their presence on that continent. The establishment of the state of Israel in 1948 was a fulfillment of the goal of *Zionism,* the belief in the need to create an autonomous Jewish state in Palestine. It demonstrated a determination that Jews not lose their identity by absorption into alien cultures and societies. It also spatially united two earlier, separated Jewish communities: the Sephardim, who were expelled from Iberia in the late 15th century, fleeing initially to North

Africa and the Near East, and the Ashkenazim, who, between the 13th and 16th centuries, sought refuge in Eastern Europe from persecutions in Western and Central Europe.

Judaism's imprint upon the cultural landscape has been subtle and unobtrusive. The Jewish community reserves space for the practice of communal burial; the spread of the cultivated citron in the Mediterranean area during Roman times has been traced to Jewish ritual needs; and the religious use of grape wine assured the cultivation of the vine in their areas of settlement. The synagogue as place of worship has tended to be less elaborate or architecturally distinctive than those of other major world religions. Synagogues feature an ark (cabinet) containing the Torah scrolls and generally face Jerusalem. However, what is essential for a religious service is merely the presence of at least 10 adults, not a specific structure.

Christianity

Christianity had its origin in the life and teachings of Jesus, a Jewish preacher of the 1st century of the common era, whom his followers believed was the messiah promised by God. The new covenant he preached was not a rejection of traditional Judaism but a promise of salvation to all humankind, rather than to just a chosen people.

Christianity's mission was conversion, and missionary work was critical in its diffusion. As a universal religion of salvation and hope, it spread quickly among the underclasses of both the eastern and western parts of the Roman Empire,

FIGURE 7.26 Religious regions of Lebanon. Long-standing religious territoriality and rivalry led, in the 1960s and 1970s, to open conflict between Muslims and Christians and among various branches of each major faith in this eastern Mediterranean country.

FIGURE 7.27 Innovation areas and diffusion routes of major world religions. The monotheistic (single deity) faiths of Judaism, Christianity, and Islam arose in southwestern Asia, the first two in Palestine in the eastern Mediterranean region, and the latter in western Arabia near the Red Sea. Hinduism and Buddhism originated within a confined hearth region in the northern part of the Indian subcontinent. Their rates, extent, and directions of spread are suggested here and detailed on later maps.

FIGURE 7.28 Jewish dispersions, A.D. 70–1500. A revolt against Roman rule in A.D. 66 was followed by the destruction of the Jewish Temple 4 years later and an Imperial decision to Romanize the city of Jerusalem. Judaism spread from the hearth region, carried by its adherents dispersing from their homeland to Europe, Africa, and eventually in great numbers to the Western Hemisphere. Although Jews established themselves and their religion in new lands, they did not lose their sense of cultural identity nor did they seek to attract converts to their faith.

carried to major cities and ports along the excellent system of Roman roads and sea lanes (Figure 7.29). In A.D. 313, Emperor Constantine proclaimed Christianity the state religion. Much later, of course, the faith was brought to the New World with European settlement (see Figure 7.27).

The dissolution of the Roman Empire into a western and eastern half after the fall of Rome also divided Christianity. The Western Church, based in Rome, was one of the very few stabilizing and civilizing forces uniting Western Europe during the Dark Ages. Its bishops became the civil as well as ecclesiastical authorities over vast areas devoid of other effective government. Parish churches were the focus of rural and urban life, and the cathedrals replaced Roman monuments and temples as the symbols of the social order.

Secular imperial control endured in the Eastern Empire, whose capital was Constantinople (now known as Istanbul). Thriving under its protection, the Eastern Church expanded into the Balkans, Eastern Europe, Russia, and the Near East. The fall of the Eastern Empire to the Turks in the 15th century opened Eastern Europe temporarily to Islam, though the Eastern Orthodox Church (the direct descendant of the state church of the Eastern Roman Empire) remains, in its various ethnic branches, a major component of Christianity.

The Protestant Reformation of the 15th and 16th centuries split the church in the west, leaving Roman Catholicism supreme in Southern Europe but installing a variety of Protestant denominations and national churches in Western and Northern Europe. The split was reflected in the subsequent

Militant Fundamentalism

The term *fundamentalism* entered the social science vocabulary in the late 20th century to describe any religious orthodoxy that is revivalist and ultraconservative. Originally, it designated an American Christian movement named after a set of volumes—*The Fundamentals: A Testimony of the Truth*—published between 1910 and 1915 and embracing both absolute religious orthodoxy and a commitment to inject its beliefs into the political and social arenas. More recently, fundamentalism has become a generic description for all religious movements that seek to regain and publicly institutionalize traditional social and cultural values that are usually rooted in the teachings of a sacred text or written dogma.

Springing from rejection of the secularist tendencies of modernity, fundamentalism is now found in every dominant religion wherever a Western-style society has developed, including Islam, Christianity, Hinduism, Judaism, Sikhism, Buddhism, Confucianism, and Zoroastrianism. Fundamentalism is, therefore, a reaction to the modern world; it represents an effort to draw upon a "golden age" religious tradition in order to cope with and counteract an already changing society that is denounced as trying to erase the true faith and traditional religious values. The near-universality of fundamentalist movements is seen by some as another expression of a widespread rebellion against the presumed evils fostered by secular globalization.

Fundamentalists always place a high priority on doctrinal conformity and its necessity for achieving salvation. Further, they are convinced of the unarguable correctness of their beliefs and the necessity of the unquestioned acceptance of those beliefs by the general society. Since the truth is knowable and indisputable, fundamentalists hold, there is no need to discuss it or argue it in open forum. To some observers, therefore, fundamentalism is, by its nature, undemocratic and states controlled by fundamentalist regimes combining politics and religion of necessity stifle debate and punish dissent. In the modern world, that rigidity seems most apparent in Islam where, it is claimed, "all Muslims believe in the absolute inerrancy of the Quran . . ." (*The Islamic Herald,* April 1995) and several countries—for example, the Islamic Republic of Iran and the Islamic Republic of Pakistan—proclaim by official name their administrative commitment to religious control.

In most of the modern world, however, such commitment is not overt or official, and fundamentalists often believe that they and their religious convictions are under mortal threat. They view modern secular society—with its assumption of equality of competing voices and values—as trying to eradicate the true faith and religious verities. Initially, therefore, every fundamentalist movement begins as an intrareligious struggle directed against its own coreligionists and countrymen in response to a felt assault by the liberal or secular society they inhabit. At first, the group may blame its own weakness and irresolution for the oppression they feel and the general social decay they perceive. To restore society to its idealized standards, the aroused group may exhort its followers to ardent prayer, ascetic practices, and physical or military training.

If it is unable to impose its beliefs on others peacefully, the fundamentalist group—seeing itself as the savior of society—may justify other, more extreme actions against perceived oppressors. Initial protests and nonviolent actions may escalate to attacks on corrupt public figures thwarting their vision and to outright domestic guerrilla warfare. That escalation is advanced and gains willing supporters when inflexible fundamentalism is combined with the unending poverty and political impotence felt in many, particularly Middle Eastern, societies today. When an external culture or power—commonly, a demonized United States—is seen as the unquestioned source of the pollution and exploitation frustrating their social vision, some fundamentalists have been able to justify any extreme action and personal sacrifice for their cause. In their struggle, it appears an easy progression from domestic dispute and disruption to international terrorism.

---

worldwide dispersion of Christianity. Catholic Spain and Portugal colonized Latin America, taking both their languages and the Roman Church to that area (see Figure 7.27), as they did to colonial outposts in the Philippines, India, and Africa. Catholic France colonized Quebec in North America. Protestants, many of them fleeing Catholic or repressive Protestant state churches, were primary early settlers of Anglo America, Australia, New Zealand, Oceania, and South Africa.

Although religious intermingling rather than rigid territorial division is characteristic of the contemporary American scene (Figure 7.30), the beliefs and practices of various immigrant groups and the innovations of domestic congregations have created a particularly varied spatial patterning of "religious regions" in the United States (Figure 7.31).

The mark of Christianity on the cultural landscape has been conspicuous and enduring. In pre-Reformation Catholic Europe, the parish church formed the center of life for small neighborhoods of every town, the village church was the centerpiece of every rural community, and in larger cities the central cathedral served simultaneously as a glorification of God, a symbol of piety, and the focus of religious and secular life (Figure 7.32a).

Protestantism placed less importance on the church as a monument and symbol, although in many communities—colonial New England, for example—the churches of the principal denominations were at the village center (Figure 7.32b). Many were adjoined by a cemetery, because Christians—in common with Muslims and Jews—practice burial in areas reserved for the dead. In Christian countries, particularly, the cemetery—whether connected to the church, separate from it, or unrelated to a specific denomination—has traditionally been a significant land use within urban areas.

Islam

Islam springs from the same Judaic roots as Christianity and embodies many of the same beliefs: there is only one God, who can be revealed to humans through prophets; Adam

FIGURE 7.29 Diffusion paths of Christianity, A.D. 100–1500. Routes and dates are for Christianity as a composite faith. No distinction is made between the Western Church and the various subdivisions of the Eastern Orthodox denominations.

FIGURE 7.30 Advertised evidence of religious diversity in the United States. The sign details only a few Christian congregations. In reality, the United States has become the most religiously diverse country in the world with essentially all of the world's faiths represented within its borders. Welcoming signs for other, particularly larger, towns might also announce Muslim, Hindu, Buddhist, and many other congregations in their varied religious mix. *Photo courtesy of Susan Reisenweaver.*

was the first human; Abraham was one of his descendants. Mohammed is revered as the prophet of *Allah* (God), succeeding and completing the work of earlier prophets of Judaism and Christianity, including Moses, David, and Jesus. The Koran, the word of Allah revealed to Mohammed, contains not only rules of worship and details of doctrine but also instructions on the conduct of human affairs. For fundamentalists, it thus becomes the unquestioned guide to matters both religious and secular. Observance of the "five pillars" (see Figure 7.24) and surrender to the will of Allah unites the faithful into a community that has no concern with race, color, or caste.

It was that law of community that unified an Arab world sorely divided by tribes, social ranks, and multiple local deities. Mohammed was a resident of Mecca but fled in A.D. 622 to Medina, where the Prophet proclaimed a constitution and announced the universal mission of the Islamic community. That flight—*Hegira*—marks the starting point of the Islamic (lunar) calendar. By the time of Mohammed's death in A.H. 11 (*Anno*—in the year of—*Hegira*, or A.D. 632), all of Arabia had joined Islam. Islam diffused rapidly through Islamic political and military expansion. It swept quickly outward from its Arabian hearth region across North African, much of Central Asia and, at the expense of Hinduism, into northern India (Figure 7.33). Later, Islam dispersed into Indonesia, southern Africa, and the Western Hemisphere. It continues its spatial spread and numerical growth as the fastest-growing major religion at the present time.

Disagreements over the succession of leadership after the Prophet led to a division between two primary groups, Sunnis and Shi'ites. Sunnis, the majority (80% to 85% of Muslims) recognize the first four *caliphs* (originally, "successor" and later the title of the religious and civil head of the Muslim state) as Mohammed's rightful successors. The Shi'ites reject the legitimacy of the first three and believe that Muslim leadership rightly belonged to the fourth caliph, the Prophet's son-in-law, Ali, and his descendants. Today, Sunnis constitute the majority of Muslims in all countries except Iran, Iraq, Bahrain, and perhaps Yemen.

The mosque—place of worship, community clubhouse, meeting hall, and school—is the focal point of Islamic communal life and the primary imprint of the religion on the cultural landscape. Its principal purpose is to accommodate the Friday communal service, mandatory for all male Muslims. It is the congregation rather than the structure that is important; small or poor communities are as well served by a bare, whitewashed room as are larger cities by architecturally splendid mosques. With its perfectly proportioned, frequently gilded or tiled domes; its graceful, soaring towers and minarets (from which the

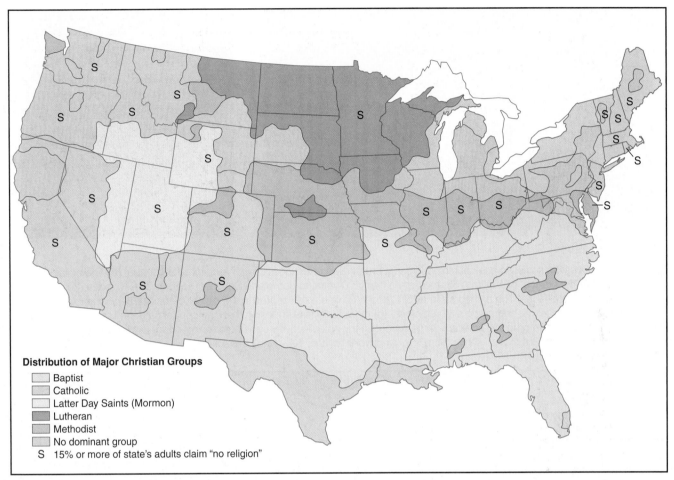

FIGURE 7.31 Religious affiliation in the conterminous United States. The greatly generalized areas of religious dominance shown conceal the reality of immense diversity of church affiliations throughout the United States. "Major" simply means that the indicated category had a higher percentage response than any other affiliation; usually that was below 50%. A sizeable number of Americans claim to have "no religion." Secularism (marked by S on the map) is particularly prominent in the western states, in the industrial Midwest, and in the Northeast. *Sources: Based on data or maps from: the 2001 "American Religious Identity Survey" by the Graduate School at City University of New York; religious denomination maps prepared by Ingolf Vogeler of the University of Wisconsin, Eau-Claire, based on data compiled by the Roper Center for Public Research; and Churches and Church Membership in the United States (Atlanta, Georgia: Glenmary Research Center, 1992).*

faithful are called to prayer); and its delicately wrought parapets and cupolas, the carefully tended mosque is frequently the most elaborate and imposing structure of the town (Figure 7.34).

Hinduism

Hinduism is the world's oldest major religion. Though it has no datable founding event or initial prophet, some evidence traces its origin back 4000 or more years. Hinduism is an ethnic religion, an intricate web of religious, philosophical, social, economic, and artistic elements constituting a distinctive Indian civilization. Its estimated 1 billion adherents are primarily Asian and largely confined to India, where it claims 80% of the population.

From its cradle area in the valley of the Indus River, Hinduism spread eastward down the Ganges River and southward throughout the subcontinent and adjacent regions by amalgamating, absorbing, and eventually supplanting earlier native religions and customs. Its practice eventually spread throughout Southeast Asia and into Indonesia, Malaysia, Cambodia, Thailand, Laos, and Vietnam, as well as into neighboring Myanmar and Sri Lanka. The largest Hindu temple complex is in Cambodia, not India, and Bali remains a Hindu pocket in dominantly Islamic Indonesia.

There is no common creed, single doctrine, or central ecclesiastical organization defining the Hindu. A Hindu is one born into a caste, a member of a complex social and economic—as well as religious—community. Hinduism accepts and incorporates all forms of belief; adherents may believe in one god or many or none. The *caste* (meaning "birth") structure of society is an expression of the eternal transmigration of souls. For Hindus, the primary aim of this life is to conform to prescribed social and ritual duties and to the rules of conduct for the assigned caste and profession. Those requirements constitute that individual's *dharma*—law and duties. Traditionally, each craft or profession is the property of a particular caste.

(a)

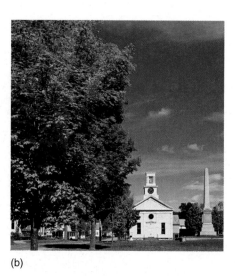

(b)

FIGURE 7.32 In Christian societies, the church assumes a prominent central position in the cultural landscape. **(a)** The building of Nôtre Dame Cathedral of Paris, France, begun in 1163, took more than 100 years to complete. Between 1170 and 1270, some 80 cathedrals were constructed in France alone. The cathedrals in all of Catholic Europe were located in the center of major cities. Their plazas were the sites of markets, public meetings, and religious ceremonies. **(b)** Individually less imposing than the central cathedral of Catholic areas, the several Protestant churches common in small and large American towns collectively constitute an important land use frequently sited in the center of the community. The church shown here is in Wentworth Village, New Hampshire. *(a) Corbis RF; (b) © Punchstock RF.*

FIGURE 7.33 Spread and extent of Islam. Islam predominates in over 35 countries along a band across northern Africa to central Asia and the northern part of the Indian subcontinent. Still farther east, Indonesia has the largest Muslim population of any country. Islam's greatest development is in Asia, where it is second only to Hinduism, and in Africa, where some observers suggest it may be the leading faith. Current Islamic expansion is particularly rapid in the Southern Hemisphere.

The practice of Hinduism is rich with rites and ceremonies, festivals and feasts, pilgrimages to holy rivers and sacred places, processions, and ritual gatherings of millions of celebrants. It involves careful observance of food and marriage rules and the performance of duties within the framework of the caste system. Worship in the temples or shrines (Figure 7.35) and the leaving of offerings to secure merit from the gods are required. The temples, shrines, daily rituals and worship, numerous

FIGURE 7.34 The Blue Mosque in Istanbul, Turkey. The common architectural features of the mosque make it an unmistakable landscape evidence of the presence of Islam in any local culture. © *Getty RF.*

FIGURE 7.35 The Chennakeshava Hindu temple complex at Belur, Karnataka, in southern India. The creation of temples and the images they house has been a principal outlet of Indian artistry for more than 3000 years. At the village level, the structure may be simple, containing only the windowless central cell housing the divine image, a surmounting spire, and the temple porch or stoop to protect the doorway of the cell. The great temples, of immense size, are ornate extensions of the same basic design. © *Allison Bohn.*

specially garbed or marked holy men and ascetics, and ever-present sacred animals mark the cultural landscape of Hindu societies, a landscape infused with religious symbols and sights that are part of a total cultural experience.

Buddhism

Numerous reform movements have derived from Hinduism over the centuries, some of which have endured to the present day as major religions on a regional or world scale. For example, *Sikhism* developed in the Punjab area of northwestern India in the late 15th century A.D., combining elements of both Hinduism and Islam and generally understood to be a syncretism of them. Sikhism rejects the formalism of both and proclaims a gospel of universal tolerance. The great majority of some 20 million Sikhs still live in India, mostly in the Punjab, though others have settled in Malaysia, Singapore, East Africa, the United Kingdom, and North America.

The largest and most influential of the dissident movements is *Buddhism*, a universalizing faith founded in the 6th century B.C. in northern India by Siddhartha Gautama, the Buddha ("Enlightened One"). The Buddha's teachings were more a moral philosophy that offered an explanation for evil and human suffering than a formal religion. He viewed the road to enlightenment and salvation to lie in understanding the "four noble truths": existence involves suffering; suffering is the result of desire; pain ceases when desire is destroyed; the destruction of desire comes through knowledge of correct behavior and correct thoughts. The Buddha instructed his followers to carry his message as missionaries of a doctrine open to all castes, for no distinction among people was recognized. In that message, all could aspire to ultimate enlightenment,

a promise of salvation that raised the Buddha in popular imagination from teacher to inspiration and Buddhism from philosophy to universalizing religion.

The belief system spread throughout India, where it was made the state religion in the 3d century B.C. It was carried elsewhere into Asia by missionaries, monks, and merchants. While expanding abroad, Buddhism began to decline at home as early as the 4th century A.D., slowly but irreversibly reabsorbed into a revived Hinduism. By the 8th century, its dominance in northern India had been broken by conversions to Islam, and by the 15th century, it had essentially disappeared from all of the subcontinent.

Present-day spatial patterns of Buddhist adherence reflect the schools of thought, or *vehicles*, that were dominant during different periods of dispersion of the basic belief system (Figure 7.36). In all of its many variants, Buddhism imprints its presence vividly on the cultural landscape. Buddha images in stylized human form began to appear in the 1st century A.D. and are common in painting and sculpture throughout the Buddhist world. Equally widespread are the three main types of buildings and monuments: the *stupa* (Figure 7.37), a commemorative shrine; the temple or pagoda enshrining an image or a relic of the Buddha; and the monastery, some of them the size of small cities.

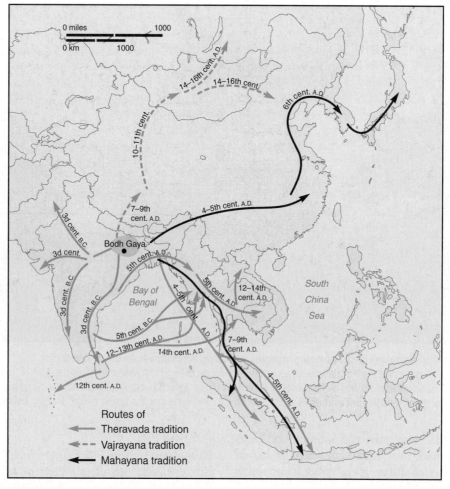

FIGURE 7.36 Diffusion paths, times, and "vehicles" of Buddhism.

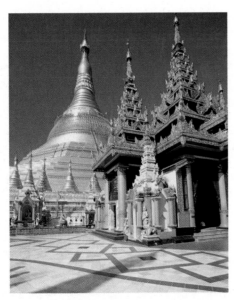

FIGURE 7.37 The gold-embellished stupa at the Swedagon pagoda in Yangon, Myanmar (Rangoon, Burma) is 98 meters (322 feet) tall. © Getty RF.

FIGURE 7.38 **Torii gate at Meiji Shrine in Tokyo, Japan.**
© Getty RF.

East Asian Ethnic Religions

When Buddhism reached China from the south some 1500 to 2000 years ago and was carried to Japan from Korea in the 6th century, it encountered and later amalgamated with already well-established ethical belief systems. The Far Eastern ethnic religions are syncretisms. In China, the union was with Confucianism and Taoism, themselves becoming intermingled by the time of Buddhism's arrival, and in Japan, it was with Shinto, a polytheistic animism and shamanism.

Chinese belief systems address not so much the hereafter as the achievement of the best possible way of life in the present existence. They are more ethical or philosophical than religious in the pure sense. Confucius (K'ung Fu-tzu), a compiler of traditional wisdom who lived about the same time as Gautama Buddha, emphasized the importance of proper conduct between ruler and subjects and between family members. The family was extolled as the nucleus of the state, and filial piety was the loftiest of virtues. There are no churches or clergy in *Confucianism*, though its founder believed in a heaven seen in naturalistic terms, and the Chinese custom of ancestor worship as a mark of gratitude and respect was encouraged.

Confucianism was joined by, or blended with, *Taoism*, an ideology that, according to legend, was first taught by Lao Tsu in the 6th century B.C. Its central theme is *Tao* (the Way), a philosophy teaching that eternal happiness lies in totally identifying with nature and deploring passion, unnecessary invention, unneeded knowledge, and governmental interference in the simple life of individuals. Buddhism, stripped by Chinese pragmatism of much of its Indian otherworldliness and defining a *nirvana* achievable in this life, was easily accepted as a companion to these traditional Chinese belief systems. Along with Confucianism and Taoism, Buddhism became one of the honored Three Teachings, and to the average person there was no distinction in meaning or importance between a Confucian temple, Taoist shrine, or Buddhist stupa.

Buddhism also joined and influenced Japanese Shinto, the traditional religion of Japan, which developed out of nature and ancestor worship. *Shinto*—the Way of the Gods—is basically a structure of customs and rituals rather than an ethical or a moral system. It observes a complex set of deities, including deified emperors, family spirits, and the divinities residing in rivers, trees, certain animals, mountains, and particularly the sun and moon. At first resisted, Buddhism was later amalgamated with traditional Shinto. Buddhist deities were seen as Japanese gods in a different form, and Buddhist priests formerly but no longer assumed control of most of the numerous Shinto shrines in which the gods are believed to dwell and which are approached through ceremonial *torii*, or gateway arches (Figure 7.38).

ETHNICITY

Any discussion of cultural diversity would be incomplete without the mention of **ethnicity.** Based on the root word *ethnos*, meaning "people" or "nation," the term is usually used to refer to the ancestry of a particular people who have in common distinguishing characteristics associated with their heritage. No single trait denotes ethnicity. Recognition of ethnic communities may be based on language, religion, national origin, unique customs, or, improperly, an ill-defined concept of "race" (see "The Matter of Race"). Whatever the unifying thread, ethnic groups may strive to preserve their special shared ancestry and cultural heritage through the collective retention of language, religion, festivals, cuisines, traditions, and in-group work relationships, friendships, and marriages. Those preserved associations are fostered by and support *ethnocentrism*, the feeling that one's own ethnic group is superior.

Normally, reference to ethnic communities is recognition of their minority status within a country or region dominated by a different, majority culture group. We do not identify Koreans living in Korea as an ethnic group because theirs is the dominant culture in their own land. Koreans living in

The Matter of Race

Human populations may be differentiated from one another on any number of bases: gender, nationality, stage of economic development, and so on. One common form of differentiation is based on recognizable inherent physical characteristics.

While humans are all one species that can freely interbreed and produce fertile offspring, there is obvious variation in our physical characteristics. The spread of human beings over the earth and their occupation of different environments were accompanied by the development of variations in visible characteristics, such as skin pigmentation, hair and eye color, and hair texture, as well as internal differences, such as blood composition or lactose intolerance. Physical differentiation among human groups is old and can reasonably be dated to the Paleolithic (100,000 to about 11,000 years ago) spread and isolation of population groups.

Geographic patterns of distinct combinations of physical traits emerged due to causative forces of evolutionary **natural selection** or **adaptation,** and **genetic drift.** Natural selection favors the transmission of characteristics that enable humans to adapt to a particular environmental feature, such as climate. Studies have suggested some plausible relationship between, for example, solar radiation and skin color and between temperature and body size. Dark skin indicates the presence of melanin, which protects against the penetration of damaging ultraviolet rays from the sun. Conversely, the production of vitamin D in the body, which is necessary to good health, is linked to the penetration of ultraviolet rays. In high latitudes where winter days are short and the sun is low in the sky, light skin confers an adaptive advantage by allowing the production of vitamin D. Genetic drift is the process by which a heritable trait appears by chance in a group and is accentuated by inbreeding. If two populations are too spatially separated for much interaction to occur (*isolation*), a trait may develop in one but not in the other. Unlike natural selection, genetic drift differentiates populations in nonadaptive ways. Natural selection and genetic drift promote differentiation. Countering them is **gene flow** via interbreeding, which homogenizes neighboring populations. Opportunities for interbreeding, always part of the spread and intermingling of human populations, have accelerated with the growing mobility and migrations of people in the past few centuries.

Racial categorization is a scientifically outdated way of making sense of human variation. A **race** is usually understood to be a population subset whose members have in common some hereditary biological characteristics that set them apart physically from other human groups. Focusing on visible physical characteristics, anthropologists in the 18th and 19th centuries created a variety of racial classification schemes, most of which derived from geographic variations of populations. Some anthropological studies at that time attempted to link physical traits with mental ability in order to construct racial hierarchies that were used to justify slavery, imperialism, immigration restrictions, anti-miscegenation laws, and eugenics. Contemporary biology has rejected racial categorization as a meaningful description of human variation. Skin color does not correspond to genetic closeness between "racial" groups. Further, pure races do not exist, and DNA-based evidence shows that there is more variation within the so-called racial groups than there is between the groups.

Living in a society where racial categorization has been widespread, we may be tempted to group humans racially and attribute intellectual ability, athletic prowess, or negative characteristics to particular racial groups. This is problematic for many reasons, the most important being that geneticists have rejected race as a scientific concept—there is only race, the human race. Second, intellectual ability as measured on standardized tests is mostly a function of socioeconomic status. Finally, the athletic abilities displayed by top athletes are the property of particular individuals, not a group trait; like intellectual ability, they are strongly influenced by social factors.

Nor does race have meaningful application to any human characteristics that are culturally acquired. That is, race is *not* equivalent to ethnicity or nationality and has no bearing on differences in religion or language. There is no "Irish" or "Hispanic" race, for example. Such groupings are based on culture, not genes. Culture summarizes the way of life of a group of people, and members of the group may adopt it irrespective of their individual genetic heritage, or race. Nevertheless, despite the fact that the older view of race as a biological category has been thoroughly discredited, race and ethnicity remain as defining and divisive realities in American society. Both are deeply rooted in individual and group consciousness, and both are strongly ingrained in the country's social and institutional life. While biological notions of race have little meaning, the society itself is extremely "racialized."

Japan, however, constitute a discerned and segregated group in that foreign country. Ethnicity, therefore, is an evidence of areal cultural diversity and a reminder that culture regions are rarely homogeneous in the characteristics displayed by all of their occupants.

Territorial segregation is a strong and sustaining trait of ethnic identity, one that helps groups retain their distinction. On the world scene, indigenous ethnic groups have developed over time in specific locations and have established themselves in their own and others' eyes as distinctive peoples with defined homeland areas. The boundaries of most countries of the world encompass a number of racial or ethnic minorities (Figure 7.39). Their demands for special territorial recognition have sometimes increased with advances in economic development and self-awareness, as Chapter 9 points out. Where clear territorial separation does not exist but ethnic identities are distinct and animosities bitter, tragic conflict within single political units can erupt. Recent histories of deadly warfare between Tutsi and Hutu in Rwanda, or Serb and Croat in Bosnia, make vivid the often continuing reality of ethnic discord and separatism.

Increasingly in a world of movement, ethnicity is less a matter of indigenous populations and more one of outsiders in an alien culture. Immigrants, legal and illegal, and refugees

(a)

(b)

FIGURE 7.39 **(a) Ethnicity in former Yugoslavia.** Yugoslavia was formed after World War I (1914–1918) from a patchwork of Balkan states and territories, including the former kingdoms of Serbia and Montenegro, Bosnia-Herzegovina, Croatia-Slavonia, and Dalmatia. The authoritarian central government created in 1945 began to disintegrate in 1991 as non-Serb minorities voted for regional independence and national separation. Religious differences between Eastern Orthodox, Roman Catholic, and Muslim adherents compounded resulting conflicts rooted in nationality and rival claims to ethnic homelands. **(b) Afghanistan** houses Pathan, Tajik, Uzbek, and Hazara ethnic groups (among others) speaking Pashto, Dari Persian, Uzbek, and several minor languages and split between majority Sunni and minority Shia Muslim believers.

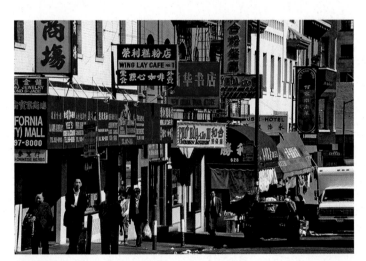

FIGURE 7.40 The advertising signs in the Chinatown area of San Francisco proclaim unmistakably the existence of a distinctive, well-established Chinese and Vietnamese community. Chinatowns, Little Italys, and other ethnic enclave counterparts in cities throughout the United States and Western Europe provide both the spatial refuge and the support systems essential to new arrivals in an alien culture realm. © Robert Moline.

from war, famine, or persecution are a growing presence in countries throughout the world. Immigrants to a country typically have two choices. They may hope for *assimilation* by giving up many of their past culture traits, losing their distinguishing characteristics and merging into the mainstream of the dominant culture, as reviewed earlier on page 212. Or they may try to retain their distinctive cultural heritage. In either

case, they usually settle initially in an area where other members of their ethnic group live, as a place of refuge and learning (Figure 7.40). With the passage of time, they may leave their protected community and move out among the general population.

The Chinatowns, Little Havanas, and Little Italys of Anglo American cities have provided the support systems essential to new immigrants in an alien culture region. Japanese, Italians, Germans, and other ethnics have formed agricultural colonies in Brazil in much the same spirit. Such ethnic enclaves may provide an entry station, allowing both individuals and the groups to which they belong to undergo cultural and social modifications sufficient to enable them to operate effectively in the new, majority society. Sometimes, of course, settlers have no desire to assimilate or are not allowed to assimilate, so that they and their descendants form a more or less permanent subculture in the larger society. The Chinese in Malaysia belong to this category. Ethnicity in the context of nationality is discussed more fully in Chapter 9.

GENDER AND CULTURE

Gender refers to socially created—not biologically based—distinctions between femininity and masculinity. Because gender relationships and role assignments differ between societies, the status of women is a cultural spatial variable and becomes, therefore, a topic of geographic interest and inquiry. Gender distinctions are complex, and the role and reward assignments of males and females differ from society to society. In many fundamental ways, those assignments are conditioned by areally different levels of economic development. Therefore, we might well assume a close similarity between the economic roles and production assignments of males and females—and the status of women—in different cultures that are at the same level of technological advancement. Indeed, it has been observed that modern African or Asian subsistence agricultural groups and those of 18th-century frontier American farm families show similarities in gender roles.

It may further be logical to believe that advancement in the technological sense would be reflected in an enhancement of the status and rewards of both men and women in all developing societies. The pattern that we actually observe is not quite that simple or straightforward, however. In addition to a culture's economic stage, religion and custom play their important roles in determining gender relationships and female prestige. Further, it appears that, at least in the earlier phases of technological change and development, women generally lose rather than gain in standing and rewards. Only recently and only in the most-developed countries have gender contrasts been reduced within and between societies.

Hunting and gathering cultures observed a general egalitarianism; each sex had a respected, productive, coequal role in the kinship group (see Figure 7.10). Gender is more involved and changeable in agricultural societies (see "Women and the Green Revolution," Chapter 10). The Agricultural Revolution—a major change in the technological subsystem—altered the earlier structure of gender-related responsibilities. In the hoe agriculture that was the first advance over hunting and gathering and is today found in much of sub-Saharan Africa and in South and Southeast Asia, women became responsible for most of the actual fieldwork, while retaining their traditional duties in child rearing, food preparation, and the like; their economic role and status remained equivalent to males. Plow agriculture, on the other hand, tended to subordinate the role of women and diminish their level of equality. Women might have hoed, but men plowed, and female participation in farmwork was drastically reduced. This is the case today in Latin America and, increasingly, in sub-Saharan Africa, where women are often more visibly productive in the market than in the field (Figure 7.41). As women's agricultural productive role declined, they were afforded less domestic authority, less control over their own lives, and few, if any, property rights independent of male family members.

At the same time, considering all their paid and unpaid labor, women spend more hours per day working than do men. In developing countries, the UN estimates, when unpaid agricultural work and housework are considered along with wage labor, women's work hours exceed men's by 30% and may involve at least as arduous—or more arduous—physical labor. The UN's Food and Agriculture Organization reports that "rural women in the developing world carry 80 tons or more of fuel, water, and farm produce for a distance of 1 km during the course of a year. Men carry much less. . . ." Everywhere, women are paid less than men for comparable employment.

Western industrial—"developed"—society emerged directly from the agricultural tradition of the subordinate female who was not considered an important element in the economically active population, no matter how arduous or essential the domestic tasks assigned. With the growth of cities and industry in 19th-century America, for example, as women began to enter the workforce in increasing numbers, a "cult of true womanhood" developed as a reaction to the competitive pressures of the marketplace and factory floor. It held that women were morally superior to men; their role was private, not public. A woman's job was to rear children, attend church, and above all keep a sober, virtuous, and cultured home, a place

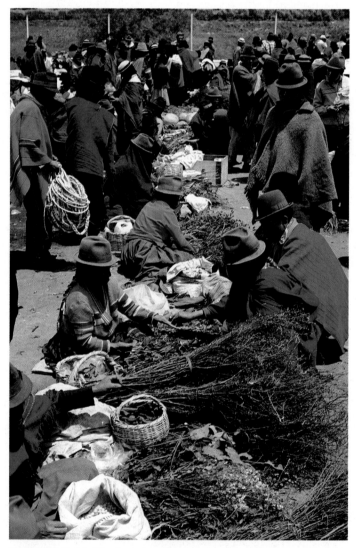

FIGURE 7.41 Women dominate the once-a-week *periodic* markets in nearly all developing countries. Here they sell produce from their gardens or the family farm and frequently offer for sale processed goods to which their labor has added value. The market shown here is in Ecuador. More than half the economically active women in the developing world are self-employed, working primarily in the informal sector. In the developed world, only about 14% of active women are self-employed. © Getty RF.

Leveling the Field

The Fourth World Conference on Women, held in Beijing during September 1995, produced the strongest and broadest declaration of women's rights and equality ever forthcoming from a series of international meetings on the subject, beginning in Mexico City in 1975. Noting that its conclusions as adopted by delegates from 185 countries were in full conformity with the Charter of the United Nations and with international law, the Beijing Conference called on all governments to formulate strategies, programs, and laws designed to assure women of their full human rights to equality and development. Its final declaration detailed recommended policies in the areas of sexuality and childbearing, violence against women, discrimination against girls, female inheritance rights, and family protection. Its particular emphasis focused on efforts to "ensure women's equal access to economic resources including land, credit, science, and technology, vocational training, information, communication and markets as a means to further advancement and empowerment of women and girls." In the opinion of one U.S. delegate, "This is a document that guarantees the same rights for women that have been long enjoyed by men." Its special economic emphasis was reinforced by the UN Food and Agriculture Organization's "Gender and Development Plan (2006–2007)," which aimed at stimulating efforts to enhance gender-based equity in control of productive resources and providing women with access to credit to enable them to engage as creators and owners of small-scale manufacturing, trade, and service businesses.

The conference did not reach its decisions and recommendations without spirited debate clearly rooted in the contrasting ways that different major cultures assign gender roles. Those contrasts, and the relationship between human rights and the national customs they imply, were put in international perspective in the preamble to the conference platform: "While the significance of national and regional particularities and various historical, cultural, and religious background must be borne in mind, it is the duty of states regardless of their political, economic, and cultural systems to promote and protect all human rights and fundamental freedoms."

All the declarations of the basic human rights of women articulated at the Beijing Conference were preserved at the "Beijing Plus Five" Conference held at the United Nations in June 2000. In addition, delegates to that meeting agreed on principles calling for the punishment of domestic violence and for the criminalization of the cross-border trafficking of women and girls for sexual and wage slavery purposes. Again, reservations to many conference proposals were voiced by different delegations that typically split into fluctuating camps of conservative countries, largely Islamic and Roman Catholic and more secular states, including most of Europe and much of Latin America. Despite the formally adopted resolutions of "Beijing Plus Five," and their reaffirmation at "Beijing Plus Ten" in New York in March 2005, those strongly ingrained reservations suggest that the playing field remains uneven.

that offered the male breadwinner refuge, security, and privacy. This Victorian ideal fostered, in America and much of Western Europe, both social and economic discrimination against working women.

Only within the later 20th century, and then only in the more-developed countries, did that subordinate role pattern change. Women became increasingly economically active and placed themselves as never before in direct competition with men for similar occupations and wages. The feminist movement in modern industrialized societies was the direct response to the barriers that formerly restricted favored economic and legal positions to men. Even though women constituted 47% of the total employed labor force in the United States in 2008, their representation in higher-paying, more-prestigious positions was lower, despite increasing acceptance of the standard of equal pay for equal work. The elimination of the remaining legal, social, and economic discriminations has been a primary objective of the North American "feminist revolution."

Such a revolution is much less likely or possible in strongly conservative and traditional economies and societies (see "Leveling the Field"). The present world pattern of gender-related institutional and economic role assignments is influenced not only by a country's level of economic development but also by the persistence of religious and customary restrictions its culture imposes on women and by the nature of its economic—particularly, agricultural—base. The first control is reflected in contrasts between the developed and developing world; the second and third are evidenced in variations within the developing world itself.

In any case, economic globalization has had a mixed impact on female participation in the paid labor force and on gender economic differentiation. On a worldwide basis, it appears that globalization's greater trade openness has increased women's share of paid employment, and in developing countries, firms that are producing for export employ more female workers, often in skilled activities. But growing labor force participation has not necessarily reduced gender discrimination. In developing countries, women also make up the largest share of workers in expanding informal sub-contracting and sweatshop piecework—often in the shifting and uncertain garment and shoe industries—with low pay and poor working conditions.

A distinct gender-specific regionalization has emerged. Among the Arab and Arab-influenced Muslim areas of western Asia and North Africa, the proportion of the female population that is economically active is low; religious tradition restricts women's acceptance in economic activities outside the home. The same cultural limitations do not apply under the different rural economic conditions of Muslims in southern and southeastern Asia, where labor force participation by women in Indonesia and Bangladesh, for example, is much higher than it is among the western Muslims. In Latin America, well known for a patriarchal social structure, women have been overcoming cultural restrictions on their growing employment outside the home.

Sub-Saharan Africa, highly diverse culturally and economically, in general is highly dependent on female farm labor and market income. The traditional role of strongly independent, property-owning women formerly encountered under traditional agricultural and village systems, however, has increasingly been replaced by the subordination of women with modernization of agricultural techniques and introduction of formal, male-dominated financial and administrative agricultural institutions. For countries for which sufficient data are available, a set of indicators has been created to establish a "gender-related development index" and ranking (Figure 7.42); it clearly displays regional differentials in the position of women in different cultures and world areas.

Regional and cultural contrasts in gender relationships are also encountered in the advanced economies and the industrial components of developing countries. In modernizing eastern Asian states, for example, women have yet to achieve the status they enjoy in most Western economies. In China, although it ranks in the second quartile in the GDI (see Figure 7.42), women are generally not effectively competitive with men and are largely absent from the highest managerial and administrative levels; in Japan, males nearly exclusively run the huge industrial and political machinery of the country. In contrast, economic and social gender equality is more advanced in the Scandinavian countries than perhaps in any other portion of the industrialized world.

OTHER ASPECTS OF DIVERSITY

Culture is the sum total of the way of life of a society. It is misleading to isolate, as we have done in this chapter, only a few elements of the technological, sociological, and ideological subsystems and imply by that isolation that they are identifying characteristics differentiating culture groups. Economic developmental levels, language, religion, ethnicity, and gender all are important and common distinguishing culture traits, but they tell only a partial story. Other suggestive, though perhaps less pervasive, basic elements exist.

Architectural styles in public and private buildings are evocative of region of origin, even when they are indiscriminately mixed together in American cities. The Gothic and New England churches, the neoclassical bank, and the skyscraper office building suggest not only the functions they house but also the culturally and regionally variant design solutions that gave them form. The Spanish, Tudor, French provincial, or ranch-style residence may not reveal the ethnic background of its American occupant, but it does constitute a culture statement of the area and the society from which it diffused.

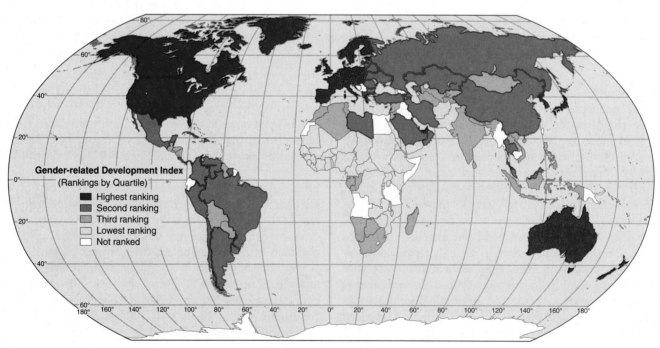

FIGURE 7.42 The gender-related development index (GDI) is a composite index that attempts to measure inequalities of achievement between men and women through differences in their life expectancies at birth, literacy levels and educational attainments, and earned income shares. The greater the gender achievement disparities, the lower is a country's GDI. In many higher-ranked countries, female life expectancy, literacy rates, and educational attainment equal or exceed those of males, while their incomes still lag significantly. The gender-related development index rankings suggest that gender equality does not necessarily depend on the overall income level of a country. *Source: 2007 rankings from United Nations Development Programme,* Human Development Report 2009. *Rankings are adjusted for each annual edition.*

Music, food, games, and other evidence of the joys of life, too, are cultural indicators associated with particular world or national areas. Music is an emotional form of communication found in all societies, but, being culturally patterned, it varies among them. Instruments, scales, and types of composition are technical forms of variants; the emotions aroused and the responses evoked to musical cues are learned behaviors among peoples. The Christian hymn means nothing emotionally to a pagan New Guinea clan. The music of a Chinese opera may be simply noise to the European ear. Where there is sufficient similarity between musical styles and instrumentation, blending (syncretism) and transferral may occur. American jazz represents a blend; calypso and flamenco music have been transferred to the Anglo American scene. Foods identified with other culture regions have similarly been transferred to become part of the culinary environment of the American "melting pot."

These are but a few additional minor statements of the variety and intricate interrelationships of that human mosaic called culture. Individually and collectively, however, in their areal expressions and variations they are only part of the subject matter of the cultural geographer. Patterns and controls of spatial interaction and behavior, national and international political structures, economic activities and orientations, and levels and patterns of urbanization—all fundamental aspects of contemporary culture—are the subjects of the following chapters.

Summary of Key Concepts

- Culture is the learned behaviors and beliefs of distinctive groups of people. Culture traits combine to shape integrated culture complexes. Together, traits and complexes in their spatial patterns create human—"cultural"—landscapes, define culture regions, and distinguish culture groups. Those landscapes, regions, and group characteristics change through time as human societies interact with their environment, develop new solutions to collective needs, or are altered through innovations adopted from outside the group.

- Understanding culture is aided by recognition of its component subsystems. The *technological subsystem* is composed of the material objects (artifacts) and techniques of livelihood. The *sociological subsystem* comprises the formal and informal institutions (sociofacts) that control the social organization of a culture group. The *ideological subsystem* consists of the ideas and beliefs (mentifacts) a culture expresses in speech and through belief systems.

- Domestication of plants and animals led to the emergence of *culture hearths* of developmental innovation and to a cultural divergence between different groups. Modern-day cultural convergence is lessened by the many distinctive elements that remain to identify and separate social groups. Among the most prominent of the differentiating culture traits are language, religion, ethnicity, and gender.

- Language and religion are both transmitters of culture and identifying traits of separate culture groups. Both have distinctive spatial patterns, reflecting past and present processes of interaction and change.

- Languages can be grouped by origins and historical development, but their world distributions depend as much on the movements of peoples and histories of conquest and colonization as they do on linguistic evolution. *Toponymy*, the study of place-names, helps document that history of movement. Linguistic geography studies spatial variations in languages, variations that may be minimized by the encouragement of standard languages or overcome by pidgins, creoles, and lingua francas.

- Spatial patterns of religion are distinct and reveal histories of migration, conquest, and diffusion. Those patterns are important components in the spatially distinctive cultural landscapes created in response to various religious belief systems. Even in secular societies, religion may influence economic activities, legal systems, holiday observances, and the like.

- Ethnicity, affiliation in a group sharing identifying culture traits, is fostered by territorial separation or isolation and is preserved in ethnically complex societies by a feeling that one's own ethnic group is superior to others. Ethnic diversity is a reality in most countries of the world and is increasing in many of them. Many ethnic minority groups seek absorption into their surrounding majority culture through acculturation and assimilation, but other groups choose to preserve their identifying distinctions through spatial separation or overt rejection of the majority culture traits.

- Gender, the culturally based social distinctions between men and women, reflects religion, custom, and, importantly, the stage of economic development of a society and the productive role assigned to women within that economy. Gender roles change as the economic structure changes, though their modification is often resisted by conservative forces within a culture.

- Culture realms are ever-changing reflections of the migrations of ethnic and cultural groups, the diffusion or adoption of languages and religions, the spread and acceptance of new technologies, and the alteration of gender relationships as economies modernize and cultural traditions respond.

Such movements, diffusions, adoptions, and responses are themselves expressions of broader concepts and patterns of the geography of spatial behavior, an essential component of the culture-environment tradition to which we next turn our attention.

Key Words

acculturation 210
amalgamation theory 211
assimilation 212
creole 218
cultural ecology 198
cultural integration 206
cultural landscape 199
culture 196
culture complex 197
culture hearth 208
culture realm 198
culture region 198
culture system 197
culture trait 197

dialect 216
environmental determinism 199
ethnicity 235
ethnic religion 224
folk culture 219
gender 237
gene flow 236
genetic drift 236
ideological subsystem 199
innovation 207
language family 214
lingua franca 219
material culture 219
natural selection (adaptation) 236

nonmaterial culture 219
pidgin 218
popular culture 219
possibilism 199
race 236
sociological subsystem 199
spatial diffusion 208
standard language 216
syncretism 210
technological subsystem 199
toponymy 221
tribal religion 224
universalizing religion 223

Thinking Geographically

1. What is included in the concept of *culture?* How is culture transmitted? What personal characteristics affect the aspects of culture that any individual acquires or fully masters?

2. What is a *culture hearth?* What new traits of culture characterized the early hearths? In the cultural geographic sense, what is meant by *innovation?*

3. Differentiate between *culture traits* and *culture complexes* and between *environmental determinism* and *possibilism.*

4. What are the components or subsystems of the three-part system of culture? What characteristics—aspects of culture—are included in each of the subsystems?

5. Why might one consider language the dominant differentiating element of culture separating societies?

6. In what way may religion affect other culture traits of a society?

7. How does the classification of religions as *universalizing, ethnic,* or *tribal* help us understand their patterns of distribution and spread?

8. How does *acculturation* occur? Is *ethnocentrism* likely to be an obstacle in the acculturation process? How do acculturation and *assimilation* differ?

9. How are the concepts of *ethnicity, race,* and *culture* related?

CHAPTER EIGHT

Spatial Interaction

CHAPTER OUTLINE

© Tim Crosby/Getty.

"For a brief 18-month period between April 1860 and October 1861, an undying blend of courage and endurance was created by the Pony Express riders. Racing through Nebraska, Wyoming, Utah, and Nevada, these horsemen carried letters written on lightweight paper (postage ranged from $2 to $10 an ounce) from one relay station to another. They covered the 1,966 miles from St. Joseph, Missouri, to Sacramento, California, in 11 days. The nature of the work is implied in the newspaper advertisements seeking riders who weighed less than 135 pounds, did not drink or carouse, and were 'daring young men—preferably orphans.' "[1] The twice-weekly trip took longer if riders had to avoid Indians or a herd of a million buffalo (Figure 8.1).

The $10 charge for an ounce of mail in 1860 is equivalent to $220 in today's money. Only such things as diamonds are as expensive to ship today. It is interesting to note that there are two nonstop and a dozen one-stop flights leaving St. Louis every day for San Francisco (cities near St. Joseph

and Sacramento, respectively), and an average one-way fare is about $150 per person (the average weight of a person with baggage is about 180 pounds). It takes approximately 4 hours for a plane to make the trip. The cost for an ounce is 5 cents by plane versus $220 by Pony Express.

This comparison shows unmistakably that the interaction between the Midwest part of the United States and the West has grown enormously over the past 144 years. The level of interaction is a function of the demand for travel, its speed, and its cost. All of these factors are conditioned by technology. In this case, the technology changed from fresh horses spaced at 16- to 24-kilometer (10- to 15-mi) intervals in the Pony Express days to jet planes. Today, with populations in each area in the millions and the cost of travel low, it is no wonder that so many planes leave daily from each city for the other.

THE DEFINITION OF *SPATIAL INTERACTION*

Spatial interaction is the term geographers use to represent the interdependence between geographic areas. Spatial interaction can be the movement of people between places, the flow of goods from one region to another, the diffusion of ideas from a center of knowledge to other areas, or the spread of a communicable disease from a group of people living in one area to those living in another area. What all of these examples have in common is that there is some sort of a flow over a distance separating people. Spatial interaction is the geographic counterpart of human interaction. The difference is that the location of those involved in the interaction can be clearly represented on maps.

If there is no one at a site (for example, on an iceberg), there can be no spatial interaction between the site and any other site. On the other hand, if there are a great number of people at one site—for example, Chicago—and a great number of people at another site—say, New York—there will be a great deal of spatial interaction between them. But if the second site is a city as far away as Tokyo is from Chicago, there will be fewer interactions between Chicago and Tokyo than between Chicago and New York. The attractive force between areas is akin to the force of gravity. Thus, the amount of spatial interaction is a function of the size of the interdependent populations and the distance between them.

FIGURE 8.1 A poster advertising the services of the Pony Express, whose riders sped across the West on horses bred to run fast. In operation from only 1860 to 1861, the Pony Express was rendered obsolete by railroads and the telegraph. In 1861, a telegraph wire strung from New York City to San Francisco reduced the time for communication between the coasts from days to seconds. *Courtesy of Pony Express Museum, St. Joseph, MO. © Bettmann/Corbis Images.*

[1]*The Story of America*, The Reader's Digest Association, Pleasantville, New York, 1975, p. 199.

DISTANCE AND SPATIAL INTERACTION

Because people make many more short-distance trips than long ones, there is greater human interaction over short distances than long distances. This is the principle of **distance decay,** the decline of an activity, a function, or an amount of interaction with increasing distance from the point of origin. The tendency is for the frequency of trips to decrease very rapidly beyond an individual's **critical distance,** the distance beyond which cost, effort, means, and perception play an

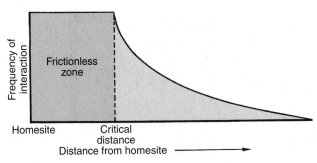

FIGURE 8.2 This general diagram indicates how most people observe distance. For each activity, there is a distance beyond which the intensity of contact declines. This is called the *critical distance*. The distance up to the critical distance is a frictionless zone, in which time or distance considerations do not effectively figure into the trip decision.

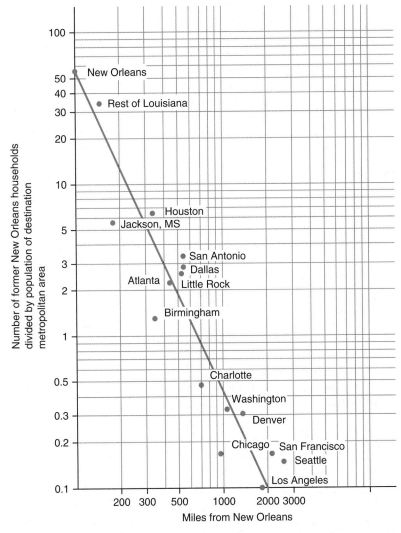

FIGURE 8.3 Migration of the victims of Hurricane Katrina. This spatial interaction diagram uses a log-log scale so that distances from New Orleans can be shown with the number of migrants divided by the populations of metropolitan areas. *Source: Data from FEMA, U.S. Census Bureau and Queens College Sociology Department.*

overriding role in our willingness to travel. Figure 8.2 illustrates this principle with regard to journeys from a homesite. The critical distance is different for each person. The variables of a person's age, mobility, and opportunity, together with an individual's interests and demands, help define how much and how far a person will travel. For example, students on campus might not think twice about visiting the campus library to do photocopying but off-campus students might wait for a convenient time to do the photocopying, or not do it at all. The campus library may be beyond the off-campus students' critical distance. Because distance retards spatial interaction, we can say there is a *friction of distance* in our lives and activities.

The amount of spatial interaction between two places is a function of the distance separating the places and the populations of the two places. Figure 8.3 shows the migration from New Orleans just after Hurricane Katrina in 2005. Because they are nearby, places in unflooded parts of New Orleans and in the state of Louisiana received most of the migrants, but many journeyed to the metropolitan areas of Houston, Dallas, Chicago, and New York.

A small child will make many trips up and down the block, but he or she will be inhibited by parental admonitions from crossing the street. Different but equally effective constraints control adult behavior. Daily or weekly shopping may be within the critical distance of an individual, and little thought may be given to the cost or effort involved. Shopping for special goods, however, is relegated to infrequent trips, and cost and effort are considered. The majority of our social contacts tend to be at a short distance within our own neighborhoods or with friends who live relatively close at hand; longer social trips to visit relatives are less frequent. In all such trips, however, the distance decay function is clearly at work.

Effort may be measured in terms of *time-distance*—that is, the time required to complete the trip. For the journey to work, time rather than cost often plays the major role in determining the critical distance. When significant differences between our cognition of distance and real distance are evident, we use the term *psychological distance* to describe our perception of distance. A number of studies show that people tend to psychologically consider known places as nearer than they really are and little-known places as farther than true distance. A humorous example of this is seen in Figure 8.4, a more serious one in Figure 8.5. Also, see "Mental Maps," pp. 248–249.

We gain information about the world from many sources. Although information obtained from radio, television, the Internet, and newspapers is important to us, face-to-face contact is assumed to be the most effective means of communication. The distance decay principle implies that, as the distance away from the home or workplace increases, the number of possible face-to-face contacts usually decreases. We expect more spatial interaction at short distances than at

FIGURE 8.4 **Psychological distance: an artist's conception of a New Yorker's view of the United States.** © *Florence Thierfeldt, Milwaukee, Wisconsin.*

long distances. Where population densities are high, such as in cities (particularly central business districts during business hours), the spatial interaction between individuals can be at a very high level, which is one reason these centers of commerce are often also centers for the development of new ideas.

BARRIERS TO INTERACTION

Recent changes in technology permit us to travel farther than ever before, with greater safety and speed, and to communicate without physical contact more easily and completely than previously possible. This intensification of contact has resulted in an acceleration of innovation and in the rapid spread of goods and ideas. Several millennia ago, innovations such as the smelting of metals took hundreds of years to spread. Today, worldwide diffusion may be almost instantaneous.

The fact that the possible number of interactions is high, however, does not necessarily mean that the effective occurrence of interactions is high. That is, a number of barriers to interaction exist. Such barriers are any conditions that hinder either the flow of information or the movement of people and thus retard or prevent the acceptance of an innovation. Distance itself is a barrier to interaction. Generally, the farther two areas are from each other, the less likely is interaction. The concept of distance decay says that, all else being equal, the amount of interaction decreases as the distance between two areas increases.

Cost is another barrier to interaction. Relatives, friends, and associates living long distances apart may find it difficult to afford to see one another. The frequency and time allocated to telephone and e-mail communication, relatively inexpensive forms of interaction, are very much a function of the location of friends and relatives—which, of course, favors short-distance interaction.

Interregional contact may also be hindered by the physical environment and by the cultural barriers of differing religions, languages, ideologies, genders, and political systems. Mountains and deserts, oceans and rivers can, and have, acted as physical barriers slowing or impeding interaction. Cultural barriers may be equally impenetrable. Those nearby who practice religions differently or speak another language may not be in touch with their neighbors. Governments (such as that of North Korea) that interfere with radio reception, control the flow of foreign literature, and discourage contact between their citizens and foreign nationals may overtly impede cultural contact.

In crowded areas, people commonly set psychological barriers around themselves, so that only a limited number of interactions take place. The barriers are raised in defense against information overload and for psychological well-being. We must have a sense of privacy in order to filter out information that does not directly concern us. As a result, we tend to reduce our interests to a narrow range when we find ourselves in crowded situations, allowing our wider interests to be satisfied by our use of the communications media.

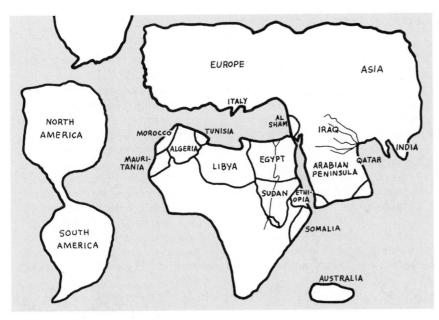

FIGURE 8.5 A mental map of the world. This map was drawn by a Palestinian high school student from Gaza. The map reflects the secondary school education the author is receiving, which conforms to the Egyptian national school curriculum and thus is influenced by the importance of the Nile River and pan-Arabism. Al Sham is the old, but still used, name for the area including Syria, Lebanon, and Palestine. The map might be quite different if the Gaza school curriculum were designed by Palestinians or if an Israeli drew it.

SPATIAL INTERACTION AND INNOVATION

The probability that new ideas will be generated out of old ideas is a function of the number of available old ideas in contact with one another. People who specialize in a particular field of interest seek out others with whom they wish to interact. Crowded central cities are characteristically composed of specialists in very narrow fields of interest. Consequently, under short-distance, high-density circumstances, the old ideas are given a hearing and new ideas are generated by the interaction. New inventions and new social movements usually arise in circumstances of high spatial interaction. An exception, of course, is the case of intensely traditional societies—Japan in the 17th and 18th centuries, for example—where the culture rejects innovation and clings steadfastly to customary ideas and methods.

The culture hearths of an earlier day (see Chapter 7) were the most densely settled, high-interaction centers of the world. At present, the great national and regional capital cities attract people who want or need to interact with others in special-interest fields. The association of population concentrations and the expression of human ingenuity have long been noted. The home addresses recorded for patent applicants by the U.S. Patent Office over the past century indicate that inventors were typically residents of major urban centers, presumably people in close contact and able to exchange ideas with those in shared fields of interest. It

still appears that the metropolitan centers of the world attract those who are young and ambitious and that face-to-face or word-of-mouth contact is important in the creation of new ideas and products. The relatively recent revolution in communications, which allows for inexpensive interaction through a variety of phone and Internet services, has suggested to some that the traditional importance of cities as collectors of creative talent may decline in the future.

INDIVIDUAL ACTIVITY SPACE

We will see in Chapter 9 that groups and countries draw boundaries around themselves to divide space into territories that are defended if necessary. The concept of **territoriality**—the emotional attachment to, and the defense of, home ground—has been seen by some as a root explanation of many human actions and responses. It is true that some collective activity appears to be governed by territorial defense responses: the conflict between street groups in claiming and protecting their "turf" (and the fear for their lives when venturing beyond it) and the sometimes violent rejection by ethnic urban neighborhoods of any different encroaching population group it considers threatening.

But for most of us, our personal sense of territoriality is a tempered one. We regard our homes and property as defensible private domains but open them to innocent visitors, known or unknown, or to those on private or official business. Nor do we confine our activities so exclusively within controlled home territories as street-gang members do within theirs. Rather, we have a more or less extended home range, an **activity space** or area within which we move freely on our rounds of regular activity, sharing that space with others who are also about their daily affairs.

Figure 8.6 suggests probable activity spaces for a family of five for 1 day. Note that the activity space for each individual for 1 day is rather limited, even though two members of the family use automobiles. If 1 week's activity were shown, more paths would have to be added to the map, and in a year's time, several long trips would probably have to be noted. Long trips are usually taken irregularly.

The kind of activities individuals engage in can be classified according to type of trip: journeys to work, school, shopping center, recreational area, and so on. People in nearly all parts of the world make the same types of journeys, though the spatially variable requirements of culture, economy, and personal circumstances dictate their frequency, duration, and significance in the time budget of an individual.

Mental Maps

Spatial interaction is affected by the way people perceive places. When information about a place is sketchy, blurred pictures develop. These influence the impression we have of places. Our willingness or ability to interact with what might be thought of as strange or unknown places cannot be discounted. We may say that each individual has a **mental map** of the world. No single person, of course, has a true and complete image of the world; therefore, having a completely accurate mental map is impossible. In fact, the best mental map that most individuals have is that of their own residential neighborhood, the place where they spend the most time.

Whenever individuals think about a place or how to get to a place, they produce a mental map. What are believed to be unnecessary details are left out, and only the important elements are incorporated. Those elements usually include awareness that the object or the destination does indeed exist, some conception of the distances separating the starting point and the named object(s), and a feeling for the directional relationships between points. A mental route map may also include reference points to be encountered on the chosen path of connection or on alternate lines of travel. Although mental maps are highly personalized, people with similar experiences tend to give similar answers to questions about the environment and to produce roughly comparable sketch maps.

Awareness of places is usually accompanied by opinions about them, but there is no necessary relationship between the depth of knowledge and the perceptions held. In general, the more familiar we are with a locale, the better is the factual basis of our mental image of it. But we form firm impressions of places

Three children, aged 6, 10, and 13, who lived in the same house, were asked to draw maps of their neighborhood. No further instructions were given. Notice how perspectives broaden and neighborhoods expand with age. For the 6-year-old (bottom left), the neighborhood consisted of the houses on each side of her own. The square block on which she lived was the neighborhood for the 10-year-old (top right). The wider activity space of the 13-year-old is also evident (bottom right). The square block that the 10-year-old drew is shaded in the 13-year-old's sketch.

10-year-old

6-year-old

13-year-old

totally unknown by us personally, and these may affect travel, migration decisions, or other forms of spatial interaction.

One way to ascertain how individuals envisage the environment is to ask them what they think of various places. For instance, they might be asked to rate places according to desirability—perhaps residential desirability—or to make a list of the best and worst places in a region such as the United States. Certain regularities appear in such studies. The accompanying figure presents some residential desirability data elicited from college students in three provinces of Canada. These and comparable mental maps suggest that near places are preferred to far places unless much information is available about the far places. Places with similar cultural forms are preferred, as are places with high standards of living. Individuals tend to be indifferent to unfamiliar places and

to dislike unfamiliar areas that have competing cultural interests (such as disliked political and military activities) or a physical environment known to be unpleasant.

On the other hand, places perceived to have superior climates or landscape amenities are rated highly in mental map studies and favored in tourism and migration decisions. The southern and southwestern coast of England is attractive to citizens of generally wet and cloudy Britain, and holiday tours to Spain, the south of France, and the Mediterranean islands are heavily booked by the English. A U.S. Census Bureau study indicates that "climate" is, after work and family proximity, the most often reported reason for interstate moves by adults of all ages. International studies reveal a similar migration motivation based not only on climate but also on concepts of natural beauty and amenities.

Each of these maps shows the residential preference of a sampled group of Canadians from the provinces of Quebec, Ontario, and British Columbia. Note that each group of respondents prefers its own area but that all like the Canadian and U.S. west coasts. *Redrawn with permission from Herbert A. Whitney, "Preferred Locations in North America: Canadians, Clues, and Conjectures," in* Journal of Geography, *Vol. 83, no. 5, p. 222. Copyright © 1984 National Council for Geographic Education, Indiana, PA.*

Preference
- ■ Strong like
- ▣ Like
- ▢ Neutral
- □ Dislike
- □ Strong dislike

ONTARIO

Toronto

QUEBEC

Montreal

BRITISH COLUMBIA

Vancouver

FIGURE 8.6 Activity space for each member of a family of five for a typical weekday. One parent commutes to work, while the other parent works at home. Routes of regular movement and areas recurrently visited help to foster a sense of territoriality and to affect one's perceptions of space.

Figure 8.7 suggests the importance of the journey to work in an urban population. The journey to work plays a decisive role in defining the activity space of most adults. Formerly restricted by walking distance or by the routes and schedules of mass transit systems, the critical distances of work trips have steadily increased in European and Anglo American cities as the private automobile has figured more importantly in the movement of workers (Figure 8.8). In more recent years, however, it has become evident that, for many, the journey to work is really a multipurpose trip, which may include side trips to day-care centers, cleaners, schools, and shops of various kinds.

The types of trips individuals make, and thus the extent of their activity space, are partly determined by three variables: people's stage in life (age); the means of mobility at their command; and the opportunities implicit in their daily activities.

Stage in Life

The first variable determining the types of trips individuals make, **stage in life,** refers to membership in specific age groups. Stages include preschool-age, school-age, young adult, adult, and elderly. Preschoolers stay close to home unless they accompany their parents or caregivers. School-age children usually travel short distances to lower-level schools and longer distances to upper-level schools. After-school activities tend to be limited to walking, bicycle, or automobile trips provided by parents to nearby locations. High school students and other

young adults are usually more mobile and take part in more activities than do younger children. They engage in more spatial interaction. Adults responsible for household duties make shopping trips and trips related to child care, as well as journeys away from home for social, cultural, and recreational purposes. Wage-earning adults usually travel farther from home than other family members. Elderly people may, through infirmity or interests, have less-extensive activity spaces.

Mobility

The second variable that affects the extent of activity space is *mobility,* or the ability to travel. An informal consideration of the cost and effort required to overcome the friction of distance is implicit. Where incomes are high, automobiles are available, and the cost of fuel is a minor item in the family budget, mobility may be great and individual action space can be large. In societies where cars are not a standard means of personal conveyance, the daily activity space may be limited to the shorter range afforded by bicycles or walking. Obviously, both intensity of purpose and the condition of the roadway affect the execution of movement decisions.

The mobility of individuals in countries or in sections of countries with high incomes is relatively great; people's activity space horizons are broad. These horizons, however, are not limitless. There is a fixed number of hours in a day, most of them consumed in performing work, preparing and eating food, and sleeping. In addition, there is a fixed number of road,

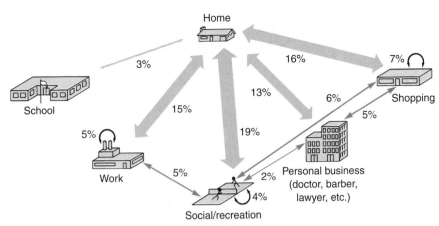

FIGURE 8.7 **Seven-county Minneapolis Metropolitan Area travel patterns.**
The numbers are the percentages of all urban trips taken on a typical weekday.
Source: Data from Metropolitan Council: The 2000 Travel Behavior Inventory.

FIGURE 8.8 The frequency distribution of work and nonwork trip lengths in minutes in the seven-county Minneapolis Metropolitan Area. Studies in various metropolitan areas support the conclusions documented by this graph: work trips are usually longer than other recurring journeys. In the United States in the early 1990s, the average work trip covered 17.1 kilometers (10.6 mi), and half of all trips to work took under 22 minutes; for suburbanites commuting to the central business district, the journey to work involved between 30 and 45 minutes. By 2000, increasing sprawl had lengthened average commuting distances and, because of growing traffic congestion, had increased the average work trip commuting time to 25 minutes; many workers had commutes of more than 45 minutes.
Source: Metropolitan Council: The 2000 Travel Behavior Inventory.

rail, and air routes, so even the most mobile individuals are constrained in the amount of activity space they can use. No one can easily claim the world as his or her activity space. An example of this limitation is that of women living in suburban communities who must balance family obligations, such as preparing meals and caring for children, with their workforce activities. In this case, women's mobility is restricted; as a result, their occupational opportunities are limited.

Opportunities

The third factor limiting activity space is the individual assessment of the availability of possible activities or *opportunities*. In the teeming cities of Asia, for example, the very poor satisfy their daily needs nearby; the impetus for journeys away from the residence is minimal. In impoverished countries and neighborhoods, low incomes limit the inducements, opportunities, destinations, and necessity of travel. Similarly, if one lives in a remote, sparsely settled area, with few or no roads, schools, factories, or stores, one's expectations and opportunities are limited, and activity space is therefore reduced. Opportunities plus mobility conditioned by life stage bear heavily on the amount of spatial interaction in which individuals engage.

DIFFUSION AND INNOVATION

As we noted in Chapter 7, **spatial diffusion** is the process by which a concept, practice, or substance spreads from its point of origin to new territories. A *concept* is an idea or invention, such as a new way of thinking—for example, deciding that shopping on the Internet is worth doing. A *practice* might be the actual process of shopping on the Internet. A *substance* is a tangible thing, such as the goods bought by means of the Internet. Diffusion is at the heart of the geography of spatial interaction.

Ideas generated in a center of activity will remain there unless some process is available for their spread. *Innovations*, the changes to a culture that result from the adoption of new ideas, spread in various ways. Some new inventions are so obviously advantageous that they are put to use quickly by those who can afford and profit from them. A new development in petroleum extraction may promise such material reward as to lead to its quick adoption by all major petroleum companies, irrespective of their distance from the point of introduction. The new strains of wheat and rice that significantly increased agricultural yields in much of the world and that were part of the Green Revolution (discussed in Chapter 10) were quickly made known to agronomists in all cereal-producing countries. However, they were more slowly taken up in poor countries, which could benefit most from them, partly because farmers had difficulty paying for them and spatial interaction was limited.

Many innovations are of little consequence by themselves, but sometimes the widespread adoption of seemingly inconsequential innovations brings about large changes when viewed over a period of time. A new musical tune, "adopted" by a few people, may lead many individuals to fancy that tune plus

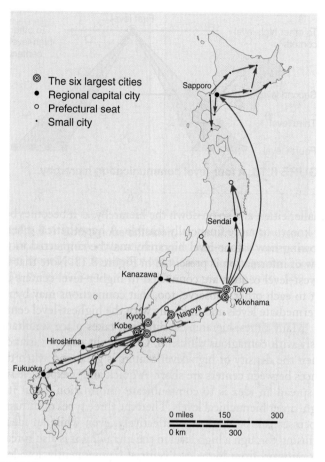

FIGURE 8.14 Rotary Clubs, members of the international service association, were established in the large cities of Japan during the 1920s. New clubs were established under the sponsorship of the original clubs. This map shows both a hierarchical and a contagious pattern of diffusion. *Redrawn with permission from Yoshio Sugiura, "Diffusion of Rotary Clubs in Japan, 1920–1940: A Case of Non-Profit Motivated Innovation Diffusion under a Decentralized Decision-Making Structure," in* Economic Geography, *Vol. 62, no. 2, p. 128. Copyright © 1986 Clark University, Worcester, MA.*

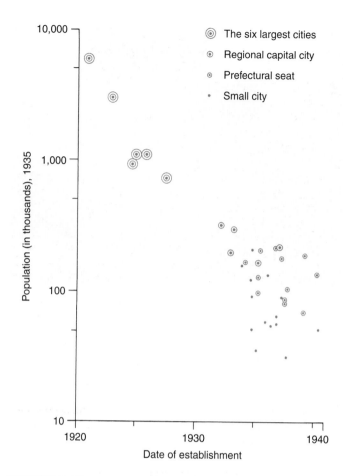

FIGURE 8.15 This diagram shows the hierarchical diffusion component of the spread of Rotary Clubs in Japan. The largest cities were the first centers of Rotary Club activity, followed by cities at lower and lower levels of urban population and city function. *Redrawn with permission from Yoshio Sugiura, "Diffusion of Rotary Clubs in Japan, 1920– 1940: A Case of Non-Profit Motivated Innovation Diffusion under a Decentralized Decision-Making Structure," in* Economic Geography, *Vol. 62, no. 2, p. 128. Copyright © 1986 Clark University, Worcester, MA.*

Automobiles

The automobile provides individuals with fast and flexible transportation on a daily basis. It has increased the ability to overcome spatial separation and has had a profound effect on the location of jobs and services. Much employment has decentralized to suburban locations, creating sprawling cities. Unfortunately, the side effects of this decentralization have been a decrease in opportunities for those without automobiles, those who must depend on public transportation. Societies have accommodated automobiles by building highways and freeways, as opposed to further developing public transportation systems. Those with automobiles are able to commute, shop, see friends and family, and engage in group activities with little inconvenience. As automobiles become more comfortable and high technology oriented, they further encourage people to seek more opportunities for interaction. Unless local governments control urban growth and development, the result is a sprawling urban environment where people appear to be

constantly on the move from one place to another. This process that increases spatial interaction has been ongoing since the automobile became affordable to large numbers of people.

Telecommunications

For information flows, space has a different meaning than it does for the movement of people or commodities. Communication, for example, does not necessarily imply the time-consuming physical relocation of things (though in the case of letters and print media, it usually does). Indeed, in modern telecommunications, the process of information flow can be instantaneous regardless of distance. The result is space-time convergence to the point of the obliteration of space. A Bell System report tells us that, in 1920, putting through a transcontinental telephone call took 14 minutes and eight operators and cost more than $15.00 for a 3-minute call. By 1940, the call completion time had been reduced to less than 1½ minutes and the cost had fallen to $4.00. In the 1960s,

Documenting Diffusion

The places of origin of many ideas, items, and technologies important in contemporary cultures are only dimly known or supposed, and their routes of diffusion are speculative at best. Gunpowder, printing, and spaghetti are presumed to be the products of Chinese inventiveness; the lateen sail has been traced to the Near Eastern culture world. The moldboard plow is ascribed to 6th-century Slavs of northeastern Europe. The sequence and routes of the diffusion of these innovations have not been documented.

In other cases, such documentation exists, and the process of diffusion is open to analysis. Clearly marked is the diffusion path of the custom of smoking tobacco, a practice that originated with Amerindians. Sir Walter Raleigh's Virginia colonists, returning home to England in 1586, introduced smoking in English court circles, and the habit very quickly spread among the general populace. England became the source region of the new custom for northern Europe; English medical students introduced smoking to Holland in 1590. Dutch and English together spread the habit to the Baltic and Scandinavian areas and overland through Germany to Russia. The innovation continued its eastward diffusion, and within 100 years, tobacco spread across Siberia and was, in the 1740s, reintroduced to the American continent at Alaska by Russian fur traders. A second route of diffusion for tobacco smoking can be traced from Spain through the Mediterranean area into Africa, the Near East, and Southeast Asia.

In more recent times, hybrid corn was originally adopted by imaginative farmers of northern Illinois and eastern Iowa in the mid-1930s. By the late 1930s and early 1940s, the new seeds were being planted as far east as Ohio and north to Minnesota,

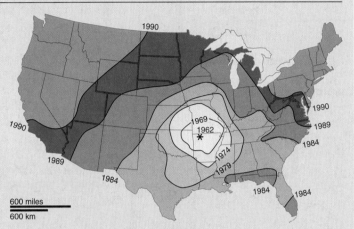

Redrawn from data in Thomas O. Graff and Dub Ashton, "Spatial Diffusion of Wal-Mart," *The Professional Geographer,* 46, no. 1, pp. 19–29. Association of American Geographers, 1994. Reprinted by permission of Blackwell Publishers.

Wisconsin, and northern Michigan. By the late 1940s, all commercial corn-growing districts of the United States and southern Canada were cultivating hybrid varieties.

A similar pattern of contagious diffusion marked the expansion of the Wal-Mart stores chain. From its origin in northwest Arkansas in 1962, the discount chain had dispersed throughout the United States by the 1990s to become the country's largest business in sales volume. In its expansion, Wal-Mart displayed a "reverse hierarchical" diffusion, initially spreading by way of small towns before opening its first stores in larger cities and metropolitan areas.

---

direct distance dialing allowed a transcontinental connection in less than 30 seconds, and electronic switching has now reduced the completion time to that involved in dialing a number and answering a phone. The price of long-distance conversation essentially disappeared with the advent of voice communication over the Internet in the late 1990s.

The Internet and communication satellites have made worldwide personal and mass communication immediate and data transfers instantaneous. The same technologies that have led to communication space-time convergence have tended toward a space-cost convergence. Domestic mail, which once charged a distance-based postage, is now carried nationwide or across town for the same price.

It is conceivable that the current revolution in telecommunications technology will have a more profound effect on people's lives, and thus social and industrial structure, than the automobile. For those with telecommunications capability, the level of spatial interaction has increased appreciably (Figure 8.16). Cellular phones, e-mail, communication on the Internet, and low-cost phone services have created lifestyles in which some people spend the better part of their days communicating with others. Because businesses have taken advantage

of the technology by offering goods and services online, the number of shopping trips of all sorts has declined. In addition, a number of individuals make a living in a telecommuting environment. That is, they conduct business on the Internet and therefore do not take part in the morning and evening journey to and from work. The implication is that many people will find it less compelling to live in a crowded urban environment, so that sprawl is likely to increase at an accelerated pace.

Many types of industries will become footloose; that is, they won't need to be tied spatially to other industries or an urban environment. Most likely, it will be low-cost wage locations that will prosper. This is due to the fact that, if industrialists and service providers have their choice of any location, they will seek one where wages are low, skills are high, and amenities, such as the existence of a warm tropical environment, are plentiful.

While automobiles foster long-distance commuting to work, telecommuting reduces the need to commute at all. Both, however, encourage urban sprawl. Because the telecommunications revolution began in the mid-1990s and is still in its infancy, we are just beginning to recognize how it affects all aspects of our lifestyles.

FIGURE 8.16 A map of the Internet i-21 network of part of Europe, a fiber optic network that connects 61 cities in 16 countries. It has the capacity to carry more than a petabit (a billion megabits) per second of communication traffic. *Source: Martin Dodge and Rob Kitchin,* An Atlas of Cyberspaces, *Copyright Martin Dodge, 2004. This work is licensed under a Creative Commons License. Available at http://www.cybergeography.org/atlas/interoute_large.gif.*

MIGRATION

An important aspect of human history has been the **migration** of peoples—that is, the permanent relocation of both place of residence and activity space. It has contributed to the evolution of separate cultures, to the relocation diffusion of those cultures, and to the complex mix of peoples and cultures found in various parts of the world. The settlement of North America, Australia, and New Zealand involved great long-distance movements of peoples. The flight of refugees from past and recent wars, the settlement of Jews in Israel, the current migration of workers to the United States from Mexico and Central

America, and innumerable other examples of mass movement come quickly to mind. In all cases, societies transplanted their cultures to the new areas, their cultures therefore diffused and intermixed, and history was altered.

Massive movements of people within countries, across national borders, and between continents have emerged as a pressing concern of recent decades. They affect national economic structures; determine population density and distribution patterns; alter traditional ethnic, linguistic, and religious mixtures; and inflame national debates and international tensions. Migration patterns and conflicts touch many aspects of social and economic relations and have become an important part of current geographic realities. In this chapter, our interest is in migration as an unmistakable, recurring, and near-universal expression of human spatial behavior.

Types of Migration

Migration flows can be discussed at different scales, from massive intercontinental torrents to individual decisions to move to a new house or apartment within the same metropolitan area. At each level, although the underlying controls on spatial behavior remain constant, the immediate motivating factors influencing the spatial interaction are different, with differing impacts on population patterns and cultural landscapes.

Naturally, the length of a move and its degree of disruption of people's lives raise distinctions important in the study of migration. A change of residence from the central city to the suburbs certainly changes the activity space of schoolchildren and of adults in many of their nonworking activities, but the workers may still retain the city—indeed, the same place of employment there—as an activity space. On the other hand, migration from Europe to the United States and the massive farm-to-city movements of rural Americans late in the 19th and early 20th centuries meant a total change of all aspects of behavioral patterns.

At the broadest scale, *intercontinental* movements range from the earliest peopling of the habitable world to the most recent flight of Asian and African refugees to countries of Europe and the Western Hemisphere. The population structure of the United States, Canada, Australia and New Zealand, Argentina, Brazil, and other South American countries is a reflection and result of massive intercontinental flows of immigrants that began as a trickle during the 16th and 17th centuries and reached a flood during the 19th and early 20th centuries. Later in the 20th century, World War II (1939–1945) and its immediate aftermath involved more than 25 million permanent population relocations, all of them international but not all intercontinental.

Intracontinental and *interregional* migrations involve movements between countries and within countries, most commonly in response to individual and group assessments of improved economic prospects, but often reflecting flight from difficult or dangerous environmental, military, economic, or political conditions. The millions of refugees leaving their homelands following the dissolution of Eastern European communist states, including the former USSR and Yugoslavia, exemplify that kind of flight. Between 1980 and 2000, Europe received some 20 million newcomers, often refugees, who joined the 15 million labor migrants ("guest workers") already in Western European countries by the early 1990s. The European Union makes it possible for labor to move easily among its many member countries (Figure 8.17). About 175 million people—3% of the world population—live in a country other than the country of their birth in the early 2000s, and migration has become a world social, economic, and political issue of first priority.

Migrations may be forced or voluntary, or, in many instances, reluctant relocations imposed on the migrants by circumstances. In *forced*, or *involuntary*, *migrations*, the relocation decision is made solely by people other than the migrants themselves (Figure 8.18). Between 10 and 12 million Africans were forcibly transferred as slaves to the Western Hemisphere from the late 16th to the early 19th centuries. Half or more were destined for the Caribbean and most of the remainder for Central and South America, though nearly a million arrived in the United States. Australia owed its earliest European settlement to convicts transported after the 1780s to the British penal colony established in southeastern Australia (New South Wales). More recent involuntary migrants include millions of Soviet citizens forcibly relocated from countryside to cities and from the western areas to labor camps in Siberia and the Russian Far East beginning in the late 1920s.

Less than fully voluntary relocation—*reluctant migration*—of some 8 million Indonesians has taken place under an aggressive governmental campaign begun in 1969 to move people from densely settled Java to other islands and territories of the country in what has been called the "biggest colonization program in history." International refugees from war and political turmoil or repression numbered some 15 million in 2003, according to the World Refugee Survey—1 out of every 415 people on the planet. In the past, refugees sought asylum mainly in Europe and other developed areas. More recently, the flight of people is primarily from developing countries to other developing regions, and many countries with the largest refugee populations are among the world's poorest. Between 2003 and 2007, Iran, Syria, and Jordan became host to millions of Iraqis fleeing persecution, terrorism, and war. Sub-Saharan Africa alone houses more than 3 million refugees (Figure 8.19). Worldwide, an additional 22 million people were "internally displaced," effectively internal refugees within their own countries. In a search for security or sustenance, they have left their home areas but not crossed an international boundary.

The great majority of migratory movements, however, are *voluntary*, representing individual response to the factors influencing all spatial interaction decisions. At root, migrations

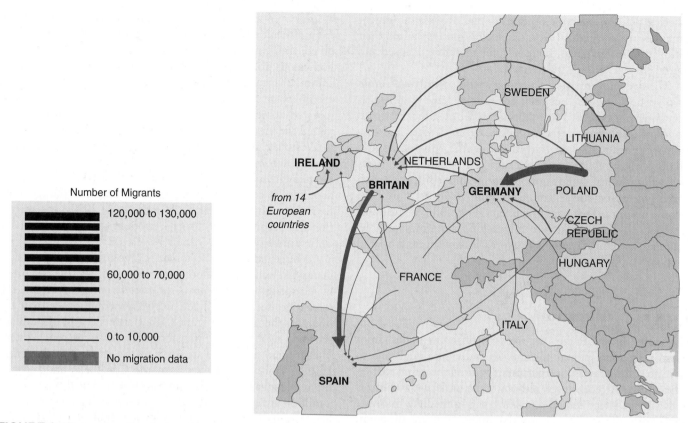

Number of Migrants

120,000 to 130,000

60,000 to 70,000

0 to 10,000

No migration data

FIGURE 8.17 Immigration to four European countries—Britain, Ireland, Germany, and Spain—from other European countries, 2003–2004. *Source: Data from Eurostat.*

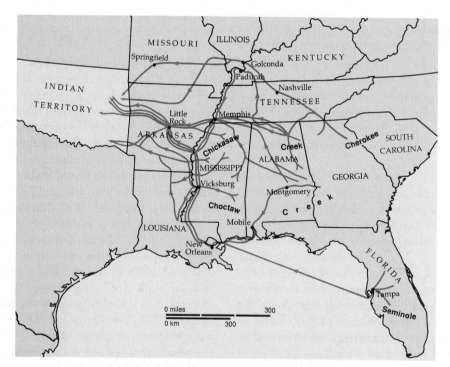

FIGURE 8.18 Forced migrations: the Five Civilized Tribes. Between 1825 and 1840, some 100,000 southeastern Amerindians were removed from their homelands and transferred by the army across the Mississippi River to "Indian Territory" in present-day Oklahoma. By far, the largest number were members of the Five Civilized Tribes of the South: Cherokees, Choctaws, Chickasaws, Creeks, and Seminoles. Settled, Christianized, literate small farmers, their forced eviction and arduous journey—particularly along what the Cherokees named their "Trail of Tears" in the harsh winter of 1837–1838—resulted in much suffering and death.

FIGURE 8.19 Major flows of refugees. The map shows the origin and destination countries of the 10 largest refugee populations as of January 1, 2006. In recent years, political upheavals have forced the migration of millions of people from their homes and across international borders. *Source: Data from United Nations High Commissioner for Refugees.*

take place because the migrants believe that their opportunities and lives will be better at their destination than they are at their present location.

Incentives to Migrate

The decision to move is a cultural and temporal variable. Nomads fleeing famine and spreading deserts in the Sahel of Africa obviously are motivated by considerations different from those of an executive receiving a job transfer to Chicago, a resident of Appalachia seeking factory employment in the city, or a retired couple searching for sun and sand. In general, people who voluntarily decide to migrate are seeking better economic, political, or cultural conditions or certain amenities. For many, the reasons for migration are frequently a combination of several of these categories.

Negative home conditions that impel the decision to migrate are called **push factors.** They include loss of job, lack of professional opportunity, overcrowding, and a variety of other influences, including poverty, war, and famine. The presumed positive attractions of the migration destination are known

as **pull factors.** They include all the attractive attributes perceived to exist at the new location—safety and food, perhaps, or job opportunities, better climate, lower taxes, more room, and so forth. Very often, migration is a result of both perceived push and pull factors (Figure 8.20). It is the perception of the opportunities and want satisfaction that is important, whether or not the perception is supported by objective reality.

Economic considerations have impelled more migrations than any other single incentive. If migrants face unsatisfactory conditions at home (e.g., unemployment or famine) and believe that the economic opportunities are better elsewhere, they will be attracted to the thought of moving. Poverty is the great motivator. Some 30% of the world's population—nearly 2 billion people—have less than $1.00 per day income. Many additionally are victims of drought, floods, and other natural catastrophes, or of wars and terrorism. Poverty in developing countries is greatest in the countryside; rural areas are home to around 750 million of the world's poorest people. Of these, 20 to 30 million move each year to towns and cities—many as "environmental refugees," abandoning land so eroded or exhausted it can no longer support them. In the cities, they join

State population growth, 2000 to 2006

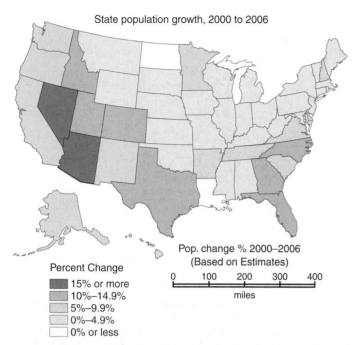

Pop. change % 2000–2006
(Based on Estimates)

0   100   200   300   400
miles

Percent Change
- 15% or more
- 10%–14.9%
- 5%–9.9%
- 0%–4.9%
- 0% or less

FIGURE 8.20 Migration in the United States. Although birth and death rates have a strong bearing on population growth, the growth pattern in the United States from 2000 to 2006 was largely a result of net migration to the West, Southwest, and Southeast. The *pull factors* included job opportunities and mild climates; the *push factors* included loss of job opportunities and harsh winters. *Source: Population Division, U.S. Census Bureau.*

FIGURE 8.21 The major paths of the early migration of Germans to America. Most emigrants left Germany because of religious and political persecution. They chose the United States not only because immigrants were made welcome but also because labor was in demand and farmland was available. The first immigrants landed, and many settled, in Boston, New York, Philadelphia, Baltimore, Charleston, and New Orleans. The migrants carried with them such aspects of their culture as religion, language, and food preferences.

the 40% or more of the labor force that is unemployed or underemployed in their home country and seek legal or illegal entry into the more promising economies of the developed world. All, rural or urban, respond to the same basic forces: the push of poverty and the pull of perceived or hoped-for opportunity.

The desire to escape war and persecution at home and to pursue the promise of freedom in a new location is a *political incentive* for migration. Americans are familiar with the history of settlers who migrated to North America seeking religious and political freedom (Figure 8.21). In more recent times, the United States has received hundreds of thousands of refugees from countries such as Hungary, following the uprising of 1956; Cuba, after its takeover by Fidel Castro; and Vietnam, after the fall of South Vietnam. The massive movements of Hindus and Muslims across the Indian subcontinent in 1947, when Pakistan and India were established as governing entities, and the exodus of Jews fleeing persecution in Nazi Germany in the 1930s are other examples of politically inspired moves. More recently, about 1 million Hutus fled into neighboring African countries after ethnic Tutsis took over Rwanda's government; ethnic Muslims living in Bosnia were pushed out of their ancestral homes by Serbs; and many Haitians, under severe economic privation during a political crisis, have left for the United States.

Migration normally but not always involves a hierarchy of decisions. Once people have decided to move and have selected a general destination (e.g., America or the Sunbelt), they must still choose a particular site in which to settle. At this scale, *cultural variables* can be important pull factors. Migrants tend to be attracted to areas where the language, religion, and racial or ethnic background of the inhabitants are similar to their own. This similarity can help migrants feel at home when they arrive at their destination, and it may make it easier for them to find a job and to become assimilated into the new culture. The Chinatowns and Little Italys of large cities attest to the drawing power of cultural factors, as discussed in Chapter 7.

Another set of inducements is grouped under the heading *amenities*, the particularly attractive or agreeable features that are characteristic of a place. Amenities may be natural (mountains, oceans, climate, and the like) or cultural (e.g., the arts and music opportunities available in large cities). They are particularly important to relatively affluent people seeking "the good life." Amenities help to account for the attractiveness of the so-called Sunbelt states in the United States for retirees; a similar movement to the southern coast has also been observed in countries such as the United Kingdom and France.

The significance of the various incentives varies according to the age, sex, education, and economic status of the migrants (see "Gender and Migration"). For the modern American, reasons to migrate have been summarized into a limited number of categories that are not mutually exclusive:

1. changes in life course, such as getting married, having children, getting a divorce, or needing less dwelling space when the children leave home

2. changes in career cycle, such as leaving college, getting a first job or a promotion, receiving a career transfer, or retiring

3. forced or reluctant migrations associated with urban development, construction projects, and the like

4. neighborhood changes from which there is flight, perhaps pressures from new and unwelcome ethnic groups, building deterioration, street gangs, or similar rejected alterations in activity space

5. changes of residence associated with individual personality (chronic mobility)

Some people simply tend to move often for no easily discernible reasons, whereas others, *stayers,* settle into a community permanently. Of course, for a country such as China, with its limitations on emigration and severe housing shortages, a totally different set of summary migration factors is present. By *emigration* we mean leaving one's country or region to settle elsewhere.

The factors that contribute to mobility tend to change over time. However, in most societies, one group has always been the most mobile: young adults (Figure 8.22). They are the members of society who are launching careers and making initial decisions about occupation and location. They have the fewest responsibilities of all adults; thus, they are not as strongly tied to family and institutions as older people are. Most of the major voluntary migrations have been composed primarily of young people who suffered from a lack of opportunities in the home area and who were easily able to take advantage of opportunities elsewhere.

The concept of **place utility** helps us understand the decision-making process that potential voluntary migrants undergo. Place utility is the value that an individual puts on a given residential site. The decision to migrate is a reflection of the appraisal—the perception—by the prospective migrant of the current homesite as opposed to other sites of which something is known or hoped for. The individual may adjust to conditions at the homesite and decide not to migrate.

In evaluating comparative place utility, the decision maker considers not only the perceived value of the present location but also the expected place utility of each potential destination. The evaluations are matched with the individual's *aspiration level*—that is, the level of accomplishment or ambition that the individual sees for himself or herself. Aspirations tend to be adjusted to what an individual considers attainable. If the person is satisfied with present circumstances, then he or she does not initiate search behavior. If, on the other hand, the person is dissatisfied with the home location, he or she assigns a utility to each possible new site. The utility is based on past

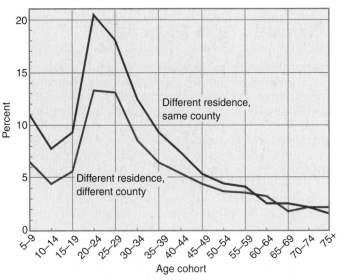

FIGURE 8.22 Percentage of 2000 population over 5 years of age with a different residence than in 1999. Young adults figure most prominently in both short- and long-distance moves in the United States, an age-related pattern of mobility that has remained constant over time. For the sample year shown, 33% of people in their twenties moved, whereas fewer than 5% of those 65 and older did so. Short-distance moves predominated; 56% of the 43 million U.S. movers between March 1999 and March 2000 relocated within the same county, and another 20% moved to another county in the same state. Some two-thirds of intracounty (mobility) moves were made for housing-related reasons; long-distance moves (migration) are likely to be made for work-related reasons. *Source: U.S. Bureau of the Census.*

or expected future rewards at the various sites. Because the new places are unfamiliar to the individual, the information received about them acts as a substitute for the personal experience of the homesite. The decision maker can do no more than sample information about the new sites, and, of course, there may be errors in both information and interpretation.

One goal of the potential migrant is to minimize uncertainty. Most decision makers either elect not to migrate or postpone the decision unless uncertainty can be lowered sufficiently. That objective may be achieved either by going through a series of transitional relocation stages or by following the example of known predecessors. **Step migration** involves the place transition from, for example, rural to central city residence through a series of less-extreme locational changes—from farm to small town to suburb and, finally, to the major central city itself. The term **chain migration** indicates that the mover is part of an established migrant flow from a common origin to a prepared destination. An advance group of migrants, having established itself in a new home area, is followed by second and subsequent migrations originating in the same home district and frequently united by kinship or friendship. Public and private services for legal migrants and informal service networks for undocumented or illegal migrants become established and contribute to the

Gender and Migration

Gender is involved in migration at every level. In a household or family, women and men are likely to play different roles regarding decisions or responsibilities for activities such as child care. These differences, and the inequalities that underlie them, help determine who decides whether the household moves, which household members migrate, and the destination for the move. Outside the household, societal norms about women's mobility and independence often restrict their ability to migrate.

The economies of both sending and receiving areas play a role as well. If jobs are available for women in the receiving area, women have an incentive to migrate, and families are more likely to encourage the migration of women as necessary and beneficial. Thousands of women from East and Southeast Asia have migrated to the oil-rich countries of the Middle East, for example, to take service jobs.

The impact of migration is also likely to be different for women and men. Moving to a new economic or social setting can affect the regular relationships and processes that occur within a household or family. In some cases, women might remain subordinate to the men in their families. A study of Greek-Cypriot immigrant women in London and of Turkish immigrant women in the Netherlands found that although these women were working for wages in their new societies, these new economic roles did not affect their subordinate standing in the family in any fundamental way.

In other situations, however, migration can give women more power in the family. In Zaire, women in rural areas move to towns to take advantage of job opportunities there, and gain independence from men in the process.

One of the keys to understanding the role of gender in migration is to disentangle household decision-making processes. Many researchers see migration as a family decision or strategy, but some family members will have more sway than others, and some members will benefit more than others will from those decisions.

For many years, men predominated in the migration streams flowing from Mexico to the United States. Women played an important role in this migration stream, even when they remained in Mexico. Mexican women influenced the migration decisions of other family members; they married migrants to gain the benefits from and opportunity for migration; and they resisted or accepted the new roles in their families that migration created.

In the 1980s, Mexican women began to migrate to the United States in increasing numbers. Economic crises in Mexico and an increase in the number of jobs available for women in the United States, especially in factories, domestic service, and service industries, have changed the backdrop of individual migration decisions. Now, women often initiate family moves or resettlement efforts.

Mexican women have begun to build their own migration networks, which are key to successful migration and resettlement in the United States. Networks provide migrants with information about jobs and places to live and have enabled many Mexican women to make independent decisions about migrating.

In immigrant communities in the United States, women are often the vital links to social institution services and to other immigrants. Thus, women have been instrumental in the way that Mexican immigrants have settled and become integrated into new communities.

Reprinted with permission from Nancy E. Riley, "Gender, Power, and Population Change," *Population Bulletin*, Vol. 52, No. 1, May 1997, pp. 32–33. Copyright © 1997 by the Population Reference Bureau, Inc.

continuation or expansion of the chain migration flow. Ethnic and foreign-born enclaves in major cities and rural areas in a number of countries are the immediate result.

Sometimes the chain migration is specific to occupational as well as ethnic groups. For example, nearly all newspaper vendors in New Delhi, in the north of India, are reported to come from one small district in Tamil Nadu, in the south of India. Most construction workers in New Delhi come either from Orissa, in the east of India, or Rajasthan, in the northwest, and taxicab drivers originate in the Punjab area. A network of about 250 related families who come from a small town several hundred miles to the north dominates the diamond trade of Mumbai (Bombay), India.

A similar domination of businesses by a single ethnic group occurs in the United States. Familiar examples of these *ethnic niche businesses* include fruit stores owned by Koreans and diners owned by Greeks, but there are many others. Female immigrants from Vietnam dominate the manicure trade, accounting for more than half the women in that profession. A large proportion of female immigrants from the Philippines find employment as nurses, particularly in New York City and the West Coast. About 30% of the Filipinos in New York City

and its suburbs work as nurses or other health practitioners, the result of their aggressive recruitment by American hospitals and the fact that U.S. immigration authorities have made it easy for nurses to obtain work visas and green cards giving them permanent resident status. Immigrants from India, mostly from the state of Gujarat, now own more than one-third of the hotels in the United States, most of them budget and midpriced franchises such as Holiday Inns, Days Inns, and Ramadas.

Another goal of the potential migrant is to avoid physically dangerous or economically unprofitable outcomes in the final migration decision. Place utility evaluation, therefore, requires assessments not only of perceived pull factors of new sites but also of the potentially negative economic and social reception the migrant might experience at those sites. An example of some of these observations can be seen in the case of the large numbers of young people from the Caribbean, Mexico, and Central America who have migrated both legally and illegally to the United States over the past 30 years (Figure 8.23).

Faced with poverty at home, these young adults regard the place utility in their own country as minimal. Their space-searching ability is limited, however, by both the lack of money and the lack of alternatives in the land of their birth. With a

(a)

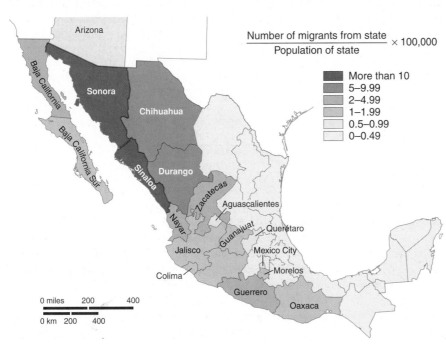

$$\frac{\text{Number of migrants from state}}{\text{Population of state}} \times 100,000$$

	More than 10
	5–9.99
	2–4.99
	1–1.99
	0.5–0.99
	0–0.49

(b)

FIGURE 8.23 (a) Illegal Mexican immigrants running from the Border Patrol. (b) Undocumented migration rate to Arizona. The Arizona region and nearby Mexican states have historical ties that go back to the early 1800s. In many respects, the international border cuts through a culture region. Note that distance plays a large role in the decision to migrate to the United States, with over half the migrants coming from four nearby Mexican states: Sonora, Sinaloa, Durango, and Chihuahua. *(a) © AP Images/ Denis Poroy; (b) Redrawn from John P. Harner, "Continuity Amidst Change," The Professional Geographer, 47, no. 4, Fig. 2, p. 403. Copyright © Association of American Geographers, 1995. Reprinted by permission of Blackwell Publishers.*

willingness to work and with aspirations for success—perhaps wealth—in the United States, they learn from friends and relatives of job opportunities north of the border, low-paying though they may be. Hundreds of thousands quickly place high utility on perhaps a temporary relocation (maybe 5 or 10 years) to the United States. Many know that dangerous risks are involved if they attempt to enter the country illegally, but even legal immigrants face legal restrictions designed to reduce the pull attractions of the United States (see "Broken Borders," pp. 264–265). The arrival of those who consider the rewards worth the risk indicate their assignment of higher utility to the new site than to the old one.

In the 20th century, nearly all countries experienced a great movement of people from agricultural areas to the cities, continuing the pattern of *rural-to-urban migration* that first became prominent during the 18th- and 19th-century Industrial Revolution

GEOGRAPHY
& Public Policy

Broken Borders

Migrants can enter a country legally—with passport, visa, working permit, or other authorization—or illegally. Some aliens enter a country legally but on a temporary basis (as a student or tourist, for example), but then remain after their official departure date. Others arrive claiming the right of political asylum but actually seeking economic opportunity. The Department of Homeland Security estimates that between one-fourth and one-third of the illegal residents in the United States entered the country legally but then overstayed their visas.

Although it is impossible to determine the precise number of people residing illegally in the United States, a number that changes daily, most authorities estimate there are anywhere from 10 to 12 million. About 55% have come from Mexico, another 20% to 25% from other Latin American countries and the Caribbean, 13% from Asia, and the remainder from Canada, Europe, and Africa. The rising tide of emotion against unauthorized immigrants is directed mainly against those from Latin America, most of whom are unskilled workers.

Once they are in the United States, Latin American immigrants find work in agricultural fields, animal slaughtering and meat packing facilities, construction, hotels, and restaurants. Many work in private residences as maids, nannies, and gardeners. While most undocumented workers initially enter California, Arizona, Texas, or Florida, and many remain in those states, they go where they find jobs. Many blend into the large migrant communities not just of Los Angeles, El Paso, and Houston, for example, but also those of Chicago and New York City. Iowa and North Carolina have some of the fastest growing populations of illegal immigrants. The demand for their labor is great enough that nearly all of the males have higher labor force participation rates than native-born men (92% versus 83%).

Concern over the growing number of illegal aliens has been reflected in a number of actions in recent years.

- Security fears since the September 11, 2001, assaults on the World Trade Center and Pentagon have led to more stringent visa applicant background checks, greater restrictions on admitting refugees and asylum seekers, stricter enforcement of Immigration and Naturalization Service (INS) rules on alien residency reports and visa time restrictions, and stricter border controls.
- Greater efforts are being made to deter illegal crossings along the 3380-kilometer (2100-mi) U.S.-Mexico border. To supplement the 120 kilometers (75 mi) of steel fences near a few U.S. cities, the Bush administration in 2007 proposed 1125 kilometers (700 mi) of new fencing, and Congress approved money for a small portion of it. The administration also increased the number of Border Patrol agents, who use automotive vehicles, helicopters, unmanned aircraft known as *drones,* night-vision cameras, and hidden electronic sensors for surveillance. In parts of Arizona and California, self-appointed

Minutemen—groups of volunteer militia—patrol the border "to protect our country from a 40-year long invasion across our southern border with Mexico," as one vigilante put it.

- Because the burden of coping with illegal immigration falls mostly on state and local governments, four states (Florida, Texas, Arizona, and California) have sued the federal government—so far unsuccessfully—to win reimbursement for the costs of illegal immigration. Similarly, the U.S.-Mexico Border Counties Coalition, composed of representatives from the 24 counties in the United States that abut Mexico, has not yet succeeded in getting the federal government to reimburse local administrations for money spent on legal and medical services for illegal aliens. These services include the detention, prosecution, and defense of immigrants; emergency medical care; ambulance service; and autopsies and burials for the hundreds who die each year while trying to cross the border.
- Concerned that large numbers of unauthorized immigrants impose a financial burden on taxpayers, congest schools and public health clinics, and result in the reduction of services to legal residents, voters in California approved Proposition 187, which barred illegal immigrants and their families from public schools, social services, and non-emergency health care. The measure also required state and local agencies to report suspected illegal immigrants to the Immigration and Naturalization Service and to certain state officials. The courts struck down Proposition 187, declaring most of the provisions to be unconstitutional, and the measure was never implemented.
- In Arizona, a law targeting employers of undocumented workers took effect on January 1, 2008. Employers are required to check the status of each worker with the federal government. A company found to have knowingly hired an illegal resident has its business license suspended for 10 days for the first offense. A second offense results in the permanent revocation of the business license. Other states are considering similar legislation.

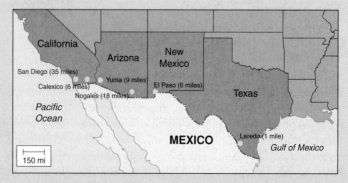

Existing miles of steel fences near U.S. cities along the Mexico border, 2007.

© AP Images/Matt York.

Millions of illegal residents managed to legalize themselves by taking advantage of government amnesties offered between 1984 and 2000. In his State of the Union address in 2005, President Bush called for a temporary-worker program that would legalize the presence of millions of undocumented workers. "We should not be content with laws that punish hard-working people who want only to provide for their families. . . . It is time for an immigration policy that permits temporary guest-workers to fill jobs that Americans will not take," he declared. Congressional efforts to pass a comprehensive immigration reform bill failed in 2007, however. It called for more border security, a guest worker program, and a path to citizenship for those already here.

Considering the Issues

1. It is estimated that some 800,000 unauthorized immigrants enter the United States each year, and most find gainful employment, yet the country issues only 5000 visas a year for unskilled foreigners seeking year-round work. Should the United States increase the number of visas available?

2. Making illegal crossings more difficult in California has not diminished the number of migrants making the journey north; it has simply pushed *coyotes,* the people who lead migrants across the border, into Arizona. Some people believe resourceful migrants will always find a way to get across the border. As one observer noted, "It's like putting rocks in a river—the water just goes around it." Do you think there is any way to seal the entire U.S.-Mexico border, or will immigration continue as long as the income gap between the United States and Latin America remains great? Could the United States reduce immigration pressures by improving the Mexican economy?

3. What reasons can you think of why anti-immigrant sentiment is directed chiefly against unauthorized immigrants from Latin America? Will such feelings eventually fade, as did earlier ones about the immigration of Irish Catholics, Chinese, Eastern Europeans, and other groups?

4. With regard to President Bush's proposal for a temporary-worker program, the libertarian Cato Institute argues that, when there is no immigration barrier, *circular migration* occurs, with migrant workers entering and leaving almost at will. It cites Puerto Rico as an example; many who move to the mainland stay for just a few years, and out-migration from the island is very low. A temporary-worker program, on the other hand, encourages migrants to move north with their entire families, and those who are already in the United States stay for good, because border crossings become more expensive and dangerous. If you were a member of Congress, would you be in favor of creating a guest-worker program? Why or why not?

5. It is often said that illegal aliens perform jobs Americans won't take. Why do you think the immigrants are willing to work for low wages, often under poor working conditions? Would Americans take the jobs if they were paid, say, $20 per hour and offered health care and other benefits?

6. What would happen if all states followed Arizona's lead in passing and enforcing laws targeting employers of undocumented workers? One in 10 or 11 workers in Arizona is undocumented, and opponents of the legislation contend that the state has put its economy in jeopardy. The workers tend to be reliable, they fill necessary jobs, they spend their wages in the communities in which they live and work, and most pay taxes because employers in the construction, hotel, restaurant, and other industries withhold taxes from paychecks.

7. Should illegal residents already here be given the opportunity to get worker permits and the possibility of eventual citizenship if they have no criminal record, pay a fine, and demonstrate that they are gainfully employed and have paid taxes?

8. Do you believe the federal government has an obligation to fully or partially reimburse state and local governments for the costs of education, medical care, incarceration, and other legal services for unauthorized immigrants? Why or why not?

9. Should the United States require citizens to have a national identification card and to present it to officials upon demand? If so, would all people who look like they may have been born abroad feel it necessary to carry proof of citizenship at all times?

in advanced economies. The migration presumably paralleled the number of perceived opportunities within cities and convictions of absence of place utility in the rural districts. Perceptions, of course, do not necessarily accord with reality. Rapid increases in impoverished rural populations of developing countries put increasing and unsustainable pressures on land, fuel, and water in the countryside. Landlessness and hunger, as well as the loss of social cohesion that the growing competition for declining resources induces, help force migration to cities. As a result, while the rate of urban growth is decreasing in the more-developed countries, urbanization in the developing world continues apace, as will be discussed more fully in Chapter 11.

Barriers to Migration

Paralleling the incentives to migration is a set of disincentives, or barriers, to migration. They help account for the fact that many people do not choose to move even when conditions are bad at home and are known to be better elsewhere. Migration depends on knowledge of the opportunities in other areas. People with a limited knowledge of the opportunities elsewhere are less likely to migrate than are those who are better informed. Other barriers include physical features, the costs of moving, ties to individuals and institutions in the original activity space, and governmental regulations.

Physical barriers to travel include seas, mountains, swamps, deserts, and other natural features. In prehistoric times, physical barriers played an especially significant role in limiting movement. Thus, the spread of the ice sheets across most of Europe in Pleistocene times was a barrier to both migration and human habitation. Physical barriers to movement have probably assumed less importance only within the past 400 years. The developments that made possible the great age of exploration, beginning about A.D. 1500, and the technological developments associated with industrialization have enabled people to conquer space more easily. With industrialization came improved forms of transportation, which made travel faster, easier, and cheaper. Even then, as the conditions the Pony Express riders experienced only a century and a half ago show, travel could be arduous, and in some parts of the world, it remains so today.

Economic barriers to migration include the cost of both traveling and establishing a residence elsewhere. Frequently, the additional expense of maintaining contact with those left behind is also a pertinent cost factor. Normally, all of these costs increase with the distance traveled and are a more significant barrier to travel for the poor than for the rich. Many immigrants to the United States were married men who came alone; when they had acquired enough money, they sent for their families to join them. This phenomenon is still evident among recent immigrants from the Caribbean area to the United States and among Turks, Yugoslavs, and West Indians who have settled in northern and Western European countries. The *cost factor* limits long-distance movement, but the larger the differential between present circumstances and perceived opportunities, the more individuals are willing to spend on moving. For many, especially older people, the differentials must be extraordinarily high for movement to take place.

Cultural factors also contribute to decisions not to migrate. Family, religious, ethnic, and community relationships defy the principle of differential opportunities. Many people will not migrate under any but the most pressing of circumstances. The fear of change and human inertia—the fact that it is easier not to move than to do so—may be so great that people consider, but reject, a move. Ties to one's own country, culture group, neighborhood, or family may be so strong as to compensate for the disadvantages of the home location. Returning migrants may convince potential leavers that the opportunities are not, in fact, better elsewhere—or that, even if they are better, they are not worth entering an alien culture or sacrificing home and family.

Restrictions on immigration and emigration constitute *political barriers* to migration. Many governments frown on movements into or outside their own borders and restrict out-migration. These restrictions may make it impossible for potential migrants to leave, and they certainly limit the number who can do so. On the other hand, countries suffering from an excess of workers often encourage emigration. The huge migration of people to the Americas in the late 19th and early 20th centuries is a good example of perceived opportunities for economic gain far greater than in the home country. Many European countries were overpopulated, and their political and economic systems stifled domestic economic opportunity at a time when people were needed by American entrepreneurs hoping to increase their wealth in untapped resource-rich areas.

The most-developed countries where per capita incomes are high, or perceived as high, are generally the most desired international destinations. In order to protect themselves against overwhelming migration streams, such countries as the United States, Australia, France, and Germany have restrictive policies on immigration. In addition to absolute quotas on the number of immigrants (usually classified by country of origin), a country may impose other requirements, such as the possession of a labor permit or sponsorship by a recognized association.

Patterns of Migration

Several geographic concepts deal with patterns of migration. The first of these is the **migration field,** an area or areas that dominate a locale's in- and out-migration patterns. For any single place, the origin of its in-migrants and the destination of its out-migrants remain fairly stable spatially over time. As would be expected, areas near the point of origin make up the largest part of the migration field (Figure 8.24). However, places far away, especially large cities, may also be prominent. These characteristics of migration fields are functions of the hierarchical movement to larger places and the fact that so many people live in large metropolitan areas that one may expect some migration into and out of them from most areas within a country.

Migration fields do not conform exactly to the diffusion concepts mentioned earlier in the section "Diffusion and Innovation." As Figure 8.25 shows, some migration fields reveal a distinctly *channelized* pattern of flow. The channels link areas that are socially and economically tied to one another by past migration patterns, economic trade considerations, or some

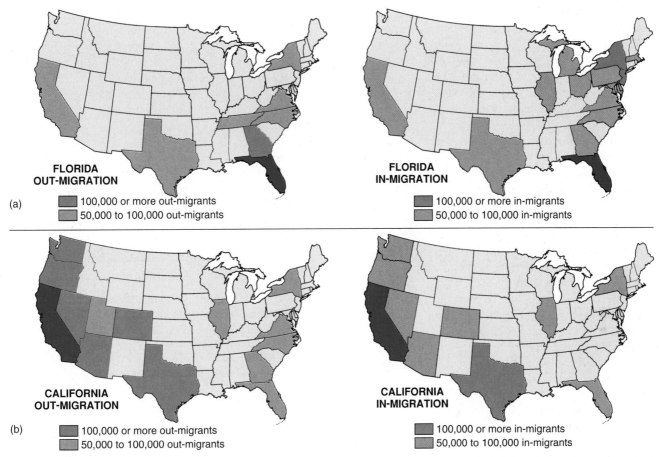

FIGURE 8.24 The migration fields of Florida and California in 1995–2000. (a) For Florida, nearby Georgia receives most out-migrants, but in-migrants originate in large numbers from the northeastern United States. **(b)** For California, the nearby western states receive large numbers of out-migrants, and there are fewer in-migrants from those states. *Source: United States Census Bureau.*

other affinity. As a result, flows of migration along these channels are greater than would otherwise be the case. The former movements of blacks from the southern United States to the North; of Scandinavians to Minnesota and Wisconsin; of Mexicans to such border states as California, Texas, and New Mexico; and of retirees to Florida and Arizona are all examples of **channelized migration** flows.

Of course, not all immigrants stay permanently at their first destination. Of the approximately 80 million newcomers to the United States between 1900 and 1980, some 10 million returned to their homelands or moved to another country. Estimates for Canada indicate that perhaps 40 of each 100 immigrants eventually leave, and about 25% of newcomers to Australia also depart permanently. A corollary of all out-migration flows is, therefore, **return migration,** or **countermigration,** the return of migrants to the regions from which they had earlier emigrated (Figure 8.26).

Within the United States, return migration—moving back to one's state of birth—makes up about 20% of all domestic moves. That figure varies dramatically among states, however. More than a third of recent in-migrants to West Virginia, for example, were returnees, as were over 25% of those moving to Pennsylvania, Alabama, Iowa, and a few other states. Such widely different states as New Hampshire, Maryland, California, Florida, Wyoming, and

Alaska were among those that found returnees were fewer than 10% of their in-migrants. Interviews suggest that states deemed attractive draw new migrants in large numbers, whereas those with high proportions of returnees in the migrant stream are not perceived as desirable destinations by other than former residents.

If freedom of movement is not restricted, it is not unusual for as many as 25% of all migrants to return to their place of origin. Unsuccessful migration is sometimes due to an inability to adjust to the new environment. More often, it is the result of false expectations based on distorted mental images of the destination at the time of the move. Myths, secondhand and false information, and people's own exaggerations contribute to what turn out to be a mistaken decision to move. Although return migration often represents the unsuccessful adjustment of individuals to a new environment, it does not necessarily mean that negative information about a place returns with the migrant. It usually means a reinforcement of the channel, as communication lines between the unsuccessful migrant and would-be migrants take on added meaning and understanding.

In addition to channelization, the influence of large cities causes migration fields to deviate from the distance-decay pattern. The concept of **hierarchical migration** assists in understanding the nature of migration fields. Earlier we noted that

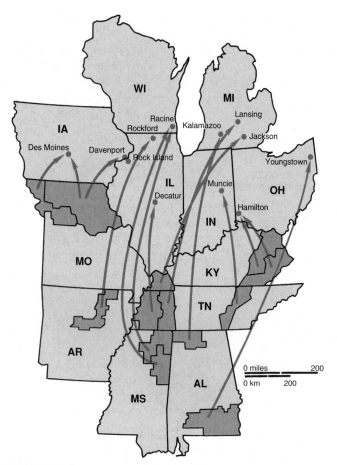

FIGURE 8.25 Channelized migration flows from the rural South to midwestern cities of medium size. Distance is not necessarily the main determinant of flow direction. Perhaps through family and friendship links, the rural southern areas are tied to particular midwestern destinations. *Redrawn by permission from* Proceedings of the Association of American Geographers, *C. C. Roseman, Vol. 3, p. 142. Copyright © Association of American Geographers. Reprinted by permission of Blackwell Publishers.*

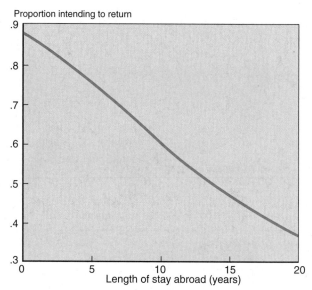

FIGURE 8.26 Migrants originally from the former Yugoslavia intending to return home from Germany. As the length of stay in Germany increases, the proportion intending to return decreases, but even after 10 years abroad, more than half intend to return. *Redrawn from B. Waldorf, "Determinants of International Return Migration Intentions,"* The Professional Geographer, *47, no. 2, Fig. 2, p. 132. Association of American Geographers, 1995.*

sometimes information diffuses according to a hierarchical rule—that is, from city to city at the highest level in the hierarchy and then to lower levels. Hierarchical migration, in a sense, is a response to that flow. The tendency is for individuals in domestic relocations to move up the level in the hierarchy, from small places to larger ones. Very often, levels are skipped on the way up; only in periods of general economic decline is there considerable movement down the hierarchy. The suburbs of large cities are considered part of the metropolitan area, so the movement from a town to a suburb is considered a move up the hierarchy. From this hierarchical pattern, we can envisage information flowing down to small places from cities and metropolitan areas, and migration flowing up from rural to urban regions.

GLOBALIZATION

We have seen how the cost of communication affects the degree of spatial interaction between places. In the past 20 years, we have witnessed the development of the Internet and have benefited from relatively low transportation costs. Increased

computerization of transactions has made it easy to buy goods from abroad and to travel abroad. During this period, there also has been a strong movement throughout the world to reduce the barriers to trade and foreign investment and ownership. The European Union is a good case in point. Its currency, the *euro*, now makes it possible to conduct financial transactions in a single currency, much as is the case in the United States. Computer technology enables investors to buy stock on foreign stock exchanges or to buy mutual funds that represent firms whose headquarters are in many parts of the world. The new technologies have helped bring about a globalizing world where people are more interdependent than ever before. **Globalization**—the increasing interconnection of all parts of the world—affects economic, political, and cultural patterns and processes.

Economic Integration

One might view the world of the 1950s through the 1980s as a period of division, when there was a wide breach between the peoples of the Western world and those of the communist world. Each side had opposing views about how economic and political systems should be organized. It was a world of division, not integration.

Integration and interdependence characterize globalization. The fact that Eastern and Western Europe are coming together as a single economic entity, and that the East and South Asian countries' economies are being integrated into those of Europe and North America, is as much a function of the revolution in communication and computer technologies as it is the will of the world's political and financial leaders. Low-cost, high-speed computers; communications satellites;

trading throughout the world. The financial balances between companies are monitored closely by brokers and traders around the world. As a result, split-second changes in all markets are possible. Within minutes of the 9/11/01 attacks on the World Trade Center and Pentagon, stock markets everywhere went down as investors sensed that the international marketplace was in jeopardy of losing its stability.

The internationalization of finance is also reflected in the immense amount of money in foreign investments. Many Americans, for example, own foreign stocks and bonds, either directly or through mutual funds and pension plans. Similarly, people outside the United States have significant holdings in U.S. companies and in U.S. treasury bonds.

Transnational Corporations

The past 20 years have seen a tremendous increase in the number of **transnational corporations (TNCs),** companies that have headquarters in one country and subsidiary companies, factories, and other facilities (laboratories, offices, warehouses, and so on) in several countries. As many as 65,000 TNCs—with several hundred thousand affiliates worldwide—engage in economic activities that are international in scope (Figure 8.28). They account for trillions of dollars in sales and, by some estimates, control about one-third of the world's productive assets (see also "Transnational Corporations" in Chapter 10).

The way that TNCs produce and provide goods and services is also a part of the globalization process. By exploiting the large differential in wage rates around the world, they keep their production costs down, which has led to the decentralization of manufacturing. More and more, American, Japanese, and Western European companies produce their manufactured goods in lower labor cost countries, such as China, Thailand, and Mexico, integrating these developing countries into the global economy.

In the United States, the service sector of employment has risen dramatically as the manufacturing sector has declined. Instead of producing heavy manufactured goods, the U.S. economy has moved toward the production of high-technology goods and services. The service sector has blossomed as the number of financial transactions has increased. With the increased wealth resulting from the effects of new technologies on production processes, Americans are able to travel more and to stay at hotels and eat out more often. This has a great bearing on the types of jobs people hold, not only in the United States but throughout the business and tourist world. These developments are discussed in more detail in Chapter 10.

Global Marketing

The greater wealth of those who have benefited from globalization has created a huge new market for goods and services. TNCs market their products around the world, whether they be goods such as Swiss watches, Italian shoes, or Coca-Cola or the services provided by, for example, worldwide hotel chains or cellular phone companies. Japanese cars are found in all parts of the world, just as are fast-food chains. Some of the ramifications of this are discussed in the section "Cultural Integration."

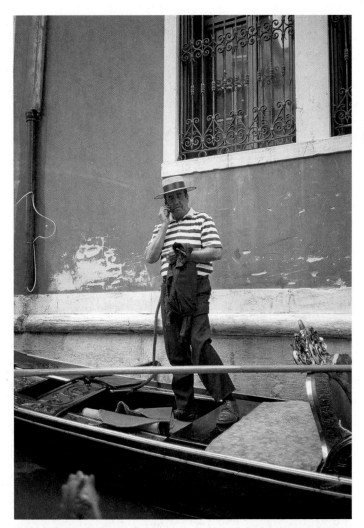

FIGURE 8.27 The old and the new: a gondolier in Venice, Italy, conducting business on a cellular phone. *Courtesy of Arthur Getis.*

fiber-optic networks; and the Internet are the main technologies of the revolution, but other technologies, such as robotics, microelectronics, electronic mail, fax machines, and cellular phones also play an important role (Figure 8.27). The fact that a consumer in Athens, Greece, can order a book from Amazon.com or clothes from Lands' End, obtain news from CNN, or engage in a transaction on the London Stock Exchange while talking on a cellular phone to a colleague in Tokyo is revolutionary. The forces at work on Americans, the Japanese, and the British have the same effect on Greek consumers as they go about their daily activities. Thus, globalization brings about greater integration and a great deal more spatial interaction.

International Banking

International banking has become a complex system of integrated and interdependent financial markets. It is no wonder that the various stock exchanges of the world tend to rise and fall together. There are exceptions, of course, but when a pharmaceutical company such as Pfizer buys Warner-Lambert Pharmaceuticals, it affects pharmaceutical stock

(a) Nokia—Finland (Pakistan)

(b) KitKat—U.K. (Bhutan)

(c) Sony—Japan (China)

(d) Ford—United States (China)

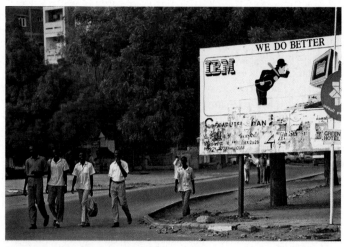

(e) IBM—United States (Sudan)

FIGURE 8.28 The number of the world's transnational corporations increased in number from about 7000 in 1970 to over 77,000 in 2005. Ninety of the top 100 TNCs are headquartered in the European Union, the United States, and Japan. Their impact, however, is global, as suggested by these billboards advertising just a sample of leading TNCs in distant settings. Corporate names and headquarters countries are followed by billboard locations in parentheses. *(a) © Robert Nickelsberg/Getty; (b) © Tim Graham/Getty; (c) © Bloomberg/Getty; (d) © Steven Harris/Newsmakers/Getty; (e) © Barry Iverson/Time Life Pictures/Getty.*

It is important to remember, however, that globalization is a fairly recent development, and at present its benefits accrue to a minority of the world's 6 billion people. Only one-tenth of those people, about 600 million, are affluent enough to live comfortably and to purchase the goods and services alluded to earlier. According to the United Nations Development Fund, one-quarter of humanity lives on less than $1 per day. An illiterate farmer in a remote village in Tibet more than likely lacks access to a telephone, much less the new technologies of the revolution in communications.

Political Integration

The flow of money (capital), goods, ideas, and information around the globe links people in ways that transcend national boundaries. One effect has been to stimulate the formation of new, supranational alliances or the restructuring of older ones. To enhance commerce, countries are signing free-trade agreements and joining economic organizations such as the North American Free-Trade Agreement (1994) and the World Trade Organization (1995). As will be discussed in Chapter 9, many other international alliances—military, political, and cultural—have been created since 1980, and some that are older, such as NATO, are enlarging their membership.

Another effect of globalization has been the enormous increase in the number of international *nongovernmental organizations* (NGOs). Their number more than quadrupled during the 1990s, from about 6000 to more than 26,000. As the names of such well-known organizations as Amnesty International, Doctors without Borders, and Greenpeace indicate, the concerns of international NGOs range widely, from human rights and acid rain to famine relief and resource depletion. What they have in common is that they bring together people in far-flung parts of the world in pursuit of mutual goals.

The transmission of news has never been wider or faster. *Time Magazine* can be bought as easily in New Delhi, India, as in New York City, and CNN broadcasts around the world, informing people about current events and, sometimes, helping bring about government intervention in places where it might not have occurred. Coverage of the wars in Bosnia and Kosovo, for example, stimulated the United Nations and NATO to send in peacekeeping troops to stop the carnage. More recently, in 2002, satellite television's graphic imagery of the havoc wrought by Palestinian suicide bombers and Israeli retaliation fueled support for the Palestinian cause throughout the Arab world.

Finally, the Internet has given people a powerful tool to affect governmental policies. To give just a few examples, in 1989, pro-democracy students in Beijing, China, used the Internet to publicize what was happening in that city and to rally support for their cause. The woman who won the Nobel Peace Prize in 1997 for her contribution to the international campaign to ban landmines, Jody Williams, used e-mail to organize 1000 human rights and arms control groups on six continents. Similarly, NGOs use the Internet to coordinate massive protests against meetings of the World Trade Organization (Figure 8.29).

FIGURE 8.29 Some of the thousands of people who demonstrated in Geneva, Switzerland, in 2009 against the World Trade Organization (WTO) and its policies. Among the protesters were those representing hundreds of NGOs. © *Fabrice Coffrini/AFP/Getty Images.*

Cultural Integration

Imagine this scene: wearing a Yankees baseball cap, a GAP shirt, Levis, and Reebok shoes, a teenager in Lima, Peru, goes with her friends to see the latest thriller. After the movie, they plan to eat at a nearby McDonald's. Meanwhile, her brother sits at home, listening to his iPod while playing a video game. Both children are evidence of the globalization of culture, particularly pop culture. That culture is Western in origin and chiefly American. U.S. movies, television shows, software, music, food, and fashion are marketed worldwide. They influence the beliefs, tastes, and aspirations of people in virtually every country, although their effect is most pronounced on young people. They, rather than their elders, are the ones who want to emulate the stars they see in movies and on YouTube and to adopt what they think are Western lifestyles, manners, and modes of dress.

Another indication of cultural integration is the worldwide spread of the English language. It has become *the* medium of communication in economics, technology, and science.

Both the dominance of English and the globalization of popular culture are resented by many people and rejected by some. Iran, Singapore, and China attempt to restrict the programming that reaches their people, although their citizens' access to satellite dishes and the Internet means those governments are not succeeding in stopping the spread of Western culture. French ministers of culture try to keep the French language pure, unadulterated by English. Other people decry what they see as the homogenization of culture, and still others find the spread of what they define as Western cultural values abhorrent. Whether or not movies, music, and other communications media accurately reflect Western culture, critics argue that they reflect values such as materialism, innovation, self-indulgence, sexuality, spontaneity, and defiance of authority and tradition. Many movies and television shows appear to glorify violence and rebellion and to promote the new over the old, leisure over work, and wealth over self-fulfillment.

I t was the autumn of 1918. War had been raging for 4 years, and Germany and its allies, the Ottoman Empire and Austria-Hungary, were suffering huge losses. In the Middle East, the British and their Arab allies had pinned down and defeated the Ottoman Turks. T. E. Lawrence, a British officer, hurried straight from the battlefields of Damascus to the British War Cabinet meeting in London, intent on arguing the cause of Arab sovereignty.

The Middle East, Lawrence knew, had been under the domination of the Ottoman Empire for centuries. He felt, however, that with British and Arab military victories the time had come to rewrite the map of the Middle East. Accordingly, Lawrence presented his map, in which he proposed new national boundaries for the Middle East (Figure 9.1).

Lawrence argued that the Kurds should have a separate state and that the people of what are now Syria, Jordan, and Saudi Arabia belonged together in one country. He felt that Sunnis and Shi'ites should not be separated in the area that is now Iraq, which is one of the issues that divides the region

today. He also placed "Palestine," or a Jewish homeland, on the map.

His reasoning fell on deaf ears. The great powers represented during the peace process carved the region up to reward war allies with resource-rich areas. The peace treaties divided the region into Greek, British, French, and Italian areas of influence and occupation. Only the areas south of what is now Iraq and Jordan were demarcated as independent Arab states.

Would Lawrence's map have changed history? There is no way to know for certain, of course, but some scholars concede that Lawrence's division of the area might have provided a more stable Middle East than the one based on the extent of influence of European powers. Between the end of the war and the current day, wars, revolutions, and alliances have redrawn the borders in the area many times. The region is home to different ethnic groups, religions, and political systems and has been a part of a continuing process of the political organization of space.

(a)

(b)

FIGURE 9.1 (a) T. E. Lawrence's Peace Map and (b) a current map of the Middle East. T. E. Lawrence's map of the Middle East was misfiled in the British national archives for decades and only recently rediscovered. Compare it to a current map of the region. Of note:

- Lawrence envisioned a Jewish state called Palestine; the state of Israel was not established until 1948, after 6 million Jews had died in the Holocaust.

- Lawrence included a separate state for Armenians; the territory of historic Armenia had been divided by the Ottomans and the Russians. Now, that area is part of Turkey.

- Lawrence included an area of French administration along the Mediterranean Sea; the British and French agreed during World War I that the French would control the area that is now made up of Lebanon and Syria. Lebanon gained independance in 1943, Syria in 1944, while France was occupied by Nazi Germany.

- Lawrence envisioned at least three Arab states under British influence; settlements at the end of World War I gave Britain a mandate over what is now Iraq, Jordan, Israel, the West Bank, and the Gaza Strip. British companies had freedom to explore and develop Iraqi oil fields.

FIGURE 9.2 These flags, symbols of separate member states, grace the front of the United Nations building in New York City. Although central to political geographic interest, states are only one level of the political organization of space. © *Corbis RF.*

The process of the political organization of space is as old as human history. From clans to kingdoms, human groups have laid claim to territory and have organized themselves and administered their affairs within it. Indeed, the political organizations of society are as fundamental an expression of culture and cultural differences as are forms of economy or religious beliefs. Geographers are interested in that structuring because it is an expression of the human organization of space and is closely related to other spatial evidences of culture, such as religion, language, and ethnicity.

Political geography is the study of the organization and spatial distribution of political phenomena. Nationality is a basic element in cultural variation among people, and political geography traditionally has had a primary interest in country units, or *states* (Figure 9.2). Of central concern have been spatial patterns that reflect the exercise of central governmental control, such as questions of boundary delimitation and effect. Increasingly, however, attention has shifted both upward and downward on the political scale. On the world scene, international alliances, regional compacts, and producer cartels have increased in prominence since 1945, representing new forms of spatial interaction. At the local level, voting patterns, constituency boundaries and districting rules, and political fragmentation have directed public attention to the significance of area in the domestic political process.

In this chapter, we discuss some of the characteristics of political entities, examine the problems involved in defining jurisdictions, seek the elements that lend cohesion to a political entity, explore the implications of partial surrender of sovereignty, and consider the significance of the fragmentation of political power. We begin with states and end with local political systems.

The emphasis in this chapter on political entities should not make us lose sight of the reality that states are rooted in the operations of the economy and society they represent, that social and economic disputes are as significant as border confrontations, and that in some regards transnational corporations and other nongovernmental agencies may exert more influence in international affairs than do the separate states in which they are housed or operate. Some of those expanded political considerations are alluded to in the discussions that follow; others are developed more fully in Chapter 10.

NATIONAL POLITICAL SYSTEMS

One of the most significant elements in cultural geography is the nearly complete division of the earth's land surface into separate national units, as shown on the Countries of the World map fold out at the end of the book. Even Antarctica is subject to the rival territorial claims of seven countries, although these claims have not been pressed because of the Antarctic Treaty of 1959 (Figure 9.3). Another element is that this division into country units is relatively recent. Although countries and empires have existed since the days of ancient Egypt and Mesopotamia, only in the past century has the world been almost completely divided into independent governing entities. Now, people everywhere accept the idea of the state, and its claim to sovereignty within its borders, as normal.

States, Nations, and Nation-States

Before we begin our consideration of political systems, we need to clarify some terminology. Geographers use the words *state* and *nation* somewhat differently than the way they are used in everyday speech; the confusion arises because each word has more than one meaning. A state can be defined as either (1) any of the political units forming a federal government (e.g., one of the United States) or (2) an independent political unit holding sovereignty over a territory (e.g., the United States). In the latter sense, *state* is synonymous with *country* or *nation*. That is, a nation can also be defined as (1) an independent political unit holding sovereignty over a territory (e.g., a member of the United Nations). But it can also be used to describe (2) a community of people with a common culture and territory (e.g., the Kurdish nation). The second definition is *not* synonymous with *state* or *country*.

To avoid confusion, we will define a **state** on the international level as an independent political unit occupying a defined, permanently populated territory and having full sovereign control over its internal and foreign affairs. We will use

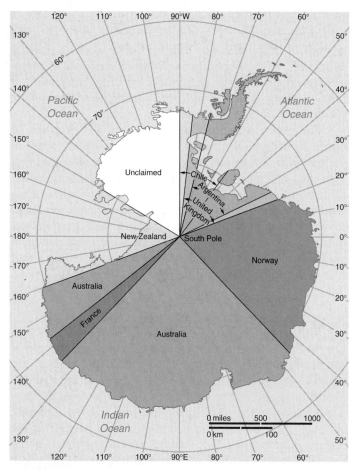

FIGURE 9.3 Territorial claims in Antarctica. Seven countries claim sovereignty over portions of Antarctica, and those of Argentina, Chile, and the United Kingdom overlap. The Antarctic Treaty of 1959 banned further land claims and made scientific research the primary use of the continent. Antarctica is neither a sovereign state—it has no permanent inhabitants or local government—nor a part of one.

country as a synonym for the territorial and political concept of "state." Not all recognized territorial entities are states. Antarctica, for example, has neither an established government nor a permanent population; it is, therefore, not a state. Nor are *colonies* or *protectorates* recognized as states. Although they have defined extent, permanent inhabitants, and some degree of separate governmental structure, they lack full control over all of their internal and external affairs.

We use *nation* in its second sense, as a reference to people, not to political structure. A **nation** is a group of people with a common culture occupying a particular territory, bound together by a strong sense of unity arising from shared beliefs and customs. Language and religion may be unifying elements, but even more important are an emotional conviction of cultural distinctiveness and a sense of ethnocentrism. For example, the Cree nation exists because of its cultural uniqueness, not by virtue of territorial sovereignty.

The composite term **nation-state** properly refers to a state whose territorial extent coincides with that occupied by a distinct nation or people or, at least, whose population shares a general sense of cohesion and adherence to a set of common values (Figure 9.4a). That is, a nation-state is an entity whose members feel a natural connection with each other by virtue of sharing language, religion, or some other cultural characteristic strong enough both to bind them together and to give them a sense of distinction from all others outside the community. In reality, very few countries can claim to be true nation-states, since few are or have ever been wholly uniform ethnically or culturally. Iceland, Slovenia, Poland, and the two Koreas are often cited as acceptable examples.

A *binational* or *multinational state* is one that contains more than one nation (Figure 9.4b). Often, no single ethnic group dominates the population. In the constitutional structure of the Soviet Union before 1988, one division of the legislative branch of the government was termed the Soviet of Nationalities. It was composed of representatives from civil divisions of the Soviet Union populated by groups of officially recognized "nations": Ukrainians, Kazakhs, Estonians, and others. In this instance, the concept of nationality was territorially less than the extent of the state.

Alternatively, a single nation may be dispersed across and be predominant in two or more states. This is the case with a *part-nation state* (Figure 9.4c). Here, a people's sense of nationality exceeds the areal limits of a single state. An example is the Arab nation, which dominates 17 states.

Finally, there is the special case of the *stateless nation*, a people without a state. The Kurds, for example, are a nation of approximately 20 million people divided among six states and dominant in none (Figure 9.4d). Kurdish nationalism has survived over the centuries, and many Kurds nurture a vision of an independent Kurdistan. Other stateless nations are the Roma (gypsies), Basques, and Palestinians.

Evolution of the Modern State

The concept and practice of the political organization of space and people arose independently in many parts of the world. Our Western orientations and biases may incline us to trace ideas of spatial political organization through their Near Eastern, Mediterranean, and Western European expressions. Mesopotamian and classical Greek city-states, the Roman Empire, and European colonizing kingdoms and warring principalities were, however, not unique. Southern, southeastern, and eastern Asia had their counterparts, as did sub-Saharan Africa and the Western Hemisphere. Although Western European models and colonization strongly influenced the forms and structures of modern states around the world, the cultural roots of statehood run deeper and reach further back in many parts of the world than the European example alone suggests.

The now universal idea of the modern state was developed by European political philosophers in the 18th century. Their views advanced the concept that people owe allegiance to a state and the people it represents, rather than to its leader, such as a king or a feudal lord. The new concept coincided in

France with the French Revolution and spread over Western Europe, to England, Spain, and Germany.

Many states are the result of European expansion during the 17th, 18th, and 19th centuries, when much of Africa, Asia, and the Americas was divided into colonies. Usually these colonial claims were given fixed and described boundaries where none had earlier been formally defined. Of course, precolonial native populations had relatively fixed home areas of control within which there was recognized dominance and border defense and from which there were, perhaps, raids of plunder or conquest of neighboring "foreign" territories. Beyond understood tribal territories, great empires arose, again with recognized outer limits of influence or control: Mogul and Chinese; Benin and Zulu; Incan and Aztec. Upon them where they still existed, and upon the less formally organized spatial patterns of effective tribal control, European colonizers imposed their arbitrary new administrative divisions of the land. In fact, groups that had little in common were often joined in the same colony (Figure 9.5). The new divisions, therefore, were not usually based on meaningful cultural or physical lines. Instead, the boundaries simply represented the limits of the colonizing empire's power.

As these former colonies have gained political independence, they have retained the idea of the state. They have generally accepted—in the case of Africa, by a conscious decision to avoid precolonial territorial or ethnic claims that could lead to war—the borders established by their former European rulers. The problem that many of the new countries face is "nation-building"—developing feelings of loyalty to the state among their arbitrarily associated citizens. Julius Nyerere, president of Tanzania, noted in 1971, "These new countries are artificial units, geographical expressions carved on the map by European imperialists. These are the units we have tried to turn into nations."

The idea of separate statehood grew slowly at first and more recently has accelerated rapidly. At the time of the Declaration of Independence of the United States in 1776, there were only about 35 empires, kingdoms, and countries in the entire world. By the beginning of World War II in 1939, their number had only doubled to about 70. Following that war, the end of the colonial era brought a rapid increase in the number of sovereign states. With the disintegration of the USSR, Czechoslovakia, and Yugoslavia, more than 20 countries were created (Figure 9.6). In 2009, there were nearly 200 independent states, and scholars predict that the number will continue to rise as small territories achieve independence, large states break up, and suppressed peoples claim autonomy.

Challenges to the State

The state and nation-state have long been the focus of political geography, and we will keep that focus in much of the following discussion. We should also realize, however, that the

(a)

(b)

(c)

(d)

FIGURE 9.4 **Types of relationships between states and nations. (a) Nation-states.** Poland and Slovenia are examples of states occupied by a distinct nation, or people. **(b) A multinational state.** Switzerland shows that a common ethnicity, language, or religion is not necessary for a strong sense of nationalism. **(c) A part-nation state.** The Arab nation extends across and dominates many states in northern Africa and the Middle East. **(d) A stateless nation.** An ancient group with a distinctive language, Kurds are concentrated in Turkey, Iran, and Iraq. Smaller numbers live in Syria, Armenia, and Azerbaijan.

Ethnic Territories
- Kurdish
- Kurdish/Sunni Arab*
- Sunni Arab*
- Sunni/Shia Arab*
- Shia Arab*
- * Within Iraq

FIGURE 9.5 The discrepancies between ethnic groups and national boundaries in Africa. Cultural boundaries were ignored by European colonial powers. The result was significant ethnic diversity in nearly all African countries and conflicts between countries over borders. *Modified from* World Regional Geography: A Question of Place *by Paul Ward English, with James Andrew Miller.*

validity of that state-centric view of the world is increasingly under assault from multiple new agents of economic and social power. These agents include the following:

- The globalization of economies and the emergence of transnational corporations whose economic and production decisions are unrelated to the interests of any single state, including their home office state. Those decisions—outsourcing of production and services, for example—may be detrimental to the employment structure, tax base, and national security of any single state and limit the applicability of national economic planning and control.

- The proliferation of international and supranational institutions initially concerned with financial or security matters but all representing the voluntary surrender of some traditional state autonomy. The World Trade

Organization, the European Union, and regional trade blocs such as the North American Free-Trade Association and a host of other international agreements all limit the independence of action of each of their members and thus diminish absolute state primacy in economic and social matters.

- The emergence and multiplication of nongovernmental organizations (NGOs) whose specific interests and collective actions cut across national boundaries and unite people sharing common concerns about issues such as globalization, AIDS efforts, and economic and social injustice. The well-publicized protests and pressures exerted by NGOs channel social pressures to influence or limit governmental actions.

- The massive international migration flows that tend to undermine the state as a cultural community with

FIGURE 9.6 By mid-1992, 15 newly independent countries had taken the place of the former USSR.

One might assume that, the larger a state's area, the greater is the chance that it will have useful resources, such as fertile soil and minerals. In general, that assumption is valid, but much depends upon accidents of location. Mineral resources are unevenly distributed, and size alone does not guarantee their presence within a state. Australia, Canada, and Russia, though large, have relatively small areas capable of supporting productive agriculture. Great size, in fact, may be a disadvantage. A very large country may have vast areas that are inaccessible, sparsely populated, and hard to integrate into the mainstream of economy and society. Small states are more apt than large ones to have a culturally homogeneous population. They find it easier to develop transportation and communication systems to link the sections of the country, and, of course, they have shorter boundaries to defend against invasion. Size alone, then, is not critical in determining a country's stability and strength, but it is a contributing factor.

assured and expected common values and loyalties. The Internet, inexpensive communication methods, and easy international travel permit immigrant retention of primary ties with their home culture and state, discouraging their full assimilation into their new social environment or the transfer of their loyalties to their adopted country.

- The increase in nationalist and separatist movements in culturally composite states, weakening through demands for independence or regional autonomy the former unquestioned primacy of the established state.

Some of these agents and developments have been touched on in earlier chapters; others will be reviewed in this chapter (see especially "Centrifugal Forces," p. 291). All represent recent and strengthening forces that, in some assessments, weaken the validity of a worldview in which national governments and institutionalized politics are all-powerful.

Geographic Characteristics of States

Every state has certain geographic characteristics by which it can be described and that set it apart from all other states. A look at the world political map inside the cover of this book confirms that every state is unique. The size, shape, and location of any one state combine to distinguish it from all others. These characteristics also affect the power and stability of states.

Size

The area that a state occupies may be large, as is true of China, or small, as is Liechtenstein. The world's largest country, Russia, occupies more than 17 million square kilometers (6.5 million sq mi), or some 11% of the land surface of the world. It is more than a million times as large as Nauru, one of the ministates found in all parts of the world (see "The Ministates," p. 280).

Shape

Like size, a country's shape can affect its well-being by fostering or hindering effective organization. Assuming no major topographical barriers, the most efficient form would be a circle, with the capital located in the center. In such a country, all places could be reached from the center in a minimal amount of time and with the least expenditure for roads, railway lines, and so on. It would also have the shortest possible borders to defend. Zimbabwe, Uruguay, and Poland have roughly circular shapes, forming a **compact state** (Figure 9.7).

Prorupt states are nearly compact but possess one or sometimes two narrow extensions of territory. Proruption may simply reflect peninsular elongations of land area, as in the case of Myanmar and Thailand. In other cases, the extensions have an economic or strategic significance, having been designed to secure state access to resources or to establish a buffer zone between states that would otherwise adjoin. Whatever their origin, proruptions tend to isolate a portion of a state.

The least-efficient shape administratively is represented by countries such as Norway and Chile, which are long and narrow. In such **elongated states,** the parts of the country far from the capital are likely to be isolated because great expenditures are required to link them to the core. These countries are also likely to encompass more diversity of climate, resources, and peoples than compact states, perhaps to the detriment of national cohesion or, perhaps, to the promotion of economic strength.

The fourth class of shapes, that of **fragmented states,** includes countries composed entirely of islands (e.g., the Philippines and Indonesia), countries that are partly on islands and partly on the mainland (Italy and Malaysia), and those that are chiefly on the mainland but whose territory is separated

The Ministates

Totally or partially autonomous political units that are small in area and population pose some intriguing questions. Should size be a criterion for statehood? What is the potential of ministates to cause friction among the major powers? Under what conditions are they entitled to representation in international assemblies such as the United Nations?

Of the world's growing number of small countries, more than 40 have less than 1 million people, the population size adopted by the United Nations as the upper limit defining "small states," though not too small to be members of that organization. Nauru has about 13,000 inhabitants on its 21 square kilometers (8.2 sq mi). Other areally small states, such as Singapore, covering 685 square kilometers (264 sq mi), have populations (4.8 million) well above the UN criterion. Many are island territories located in the Caribbean and the Pacific Ocean (such as Grenada and Tonga Islands), but Europe (Vatican City and Andorra), Asia (Bahrain and Brunei), and Africa (Djibouti and Equatorial Guinea) have their share.

Many ministates are vestiges of colonial systems that no longer exist. Some of the small countries of West Africa and the Arabian peninsula fall into this category. Others, such as Mauritius, served primarily as refueling stops on transoceanic voyages.

However, some occupy strategic locations (such as Bahrain, Malta, and Singapore), and others contain valuable minerals (Kuwait and Trinidad). The possibility of claiming 370-kilometer-wide (200-nautical-mile) zones of adjacent seas (see p. 299) adds to the attraction of yet others.

Their strategic or economic value can expose small islands and territories to unwanted attention from larger neighbors. The 1982 war between Britain and Argentina over the Falkland Islands (called the Islas Malvinas by Argentina) and the Iraqi invasion of Kuwait in 1990 demonstrate the ability of such areas to bring major powers into conflict and to receive world attention that is out of proportion to their size and population.

The proliferation of tiny countries raises the question of their representation and their voting weight in international assemblies. Should there be a minimum size necessary for participation in such bodies? Should countries receive a vote proportional to their population? New members accepted into the United Nations in 1999 and 2000 included four small Pacific island countries, all with populations under 100,000: Nauru, Tonga, Kiribati, and Tuvalu. Within the United Nations, the Alliance of Small Island States (AOSIS) has emerged as a significant power bloc, controlling more than one-fifth of UN General Assembly votes.

Pacific Ocean ministates.

FIGURE 9.7 Shapes of states. The sizes of the countries should not be compared. Each is drawn on a different scale.

by another state (the United States). Fragmentation makes it harder for the state to impose centralized control over its territory, particularly when the parts of the state are far from one another. This is a problem in Indonesia, which is made up of more than 13,000 islands, stretched out along a 5100-kilometer (3200-mi) arc. Fragmentation helped lead to the disintegration of Pakistan. It was created in 1947 as a fragmented state, but East and West Pakistan were 1610 kilometers (1000 mi) from one another. That distance exacerbated economic and cultural differences between the two, and when the eastern part of the country seceded in 1971 and declared itself the independent state of Bangladesh, West Pakistan was unable to impose its control.

A special case of fragmentation occurs when a territorial outlier of one state, an **exclave,** is located within another state. Before German unification, West Berlin was an outlier of West Germany within East Germany (the German Democratic Republic). Europe has many such outlying bits of one country inside another. Kleinwalsertal, for example, is a piece of Austria accessible only from Germany. Baarle-Hertog is a fragment of Belgium inside Holland. Llivia is a Spanish town just inside France. Exclaves are not limited to Europe: African examples include Cabinda, an exclave of Angola, and Melilla and Ceuta, two Spanish exclaves in Morocco (Figure 9.8).

The counterpart of an exclave, an **enclave,** helps to define the fifth class of shapes, the **perforated state.** A perforated state completely surrounds a territory that it does not rule, as the Republic of South Africa surrounds Lesotho. The enclave, the surrounded territory, may be independent or may be part of another state. Two of Europe's smallest independent states, San Marino and Vatican City, are enclaves that perforate Italy. As an *exclave* of West Germany, West Berlin perforated the national territory of former East Germany and was an *enclave* in it. The stability of the perforated state can be weakened if the enclave is occupied by people whose value systems differ from those of the surrounding country.

Location

The significance of size and shape as factors in national well-being can be modified by a state's location, both absolute and relative. Although both Canada and Russia are extremely large, their *absolute* location in the upper-middle latitudes reduces their size advantages when agricultural potential is considered. For another example, Iceland has a reasonably compact shape, but its location in the North Atlantic Ocean, just south of the Arctic Circle, means that most of the country is barren. Settlement is confined to the rims of the island.

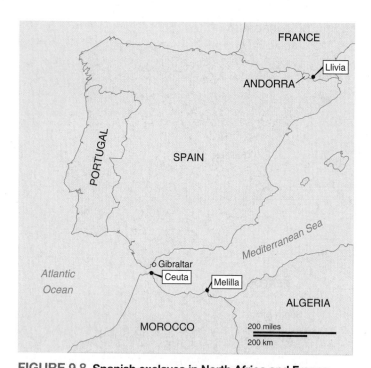

FIGURE 9.8 Spanish exclaves in North Africa and France.
Although Spanish troops seized the garrison towns of Melilla and Ceuta almost 500 years ago, and a majority of the exclaves's residents are of Spanish descent, Morocco still claims sovereignty over the towns. In recent years, Ceuta and Melilla have become the temporary stopping points for tens of thousands of would-be migrants to Spain. Emigrants from Mali, Nigeria, and as far away as Kashmir and Iraq enter Ceuta and Melilla requesting political asylum and seeking work permits or visas to enter Europe. Today the enclaves are surrounded by fences. Llivia became an exclave in 1660 when Spain ceded the surrounding area to France in the Treaty of the Pyrenees. Gibraltar is a British colony, and Andorra is an independent ministate.

A state's *relative* location, its position compared to that of other countries, is as important as its absolute location. *Landlocked* states, those lacking ocean frontage and surrounded by other states, are at a geographic disadvantage (Figure 9.9). They lack easy access to maritime (seaborne) trade and to the resources found in coastal waters and submerged lands. Bolivia gained 480 kilometers (300 mi) of sea frontier along with its independence in 1825, but lost its ocean frontage by conquest to Chile in 1879. Its annual Day of the Sea ceremony reminds Bolivians of their loss and of continuing diplomatic efforts to secure an alternate outlet. The number of landlocked states—about 40—increased greatly with the dissolution of the Soviet Union and the creation of new, smaller countries out of such former multinational countries as Yugoslavia and Czechoslovakia.

In a few instances, a favorable relative location constitutes the primary resource of a state. Singapore, a state of only 685 square kilometers (264 sq mi) and 4.8 million people, is located at a crossroads of world shipping and commerce. Based on its port and commercial activities, and buttressed by its more recent industrial development, Singapore has become a notable Southeast Asian economic success. In general, history has shown that countries benefit from a location on major trade routes, not only from the economic advantages such a location carries, but also because they are exposed to the diffusion of new ideas and technologies.

Cores and Capitals

Many states have come to assume their present shape, and thus the location they occupy, as a result of growth over centuries. They grew outward from a central region, gradually expanding

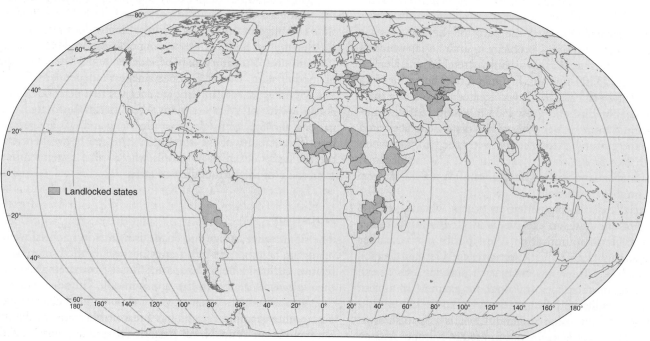

FIGURE 9.9 Landlocked states. Landlocked states are at a commercial and strategic disadvantage, compared to countries that have ocean frontage.

into surrounding territory. The original nucleus, or **core area,** of a state usually contains its densest population and largest cities, the most highly developed transportation system, and the most developed economic base. All of these elements become less intense away from the national core. Urbanization ratios and city sizes decline, transport networks thin, and economic development is less intensive on the periphery than in the core.

Easily recognized and unmistakably dominant national cores include the Paris Basin of France; London and southeastern England; Moscow and the major cities of European Russia; northeastern United States and southeastern Canada; and the Buenos Aires megalopolis in Argentina. Not all countries have such clearly defined cores, and some may have two or more rival core areas. Chad, Mongolia, and Saudi Arabia have no clearly defined core, for instance, whereas Ecuador, Nigeria, Democratic Republic of the Congo, and Vietnam are examples of multicore states.

The capital city of a state is usually within its core region and frequently is the very focus of it, dominant not only because it is the seat of central authority but because of the concentration of population and economic functions as well. That is, in many countries, the capital city is also the largest, or *primate* city, dominating the structure of the entire country. Paris in France, London in the United Kingdom, and Mexico City are all examples of that kind of political, cultural, and economic primacy.

This association of capital with core is common in what have been called the *unitary states,* countries with highly centralized governments, relatively few internal cultural contrasts, a strong sense of national identity, and borders that are clearly cultural as well as political boundaries. Most European cores and capitals are of this type. This association is also found in many newly independent countries whose former colonial occupiers established a primary center of exploitation and administration and developed a functioning core in a region that lacked an urban structure or organized government. With independence, the new states retained the established infrastructure, added new functions to the capital, and, through lavish expenditures on governmental, public, and commercial buildings, sought to create prestigious symbols of nationhood.

In *federal states,* associations of more or less equal provinces or states with strong regional governmental responsibilities, the capital city may have been newly created to serve as the administrative center. Although part of a generalized core region of the country, the designated capital was not its largest city and acquired few of the additional functions to make it so. Ottawa, Canada; Washington, D.C.; and Canberra, Australia, are examples (Figure 9.10).

A new form of state organization—*regional* government, or *asymmetric federalism*—is emerging in Europe as formerly strong unitary states acknowledge the autonomy aspirations of their several subdivisions and grant to them varying degrees of local administrative control while retaining in central hands authority over matters of nationwide concern, such as monetary policy, defense, and foreign relations. Autonomy is most likely to be granted to regions with the most outspoken

FIGURE 9.10 Canberra, the planned capital of Australia, was deliberately sited away from the country's two largest cities, Sydney and Melbourne. Planned capitals are often architectural showcases, providing a focus for national pride. © *Chris Groenhout.*

residents, who claim that their region is different from the national whole. Such claims are mostly based on differences in religions, languages, or economic centers and interests. National governments may recognize regional capitals, legislative assemblies, and administrative bureaucracies. The asymmetric federalism of the United Kingdom, for example, now involves separate status for Scotland, Wales, and Northern Ireland, with their own capitals at Edinburgh, Cardiff, and Belfast. That of Spain recognizes Catalonia and the Basque country, with capitals in Barcelona and Vitoria, respectively.

All other things being equal, a capital located in the center of the country provides equal access to the government, facilitates communication to and from the political hub, and enables the government to exert its authority easily. Many capital cities, such as Washington, D.C., were centrally located when they were designated as seats of government, but lost their centrality as the state expanded.

Some capital cities have been relocated outside of peripheral national core regions, at least in part to achieve the presumed advantages of centrality. Two examples of such relocation are from Karachi inland to Islamabad in Pakistan and from Istanbul to Ankara, in the center of Turkey's territory. A particular type of relocated capital is the *forward-thrust capital* city, one that has been deliberately sited in a state's frontier zone to signal the government's awareness of regions away from the core and its interest in encouraging more uniform development. In the late 1950s, Brazil moved its capital from Rio de Janeiro to the new city of Brasília to demonstrate its intent to develop the vast interior of the country. The West African country of Nigeria has been building the new capital of Abuja near its geographic center since the late 1970s, with the relocation there of government offices and foreign embassies in the early 1990s. The British colonial government relocated Canada's capital six times between 1841 and 1865, in part seeking centrality to the mid-19th-century population pattern and in part seeking a location that bridged that country's cultural divide (Figure 9.11).

Boundaries: The Limits of the State

Recall that no portion of the earth's land surface is outside the claimed control of a national unit, that even uninhabited Antarctica has had territorial claims imposed upon it (see Figure 9.3). Each of the world's states is separated from its neighbors by *international boundaries,* or lines that establish the limit of each state's jurisdiction and authority. Boundaries indicate where the sovereignty of one state ends and that of another begins.

Within its own bounded territory, a state administers laws, collects taxes, provides for defense, and performs other

FIGURE 9.11 Canada's migratory capital. Kingston was chosen as the first capital of the united Province of Canada in preference to either Quebec, capital of Lower Canada, or Toronto, that of Upper Canada. In 1844, governmental functions were relocated to Montreal, where they remained until 1849, after which they shifted back and forth—as the map indicates—between Toronto and Quebec. An 1865 session of the provincial legislature was held in Ottawa, the city that became the capital of the Confederation of Canada in 1867. *Redrawn with permission from David B. Knight,* A Capital for Canada. *Chicago: University of Chicago, Department of Geography, Research Paper no. 182, 1977, Fig. 1, p. vii.*

such governmental functions. Thus, the location of the boundary determines the kind of money people in a given area use, the legal code to which they are subject, the army they may be called upon to join, and the language and perhaps the religion children are taught in school. These examples suggest how boundaries serve as powerful reinforcers of cultural variation over the earth's surface.

Territorial claims of sovereignty are three-dimensional. International boundaries not only mark the outer limits of a state's claim to land (or water) surface but also are projected downward to the center of the earth in accordance with international consensus allocating rights to subsurface resources. States also project their sovereignty upward, but with less certainty because of a lack of agreement on the upper limits of territorial airspace. Properly viewed, then, an international boundary is a line without breadth; it is a vertical interface between adjacent state sovereignties.

Before boundaries were delimited, nations or empires were likely to be separated by *frontier zones,* ill-defined and fluctuating areas marking the effective end of a state's authority. Such zones were often uninhabited or only sparsely populated and were liable to change with shifting settlement patterns. Many present-day international boundaries lie in former frontier zones, and in that sense, the boundary line has replaced the broader frontier as a marker of a state's authority.

Natural and Artificial Boundaries

Geographers have traditionally distinguished between "natural" and "artificial" boundaries. **Natural** (or *physical*) **boundaries** are those based on recognizable physiographic features such as mountains, rivers, and lakes. Although they might seem to be attractive as borders because they actually exist in the landscape and are visible dividing elements, many natural boundaries have proved to be unsatisfactory. That is, they do not effectively separate states.

Many international boundaries lie along mountain ranges—for example, in the Alps, Himalayas, and Andes. Some have proved to be stable; others have not. Mountains are rarely total barriers to interaction. Although they do not invite movement, they are crossed by passes, roads, and tunnels. High pastures may be used for seasonal grazing, and a mountain region may be a source of water for hydroelectric power. Nor is the definition of a boundary along a mountain range a simple matter. Should it follow the crests of the mountains or the *water divide* (the line dividing two drainage areas)? The two are not always the same. Border disputes between China and India are, in part, the result of the failure of mountain crests and headwaters of major streams to coincide. Recently, glaciers shrinking in the Alps have forced Italy to renegotiate its borders with Switzerland, France, and Austria, as the original borders were drawn along the ridge of the glaciers (Figure 9.12).

Rivers can be even less satisfactory as boundaries. In contrast to mountains, rivers foster interaction. River valleys are likely to be agriculturally or industrially productive and to be densely populated. For example, for hundreds of miles the

FIGURE 9.12 Several international borders run through the jumble of the Alps. © *Martial Colomb/Getty RF.*

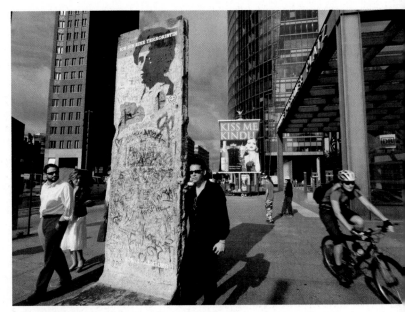

FIGURE 9.13 Since the reunification of Germany, the portions of the Berlin Wall still standing are a relic boundary. Here, a section of the wall stands in Potsdamer Platz. © *Iain Masterton/Alamy.*

Rhine River serves as an international boundary in Western Europe. It is also a primary traffic route lined by chemical plants, factories, and power stations and dotted by the castles and cathedrals that make it one of Europe's major tourist attractions. It is more a common, intensively used resource than a barrier in the lives of the states it borders.

The alternative to natural boundaries are **artificial,** or **geometric, boundaries.** Frequently delimited as sections of parallels of latitude or meridians of longitude, they are found chiefly in Africa, Asia, and the Americas. The western portion of the United States–Canada border, which follows the 49th parallel, is an example of a geometric boundary. Many such boundaries were established when the areas in question were colonies, the land was only sparsely settled, and detailed geographic knowledge of the frontier region was lacking.

Boundaries Classified by Settlement

Boundaries can also be classified according to whether they were laid out before or after the principal features of the cultural landscape developed. An **antecedent boundary** is one drawn across an area before it is well populated—that is, before most of the cultural landscape features developed. To continue our earlier example, the western portion of the United States-Canada boundary is such an antecedent line, having been established by a treaty between the United States and Great Britain in 1846.

Boundaries drawn after the development of the cultural landscape are termed **subsequent boundaries.** One type of subsequent boundary is a **consequent** (also called *ethnographic*) **boundary,** a border drawn to accommodate existing religious, linguistic, ethnic, or economic differences between countries. An example is the boundary drawn between Northern Ireland and Eire (Ireland). Subsequent **superimposed boundaries** may also be forced upon existing cultural landscapes,

a country, or a people by a conquering or colonizing power that is unconcerned about preexisting cultural patterns. The colonial powers in 19th-century Africa superimposed boundaries upon established African cultures without regard to the tradition, language, religion, or ethnic affiliation of those whom they divided (see Figure 9.5).

When Great Britain prepared to leave the Indian subcontinent after World War II, it was decided that two independent states would be established in the region: India and Pakistan. The boundary between the two countries, defined in the partition settlement of 1947, was thus both a *subsequent* and a *superimposed* line. As millions of Hindus migrated from the northwestern portion of the subcontinent to seek homes in India, millions of Muslims left what would become India for Pakistan. In a sense, they were attempting to ensure that the boundary would be *consequent*—that is, that it would coincide with a division based on religion. This boundary example is more fully discussed in "Political Regions in the Indian Subcontinent," p. 445 in Chapter 13.

If a former boundary line that no longer functions as such is still marked by some landscape features or differences on the two sides, it is termed a *relic boundary.* The abandoned castles dotting the former frontier zone between Wales and England are examples of a relic boundary. They are also evidence of the disputes that sometimes attend the process of boundary making. A more recent example is the Berlin Wall, built by communist East Germany in 1961 to seal off the border between East and West Berlin. With the reunification of Germany in 1990, the wall was mostly dismantled. Berliners have chosen to preserve some pieces of the wall as historical monuments; elsewhere, the course of the wall is marked by a double row of paving stones, another form of relic boundary (Figure 9.13).

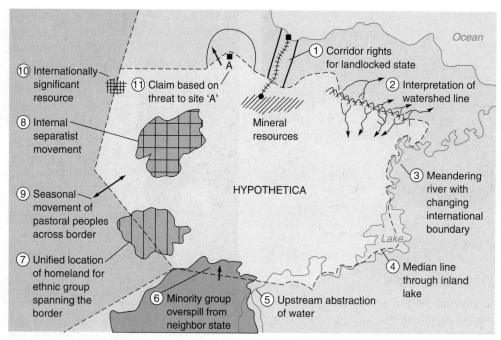

FIGURE 9.14 Geographic sources of international stress. To illustrate the conditions that can give rise to conflicts between states, eminent British geographer Peter Haggett drew this map of a hypothetical state and identified potential trouble spots. Real-world examples of the stress points and disputes shown in this map are discussed in the text. *Redrawn from Peter Haggett,* Geography, a Global Synthesis *(Prentice Hall, 2001). Figure 17.10, p. 522.*

Boundaries as Sources of Conflict

Boundaries create many possibilities for conflict between countries. At the start of the 21st century, about 80 countries are involved in disputes with one or more of their neighbors. Although the causes of conflict are varied, geographic considerations underlie many of them. Figure 9.14 shows for an imaginary state, Hypothetica, the spatial conditions that could give rise to conflict with its neighbors. Each condition is identified by number, and each is illustrated by real-world examples in the discussion that follows.

Landlocked States (Potential Trouble Spot #1) Hypothetica is a landlocked country, as are about one-fifth of the world's states (see Figure 9.9). To trade with overseas markets, landlocked states have to import and export their goods by land-based modes of transportation. They must cooperate with neighboring states and arrange for the goods to travel across a foreign country, and cooperation may be difficult.

Access to the sea usually is gained in one of two ways. Typically, the landlocked country arranges to use facilities at a foreign port and to have the right to travel to that port, but such arrangements are not without their problems. For centuries, landlocked countries have had to contend with restrictions, tolls, high fees for transit and storage, complicated customs formalities, the risk that the goods will be lost or damaged, and other obstructions to the easy movement of goods to and from the sea. In addition, they have had little or no control over the availability and efficiency of the transport and port facilities outside their borders, and they face the possibility that war will close their access to the sea. However, the situation

has improved in recent decades for countries that have signed international conventions permitting the movement of goods across intervening territories without discriminatory taxes, tolls, or freight charges. Bolivia, for example, has access to the Chilean port of Arica, the Peruvian port of Ilo, and the Argentinian city of Rosario on the Parana River (Figure 9.15).

Rather than depend on another country's port and goodwill, some landlocked states have gained access to the sea through a narrow corridor of land that reaches either the sea or a navigable river. Examples include the Congo Corridor of the Democratic Republic of Congo and the Caprivi Strip of Namibia, which was designed by the Germans to give what was then their colony of Southwest Africa access to the Zambezi River and Indian Ocean. Although these corridors have endured, others—such as the Polish and Finnish Corridors established after World War I—were short-lived.

Waterbodies as National Boundaries (#2, #3, #4, #5) As we noted earlier (p. 284), although rivers and lakes form parts of many national borders, they create many opportunities for conflict. Any body of water that forms part of a border requires agreement on where the boundary line should lie: along the right or left bank or shore, along the center of the waterway, or perhaps along the middle of the navigable channel. Soviet insistence that its sovereignty extended to the Manchurian (Dongbei) bank of the Amur and Ussuri Rivers was a long-standing matter of dispute and border conflict between the USSR and the People's Republic of China, only resolved with Russian agreement in 1987 that the boundary should pass along the main channel of the rivers. Even an agreement in

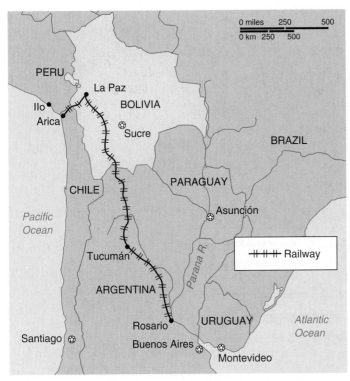

FIGURE 9.15 Like many other landlocked countries, Bolivia has gained access to the sea through arrangements with neighboring states. Unlike most landlocked countries, however, Bolivia can access ports on two oceans.

FIGURE 9.16 The disputed boundary between Argentina and Chile in the southern Andes. The treaty establishing the boundary between the two countries preceded adequate exploration and mapping of the area, leaving its precise location in doubt. After years of friction, the last remaining territorial dispute between Chile and Argentina in the Andes was settled in an accord signed in late 1998.

accordance with international custom that the boundary be drawn along the main channel may be impermanent if the river changes its course, floods, or dries up.

Potential trouble spot #2 relates to the use of a watershed boundary in defining an international dividing line—that is, one that runs along a ridge or crest dividing two drainage areas. Disputes occur when states disagree about the interpretation of documents that define a boundary and/or the way the boundary was delimited. The boundary between Argentina and Chile, originally defined during Spanish colonial rule and then established by treaty in 1881, was to follow "the most elevated crests of the Andean Cordillera dividing the waters" (Figure 9.16). Because the southern Andes had not been adequately explored and mapped, it wasn't apparent that the crestlines (highest peaks) and the watershed divides between east- and west-flowing rivers do not always coincide. In some places, the water divide is many miles east of the highest peaks, leaving a long, narrow area of about 52,000 square kilometers (20,000 sq mi) in dispute. The discrepancies in claims made for difficult relations between Argentina and Chile for nearly a century.

Pressure point #3 shows a meandering river (one that changes its course). If the river constitutes part of the international boundary, as it does here, the border will change over time. The boundary between the United States and Mexico, for example, which runs along the main channel of the Rio Grande, has changed as the river has altered its course.

Similarly, a lake (#4) requires agreement on where the boundary between two countries lies. In the case of the United States and Canada, the two countries agreed that a line equidistant from the shores of Lake Erie and Ontario would form part of the international border.

Another trouble spot (#5) relates to Hypothetica's use of the river that flows downstream into it from another country. Water use is an increasing source of conflict among countries, particularly in arid or semiarid regions. When water is scarce, its abstraction, diversion, or pollution by one country can significantly affect the quantity and quality of water available to those downstream. Growing shortages of fresh water are leading to tensions along many rivers, including the Jordan, Tigris and Euphrates, Nile, Indus, Ganges, and Brahmaputra.

Minority Group Identification (#6, #7, #8) Like nearly all countries, Hypothetica contains more than one culture group. In the real world, the locations of minority groups have led to international tensions, civil wars, wars of liberation, and international strife around the globe. As one of the most difficult problems with which countries must deal, minority group identification is discussed in more detail in the section "Centrifugal Forces," but brief examples of pressure points #6, #7, and #8 are provided in the following paragraphs.

Conflicts can arise if the people of one state claim and seek to acquire a territory whose population is historically or ethnically related to that of the state but is now subject to a foreign government. This condition is represented by pressure point #6, minority group overspill from a neighboring state. Under these conditions, the desire to expand the country's borders is called **irredentism,** from the Italian word for "unredeemed." Since 1950, both India and Pakistan have claimed Jammu and Kashmir as part of their own national territory, based upon the fact that the area contains substantial Muslim and Hindu populations.

Hungary's claims to Transylvania, a Romanian province, are based on both historical and ethnic ties. The two countries have quarreled over it for centuries. Transylvania was under Hungarian control from 1649 until 1920, when—as part of the reordering of the political map of Europe that followed World War I—it became part of Romania. In 1940, Germany and Italy forced Romania to give the province back to Hungary, but the country had to surrender it again after World War II.

We earlier discussed the case of the stateless nation (p. 276), a people without a state, and cited as examples Kurds, Roma, Basques, and Palestinians. Pressure point #7 shows a distinct ethnic group or nation located in both Hypothetica and a neighboring state. Conflict occurs when nations seek to govern themselves in their own state and try to carve out a new nation-state from portions of existing countries. As the example of the Basques indicates, they need not represent a majority of their residents in order to foment discord.

Basques live in a region overlapping France and Spain (Figure 9.17). In an attempt to dampen the separatist fires that had burned there since the 1960s, Spain granted its three Basque provinces a significant degree of self-rule in 1978, but that has failed to satisfy the extreme separatist movement Euskadi ta Askatasuna (ETA), which means "Basque Homeland and Liberty." The separatists contend that the Spanish state has attempted to destroy the Basques's unique cultural identity and to suppress their language, Euskadi, which is unrelated to any other language on Earth. They demand an independent, unified Basque state, not only for the Basque region of Spain but for a portion of southern France as well. Even though the Basques in Spain already possess far more autonomy than those in France, Spain has been the site of more agitation and violence than France, leading scholars to theorize that in this instance the influence of place—in addition to the stronger nation-state history of France—has resulted in differential identification with the proposed state. The ETA observed a unilateral cease-fire for 14 months following the 1998 Good Friday accords in Ireland, but after Spain cracked down on the group militarily, and then a second cease-fire, the group

FIGURE 9.17 The Basque region straddles the border between Spain and France. Although the Basques have been granted a measure of self-rule for their region, militant separatists in the Euskadi ta Askatasuna (ETA) want to see the establishment of an independent state for the Basque region of Spain and a portion of southern France.

has taken up sporadic violence again, mainly aimed at hurting Spain's tourist economy.

In the case of pressure point #8, an internal separatist movement, the group seeking independence is totally contained within Hypothetica. The Civil War in the United States in the 19th century is one example of a secessionist conflict, but wars of secession were numerous in the 20th century, particularly in Africa and Asia. The 1967–1970 civil war in Nigeria is one example.

Resource Disputes (#9, #10, #11) Neighboring states are likely to covet the resources—whether they be valuable mineral deposits, rich fishing grounds, or a cultural resource, such as a site of religious significance—lying in border areas and to disagree over their use. In recent years, for example, the United States has been involved in resource disputes with both its immediate neighbors: with Mexico over the shared resources of the Colorado River and Gulf of Mexico and with Canada over the Georges Bank fishing grounds in the Atlantic Ocean.

Conflicts arise when neighboring states disagree over policies to be applied along a border. Such policies may concern the movement of traditionally nomadic groups (#9), immigration, customs regulations, and the like. U.S. relations with Mexico, for example, have been affected by the increasing number of illegal aliens and the flow of drugs entering the United States from Mexico (Figure 9.18). (See "Broken Borders," pp. 264–265, for more information on the U.S.-Mexico boundary.)

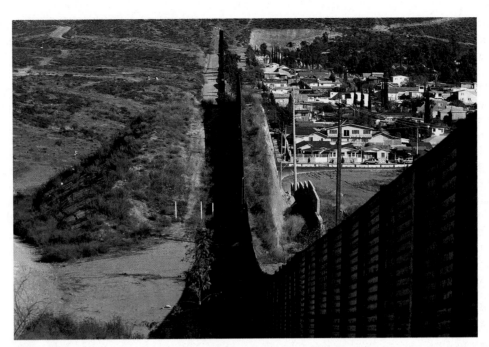

FIGURE 9.18 To stem the flow of undocumented migrants entering California from Baja California, the United States constructed a fence 3 meters (10 ft) high along the border in 1993. Since then, the fence has been extended and reinforced. Parts of the borders of Texas and California and Mexico now have 4.6-meter (15-ft)-high double fences. © *Hector Mata/AFP/Getty.*

The location of an internationally significant resource in a border region (#10) provides another opportunity for conflict. One of the causes of the 1990–1991 war in the Persian Gulf was the huge oil reservoir known as the Rumaila field, which lies mainly in Iraq, with a small extension into Kuwait (Figure 9.19). Because the two countries had been unable to agree on percentages of ownership, or a formula for sharing production costs and revenues, Kuwait pumped oil from Rumaila without any international agreement. Iraq helped justify its invasion of Kuwait by contending that the latter had been stealing Iraqi oil in what amounted to economic warfare.

As global warming shrinks polar ice in the Arctic, a new area of conflict develops. Not only might the melting ice provide a quicker sea route from the Atlantic to the Pacific than the Panama Canal, but scientists estimate that the seabed might also contain as much as a quarter of the world's undiscovered oil, gas, and minerals. Countries bordering the region, including Russia, Denmark, the United States, and Canada, are racing to establish claims to the area. Recently, a Russian submarine planted a titanium Russian flag on the seabed under the North Pole; a Danish expedition used crews of icebreakers to map the seabed; and Canada established two new military bases in the Canadian Arctic.

A final potential trouble spot is represented by site A on the map in Figure 9.14 (#11), the location of a resource that the state believes is crucial to its survival and that must be defended, even if it means claiming an adjacent piece of

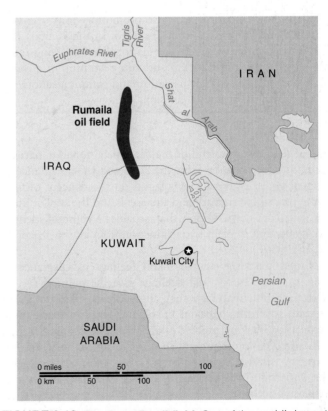

FIGURE 9.19 The Rumaila oil field. One of the world's largest oil reservoirs, Rumaila straddles the Iraq-Kuwait border. Iraqi grievances over Kuwaiti drilling were partly responsible for Iraq's invasion of Kuwait in 1990.

land in a neighboring state. The resource might be physical, such as a military post, or cultural, such as a holy city. Syria and Israel, for example, dispute the ownership of the Golan Heights, which contains water and is high ground. It allows the country that controls it to look down upon and listen to the country on the other side—Israelis can literally look at Damascus from Mount Hermon. A disputed cultural resource is represented by Jerusalem, a site of great religious significance to Christians, Jews, and Muslims. It has been the source of conflicts since at least the beginning of the first crusade in A.D. 1096. Believing that Jerusalem is vital to its own identity, Israel has in recent years effectively annexed much of Muslim East Jerusalem. Currently, one of the principal points of contention between the Israeli government and Palestinians is access to and the control of holy sites in the city.

Centripetal Forces: Promoting State Cohesion

At any moment in time, a state is characterized by forces that promote unity and national stability and by others that disrupt them. Political geographers refer to the unifying factors as **centripetal forces;** they bind together the people of a state, enable it to function, and give it strength. **Centrifugal forces,** on the other hand, destabilize and weaken a state. If centrifugal forces are stronger than those promoting unity, the very existence of the state will be threatened. In the sections that follow, we examine four forces—nationalism, unifying institutions, effective organization and administration of government, and systems of transportation and communication—to see how they can promote cohesion.

Nationalism

One of the most powerful of the centripetal forces is **nationalism,** an identification with the state and the acceptance of national goals. Nationalism is based on the concept of allegiance to a single country and the ideals and the way of life it represents. It is an emotion that provides a sense of identity and loyalty and of collective distinction from all other peoples and lands.

States purposely try to instill feelings of allegiance in their constituents, for such feelings give the political system strength. People who have such allegiance are likely to accept the rules governing behavior in the area and to participate in the decision-making process establishing those rules. In light of the divisive forces present in most societies, not everyone, of course, will feel the same degree of commitment or loyalty. The important consideration is that the majority of a state's population accept its ideologies, adhere to its laws, and participate in its effective operation. For many countries, such acceptance and adherence has come only recently and partially; in some, it is frail and endangered.

Recall that true nation-states are rare; in only a few countries do the territory occupied by the people of a particular nation and the territorial limits of the state coincide. Most countries have more than one culture group that considers itself separate in an important way from other citizens. In a multicultural society, nationalism helps integrate different groups into a unified population. This kind of consensus nationalism has emerged in countries such as the United States and Switzerland, where different culture groups have joined together to create political entities commanding the loyalties of all of their citizens.

States promote nationalism in a number of ways. *Iconography* is the study of the symbols that help unite people. National anthems and other patriotic songs, flags, national sports teams, rituals, and holidays are all developed as symbols of a state in order to promote nationalism and attract allegiance (Figure 9.20). By ensuring that all citizens, no matter how diverse the population, will have at least these symbols in common, they impart a sense of belonging to a political entity, called, for example, Japan or Canada. In some

FIGURE 9.20 The ritual of the Pledge of Allegiance is just one way in which schools in the United States seek to instill a sense of national identity in students. © *PictureQuest RF.*

countries, certain documents, such as the Magna Carta in England or the Declaration of Independence in the United States, serve the same purpose. Royalty may fill the need: in Sweden, Japan, and Great Britain, the monarchy functions as the symbolic focus of allegiance. Symbols and beliefs are major components of every culture. When a society is very heterogeneous, composed of people with different customs, religions, and languages, belief in the national unit can help weld them together.

Unifying Institutions

Institutions as well as symbols help develop the sense of commitment and cohesiveness essential to the state. Schools, particularly elementary schools, are among the most important of these. Children learn the history of their own country and relatively little about other countries. Schools are expected to instill the society's goals, values, and traditions; to teach the common language that conveys them; and to guide youngsters to identify with their country.

Other institutions that promote nationalism are the armed forces and, sometimes, a state church. The armed forces are, of necessity, taught to identify with the state. They see themselves as protecting the state's welfare from what are perceived to be its enemies.

In about one-quarter of the world's countries, the religion of the majority of the people has by law been designated a state church. In such cases, the church sometimes becomes a force for cohesion, helping unify the population. This is true of Islam in Pakistan, Judaism in Israel, Buddhism in Thailand, and Hinduism in Nepal. In countries such as these, the religion and the church are so identified with the state that belief in one is transferred to allegiance to the other.

The schools, the armed forces, and the church are just three of the institutions that teach people to be members of a state. As institutions, they operate primarily on the level of the sociological subsystem of culture, helping structure the outlooks and behaviors of the society. But by themselves, they are not enough to give cohesion, and thus strength, to a state. Indeed, each of the institutions we have discussed can be a destabilizing centrifugal force.

Organization and Administration

A further bonding force is public confidence in the effective organization of the state. Can it provide security from external aggression and internal conflict? Are its resources distributed and allocated in such a way as to be perceived to promote the economic welfare of all its citizens? Are all citizens afforded equal opportunity to participate in governmental affairs (see "Legislative Women," p. 292)? Do institutions that encourage consultation and the peaceful settlement of disputes exist? How firmly established are the rule of law and the power of the courts? Is the system of decision making responsive to the people's needs?

The answers to these questions and the relative importance of the answers vary from country to country, but they and similar ones are implicit in the expectation that the state will, in the words of the Constitution of the United States, "establish justice, insure domestic tranquillity, provide for the common defense, [and] promote the general welfare. . . ." If those expectations are not fulfilled, the loyalties promoted by national symbols and unifying institutions may be weakened or lost.

Transportation and Communication

A state's transportation network fosters political integration by promoting interaction between areas and by joining them economically and socially. The role of a transportation network in uniting a country has been recognized since ancient times. The saying that all roads lead to Rome had its origin in the impressive system of roads that linked Rome to the rest of the empire. Centuries later, a similar network was built in France, linking Paris to the various departments of the country. Often, the capital city is better connected to other cities than the outlying cities are to one another. In France, for example, it can take less time to travel from one city to another by way of Paris than by direct route.

Roads and railroads have played a historically significant role in promoting political integration. In the United States and Canada, they not only opened up new areas for settlement but also increased interaction between rural and urban areas. Because transportation systems play a major role in a state's economic development, it follows that, the more economically advanced a country is, the more extensive its transport network is likely to be. At the same time, the higher the level of development, the more money there is to be invested in building transport routes. The two reinforce one another.

Transportation and communication, although encouraged within a state, are frequently curtailed or at least controlled between states as a conscious device for promoting state cohesion through limitation on external spatial interaction (Figure 9.21). The mechanisms of control include restrictions on trade through tariffs and embargoes, legal barriers to immigration and emigration, and limitations on travel through passports and visa requirements.

Centrifugal Forces: Challenges to State Authority

State cohesion is not easily achieved or, once gained, invariably retained. Destabilizing centrifugal forces are ever-present, sowing internal discord and challenges to the state's authority (see "Terrorism and Political Geography," pp. 294–295). Transportation and communication may be hindered by a country's shape or great size, leaving some parts of the country not well integrated with the rest. A state that is not well organized or administered stands to lose the loyalty of its citizens. Institutions that in some states promote unity can be a divisive force in others.

FIGURE 9.22 **(a) Regions with active autonomous movement.** Despite long-standing state attempts to culturally assimilate these historic nations, each contains a political movement that has recently sought or is currently seeking a degree of self-rule that recognizes its separate identity. Separatists on the island of Corsica, for example, want to secede from France, and separatists in Catalonia demand independence from Spain. The desires of nationalist parties in both Wales and Scotland were partially accommodated by the creation in 1999 of their own parliaments and a degree of regional autonomy, an outcome labeled "separation but not a divorce" from the United Kingdom. **(b)** Demonstrators carry a giant Basque flag during a march to call for independence for the Basque region. Spain has granted limited independence to the Basque region in an example of asymmetric federalism. *(b) © AP Images/Aranberri*

containing disparate groups that are more motivated by enmity than affinity have powerful centripetal tendencies. The Basques of Spain and the Bretons of France have their counterparts in the Palestinians in Israel, the Sikhs in India, the Tamils in Sri Lanka, the Moros in the Philippines, and many others.

The countries of Eastern Europe and the republics of the former Soviet Union have seen many instances of regionally rooted nationalist feelings. Now that the forces of ethnicity, religion, language, and culture are no longer suppressed by communism, ancient rivalries are more evident than at any-time since World War II. The end of the Cold War aroused hopes of decades of peace. Instead, the collapse of communism and the demise of the USSR spawned many smaller wars. Numerous ethnic groups, large and small, are asserting their

identities and what they perceive to be their right to determine their own political status.

The national independence claimed in the early 1990s by the 15 former Soviet republics did not assure the satisfaction of all separatist movements within them (see Figure 9.6). Many of the new individual countries are subject to strong destabilizing forces that challenge their territorial integrity and survival. The Russian Federation itself, the largest and most powerful remnant of the former USSR, has 89 components, including 21 "ethnic republics" and a number of other nationality regions. Many are rich in natural resources, have non-Russian majorities, and seek greater autonomy within the federation. Some, indeed, want total independence. One, the predominantly Muslim republic of Chechnya, in 1994 claimed the right of self-determination and attempted to secede from the federation, provoking a bloody war that escalated again in 1996 and 1999. The indiscriminate violence of Russia's reaction spilled over to neighboring regions, making the entire area a tinderbox.

As the USSR declined and eventually disbanded, it lost control of its communist satellites in Eastern Europe. That loss and resurgent nationalism led to a dramatic reordering of the region's political map. East Germany was reunified with West Germany in 1990, and 3 years later, the people of Czechoslovakia agreed to split their country into two separate, ethnically based states: the Czech Republic and Slovakia. More violently, Yugoslavia shattered into five pieces in 1991–1992, but with the exception of Slovenia, the boundaries of the five new republics did not match the territories occupied by nationalities, a situation that plunged the region into war as nations fought to redefine the boundaries of their countries. One tactic used to transform a multinational area into one containing only one nation is **ethnic cleansing,** the killing or forcible relocation of less-powerful minorities. It occurred in Croatia, Bosnia-Herzegovina, and the Kosovo province of southern Serbia. An uneasy truce now prevails in each of these regions, enforced in Bosnia and Kosovo by NATO peacekeeping forces. Few doubt that, if the soldiers were withdrawn, fighting would erupt again.

It is too early to tell whether these new states and others will be viable political entities. We can, however, make some generalizations about nationalist challenges to state authority.

The two preconditions common to all separatist movements are *territory* and *nationality*. First, the group must be concentrated in a core region that it claims as a national homeland. It seeks to regain control of land and power that it believes were unjustly taken by the ruling party. Second, certain cultural characteristics must provide a basis for the group's perception of separateness, identity, and cultural unity. These might be language, religion, or distinctive group customs, which promote feelings of group identity at the same time that they foster exclusivity. Normally, these cultural differences have persisted over several generations and have survived despite strong pressures toward assimilation.

Other characteristics common to many separatist movements are a *peripheral location* and *social and economic inequality*. Troubled regions tend to be peripheral, often isolated in rural pockets, and their location away from the seat of central government engenders feelings of alienation, exclusion, and neglect. Second, the dominant culture group is often seen as an exploiting class that has suppressed the local language, controlled access to the civil service, and taken more than its share of wealth and power. Poorer regions complain that they have lower incomes and greater unemployment than prevail in the rest of the state and that "outsiders" control key resources and industry. Separatists in relatively rich regions believe that they could exploit their resources for themselves and do better economically without the constraints imposed by the central state.

COOPERATION AMONG STATES

The modern state is fragile and, as we have seen, its primacy may be less assured in recent years. In many ways, countries are now weaker than ever before. Many are economically frail, others are politically unstable, and some are both. Strategically, no state is safe from military attack, for technology now enables countries to shoot weapons halfway around the world. Is national security possible in the nuclear age?

Recognizing that a country cannot by itself guarantee either its prosperity or its own security, many states have opted to cooperate with others. These cooperative ventures are proliferating quickly, and they involve countries everywhere. They are also adding a new dimension to the concept of political boundaries, because the associations of states have borders of a higher spatial order than those between individual states. Such boundaries as the current division between North Atlantic Treaty Organization (NATO) and non-NATO states, or between the European Union area and other European countries, represent a different scale of the political ordering of space.

Supranationalism

Associations among states represent a new dimension in the ordering of national power and national independence. Recent trends in economic globalization and international cooperation suggest to some that the sovereign state's traditional responsibilities and authorities are being diluted by a combination of forces and partly delegated to higher-order political and economic organizations. Corporations and even nongovernmental agencies often operate in controlling ways outside of nation-state jurisdiction.

The rise of transnational corporations dominant in global markets, for example, limits the economic influence of individual countries. Cyberspace and the Internet are controlled by no one and are largely immune to the state restrictions on the flow of information exerted by many governments. And increasingly, individual citizens of any country have their lives and actions shaped by decisions not only of local and national authorities but also of regional economic associations (e.g., the North American Free-Trade Agreement), of multiparty military alliances (e.g., NATO), and of global political agencies (e.g., the United Nations).

The roots of such multistate cooperative systems are ancient—for example, the leagues of city-states in the ancient Greek world or the Hanseatic League of free German cities in Europe's medieval period. New cooperative systems have proliferated since the end of World War II. They represent a world trend toward a **supranationalism** composed of associations of three or more states created for mutual benefit and the achievement of shared objectives. Although many individuals and organizations decry the loss of national independence that supranationalism entails, the many supranational associations in existence early in the 21st century are evidence of their attraction and pervasiveness. Nearly all countries, in fact, are members of at least one—and most are members of many—supranational groupings.

The United Nations and Its Agencies

The United Nations (UN) is the only organization that tries to be universal. Its membership has expanded from 51 countries in 1945 to 192 in 2009. The most recent state to be recognized as a member is Montenegro (2006).

The UN is the most ambitious attempt ever undertaken to bring together the world's countries in international assembly and to promote world peace. Stronger and more representative than its predecessor, the League of Nations, it provides a forum where countries can discuss international problems and regional concerns and a mechanism, admittedly weak but still significant, for forestalling disputes or, when necessary, for ending wars (Figure 9.23). The United Nations also sponsors 40 programs and agencies aimed at fostering international cooperation with respect to specific goals. Among these are the World Health Organization (WHO); the Food and Agriculture Organization (FAO); and the United Nations Educational, Scientific, and Cultural Organization (UNESCO). Many other UN agencies and much of the UN budget are committed to assisting member states with matters of economic growth and development.

Member states have not surrendered sovereignty to the UN, and the world body is legally and effectively unable to make or enforce a world law. Nor is there a world police force. Although there is recognized international law adjudicated by the International Court of Justice, rulings by this body are sought only by countries agreeing beforehand to abide by its arbitration. Finally, the United Nations has no authority over the military forces of individual countries.

A pronounced change both in the relatively passive role of the United Nations and in traditional ideas of international relations has begun to emerge, however. Long-established rules of total national sovereignty that allowed governments to act internally as they saw fit, free of outside interference, are fading as the United Nations increasingly applies a concept of "interventionism." The Persian Gulf War of 1991 was UN-authorized under the old rules prohibiting one state (Iraq) from violating the sovereignty of another (Kuwait) by attacking it. After the war, the new interventionism sanctioned UN operations within Iraq to protect Kurds within that country. Later, the UN intervened with troops and relief agencies in Somalia, Bosnia, and elsewhere, invoking an "international jurisdiction over inalienable human rights" that prevails without regard to state frontiers or sovereignty considerations. In 2008, the UN had 116,000 personnel serving on 17 peacekeeping operations on four continents.

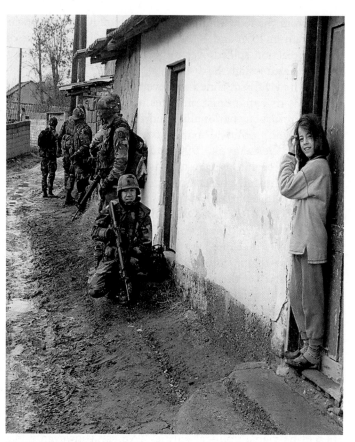

FIGURE 9.23 **U.S. soldiers in Kosovo, 2000.** A United Nations Security Council resolution established a civilian administration in the war-torn province. Under the auspices of the UN, soldiers from many countries staff peacekeeping forces and military observer groups in many world regions in an effort to halt or mitigate conflicts. The demand for peacekeeping and observer operations is indicated by the recent deployment of UN forces in the Congo, Sudan, and South Lebanon. © *Historicus, Inc.*

Whatever the long-term prospects for interventionism replacing absolute sovereignty, for the short term the UN remains the only institution where the vast majority of the world's countries can collectively discuss international political and economic concerns and attempt peacefully to resolve their differences. It has been particularly influential in formulating a law of the sea.

Maritime Boundaries

Boundaries define political jurisdictions and areas of resource control, but claims of national authority are not restricted to land areas alone. Water covers about two-thirds of the earth's surface, and increasingly countries have been projecting their sovereignty seaward to claim adjacent maritime areas and resources. A basic question involves the right of states to control water and the resources it contains. The inland waters of a country, such as rivers and lakes, have traditionally been regarded as being within the sovereignty of that country. Oceans, however, are not within any country's borders.

Are they, then, to be open to all states to use, or may a single country claim sovereignty and limit access and use by other countries?

For most of human history, the oceans remained effectively outside individual national control or international jurisdiction. The seas were a common highway for those daring enough to venture on them, an inexhaustible larder for fishermen, and a vast refuse pit for the muck of civilization. By the end of the 19th century, however, most coastal countries claimed sovereignty over a continuous belt 3 or 4 nautical miles wide (a *nautical mile*, or *nm*, equals 1.15 statute miles, or 1.85 kilometers). At the time, the 3-nm limit represented the farthest range of artillery and thus the effective limit of control by the coastal state. Though recognizing the rights of others to innocent passage, such sovereignty permitted the enforcement of quarantine and customs regulations, allowed national protection of coastal fisheries, and made claims of neutrality effective during other people's wars. The primary concern was with security and unrestricted commerce. No separately codified law of the sea existed, however, and none seemed to be needed until after World War I.

A League of Nations Conference for the Codification of International Law, convened in 1930, inconclusively discussed maritime legal matters and identified areas of concern that were to become increasingly pressing after World War II. Important among these was an emerging shift from interest in commerce and national security to a preoccupation with the resources of the seas, an interest fanned by the *Truman Proclamation* of 1945. Motivated by a desire to exploit offshore oil deposits, the U.S. federal government, under this doctrine, laid claim to all resources on the continental shelf contiguous to its coasts. Other states, many claiming even broader areas of control, hurried to annex marine resources. Within a few years, a quarter of the earth's surface was appropriated by individual coastal countries.

An International Law of the Sea

Unrestricted extensions of jurisdiction and territorial disputes over proliferating claims to maritime space and resources led to a series of United Nations conferences on the Law of the Sea. Meeting over a period of years, delegates from more than 150 countries attempted to achieve consensus on a treaty that would establish an internationally agreed-upon "convention dealing with all matters relating to the Law of the Sea." The meetings culminated in a draft treaty in 1982, the **United Nations Convention on the Law of the Sea (UNCLOS).**

The convention delimits territorial boundaries and rights by defining four zones of diminishing control (Figure 9.24).

1. A *territorial sea* of up to 12 nm (19 km) in breadth, over which coastal states have sovereignty, including exclusive fishing rights. Vessels of all types normally have the right of innocent passage through the territorial sea, although under certain circumstances noncommercial vessels (primarily military and research) can be challenged.

2. A *contiguous zone* of up to 24 nm (38 km). Although a coastal state does not have complete sovereignty in this zone, it can enforce its customs, immigration, and sanitation laws and has the right of hot pursuit out of its territorial waters.

3. An **exclusive economic zone (EEZ)** of up to 200 nm (370 km), in which the state has recognized rights to explore, exploit, conserve, and manage the natural resources, both living and nonliving, of the seabed and waters (Figure 9.25). Countries have exclusive rights to the resources lying within the continental shelf when this extends farther, up to 350 nm (560 km) beyond their coasts. The traditional freedoms of the high seas are to be maintained in this zone.

4. The *high seas* beyond the EEZ. Outside any national jurisdiction, they are open to all states, whether coastal or landlocked. Freedom of the high seas includes the right to sail ships, fish, fly over, lay submarine cables and pipelines, and pursue scientific research. Mineral resources in the international deep seabed area beyond national jurisdiction are declared the common heritage of humankind, to be managed for the benefit of all the peoples of the earth.

By the end of the 1980s, most coastal countries, including the United States, had used the UNCLOS provisions to

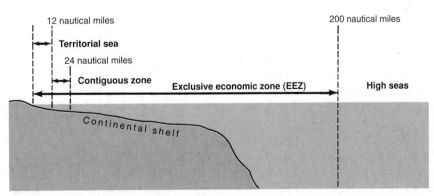

FIGURE 9.24 Territorial claims permitted by the 1982 United Nations Convention on the Law of the Sea (UNCLOS).

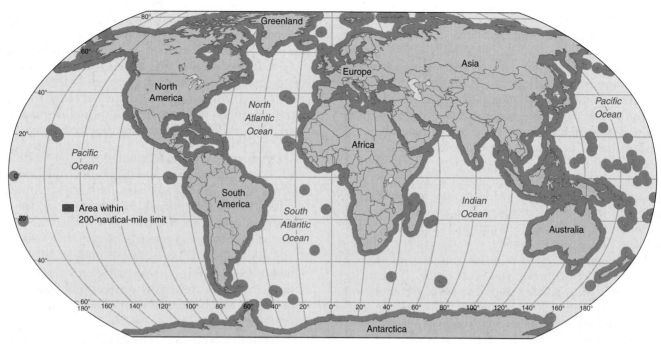

FIGURE 9.25 **The 200-nautical-mile exclusive economic zone (EEZ) claims of coastal states.** The provisions of the Law of the Sea Convention, in effect, changed the maritime map of the world. Three important consequences flowed from the 200-nm EEZ concept: (1) islands gained a new significance; (2) countries gained a host of new neighbors; and (3) the EEZ lines resulted in overlapping claims. EEZ lines are drawn around a country's possessions as well as around the country itself. Every island, no matter how small, has its own 200-nm EEZ. This means that, although the United States shares continental borders only with Canada and Mexico, it has maritime boundaries with countries in Asia, South America, and Europe. All told, the United States may have to negotiate some 30 maritime boundaries, which is likely to take decades. Other countries, particularly those with many possessions, will have to engage in similar lengthy negotiations.

proclaim and reciprocally recognize jurisdiction over 12-nm (19-km) territorial seas and 200-nm (370-km) economic zones. Despite reservations held by the United States and a few other industrial countries about the deep seabed mining provisions, the convention received the necessary ratification by 60 states and became international law in 1994.

UN Affiliates

Other fully or essentially global supranational organizations with influences on the economic, social, and cultural affairs of states and individuals have been created. Most are specialized international agencies, autonomous and with their own memberships but with affiliated relationships with the United Nations and operating under its auspices. Among them are the Food and Agriculture Organization (FAO), the World Bank, the International Labor Organization (ILO), the United Nations Children's Fund (UNICEF), the World Health Organization (WHO), and—of growing economic importance—the World Trade Organization (WTO).

The World Trade Organization, which came into existence in 1995, has become one of the most significant of the global expressions of supranational economic control. It is charged with enforcing the global trade accounts that grew out of years of international negotiations under the terms of the General Agreement on Tariffs and Trade (GATT). The basic principle behind the WTO is that the 153 members as of 2010

member countries should work to cut tariffs, dismantle non-tariff barriers to trade, liberalize trade in services, and treat all other countries uniformly in matters of trade. Any preference granted to one should be available to all.

Increasingly, however, regional rather than global trade agreements are being struck, and free-trade areas are proliferating. Only a few WTO members are not already part of another regional trade association. Some argue that such regional alliances make world trade less free by scrapping tariffs on trade among member states but retaining them on exchanges with nonmembers.

Regional Alliances

In addition to their membership in international agencies, countries have shown themselves willing to relinquish some of their independence to participate in smaller, multinational systems. These groupings can be economic, military, or political. Cooperation in the economic sphere seems to come more easily to states than does political or military cooperation.

Economic Alliances

Among the most powerful and far-reaching of the economic alliances are those that have evolved in Europe, particularly the **European Union (EU).** The EU grew out of the

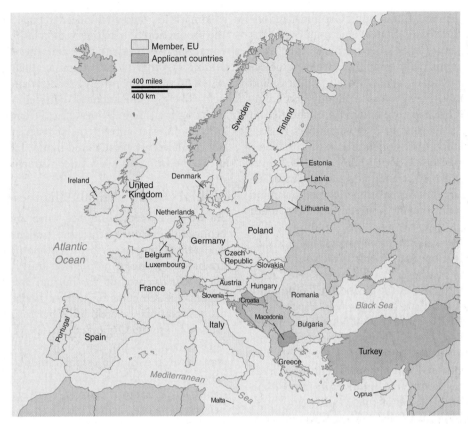

FIGURE 9.26 The members of the European Union (EU) as of September 2009. Bulgaria and Romania joined the EU on January 1, 2007. Turkey, whose application has been pending since 1987, is also a candidate for membership; formal talks are underway. Other candidate countries include Croatia and the former Yugoslav Republic of Macedonia. The EU has stipulated that, in order to join, a country must have stable institutions guaranteeing democracy, the rule of law, human rights, and protection of minorities; a functioning market economy; and the ability to accept the obligations of membership, including the aims of political, economic, and monetary union.

Common Market, which was established in 1957 and was composed at first of only six states: France, Italy, West Germany, Belgium, the Netherlands, and Luxembourg. It added new members slowly at the outset, as the United Kingdom, Denmark, and Portugal joined the organization between 1973 and 1986; Greece, Spain, and Portugal joined during the 1980s; Austria, Finland, and Sweden joined in 1995. As it gathered momentum, more countries were admitted to the EU during the early 2000s, including the island states of Malta and Cyprus and eight former Soviet bloc nations, from Estonia in the north to Slovenia in the south (Figure 9.26). These additions brought the number of member nations to 27, increased the EU's landmass by 23%, raised its total population to more than 495 million people, and expanded its economy to rival that of the United States. The EU is the world's largest and richest bloc of countries.

Over the years, members of the European Union have taken many steps to integrate their economies and coordinate their policies in such areas as transportation, agriculture, and fisheries. A council of ministers, a commission, a European parliament, and a court of justice give the European Union supranational institutions with effective ability to make and enforce laws. By January 1, 1993, the EU had abolished most remnant barriers to free trade and the free movement of capital

and people among its members, creating a single European market. In another step toward economic and monetary union, the EU's single currency, the *euro,* replaced separate national currencies in 1999. Notes and coins in 12 national currencies—such as the Portuguese escudo and the deutsche mark—were withdrawn in 2002. Some countries within the EU such as Sweden and the United Kingdom have elected to delay moving to the single currency.

Countries outside of Europe join together in regional alliances as well. In a fluid process, countries come together in an association to achieve economic and political goals. Sometimes members drop out, while others join. New treaties are made, and new coalitions emerge. Indeed, a number of such regional economic and trade associations have been added to the world supranational map. None are as encompassing in power and purpose as the EU, but all represent a cession of national independence to achieve broader regional goals.

NAFTA, the North American Free-Trade Agreement, was launched in 1994 and links Canada, the United States, and Mexico in an economic community aimed at lowering or removing trade and movement restrictions between the countries. A new agreement, CAFTA (United States–Central America–Dominican Republic Free-Trade Agreement), is a comprehensive trade agreement between Costa

Rica, the Dominican Republic, El Salvador, Guatemala, Honduras, Nicaragua, and the United States. Free trade is not the only reason states cooperate. The Americas have other, similar associations with comparable trade-enhancement objectives, though frequently they also have social, political, and cultural interests in mind. Caribbean Community and Common Market (CARICOM), for example, was established in 1974 to further cooperation among its 15 members in economic, health, cultural, and foreign policy arenas. The Common Market of the Southern Cone (MERCOSUR), which unites Brazil, Argentina, Uruguay, and Paraguay (and associate members Bolivia and Chile) in the creation of a customs union to eliminate levies on goods moving between them, is a South American example.

A similar interest in promoting economic, social, and cultural cooperation and development among its members underpins the Association of Southeast Asian Nations (ASEAN). A less-wealthy African example is the Economic Community of West African States (ECOWAS). The Asia Pacific Economic Cooperation (APEC) forum includes China, Japan, Australia, Canada, and the United States among its 21 members and has a grand plan for "free trade in the Pacific" by 2020. More restricted bilateral and regional preferential trade arrangements have also proliferated, numbering more than 400 in 2010 and creating a maze of rules, tariffs, and commodity agreements that result in trade restrictions and preferences contrary to the free-trade intent of the World Trade Organization.

Economic interests, then, motivate the establishment of most international alliances, though political, social, and cultural objectives also figure largely in many. Although the alliances themselves will change, the idea of supranational associations appears to have been permanently added to the national political and global realities of the 21st century. The world map pattern those alliances create must be recognized to understand the current international order.

Three further points about regional international alliances are worth noting. The first is that the formation of a coalition in one area often stimulates the creation of another alliance by countries left out of the first. Thus, the creation of NAFTA was a precedent for CAFTA.

Second, the new economic unions tend to be composed of contiguous states (Figure 9.27). This was not the case with the recently dissolved empires, which included far-flung territories. Contiguity facilitates the movement of people and goods. Communication and transportation are simpler and more effective among adjoining countries than among those far removed from one another, and common cultural, linguistic, and political traits and interests are more to be expected in countries adjacent to one another.

Finally, it does not seem to matter whether countries are alike or distinctly different in their economies, as far as joining economic unions is concerned. There are examples of both. If the countries are dissimilar, they may complement each other. This was one basis for the European Common Market, which preceded the EU. Dairy products and furniture from Denmark are sold in France, freeing France to specialize in the production of machinery and clothing. On the other hand, countries that produce the same raw materials hope that, by joining together in an economic alliance, they might be able to enhance their control of markets and prices for their products. The Organization of Petroleum Exporting Countries (OPEC) is a case in point. Other attempts to form commodity cartels and price agreements between producing and consuming countries are represented by the International Tin Agreement, the International Coffee Agreement, and others.

Military and Political Alliances

As we have seen, countries form alliances for other than economic reasons. Strategic, political, and cultural considerations may also foster cooperation. *Military alliances* are based on the principle that unity brings strength. Such pacts usually provide for mutual assistance in the case of aggression. Once again, action breeds reaction when such an association is created. The formation of the North Atlantic Treaty Organization (NATO), a defensive alliance of many European countries and the United States, was countered by the establishment of the Warsaw Treaty Organization, which joined the USSR and its satellite countries of Eastern Europe. Both pacts allowed the member states to base armed forces in one another's territories,

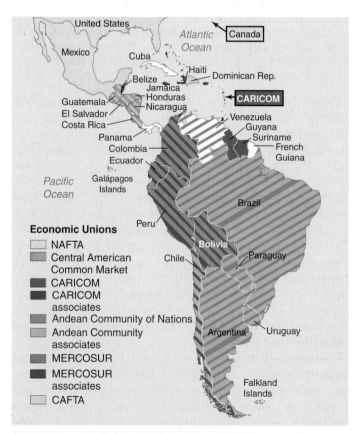

FIGURE 9.27 Western Hemisphere economic unions in 2009. The number of international trade organizations has risen rapidly since the 1960s.

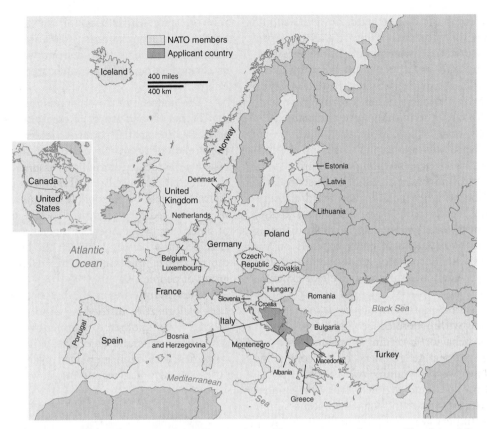

FIGURE 9.28 The NATO military alliance as of 2010 had 28 members. The newest members are Albania and Croatia; the Former Yugoslav Republic of Macedonia, Montenegro, and Bosnia and Herzegovina are applicants for membership. Proponents of expansion argue that it is necessary to create a zone of stability and security throughout Europe. Opponents contend that enlargement is a divisive move that will cast a shadow over the future of relations with Russia, which is opposed to expansion so close to its borders.

a relinquishment of a certain degree of sovereignty uncommon in the past.

Military alliances depend on the perceived common interests and political goodwill of the countries involved. As political realities change, so, too, do the strategic alliances. NATO was created to defend Western Europe and North America against the Soviet military threat. When the dissolution of the USSR and Warsaw Pact removed that threat, the purpose of the NATO alliance became less clear. Since the 1990s, however, the organization has added seven members and has taken on a greater role in peacekeeping activities (Figure 9.28).

All international alliances recognize communities of interest. In economic and military associations, common objectives are clearly seen and described, and joint actions are agreed upon with respect to the achievement of those objectives. More-generalized mutual concerns or appeals to historical interest may be the basis for primarily *political alliances*. Such associations tend to be rather loose, not requiring their members to yield much power to the union. Examples are the Commonwealth of Nations (formerly the British Commonwealth), composed of many former British colonies and dominions, and the Organization of American States (OAS), both of which offer economic as well as political benefits.

There are many examples of abortive political unions that have foundered because the individual countries could not agree on questions of policy and were unwilling to subordinate individual interests to make the union succeed. The United Arab Republic, the Central African Federation, the Federation of Malaysia and Singapore, and the Federation of the West Indies fall within this category.

Although many such political associations have failed, observers of the world scene speculate about the possibility that "superstates" will emerge from one or more of the international alliances that now exist. Will a "United States of Europe," for example, under a single common government, be the logical outcome of the successes of the EU? No one knows, but as long as the individual state is regarded as the highest form of political and social organization (as it is now) and as the body in which sovereignty rests, such total unification is unlikely.

LOCAL AND REGIONAL POLITICAL ORGANIZATION

The most profound contrasts in cultures tend to occur between, rather than within, states, one reason political geographers traditionally have been interested primarily in country units. The emphasis on the state, however, should not obscure the fact that, for most of us, it is at that local level that we find our most intimate and immediate contact with government and its influence on the administration of our affairs. In the United States, for example, an individual is subject to the decisions and regulations made by the local school board, the municipality, the county, the state, and perhaps, a host of special-purpose districts—all in addition to the laws and regulations issued by the federal government and its agencies. Among other things, local political entities determine where children go to school, the minimum size lot on which a person may build a house, and where one may legally park a car. Adjacent states of the United States may be characterized by sharply differing personal and business tax rates; differing controls on the sale of firearms, alcohol, and tobacco; variant administrative systems for public services; and different levels of expenditures for them.

All of these governmental entities are *spatial systems.* Because they operate within defined geographic areas, and because they make behavior-governing decisions, they are topics of interest to political geographers. In the concluding sections of this chapter, we will examine two aspects of political organization at the local and regional level. Our emphasis will be on the United States and Canadian scene simply because their local political geography is familiar to most of us. We should remember, however, that the North American structure of municipal governments, minor civil divisions, and special-purpose districts has counterparts in other regions of the world.

The Geography of Representation: The Districting Problem

There are more than 85,000 local governmental units in the United States. Slightly more than half of these are municipalities, townships, and counties. The remainder are school districts, water-control districts, airport authorities, sanitary districts, and other special-purpose bodies. Boundaries have been drawn around each of these districts. Although the number of districts does not change greatly from year to year, many boundary lines are redrawn in any single year. Such *redistricting,* or *reapportionment,* is made necessary by shifts in population, as areas gain or lose people.

Every 10 years, following the United States census, updated figures are used to redistribute the 435 seats in the House of Representatives among the 50 states. Redrawing the congressional districts to reflect population changes is required by the Constitution, the intention being to make sure that each legislator represents roughly the same number of people. Since 1964, Canadian provinces and territories have entrusted redistricting for federal offices to independent electoral boundaries commissions. Although a few states in the United States also have independent, nonpartisan boards or commissions draw district boundaries, most

rely on state legislatures for the task. Across the United States, the decennial census data are also used to redraw the boundaries of legislative districts within each state as well as those for local offices, such as city councils and county boards.

The analysis of how boundaries are drawn around voting districts is one aspect of **electoral geography,** which also addresses the spatial patterns yielded by election results and their relationship to the socioeconomic characteristics of voters. In a democracy, it might be assumed that election districts should contain roughly equal numbers of voters, that electoral districts should be reasonably compact, and that the proportion of elected representatives should correspond to the share of votes cast by members of a given political party. Problems arise because the way in which the boundary lines are drawn can maximize, minimize, or effectively nullify the power of a group of people.

Gerrymandering is the practice of drawing the boundaries of legislative districts so as to unfairly favor one political party over another, to fragment voting blocs, or to achieve other nondemocratic objectives (Figure 9.29). A number of strategies have been employed over the years for that purpose. *Stacked* gerrymandering involves drawing circuitous

THE GERRY-MANDER.   (Boston, 1811.)

FIGURE 9.29 The original gerrymander. The term *gerrymander* originated in 1811 from the shape of an electoral district formed in Massachusetts while Elbridge Gerry was governor. When an artist added certain animal features, the district resembled a salamander and quickly came to be called a gerrymander. *Source: © Bettmann/Corbis Images.*

boundaries to enclose pockets of strength or weakness of the group in power; it is what we usually think of as gerrymandering. The *excess vote* technique concentrates the support of the opposition in a few districts, which it can win easily, but leaves it few potential seats elsewhere. Conversely, the *wasted vote* strategy dilutes the opposition's strength by dividing its votes among a number of districts.

Assume that X and O represent two groups with an equal number of voters but different policy preferences. Although there are equal numbers of Xs and Os, the way electoral districts are drawn affects voting results. In Figure 9.30a, the Xs are concentrated in one district and will probably elect only one representative of four. The power of the Xs is maximized in Figure 9.30b, where they may control three of the four districts. The voters are evenly divided in Figure 9.30c, where the Xs have the opportunity to elect two of the four representatives. Finally, Figure 9.30d shows how both political parties may agree to delimit the electoral districts to provide "safe seats" for incumbents. Such a partitioning offers little chance for change.

Figure 9.30 depicts a hypothetical district, compact in shape with an even population distribution and only two groups competing for representation. In actuality, American municipal voting districts are often oddly shaped because of such factors as the city limits, historic settlement patterns, current population distribution, and transportation routes—as well as past gerrymandering. Further, in any large area, many groups vie for power. Each electoral interest group promotes its version of "fairness" in the way boundaries are delimited. Minorities seek representation in proportion to their numbers, so that they will be able to elect representatives who are concerned about and responsive to their needs.

Gerrymandering is not automatically successful. First, a districting arrangement that appears to be unfair may be appealed to the courts. In addition, many factors other than political party affiliation influence voting decisions. Key issues may cut across party lines, scandal may erode (or personal charm increase) votes unexpectedly, and the amount of candidate financing or the number of campaign workers may determine election outcomes if compelling issues are absent.

The Fragmentation of Political Power

Boundary drawing at any electoral level is never easy, particularly when political groups want to maximize their representation and minimize that of opposition groups. Furthermore, the boundaries that we may want for one set of districts may *not* be those that we want for another. For example, sewage districts must take natural drainage features into account, whereas police districts may be based on the distribution of the population or the number of miles of street to be patrolled. And school attendance zones must consider the numbers of school-aged children and the capacities of individual schools.

As these examples suggest, the United States is subdivided into great numbers of political administrative units whose areas of control are spatially limited. The 50 states are partitioned into more than 3000 counties ("parishes" in Louisiana), most of which are further subdivided into townships, each with a still lower level of governing power. This political fragmentation is further increased by the existence of nearly innumerable special-purpose districts whose boundaries rarely coincide with the standard major and minor civil divisions of the country, or even with each other (Figure 9.31). Each district represents a form of political allocation of territory to achieve a specific aim of local need or legislative intent.

Canada, a federation of 10 provinces and 3 territories, has a similar pattern of political subdivision. Each of the provinces contains minor civil divisions—municipalities—under provincial control, and all (cities, towns, villages, and rural municipalities) are governed by elected councils. Ontario and Quebec also have counties that group smaller municipal units for certain purposes. In general, municipalities are responsible for police and fire protection, local jails, roads and hospitals, water supply and sanitation, and schools, duties that are discharged either by elected agencies or by appointed commissions.

Most North Americans live in large and small cities. In the United States, these, too, are subdivided, not only into wards or precincts for voting purposes but also into special districts for such functions as fire and police protection, water and electricity supply, education, recreation, and sanitation.

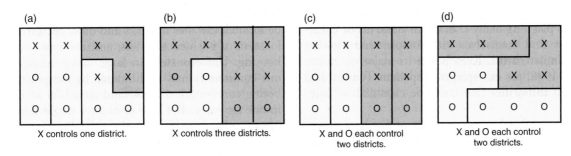

(a) X controls one district.
(b) X controls three districts.
(c) X and O each control two districts.
(d) X and O each control two districts.

FIGURE 9.30 Alternative districting strategies. Xs and Os might represent Republicans and Democrats, urban and rural voters, blacks and whites, or any other distinctive groups.

FIGURE 9.31 Political fragmentation in Champaign County, Illinois. The map shows a few of the independent administrative agencies with separate jurisdictions, responsibilities, and taxing powers in a portion of a single Illinois county. Among the other such agencies forming the fragmented political landscape are Champaign County itself, a forest preserve district, a public health district, a mental health district, the county housing authority, and a community college district.

Summary of Key Concepts

- The sovereign state is the dominant entity in the political subdivision of the world. It constitutes an expression of cultural separation and identity as pervasive as that inherent in language, religion, or ethnicity. A product of 18th-century political philosophy, the idea of the state was diffused globally by colonizing European powers. In most instances, the colonial boundaries they established have been retained as their international boundaries by newly independent countries.

- The greatly varying geographic characteristics of states contribute to national strength and stability. Size, shape, and relative location influence countries's economies and international roles, while national cores and capitals are the heartlands of states. Boundaries, the legal definition of a state's size and shape, determine the limits of its sovereignty. They may or may not reflect preexisting cultural landscapes and, in any given case, may or may not prove to be viable. Whatever their nature, boundaries are at the root of many international conflicts. Maritime boundary claims, particularly as reflected in the United Nations Convention on the Law of the Sea, add a new dimension to traditional claims of territorial sovereignty.

- State cohesiveness is promoted by a number of centripetal forces. Among these are national symbols; a variety of institutions; and confidence in the aims, organization, and administration of government. Also helping foster political and economic integration are transportation and communication connections. Destabilizing centrifugal forces, particularly ethnically based separatist

movements, threaten the cohesion and stability of many states.

- Although the state remains central to the partitioning of the world, a broadening array of political entities affects people individually and collectively. Recent decades have seen a significant increase in supranationalism, in the form and variety of global and regional alliances, to which states have surrendered some sovereign powers. At the other end of the spectrum, expanding Anglo American urban areas and governmental responsibilities raise questions of fairness in districting procedures and of effectiveness when political power is fragmented.

Key Words

antecedent boundary 285
artificial (geometric) boundary 285
centrifugal force 290
centripetal force 290
compact state 279
consequent boundary 285
core area 283
devolution 295
electoral geography 304
elongated state 279
enclave 281
ethnic cleansing 297

European Union (EU) 300
exclave 281
exclusive economic
    zone (EEZ) 299
fragmented state 279
gerrymandering 304
irredentism 288
nation 276
nationalism 290
nation-state 276
natural boundary 284
perforated state 281

political geography 275
prorupt state 279
regionalism 293
state 275
subnationalism 393
subsequent boundary 285
superimposed boundary 285
supranationalism 297
terrorism 294
United Nations Convention on the
    Law of the Sea (UNCLOS) 299

Thinking Geographically

1. What are the differences among a *state*, a *nation*, and a *nation-state?* Why is a colony not a state? How can one account for the rapid increase in the number of states since World War II?

2. What attributes differentiate states from one another? How do a country's size and shape affect its power and stability? How can a piece of land be both an *enclave* and an *exclave?*

3. How can boundaries be classified?

4. How do borders create opportunities for conflict? Describe and give examples of three types of such conflicts.

5. Distinguish between *centripetal* and *centrifugal* political forces. Why is nationalism both a centripetal and a centrifugal force? What are some of the ways national cohesion and identity are achieved?

6. What characteristics are common to all or most separatist movements? Where are some of these movements active?

Why do they tend to be located on the periphery rather than at the national core?

7. What types of international organizations and alliances can you name? What were the purposes of their establishment? What generalizations can you make regarding economic alliances?

8. How does the *United Nations Convention on the Law of the Sea* define zones of diminishing national control? What are the consequences of the concept of the 200-nm *exclusive economic zone?*

9. Why does it matter how boundaries are drawn around electoral districts? Theoretically, is it always possible to delimit boundaries "fairly"? Support your answer.

10. What reasons can you suggest for the great political fragmentation of the United States? What problems stem from such fragmentation?

PART
THREE

The Location Tradition

Given, then, our population map, what has it to show us? Starting from the most generally known before proceeding towards the less familiar, observe first the mapping of London—here plainly shown, as it is properly known, as Greater London—with its vast population streaming out in all directions—east, west, north, south—flooding all the levels, flowing up the main Thames valley and all the minor ones, filling them up, crowded and dark, and leaving only the intervening patches of high ground pale. . . . This octopus of London, polypus rather, is something curious exceedingly, a vast irregular growth without previous parallel in the world of life—perhaps likest to the spreading of a great coral reef. Like this, it has a stony skeleton, and living polypes—call it, then, a "man-reef" if you will. Onward it grows, thinly at first, the pale tints spreading further and faster than the others, but the deeper tints of thicker population at every point steadily following on. Within lies a dark crowded area; of which, however, the daily pulsating centre calls on us to seek some fresh comparison to higher than corraline life.[a]

Thus, in the lavish prose of the early 20th century, did Patrick Geddes, "spokesman for man and the environment," capsulize the spread of people in the London region. The physical environment, the vibrant human life of cities, and the change in human settlement patterns are all implicit in his remarks, as they are in the locational tradition of geography.

A theme that has run like a thread through the first two parts of this book may aptly be termed the *theme of location.* Distributions of climates, landforms, culture hearths, and religions were points of interest in our examinations of physical and cultural landscapes. In Part Three of our study, the analysis of location becomes our central concern rather than just one strand among many, and the locational tradition of geography is brought to the fore.

In the study of economic or urban geography or of the varied impacts of humans on the environments they occupy and exploit, a central question has to do with *where* certain types of human activities take place, not just in absolute terms

but also in relation to one another. In studying the distribution of a given activity, such as commercial grain farming, the concern is with identifying the locational pattern, analyzing it to see why it is arranged the way it is, and searching for underlying principles of location. Because the elements of culture are integrated, such a study often must take into consideration the ways in which the location of one element affects the locations of others. For example, certain characteristics of the labor pool helped alter the distribution of the athletic footwear industry worldwide, and that alteration had economic consequences for both the United States and Asia.

In Chapter 10, "Economic Geography," our attention is directed to the location of economic activities as we seek to answer the question of why they are distributed as they are. What forces operate to make some regions extremely productive and others less so, or some enterprises successful and others not? The stages of economic activities from primary production to sophisticated technical services are examined.

The increasing urbanization of the world's population represents another stage of the process of cultural development, economic change, and environmental control, aspects of which have been the topics of earlier separate chapters. In Chapter 11, "An Urban World" urban areas themselves are viewed in two ways. First, we focus on cities as points in space with patterns of distribution and specializations of function that invite analysis. Second, we look inside cities at the specialized arrangements of land uses resulting from recognizable processes of urban growth and development.

Part Three concludes with a critical look at the imprint humans have made on the earth's surface and its environments. Chapter 12, "Human Impact on the Environment," explores some of the worldwide and regionally specific implications of a basic geographic observation: in the interaction between humans and the physical environment, humans are the active and frequently destructive agents of change.

Human exploitation of the earth results in both intended and unanticipated alterations to the natural world—to water resources, world and regional climates, soils, plant and animal life, and the like. Ecological damage or change is no longer occasional and localized; it has become permanent and generalized and of growing concern to people and governments everywhere. The structure of this book separates the discipline into its physical and cultural components. That final chapter of "The Location Tradition" reminds us of the inseparable unity of physical and human geography.

[a]From *Patrick Geddes: Spokesman for Man and the Environment,* ed. by Marshall Stalley. New Brunswick, N.J.: Rutgers University Press, 1972, p. 123.

Opposite page: The Rock of Ages granite quarry in Barre, Vermont, shows a form of economic development leaving a lasting impact on the physical environment. © *The McGraw-Hill Companies, Inc./Photo by Doug Sherman.*

CHAPTER TEN

Economic Geography

CHAPTER OUTLINE

Digital communication technologies have allowed the globalization of service industries. These New Delhi, India, call center workers are recent college graduates and often must work night shifts to cater to customers in Europe and North America. © Sondeep Shankar/Bloomberg/Getty.

The crop bloomed luxuriantly that summer of 1846. The disaster of the preceding year seemed over and the potato, the sole sustenance of some 8 million Irish peasants, would again yield in the bounty needed. However, within a week, wrote Father Mathew, "I beheld one wide waste of putrefying vegetation. The wretched people were seated on the fences of their decaying gardens . . . bewailing bitterly the destruction that had left them foodless." Colonel Gore found that "every field was black," and an estate steward noted that "the fields . . . look as if fire has passed over them." The potato was irretrievably gone for a second year; famine and pestilence were inevitable.

Within 5 years, the settlement geography of the most densely populated country in Europe was forever altered. The United States received a million immigrants, who provided the cheap labor needed for the canals, railroads, and mines that it was creating in its rush to economic development. New patterns of commodity flows were initiated as American maize for the first time found an Anglo-Irish market—as part of Poor Relief—and then entered a wider European market that had also suffered general crop failure in that bitter year. Within days, a microscopic organism, the cause of the potato blight, had altered the economic and human geography of two continents.

That alteration resulted from a complex set of intertwined causes and effects that demonstrates once again our repeated observation that apparently separate physical and cultural geographic patterns are really interconnected parts of a single reality. Central among those patterns are the ones the economic geographer isolates for special study.

Simply stated, **economic geography** is the study of how people earn their living, how livelihood systems vary by area, and how economic activities are spatially interrelated and linked. Of course, we cannot really comprehend the totality of the economic pursuits of approximately 7 billion human beings. We cannot examine the infinite variety of production and service activities found everywhere on the earth's surface; nor can we trace all their innumerable interrelationships, linkages, and flows. Even if that level of understanding were possible, it would be valid for only a fleeting instant of time, for economic activities are constantly undergoing change.

Economic geographers seek consistencies. They attempt to develop generalizations that will aid in the comprehension of the maze of economic variations characterizing human existence. From their studies emerges a deeper awareness of the dynamic, interlocking diversity of human enterprise, of the impact of economic activity on all other facets of human life and culture, and of the increasing interdependence of differing national and regional economic systems (see "Economic Regions" in Chapter 13). The potato blight, although it struck only one small island, ultimately affected the economies of continents. In like fashion, the depletion of America's natural resources and the "deindustrialization" of its economy and conversion to postindustrial service and knowledge-based activities are altering the relative wealth of countries, flows of international trade, domestic employment and income patterns, and more (Figure 10.1).

FIGURE 10.1 This derelict, abandoned farm equipment factory in Brantford, Canada—a brownfield site—typifies the structural changes occurring in postindustrial economies. Established patterns of production and exchange are constantly subject to change in a world of increasing economic and cultural interdependence. *Photo by Mark Bjelland.*

THE CLASSIFICATION OF ECONOMIC ACTIVITY AND ECONOMIES

Understanding livelihood patterns is made more difficult by five major environmental and cultural realities controlling the economic activities of humans. Many production patterns are rooted in the spatially variable circumstances of the *physical environment*. The staple crops of the humid tropics, for example, are not part of the agricultural systems of the midlatitudes; livestock types that thrive in American feedlots or on western ranges are not adapted to the Arctic tundra or the margins of the Sahara Desert. The unequal distribution of useful mineral deposits gives some regions and countries economic prospects and employment opportunities denied to others. Forestry and fishing depend on still other natural resources unequal in occurrence, type, and value.

Within the bounds of the environmentally possible, economic or production decisions may be conditioned by *cultural considerations*. For example, culturally based food preferences rather than environmental limitations may dictate the choice of crops or livestock. Maize is a preferred grain in Africa and the Americas; wheat in North America, Australia, Argentina, southern Europe, and Ukraine; and rice in much of Asia. Pigs are not produced in Muslim areas. The level of *technological development* of a culture will affect its recognition of resources or its ability to exploit them. Preindustrial societies do not know of, or need, iron ore or coal deposits that may underlie their hunting, gathering, or gardening grounds. *Political decisions* may encourage or discourage—through subsidies, protective tariffs, or production restrictions—patterns of economic activity. And, ultimately, production is controlled by *economic factors* of demand, whether that demand is expressed through a free market mechanism, through government intervention, or through the consumption requirements of a single family producing for its own needs.

Categories of Activity

Such regionally varying environmental, cultural, technological, political, and market conditions add spatial details to more generalized ways of categorizing the world's productive work. One approach to that categorization is to view economic activity as ranged along a continuum of both increasing complexity of product or service and increasing distance from the natural environment. Seen from that perspective, a small number of distinctive stages of production and service activities can be distinguished (Figure 10.2).

Primary activities are those that harvest or extract something from the earth. They are at the beginning of the production cycle, where humans are in closest contact with the resources and potentialities of the environment. Such primary activities involve basic foodstuffs and raw material production. Hunting and gathering, grazing, agriculture, fishing, forestry, and mining and quarrying are examples.

FIGURE 10.2 The categories of economic activity. The five main sectors of the economy do not stand alone. They are connected and integrated by transportation and communication services and facilities not assigned to any single sector but common to all.

Secondary activities are those that add value to materials by changing their form or combining them into more useful, and therefore more valuable, commodities. That provision of *form utility* ranges from the simple handicraft production of pottery or woodenware to the delicate assembly of electronic goods or space vehicles (Figure 10.3). Copper smelting, steel-making, metalworking, automobile production, the textile and chemical industries—indeed, the full array of *manufacturing* and *processing industries*—are included in this phase of the production process. Also included are the production of *energy* (the "power company") and the *construction* industry.

Tertiary activities consist of those business and labor specializations that provide *services* to the primary and secondary sectors and *goods* and *services* to the general community and to the individual. These include professional, clerical, and personal services. They constitute the vital link between producer and consumer, for tertiary occupations importantly include the wholesale and retail *trade* activities—including "dot-com" Internet sales—necessary in highly interdependent societies.

In economically advanced societies, a growing number of individuals and entire organizations are engaged in the processing and dissemination of information and in the administration and control of their own or other enterprises. The term **quaternary activity** is applied to this fourth class of economic activities, which is composed entirely of services rendered by white collar professionals working in education, government, management, information processing, and research. Sometimes, a subdivision of these management functions—**quinary activities**—is distinguished to recognize high-level decision-making roles in all types of large organizations, public or

FIGURE 10.3 These logs entering a lumber mill are products of *primary production*. Processing them into boards, plywood, or prefabricated houses is a *secondary activity* that increases their value by altering their form. The products of many secondary industries— sheet steel from steel mills, for example—constitute "raw materials" for other manufacturers. © *Mark E. Gibson.*

private. The distinctions between tertiary, quaternary, and quinary activities are further developed later in this chapter under the section "Tertiary and Beyond." As Figure 10.2 further suggested, transportation and communication services cut across the general activity categories, unite them, and make possible the spatial interactions that all human enterprise requires.

These categories of production and service activities help us see an underlying structure to the nearly infinite variety of things people do to earn a living and to sustain themselves. But they tell us little about the organization of the larger economy of which the individual worker or enterprise is a part. For that wider organizational understanding of world and regional economies, we look to *systems* rather than *components* of economies.

Types of Economic Systems

Broadly viewed, national economies in the early 21st century fall into one of three major types of system: *subsistence, commercial,* or *planned.* None of these economic systems is or has

been "pure." That is, none exists in isolation in an increasingly interdependent world. Each, however, displays certain underlying characteristics based on its distinctive forms of resource management and economic control.

In a **subsistence economy,** goods and services are created for the use of the producers and their kinship groups. Therefore, there is little exchange of goods and only limited need for markets. In the **market (commercial) economies** that have become dominant in nearly all parts of the world, producers or their agents in theory freely market their goods and services, the laws of supply and demand determine price and quantity, and market competition is the primary force shaping production decisions and distributions. In **planned economies** associated with communist-controlled societies, producers or their agents dispose of goods and services through governmental agencies that control both supply and price. The quantities produced and the locational patterns of production are tightly programmed by central planning departments.

With a few exceptions—such as Cuba and North Korea— rigidly planned economies no longer exist in their classical form; they have been modified or dismantled in favor of free market structures or are only partially retained in the lesser degree of economic control associated with governmental supervision or ownership of selected sectors of increasingly market-oriented economies. Nevertheless, their landscape evidence lives on. The physical structures, patterns of production, and imposed regional interdependencies they created remain to influence or distort the economic decisions of successor societies.

In actuality, few people are members of only one of these systems, although one may be dominant. A farmer in India may produce rice and vegetables primarily for the family's consumption but also save some of the produce to sell. In addition, members of the family may market cloth or other handicrafts they make. With the money derived from those sales, the Indian peasant is able to buy, among other things, clothes for the family, tools, or fuel. Thus, that Indian farmer is a member of at least two systems: subsistence and commercial.

In the United States, government controls on the production of various types of goods and services (such as growing wheat or sugarcane, producing alcohol, constructing and operating nuclear power plants, or engaging in licensed personal and professional services) mean that the country does not have a purely market economy. To a limited extent, its citizens participate in a controlled and planned as well as in a free market environment. Many African, Asian, and Latin American market economies have been decisively shaped by governmental policies encouraging or demanding the production of export commodities rather than domestic foodstuffs or promoting through import restrictions the development of domestic industries not readily supported by the national market alone. Example after example would show that there are very few people in the world who are members of only one type of economic system (Figure 10.4).

Inevitably, spatial patterns, including those of economic systems and activities, are subject to change. For example, the commercial economies of Western European countries, some with sizeable infusions of planned economy controls, are being restructured by both increased free market competition and supranational regulation under the World Trade Organization and the European Union (see p. 300). Many of the countries of Latin America, Africa, Asia, and the Middle East that traditionally were dominated by subsistence economies are now benefiting from technology transfer from advanced economies and integration into expanding global production and exchange patterns.

Stages of Development

Despite such changes and global convergences, disparities between regions and countries in observable economic and social conditions obviously exist and, since the middle of the 20th century, have been the subject of theories and measurements of development and underdevelopment. We noted in Chapter 7 (pp. 199–204) that development implies the full

FIGURE 10.4 Independent street merchants, shop owners, and peddlers in modern China are members of both a planned and a market system. Free markets and private vendors multiplied after the government removed price controls on most food items in May 1985. Increasingly, nonfood trade and manufacturing, too, are being freed from central government control and are thriving in the private sector. As state-run companies shrank and laid off workers, privately owned businesses in 2007 accounted for well over two-thirds of China's gross domestic product and the private sector was growing twice as fast as the rest of the economy. The photo shows a row of outdoor poultry merchants in Wanxian, Sichuan Province. © *Jon C. Malinowski.*

productive use of a country's natural and human resources, and we traced the emergence of such comparative labels as *developed, less-developed, developing, newly industrializing,* and similar descriptors. There, too, we reviewed the UN-sanctioned recognition of a global contrast (Figure 7.8) between an economically advanced industrialized "North" with relatively high per capita incomes and a "South" with little or no industrialization and low income levels (Figure 7.7). In that contrast, a key indicator was the degree of an economy's industrialization and progression beyond a largely subsistence livelihood system.

In the 1960s, a dominant theory described normal development as a progression from the limitations of a traditional society of subsistence agriculture, low technology levels, and poorly developed commercial exchanges through "takeoff" stages of increasing investment in infrastructure and human capital, application of modern technology to resource exploitation, and a gradually expanding and maturing industrial base. Eventually, the developing state would achieve an "age of mass production and consumption" and, ultimately, the postindustrial status of the most-advanced, Western economies.

That theoretically expected progression proved illusory; many less- and least-developed countries remained locked in the pre-takeoff stage, despite infusions of loans, investments, and technology transfers from the more-developed states. The 1960s, 1970s, and 1980s—all proclaimed by the United Nations as "Development Decades"—proved instead to be decades of disappointment, at least by economic measures. However, substantial economic growth in the developing world between 1990 and 2007 revived faith for many in the "stages of development." Average per capita income growth in developing countries in the 1990s was 1.5%, about three times the rate in the 1980s; between 2000 and 2005, their average per capita income growth increased to 3.5%, about double the rate for high-income states. Even sub-Saharan Africa posted an increase of 1.3% a year in the 2000–2005 period. The food and fuel crises that hit hard in many developing countries in 2007 and the financial crisis and recession that spread from the United States to many other countries dampened what had been a long period of global economic expansion.

Other developmental theories and models were proposed to supplement or replace the 1960s original. The concept of the "Big Push" concludes that underdeveloped economies can break out of poverty by coordinated investment in both basic (but high-wage) industries and infrastructure, expanding the consumer base while ensuring the volume production of lower-cost consumer goods. Another viewpoint holds that differing national growth rates are rooted in differing investments in human capital—a composite of skills, habits, education, and health—deemed essential to effectively adopt advanced technologies and entrepreneurial skills. A corollary concept concludes that, for least-developed and newly industrializing countries, incentives encouraging foreign direct investment (see p. 346) and technology transfer are the most effective way to jump-start economic growth.

Although frequently criticized for their Western market economy biases, assessments of stages of economic development understandably emphasize standardized, easily obtainable measures of country contrasts. Besides the obvious per capita income distinctions, attention is often concentrated on the allocation of the labor force of different countries among the several categories of activities (primary, secondary, and so on, as outlined at the beginning of this chapter) and the relative contribution of agriculture, industry, and services to their gross domestic product (GDP). Degree of development, it is held, can be traced through the reallocation of labor resources from the basic primary (largely agricultural) activities to a rising share of workers engaged in secondary, and then tertiary and quaternary endeavors. Underdeveloped Bhutan (a small Himalayan state), with 93% of its labor force in agriculture, 2% in industry, and 5% in services, stands in obvious contrast to highly developed Australia, with only 1.5% of labor force involvement in agriculture, 19% in industry, and nearly 80% in services. In a similar way, using the relative contributions of the different categories of activity to GDP reveals meaningful contrasts between levels of national development. A sizeable contribution to GDP from agriculture, for example, coupled with only a small input from services suggests a dependence on subsistence agriculture and a paucity or only low level of retail, personal, and professional services—unmistakable indicators of economic underdevelopment (Table 10.1). Highly advanced, postindustrial societies, on the other hand, have relatively small inputs from primary production (including agriculture) and a dominating GDP input from the personal and professional services, marking their highly integrated knowledge-based exchange economies.

No matter what economic system locally prevails, in all instances transportation is a key variable. No advanced economy can flourish without a well-connected transport network. All subsistence societies—and subsistence areas of developing countries—are characterized by their isolation from regional and world routeways (Figure 10.5), and that isolation restricts their progression to more-advanced forms of economic structure.

Former sharp contrasts in economic organization are becoming blurred and countries' economic orientations are changing as globalization reduces structural contrasts in national economies. Still, both approaches to economic classification—by type of activity and by organization of economies—help us visualize and understand world economic geographic patterns. In this chapter, our path to that understanding leads through the successive categories of economic activity, from primary to quinary, with emphasis on the technologies, spatial patterns, and organizational systems that are involved in each category.

PRIMARY ACTIVITIES: AGRICULTURE

Humankind's basic economic concern is producing or securing food resources sufficient to meet individual daily energy requirements and so balanced as to satisfy normal nutritional

TABLE 10.1
Stage of Economic Development and the Structure of Output

Country Category	PERCENT OF GROSS DOMESTIC PRODUCT, 2006			
	Agriculture	Industry [a]	Manufacturing [b]	Services
Least-Developed				
Central African Republic	56	15	8	29
Mali	37	24	3	39
Newly Industrialized				
Malaysia	9	50	30	41
Thailand	11	45	35	45
Industrial				
Czech Republic	3	39	27	58
South Korea	3	40	28	57
Postindustrial				
Australia	3	28	11	69
United States	1	23	14	76

Source: The World Bank, *World Development Indicators* 2008.
[a]Includes mining, manufacturing, construction, and utilities.
[b]Also included in "Industry."

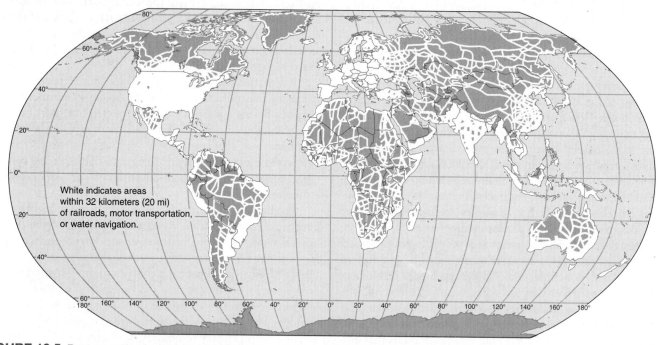

White indicates areas within 32 kilometers (20 mi) of railroads, motor transportation, or water navigation.

FIGURE 10.5 Patterns of access and isolation. Accessibility is a key measure of economic development and of the degree to which a world region can participate in interconnected market activities. Isolated areas of countries with advanced economies suffer a price disadvantage because of high transportation costs. Lack of accessibility in subsistence economic areas slows their modernization and hinders their participation in the world market. *Source: Copyright Permission: Hammond Incorporated, Maplewood, NJ 07040.*

needs. Those supplies may be acquired by the consumer directly through the primary economic activities of hunting, gathering, farming, and fishing (a form of "gathering") or indirectly through the performance of other primary, secondary, or higher-level economic endeavors that yield income sufficient to provide the earner and the earner's family with income to obtain needed daily sustenance.

Since the middle of the 20th century, a recurring but unrealized fear has been that the world's steadily increasing population would exceed available or potential food supplies.

Instead, although global population has more than doubled since 1950, the total amount of human food produced worldwide since then has also more than doubled. The Food and Agriculture Organization (FAO) of the United Nations has set the minimum daily requirement for caloric intake per person at 2350. By that measure, annual food supplies are more than sufficient to meet world needs. That is, if total food resources were evenly distributed, everyone would have access to amounts sufficient for adequate daily nourishment. In reality, however, the number of undernourished people worldwide has climbed to over 1 billion—almost all in the developing countries (Figure 10.6). A 30-year trend of reduced global hunger was reversed with the economic crisis that began in 2007. Because the world economy is closely interlinked, the recession in developed countries meant less money sent home from immigrant workers, and higher energy costs translated into higher food costs, which pushed many of the world's poor into the ranks of the chronically hungry.

This stark contradiction between sufficient worldwide food supplies and widespread malnutrition reflects inequalities in national and personal incomes; population growth rates; lack of access to fertile soils, credit, and education; local climatic conditions or catastrophes; and lack of transportation and storage facilities, among other reasons. By mid-century, the increasingly interconnected world population will expand to more than 9 billion and concerns with individual states'

food supplies will inevitably continue and remain a persistent international issue.

Before there was farming, *hunting* and *gathering* were the universal forms of primary production. These preagricultural pursuits are now practiced by at most a few thousand persons worldwide, primarily in isolated and remote pockets within the low latitudes and among the sparse populations of very high latitudes. The interior of New Guinea, rugged areas of interior Southeast Asia, diminishing segments of the Amazon rain forest, a few districts of tropical Africa and northern Australia, and parts of the Arctic regions still contain such preagricultural people. Their numbers are few and declining, and wherever they are brought into contact with more-advanced cultures, their way of life is eroded or lost.

Agriculture, defined as the growing of crops and the tending of livestock, whether for the subsistence of the producers or for sale or exchange, has replaced hunting and gathering as economically the most significant of the primary activities. It is spatially the most widespread, found in all world regions where environmental circumstances—including adequate moisture, good growing season length, and productive soils—permit (Figure 10.7). Crop farming alone covers some 15 million square kilometers (5.8 million sq mi) worldwide, about 10% of the earth's total land area. In many developing economies, at least two-thirds of the labor force is directly involved in farming and herding. In some, such as Bhutan in Asia and Burkina

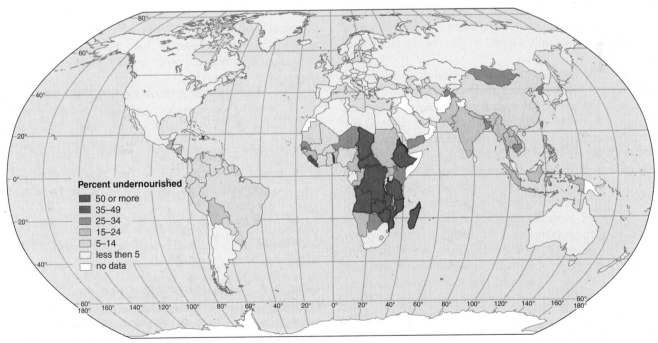

FIGURE 10.6 Percent of national population that was undernourished, 2004–2006. According to the FAO, in 2009 there were about 1.02 billion people worldwide facing chronic hunger or starvation, undernutrition, and deficiencies of essential iron, iodine, Vitamin A, and other micronutrients. More than one-third of people living in poor countries in 1970 were undernourished: by 2008, that figure had fallen to about 17%. Numerically, however, the total of malnourished people across the developing world began to grow after 1995. Sub-Saharan Africa's incidence of undernourishment has remained constant, a reflection of the region's continuing poverty and progressive drop in per capita food production since the 1960s. In contrast, the FAO indicates that all industrialized countries have average daily per capita caloric intake above 110% of physiological requirements, although that generalization masks troubling incidences of areal and household hunger and malnutrition. *Source: FAO, 2009.*

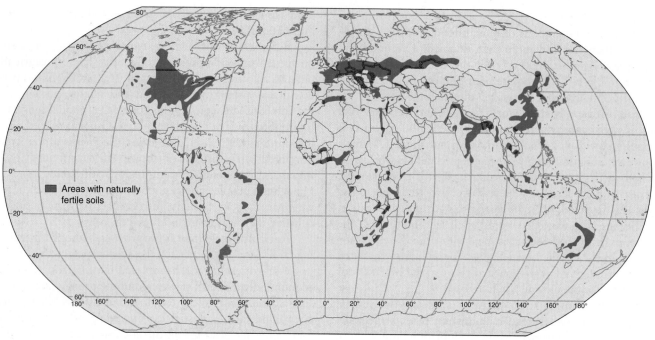

FIGURE 10.7 Areas with naturally fertile soils account for much of the world's grain production and include the corn and wheat belts of North America, Ukraine, and southern Siberia and the rice-producing regions of India and Southeast Asia. A comparison of this map with Figure 10.6 will help explain the prevalence of undernourishment in sub-Saharan Africa.

Faso and Burundi in Africa, the figure is more than 90%. Overall, however, employment in agriculture is steadily declining in developing countries, echoing but trailing the trend in highly developed market economies, where direct employment in agriculture involves only a small fraction of the labor force (see Figure 7.6).

It has been customary to classify agricultural societies on the twin bases of the importance of off-farm sales and the level of mechanization and technological advancement. *Subsistence, traditional* (or *intermediate*), and *advanced* (or *modern*) are the terms usually employed to recognize both aspects. These are not mutually exclusive but, rather, are stages along a continuum of farm economies. At one end lies production solely for family sustenance, using simple tools and native plants. At the other is the specialized, highly capitalized, industrialized agriculture for off-farm delivery that marks advanced economies. Between these extremes is the middle ground of traditional agriculture, where farm production is in part destined for home consumption and in part oriented toward off-farm sale, either locally or in national and international markets. We can most clearly see the variety of agricultural activities and the diversity of controls on their spatial patterns by examining the "subsistence" and "advanced" ends of the agricultural continuum.

Subsistence Agriculture

A *subsistence* economic system involves nearly total self-sufficiency on the part of its members. Production for exchange is minimal and any exchange is noncommercial. Each family or close-knit social group relies on itself for its food and other most-essential requirements. Farming for the immediate needs of the family is, even today, the predominant occupation of humankind. In most of Africa, much of Latin America, and most of southern and eastern Asia, the majority of the people are primarily concerned with feeding themselves from their own land and livestock.

Two chief types of subsistence agriculture can be recognized: *extensive* and *intensive*. Although each type has several variants, the essential contrast between them is yield per unit of land used and, therefore, population-supporting potential. **Extensive subsistence agriculture** involves large areas of land and minimal labor input per hectare. Both product per land unit and population densities are low. **Intensive subsistence agriculture** involves the cultivation of small land holdings through the expenditure of great amounts of labor per acre. Yields per unit area and population densities are both high (Figure 10.8).

Extensive Subsistence Agriculture

Of the several types of *extensive subsistence* agriculture—varying one from another in their intensities of land use—two are of particular interest: nomadic herding and shifting cultivation.

Nomadic herding, the wandering but controlled movement of livestock solely dependent on natural forage, is the most extensive type of land use system (Figure 10.8). That is, it requires the greatest amount of land area per person sustained. Over large portions of the Asian semidesert and desert areas, in certain highland areas, and on the fringes of and within the Sahara, a relatively small number of people graze animals for

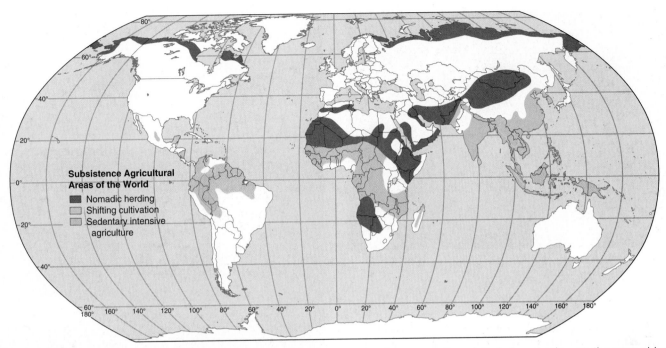

FIGURE 10.8 Subsistence agricultural areas of the world. Nomadic herding, supporting relatively few people, was the ages-old way of life in large parts of the dry and cold world. Shifting cultivation, or swidden agriculture maintains soil fertility by tested traditional practices in tropical wet and wet-and-dry climates. Large parts of Asia support millions of people engaged in sedentary intensive cultivation, with rice and wheat the chief crops.

consumption by the herder group, not for market sale. Sheep, goats, and camels are most common, while cattle, horses, and yaks are locally important. The reindeer of Lapland were formerly part of the same system.

Whatever the animals involved, their common characteristics are hardiness, mobility, and an ability to subsist on sparse forage. The animals provide a variety of products: milk, cheese, yogurt, and meat for food; hair, wool, and skins for clothing; skins for shelter; and excrement for fuel. For the herder, they represent primary subsistence. Nomadic movement is tied to sparse and seasonal rainfall or to cold temperature regimes and to the areally varying appearance and exhaustion of forage. Extended stays in a given location are neither desirable nor possible. *Transhumance* is a special form of seasonal movement of livestock to exploit specific locally varying pasture conditions. Used by permanently or seasonally sedentary pastoralists and pastoral farmers, transhumance involves either the regular vertical movement from mountain to valley pastures between summer and winter months or horizontal movement between established lowland grazing areas to reach pastures temporarily lush from monsoonal (seasonal) rains.

As a type of economic system, nomadic herding is declining. Many economic, social, and cultural changes are causing nomadic groups to alter their way of life or to disappear entirely. On the Arctic fringe of Russia, herders under communism were made members of state or collective herding enterprises. In northern Scandinavia, Lapps (Saami) are engaged in commercial more than in subsistence livestock farming. In the Sahel region of Africa on the margins of the Sahara, oases

once controlled by herders have been taken over by farmers, and the great droughts of recent decades have forever altered the formerly nomadic way of life of thousands.

A much differently based and distributed form of extensive subsistence agriculture is found in all of the warm, moist, low-latitude areas of the world. There, many people engage in a kind of nomadic farming. In these warm, wet tropical climates, once a field is put into production, dead plant matter decomposes rapidly and soil nutrients are quickly leached—washed away by surface water or groundwater. Thus, soil fertility declines rapidly and, after harvesting several crops, the farmer is forced to move on. In a sense, they rotate fields rather than crops to maintain productivity. This type of **shifting cultivation** has a number of names, the most common of which are *swidden* (an English localism for "burned clearing") and *slash-and-burn*. Each region of its practice has its own name—for example, *milpa* in Middle and South America, *chitemene* in Africa, and *ladang* in Southeast Asia.

Characteristically, the farmers hack down the natural vegetation and burn the cuttings, which puts nutrients into the soil. Then they plant such crops as maize (corn), millet (a cereal grain), rice, manioc or cassava, yams, and sugarcane (Figure 10.9). Increasingly included in many of the crop combinations are such high-value, labor-intensive commercial crops as coffee, providing the cash income that is evidence of the growing integration of all peoples into exchange economies. Initial yields—the first and second crops—may be very high, but they quickly become lower with each successive planting on the same plot. As that occurs, cropping ceases,

FIGURE 10.9 Preparation of a swidden plot in Liberia, Africa. (a) First the vegetation is hacked down. **(b)** Then the field is planted. Stumps and trees left in the clearing will remain after the burn. © *Albert Swingle.*

native vegetation is allowed to reclaim the clearing, and gardening shifts to another newly prepared site. The first clearing will ideally not be used again for crops until, after many years, natural fallowing replenishes its fertility (see "Swidden Agriculture," p. 323).

Less than 3% of the world's people are still predominantly engaged in tropical shifting cultivation on about one-seventh of the world's land area (see Figure 10.8). Because the essential characteristic of the system is the intermittent cultivation of the land, each family requires a total occupance area equivalent to the garden plot in current use plus all land left fallow for regeneration. Population densities are characteristically low, because much land is needed to support few people. It may be argued that shifting cultivation is a highly efficient cultural adaptation where land is abundant in relation to population, and levels of technology and capital availability are low. As those conditions change, the system becomes less viable.

Intensive Subsistence Agriculture

About 45% of the world's people are engaged in intensive subsistence agriculture, which predominates in the areas shown in Figure 10.8. As a descriptive term, *intensive subsistence* is no longer fully applicable to a changing way of life and economy in which the distinction between subsistence and commercial is decreasingly valid. Although families may still be fed primarily with the produce of their individual plots, the exchange of farm commodities within the system is considerable. Production of foodstuffs for sale in rapidly growing urban markets is increasingly vital for the rural economies of subsistence

farming areas and for the sustenance of the growing proportion of national and regional populations no longer themselves engaged in farming.

Nevertheless, hundreds of millions of Indians, Chinese, Pakistanis, Bangladeshis, and Indonesians, plus further millions in other Asian, African, and Latin American countries remain small-plot, mainly subsistence producers of rice, wheat, maize, millet, or pulses (peas, beans, and other legumes). Most live in monsoon Asia, where warm, moist districts are well suited to the production of rice, a crop that under ideal conditions can provide large amounts of food per unit of land. Rice also requires a great deal of time and attention, for planting rice shoots by hand in standing fresh water is a tedious art (Figure 10.10). In the cooler and drier portions of Asia north of 20°N, wheat is grown intensively, along with millet and, less commonly, upland rice.

Intensive subsistence farming is characterized by large inputs of labor per unit of land; by small plots; by the intensive use of fertilizers, mostly animal manure (see "The Economy of a Chinese Village," p. 324); and by the promise of high yields in good years. For food security and dietary custom, *polyculture*—production of several different crops, often in the same field—is practiced. Vegetables and some livestock are part of the agricultural system, and fish may be reared in rice paddies and ponds. Food animals include swine, ducks, and chickens, but since Muslims eat no pork, hogs are absent in their areas of settlement. Hindus generally eat little meat, mainly goat and lamb but not pork or beef. The large numbers of cattle in India are vital for labor and are a source of milk and cheese, as well as producers—through excrement—of fertilizer and fuel.

Swidden Agriculture

The following account describes shifting cultivation (swidden agriculture) among the Hanunóo people of the Philippines. Nearly identical procedures are followed in all swidden farming regions.

When a garden site of about one-half hectare (a little over one acre) has been selected, the swidden farmer begins to remove unwanted vegetation. The first phase of this process consists of slashing and cutting the undergrowth and smaller trees with bush knives. The principal aim is to cover the entire site with highly inflammable dead vegetation so that the later stage of burning will be most effective. Because of the threat of soil erosion the ground must not be exposed directly to the elements at any time during the cutting stage. During the first months of the agricultural year, activities connected with cutting take priority over all others.

Once most of the undergrowth has been slashed, the larger trees must be felled or killed by girdling (cutting a complete ring of bark) so that unwanted shade will be removed. Some trees, however, are merely trimmed but not killed or cut, both to reduce labor and to leave trees to reseed the swidden during the subsequent fallow period.

The crucial and most important single event in the agricultural cycle is swidden burning. The main firing of a swidden is the culmination of many weeks of preparation in spreading and leveling chopped vegetation, preparing firebreaks to prevent flames escaping into the jungle, and allowing time for the drying process. An ideal burn rapidly consumes every bit of litter; in no more than an hour or an hour and a half, only smoldering remains are left.

Swidden farmers note the following as the benefits of a good burn: (1) removal of unwanted vegetation, resulting in a cleared swidden; (2) extermination of many animal and some weed pests; (3) preparation of the soil for dibble (any small hand tool or stick to make a hole) planting by making it softer and more friable; (4) provision of an evenly distributed cover of wood ashes, good for young crop plants and protective of newly planted grain seed. Within the first year of the swidden cycle, an average of between 40 and 50 different types of crop plants have been planted and harvested.

The most critical feature of swidden agriculture is the maintenance of soil fertility and structure. The solution is to pursue a system of rotation of one to three years in crop and ten to twenty in woody or bush fallow regeneration. When population pressures mandate a reduction in the length of fallow period, productivity tends to drop as soil fertility is lowered, marginal land is utilized, and environmental degradation occurs. The balance is delicate.

Source: Adapted from Hanunoo Agriculture, *by Harold C. Conklin (FAO Forestry Development Paper No. 12), 1957.*

FIGURE 10.10 Transplanting rice seedlings requires arduous hand labor by all members of the family. The newly flooded diked fields, previously plowed and fertilized, will have their water level maintained until the grain is ripe. The scene in this photograph is repeated wherever subsistence wet-rice agriculture is practiced.
© *Corbis RF.*

Not all of the world's subsistence farming is based in rural areas. Urban agriculture is a rapidly growing activity, with some 800 million city farmers worldwide providing, according to United Nations figures, one-seventh of the world's total food production. Occurring in all regions of the world, developed and underdeveloped, but most prevalent in Asia, urban agricultural activities range from small garden plots to backyard livestock breeding to fish raised in ponds and streams. Using the garbage dumps of Jakarta, the rooftops of Mexico City, and meager dirt strips along roadways in Kolkata or Kinshasa, millions of people are feeding their own families and supplying local markets with vegetables, fruit, fish, and even meat—all produced within the cities themselves and all without the expense and spoilage of storage or long-distance transportation.

In Africa, a reported 20% of urban nutritional requirement is produced in the towns and cities; two of three Kenyan and Tanzanian urban families engage in farming, for example, and in Accra, Ghana's capital, urban farming provides the city with 90% of its fresh vegetables. In all parts of the developing world, urban-origin foodstuffs have reduced the incidence of adult and child malnutrition in rapidly expanding cities.

The Economy of a Chinese Village

The village of Nanching is in subtropical southern China on the Zhu River delta near Guangzhou (Canton). Its traditional subsistence agricultural regime was described by a field investigator, whose account is condensed here. The system is still followed in its essentials in other rice-oriented societies.

In this double-crop region, rice was planted in March and August and harvested in late June or July and again in November. March to November was the major farming season. Early in March the earth was turned with an iron-tipped wooden plow pulled by a water buffalo. The very poor who could not afford a buffalo used a large iron-tipped wooden hoe for the same purpose.

The plowed soil was raked smooth, fertilizer was applied, and water was let into the field, which was then ready for the transplanting of rice seedlings. Seedlings were raised in a seedbed, a tiny patch fenced off on the side or corner of the field. Beginning from the middle of March, the transplanting of seedlings took place. The whole family was on the scene. Each took the seedlings by the bunch, ten to fifteen plants, and pushed them into the soft inundated soil. For the first thirty or forty days the emerald green crop demanded little attention except keeping the water at a proper level. But after this period came the first weeding; the second weeding followed a month later. This was done by hand, and everyone old enough for such work participated. With the second weeding went the job of adding fertilizer. The grain was now allowed to stand to "draw starch" to fill the hull of the kernels. When the kernels had "drawn enough starch," water was let out of the field, and both the soil and the stalks were allowed to dry under the hot sun.

Then came the harvest, when all the rice plants were cut off a few inches above the ground with a sickle. Threshing was done on a threshing board. Then the grain and the stalks and leaves were taken home with a carrying pole on the peasant's shoulder. The plant was used as fuel at home.

As soon as the exhausting harvest work was done, no time could be lost before starting the chores of plowing, fertilizing, pumping water into the fields, and transplanting seedlings for the second crop. The slack season of the rice crop was taken up by chores required for the vegetables which demanded continuous attention, since every peasant family devoted a part of the farm to vegetable gardening. In the hot and damp period of late spring and summer, eggplant and several varieties of squash and beans were grown. The green-leafed vegetables thrived in the cooler and drier period of fall, winter, and early spring. Leeks grew the year-round.

When one crop of vegetables was harvested, the soil was turned and the clods broken up by a digging hoe and leveled with an iron rake. Fertilizer was applied, and seeds or seedlings of a new crop were planted. Hand weeding was a constant job; watering with the long-handled wooden dipper had to be done an average of three times a day, and in the very hot season when evaporation was rapid, as frequently as six times a day. The soil had to be cultivated with the hoe frequently as the heavy tropical rains packed the earth continuously. Instead of the two applications of fertilizer common with the rice crop, fertilizing was much more frequent for vegetables. Besides the heavy fertilizing of the soil at the beginning of a crop, usually with city garbage, additional fertilizer, usually diluted urine or a mixture of diluted urine and excreta, was given every ten days or so to most vegetables.

Adapted from C. K. Yang, A Chinese Village in Early Communist Transition. The MIT Press, Cambridge, Mass. Copyright © 1959 by the Massachusetts Institute of Technology.

Expanding Crop Production

Continuing population pressures on existing resources are a constant spur for seeking ways to expand the food supply available both to the subsistence farmers of the developing economies and to the wider world as a whole. Two paths to promoting increased food production are apparent: (1) expand the land area under cultivation and (2) increase crop yields from existing farmlands.

The first approach—increasing cropland area—is not a promising strategy. Approximately 70% of the world's land area is agriculturally unsuitable, being too cold, too dry, too steep, or totally infertile. Of the remaining 30%, most of the area well suited for farming is already under cultivation, and of that area, millions of hectares annually are being lost through soil erosion, salinization, desertification, and the conversion of farmland to urban, industrial, and transportation uses in all developed and developing countries. Only the rain forests of Africa and the Amazon Basin of South America retain sizeable areas of potentially farmable land. The soils of those regions, however, are fragile, are low in nutrients, have poor water retention, and are easily eroded or destroyed following deforestation. By most accounts, then, world food output cannot reasonably be increased by simple expansion of cultivated areas.

Intensification and the Green Revolution

Increased productivity of existing cropland rather than expansion of cultivated area has been the key to the growth of agricultural output over the past few decades. Between 1975 and 2005, world total grain production rose more than 62%. Despite some 2.3 billion more people in the world, grain production per capita for the period 2004–2005 was nearly 5% above the 1974–1975 level. The vast majority of that production growth was due to increases in yields rather than expansions in cropland. For Asia as a whole, cereal yields grew by more than 40% between 1980 and the early 21st century, accounted for largely by increases in China and India; they increased by more than 35% in South America. Two interrelated approaches to those yield increases mark recent farming practices.

First, throughout much of the developing world production inputs such as water, fertilizer, pesticides, and labor have been increased to expand yields on a relatively constant supply of cultivable land. Irrigated area, for example, has nearly doubled since 1960 to comprise by 2007 some 19% of the world's cropland. Global consumption of fertilizers has dramatically increased since the 1950s, and inputs of pesticides and herbicides have similarly grown. Traditional practices of leaving land fallow (uncultivated) to renew its fertility have been largely abandoned, and double and triple cropping of land where climate permits has increased in Asia and even in Africa, where marginal land is put to near-continuous use to meet growing food demands.

Many of these intensification practices are part of the second approach, linked to the **Green Revolution**—a complex of seed and management improvements adapted to the needs of intensive agriculture and designed to bring larger harvests from a given area of farmland. Genetic improvements in rice and wheat have formed the basis of the Green Revolution. Dwarfed varieties have been developed that respond dramatically to heavy applications of fertilizer, that resist plant diseases, and that can tolerate much shorter growing seasons than traditional native varieties. Adopting the new varieties and applying the irrigation, mechanization, fertilization, and pesticide practices they require have created a new "high-input, high-yield" agriculture.

But a price has been paid. The Green Revolution is commercially oriented and demands high inputs of costly hybrid seeds, mechanization, irrigation, fertilizers, and pesticides. As the Green Revolution is adopted, traditional and subsistence agriculture are being displaced. Lost, too, are the food security that distinctive locally adapted native crop varieties provide and the nutritional diversity and balance that multiple-crop intensive gardening assure. Subsistence farming, wherever practiced, is oriented toward risk minimization. Many differentially hardy varieties of a single crop guarantee some yield whatever adverse weather, disease, or pest problems might occur. Commercial agriculture, however, aims at profit maximization, not minimal food security.

There are other costs for Green Revolution successes. For example, irrigation, responsible for an important part of increased crop yields, has destroyed large tracts of land; excessive salinity of soils resulting from poor irrigation practices is estimated to have a serious effect on the productivity of more than 10% of all the world's irrigated land. And the huge amount of water required for Green Revolution irrigation has led to serious groundwater depletion; to conflict between agricultural and growing urban and industrial water needs in developing countries, many of which are in subhumid climates; and to worries about scarcity and future wars over water.

The presumed benefits of the Green Revolution are not available to all subsistence agricultural areas or advantageous to everyone engaged in farming. Most poor farmers on marginal and rain-fed (nonirrigated) lands, for example, have not benefited from the new plant varieties requiring irrigation and high chemical inputs, and women have often been losers in the transition from traditional to the more-industrialized farming practices of the Green Revolution (see "Women and the Green Revolution," p. 326). Africa is a case in point. Green Revolution crop improvements have concentrated on wheat, rice, and maize. Of these, only maize is important in Africa, where principal food crops include millet, sorghum, cassava, manioc, yams, cowpeas, and peanuts.

In many areas showing greatest past successes, Green Revolution gains are leveling off. Recent cereal yields in Asia, for example, are growing at only two-thirds of their 1970s rate; the UN's Food and Agriculture Organization now considers Green Revolution technologies "almost exhausted" of any further productivity gains in Asian rice cultivation. Little prime land and even less water remain to expand farming in many developing countries, and the adverse ecological and social consequences of industrial farming techniques arouse growing resistance. Nor does biotechnology—which many have hailed as a promising new Green Revolution approach—seem likely to fill the gap. Consumer resistance to genetically modified (GM) food crops, fear of the ecological consequences of such modification, the continuing partial rejection of GM foods in the European Union market, and the high cost of and restrictions on the new biotechnologies imposed by their corporate developers all conspire to inhibit the widespread adoption of the new technologies.

Nevertheless, the production of engineered crops is spreading rapidly. In 1996, the first year GM crops were commercially available, about 1.7 million hectares (4.3 million acres) were placed in biotechnology cultivation. That total had grown to 125 million hectares (309 million acres) by 2008. GM technology is rapidly diffusing to developing countries—a total of 25 countries used commercial GM crops in 2008. However, half the world's acreage of GM crops in 2008 was in the United States. Other top producers of GM crops included Argentina, Brazil, India, Canada, and China. The crops for which GM seeds are most prevalent are soybeans, cotton, corn, and rapeseed. Of all the genetic crop modifications recently introduced, herbicide resistance (Roundup Ready soybeans) and insect resistance (Bt corn and cotton) have been the most important and the most responsible for the significant increase in productivity and reduction in costs of the crops involved. GM crop opponents note, indeed, that no engineered crops so far introduced have featured added nutrients or other attributes that could fight developing-world malnutrition. Rather, they have been genetically altered in ways that benefit farmers instead of consumers.

Women and the Green Revolution

Women farmers grow at least half of the world's food and up to 80% in some African countries. They are responsible for an even larger share of food consumed by their own families: 80% in sub-Saharan Africa, 65% in Asia, and 45% in Latin America and the Caribbean. Further, women comprise between one-third and one-half of all agricultural laborers in developing countries. For example, African women perform about 90% of the work of processing food crops and 80% of the work of harvesting and marketing.

Women's agricultural dominance in developing states is increasing, in fact, as male family members continue to leave for cities in search of paid urban work. In Mozambique, for example, for every 100 men working in agriculture, there are 153 women. In nearly all other sub-Saharan countries, the female component runs between 120 and 150 per 100 men. The departure of men for near or distant cities means, in addition, that women must assume the effective management of their families' total farm operations.

Despite their fundamental role, however, women do not share equally with men in the rewards from agriculture, nor are they always beneficiaries of presumed improvements in agricultural technologies and practices. Often, they cannot own or inherit the land on which they work and frequently have difficulty in obtaining improved seeds or fertilizers available to male farmers.

As a rule, women farmers work longer hours and have lower incomes than do male farmers. This is not because they are less competent. Rather, it is due to restricting cultural and economic factors. First, most women farmers are involved in subsistence farming and food production for the local market, which yields little cash return. Second, they have far less access than men to credit at bank or government-subsidized rates that would make it possible for them to acquire the Green Revolution technology, such as hybrid seeds and fertilizers. Third, in some cultures women cannot own land and so are excluded from agricultural improvement programs and projects aimed at landowners. For example, many African agricultural development programs are based on the conversion of communal land, to which women have access, to private holdings, from which they are excluded. In Asia, inheritance laws favor male over female heirs, and female-inherited land is managed by husbands; in Latin America, discrimination results from the more-limited status held by women under the law.

At the same time, the Green Revolution and its greater commercialization of crops have generally required an increase in labor per hectare, particularly in tasks typically reserved for women, such as weeding, harvesting, and postharvest work. If women are provided no relief from their other daily tasks, the Green Revolution for them may be more burden than blessing. But when mechanization is added to the new farming system, women tend to be losers. Frequently, such predominantly female tasks as harvesting or dehusking and polishing of grain—all traditionally done by hand—are given over to machinery, displacing rather than employing women. Even the application of chemical fertilizers ("a man's task") instead of cow dung ("women's work") has reduced the female role in agricultural development programs. The loss of those traditional female wage jobs means that already poor rural women and their families have insufficient income to improve their diets even in the light of substantial increases in food availability through Green Revolution improvements.

If women are to benefit from the Green Revolution, new cultural norms—or culturally acceptable accommodations within traditional household, gender, and customary legal relations—will be required. These must permit or recognize women's landowning and other legal rights not now clearly theirs, access to credit at favorable rates, and admission on equal footing with males to government assistance programs.

Recognition of those realities fostered the Food and Agriculture Organization of the United Nations's "FAO Plan of Action for Women in Development (1996–2001)" and its "Gender and Development Plan (2002–2007)." Both aimed at stimulating and facilitating efforts to enhance the role of women as contributors and beneficiaries of economic, social, and political development. Objectives of the plans included promoting gender-based equity in control of productive resources; enhancing women's participation in decision- and policy-making processes at all levels, local and national; and providing women with access to credit to enable them to engage as creators and owners of small-scale manufacturing, trade, or service businesses.

The model for that credit access is the Grameen Bank, established by a Bangladeshi economist in 1976. Based on the conviction that access to credit should be a basic human right, the bank extends "microcredit"—the average loan is U.S. $160—for "microenterprises," with women the primary borrowers. The Grameen concept has spread from its Bangladesh origins to elsewhere in Asia and to Eastern Europe, Latin America, and Africa. Figures for worldwide microloans vary widely; in 2007 the UN guessed that a total of 70 million to 200 million or more loans had been made, granted to some of the world's poorest people in programs encouraged by the designation of 2005 as the "International Year of Microcredit" by the UN General Assembly.

Commercial Agriculture

Few people or areas still retain the isolation and self-sufficiency characteristic of pure subsistence economies. Nearly all have been touched by a modern world of trade and exchange and, in response, have adjusted their traditional economies. Modifications of subsistence agricultural systems have inevitably made them more complex by imparting to them at least some of the diversity and linkages of activity that mark the advanced economic systems of the more-developed world. Farmers in those systems produce not for their own subsistence but primarily for a market off the farm itself. They are part of integrated exchange economies in which agriculture is but one element in a complex structure that includes employment in mining, manufacturing, processing, and the service activities of the tertiary, quaternary, and quinary sectors. In those economies, farming activities presumably reflect production responses to market demand expressed through price and are related to the consumption requirements of the larger society, rather than to the immediate needs of farmers themselves.

Production Controls

Agriculture within modern, developed economies is characterized by specialization—by enterprise (farm), by area, and even by country; by *off-farm sale* rather than subsistence production; and by *interdependence* of producers and buyers linked through markets. Farmers in a free market economy supposedly produce the crops that their estimates of market price and production cost indicate will yield the greatest return. Supply, demand, and the market price mechanism are the presumed controls on agricultural production in commercial economies.

Total production costs, eventual harvest yields, and future market prices are among the many uncertainties that individual farmers must face. Beginning in the 1950s in the United States, specialist farmers and corporate purchasers developed strategies for minimizing those uncertainties. Processors sought uniformity of product quality and timing of delivery. Vegetable canners—of tomatoes, sweet corn, and the like—required volume delivery of raw products of uniform size, color, and ingredient content on dates that accorded with cannery and labor schedules. And farmers wanted the support of a guaranteed market at an assured price to minimize the uncertainties of their specialization and to stabilize the return on their investment.

The solution was contractual arrangements or vertical integrations (where production, processing, and sales are all coordinated within one firm) uniting contracted farmer with purchaser-processor. Broiler chickens of specified age and weight, cattle fed to an exact weight and finish, wheat with a minimum protein content, popping corn with prescribed characteristics, potatoes of the kind and quality demanded by particular fast-food chains, and similar product specifications became part of production contracts between farmer and buyer-processor. In the United States, the percentage of total farm output produced under contractual arrangements or by vertical integration rose from 19% in 1960 to well over one-third by the turn of the century. For example, in 2003 about 72% of hogs were sold under some form of contract; in 1980 only 5% were sold that way. The term *agribusiness* is applied to the growing merging of older, farm-centered crop economy and newer patterns of more integrated production and marketing systems.

Even for family farmers not bound by contractual arrangements to suppliers and purchasers, the older assumption that supply, demand, and the market price mechanism are effective controls on agricultural production is not wholly valid. In reality, those theoretical controls are joined by a number of nonmarket governmental influences that may be as decisive as market forces in shaping farmers' options and spatial production patterns. If there is a glut of wheat on the market, for example, the price per ton will come down and the area sown to it should diminish. It will also diminish regardless of supply if governments, responding to economic or political considerations, impose acreage controls.

Distortions of market control may also be introduced to favor certain crops or commodities through subsidies, price supports, market protections, and the like. The political power of farmers in the European Union, for example, secured generous product subsidies and, for the Union, immense unsold stores of butter, wine, and grains until 1992, when reforms began to reduce the surplus stockpiles even while increasing total farm spending. In Japan, the home market for rice is largely protected and reserved for Japanese rice farmers, even though their production efficiencies are low and their selling price is high by world market standards. In the United States, programs of farm price supports, acreage controls, financial assistance, and other governmental involvements in agriculture have given recurring and equally distorting effects.

A Model of Agricultural Location

Early in the 19th century, when transportation systems were less efficient and before such governmental influences were the norm, Johann Heinrich von Thünen (1783–1850) observed that lands of apparently identical physical properties were used for different agricultural purposes. Around each major urban market center, he noted, developed a set of concentric rings of different farm products (Figure 10.11a). The ring closest to the market specialized in perishable commodities that were both expensive to ship and in high demand. The high prices they could command in the urban market made their production an appropriate use of high-valued land near the city. Rings of farmlands farther away from the city were used for less-perishable commodities with lower transport costs, reduced demand, and lower market prices. General farming and grain farming replaced the market gardening of the inner ring. At the outer margins of profitable agriculture, farthest from the single central market, livestock grazing and similar extensive land uses were found.

To explain why this should be so, von Thünen proposed a formal spatial model, perhaps the first developed to analyze human activity patterns. He concluded that the uses to which parcels were put were a function of the differing "rent" values placed on seemingly identical lands. Those differences, he claimed, reflected the cost of overcoming the distance separating a given farm from a central market town. ("A portion of each crop is eaten by the wheels," he observed.) The greater the distance, the higher was the operating cost to the farmer, since transport charges had to be added to other expenses. When a commodity's production costs plus its transport costs just equaled its value at the market, a farmer was at the economic margin of its cultivation. Because in this model transport costs are uniform in all directions away from the center, the concentric zonal pattern of land use called the **von Thünen rings** results (Figure 10.11a).

1. Dairying and market gardening
2. Specialty farming
3. Cash grain and livestock
4. Mixed farming
5. Extensive grain farming or stock raising

(a)

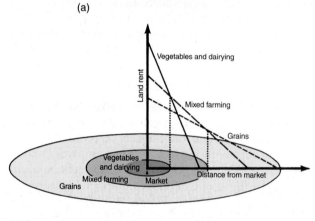

(b)

FIGURE 10.11 (a) von Thünen's model. Recognizing that, as distance from the market increases, the value of land decreases, von Thünen developed a descriptive model of intensity of land use that holds up reasonably well in practice. The most intensively produced agricultural crops are found on land close to the market; the less intensively produced commodities are located at more-distant points. The numbered zones of the diagram represent modern equivalents of the theoretical land use sequence von Thünen suggested some 175 years ago. As the metropolitan area at the center increases in size, the agricultural specialty areas are displaced outward, but the relative position of each is retained.
(b) Transport gradients and agricultural zones. In the model, perishable commodities such as fruits and vegetables have high transport rates per unit of distance; grain and other crops have lower rates. Land rent for any farm commodity decreases with increasing distance from the central market, and the rate of decline is determined by the *transport gradient* for that commodity. Crops that have both the highest market price and the highest transport costs will be grown nearest to the market. Less-perishable crops with lower production and transport costs will be grown at greater distances away.

The von Thünen model may be modified by introducing ideas of differential transport costs, variations in topography or soil fertility, or changes in commodity demand and market price. With or without such modifications, von Thünen's analysis helps explain the changing crop patterns and farm sizes

evident on the landscape at increasing distance from major cities, particularly in regions dominantly agricultural in economy. Farmland close to markets takes on high value, is used *intensively* for high-value crops, and is subdivided into relatively small units. Land far from markets is used *extensively* and in larger units (Figure 10.11b).

With improved transportation systems for perishable products and higher standards of living in industrial and postindustrial economies, the von Thünen regularities have undergone change. Today, for example, the presence of the nearby city may be felt in the form of market gardens and orchards (often community-supported organic agriculture or pick-your-own), nursery and bedding plant operations, hobby farms (frequently with horses), and land withheld from farming by developers who have purchased the land in anticipation of future subdivision.

Intensive Commercial Agriculture

Following World War II, agriculture in the developed world's market economies turned increasingly to concentrated methods of production. Machinery, chemicals, irrigation, and dependence on a restricted range of carefully selected and bred plant varieties and animal breeds all were employed in a concerted effort to wring more production from each unit of farmland.

The goal, of course, was to increase off-farm sales as American agriculture increasingly shifted from an objective of self-sufficiency to total commitment to a fully commercial, exchange-economy stance. Prior to 1950 most U.S. farms had a significant subsistence orientation; they were "general farms" growing a variety of crops, some for sale and some for feed for farmstead livestock—a milk cow or two, chickens for the pot and for household eggs, a few hogs and steers, partly for farm slaughter and use. Their extensive kitchen gardens supplied vegetables and fruits for farm family seasonal consumption and home canning. In 1949 the average American farm sold only $4100 worth of products. By 2007, however, most farms had a full commitment to the market, average off-farm sales rose to more than $135,000, and farm families—like other Americans—shopped the supermarkets for their food needs. With the increases in capital investment and the need for larger farms to maximize return on that investment, many inefficient small farms have been abandoned. Consolidation has reduced the number and enlarged the size of farms still in production. From a high of 6.8 million in 1934, the number of U.S. farms of all sizes dropped to 2.1 million in 2002 and then increased to 2.2 million in 2007. The recent increase in the number of farms was due to more small farms, many of which were classified as lifestyle or retirement farms, in which farm products were not the primary source of income for the farmer. Small farms have also increased in part as a response to consumers' desire for organic and local food.

The reorientation of farm production goals in the United States and in most other highly developed market economies has led to significant changes in regional farm production patterns. Reflecting the drive for enhanced and more specialized output and the investment of large amounts of capital (for machinery, fertilizers, and specialized buildings, for example), all modern agriculture is "intensive." But the several types of farm specialization differ in how much capital is invested per hectare of farmed land (and, of course, in the specifics of those capital inputs). Those differences underlie generalized distinctions between traditional intensive and extensive commercial agriculture.

The term **intensive commercial agriculture** is now usually understood to refer specifically to the production of crops that give high yields and high market value per unit of land. These include fruits, vegetables, and dairy products, all of which are highly perishable, as well as some "factory farm" production of livestock. Dairy farms and *truck farms* (horticultural, or "market garden," farms that produce a wide range of vegetables and fruits) are found near most medium-size and large cities. Because their products are perishable, transport costs increase because of the special handling that is needed, such as the use of refrigerated trucks and custom packaging. This is another reason for locations close to market.

Livestock-grain farming involves the growing of grain to be fed on the producing farm to livestock, which constitute the farm's cash product. In Western Europe, three-fourths of cropland is devoted to production for animal consumption; in Denmark, 90% of all grains are fed to livestock for conversion into meat, butter, cheese, and milk. Although livestock-grain farmers work their land intensively, the value of their product per unit of land is usually less than that of the truck farm. Consequently, in North America at least, livestock-grain farms are farther from the main markets than are horticultural and dairy farms. In general, the livestock-grain belts of the world are close to the great coastal and industrial zone markets. The Corn Belt of the United States and the livestock region of Western Europe are two examples.

In the United States—and commonly in all developed countries—the traditional livestock and grain operations of small and family farms have been largely supplanted by very large-scale, concentrated animal-feeding operations involving thousands or tens of thousands of closely quartered animals (Figure 10.12). From its inception in the 1920s, the intensive, industrialized rearing of livestock, particularly beef and dairy cattle, hogs, and poultry, has grown to dominate meat, dairy, and egg production. To achieve their objective of producing a large-volume, uniform product at the lowest possible cost, operators of livestock factory farms confine animals to pens or cages, treat them with antibiotics and vitamins to maintain health and speed growth, provide processed feeds that often contain low-cost animal by-products or crop residue, and deliver them under contract to processors, packers, or their parent company. Although serious concerns have been voiced about animal waste management and groundwater, stream, and atmospheric pollution, contract-based concentrated feeding operations now provide almost all supermarket meat and dairy products. The location of this form of intensive commercial farming is often determined

FIGURE 10.12 This concentrated animal-feeding operation in Kansas exemplifies the changing scale of American agriculture. © Cathryn Dowd.

not by land value or proximity to market but by land use restrictions and environmental standards imposed by state and county governments.

Extensive Commercial Agriculture

Farther from the market, on less-expensive land, there is less need to use the land intensively. Cheaper land gives rise to larger farm units. **Extensive commercial agriculture** is typified by large wheat farms and livestock ranching.

Large-scale wheat farming requires sizeable capital inputs for planting and harvesting machinery, but the inputs per unit of land are low; wheat farms are very large. Nearly half the farms in Saskatchewan, for example, are more than 400 hectares (1000 acres). The average farm in Kansas is more than 300 hectares; in North Dakota, more than 525 (1300 acres). In North America, the spring wheat (planted in spring, harvested in autumn) region includes the Dakotas, eastern Montana, and the southern parts of the Prairie Provinces of Canada. The winter wheat (planted in fall, harvested in midsummer) belt focuses on Kansas and includes adjacent sections of neighboring states (Figure 10.13). Argentina is the only South American country to have comparable large-scale wheat farming. In the Eastern Hemisphere, the system is fully developed only east of the Volga River in northern Kazakhstan and the southern part of West Siberia, and in southeastern and western Australia.

Livestock ranching differs significantly from livestock-grain farming and, by its commercial orientation and distribution, from the nomadism it superficially resembles. A product of the 19th-century growth of urban markets for beef and wool in Western Europe and the northeastern United States, ranching has been primarily confined to areas of European settlement. It is found in the western United States and adjacent sections of Mexico and Canada (Figure 10.13); the grasslands of Argentina, Brazil, Uruguay, and Venezuela; the interior of Australia;

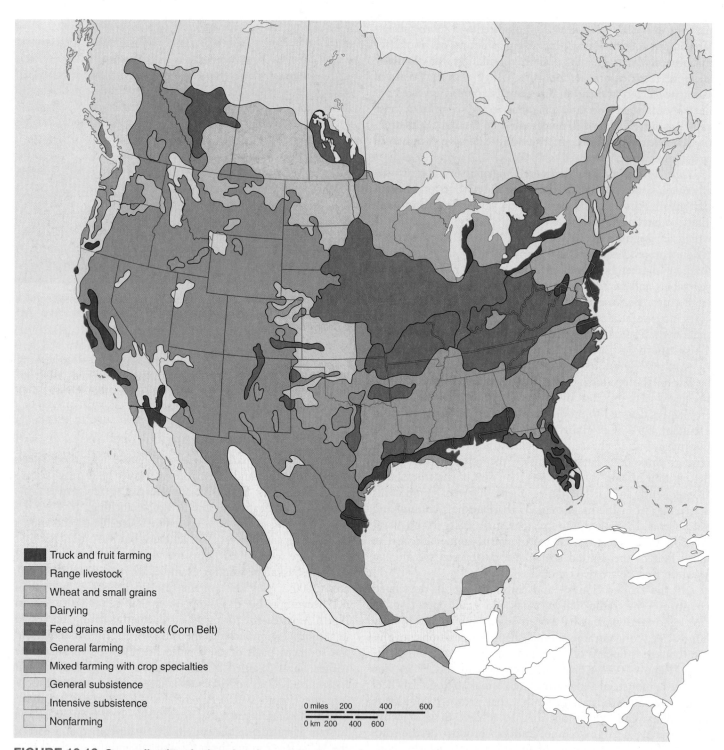

FIGURE 10.13 Generalized agricultural regions of North America. *Sources: U.S. Bureau of Agricultural Economics; Agriculture Canada; Mexico, Secretaría de Agricultura y Recursos Hidráulicos.*

Legend:
- Truck and fruit farming
- Range livestock
- Wheat and small grains
- Dairying
- Feed grains and livestock (Corn Belt)
- General farming
- Mixed farming with crop specialties
- General subsistence
- Intensive subsistence
- Nonfarming

the uplands of South Island, New Zealand; and the Karoo and adjacent areas of South Africa (Figure 10.14). All except New Zealand and the humid pampas of South America have semi-arid climates. All, even the most remote from markets, were a product of improvements in transportation by land and sea, the refrigeration of carriers, and meat-canning technology. In all, introduced beef cattle or sheep replaced original native fauna,

such as bison on North America's Great Plains, almost always with eventual severe environmental deterioration. More recently, the midlatitude demand for beef has been blamed for expanded cattle production and the extensive destruction of tropical rain forests in Central America and the Amazon Basin, though in recent years Amazon Basin deforestation has reflected more the expansion of soybean farming than of beef production.

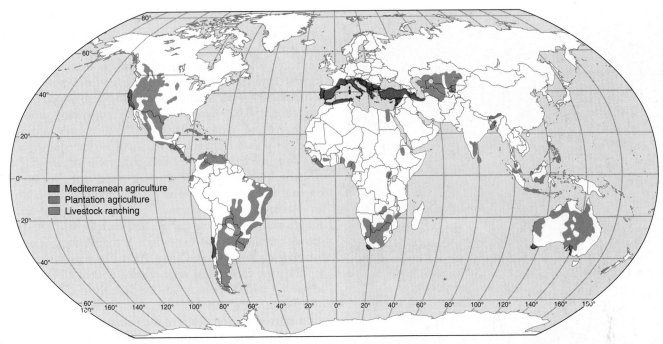

FIGURE 10.14 Livestock ranching and special crop agriculture. Livestock ranching is primarily a midlatitude enterprise catering to the urban markets of industrialized countries. Mediterranean and plantation agriculture are similarly oriented to the markets provided by advanced economies of Western Europe and North America. Areas of Mediterranean agriculture—all of roughly comparable climatic conditions—specialize in similar commodities, such as grapes, oranges, olives, peaches, and vegetables. The specialized crops of plantation agriculture are influenced by both physical geographic conditions and present or, particularly, former colonial control of areas.

In all of the ranching regions, livestock range (and the area exclusively in ranching) has been reduced as crop farming has encroached on its more humid margins, as pasture improvement has replaced less-nutritious native grasses, and as grain fattening has supplemented traditional grazing. Since ranching can be an economic activity only where alternative land uses are nonexistent and land quality is low, ranching regions of the world characteristically have low population densities, low capitalization per land unit, and relatively low labor requirements.

Special Crops

Proximity to the market does not guarantee the intensive production of high-value crops, should terrain or climatic circumstances hinder it. Nor does great distance from the market inevitably determine that extensive farming on low-priced land will be the sole agricultural option. Special circumstances, most often climatic, make some places far from markets intensively developed agricultural areas. Two special cases are agriculture in Mediterranean climates and in plantation areas (Figure 10.14).

Most of the arable land in the Mediterranean Basin itself is planted to grains, and much of the agricultural area is used for grazing. *Mediterranean agriculture* as a specialized farming economy, however, is known for grapes, olives, oranges, figs, vegetables, and similar commodities. These crops need warm temperatures all year-round and a great deal of sunshine in the summer. The Mediterranean agricultural lands indicated in Figure 10.14 are among the most productive agricultural lands

in the world. The precipitation regime of Mediterranean climate areas—winter rain and summer drought—lends itself to the controlled use of water. Of course, much capital must be spent for the irrigation systems, another reason for the intensive use of the land for high-value crops that are, for the most part, destined for export to industrialized countries or areas outside the Mediterranean climatic zone and even, in the case of Southern Hemisphere locations, to markets north of the equator.

Climate is also considered the vital element in the production of what are commonly but imprecisely known as *plantation crops*. The implication of **plantation** is the introduction of a foreign element—investment, management, and marketing—into an indigenous culture and economy, often employing an introduced alien labor force. The plantation itself is an estate whose resident workers produce one or two specialized crops. Those crops, although native to the tropics, were frequently foreign to the areas of plantation establishment: African coffee and Asian sugar in the Western Hemisphere and American cacao, tobacco, and rubber in Southeast Asia and Africa are examples (Figure 10.15). Entrepreneurs in Western countries such as England, France, the Netherlands, and the United States became interested in the tropics partly because they afforded them the opportunity to satisfy a demand in temperate lands for agricultural commodities not producible in the market areas. Custom and convenience usually retain the term *plantation*, even where native producers of local crops dominate, as they do in cola nut production in Guinea, spice growing in India and Sri Lanka, and sisal production in the Yucatán. As Figure 10.14 suggested, for ease of

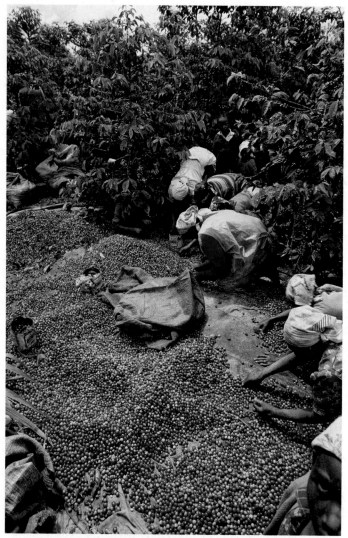

FIGURE 10.15 Women picking coffee beans in Kenya.
Here the women are also responsible for child care while working in the fields. Coffee is a classic plantation crop, with operations typically established by foreign capital in locations offering a suitable physical environment (climate and soils) and producing an introduced crop for a distant market. While coffee was first domesticated in East Africa, it is grown in many tropical countries, mostly for export to developed countries located in the midlatitudes. © Christopher Pillitz/The Image Bank/Getty.

access to shipping most plantation crops are cultivated along or near coasts, since production for export rather than for local consumption is the rule.

Agriculture in Planned Economies

As their name implies, planned economies have a degree of centrally directed control of resources and of key sectors of the economy that permits the pursuit of governmentally determined objectives. When that control is extended to the agricultural sector, state and collective farms and agricultural communes replace private farms, crop production is divorced from market control or family need, and prices are established by plan rather than by demand or production cost. Although

such extremes of rural control have in recent years been relaxed or abandoned in most formerly strictly planned economies, past centralized control of agriculture altered traditional rural landscapes. Before the former Soviet Union collapsed in 1991, its rural landscape had been transformed from millions of pre-revolutionary small farm holdings to a consolidated pattern of fewer than 50,000 centrally controlled operating units. Even today, because of inadequacies in farm registry and boundary descriptions and because of clouded ownership rights, the remnants of the old Soviet collective farm system still operate more than 90% of the country's farmlands, but now they respond to market opportunities, not centralized directives.

An incomplete progression from private and peasant agriculture, through collectivization, and back to what is virtually a private farming system took place in the planned economy of the People's Republic of China. After its assumption of power in 1949, the communist regime redistributed all farmlands to some 350 million peasants in inefficiently small (0.2-hectare, or 0.5-acre) subsistence holdings that were totally inadequate for the growing food needs of the country. Later, by the end of 1957, some 90% of peasant households had been collectivized into about 700,000 communes, a number further reduced in the 1970s to 50,000 communes averaging some 13,000 members.

After the death of Chairman Mao in 1976, what became effectively a private farming system was reintroduced when 180 million new farms were allocated to peasant families. Currently, peasants have renewable land use contracts valid for 30 years, but they cannot own the land or sell their leases. Farmland remains owned and controlled by the state, and most staple crops are still sold at fixed prices to government purchasers. Today, production decisions are generally made by the individual farmer, based on the same market assessments that control capitalistic economies. Increasingly, China's farmers have turned to the production of labor-intensive specialty crops, such as fruits, vegetables, meat, and pond-raised fish—not only for the country's rapidly expanding domestic market but for export as well. China's per capita food production and availability have increased dramatically as this conversion to an agricultural market economy, rather than a subsistence or planned economy, has progressed.

OTHER PRIMARY ACTIVITIES

In addition to agriculture, primary economic activities include fishing, forestry, and the mining and quarrying of minerals. These industries involve the direct exploitation of natural resources that are unequally available in the environment and differentially evaluated by different societies. Their development, therefore, depends on the occurrence of perceived resources, the technology to exploit their natural availability, and the cultural awareness of their value. (The definition, perception, and utilization of resources are explored in depth in Chapter 5.)

Two of them—fishing and forestry—are **gathering industries** based on harvesting the natural bounty of renewable resources, though ones in serious danger of depletion through overexploitation. Mining and quarrying are **extractive industries,** removing nonrenewable metallic and nonmetallic minerals, including the mineral fuels, from the earth's crust. They are the initial raw material phase of modern industrial economies.

Fishing

Although fish and shellfish account for only about 15% of all human animal protein consumption, an estimated 1 billion people—primarily in the developing countries of eastern and southeastern Asia, Africa, and parts of Latin America—depend on fish as their primary source of protein. Fish are also very important in the diets of most advanced states, both those with and without major domestic fishing fleets. Although about 80% of the world annual fish harvest is consumed by humans, the remainder is processed into fish meal to be fed to livestock or used as fertilizer. Those two quite different markets have increased both the demand for and the annual harvest of fish. Indeed, so rapidly have pressures on the world's fish stocks increased that evidence is unmistakable that, at least locally, their *maximum sustainable yield* is actually or potentially being exceeded. The **maximum sustainable yield** of a resource is the largest volume or rate of use that will not impair its ability to be renewed or to maintain the same future productivity. For fishing, that level is marked by a catch or harvest equal to the net growth of the replacement stock.

The annual fish supply comes from three sources:

1. the *inland catch,* from ponds, lakes, and rivers
2. *fish farming,* where fish are produced in a controlled and contained environment
3. the *marine catch,* all wild fish harvested in coastal waters or on the high seas

Fish capture (catch) is responsible for two-thirds of the total annual fish harvest. Inland waters supply less than 10% of that catch. Fish farming, both inland and marine, accounts for about one-third of total global production (Figure 10.16). Most of that marine capture is made in coastal wetlands, estuaries, and the relatively shallow coastal waters above the continental shelf. Near shore, shallow embayments and marshes provide spawning grounds and river waters supply nutrients to an environment highly productive of fish. Increasingly, these are also areas seriously affected by pollution from runoff and ocean dumping, an environmental assault so devastating in some areas that fish and shellfish stocks have been destroyed with little hope of revival.

Commercial marine fishing is largely concentrated in northern waters, where warm and cold currents join and mix and where such familiar food species as herring, cod, mackerel, haddock, and flounder congregate, or "school," on the broad continental shelves (Figure 10.17). Two of the most heavily fished regions are the Northeast Pacific and Northwest Atlantic. Tropical fish species tend not to school and, because of their high oil content and unfamiliarity, are less acceptable in the commercial market. They are, however, of great importance for local consumption. Only a very small percentage of total

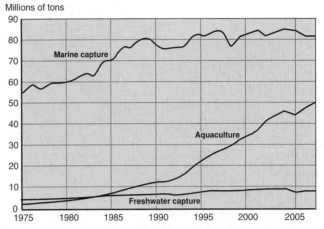

FIGURE 10.16 Officially recorded annual fish harvests, 1975–2007 rose irregularly from 66 million tons in 1975 to some 140 million tons in 2007. The 1993 and 1998 dips are associated with ocean temperature changes produced by El Niño. Chinese admission of regular overreporting of, particularly, their marine capture suggests that world marine catch and composite harvest totals actually registered an irregular downward trend each year since 1988. The FAO estimates that 20 to 40 million tons per year of unintended marine capture of juvenile or undersized fish and nontarget species are discarded each year. *Source: Food and Agriculture Organization (FAO).*

marine catch comes from the open seas that make up more than 90% of the world's oceans.

Modern technology and more aggressive fishing fleets of more countries greatly increased annual marine capture in the years after 1950. That technology included the use of sonar, radar, helicopters, and satellite communications to locate schools of fish; more efficient nets and tackle; and factory trawlers to follow fishing fleets to prepare and freeze the catch. In addition, more nations granted ever-larger subsidies to expand and reward their marine trawler operations. The rapid rate of increase led to inflated projections of continuing or growing fisheries productivity and to optimism that the resources of the oceans were inexhaustible.

Quite the opposite has proved to be true. In fact, in recent years, the productivity of marine fisheries has declined because *overfishing* (catches above reproduction rates) and the pollution of coastal waters have seriously endangered the supplies of traditional and desirable food species. Adjusted world total catch figures indicate that, rather than the steady increase in capture rates shown in Figure 10.16, there has really been a decline of more than 660,000 tons per year since the late 1980s. The decline, coupled with a growing world population, has caused a serious drop in the average per capita marine catch. The UN reports that all 17 of the world's major oceanic fishing areas are being fished at or beyond capacity; 13 are in decline. The plundering of Anglo American coastal waters has imperiled a number of the most desirable fish species; in 1993, Canada shut down its cod industry to allow stocks to recover, and U.S. authorities report that 67 North American species are overfished and 61 harvested to capacity.

FIGURE 10.17 The major commercial marine fisheries of the world. The waters within 325 kilometers (200 miles) of the U.S. coastline account for almost one-fifth of the world's annual fish and shellfish harvests. Overfishing, urban development, and the contamination of bays, estuaries, and wetlands have contributed to the depletion of the fish stocks in those coastal waters.

Overfishing is partly the result of the accepted view that the world's oceans are common property, a resource open to anyone's use, with no one responsible for its maintenance, protection, or improvement. The result of this "open seas" principle is but one expression of the so-called **tragedy of the commons**[a]—the economic reality that, when a resource is available to all, each user, in the absence of collective controls, thinks he or she is best served by exploiting the resource to the maximum, even though this means its eventual depletion. In 1995, more than 100 countries adopted a treaty that became legally binding in December 2001, to regulate fishing on the open oceans outside territorial waters. Applying to such species as cod, pollock, and tuna—that is, to migratory and high-seas species—the treaty requires fishermen to report the size of their catches to regional organizations that would set quotas and subject vessels to boarding to check for violations. These and other fishing control measures could provide the framework for the future sustainability of important food fish stocks, though they appear to be too late to save or revive the marine food chain in such formerly important fisheries as the Atlantic coast of Canada.

One approach to increasing the fish supply is through *fish farming,* or **aquaculture,** the breeding of fish in freshwater ponds, lakes, and canals or in fenced-off coastal bays and estuaries or enclosures. Aquaculture production has provided a growing share of the total fish harvest in recent years; its contribution to the human food supply is even greater than raw production figures suggest. Whereas one-third of the conventional fish catch is used to make fishmeal and fish oil, virtually all farmed fish are used as human food. Fish farming has long been practiced in Asia, where fish are a major source of protein, but now takes place on every continent. Critical environmental problems associated with marine aquaculture exist: pollution from fish wastes and chemicals and drugs; transference of disease to wild fish stocks; depletion of wild stock to provide feed for farmed fish; genetic damage to wild stock from escaped alien or genetically altered farmed fish; and more. Despite concerns about its potential adverse consequences, its rapid and continuing production increase makes aquaculture the fastest-growing sector of the world food economy.

Forestry

Forests, like fish, are a heavily exploited renewable resource. Even after millennia of land clearance for agriculture and, more recently, commercial lumbering, cattle ranching, and fuelwood gathering, forests still cover nearly a third of the world's land area. Livelihoods based on forest resources are spatially widespread and parts of both subsistence and commercial economies. A full treatment of forest resources and their nature, distribution, and exploitation appears in Chapter 5.

Mining and Quarrying

Societies at all stages of economic development engage in agriculture, fishing, and forestry. The extractive industries—mining and drilling for nonrenewable mineral wealth—emerged only when cultural advancement and economic necessity made

[a]The *commons* refers to undivided land available for the use of everyone; usually, it meant the open land of a village that all used as pasture. The *Boston Common* originally had this meaning.

possible a broader understanding of the earth's resources. Now those extractive industries provide the raw material and energy base for the way of life experienced by people in the advanced economies and are the basis for an important part of the international trade connecting the developed and developing countries of the world.

Extractive industries depend on the exploitation of minerals unevenly distributed in amounts and concentrations determined by past geologic events, not by contemporary market demand. Because usable deposits are the result of geologic accident, there is no necessary relationship between the size and wealth of a country and the resources its territory contains. Although larger states are more likely to be the beneficiaries of such "accidents," many smaller developing countries are major sources of one or more critical raw materials and, therefore, are important participants in the growing international trade in minerals.

Transportation costs play a major role in determining where *low-value minerals* will be mined. Materials such as gravel, limestone for cement, and aggregate are found in such abundance that they have value only when they are near the site where they are to be used. For example, gravel for road building has value if it is near the road-building site, not otherwise. Transporting gravel hundreds of miles is an unprofitable activity.

The production of other minerals—especially *metallic minerals* such as copper, lead, and iron ore—is affected by a balance of three forces: the quantity available, the richness of the ore, and the distance to markets. Another factor, land acquisition and royalty costs, may equal or exceed other considerations in mine development decisions (see "Public Land, Private Profit," p. 336). Even if these conditions are favorable, mines may not be developed or even remain operating if supplies from competing sources are more cheaply available in the market. In the 1980s, more than 25 million tons of iron ore-producing capacity was permanently shut down in the United States and Canada as a result of such price competition. Similar declines occurred in North American copper, nickel, zinc, lead, and molybdenum mining as market prices fell below domestic production costs. Beginning in the early 1990s, as a result of both resource depletion and the availability of low-cost imports, the United States became a net importer of non-fuel minerals for the first time. Of course, increases in mineral prices may be reflected in opening or reopening mines that, at lower returns, were deemed unprofitable. However, the developed industrial countries of commercial economies, whatever their former or even present mineral endowment, frequently find themselves at a competitive disadvantage against producers in developing countries with lower-cost labor and state-owned mines with abundant, rich reserves.

When the ore is rich in metallic content, it is profitable (in the case of iron and aluminum ores) to ship it directly to the market for refining. But, of course, the highest-grade ores tend to be mined first. Consequently, the demand for low-grade ores has been increasing in recent years as richer deposits have been depleted. Low-grade ores are often upgraded by various types of separation treatments at the mine site to avoid the cost of transporting waste materials not wanted at the market. Concentration of copper is nearly always mine-oriented (Figure 10.18); refining takes place near areas of consumption.

The large amount of waste in copper (98% to 99% or more of the ore) and in most other industrially significant ores should not be considered the mark of an unattractive deposit. Indeed, the opposite may be true. Many higher-content ores are left unexploited—because of the cost of extraction or the smallness of the reserves—in favor of the use of large deposits of even very low-grade ore. The attraction of the latter is

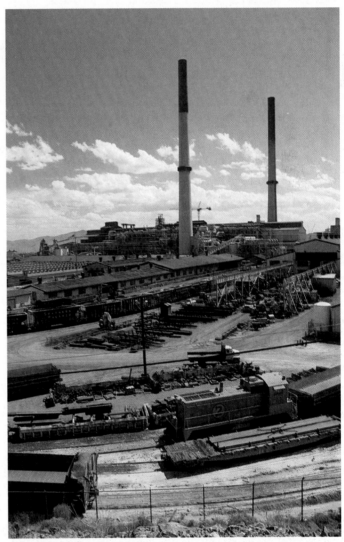

FIGURE 10.18 Copper ore concentrating and smelting facilities at the Phelps-Dodge mine in Morenci, Arizona. Concentrating mills crush the ore, separating copper-bearing material from the rocky mass containing it. The great volume of waste material removed assures that most concentrating operations are found near the ore bodies. Smelters separate concentrated copper from other, unwanted, compounds containing iron or sulfur. Because smelting is also a "weight-reducing" (and, therefore, transportation cost–reducing) activity, it is frequently—though not invariably—located close to the mine as well. © Cameramann International.

GEOGRAPHY
& Public Policy

Public Land, Private Profit

When President Ulysses S. Grant signed the Mining Act of 1872, the presidential and congressional goal was to encourage Western settlement and development by allowing any "hard-rock" miners (including prospectors for silver, gold, copper, and other metals) to mine federally owned land without royalty payment. It further permitted mining companies to gain clear title to publicly owned land and all subsurface minerals for no more than $12 a hectare ($5 an acre). Under those liberal provisions, mining firms have bought 1.3 million hectares (3.2 million acres) of federal land since 1872 and each year remove some $1.2 billion worth of minerals from government property. In contrast to the royalty-free extraction privileges granted to metal miners, oil, gas, and coal companies pay royalties of as much as 12.5% of their gross revenues for exploiting federal lands.

Whatever the merits of the 1872 law in encouraging the economic development of lands otherwise unattractive to homesteaders, modern-day mining companies throughout the Western states have secured enormous actual and potential profits from the law's generous provisions. In Montana, a company claim to 810 hectares (2000 acres) of land would cost it less than $10,000 for an estimated $4 billion worth of platinum and palladium; in California, a gold mining company in 1994 sought title to 93 hectares (230 acres) of federal land containing a potential of $320 million of gold for less than $1200. Foreign as well as domestic firms may be beneficiaries of the 1872 law. In 1994, a South African firm arranged to buy 411 hectares (1016 acres) of Nevada land with a prospective $1.1 billion in gold from the government for $5100. And a Canadian firm in 1994 received title to 800 hectares (nearly 2000 acres) near Elko, Nevada, that cover a likely $10 billion worth of gold—a transfer that Interior Secretary Bruce Babbitt dubbed "the biggest gold heist since the days of Butch Cassidy." And in 1995 Mr. Babbitt conveyed about $1 billion worth of travertine (a mineral used in whitening paper) under 45 hectares (110 acres) of Idaho to a Danish-owned company for $275.

The "gold heist" characterization summarized a growing administration and congressional feeling that what was good in 1872 and today for metal mining companies was not necessarily beneficial to the American public, who own the land. In part, that feeling results from the fact that mining companies commit environmental sins that require public funding to repair or public tolerance to accept. The mining firms may destroy whole mountains to gain access to low-grade ores and leave toxic mine tailings, surface water contamination, and open-pit scarring of the landscape as they move on or disappear. The projected public costs of cleaning up more than 50,000 abandoned mine sites, thousands of miles of damaged or dead streams, and several billion tons of contaminated waste are estimated at a minimum of $35 billion.

A congressional proposal introduced, but defeated, in 1993 would have required mining companies to pay royalties of 8% on gross revenues for all hard-rock ores extracted and would have prohibited them from outright purchase of federal land. The royalty provision alone would have yielded nearly $100 million annually at 1994 levels of company income. Mining firms claim that an imposition of royalties might well destroy America's mining industry. They stress both the high levels of investment they must make to extract and process frequently low-grade ores and the large number of high-wage jobs they provide as their sufficient contribution to the nation. The Canadian company involved in the Elko site, for example, reports that, since it acquired the claims in 1987 from their previous owner, it has expended more than $1 billion, plus has made additional donations for town sewer lines and schools and has created 1700 jobs. The American Mining Congress estimates that the proposed 8% royalty charge would have cost 47,000 jobs out of 140,000, and even the U.S. Bureau of Mines assumes a loss of 1100 jobs.

Public resistance to Western mining activities are taking their toll. State and federal regulatory procedures, many dragging on for a decade or more, have discouraged opening new mines; newly enacted environmental regulations restricting current mining operations (for example, banning the use of cyanide in gold and silver refining) reduce their economic viability. In consequence, both investment and employment in U.S. mining are in steady decline, eroding the economic base of many Western communities.

Considering the Issues

1. Do you believe the 1872 Mining Act should be repealed or amended? If not, what are your reasons for arguing for retention? If so, would you advocate the imposition of royalties on mining company revenues? At what levels, if any, should royalties be assessed? Should hard-rock and energy companies be treated equally for access to public land resources? Why or why not?

2. Would you propose to prohibit outright land sales to mining companies? If not, should sales prices be determined by the surface value of the land or by the estimated (but unrealized) value of mineral deposits it contains?

3. Do you think that cleanup and other charges now borne by the public are acceptable in view of the capital investments and job creation of hard-rock companies? Do you accept the industry's claim that an imposition of royalties would destroy American metal mining? Why or why not?

4. Do you favor continued state and federal restrictions on mining operations, even at the cost of jobs and community economies? Why or why not?

a size of reserve sufficient to justify the long-term commitment of development capital and, simultaneously, to assure a long-term source of supply. At one time, high-grade magnetite iron ore was mined and shipped from the Mesabi area of Minnesota. Those deposits are now exhausted. However, immense amounts of capital (including, since 2003, Chinese capital) have been invested in the mining and processing into high-grade iron ore pellets of the virtually unlimited supplies of low-grade iron-bearing rock (taconite) still remaining.

Such investments do not assure the profitable exploitation of the resource. The metals market is highly volatile. Rapidly and widely fluctuating prices can quickly change profitable mining and refining ventures to losing undertakings. Marginal gold and silver deposits are opened or closed in reaction to trends in precious metals prices. Taconite beneficiation (waste material removal) in the Lake Superior region has materially slowed in response to the decline of the U.S. steel industry and the price advantage of imported ores. In market economies, cost and market controls dominate economic decisions. In planned economies, cost may be a less-important consideration than are such other concerns as goals of national development and resource independence.

The advanced economies have reached that status through their control and use of energy. Domestic supplies of mineral fuels, therefore, are often considered basic to national strength and independence. When those supplies are absent, developed countries are concerned with the availability and price of coal, oil, and natural gas in international trade. Mineral fuels and other energy sources are given extended discussion in Chapter 5.

TRADE IN PRIMARY PRODUCTS

With the liberalization of international trade policies that began in the 1980s, international trade has undergone massive expansion, so that it accounts for a significant fraction of the world's economic activity. Primary commodities—agricultural goods, minerals, and fuels—made up one-quarter of the total dollar value of those international flows. During much of the first half of the 20th century, the world distribution of supply and demand for those items in general resulted in an understandable pattern of commodity flow: from raw material producers located within less-developed countries to the processors, manufacturers, and consumers in the more-developed ones (Figure 10.19). The reverse flow carried manufactured goods processed in the industrialized states back to the developing countries. That two-way trade presumably benefited the developed states by providing access to a continuing supply of industrial raw materials and foodstuffs not available domestically and gave less-developed countries needed capital to invest

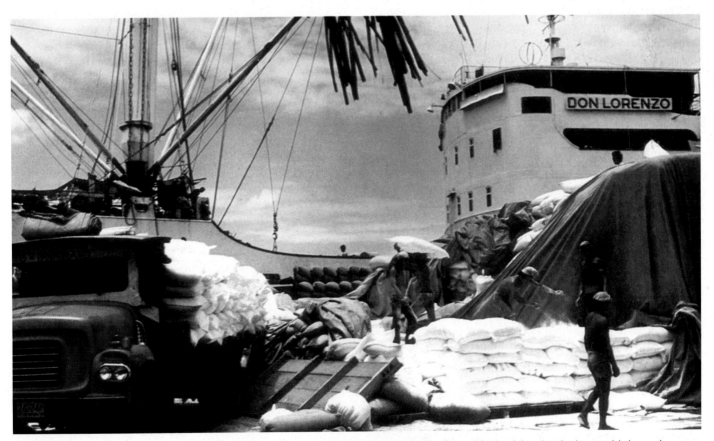

FIGURE 10.19 Sugar being loaded for export at the port of Cebu in the Philippines. Much of the developing world depends on exports of mineral and agricultural products to the developed countries for the major portion of its income. Fluctuations in market demand and price of some of those commodities can have serious consequences for the economies of exporting states. © UN/DPI Photo.

in their own development or to expend on the importation of the manufactured goods, food supplies, or commodities—such as petroleum—they did not themselves produce.

By the end of the 20th century, however, world trade flows and export patterns of the emerging economies were radically changing. Raw materials greatly decreased and manufactured goods increased in the export flows from developing states. Even with the overall decline in raw material exports, however, trade in unprocessed goods remains dominant in the economic well-being of many of the world's poorer economies. Increasingly, the terms of the traditional trade flows on which they depend have been criticized as unequal and damaging to commodity-exporting countries.

Countries that depend on primary commodities for most of their export earnings are vulnerable to price volatility and technological substitutes. Prices may rise sharply in periods of product shortage or international economic growth and swiftly decline when the world economy slows. During much of the 1980s and 1990s, commodity prices moved downward, to the great detriment of material-exporting economies. Prices for agricultural raw materials, for example, dropped by 30% between 1975 and 2000, and those for metals and minerals decreased by almost 40%. Such price declines cut deeply into the export earnings of many emerging economies.

Whatever the current world prices of raw materials may be, as a group, raw material exporting states have long expressed resentment at what they perceive as commodity price manipulation by rich countries and corporations to ensure low-cost supplies. Although collusive price fixing has not been demonstrated, technological substitutes can reduce demand for primary commodities. Glass fibers replace copper wire in telecommunications applications; synthetic rubber replaces natural rubber; glass and carbon fibers provide the raw material for rods, tubes, and sheet panels and other products superior in performance and strength to the metals they replace; and a vast and enlarging array of plastics are the accepted raw materials for commodities and uses for which natural rivals are not even considered. That is, even as the world industrial economy expands, demands and prices for traditional raw materials may remain depressed.

While prices paid for developing country commodities tend to be low, prices charged for the manufactured goods offered in exchange by the developed countries tend to be high. To capture processing and manufacturing profits for themselves, some developing states have placed restrictions on the export of unprocessed commodities. Malaysia, the Philippines, and Cameroon, for example, have limited the export of logs in favor of increased domestic processing of sawlogs and exports of lumber. Some developing countries have also encouraged domestic manufacturing to reduce imports and to diversify their exports. Frequently, however, such exports meet with tariffs and quotas protecting the home markets of the industrialized states.

Many developing regions heavily dependent on commodity sales saw their share of global trade fall materially between 1970 and the early 21st century. Those declines are understandable in the light of greatly expanding international trade

in manufactured goods from China, Korea, Mexico, and other rapidly industrializing states and from the expansion of trade in both manufactured goods and primary products between the industrialized countries themselves within newly established regional free-trade zones.

In 1964, in reaction to the whole range of perceived trade inequities, developing states promoted the establishment of the United Nations Conference on Trade and Development (UNCTAD). Its central constituency—the "Group of 77," which had expanded to 130 developing states by 2008—continues to press for a new world economic order based, in part, on an increase in the prices and values of exports from developing countries, a system of import preferences for their manufactured goods, and a restructuring of international cooperation to stress trade promotion and recognition of the special needs of poor countries. The World Trade Organization, established in 1995 (and discussed in detail in Chapter 9) was designed, in part, to reduce trade barriers and inequities. It has, however, been judged by its detractors as ineffective on issues of importance to developing countries. Chief among the complaints is the continuing failure of the industrial countries significantly (or at all) to reduce protections for their own agricultural and mineral industries. The World Bank has calculated, for example, that agricultural trade barriers and subsidies in rich countries reduce incomes in developing countries by at least $20 billion a year.

In 2001, members of the World Trade Organization met in Doha, Qatar, to begin negotiations on opening world markets in agriculture—of primary concern to developing states—and in industrial goods and trade in services—the principal interest of the fully developed countries. The "Doha Round" of discussions, with an original December 2004 deadline, continued over the next 4 years without reaching agreement. Despite the fact that agriculture makes up less than 10% of world trade, it has been the roadblock in all global trade talks. Although the trade ministers of 149 countries at the December 2005 WTO meeting in Hong Kong did agree to the elimination of export subsidies on farm goods by the end of 2013, the agreement was criticized by developing states as insufficient and incomplete. In turn, the rich economies wanted reciprocal concessions on trade in manufactured goods and services. After 7 years, the Doha Round talks collapsed in July 2008. The goals of greater equity in freer world trade flows, special consideration for the economic and developmental needs of poorer countries, and more fairness in international trade in primary products are yet to be achieved to the satisfaction of all parties.

SECONDARY ACTIVITIES: MANUFACTURING

Since the Industrial Revolution and introduction of the factory system in late 18th-century England, manufacturing and heavy industry have been seen as the measures and symbols of economic development. Wherever introduced, manufacturing has been the catalyst for the whole range of economic and social changes recognized as modernization and the eagerly sought escape from traditional subsistence economies. The factory system and mass production of standardized, lower-cost goods were the spur to inventions and improvements in transportation and to the urbanization of populations and their release from peasant agricultural drudgery. Wages and a money economy became the norm. Wholesale and retail trade expansion, increased labor specialization, the rise of an economic middle class, and social and political movement away from rigid class divisions were the near-universal attributes of the changes flowing from the introduction and expansion of manufacturing—first in continental Europe and Anglo America and now throughout the world. And everywhere the new industrial economy was introduced, it prospered or faltered to the extent that it observed the new sets of controls on location and spatial behavior implicit in the new economic structure.

Although primary industries are locationally tied to the natural resources they gather or exploit, secondary and later stages of economic activity are less concerned with conditions of the physical environment. For them, location is more closely related to cultural and economic than to physical circumstances. They are movable rather than spatially tied and are assumed to respond to recurring locational requirements and controls.

Those controls are rooted in observations about human spatial behavior in general and economic behavior in particular. We have already explored some of those assumptions in earlier discussions. We noted, for example, that the intensity of spatial interaction decreases with distance—distance decay, we called it. Recall that von Thünen's model of agricultural land use was rooted in conjectures about transportation cost and land value relationships.

Such simplifying assumptions help us understand an accepted common set of controls and motivations guiding human economic behavior. We assume, for example, that people are *economically rational;* that is, given the information at their disposal, they make locational, production, or purchasing decisions in light of a perception of what is most cost-effective and advantageous. From the standpoint of producers or sellers of goods or services, it is further assumed that each is intent on *maximizing profit.* To reach that objective, a host of production and marketing costs and political, competitive, and other limiting factors may be considered, but the ultimate goal of profit-seeking remains clear. Finally, in commercial economies it has been accepted that the best measure of the correctness of economic decisions is afforded by the market mechanism and the equilibrium between supply and demand that market prices establish (Figure 10.20). Although increasingly challenged as too rigid and unrealistic as explanations of actual human behavior and economic decision making, those assumptions still underlie most current analyses of the spatial patterns of industry.

Industrial Locational Models

When market principles are controlling, entrepreneurs seek to maximize profits by locating manufacturing activities at sites of lowest total input costs (and high revenue yields). In order

FIGURE 10.20 Supply, demand, and market equilibrium. The regulating mechanism of the market may be visualized graphically. **(a)** The *supply curve* tells us that, as the price of a good increases, more of that good will be made available for sale. Countering any tendency for prices to rise to infinity is the market reality that, the higher the price, the smaller the demand as potential customers find other purchases or products more cost-effective. **(b)** The *demand curve* shows how the market will expand as prices drop and the good becomes more affordable and attractive to more customers. **(c)** *Market equilibrium* is marked by the point of intersection of the supply and demand curves and determines the price of the good, the total demand, and the quantity bought and sold.

to assess the advantages of one location over another, industrialists must evaluate the most important **variable costs.** They subdivide their total costs into categories and note how each cost will vary from place to place. In different industries, transportation charges, labor rates, power costs, plant construction or operation expenses, the interest rate of money, or the price of raw materials may be the major variable cost. The industrialist must look at each of these and, by a process of elimination, eventually select the lowest-cost site. If the producer then determines that a large enough market can be reached cheaply enough, the location promises to be profitable.

In the economic world, nothing remains constant. Because of a changing mix of input costs, production techniques, and marketing activities, many initially profitable locations do not remain advantageous. Migrations of population, technological advances, and changes in the demand for products affect industrialists and industrial locations greatly. The abandoned mills and factories of New England or steel towns of Pennsylvania, even the "deindustrialization" of America itself in the face of changing domestic economy and foreign industrial cost advantages and competition, are testimony to the impermanence of the "best" locations. Similarly, the spread of manufacturing from the more-developed to the less-developed regions of the world since World War II testifies to changing perceptions of manufacturing costs and locational advantages.

The concern with variable costs as a determinant in industrial location decisions has inspired an extensive theoretical literature. Much of it is based on industrial patterns and economic assessments seen as controlling during the later 19th and early 20th centuries and extends the **least-cost theory** proposed by German location economist Alfred Weber (1868–1958), and sometimes called *Weberian analysis.* Weber explained the optimum location of a manufacturing establishment in terms of the minimization of three basic expenses: relative transport costs, labor costs, and agglomeration costs. **Agglomeration** refers to the clustering of productive activities and people for mutual advantage. Such clustering can produce *agglomeration economies* through shared facilities and services. Diseconomies such as higher rents or wage levels resulting from competition for these localized resources may also occur.

Weber concluded that transport costs were the major consideration determining location. That is, the optimum location would be found where the costs of transporting raw materials to the factory and finished goods to the market were at their lowest (Figure 10.21). He noted, however, that, if variations in labor or agglomeration costs were sufficiently great, a location determined solely on the basis of transportation costs might not, in fact, be the optimum one.

Assuming, however, that transportation costs determine the "balance point," optimum location will depend on distances, the respective weights of the raw material inputs, and the final weight of the finished product. It may be either *material-oriented* or *market-oriented*. Material orientation reflects a sizeable weight loss during the production process; market orientation indicates a weight gain (Figure 10.22).

For many theorists, Weber's least-cost analysis is unnecessarily rigid and restrictive. They propose instead a *substitution principle* which recognizes that in many industrial processes it is possible to replace a declining amount of one input (e.g., labor) with an increase in another (e.g., capital for automated equipment) or to increase transportation costs while simultaneously reducing land rent. With substitution, a number of different points may be optimal manufacturing

locations. Further, they suggest, a whole series of points may exist where total revenue of an enterprise just equals its total cost of producing a given output. These points, connected, mark the *spatial margin of profitability* and define the area within which profitable operation is possible (Figure 10.23). Location anywhere within the margin assures some profit and tolerates both imperfect knowledge and personal (rather than economic) considerations.

Other Locational Considerations

The behavior of individual firms seeking specific production sites under competitive conditions forms the basis for most classical industrial location theory. But such theory no longer fully explains world or regional patterns of industrial localization or specialization, nor does it account for locational behavior that is uncontrolled by objective "factors," that are influenced by new production technologies and corporate structures, or that are directed by noncapitalistic planning goals.

Traditional theories sought to explain locational decisions for plants engaged in mass production for mass markets where transportation lines were fixed and transport costs were

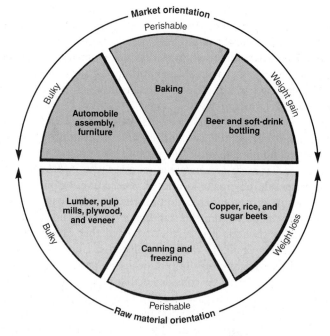

FIGURE 10.22 Spatial orientation tendencies. *Raw material orientation* is presumed to exist when there are limited alternative material sources, when the material is perishable, or when, in its natural state, it contains a large proportion of impurities or nonmarketable components. *Market orientation* represents the least-cost solution when manufacturing uses commonly available materials that add weight to the finished product, when the manufacturing process produces a commodity much bulkier or more expensive to ship than its separate components, or when the perishable nature of the product demands processing at individual market points. *Redrawn with permission from Truman A. Hartshorn,* Interpreting the City. *Copyright © 1980 John Wiley & Sons, Inc., New York, NY.*

FIGURE 10.21 Plane table solution to a plant location problem. This mechanical model, suggested by Alfred Weber, uses weights to demonstrate the least transport cost point where there are several sources of raw materials. When a weight is allowed to represent the "pull" of raw material and market locations, an equilibrium point is found on the plane table. That point is the location at which all forces balance each other and represents the least-cost plant location.

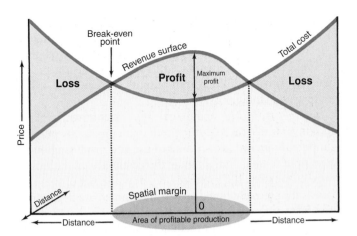

FIGURE 10.23 The spatial margin of profitability. In the diagram, **0** is the single optimal profit-maximizing location, but location anywhere within the area defined by the intersects of the total cost and total revenue surfaces will permit profitable operation. Some industries will have wide margins; others will be more spatially constricted. Skilled entrepreneurs may be able to expand the margins farther than less-able industrialists. Importantly, a *satisficing* location may be selected by reasonable estimate even in the absence of the totality of information required for an *optimal* decision.

relatively high. Both conditions began to change significantly during the last years of the 20th century. Assembly line production of identical commodities by a rigidly controlled and specialized labor force for generalized mass markets—known as **Fordism** to recognize Henry Ford's pioneering development of the system—became less realistic in both market and technology terms. In its place, post-Fordist *flexible manufacturing* processes based on smaller production runs of a greater variety of goods aimed at smaller, niche markets than were catered to by traditional manufacturing have become common. At the same time, information technology applied to machines and operations, increasing flexibility of labor, and declining costs for transportation services that were increasingly viewed from a cost-time rather than a cost-distance standpoint have materially altered underlying assumptions of the classical theories.

Transport Characteristics

Within both national and international economies, the type and efficiency of transport modes, as well as transportation costs, have been central to the spatial patterning of production, explaining the location of a large variety of economic activities. Waterborne transportation is nearly always cheaper than any other mode of conveyance, and the enormous amount of commercial activity that takes place on coasts or on navigable rivers leading to coasts is an indication of that cost advantage. When railroads were developed and the commercial exploitation of inland areas could begin, coastal sites continued to be important as more and more goods were transferred there between low-cost water and land modes. The advent of highway transportation vastly increased the number of potential "satisficing" manufacturing locations by freeing the locational

decision from fixed-route production sites. Every change in carrier mode, efficiency, or cost structure has direct implications for locations of economic activity.

In the rare instance when transportation costs become a negligible factor in production and marketing, an economic activity is said to be *footloose*. Some manufacturing is located without reference to raw materials; for example, the raw materials for electronic products such as computers are so valuable, light, and compact that transportation costs have little bearing on where production takes place. Others are inseparable from the markets they serve and are so widely distributed that they are known as *ubiquitous industries*. Newspaper publishing, bakeries, and dairies, all of which produce a highly perishable commodity designed for immediate consumption, are examples.

Overall, transportation costs have been declining and efficiencies have been increasing. The advent of near-universal commercial jet aircraft service, the development of large ocean-going superfreighters, and the introduction of containerization and intermodal transfers in both water and land shipments of goods have reduced the costs and increased the speed of freight services. As those costs have decreased, manufacturing location has become more influenced by nontransport locational factors. To that extent, Weberian location theories have reduced applicability to the modern global space economy.

Agglomeration Economies

The geographic concentration of economic, including industrial, activities is the norm at the local or regional scale. The cumulative and reinforcing attractions of industrial concentration and urban growth are recognized locational factors, but ones not easily quantified. Both cost-minimizing and profit-maximizing theories make provision for *agglomeration*, the spatial concentration of people and activities for mutual benefit. That is, both recognize that the areal grouping of industrial activities may produce benefits for individual firms that they could not experience in isolation. Those benefits—**external economies,** or *agglomeration economies*—accrue in the form of savings from shared transport facilities, social services, public utilities, communication facilities, and the like. Collectively, these and other installations and services needed to facilitate industrial and other forms of economic development are called **infrastructure.** Areal concentration may also create pools of skilled and ordinary labor; of capital, ancillary business services; and, of course, a market built of other industries and urban populations. New firms, particularly, may find significant advantages in locating near other firms engaged in the same activity, for labor specializations and support services specific to that activity are already in place. Some may find profit in being near other firms with which they are linked either as customers or suppliers.

A concentration of capital, labor, management skills, customer base, and all that is implied by the term *infrastructure* tends to attract still more industries from other locations to the agglomeration. In Weber's terms, that is, economies of association distort or alter locational decisions that otherwise would be based solely on transportation and labor costs, and once in existence, agglomerations tend to grow (Figure 10.24). Through a *multiplier effect,* each new firm added to the agglomeration will lead to the further development of infrastructure and linkages. As we will see in Chapter 11, the multiplier effect also implies total (urban) population growth and thus the expansion of the labor pool and the localized market that are part of agglomeration economies.

Just-in-Time and Flexible Production

Agglomeration economies and tendencies are also encouraged by newer manufacturing policies practiced by both older, established industries and by newer, post-Fordist plants.

Traditional Fordist industries required the on-site storage of large lots of materials and supplies ordered and delivered well in advance of their actual need in production. That

practice permitted cost savings through infrequent ordering and reduced transportation charges, and it made allowances for delayed deliveries and for the inspection of received goods and components. The assurance of supplies on hand for long production runs of standardized outputs was achieved at high inventory and storage costs.

Just-in-time (JIT) manufacturing, in contrast, seeks to reduce inventories through the production process by purchasing inputs for arrival just in time to use and producing output just in time to sell. Rather than the costly accumulation and storage of supplies, JIT requires frequent ordering of small lots of goods for precisely timed arrival and immediate deployment to the factory floor. Such "lean manufacturing" based on the frequent purchasing of immediately needed goods demands rapid delivery by suppliers and encourages them to locate near the buyer. Recent manufacturing innovations thus reinforce and augment the spatial agglomeration tendencies evident in

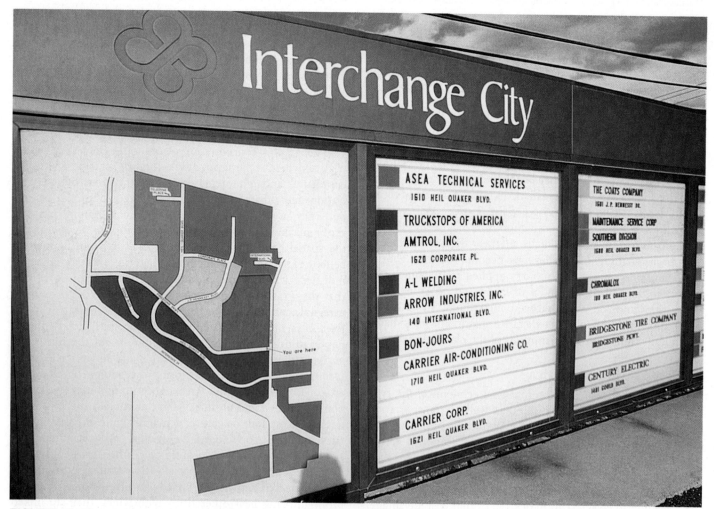

FIGURE 10.24 On a small scale, the planned industrial park furnishes its tenants external agglomeration economies similar to those offered by large urban concentrations to industry in general. An industrial park provides a subdivided tract of land developed according to a comprehensive plan for the use of (frequently) otherwise unconnected firms. Since the park developers, whether private companies or public agencies, supply the basic infrastructure of streets, water, sewage disposal, power, transport facilities, and, perhaps, private police and fire protection, park tenants are spared the additional cost of providing these services themselves. In some instances, factory buildings are available for rent, still further reducing firm development outlays. Counterparts of industrial parks for manufacturers are the office parks, research parks, science parks, and the like for "high-tech" firms and for enterprises in tertiary and quaternary services. © *Cameramann International.*

the older industrial landscape and deemphasize the applicability of older, single-plant location theories.

JIT is one expression of a transition from mass production Fordism to more *flexible production systems*. That flexibility is designed to allow producers to shift quickly and easily between different levels of output and, importantly, to move from one factory process or product to another as market demand dictates. Flexibility of that type is made possible by new technologies of easily reprogrammed computerized machine tools and by computer-aided design and computer-aided manufacturing systems. These technologies permit small-batch, just-in-time production and distribution responsive to current market demand as monitored by computer-based information systems.

Flexible production, to a large extent, requires significant acquisition of components and services from outside suppliers rather than from in-house production. For example, modular assembly, in which many subsystems of a complex final product enter the plant already assembled, reduces factory space and worker requirements. The premium that flexibility places on proximity to component suppliers adds still another dimension to industrial agglomeration tendencies. "Flexible production regions" have, according to some observers, emerged in response to the new flexible production strategies and interfirm dependencies. Those regions, it is claimed, are usually some distance—spatially or socially—from established concentrations of Fordist industrialization.

Comparative Advantage, Outsourcing, and Offshoring

The principle of *comparative advantage* and the practices of *outsourcing* and *offshoring* are of growing international importance in decisions regarding industrial location. They are interconnected in that each reflects cost advantages of specialization and each is dependent on free trade and the free flow of information. **Comparative advantage** tells us that areas and countries can best improve their economies and living standards through specialization and trade. These benefits will follow if each area or country concentrates on the production of those items for which it has the greatest relative advantage over other areas or for which it has the least relative disadvantage and imports all other goods. This principle is basic to the understanding of regional specialization, and it applies as long as areas have different relative advantages for two or more goods and free trade exists between them.

The logic of comparative advantage was recognized by economists in the 19th century when specialization and exchange involved shipments of grain, coal, or manufactured goods whose relative costs of production in different areas were clearly evident. Today, when other countries's comparative advantages may reflect lower costs for labor, land, and capital, the application of the principle is seen in a much less favorable light by some critics. They observe that manufacturing activities may relocate from higher-cost market-country locations to lower-cost foreign production sites, taking jobs and income away from the consuming country to the apparent detriment of that country's prosperity.

However, other observers argue that the domestic economic consequences of such voluntary **outsourcing**—producing parts or products abroad for domestic sale—by American manufacturers are no different from those resulting from successful competition by foreign companies or from industrial locational decisions favoring one section of the country over others.

Outsourcing has also come to mean subcontracting production and service sector work to outside, often nonunion, domestic companies. In 2006, U.S. companies outsourced more than $4 trillion in goods and services, a 50% increase since the start of the century; outsourcing in that purely American context is growing at an estimated pace of 15% to 20% per year. Roughly one-half of the 2005 total value of outsourcing related to manufacturing; about one-third of that share involves foreign, not domestic, suppliers. In manufacturing, outsourcing has become an important element in just-in-time acquisition of preassembled components for snap-together fabrication of finished products. When comparative advantage and outsourcing are exploited by individual corporations, one expression of flexible production systems is evident in the erosion of the rigid spatial concentration of manufacturing assumed by classical location theory.

A distinctive regional illustration of more-diversified industrial deconcentration through outsourcing is found along the northern border of Mexico. In the 1960s, Mexico enacted legislation permitting foreign (specifically, American) companies to establish "sister" plants, called *maquiladoras*, within 20 kilometers (12 mi) of the U.S. border for the duty-free assembly of products destined for re-export. By 2003 more than 3000 such assembly and manufacturing plants had been established to produce a diversity of goods, including electronic products, textiles, furniture, leather goods, toys, and automotive parts. The plants generated direct and indirect employment for more than a million Mexican workers (Figure 10.25) and for large numbers of U.S. citizens, employees of growing numbers of American-side *maquila* suppliers and of diverse service-oriented businesses spawned by the "multiplier effect."

On the broader world scene, outsourcing often involves production of commodities by developing countries that have benefited from the transfer of technology and capital from industrialized states and that use their new facilities and skills to improve productivity in areas formerly dominated by the profitable home products and exports of a rich world state. For example, electrical and electronic goods from China and Southeast Asia compete with and replace in the market similar goods formerly produced by Western firms. Such replacements, multiplied by numerous new country origins of the whole range of producer and consumer goods in world trade, have resulted in new global patterns of industrial regions and specializations. They have also strikingly changed the developing world's share of gross global output from an estimated 20% in the mid-20th century to more than one-half in 2006, measured in purchasing power parity (see Figure 7.7b). That improvement reflected, in part, growth in manufactures share of their exports. For some observers, that change is ample proof of the beneficial impact of comparative advantage on the world economy.

the *rationalization* of industry through full development of the resources of the country wherever they were found and without regard to the cost or competitiveness of such development. Inevitably, although the factors of industrial production are identical in capitalist and noncapitalist economies, the philosophies and patterns of industrial location and areal development will differ between them. Because major capital investments are relatively permanent additions to the landscape, the results of their often noneconomic political or philosophical decisions are fixed and will long remain to influence industrial regionalism and competitive efficiencies into the postcommunist present and future. Those same decisions and rigidities continue to inhibit the transition by the formerly fully planned economies to modern capitalist industrial techniques and flexibilities.

Transnational Corporations (TNCs)

Outsourcing is but one small expression of the growing international structure of modern manufacturing and service enterprises. Business and industry are increasingly stateless and economies borderless as giant **transnational corporations (TNCs)**—private firms that have established branch operations in nations foreign to their headquarter's country—become an ever-more important driving force in the globalizing world space economy. By 2006 there were about 78,000 transnational (or *multinational*) companies (briefly introduced in Chapter 8) controlling more than 900,000 foreign affiliates employing about 62 million workers. Excluding the parent companies themselves, the TNC affiliates accounted for some one-ninth of world GDP, and more than one-third of world exports.

The largest transnational corporations have annual revenues larger than the GDP of many sizeable, developed or developing countries. For example, in 2008 Walmart Stores had 2.1 million employees and annual revenues of $406 billion (U.S.). If Walmart were a country, it would be ranked the 26th-largest economy in the world, just ahead of Iran, Greece, Denmark, and Argentina. The great majority of large TNCs are headquartered in the United States, Europe, or East Asia. With the exception of Walmart, most of the largest TNCs are involved in manufacturing or petroleum extraction and refining. Ranked by foreign assets, the largest TNCs in 2007 were General Electric and Vodafone, while a ranking by total revenues would put Royal Dutch Shell, Exxon Mobil, Walmart Stores, BP, and Chevron in the top five positions. Although tertiary and quaternary activities have also become international in scope and transnational in corporate structure, the locational and operational advantages of multicountry operation were first discerned and exploited by manufacturers.

The direct impact of TNCs was earlier limited to relatively few countries and regions. **Foreign direct investment (FDI)**—the purchase or construction of factories and other fixed assets by TNCs—has been a significant engine of globalization. About one-third of FDI flows go to developing countries and the majority of that share is concentrated in 10 to 15 states, mainly in South, Southeast, and East Asia (China was the largest developing country recipient) and in Latin America and the Caribbean. The portion of FDI going to the 50 least-developed countries as a group, however—including nearly all African states—has been, and stays, consistently small, amounting to only 1% global FDI inflows in 1994 and remaining at that level in 2007, though in 2007 the inflows were at their highest ever amounts of $20 billion.

Because 80% of the world's approximately 7 billion consumers live in the expanding developing nations, TNCs based in newly industrializing countries have the strength of familiarity with those markets and have an advantage in supplying them with goods and services that are usually cheaper to purchase, simpler and more familiar in operation, and more effectively distributed than those of many Western rival TNCs. Nevertheless, despite poor countries's hopes for foreign investment to spur their economic growth, the vast majority of FDI flows not to the poor or developing worlds but to the rich.

The advanced-country destination of those capital flows is understandable: TNCs are actively engaged in merging with or purchasing competitive established firms in already developed foreign market areas, and cross-border mergers and acquisitions have been the main stimulus behind FDI. Because most transnational corporations operate in only a few industries—computers, electronics, petroleum and mining, motor vehicles, chemicals, and pharmaceuticals—the worldwide impact of their consolidations is significant. Some dominate the marketing and distribution of basic and specialized commodities. In raw materials, a few TNCs account for 85% or more of world trade in wheat, maize, coffee, cotton, iron ore, and timber, for example. In manufactures, the highly concentrated world pharmaceutical industry is dominated by just six firms.

Because they are international in operation with multiple markets, plants, and raw material sources, TNCs actively exploit the principle of comparative advantage and seize opportunities for outsourcing and offshoring. In manufacturing, they have internationalized the plant-siting decision process and have multiplied the number of locationally separated operations that must be assessed. TNCs produce in that country or region where the costs of materials, labor, or other production inputs are minimized, or where existing efficient company-owned factories can be easily expanded to produce for a global, rather than simply a national, market. At the same time, they can maintain operational control and declare taxes in localities where the economic climate is most favorable. Research and development, accounting, and other corporate activities are placed wherever economical and convenient.

TNCs have become global entities because global communications make it possible. Many have lost their original national identities and are no longer closely associated with or controlled by the cultures, societies, and legal systems of a nominal home country. At the same time, their multiplication of economic activities has reduced any earlier identifications with single products or processes and has given rise to "transnational integral conglomerates" spanning a large spectrum of both service and industrial sectors.

World Manufacturing Patterns and Trends

Whether locational decisions are made by private entrepreneurs or by central planners—and on whatever considerations those decisions are based—the results over many years have produced a distinctive world pattern of manufacturing. Figure 10.26 suggests the striking prominence of a relatively small number of major industrial concentrations localized within relatively few countries primarily but not exclusively parts of the "industrialized" or "developed" world. These can be roughly grouped into four commonly recognized major manufacturing regions: *Eastern Anglo America, Western and Central Europe, Eastern Europe,* and *Eastern Asia.* Together, the industrial plants within these established concentrations account for an estimated three-fifths of the world's manufacturing output by volume and value.

Their continuing dominance is by no means assured. The first three—those of Anglo America and Europe—were the beneficiaries of an earlier phase in the development and spread of manufacturing following the Industrial Revolution of the 18th century and lasting until after World War II. The countries within them now are increasingly developing postindustrial economies in which traditional manufacturing and processing are of declining relative importance.

The fourth—the East Asian industrial region—is a part and forerunner of the wider, new pattern of world industrialization that has emerged in recent years, the result of international cultural convergence and technology transfers in the latter half of the 20th century, as briefly reviewed in Chapter 7. The older, rigid industrial "North–South" split between the developed and developing worlds has rapidly weakened as the full range of industrial activities from primary metal processing (e.g., the iron and steel industries) through advanced electronics assembly has been dispersed from, or separately established within, an ever-expanding list of countries.

Such states as Mexico, Brazil, China, and others of the developing world have created industrial regions of international significance, and the contribution to world manufacturing activity of the smaller, newly industrializing countries (NICs) has been growing significantly. Even economies that until recently were overwhelmingly subsistence or dominated by agricultural or mineral exports have become important players in the changing world manufacturing scene. Foreign branch plant investment in low-wage Asian, African, and Latin American states has not only created their industrial infrastructures but also increased their gross national products and per capita incomes sufficiently to permit expanded production for growing domestic—not just export—markets.

In Malaysia, for example—one of the rapidly growing Southeast Asian economies—agriculture's share of gross domestic product was cut by nearly 60% between 1981 and 2006, and the share of merchandise exports from manufacturing rose from 19% to 75%. For Pakistan in South Asia, manufactured goods jumped from less than half to 85% of export values in that period. Collectively, the "developing world" accounted for nearly 30% of *gross world product* in 2008 using current exchange rates and closer to 50% measured at purchasing power parity. Increasingly, their share of that output is comprised of the manufactured goods that formerly were nearly exclusively the product of the "advanced world" of the North.

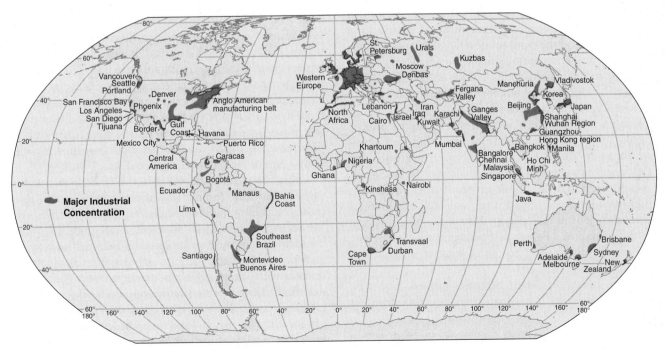

FIGURE 10.26 World industrial regions. Industrial districts are not as continuous or "solid" as the map suggests. Manufacturing is a relatively minor user of land even in areas of its greatest concentration.

High-Tech Patterns

Major industrial districts of the world developed over time as entrepreneurs and planners established traditional secondary industries according to the pulls and orientations predicted by classical location theories. Those theories are less applicable in explaining the location of the latest generation of manufacturing activities: the high-technology—or *high-tech*—processing and production that is increasingly part of the advanced economies. For these firms, new and different patterns of locational orientation and advantage have emerged, based on other than the traditional regional and site attractions.

High technology is more an ambiguous concept than a precise definition. Today's high-tech fields may become standard in just a few years and old, obsolete fields within a few decades. It probably is best understood as the application of intensive research and development efforts to the creation and manufacture of new products of an advanced scientific and engineering character.[b] Professional—"white-collar"—workers make up a large share of the total workforce. They include research scientists, engineers, and skilled technicians. When these high-skill specialists are added to administrative, supervisory, marketing, and other professional staffs, they may greatly outnumber actual production workers in a firm's employment structure. In the world of high tech, that is, the distinction between secondary (manufacturing) and quaternary (knowledge) activities and workers is increasingly blurred.

Although only a few types of industrial activity are generally reckoned as exclusively high tech—electronics, communications, computers, software, pharmaceuticals and biotechnology, aerospace, and the like—advanced technology is increasingly a part of the structure and processes of all forms of industry. Robotics on the assembly line, computer-aided design and manufacturing, electronic controls of smelting and refining processes, and the constant development of new products of the chemical and pharmaceutical industries are cases in point. Indeed, in the United States in 2006 an estimated average of more than 5% of total employment among all industry was in technology-oriented occupations.

The impact of high-tech industries on patterns of economic geography is expressed in several ways. High-tech activities are becoming major factors in employment growth and manufacturing output in the advanced and newly industrializing economies. Restricting the count only to those defined as truly high-tech industries, there were 14.4 million American wage and salary jobs in 2002, about 11% of the total nonfarm jobs in the economy. High-tech employment is important, but it is not the dominating economic force it is sometimes claimed to be.

The U.S. Bureau of Labor Statistics foresees high-tech manufacturing declining faster than overall manufacturing as physical production continues to move out of the country. The United Kingdom, Germany, Japan, and other advanced countries have had similar high-tech employment courses, while high-tech manufacturing has been established and grown most dramatically in the newly industrializing countries of South, Southeast, and East Asia, beneficiaries initially of outsourcing and offshoring but also, more recently, of independent, vigorous, and successful competition in the world market.

High-tech industries have tended to become regionally concentrated in their countries of development, and within those regions they frequently form self-sustaining, highly specialized agglomerations in hubs of technological innovation (Figure 10.27). California, for example, has a share of U.S. high-tech employment far in excess of its share of American population. Along with California, the Pacific Northwest (including British Columbia), New England, New Jersey, Texas, and Colorado all have proportions of their workers in high-tech industries above the national average. And within these and other states or regions of high-tech concentration, specific locales have achieved prominence: Silicon Valley of Santa Clara County near San Francisco; Irvine and Orange County south of Los Angeles; the Silicon Forest near Seattle; North Carolina's Research Triangle; Utah's Software Valley; Routes 128 and 495 around Boston; Silicon Swamp of the Washington, D.C., area; Ottawa, Canada's, Silicon Valley North; and the Canadian Technology Triangle west of Toronto are familiar Anglo American examples.

Within such concentration, specialization is often the rule: medical technologies in Minneapolis and Philadelphia; biotechnology around San Antonio; computers and semiconductors in eastern Virginia and at "Silicon Hills" in Austin, Texas; biotechnology and telecommunications in New Jersey's Princeton Corridor; and telecommunications and Internet industries near Washington, D.C. Elsewhere, Scotland's Silicon Glen, England's Sunrise Strip and Silicon Fen, Wireless Valley in Stockholm, Zhong Guancum in suburban Beijing and the high-tech industries zone in Xian, and High-Tec city, Pune, and Bangalore, India, are other examples of industrial landscapes characterized by low, modern, dispersed office-plant-laboratory buildings rather than by massive factories, mills, or assembly structures, freight facilities, and storage areas. Planned business parks catering to the needs of smaller companies are increasingly a part of regional and local economic planning.

The older distributional patterns of high-tech industries suggest that they respond to different localizing forces than those controlling traditional manufacturing industries. At least five locational tendencies have been recognized: (1) proximity to major universities or research facilities and to a large pool of scientific and technical labor skills; (2) the avoidance of areas with strong labor unionization where contract rigidities might slow process innovation and workforce flexibility; (3) locally available venture capital and entrepreneurial daring; (4) location in regions and major metropolitan areas with favorable "quality of life" reputations—climate, scenery, recreation, good universities, and an employment base sufficiently large to supply needed workers and provide job opportunities

---

[b]The Congressional Office of Technology describes high-technology firms as those "engaged in the design, development, and introduction of new products and/or innovative manufacturing processes through the systematic application of scientific and technical knowledge."

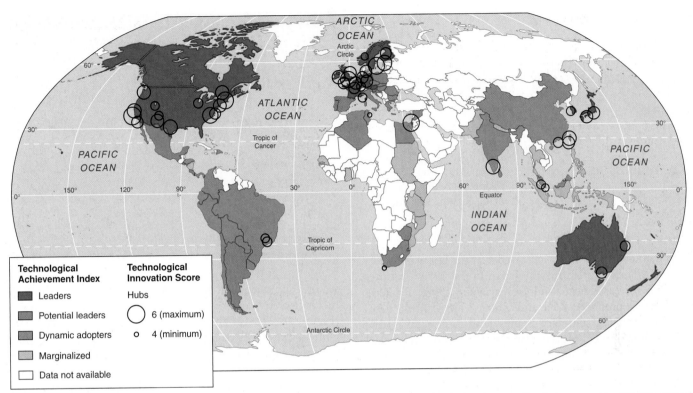

FIGURE 10.27 Global hubs of technological innovation. The technology innovation hubs shown with circles were identified by *Wired* magazine in 2000 based on the presence of research universities, research laboratories, established technology companies, venture capital, and entrepreneurial activity. The highest-scoring regions were Silicon Valley (California), Boston (Massachusetts), Stockholm (Sweden), Israel, Research Triangle (North Carolina), and London (U.K.). The technological achievement index was generated by the United Nations. *Source: United Nations Development Report, 2001. Adapted by permission from Bradshaw, White, Dymond, and Chacko, Contemporary World Regional Geography, 2009.*

for professionally trained spouses; (5) the availability of first-quality communication and transportation facilities to unite separated stages of research, development, and manufacturing and to connect the firm with suppliers, markets, finances, and the governmental agencies so important in supporting research. Essentially all the major high-tech agglomerations have developed on the semirural peripheries of metropolitan areas but far from inner-city problems and disadvantages. Many have emerged as self-sufficient areas of subdivisions, shopping centers, schools, and parks in close proximity to the company locations and business parks that form their core. Although the New York metropolitan area is a major high-tech concentration, most of the technology jobs are suburban, not in Manhattan, which is more attractive to financial services and creative service industries, such as advertising and Web design.

Agglomerating forces are also important in this new industrial locational model. The formation of new firms is frequent and rapid in industries where discoveries are constant and innovation is continuous. Because many are "spin-off" firms founded by employees leaving established local companies, areas of existing high-tech concentration tend to spawn new entrants and to provide the necessary labor skills. Agglomeration, therefore, is both a product and a cause of spatial associations.

Not all phases of high-tech production must be concentrated, however. The spatial attractions affecting the

professional, scientific, and knowledge-intensive aspects of high tech have little meaning for many of the component manufacturing and assembly operations, which may be highly automated or require little in the way of labor skills. These tasks, in our earlier locational terminology, are "footloose"; they require highly mobile capital and technology investments but may be advantageously performed by young women in low-wage areas at home or—more likely—in countries such as Taiwan, Hong Kong, Malaysia, China, and Mexico. Contract manufacturers totally divorced spatially and managerially from the companies whose products they produce accounted in 2006 for an estimated 15% to 20% of the output of all electronics hardware. Most often, the same factory produces similar or identical products under a number of different brand names.

Through manufacturing transfers of technology and outsourcing, therefore, high-tech activities are spread to newly industrializing countries. This globalization through areal transfer and dispersion represents another impact of high-tech activities on world economic geographic patterns already undergoing significant but variable change in response to the new technologies. The United States was consistently the world's leading producer of high-tech products from 1980 to 2002, contributing about one-third of the total world high-tech output. In the early 21st century, the European Union remained in second place but was losing share to fast-rising Asian countries.

Percent of U.S. labor force

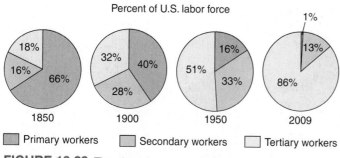

FIGURE 10.28 The changing sectoral allocation of the U.S. labor force is a measure of the economic development of the country. Its progression from a largely agricultural to postindustrial status is clearly evident.

	TABLE 10.2		
Contribution of the Service Sector to Gross Domestic Product			
	PERCENTAGE OF GDP		
Country Group	**1960**	**1980**	**2006–2008**
Low-income	32	29	46
Middle-income	47	48	53
High-income	54	61	73
United States	58	63	77
World		55	69

Source: Data from World Bank.

Asia's market share steadily increased over the last two decades of the 20th century, led first by Japan in the 1980s and then by South Korea, Taiwan, and China in the 1990s. By 2001, South Korea produced 7.1% and China 8.7% of world high-tech output. Such summary figures tend to conceal relative national importance in particular types of high-tech production and trade. For example, by 2004 China had surpassed the United States in exporting information-technology goods, such as laptop computers, mobile phones, and digital cameras and in 2007 30% of its manufacturing exports were in high technology.

TERTIARY AND BEYOND

Primary activities, you will recall, gather, extract, or grow things. *Secondary* industries give *form utility* to the products of primary industry through manufacturing and processing efforts. A major and growing segment of both domestic and international economic activity, however, involves *services* rather than the production of commodities. These *tertiary* activities consist of those business and labor specializations that provide services to the primary and secondary sectors, to the general community, and to individuals. They imply pursuits other than the actual production of tangible commodities.

As we saw earlier in this chapter, regional and national economies undergo fundamental changes in emphasis in the course of their development. Subsistence societies exclusively dependent on primary industries may progress to secondary-stage processing and manufacturing activities. In that progression, the importance of agriculture, for example, as an employer of labor or as a contributor to national income declines as that of manufacturing expands. As economic growth continues, secondary activities in their turn are replaced by service, or tertiary, functions as the main support of the economy. Advanced economies that have made that transition are often referred to as *postindustrial* because of the dominance of their service sectors and the significant decline of manufacturing as a generator of employment and national income.

Perhaps more than any other major country economy, the United States has reached postindustrial status. Its primary sector component fell from 66% of the labor force in 1850 to 1% in 2009, and the service sector rose from 18% to 86% (Figure 10.28). Of the 15 million new jobs created in the United States between 1997 and 2009, nearly all of them, after discounting for job losses in other employment sectors, occurred in services. Comparable changes are found in other countries. Early in the 21st century, between 65% and 80% of jobs in such developed economies as Japan, Canada, Australia, Israel, and all major Western European countries were also in the service sector.

The significance of tertiary activities to national economies and the contrast between more-developed and less-developed states are made clear not just by employment but also by the differential contribution of services to the gross domestic products of states. The relative importance of services displayed in Figure 10.29 shows a marked contrast between advanced and subsistence societies. The greater the service share of an economy, the greater are the integration and interdependence of that society. That share has grown over time among most regions and all national income categories because all economies have shared to some degree in world developmental growth (Table 10.2). Indeed, the expansion of the tertiary sector in modernizing East Asia, South Asia, and the Pacific was more than twice the world average in the 1990s. In Latin America and the Caribbean, services accounted for 60% of total output in 2005.

Tertiary and *service,* however, are broad and imprecise terms that cover a range of activities from neighborhood barber to World Bank president. The designations are equally applicable to traditional, low-order personal and retail activities and to higher-order, knowledge-based professional services performed primarily for other businesses, not for individual consumption.

Logically, the composite service category should be subdivided to distinguish between those activities answering to the daily living and support needs of individuals and local communities and those involving professional, administrative, or financial management tasks on regional, national, and international scales. Those different levels of activity and scope

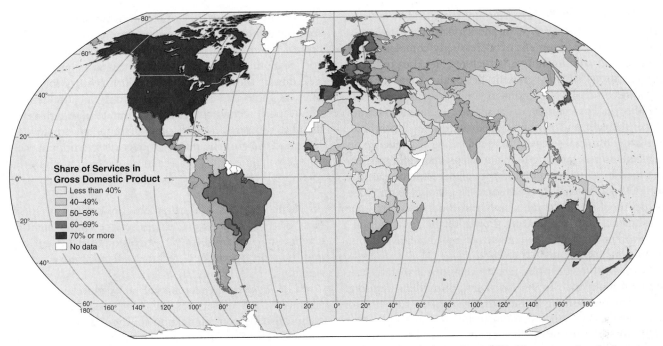

FIGURE 10.29 Services accounted for almost 70% of global GDP in 2006, up sharply from about 50% 20 years earlier. As the map documents, the contribution of services to individual national economies varied greatly; Table 10.2 indicates all national income categories shared to some degree in the expansion of service activities. *Source: World Bank,* World Development Indicators 2008 *and CIA,* World Fact Book 2008.

represent different locational principles and quite different roles in their contribution to domestic and world economies.

To recognize such fundamental contrasts, we can usefully restrict the term *tertiary* specifically to the lower-level activities largely related to the day-to-day needs of people and to the usual range of functions found in smaller towns and cities worldwide. We can then assign higher-level, more-specialized information, research, and management activities to distinctive *quaternary* and *quinary* categories (see Figure 10.2) with quite different and distinctive characteristics and significance.

Tertiary Services

Some essential services are concerned with the wholesaling or retailing of goods, providing what economists call *place utility* to items produced elsewhere. They fulfill the exchange function of advanced economies and provide the market transactions necessary in highly interdependent societies. In commercial economies, tertiary activities also provide vitally needed information about market demand without which economically justifiable production decisions are impossible.

Most tertiary activities, however, are concerned with personal and business services performed in shops and offices that, typically, cluster in cities large and small. The supply of those kinds of low-level services of necessity must be identical to the spatial distribution of *effective demand*—that is, wants made meaningful through purchasing power. Retail and personal service activities are localized by their markets, for the production of the service and its consumption are simultaneous

FIGURE 10.30 Low-level services are most efficiently and effectively performed where demand and purchasing power are concentrated, as this garment repairperson working in a street in central Kathmandu, Nepal, demonstrates. Such "informal sector" employment—street vendors, odd-job handymen, open-air dispensers of such personal services as barbering, shoe shining, clothes mending, and the like—usually escapes governmental registration and is not included in official service employment totals. © *Mark Bjelland.*

occurrences. Retailers and personal service providers tend to locate, therefore, where market density is greatest and multiple service demands are concentrated (Figure 10.30). Their locational patterns and the employment support they imply are important aspects of urban economic structure and are dealt with in Chapter 11.

In all of the world's increasingly interdependent postindustrial societies, the growth of the service component not only reflects the development of increasingly complex social, economic, and administrative structures; it also indicates changes made possible by growing personal incomes or possible and necessary by alterations in family structure and individual lifestyle. For example, in subsistence economies families produce, prepare, and consume food within the household. Urbanizing industrial societies have increasing dependence on specialized farmers growing food and wholesalers and retailers selling food to households that largely prepare and consume it at home. Postindustrial America increasingly opts to purchase prepared foods in restaurants and fast-food and carry-out establishments with accelerating growth of the tertiary food-service workers that change demands. People are still fed, but the employment structure has changed.

Part of the growth in the tertiary component is statistical, rather than functional. In our discussion of modern industry, we saw that outsourcing is increasingly used as a device to reduce costs and enhance manufacturing and assembly efficiencies. In the same way, outsourcing of services formerly provided in-house is also characteristic of current business practice. Cleaning and maintenance of factories, shops, and offices—formerly done by the company itself as part of internal operations—now are subcontracted to specialized service providers. The jobs are still done, perhaps even by the same personnel, but worker status has changed from "secondary" (as employees of a manufacturing plant, for example) to "tertiary" (as employees of a service company).

Special note should be made of *tourism*—travel undertaken for the purposes of recreation rather than business. It has become not only the most important single tertiary sector activity but also the world's largest industry in jobs and total value generated. On a worldwide basis, tourism accounts for some 250 million recorded jobs and untold additional numbers in the informal economy. Altogether, 15% or more of the world's workforce is engaged in providing services to recreational travelers, and in 2005 the total economic value of tourism goods and services reached about $4.5 trillion, or 10% of the world's gross domestic product. In middle- and high-income countries, tourism supports a diversified share of domestic expenditures through transportation-related costs, roadside services, entertainment, national park visits, and the like. International tourism, on the other hand, generates new income and jobs of growing importance in developing states. Altogether, worldwide international tourist visits numbered about 920 million in 2008, more than a third of them destined for the less-developed low- and middle-income countries. International tourism, accounting for 40% of global services trade in 2005, produced some 7% of all foreign earnings of developing states and—in the form of goods and services, such as meals, lodging, and transport consumed by foreign travelers—constituted more than 45% of their total "service exports." For half of the world's 50 poorest countries, tourism had become the leading service export sector.

Whatever the origins of tertiary employment growth, the social and structural consequences are comparable. The process of development leads to increasing labor specialization and economic interdependence within a country. That was true during the latter part of the 20th century for all economies, as Table 10.2 attests. Carried to the postindustrial stage of advanced technology-based economies and high per capita income, the service component of both the employed labor force and the gross domestic product rises to dominance.

Beyond Tertiary

Available statistics, unfortunately, do not always permit a clear distinction between *tertiary* service employment that is a reflection of daily lifestyle or corporate structural changes and the more-specialized, higher-level *quaternary* and *quinary* activities.

The *quaternary* sector can be seen realistically as an advanced form of services involving specialized knowledge, technical skills, communication ability, or administrative competence. These are the tasks carried out in office buildings, elementary and university classrooms, hospitals and doctors's offices, theaters, accounting and brokerage firms, and the like. With the explosive growth in the demand for and consumption of information-based services—mutual fund managers, tax consultants, Internet and software developers, statisticians, and more—the quaternary sector in the most highly developed economies has unmistakably replaced all primary and secondary employment as the basis for economic growth. In fact, over half of all workers in rich economies are in the "knowledge sector" alone—in the production, storage, retrieval, or distribution of information.

Quaternary activities performed for other business organizations often embody the "externalization" of specialized services similar to the outsourcing of low-level tertiary functions. The distinction between them lies in the fact that knowledge- and skill-based free-standing quaternary service establishments can be spatially divorced from their clients; they are not tied to resources, affected by the environment, or necessarily localized by market. They can realize cost reductions through serving multiple clients in highly technical areas and permit client firms to use specialized skills and efficiencies to achieve competitive advantage without the expense of adding to their own labor force.

Often, of course, when high-level personal contacts are required, the close functional association of client and service firms within a country encourages quaternary establishment locational and employment patterns similar to those of the headquarters distribution of the primary and secondary industries served. But the transportability of quaternary services also means that many quaternary activities can be spatially isolated from their client base. In the United States, at least, these combined trends have resulted both in the concentration of certain specialized services—merchant banking or bond underwriting, for example—in major metropolitan areas and in a regional diffusion of the quaternary sector to accompany the growing regional deconcentration of the client firm base. Similar locational tendencies have been noted even for the spatially more-restricted advanced economies of, for example, England and France.

Information, administration, and the "knowledge" activities in their broadest sense are dependent on communication. Their spatial dispersion, therefore, has been abetted by the underlying technological base of most quaternary activities: electronic digital processing and telecommunications transfer of data. That technology permits many "back-office" tasks to be spatially distant from the home office locations of either the service or the client firms. Insurance claims, credit card charges, mutual fund and stock market transactions, and the like are more efficiently and economically recorded or processed in low-rent, low-labor cost locations—often in suburbs or small towns and in rural states—than in the financial districts of major cities. The production and consumption of such services can be spatially separated in a way not feasible for tertiary, face-to-face activities.

Finally, there are the *quinary* activities, another separately recognized subdivision of the tertiary sector representing the special and highly paid skills of top business executives, government officials, research scientists, financial and legal consultants, and so on. These people find their place of business in major metropolitan centers, in and near major universities and research parks, at first-rank medical centers, and in cabinet- and department-level offices of political capitals. Within their cities of concentration, they may be highly localized by prestigious street addresses (Park Avenue, Wall Street) or post offices (Princeton, New Jersey) or by notable "signature" office buildings (Transamerica Building, Sears Tower, or John Hancock Building). Their importance in the structure of advanced economies far outweighs their numbers.

SERVICES IN WORLD TRADE

Just as service activities have been major engines of national economic growth within the most-advanced states, so, too, have they become an increasing factor in international trade flows and economic interdependence. Between 1980 and 2006, services increased from 15% of total world trade to 23%. The fastest-growing segment of that increase was in such private services as financial, brokerage, and leasing activities, which had grown to 50% of all commercial services trade by 2005. As in the domestic arena, rapid advances in information technology and electronic data transmission have been central elements in the internationalization of services as wired and wireless communication costs have been reduced to negligible levels. Many services considered nontradable even late in the 1990s are now actively traded at long distance, as the growth of services offshoring clearly shows.

Developing countries have been particular beneficiaries of the new technologies. Their exports of commercial services—valued at nearly $870 billion in 2006—grew at an annual 15% rate in the 1990s, twice as fast as service exports from industrial regions. The increasing tradability of services has expanded the international comparative advantage of developing states in relatively labor-intensive long-distance service activities such as mass data processing and computer software development. At the same time, they have benefited from increased access to efficient, state-of-the-art equipment and techniques transferred from advanced economies.

The concentration of computer software development around Bangalore, Pune, and Hyderabad has made India a major world player in software innovation, for example, whereas elsewhere in that country increasing volumes of back-office work for Western insurance companies and airlines is being performed. Claims processing for life and health insurance firms have become concentrated in English-speaking Caribbean states to take advantage of lower wages and the availability of a large pool of educated workers there. In all such cases, the result is an acceleration in the transfer rate of technology in such expanding areas as information and telecommunications services and an increase in the rate of developing-country integration in the world economy.

That integration has increasingly moved to higher levels of economic and professional services. The cost and efficiency advantages of outsourcing such skilled functions as paralegal and legal services, accountancy, medical analysis and technical services, and research and development work in a nearly unlimited range of businesses are now widely understood and appreciated. Wired and wireless transmission of data, documents, medical and technical records, charts, X rays, and the like make distant quaternary and higher-level services immediately and efficiently accessible. Further, many higher-level services are easily subdivided and performable in sequence or simultaneously in multiple locations. The well-known "follow the sun" practices of software developers who finish a day's tasks only to pass on work to colleagues elsewhere in the world are now increasingly used by professionals in many other fields. When the practice involves highly educated and talented specialists receiving developing-world compensation levels, the cost attractions for developed country companies are irresistible. The necessary levels of education and technical expertise are, to an ever-greater extent, more apt to have been acquired not by expensive training in European or North American universities but, rather, through distant learning programs and professional school contacts through the Internet.

Many of the current developing-country gains in international quaternary services are the result of increased foreign direct investment (FDI) in the services sector. Those flows accounted for three-fifths of all FDI in the early years of the 21st century. The majority of such investment, however, is transferred within the advanced countries themselves rather than between industrial and developing states. In either case, as transnational corporations use mainframe computers around the clock for data processing, they can exploit or eliminate time zone differences between home office countries and host countries of their affiliates. Such cross-border intrafirm service transactions are not usually recorded in balance of payment or trade statistics but materially increase the volume of international services flows.

Despite the increasing share of global services trade held by developing countries, world trade—imports plus exports—in services is still overwhelmingly dominated by a very few (Table 10.3). The country and category contrasts are great, as a comparison of the "high-income" and "low-income" groups documents. At a different level, in 2005, the single small island state of Singapore had a greater share (2.1%) of world services trade than did all of sub-Saharan Africa (1.2%).

The same cost and skill advantages that enhance the growth and service range of quaternary firms and quinary activities on the domestic scene also operate internationally.

(a)

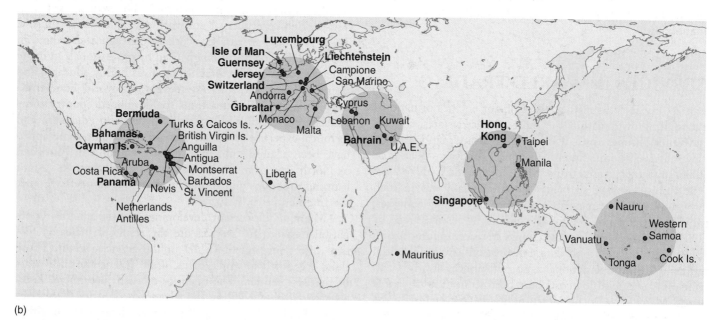

(b)

FIGURE 10.31 (a) The hierarchy of international financial centers, topped by New York and London, indicates the tendency of highest-order quaternary activities to concentrate in a few world and national centers. **(b)** At the same time, the multiplication of offshore locations where "furtive money" avoiding regulatory control and national taxes finds refuge, suggests that dispersed convenience sites also serve the international financial community. *Source: Peter Dicken.* Global Shift. *4th ed. Guilford Press, 2003, Figures 13.8 and 13.10.*

TABLE 10.3
Shares of World Trade in Commercial Services (Exports, 2006)

Country or Category	Percent of World Trade in Services
United States	14.4
United Kingdom	8.2
Germany	6.0
China (incl Hong Kong)	3.3
Japan	4.2
France	4.2
Italy	3.5
Spain	3.8
Total	**60.0**
High-income states	72.4
Low-income states	4.0
Sub-Saharan Africa	1.3
European Monetary Union	31.5

Source: Data from World Bank, *World Development Indicators 2008*.

The principal banks of all the advanced countries have established foreign branches, and the world's leading banks have become major presences in the primary financial capitals. In turn, a relatively few world cities have emerged as international business and financial centers whose operations and influences are continuous and borderless, while a host of offshore banking havens have emerged to exploit gaps in regulatory controls and tax laws (Figure 10.31). Accounting firms, advertising agencies, management consulting companies, and similar quaternary sector establishments of North American or European origin primarily have increasingly established their international presence, with main branches located in principal business centers worldwide.

The list of tertiary, quaternary, and quinary employment is long. Its diversity and familiarity remind us of the complexity of modern life and of how far removed we are from the subsistence economies. As societies advance economically, the shares of employment and national income generated by the primary, secondary, and composite tertiary sectors continually change, and spatial patterns of human activity reflect those changes. The shift is steadily away from primary production and secondary processing and toward the trade, personal, and professional services of the tertiary sector and the information and control activities of the quaternary and quinary.

Summary of Key Concepts

- Three recognized types of economic systems are *subsistence, commercial,* and *planned*. The first is concerned with production for the immediate consumption of individual producers and family members. In the second, economic decisions ideally respond to impersonal market forces and reasoned assessments of monetary gain. In the third, at least some nonmonetary social or political goals influence production decisions.

- Economic activities may be grouped by the stages of production and the degree of specialization they represent into *primary* activities (food and raw material production), *secondary* industries (processing and manufacturing), *tertiary* activities (distribution and general professional and personal service), and the administrative, informational, and technical specializations (*quaternary* and *quinary* activities) that mark highly advanced societies of either planned or commercial systems.

- Different countries and regions display different stages of economic development; there is no single, inevitable pattern of progression from underdeveloped subsistence status to the advanced integration of secondary, tertiary, and quaternary activities that marks a modern market economy.

- Agriculture, the most extensively practiced of the primary industries, is part of the spatial economy of both subsistence and advanced societies. In the first instance, it is responsive to the immediate consumption needs of the producer group and reflective of the environmental conditions under which it is practiced. In the second, agriculture reacts to consumer demand expressed through free or controlled markets.

- Manufacturing is the dominant form of secondary activity and is evidence of economic advancement beyond the subsistence level. Location theories help explain observed patterns of industrial development. Those theories are based on simplifying assumptions about fixed and variable costs of production and distribution, including costs of raw materials, power, labor, market accessibility, and transportation.

- Agglomeration economies and the multiplier effect may make attractive locations not otherwise predicted for individual firms, while comparative advantage may influence production decisions of entrepreneurs. Just-in-time and flexible productions systems introduce different locational considerations than those shaping traditional theories. A growing number of transnational corporations (TNCs) with multiple markets, plants, and raw material sources actively exploit advantages of outsourcing and offshoring in making foreign direct investments away from their home country base.

- A large share of global manufacturing activity is found within a relatively small number of major industrial

Cairo was a world-class city in the 14th century. Situated at the crossroads of Africa, Asia, and Europe, it dominated trade on the Mediterranean Sea. By the early 1300s, it had a population of half a million or more, with 10- to 14-story buildings crowding the city center. There were more than 12,000 shops, some of which specialized in luxury goods from all over the world—Siberian sable, chain mail, musical instruments, cloth, songbirds. Travelers marveled at the size, density, and variety of Cairo, comparing it favorably with cities such as Venice, Paris, and Baghdad. Cairo's chronicler of the period, Taqui-al-Din-Al-Maqrizi, recorded the construction of a huge building with shops on the first floors and apartments housing 4000 people. One Florentine visitor estimated that more people lived on a single Cairo street than in all of Florence. Travelers from all over Europe and Asia made their way through Cairo, and the shipping at the port of Bulaq outdistanced those of Venice and Genoa combined.

Today, Cairo is a vast, sprawling metropolis representative of several recent trends in urbanization in developing countries where population growth far outstrips economic development. The population of Egypt was measured at 35 million in 1970. In recent decades, better health care has led to a big drop in infant mortality, and the result is a country of 83 million people. Some 12 million reside in the Cairo greater metropolitan area. Greater Cairo now extends more than 450 square kilometers (175 sq mi) and has a population density of about 27,000 per square kilometer (70,000 per sq mi). Population trends are expected to continue, with a predicted population of around 13.5 million by 2015.

A steady stream of migrants arrives in Cairo daily because it is the place where people think opportunities are available, where life will be better and brighter than in the crowded countryside. Cairo is the symbol of modern Egypt, a place where young people are willing to undergo deprivation for the chance to "make it." But real opportunities continue to be scarce. The poor, of whom there are millions, crowd into row after row of apartment houses, many of them poorly constructed. Tens of thousands more live in rooftop sheds or small boats on the Nile; a half million find shelter in the Northern and Southern Cemeteries—known as the Cities of the Dead—on Cairo's eastern edge. On occasion, buildings collapse; the earthquake of October 12, 1992, measured 5.9 on the Richter scale but caused enormous damage, leveling thousands of buildings. Yet the city continues to grow, spreading onto valued farmland, thus decreasing food availability for the country's increasing population.

One's first impression when arriving in central Cairo is of opulence, a stark contrast to what lies outside the center. High-rise apartments, regional headquarters buildings of multinational corporations, and modern hotels stand amid clogged streets, symbols of the new Egypt (Figure 11.1). The well-to-do can eat at McDonald's, Pizza Hut, Taco Bell, or Chili's; new suburban developments and exclusive residential communities create enclaves for the wealthy. The plush apartments and expensive cars, however, are only a short distance from the slums that are home to masses of underemployed people, perhaps as much as 20% of Cairo's population. The contrasts evident in Cairo between wealth and poverty, between modern structures and slums, between space and overcrowding are profound. Like a number of large cities, Cairo has witnessed an urban explosion, one that sees an increasing proportion of the world's population housed in cities without the structures to support them all.

FIGURE 11.1 Cairo, Egypt. The population growth in the greater metropolitan area—from some 3 million in 1970 to 12 million today—has been mirrored in many developing countries. The rapid growth of urban areas brings with it housing shortages, inadequate transportation and other infrastructure development, unemployment, poverty, and environmental deterioration. © Corbis RF.

Because of its rapid growth, Cairo has not been able to plan and create an adequate infrastructure for its inhabitants. The 1992 earthquake prompted the city's adoption of its first development plan. Traffic is always a problem in Cairo, despite recent improvements, such as a ring road around the city and the construction of a metro. Vehicles idle in traffic, consuming large amounts of fuel; 10% of Cairenes suffer respiratory illnesses due to air pollution. In fact, Cairo's air pollution is worse than that of Mexico City, long thought to be the world's worst. The traffic and the crowding contribute to noise pollution, in which noise levels often reach 80 decibels or more. Water pollution both in the Nile and in treated drinking water shows dangerous levels of lead and cadmium, whose health effects will be borne for years to come. These problems of size, population, poverty, planning, and infrastructure face all cities to some degree and are some of the topics we consider in this chapter.

AN URBANIZING WORLD

Cities today are growing at a phenomenal rate. In 1900 only 13 cities had a population of more than 1 million people; in 2008 there were 455 such cities (Figure 11.2). It has been projected that by 2015 there will be 564 cities with population exceeding 1 million.

In 1900, no cities had a population of more than 10 million people. Nineteen metropolises had 10 million or more people in 2008 (Table 11.1 and Figure 11.3). The United Nations calls these *megacities*. Of course, as we saw in Chapter 6, we would expect the urban component to have increased as the world's population has greatly increased. Urbanization and metropolitanization have increased more rapidly than the growth of total population, however. In the year 1800, only 3% of the world's population lived in cities; now, the figure is about 50%. The amount of urban growth differs from continent to continent and from country to country, but all countries have one thing in common: the proportion of the people living in cities is rising.

Table 11.2 shows world urban population by region. Note that the most industrialized parts of the world, North America and Western Europe, are the most urbanized in terms of percentage of people living in cities, while Asia and Africa have lower proportions of urban population. Industrialization fosters urbanization, but in developing countries, urbanization has resulted only partly from industrialization. People flock to the cities seeking a better life than they can find in rural areas, but they often do not find it. The cities of sub-Saharan Africa are growing at a rapid rate, largely due to rural-to-urban migration. However, the urban growth is beyond the capability of the economic system to create employment, housing, and social services. Shantytowns and squatter settlements, in addition to unemployment and underemployment, are characteristic of cities such as Lagos, Nigeria, and Dakar, Senegal (see Figure 11.33 on page 389).

It is interesting to note in Table 11.2 that China and Southeast Asia (Vietnam, Indonesia, etc.) have relatively low proportions of people in urban regions. Their absolute number of people in urban areas, however, is among the highest in the world. Given the huge populations in Asia, and the relatively heavy emphasis on agriculture (excluding Japan and Korea), it sometimes escapes us that many large cities exist throughout parts of the world where most people are still engaged in subsistence agriculture.

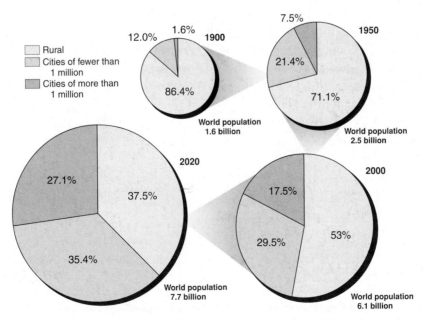

FIGURE 11.2 Trends in world urbanization. Note the steady decline in the proportion of people living in rural areas. The United Nations predicts that virtually all of the population growth during 2000–2020 will be concentrated in the urban areas of the world. *Sources: Estimates and projections from Population Reference Bureau and other sources.*

TABLE 11.1

Cities with 10 Million or More Inhabitants (Megacities), 2007 (Population in Millions)

City	Country	POPULATION 2007	RANK 2007
Tokyo	Japan	35.68	1
New York	United States	19.04	2
Mexico City	Mexico	19.03	3
Mumbai (Bombay)	India	18.98	4
São Paulo	Brazil	18.85	5
Delhi	India	15.93	6
Shanghai	China	14.99	7
Kolkata (Calcutta)	India	14.79	8
Dhaka	Bangladesh	13.49	9
Buenos Aires	Argentina	12.80	10
Los Angeles	United States	12.50	11
Karachi	Pakistan	12.13	12
Cairo	Egypt	11.89	13
Rio de Janeiro	Brazil	11.75	14
Osaka-Kobe	Japan	11.29	15
Beijing	China	11.11	16
Manila	Philippines	11.10	17
Moscow	Russian Federation	10.45	18
Istanbul	Turkey	10.06	19

Source: The UN Population Division.

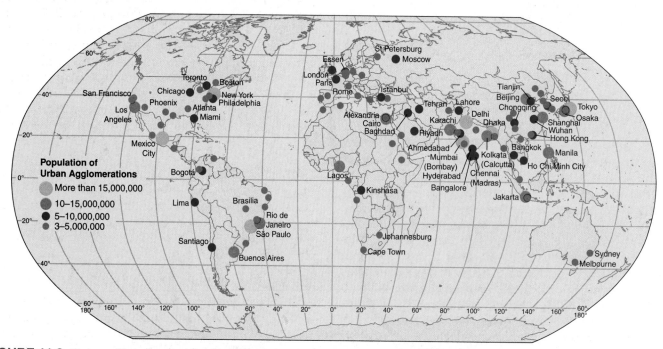

FIGURE 11.3 Metropolitan areas of 3 million or more in 2005. Only metropolitan areas with a population of 5 million or more are named. Massive urbanized districts are no longer characteristic only of the industrialized, developed countries. Note the clusters of large metropolitan areas in developing countries, such as Rio de Janeiro–São Paulo in Brazil, Beijing-Tianjin in China, and the Mumbai (Bombay) region of India. *Source: Population projections from United Nations Population Division.*

TABLE 11.2

Estimated Urban Share of Total Population for Selected Regions and Countries, 1950 and 2000, with Projections to 2030

Region or Country	1950	2000	2030
North America	64	79	87
Latin America	42	76	84
Europe	51	72	78
Russia	45	73	76
Oceania	61	71	74
Japan	35	65	74
China	13	36	60
Southeast Asia	15	40	61
Africa	15	36	51
World	29	47	60

Source: United Nations Population Division.

In this chapter, our first objective is to consider the major factors responsible for the development, location, and functions of urban areas. Our second goal is to examine the systems of urban areas—the relationships they bear to one another. The third goal is to identify the nature of land use patterns within those areas. Fourth, we attempt to differentiate cities around the world by reviewing some of the factors that help explain their special nature.

ORIGINS AND EVOLUTION OF CITIES

People need to be near one another: they gather together to form couples, families, groups, organizations, and towns. Beyond companionship, people need each other to sustain important support systems. The origins of towns lie in several factors: the existence of a settled community (not a hunter-gatherer society); a concentration of people; groups not directly engaged in agriculture; and the existence and governance of an elite group. These factors are the basis for urban settlement and the underpinnings of civilization (note that *city* and *civilization* have the same Latin root, *civis*). Although civilization was necessary before the first towns and cities emerged, the development of cities depended on favorable circumstances, including fertile soil, the presence of water for transportation, building materials, and a defensible situation. Technology in the form of agricultural production and food transport and storage was also necessary for urban development. Given these conditions, how did cities begin in the ancient world?

First and foremost, the earliest cities depended on the existence of an agricultural surplus. Many early cities included farms within their walls, but the main distinction between the city and the countryside stemmed from the nonagricultural aspect of most urban dwellers. This meant that food had to be provided to the urban population by the **hinterland** surrounding the city. Advances in agriculture, stemming from fortunate circumstances and improvements in technology, created a food surplus in an area surrounding a population center. Those in the nascent town who were not involved in agriculture were free to specialize in other occupations—metalsmithing, perhaps—that in turn helped further the technology important in creating the food surplus. Others might become part of the ruling elite or priestly castes, helping to refine the power structure and civilization that organized residents' lives.

Social organization and power, often reflected in religion, were the second necessary precursor to urban development. Most ancient cities centered on a temple or a palace, which housed the priests, the granary, the schools, and often the ruler. Cities became the seats of central power, cementing the relationship to the hinterland and allowing the extraction of the agricultural surplus from the hinterland and its redistribution in the city.

Ancient cities grew in spots that were easy to defend. Positions along rivers aided in transportation, but hilltops offered defensive advantages. Often residents built walls to surround the town and aid in its defense. Building walls and sometimes moats was a strategy used in much of Europe, but these defensive frameworks could also limit city expansion. Some cities, such as Rome, went through multiple rounds of wall construction, with each addition extending the area in which residents could live.

The fourth factor in the emergence of urban areas was the development of a more-complex economy. Cities extracted their sustenance from the surrounding hinterland. As the city extended its power and organization, it could extend its hold over a wider hinterland. As agricultural technology improved, the hinterland could produce more food, and as methods of transportation and storage improved, cities could bring in more food and store it safely for eventual redistribution to the urban population. The size of a hinterland could limit urban growth, as cities could grow only if the agricultural surplus also grew.

In Europe and Asia, from about the 10th to the 18th century, shifts in economic relationships changed the simple extractive relationship between the city and its hinterland. As trade became the engine of the economy, urban merchants began to buy and sell. In general, they traded raw materials—wool, wood, spices—which were then used to produce finished goods, such as textiles, boats, and food.

With the Industrial Revolution, another shift in economic organization took place. The Industrial Revolution accelerated urbanization, especially in Europe. Powered by water or coal, new machinery in factories, operated by growing working populations, fostered mass production. Cities, once centered on the temple or the palace, once surrounded by walls, once focused on the marketplace and the river, changed utterly: their economic fortunes centered on the factories, the railroads, and housing for the factory workers.

(a)

(b)

FIGURE 11.4 The differences in size, density, and land use complexity are immediately apparent between **(a)** New York City and **(b)** a small town (Camden, Maine). One is a city, one is a town, but both are urban areas. *(a) © Getty RF; (b) Corbis RF.*

This very brief overview of the development of urban areas only scratches the surface of a very complex phenomenon and a very long history, but it is important to understand the origins of cities before examining other aspects of cities. First, we will start with some definitions, then turn to the factors influencing the location of urban settlement and the economic structure of cities.

Defining the City Today

Urban areas are not of a single type, structure, or size. Their common characteristic is that they are nucleated, nonagricultural settlements. At one end of the size scale, urban areas are small towns with perhaps a single main street of shops; at the opposite end, they are complex, multifunctional metropolitan areas or megacities (Figure 11.4). The word *urban* is often used to describe such places as a town, city, suburb, or metropolitan area, but it is a general term, not used to specify a particular type of settlement. People use common terms differently. What a resident of rural Vermont or West Virginia calls a city may not at all be afforded that name and status by an inhabitant of California or New Jersey. In addition, one should keep in mind that the term *urban* differs the world over: in the United States, the Census Bureau describes *urban* places as having 2500 or more inhabitants; in Greece, *urban* is defined as municipalities in which the largest population center has 10,000 or more inhabitants; in Nicaragua, it denotes administrative centers of localities with streets, electric lights, and at least 1000 inhabitants. It is necessary in this chapter to agree

on the meanings of terms commonly employed but interpreted in different ways.

The words **city** and **town** denote nucleated settlements, multifunctional in character, including an established central business district and both residential and nonresidential land uses. Towns are smaller in size and have less functional complexity than cities, but they still have a nuclear business concentration. **Suburb** denotes a subsidiary area, a functionally specialized segment of a large urban complex, dependent on an urban area. It may be dominantly or exclusively residential, industrial, or commercial. Suburbs, however, can be independent political entities. The **central city** is the part of the urban area contained within the suburban ring; it usually has official boundaries.

Some or all of these urban types may be associated into larger units. An **urbanized area** is a continuously built-up landscape defined by building and population densities with no reference to political boundaries. It may contain a central city and many contiguous cities, towns, suburbs, and other urban tracts. A **metropolitan area,** on the other hand, refers to a large-scale *functional* entity, perhaps containing several urbanized areas, discontinuously built up but nonetheless operating as an integrated economic whole (Figure 11.5).

The Location of Urban Settlements

Urban centers are connected to other cities and rural areas as they provide services for themselves and for others and rely on outside areas for goods and services not produced locally and

FIGURE 11.5 A hypothetical spatial arrangement of urban units within a metropolitan area. Sometimes the official limits of the central city are very expensive and contain areas commonly thought of as suburban or even rural. On the other hand, older eastern U.S. cities and some, such as San Francisco, in the West more often have official limits that contain only part of the high-density land uses and populations of their metropolitan areas.

FIGURE 11.6 The site of Philadelphia.

as markets for their products and activities. To perform the tasks that support it and to add new functions as demanded by the larger economy, the urban unit must be efficiently located. Efficiency may derive from its centrality, from the physical characteristics of its site, or from its location relative to the resources, productive regions, and a transportation network connecting it to its markets.

In discussing urban settlement location, geographers frequently differentiate between site and situation, concepts introduced in Chapter 1. You will recall that **site** refers to the exact location of a settlement and can be described either in terms of latitude and longitude, or in terms of the physical characteristics of the site. For example, the site of Philadelphia is an area bordering and west of the Delaware River north of the intersection with the Schuylkill River in southeast Pennsylvania (Figure 11.6).

The description can be more or less exhaustive, depending on the purpose it is meant to serve. In the Philadelphia case, the fact that the city is partly on the Atlantic coastal plain, is partly in the piedmont (foothills), and is served by a navigable river is important if one is interested in the development of the city during the Industrial Revolution. As Figure 11.7 suggests, water transportation and power were important localizing factors when major American cities were established on the East Coast.

Classifications of cities according to site characteristics have been proposed, recognizing special placement circumstances. These include *break-of-bulk* locations, such as river crossing points where cargoes and people must interrupt a journey; *head-of-navigation* or *bay head* locations where the limits of water transportation are reached; and *railhead* locations where a railroad ends. In Europe, security and defense—island locations or elevated sites—were considerations in earlier settlement locations.

Whereas *site* suggests absolute location, **situation** indicates relative location; it places a settlement in relation to the physical and cultural characteristics of the surrounding areas. Very often it is important to know what kinds of possibilities and activities exist in the area near a settlement, such as the distribution of raw materials, market areas, agricultural regions, mountains, and oceans.

The site of central Chicago is 41°52′N, 87°40′W, on a lake plain. More important, however, is its situation close to the deepest penetration of the Great Lakes system into the interior of the country, astride the Great Lakes–Mississippi waterways, and near the western margin of the manufacturing belt, the northern boundary of the Corn Belt, and the southeastern reaches of a major dairy region. References to railroads, coal deposits, and ore fields would amplify its situational characteristics (Figure 11.8). As a gateway to the West from the East and vice versa, Chicago's O'Hare International Airport is one of the busiest in the United States. From this description of Chicago's situation, implications relating to market, to raw materials, and to transportation centrality can be drawn.

FIGURE 11.7 The fall line separates hard Paleozic metamorphic rocks to the west from the softer sedimentary rocks of the coastal plain. Rivers flowing from the west move powerfully over this erosional scarp. The fall line hosted waterwheel powered industries in colonial times and helped to determine the location of major cities such as Philadelphia, Richmond, and Baltimore. *Source: Data from USGS.*

Dairying
Corn Belt
Major coal-mining area
······ Manufacturing belt
〰〰 Waterway
—— Railroad

FIGURE 11.8 The situation of Chicago helps to suggest the reasons for its functional diversity and size. Railroad development in the Midwest and the West was an important factor in determining the growth or decline of a settlement.

The site or situation that originally gave rise to an urban unit may not remain the essential ingredient for its growth and development for very long. The already existing markets, labor force, and urban facilities of a successful city may attract people and activities totally unrelated to the initial localizing forces. For instance, although coal mining had much to do with Pittsburgh's early growth, other factors are more important to its well-being today.

The Economic Base

Every urban area has an **economic base,** the activities people do to support the urban population. These are activities such as manufacturing goods, repairing roads, managing stores, tending to the sick, and teaching children. The economic base of an urban area can be categorized in terms of basic and nonbasic sectors.

The **basic sector** of an urban area's economic structure is made up of the activities of people that bring in money from outside the community. People who produce goods or perform services bought by those outside the urban area are engaged in "export" activities. For example, people manufacture computer chips in Hillsboro, Oregon. The chips are bought by computer manufacturers all over the world, making the chip manufacturers part of the basic sector of the economic structure of Hillsboro.

Other workers produce goods or services for residents of the city itself. They are not bringing new money into the community, as their goods and services are not being exported. This is the **nonbasic sector** of a city's economy, which is crucial for its internal functioning. It includes the operation of stores, offices, city government, local transit, and school systems.

The total economic structure of an urban area equals the sum of its basic and nonbasic activities. It is difficult to classify work as belonging exclusively to one sector or the other, however. Doctors, for example, may have mainly local patients and thus are members of the nonbasic sector, but

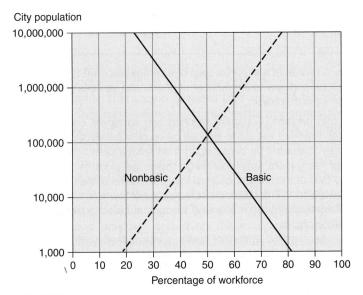

City population

Percentage of workforce

FIGURE 11.9 A generalized representation of the proportion of the workforce engaged in basic and nonbasic activities. As settlements become larger, a greater proportion of the workforce is employed in nonbasic activities. A city of 10 million will have about one-quarter of the workforce engaged in basic activities, whereas one with only 100,000 residents will have more than half the workforce so employed.

the moment they treat someone from outside the community, they bring new money into the city and become part of the basic sector.

Variations in basic employment structure among urban units characterize the specific functional role played by individual cities. Most centers perform many export functions, and the larger the urban unit, the more multifunctional it becomes. Nonetheless, even in cities with a diversified economic base, one export activity, or a very small number of export activities, tends to dominate the structure of the community. Such functional specialization permits the classification of cities into categories: manufacturing, retailing, wholesaling, transportation, government, and so on.

Economic growth has a **multiplier effect:** as a city adds basic sector employment, it will acquire people filling both basic sector and nonbasic sector positions, in addition to their dependents, fueling population growth. Dividing the employed population of an urban area into separate basic and nonbasic sectors makes it possible to establish a ratio between the two employment groups. The basic/nonbasic ratio shown in Figure 11.9 indicates that, as a settlement increases in size, the number of nonbasic personnel grows faster than the number of basic workers. This is because the more basic workers an urban area has, the more nonbasic workers are needed to support them. In cities with a population of 1 million, the ratio is about 2 nonbasic workers for every basic worker. This means that adding 10 new basic employees expands the labor force by 30 (10 basic, 20 nonbasic). For example, if the computer chip manufacturer in Hillsboro, Oregon, hires new technicians, they and their dependents will create a demand for more doctors, teachers, and lawyers.

FUNCTIONS OF CITIES

Most modern cities take on multiple functions. These include manufacturing, retailing, transportation hub, public administration, military uses, and site of major universities. Yet most cities specialize in categories, and even for truly diversified cities it can help to consider cities in regard to their relationship to markets, sites of production, or administration and other services.

No matter what their size, urban settlements exist for the efficient performance of necessary functions. They have three main functions: (1) central place functions, or providing general services for a surrounding area; (2) transport functions; and (3) special functions, or singular functions not necessarily geared to the local area. All towns provide the first two functions, but not necessarily the third.

Detroit, for example, grew to a population of 1,849,568 at its height in 1950 as it provided a point of general merchandise services, convenient transportation on the Great Lakes and the web of railroad networks crisscrossing the Midwest, and a specialized function of manufacturing automobiles. Now, there is only one automobile assembly plant in Detroit, but the city's metropolitan area continues to grow. Other examples of specialized functions are those of Washington, D.C., which provides government services to the whole United States, and the Mayo Clinic in Rochester, Minnesota, which provides specialized health services to all who seek them.

Cities as Central Markets

When people want to buy an item or purchase a service, they go to the city. For as long as cities have existed, they have served as marketplaces, not only for their own residents but also for the population beyond the city limits. Small cities provide a range of goods and services that suffice for most people's needs. But truly unique items or special services can be found only in the biggest cities.

The geographer Walter Christaller developed **central place theory** (see "Central Place Theory," p. 366) to explain the size and location of settlements. He detected a pattern of small, medium, and larger settlements that were dependent on each other. Smalls towns, he postulated, would serve as marketplaces for the surrounding populations, while expensive luxury goods would be available in the large cities that served the surrounding small towns. People would have to travel short distances for basic goods, such as groceries, and longer distances for rarer items, such as luxury cars. Christaller's theories have been shown to be generally valid in widely differing areas within the commercial world. When varying incomes, cultures, landscapes, and transportation systems are taken into consideration, the theories hold up rather well. They are particularly applicable to agricultural areas, especially with regard to the size and spacing of cities and towns. If we combine a Christaller-type approach with the ideas that help us understand industrial location and transportation alignments (see Chapter 10), we have a fairly good understanding of the location of most cities and towns.

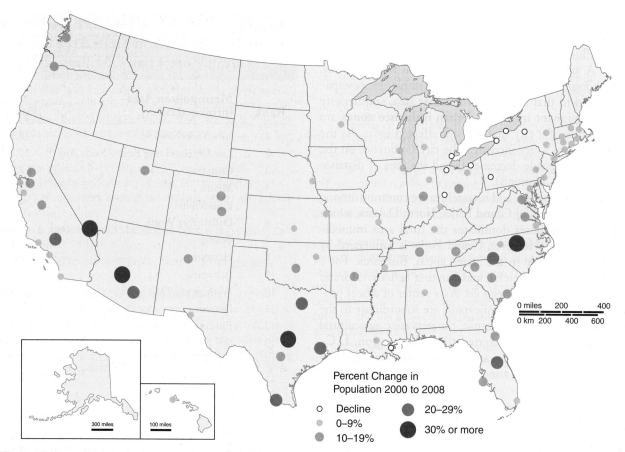

FIGURE 11.10 The pattern of metropolitan growth and decline in the United States, 2000–2008. Shown are metropolitan areas with 600,000 or more people in 2008. The cities of the southern and southwestern Sunbelt showed the greatest relative growth. Only modest growth, stability, or decline generally marked the Northeast and Midwest. *Source: Data from U.S. Bureau of the Census.*

grow substantially once the government is in place, as governments are important employers.

In cities of all sizes, some proportion of the population is employed in government services. In addition to those in the government, whether it is federal, state, metropolitan, or local, educators and health care workers are often government employees as well. Within the education sector, people are employed in primary and secondary schools and in postsecondary, technical, and professional education. Within the health care sector, the government may employ people in social agencies, hospitals, and therapy facilities. Education and health care services must be accessible and thus must be located where the population is. Therefore, the size of the government sector of employment is usually proportional to the size of the urban population.

The relationship between the size of government sector employment and the size of the local population does not necessarily hold for governmental services, which tend to be concentrated in capitals. Educational services will be closely linked to distribution of population, but some cities have a disproportionate education sector population, especially cities that are home to a university or college. Madison, Wisconsin, for example, has large government sector employment numbers, as it is the state capital and home to a large public university.

SYSTEMS OF CITIES

Cities today are interdependent. Any given city may have few or multiple functions, and these will be influenced by its location and size. It will also be affected by the distance from, size of, and functions of other cities. Taken together, cities are part of a system of urban settlement.

The Urban Hierarchy

Perhaps the most effective way to recognize how systems of cities are organized is to consider the **urban hierarchy,** a ranking of cities based on their size and functional complexity. One can measure the numbers and kinds of services each city or metropolitan area provides. The hierarchy is then like a pyramid; a few large and complex cities are at the top, and many smaller ones are at the bottom. There are always more smaller cities than larger ones.

When a spatial dimension is added to the hierarchy, as in Figure 11.11, it becomes clear that an areal system of metropolitan centers, large cities, small cities, and towns exists. Goods, services, communications, and people flow up and down the hierarchy. The few high-level metropolitan areas provide specialized functions for large regions, while the smaller cities serve

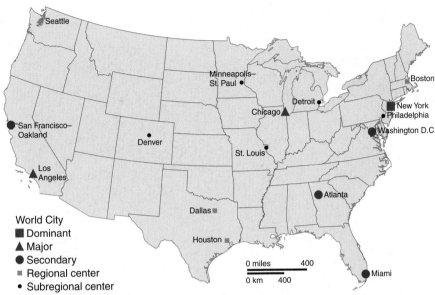

FIGURE 11.11 The global network connectedness of U.S. cities. Only the major metropolitan areas are shown. The network includes smaller urban areas (not shown) that depend on or serve the larger centers. *Source: Data from P. J. Taylor and Robert E. Lang, "U.S. Cities in the 'World City Network,'" Metropolitan Policy Program, The Brookings Institutions (Feb. 2005).*

than 40% of the total population of South Korea. Bangkok is home to more than half of the urban residents of Thailand.

The capital cities of many developing countries display this kind of overwhelming primacy. In part, their primate city pattern is a heritage of their colonial past, when economic development, colonial administration, and transportation and trade activities were concentrated at a single point. Dakar (Senegal), Luanda (Angola), and many other capital cities of African countries are examples.

In other instances, development and population growth have tended to concentrate disproportionately in a capital city whose very size attracts further development and growth. Many European countries (e.g., the United Kingdom, France, and Austria) show a primate structure, often ascribed to the former concentration of economic and political power around the royal court in a capital city that was, perhaps, also the administrative and trade center of a larger colonial empire.

Rank-Size Relationships

The development of city systems on a global scale raises the question of the organization of city systems within regions or countries. In some countries, especially those with complex economies and a long urban history, the **rank-size rule** describes the urban system. It tells us that the nth largest city of a national system of cities will be $1/n$ the size of the largest city. That is, the second-largest settlement will be half the size of the largest, the tenth-biggest will be 1/10 the size of the first ranked city, and so on. Although no national urban system exactly meets the requirement of the rank-size rule, those of Russia and the United States closely approximate it.

The rank-size ordering is less applicable to countries with developing economies and those in which the urban system is dominated by a **primate city,** one that is far more than twice the size of the second ranked city. In fact, there may be no obvious "second city" at all, for a characteristic of a primate city hierarchy is one very large city, few or no intermediate-size cities, and many subordinate smaller settlements. For example, metropolitan Seoul (with 9.8 million in 2000) contains more

smaller districts. The separate centers interact with the areas around them, but because cities of the same level provide roughly the same services, those of the same size tend not to serve each other unless they provide a specialized service, such as a major hospital or a research university. Thus, the settlements of a given level in the hierarchy are not independent but interrelated with communities of other levels in that hierarchy. Together, all centers at all levels in the hierarchy constitute an urban system.

World Cities

Standing at the top of national systems of cities are a relatively few centers that may be called **world cities.** These large urban centers are the "control and command" centers of the global economy. They are control points for international advanced producer services, including finance, advertising, banking, and law.

London, New York, and Tokyo are the dominant world cities. They contain the highest number of transnational service offices and the headquarters of multinational corporations, and they dominate commerce in their respective parts of the world. Each is directly linked to a number of other world cities. All are bound together in complex networks that control the organization and management of the global system of finance, manufacturing, and trade. They are key to the globalization of the economy. Figure 11.12 shows the links among the dominant centers and the suggested major and secondary world cities, which include Paris, Frankfurt, Hong Kong, Singapore, Milan, Toronto, Chicago, and Los Angeles. These cities are all interconnected by advanced communications systems among governments, major corporations, stock and futures exchanges, securities and commodity markets, major banks, and international organizations.

Major international corporations spur world city development and dominance. The growing size and complexity of transnational corporations dictate their need to outsource central managerial functions to specialized service firms to minimize the complexity of control over dispersed operations. Those specialized service agencies—legal, accounting, financial, and so on—in their turn need to draw on the very large pools of expertise, information, and talent available only in world cities.

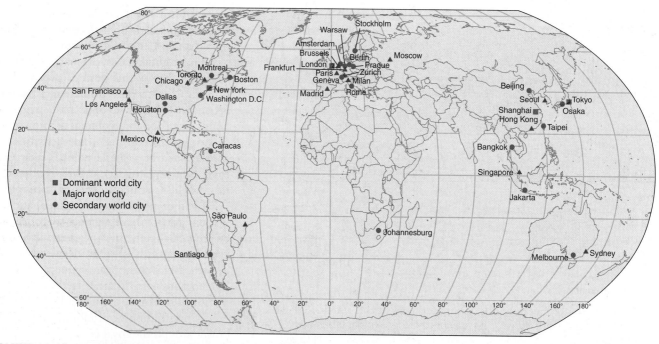

FIGURE 11.12 A classification of world cities. World cities are centers of international production, marketing, and finance. They are bound together in complex networks and all are interconnected in many different ways. *Source: Data from J. V. Beaverstock, P. J. Taylor, and R. G. Smith, "A Roster of World Cities," Cities (1999).*

INSIDE THE CITY

Urban areas have distinct physical and cultural landscapes, so an understanding of the nature of cities is incomplete without a knowledge of their internal characteristics. So far, we have explored the origins and functions of cities within hierarchical urban systems. Now we turn to the urban patterns of land use, changes in urban form, the social areas of cities, and the institutional controls that determine much of the character of an urban area. This discussion will primarily relate to cities in the United States, although most cities of the world have many of the same elements.

Patterns of Land Use

Think about a city you know well. What businesses are in the center of the town? Why are they there? Many store owners wish to locate where they can be reached easily by potential customers, as the commercial activity needs to be accessible to thrive. The central city generally is dominated by stores or administrative functions that depend on easy access for large numbers of people. Factories and residents generally locate outside the central city, as they have different needs. Factories need a convenient meeting point for their workers and their materials. Residents desire easy access to jobs, stores, and schools. Accessibility is one key to understanding land use inside the city.

A recurring pattern of land use arrangements and population densities exists within urban areas. There is a certain sameness to the way cities are internally organized, especially within one particular culture sphere, such as North America or Western Europe. The major variables shaping internal land use patterns are accessibility, a competitive market in land, and the transportation technologies available during the periods of urban growth.

The Central Business District

In the United States, the first cities grew up around pedestrian movement and pack-animal haulage. Populations were small and the cities compact. During the late 19th and early 20th centuries, cities installed mass-transit systems, which were costly but efficient. Even with their introduction, however, only land within walking distance of the mass-transit routes could be incorporated successfully into the expanding urban structure. Within the older central city, locations at the city core, called the **central business district (CBD),** had the highest accessibility and were therefore the most desirable for many functions. The central business district was located at the convergence of mass-transit lines (in European cities and large U.S. cities) or the central roads of the city (in smaller cities).

Land parcels at the city center had high value in addition to their high accessibility. Business owners who demanded the greatest accessibility for their establishments bid the most for land parcels within the CBD. The slightly less accessible CBD parcels generally became sites for tall office buildings (skyscrapers), the principal hotels, and similar land uses that helped produce the skyline of the commercial city. Public uses, such as parks and schools, were allocated land according to criteria other than ability to pay.

Land in the CBD was a scarce commodity, and its scarcity made it expensive, demanding intensive, high-density utilization. Because of its limited supply of usable land, the industrial

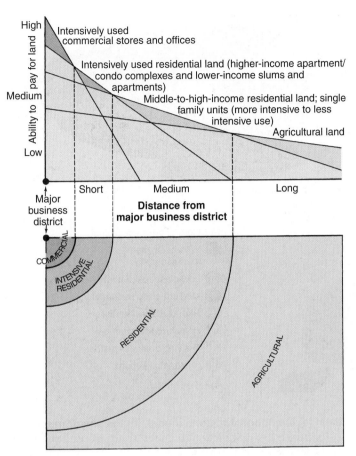

FIGURE 11.13 A generalized urban land use pattern. The model depicts the location of various land uses in an idealized urban area where the highest bidder gets the most accessible land.

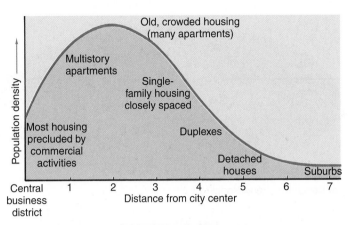

FIGURE 11.14 A generalized population density curve. As distance from the area of multistory apartment buildings increases, the population density declines.

city of the mass-transit era was compact. It was characterized by high residential and structural densities, and at its margins there was a sharp break between urban and nonurban uses. The older central cities of the northeastern United States and southeastern Canada display this pattern.

Outside the Central Business District

Outside the core area of the city, comparable but lower-order commercial aggregations developed at the outlying intersections—transfer points—of the mass-transit system. Industry controlled parcels adjacent to essential cargo routes: rail lines, waterfronts, rivers, and canals. Strings of stores, light industries, and high-density apartment structures could afford and benefit from location along high-volume transit routes. The least accessible locations within the city were left for the least-competitive users: low-density residences. A diagrammatic summary of this repetitive allocation of space among competitors for urban sites is shown in Figure 11.13.

The competitive bidding for land should yield—in theory, at least—two separate but related distance-decay patterns. Both land value and population density decrease as distance from the CBD increases. Land value declines in a distinct pattern: there is a sharp drop in land value a short distance from the *peak land value intersection,* the most accessible and

costly parcel of the central business district, and then the value declines less steeply to the margins of that built-up area. The population density pattern of the central city shows a comparable distance-decay arrangement, as suggested by Figure 11.14.

The land use regularities of the older, eastern mass-transit central cities were not fully replicated in the 20th-century urban centers of the western United States. The density and land use structures of those newer cities have been influenced more by the automobile than by mass-transit systems. They spread more readily, evolved at lower densities, and therefore display less tightly structured and standardized land use patterns than do their eastern predecessors. Even so, the patterns we have been discussing here have been recognized since the early 20th century by sociologists and geographers alike.

Models of Urban Form

Generalized models—simplified graphic summaries—of urban growth and land use patterns were proposed during the 1920s and 1930s. While such models generalize what admittedly is a tremendous degree of variation in cities, they also help us understand some regularities in urban shape. More recently, urban geographers have begun to employ models that help us better understand a decentralized city.

The common starting point of the classic models is the distinctive central business district found in every older central city. The core of this area displays intensive land use development: tall buildings, many stores and offices, and crowded streets. Framing the core is a fringe area of warehousing, transportation terminals, and light industries (as long as they require few raw materials and pollute very little). Just beyond the urban core, residential land uses begin.

The **concentric zone model** (Figure 11.15a) was developed by a sociologist, Ernest Burgess, in the 1920s. He described five zones, radiating outward from the first, the CBD. The second ring, the zone of transition, is characterized by stagnation and deterioration and contains high-density, low-income slums, rooming houses, and perhaps ethnic ghettoes. The third is a zone of workers' homes, usually smaller,

(a) Concentric Zone Model

(b) Sector Model

(c) Multiple-Nuclei Model

1. Central business district
2. Wholesale, light manufacturing
3. Low-class residential
4. Medium-class residential
5. High-class residential
6. Heavy manufacturing
7. Outlying business district
8. Residential suburb
9. Industrial

FIGURE 11.15 Three classic models of the internal structure of cities: (a) the concentric zone model, (b) the sector model, and (c) the multiple-nuclei model. *Redrawn from "The Nature of Cities" by C. D. Harris and E. L. Ullman in volume no. 242 of The Annals of the American Academy of Political and Social Science. Copyright © 1945 The American Academy of Political and Social Science, Philadelphia, PA.*

older homes on modest lots; the fourth and fifth zones are areas of middle-class and well-to-do houses and apartments.

The concentric zone model is dynamic. Each type of land use and each group tends to move outward into the next outer zone. The movement is part of a ceaseless process of invasion and succession that yields a restructured land use pattern and population segregation by income level. The development of Chicago (Figure 11.16) shows some accordance with this model.

The **sector model** (see Figure 11.15b), developed in the 1930s, focuses on transportation arterials. It states that high-rent residential areas expand outward from the city center along major transportation routes such as suburban commuter rail lines. As cities grow, this model proposes, the highest-income groups move into new homes in new neighborhoods that are located along existing transportation routes radiating outward from the center of the city. Middle-income housing clusters around the housing for the wealthy, and low-income housing occupies land adjacent to the areas of industry and associated transportation, such as freight railroad lines.

The sector model is also dynamic, as there tends to be a filtering-down process as older areas are abandoned by the outward movement of their original inhabitants, with the lowest-income populations (closest to the center of the city and farthest from the current location of the wealthy) becoming the dubious beneficiaries of the least-desirable vacated areas. The expansion of the city is radial, not zonal, as in the concentric zone model.

The accordance of the sector model with the actual pattern that developed in Calgary, Canada, is suggested in Figure 11.17.

The third model of urban land use patterns, the **multiple-nuclei model** (see Figure 11.15c), counters the central assumption of the concentric zone and sector models—that urban growth and development spread outward from a single central core. This model states that large cities develop by peripheral spread from several nodes of growth, not just one. Certain activities are limited to specific sites based on their needs: the retail district needs accessibility, whereas a port needs a waterfront location, for example. Peripheral expansion of the separate nuclei eventually leads to coalescence and the meeting of incompatible land uses along the lines of juncture. The urban land use pattern, therefore, is not regularly structured from a single center in a sequence of circles or a series of sectors but is based on separately expanding clusters of contrasting activities.

Although the culture, society, economy, and technology these three models summarized have now been superseded, the physical patterns they explained remain as vestiges and controls on the current landscape. Many cities prior to 1950 resembled the concentric zone or the sector models in that they had a clearly defined and dominant CBD, but cities grew more and more complex in the years following World War II. The multiple-nuclei model may more closely accord with urban development in the recent past, but it should be supplemented by a fourth, the peripheral model.

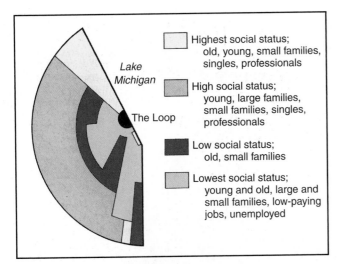

FIGURE 11.16 **A diagrammatic representation of the major social areas of the Chicago region.** The central business district is known as The Loop. *Redrawn with permission from Philip Rees, "The Factorial Ecology of Metropolitan Chicago," M. A. Thesis, University of Chicago, 1968.*

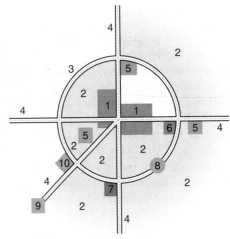

1. Central city
2. Residential area
3. Circumferential highway
4. Radial highway
5. Shopping mall
6. Industrial district
7. Office park
8. Service center
9. Airport complex
10. Combined employment and shopping center

FIGURE 11.18 **The peripheral model of urban form.** This model supplements the concentric zone, sector, and multiple-nuclei models.

FIGURE 11.17 **The land use pattern in and around Calgary, Alberta, Canada, in 1981.** Physical and cultural barriers and the evolution of urban areas over time tend to result in a sectoral pattern of similar land uses. Calgary's central business district is the focus for many of the sectors. *Revised and redrawn with permission from P. J. Smith, "Calgary: A Study in Urban Patterns,"* Economic Geography, 38, *no. 4, p. 328. Copyright © 1962 Clark University, Worcester, MA.*

The **peripheral model** takes into account the major changes in urban form that have taken place since World War II, especially suburbanization. The peripheral model supplements rather than supplants the three earlier models of urban land use patterns (Figure 11.18). It focuses on the peripheral belt that lies within the metropolitan area, but outside the central city. Functions of the peripheral belt are defined not by their relationship to the center, but to other parts of the peripheral zone. In this model, a circumferential highway outside the center city makes available large tracts of land to development. Residences are relatively homogeneous and are located in large

developments. Nodes on the peripheral belt are centers for employment or services. These include shopping malls, industrial parks, distribution and warehouse clusters, office parks, and airport clusters (including hotels, meeting facilities, and car rental agencies). Much of the life of the residents of the periphery takes place on the periphery, not in the city, as they shop for food, clothing, and services in the shopping malls, find recreation in country clubs and entertainment complexes, and find employment in the industrial or office parks.

Observers of the urban scene disagree over the direction of the U.S. peripheral city. Those who first proposed the peripheral pattern felt that the periphery of the city is not completely separate from the city; it is still a functional part of the metropolitan area. More recently, some scholars have argued that U.S. cities are developing complex suburban downtowns that compete with the CBD. They find that the metropolis is dividing into a set of increasingly self-contained urban realms, each served more or less by its own downtown. This trend relegates the influence of the CBD to the status of one of many urban centers within the metropolis. The new polycentric metropolis shows a CBD and a surrounding constellation of suburban downtowns, which are vitally important to the metropolitan, and indeed the national, economy.

The models of urban form discussed in this section aid our understanding of urban structure and development, but it must be stressed that a model is not a map and that many cities have some of the characteristics of several models.

Changes in Urban Form

The 20th century saw massive change in U.S. urban patterns. This was the consequence of the creation of a technological, physical, and institutional structure that fostered change. First, the improvement of the automobile increased its reliability, range, and convenience, freeing its owner from dependence on fixed-route public transit for access to home, work, or shopping. Then, the acceptance of a maximum 40-hour workweek in 1938 guaranteed millions of Americans the time for a commuting journey not possible when workdays of 10 or more hours were common.

After World War II, the United States witnessed a significant increase in the number of its citizens owning their own homes, from below 50% in 1945 to 60% in 1960. The government stimulated this boom by authorizing increased spending for home loans by the Federal Housing Administration (FHA) and the Veterans Administration (VA). These agencies offered much more generous terms than private bankers had before the war, when buyers had to put down large down payments (sometimes 50% or more) and repay their loans in a short time, often 10 years. The FHA and VA revolutionized homebuying, offering mortgages of up to 90% of a home's value and up to 30 years to pay off loans. The VA permitted many veterans to purchase homes with virtually no down payment.

In addition, the development of the interstate highway system made commuting long distances more feasible. During the 1970s, the interstate highway system was substantially completed and major metropolitan expressways were put in place, allowing sites 30 to 45 kilometers (20 to 30 mi) or more to be considered commuting distance between workplace and home.

The combination of new transportation flexibility, widespread homeownership, shorter workweeks, and new roads opened up vast new acreages of nonurban land to urban development. These developments changed the prevailing patterns of population growth. Over the past 60 to 70 years, U.S. cities have experienced a depopulation at the center as residents, businesses, and industry moved outward into suburbs; then a consequent decline at the city center; and recently a slight reversal of these trends as some people have returned to the core areas of many cities.

Suburbanization

Demands for housing, pent up by years of economic depression and wartime restrictions, were loosed in a flood after 1945, and a massive suburbanization altered the existing pattern of urban America. Between 1950 and 1970, the two most prominent patterns of population growth were the *metropolitanization* of people and, within metropolitan areas, their *suburbanization*. The 2000 census showed that the United States' 100 largest cities had twice as great a population growth rate in their suburbs as in the cities themselves over the previous 10 years (18% versus 9%). Nearly two-thirds of city growth occurred on the suburban edge.

Residential land uses led the rush to the suburbs. Typically, uniform but spatially discontinuous housing developments were built beyond the boundaries of most older central cities. The new design was an unfocused sprawl because it was not tied to mass-transit lines. It also represented a massive

FIGURE 11.19 A history of urban sprawl. In Chicago, as in most larger and older U.S. cities, the slow peripheral expansion recorded during the late 19th and early 20th centuries suddenly accelerated as the automobile suburbs began developing after 1945. The red line indicates the Chicago city boundaries. *Revised with permission from B. J. L. Berry,* Chicago: Transformation of an Urban System, *Ballinger Publishing Co., Cambridge, Mass. 1976, with additions from other sources.*

relocation of purchasing power to which retail merchants were quick to respond. The planned major regional shopping center became the suburban counterpart of higher-order central places and the outlying commercial districts of the central city. Smaller shopping malls and strip shopping centers gradually completed the retailing hierarchy.

Faced with a newly suburbanized labor force, industry followed the outward move, attracted as well by the economies derived from modern single-story plants with plenty of parking space for employees. Industries no longer needed to locate near railway facilities; freeways presented new opportunities for lower-cost, more-flexible truck transportation. Service industries were also attracted by the purchasing power and large, well-educated labor force now living in the suburbs, and complexes of office buildings developed, like the shopping malls, at freeway intersections and along freeway frontage roads and major connecting highways.

The major metropolitan areas rapidly expanded in area and population. Growth patterns for the Chicago area are shown in Figure 11.19. Cities grew outward, drawing populations away from the central core. Figure 11.20 illustrates population density change over time. It is a time-series graph of population density patterns for Cleveland, Ohio, over a 50-year period. The peak density was 2.8 miles from the CBD

FIGURE 11.20 Population density gradients for Cleveland, Ohio, 1940–1990. The progressive depopulation of the central core and flattening of the density gradient to the margin of the city are clearly seen, as Cleveland passed from mass-transit to automobile domination. The Cleveland pattern is consistent with conclusions drawn from other studies of urban density: density gradients tend to flatten over time, and the larger the city, the flatter the gradient. *Source: Anupa Mukhopadhyay and Ashok K. Dutt, "Population Density Gradient Changes for a Postindustrial City—Cleveland, Ohio 1940–1990," GeoJournal 34:517, no. 4, 1994. Redrawn by permission of Kluwer Academic Publishers and Ashok K. Dutt.*

in 1940, but in 1990 it was 5.8 miles. As the city expanded, density close to the center decreased. By 2000, however, this pattern had reversed as affluent younger people opted to live in the most accessible locations.

By the 1990s, a new urban America had emerged on the perimeters of the major metropolitan areas. With increasing sprawl and the rising costs implicit in the ever-greater spatial separation of the functional segments of the fringe, peripheral expansion slowed, the supply of developable land was reduced, and the intensity of land development grew. No longer dependent on the central city, the suburbs were reborn as vast, collectively self-sufficient outer cities, marked by landscapes of industrial parks, skyscraper office parks, massive retailing complexes, and a proliferation of gated communities and apartment complexes.

The new suburbia began to rival the older central business district in size and complexity. Collectively, the new centers surpassed the central cities as generators of employment and income. Together with the older CBDs, the suburbs perform the tertiary and quaternary services that mark the postindustrial metropolis. During the 1980s, more office space was created in the suburbs than in the central cities of America. Tysons Corner, Virginia (between Arlington and Reston), for example, became the ninth-largest central business district in the United States. Regional and national headquarters of leading corporations, banking, professional services of all kinds, major hotel complexes, and recreational centers became parts of the new outer cities, sometimes called **edge cities**: large nodes of office and retail activities at the margin of an urban area.

Edge cities now exist in all regions of urbanized North America. The South Coast Metro Center in Orange County, California; the City Post Oak–Galleria center on Houston's west side; King of Prussia and the Route 202 corridor northwest of Philadelphia; the Meadowlands, New Jersey, west of New York City; and Schaumburg, Illinois, in the western Chicago suburbs are a few examples of the new urban forms. There is even a suburb of Atlanta named Periphery Center.

In recent years, suburban areas have expanded to the point where metropolitan areas are coalescing. The Boston-to-Washington corridor, often called a **megalopolis**, is a continuously built-up region with many new centers that compete with the business districts of Boston, Providence, New York, Philadelphia, Baltimore, and Washington, D.C. A further analysis of the northeastern U.S. urban corridor appears in "Megalopolis" in Chapter 13.

Decline of the Central City

Changing patterns of accessibility have had a tremendous effect on the vitality of the central business district and of the inner city surrounding it. The CBD once enjoyed high levels of accessibility, at the center of streetcar and intercity rail lines. With the coming of the interstate highway system and widespread air transportation, central cities are increasingly viewed as overly congested and relatively inaccessible. The dynamic that provided economic advantages to central cities now works to their detriment. Many jobs have moved from the central city to the urban periphery, along with much of the prosperous population.

The upwardly mobile residents of the city—younger, wealthier, and better educated—took advantage of the automobile and the freeway to leave the central city. The poorer, older, least-advantaged urbanites were left behind (Figure 11.21). The central cities and suburbs became increasingly differentiated. Large areas within the cities now contain only the poor and minority groups, a population barely able to pay the rising costs of social services that their numbers, neighborhoods, and condition require.

The services needed to support the poor include welfare payments, social workers, police and fire protection, health delivery systems, and subsidized housing. Central cities, by themselves, are unable to raise the taxes needed to support such an array and intensity of social services because they have lost the tax bases represented by suburbanized commerce, industry, and social services their far-flung populations require. Schools remain unbuilt and underfunded; water supplies are increasingly difficult and expensive to obtain; open-space requirements for parkland are ignored; street and highway improvements and repairs are inadequate even as demand for them increases. Each additional unit of unrestricted growth costs the municipality more than the additional development generates in tax revenue.

Increasingly, central cities and metropolitan areas of both the eastern and the western United States are seeking to restrain rather than encourage physical growth. Portland, Oregon, drew a "do not pass" line around itself in the late 1970s, prohibiting urban conversion of surrounding forests, farmlands, and open space. Rather than losing people and functions, it has added both while preserving and increasing parklands and other urban amenities.

Other cities, metropolitan areas, and states are also beginning to resist and restrict urban expansion. "Smart growth" programs have been adopted by Colorado, Delaware, Minnesota, and Washington. These programs encourage governments and private developers to build a range of housing types, create walkable neighborhoods, mix land uses, preserve open space, provide a variety of transportation options, and direct support toward existing communities rather than continuing city sprawl. Developers generally find it easier to build large developments on new land rather than filling in or rehabilitating city neighborhoods. In both the West and the East, U.S. cities are beginning to tighten controls on unrestricted growth, but private sector resistance to controlling sprawl is still an important factor.

Social Areas of Cities

The larger and more economically and socially complex cities are, the stronger is the tendency for city residents to segregate themselves into groups on the basis of *social status, family status,* and *ethnicity.* In a large metropolitan region with a diversified population, this territorial behavior may be a defense against the unknown or unwanted; a desire to be among similar kinds of people; a response to income constraints; or a result of social and institutional barriers. Most people feel more at ease when they are near those with whom they can easily identify. In cities, people tend to group according to income or occupation (social status), stage in the life cycle (family status), and language or race (ethnic characteristics) (see "Birds of a Feather," p. 381).

Many of these groupings are fostered by the size and value of available housing. Land developers, especially in cities, produce homes of similar quality in specific areas. Of course, as time elapses, there is a change in the quality of houses. Land uses may change and new groups may replace old groups, leading to the evolution of new neighborhoods of similar social characteristics.

Family Status

As the distance from the city center increases, the average age of the head of the household declines, the size of the family increases, or both. Wealthy older people whose children do not live with them and young professionals without families tend to live close to the city center. The young families seek space

FIGURE 11.25 The social geography of American and Canadian urban areas. *Redrawn with permission from Robert A. Murdie, "Factorial Ecology of Metropolitan Toronto," Research Paper 116, Department of Geography Research Series, University of Chicago, 1969.*

for child rearing, and older people covet more access to the cultural and business life of the city. Where inner-city life is unpleasant, there is a tendency for older people to migrate to the suburbs or to retirement communities.

Within lower-status populations, the same pattern tends to emerge. Transients and single people are housed in the inner city, and families, if they find it possible or desirable, live farther from the center. The arrangement that emerges is a concentric-circle patterning according to family status (Figure 11.25). In general, inner-city areas house older people and outer-city areas house younger people.

As the structure of American cities has changed over the past half-century, more and more jobs have moved from central cities to the suburbs. This has had long-reaching effects on those living in the central cities, where work opportunities are now more limited.

Many large urban areas, such as Detroit, have no mass transit besides a metropolitan bus service—and many more have minimal systems providing meager access to only certain parts of a city. In Detroit, it can take 3 hours and 3 buses to travel from the downtown to a job in the suburbs. This particularly affects those without the means to own or maintain an automobile, especially women and minorities. Recent studies of poverty have shown the following:

- The central cities of the United States have more households headed by women than by men.
- Women constitute the majority of poor people.

Birds of a Feather . . . , or Who Are the People in Your Neighborhood?

How does a McDonald's or Burger King decide which $1 menu items to promote at a certain site, or whether it can profitably offer salads at that franchise? Are there enough families with children to justify building a play area? On what basis does a Starbucks or an Easy Lube determine in what neighborhood to open a new store?

Many businesses, large and small, base their decisions on a marketing analysis system developed by the San Diego-based Claritas, Inc. The system is based on census data and uses zip codes to categorize Americans by where they live, work, and spend their money. People tend to cluster together in roughly homogeneous areas based on social status, family status, ethnicity, and other cultural markers. People in any one cluster tend to have or adopt similar lifestyles—as Claritas puts it, "You are where you live." Residents of a cluster read the same kinds of books, subscribe to the same magazines and newspapers, and watch the same movies and television shows. They exhibit similar preferences in food and drink, clothes, furniture, cars, and all the other goods a consumer society offers.

Claritas uses a number of variables to classify areas of the country: household density per square mile; area type (city, suburb, town, farm); degree of ethnic diversity; family type (married with children, single, and so on); predominant age group; extent of education; type of employment; housing type; and neighborhood quality. After analyzing the data, the firm characterizes each zip code as belonging to from 1 to 5 of 67 possible neighborhood lifestyle categories. Claritas has given catchy names to these clusters, ranging from "Blueblood Estates" (elite, super-rich families) to "Golden Ponds" (older singles in small towns, who belong to veterans clubs and watch *The Price Is Right*) to "Shotguns and Pickups" (young rural families who go to auto races and drive Dodge Rams). Some of the others are "Winner's Circle" (executive suburban families); "Pools and Patios" (established empty-nesters); "American Dreams" (children of immigrants in multilingual neighborhoods); and "Young Digerati" (tech-savvy college graduates living on the urban fringe).

The company realizes that the designations don't define the tastes and habits of every person in a community, but they do identify the behavior that most people are apt to follow. In the zip code area for "Boomtown Singles" (college-town singles younger than 45), for example, residents are likely to go snowboarding, read *The Source* magazine, watch *Futurama* (a Matt Groening television show), and drive a Nissan Sentra. But in the zip code area for "Money and Brains" (older, sophisticated townhouse couples predominantly employed in white-collar jobs), residents are most likely to support the arts, shop at Nordstrom's, read the Sunday newspaper, watch *Wall Street Week* on TV, and drive a Mercedes-Benz E-class.

If you want to know how Claritas marketing analysts have categorized your neighborhood, go to www.claritas.com/MyBestSegments/Default.jsp and enter your zip code.

- The vast majority of poor people live in central cities.
- Downtowns also house more elderly, among whom women predominate.
- Women depend on public transportation more than men do.
- Minorities are more likely than whites to use public transportation.

Access to jobs is determined by the location of the job, the location of other necessary facilities such as child-care facilities, and the constraints on nonwork hours. Such constraints include responsibilities to other family members and an ability to respond quickly in case of an emergency. Rents in the suburbs are unaffordable to those in low-wage positions, making long commutes common for those who are least able to afford them.

Social Status

The social status of an individual or a family is determined by income, education, occupation, and home value. In the United States, high income, a college education, a professional or managerial position, and high home value constitute high status. High home value can mean an expensive rented apartment or a large house with extensive grounds.

A good housing indicator of social status is people per room. A low number of people per room tends to indicate high status. Low status characterizes people with low-income jobs living in low-value housing. There are many levels of status, and people tend to filter out into neighborhoods where most of the heads of households are of similar rank.

Social-status patterning agrees with the sector model. In most cities, people of similar social status are grouped in sectors that fan out from the innermost urban residential areas (Figure 11.25). The pattern in Chicago was illustrated in Figure 11.16. If the number of people within a given social group increases, they tend to move away from the central city along an arterial connecting them with the old neighborhood. Major transport routes leading to the city center are the usual migration routes out from the center.

Today, social-status divisions are often perpetuated between separate municipalities, which may differ greatly in relative income. Many residential developments are also income segregated, because the houses are of similar value. To preserve the upscale nature of a development and protect land values, self-governing community associations enact conditions and restrictions (see "The Gated Community," p. 383). Pervasive and detailed, these conditions specify such things as the size, construction, and color of walls and fences; the size and permitted uses of rear and side yards; and the design of lights and mailboxes. Some go so far as to tell residents what trees they may plant, what pets they may raise, and where they may park their boats or recreational vehicles.

FIGURE 11.26 Racial/ethnic patterns in Los Angeles, 2000. Although Los Angeles County has an extremely diverse population, people tend to cluster in distinct neighborhoods by race and ethnicity. Between 1990 and 2000, the Hispanic population of Los Angeles County increased from 38% to 45%, and the proportion of Asians grew from 10% to 12%. The proportion of blacks in the population decreased from 11% to 9%, while the proportion of whites declined from 41% to 31%. *Source: U.S. Census Bureau as published in* The New York Times, *March 30, 2001, p. A16.*

Ethnicity

For some groups, ethnicity is a more-important residential location determinant than social or family status. Areas of homogeneous ethnic identification appear in the social geography of cities as separate clusters or nuclei reminiscent of the multiple-nuclei concept of urban structure. For some ethnic groups, cultural segregation is both sought and vigorously defended, even in the face of pressures for neighborhood change exerted by potential competitors for housing space. The durability of "Little Italys" and "Chinatowns" and of Polish, Greek, Armenian, and other ethnic neighborhoods in many American cities is evidence of the persistence of self-maintained segregation.

Certain ethnic or racial groups, especially blacks, have been segregated in nuclear communities. Every city in the United States has one or more black areas that, in many respects, may be considered cities within a city. Figure 11.26 illustrates the concentration of blacks, Hispanics, and other racial/ethnic groups in

distinct neighborhoods in Los Angeles. The social and economic barriers to movement outside the area have always been high. In many American cities, the poorest residents are the blacks, who are often relegated to the lowest-quality housing in the least-desirable areas of the city. Similar restrictions have been placed on Hispanics and other non-English-speaking minorities.

Institutional Controls

The governments—local and national—of most Western urbanized societies have instituted innumerable laws to control all aspects of urban life, including the rules for using streets, the provision of sanitary services, and the use of land. In this section, we touch only upon land use.

Institutional and governmental controls have strongly influenced the land use arrangements and growth patterns of most cities in the world. Cities have adopted land use plans and enacted subdivision control regulations and zoning

The Gated Community

Approximately one in six Americans—some 48 million people—lives in a *master-planned community*. Particularly characteristic of the fastest-growing parts of the country, most of these communities are in the South and West, but they occur everywhere. Master-planned communities date back to the 1960s, when Irvine, California, and Sun City, Arizona, were built.

A subset of the master-planned community is the **gated community,** a fenced or walled residential area where access is limited to designated individuals. More than 9 million Americans live in these middle- and high-income developments. Entry to these communities within communities is restricted; gates are manned by security guards or are accessible only by computer key card or telephone. Some of the communities hire private security forces to patrol the streets. Surveillance systems monitor common recreational areas, such as community swimming pools, tennis courts, and health clubs. Houses are commonly equipped with security systems. Troubled by the high crime rates, drug abuse, gangs, and drive-by shootings that characterize many urban areas, people seek safety within their walled enclaves.

Gated and sheltered communities are not just an American phenomenon but are increasingly found in all parts of the world. More and more guarded residential enclaves have been sited in such stable Western European states as Spain, Portugal, and France. Developers in Indian cities have also used gated communities to attract wealthy residents. Trying to appeal to Indians returning to that country after years in areas such as the Boston high-tech corridor and Silicon Valley, developers have built enclaves, with names such as Regent Place and Golden

Gated community. *Courtesy of Arthur Getis.*

Enclave, that boast two-story houses and barbecues in the backyards.

Elsewhere, as in Argentina or Venezuela in South America or Lebanon in the Middle East—with little urban planning, unstable city administration, and inadequate police protection—not only rich but also middle-class citizens are opting for protected residential districts. In China and Russia, the sudden boom in private and guarded settlements reflects in part a new form of postcommunist social class distinction, while in South Africa gated communities serve as effective racial barriers.

---

ordinances to realize those plans. They have adopted building, health, and safety codes to assure legally acceptable urban development and maintenance. All such controls are based on broad applications of the police powers of municipalities and their rights to assure public health, safety, and well-being even when private-property rights are infringed.

These nonmarket controls on land use are designed to minimize incompatibilities (residences adjacent to heavy industry, for example) and provide for the creation in appropriate locations of public uses (the transportation system, waste disposal, government buildings, prisons, and parks) and private uses (colleges, shopping centers, and housing) needed for and conducive to a balanced, orderly community. In theory, such careful planning should preclude the emergence of slums, so often the result of undesirable adjacent uses, and should stabilize neighborhoods by reducing market-induced pressures for land use change.

In the United States, zoning ordinances and subdivision regulations have been used to exclude "undesirable" uses—apartments, special housing for the aged, low-income housing, half-way homes—from upper-income areas. Bitter court battles have been waged over "exclusionary" zoning practices: while proponents contend that the undesirable uses will harm the city and, more importantly, property values, opponents argue that such uses are important to the city as a whole. In

recent years, some newly incorporated suburbs have sought to reduce the costs of growth—such as developing infrastructure and building schools and playgrounds—by zoning out housing that would bring in children.

In most of Asia, there is no zoning, and it is quite common to have small-scale industrial activities operating in residential areas. Even in Japan, a house may contain several people doing piecework for a local industry. In both Europe and Japan, neighborhoods have been built and rebuilt gradually over time, and it is usual to have a wide variety of building types from various eras mixed together on the same street. In the United States and Canada, such mixing is much rarer and is often viewed as a temporary condition as areas are in transition toward total redevelopment. Perhaps the only exception to this in a large city is Houston, Texas, which has no zoning regulations.

GLOBAL URBAN DIVERSITY

The structure, form, and functions of cities differ between regions, reflecting diverse heritages and economies. Much of the discussion in this chapter has dwelt on models of the city in the United States. But the models and descriptions of the U.S. city do not generally apply to cities in other parts of the world. Those cities have developed different functional and structural patterns, some so radically different from the models we have explored that we would find them unfamiliar and uncharted landscapes, indeed. The city is universal; its characteristics are cultural and regional.

Western European Cities

Although each is unique historically and culturally, Western European cities as a group share certain common features. They have a much more compact form and occupy less total area than American cities of comparable population, and most of their residents are apartment dwellers. Residential streets of the older sections tend to be narrow, and front, side, or rear yards or gardens are rare.

European cities also enjoy a long historical tradition. A generally common heritage of medieval origins, Renaissance restructurings, and industrial-period growth has given the cities of Western Europe distinct features. Despite wartime destructions and postwar redevelopments, many still bear the impress of past occupants and technologies, even as far back as Roman times. An irregular system of narrow streets may be retained from the random street pattern developed in medieval times of pedestrian and pack-animal movement. Main streets radiating from the city center and cut by circumferential "ring roads" tell us the location of high roads leading into town through the gates in city walls now gone and replaced by circular boulevards. Broad thoroughfares, public parks, and plazas mark Renaissance ideals of city beautification and the aesthetic need for processional avenues and promenades.

European cities were developed for pedestrians and still retain the compactness appropriate to walking distances. The sprawl of American peripheral or suburban zones is generally absent. At the same time, compactness and high density do not mean skyscraper skylines. Much of urban Europe predates the steel-frame building and the elevator. City skylines tend to be low, three to five stories in height, sometimes (as in central Paris) held down by building ordinance or by prohibitions against private structures exceeding the height of a major public building, often the central cathedral (Figure 11.27). Where those restrictions have been relaxed, however, tall office buildings have been erected.

Compactness, high densities, and apartment dwelling encouraged the development and continued importance of public transportation, including well-developed subway systems. The private automobile has become much more common of late, though most central-city areas have not yet been significantly restructured with wider streets and parking facilities to accommodate it. For instance, private autos are charged a high fee to enter the central business district of London. The automobile is not the universal need in Europe that it has become in American cities, as home and work are generally more closely spaced. Even though most European cities have core areas that tend to be stable in population and attract, rather than repel, the successful middle class and the upwardly mobile, they are also affected by the processes of decentralization. Many residents choose to live in suburban locations as car ownership and use become more commonplace, a pattern also seen in Canada (see "The Canadian City," p. 385).

FIGURE 11.27 Even in their central areas, many European urban centers show a low profile, like that of Budapest, seen here. Although taller buildings—20, 30, and even 50 or more stories in height—have become more common in major urban areas since World War II, they are not the universal mark of the central business districts they have become in the United States, nor the generally welcomed symbols of progress and pride. © *Arthur Getis.*

The old city fortifications may mark the boundary between the core and the surrounding transitional zone of substandard housing, 19th-century industry, and recent immigrants. European governments used the strategy of grouping industrial developments and working-class homes in suburban areas outside the city core; these have been the areas in which immigrants, often from North Africa and Turkey, have found housing. Some of these areas have been neglected and suffer decline, especially when unemployment rates are high.

Eastern European Cities

Most of the cities that were once part of the communist world are located in Eastern Europe and the former European republics of the Soviet Union. The postcommunist city shares many of the traditions and practices of Western European cities, but it differs from them in the centrally administered planning principles that were, in the communist period (1945–1990), designed to shape and control both new and older settlements. The governments' goals were, first, to limit city size to avoid metropolitan sprawl; second, to ensure an internal structure of neighborhood equality and self-sufficiency; and third, to segregate land uses. The planned communist city fully achieved none of these objectives, but by attempting them it has emerged as a distinctive urban form.

The postcommunist city is compact, with relatively high building and population densities reflecting the nearly universal apartment dwelling, and with a sharp break between urban and rural land uses on its periphery. The postcommunist city depends nearly exclusively on public transportation.

During the communist period, the Eastern European city differed from its Western counterpart in its purely governmental, rather than market, control of land use and functional

The Canadian City

In 1900, only 37% of Canadians lived in urban areas; in 2005, some 81% of the population was urban. Cities in the wealthiest provinces of the country, such as Alberta and Ontario, have seen population growth rates above 30% in the last 10 years; poorer regions have seen a decline similar to that of declining U.S. industrial cities.

While urban forms are similar, there are some subtle but significant differences between Canadian and U.S. cities. The Canadian city, for example, is more compact than its U.S. counterpart of equal population size, with a higher density of buildings and people and a lesser degree of suburbanization of populations and functions.

Space-saving and multiple-family housing units are more the rule in Canada, so a similar population size is housed on a smaller land area with much higher densities within the central area of cities. The Canadian city is better served by and more dependent on mass transportation than is the U.S. city. Because Canadian metropolitan areas have only one-fourth as many miles of expressway lanes per capita as U.S. metropolitan areas, suburbanization is less extensive north of the border than south of it. As in the United States, some Canadian suburbs, such as those of Calgary, are contiguous to the city itself; others, such as those surrounding Vancouver and Toronto, are detached.

The differences are cultural as well. Cities in both countries are ethnically diverse (Canadian communities, in fact, have a higher proportion of foreign born), but U.S. central cities exhibit far greater internal distinctions in race, income, and social status and more pronounced contrasts between central-city and suburban residents. That is, there has been much less "flight to the suburbs" by middle-income Canadians. As a result, the Canadian city shows greater social stability, higher per capita average income, more retention of shopping facilities, and more employment opportunities and urban amenities than its U.S. central-city counterpart. In particular, it does not have the rivalry from the well-defined, competitive, edge cities of suburbia that fragment U.S. metropolitan complexes.

The central and outlying central business districts of Toronto, easily visible in this photo, are still rooted firmly by mass-transit convergence and mass-transit usage. On average, Canadian metropolitan areas are almost twice as densely populated as metropolitan areas in the United States. On a per capita basis, Canadian urbanites are two and a half times more dependent on public transportation than are American city dwellers. That reliance gives form, structure, and coherence to the Canadian central city, qualities now irretrievably lost in the sprawled and fragmented U.S. metropolis. © Getty RF.

patterns. This control dictated that the central area of cities should be reserved for public use, not occupied by retail establishments or office buildings on the Western, capitalist model. Eastern European governments preferred a large central square ringed by administrative and cultural buildings with space nearby for a large recreational and commemorative park. They emphasized industrial development of cities and marginalized consumer services. Residential areas were expected to be largely self-contained in the provision of low-order goods and services, minimizing the need for a journey to centralized shopping locations.

Residential areas are made up of *microdistricts*, assemblages of uniform apartment blocks housing perhaps 10,000 to 15,000 people, surrounded by broad boulevards, and containing centrally sited nursery and grade schools, grocery and department stores, theaters, clinics, and similar neighborhood necessities and amenities (Figure 11.28). Plans called for the effective separation of residential quarters from industrial districts by landscaped buffer zones, but in practice many microdistricts were built by factories for their own workers and were located immediately adjacent to the workplace. Because microdistricts were most easily and rapidly constructed on open land at the margins of expanding cities, high residential densities have been carried to the outskirts of town.

This pattern will change in the decades to come, as capitalist principles of land allocation are adopted. Now that private interests can own land and buildings, the urban areas in postcommunist Eastern Europe may take on the basic form of the Western European city. The weighting of the economy is changing, with less emphasis on industry and more on the

FIGURE 11.28 This scene from Bratislava, Slovakia, shows "superblocks" of self-contained apartment housing microdistricts that contain their own shopping areas, schools, and other facilities. © Getty RF.

service sector. The socioeconomic divisions in cities are increasing as the newly rich can afford spacious, privately owned apartments and newly constructed single-family homes, while housing shortages for the less well off have become acute.

Rapidly Growing Cities in the Developing World

The fastest-growing cities, and the fastest-growing urban populations, are found in the developing world (Figure 11.29). Industrialization has come to most of them only recently.

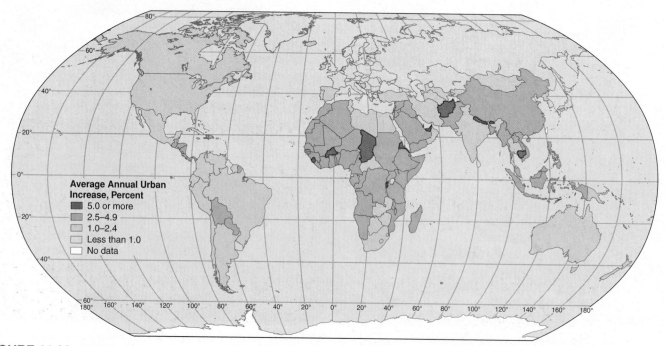

FIGURE 11.29 Average annual urban population growth rates, 2000–2005. In general, developing countries show the highest percentage increases in their urban populations, and the already highly urbanized and industrialized countries have the lowest—less than 1% per year in most of Europe. Demographers predict that population increase in cities in developing countries will be the distinguishing demographic trend of the 21st century, with the most-explosive growth expected in Africa and Asia. An urban growth rate of 5% means that a city's population will double in just 14 years. *Source: Data from United Nations Population Division.*

Modern technologies in transportation and public facilities are sparsely available, and the structures of cities and the cultures of their inhabitants are far different from the urban world familiar to North Americans. The developing world is vast in extent and diverse in its physical and cultural landscapes.

The backgrounds, histories, and current economies and administrations of developing-world cities vary so greatly that it is impossible to generalize about their internal structure. Some are ancient, having been established centuries before the more-developed cities of Europe and North America. Some are still preindustrial, with only a modest central commercial core; they lack industrial districts, public transportation, or any meaningful degree of land use separation. Others, though increasingly Western in form, are only beginning to industrialize.

Despite the variety of urban forms found in such diverse regions as Latin America, Africa, the Middle East, and Asia, we can identify some features common to most of them. First, most of what are currently categorized as developing countries have a colonial legacy, and several major cities were established principally to serve the needs of the colonizing country. The second aspect is that urban primacy and the tremendous growth these cities are generally experiencing as their societies industrialize have left many of these cities with inadequate facilities and no way to keep up with population growth. Third, most cities in developing countries are now characterized by neighborhoods hastily built by new migrants, away from city services, and often occupying land illegally. Such squatter settlements are a large and growing component of these cities and reflect both the city's relative opportunity and poverty. Finally, in many cases, the government has responded with greater planning, sometimes going so far as to move the national capital away from the overcrowded primate city to a new location or to create entirely new cities to house industrial or transport centers.

Colonial and Noncolonial Antecedents

Cities in developing countries originated for varied reasons and continue to serve several functions based on their position as market, production, government, or religious centers. Their legacy and purpose influence their urban form.

Many cities in developing countries are products of colonialism, established as ports or outposts of administration and exploitation, built by Europeans on a Western model. For example, the British built Kolkata (Calcutta), New Delhi, and Mumbai (Bombay) in India and Nairobi and Harare in Africa. The French developed Hanoi and Ho Chi Minh City (Saigon) in Vietnam, Dakar in Senegal, and Bangui in the Central African Republic. The Dutch used Jakarta as their main outpost, Belgium had Kinshasa (formerly Leopoldville) in what is now the Democratic Republic of the Congo, and the Portuguese founded a number of cities in Angola and Mozambique. Colonialists controlled the economies of the regions from these urban centers.

Urban structure is a function not just of the time when a city was founded, or of who the founder was, but also of the role a city plays in its own cultural milieu. Land use patterns in capital cities reflect the centralization of government functions and the concentration of wealth and power in a single city of a country (Figure 11.30a). The physical layout of a religious center, or sacred city, is conditioned by the religion it serves, whether it is Hinduism, Buddhism, Islam, Christianity, or another faith. Typically, a monumental structure—such as a temple, mosque, or cathedral—and associated buildings rather than government offices occupy the city center (Figure 11.30b). Traditional market centers for a wide area (Timbuktu in Mali and Lahore in Pakistan) or cultural capitals (Addis Ababa in Ethiopia and Cuzco in Peru) have land use patterns that reflect their special functions. Likewise,

(a)

(b)

FIGURE 11.30 Developing-world cities. Compare the monumental government buildings in **(a)** the capital city of Brasília, Brazil, with **(b)** a state capital, Guanajuato, Mexico, which is dominated by religious structures. *(a) © Julia Waterlow/Corbis Images; (b) © Jose Fuste Raga/Corbis Images.*

FIGURE 11.31 **High-rise buildings in São Paulo, Brazil.** Contrast this photo with that of *favelas* in Rio de Janeiro in Figure 11.33. © *Yann Arthus-Bertrand/ Corbis Images.*

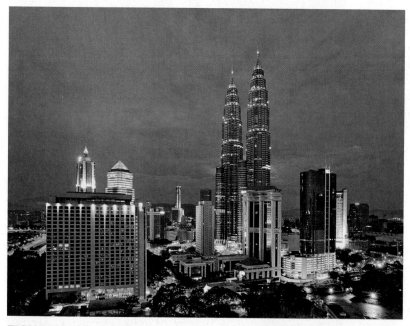

FIGURE 11.32 **The Petronas Twin Towers in Kuala Lumpur, Malaysia.** © *Getty RF.*

Urban Primacy and Rapid Growth

The developing countries have experienced disproportionate population concentrations in their national and regional capitals. Few developing countries have mature, functionally complex small- and medium-size centers. The primate city dominates their urban systems. More than a quarter of all Nicaraguans live in Managua, and Libreville contains one-third of the population of Gabon.

Many cities in developing countries with rapidly growing economies have a vibrant and modern city center (Figure 11.31). Such districts contain amenities that could be found in many cosmopolitan centers and are the places where the wealthiest members of society work and often live. This is also the part of the city that businesspeople, officials, tourists, and other visitors are most likely to see. Some cities have poured enormous efforts into these city centers: for example, the Petronas Towers in Kuala Lumpur, Malaysia, rank among the tallest buildings in the world and were completed in 1998 after 6 years of planning and construction (Figure 11.32).

However, the presence of gleaming downtowns cannot disguise the fact that most of these cities simply cannot keep pace with the massive growth they are experiencing. The United States and other Western nations are about 76% urban; developing nations are about 40% urban. That statistic is changing rapidly, as it is expected that 60% of the world population will be urban by 2030, with most of that urban growth occurring in developing countries. Many cities in Latin America, Africa, and Asia are adding population at terrific rates: in India, rural-to-urban migration is proceeding at such a pace that observers predict that 31 villagers will continue to arrive in an Indian city every minute over the next 43 years—700 million people altogether. They leave their villages to become their family breadwinners; they will become the cities' underclass, driving taxis, parking cars, or selling tea on street corners.

Lagos, Nigeria, is the second most populous city in Africa, following Cairo, Egypt. It has a current population of nearly 10 million and a growth rate between 6% and 8% yearly, which means it is growing 10 times faster than New York or Los Angeles. It adds 600,000 people each year, or 1644 daily. Although most of the population of Lagos has access to electricity, only 65% of households are connected to a water source and only 2% are connected to a sewage or telephone system. Much of the city's human waste is disposed of through open ditches that discharge onto the city's waterfront.

Nigeria and other developing countries are experiencing urban growth that is spurred by rural-to-urban migration. In

port cities such as Dubai (UAE), Haifa (Israel), and Shanghai (China) have a land use structure different from that of an industrial or mining center such as Johannesburg (South Africa). Adding to the complexity are the facts that cities with a long history reflect the changes wrought by successive rulers and/or colonial powers and that as some of the megacities in the developing world have grown, they have engulfed nearby towns and cities.

2005, China had 114 to 150 million rural-to-urban migrants, at least 25 times the number of Irish immigrants to the United States from 1820 to 1930. The government allows such migration to promote cheap factory and construction labor and its long-term goal of turning its mostly rural economy into an urban economy.

Traffic in these rapidly growing cities is almost always a problem. Most people do not own cars and must rely on public transportation. Where the public transport system is limited, the result has been an overcrowded city centered on a single major business district in the old tradition. In Lagos, it takes an average of 2 to 3 hours to travel 10 to 20 kilometers (6–12 mi), as there are only three bridges connecting the city's four islands to the mainland. In cities with expanded automobile use, congestion and air pollution have become severe. Mexico City and Bangkok are especially plagued by traffic-choked streets and bad air.

For those who are well off, living in many of these cities can present a series of challenges. Unlike residents of cities in more-developed countries, they cannot take urban planning, a stable city administration, and adequate protection for granted.

Squatter Settlements

The developing countries have experienced massive in-migrations from rural areas as vast numbers of low-income residents have migrated to cities with the hope of finding jobs and improving their socioeconomic condition. That hope is rarely realized because the cities already have populations greater than their formal functions and employment bases can support. In all of them, large numbers of people support themselves in the "informal" sector—as food vendors, peddlers of cigarettes or trinkets, streetside barbers or tailors, errand runners, or package carriers—outside the usual forms of wage labor.

Most of the new urbanites have little choice but to pack themselves into shantytowns and squatter settlements on the fringes of the city, isolated from sanitary facilities, public utilities, and job opportunities found only at the center. In some cities, one-third to two-thirds of the population live in shantytowns, often in defiance of the law.

Impoverished squatter districts exist around most major cities in Africa, Asia, and Latin America (Figure 11.33). In the vignette that opened this chapter, you read that one-half million people are estimated to live in Cairo's Northern and Southern Cemeteries. In the sprawling slum district of Nairobi, Kenya, called Mathare Valley, a quarter-million people are squeezed into 15 square kilometers (6 sq mi) with little or no access to public services such as water, sewers and drains, paved roads, and garbage removal. Similar shantytowns and squatter settlements house approximately one-fourth of the population of such Asian cities as Bangkok (Thailand), Kuala Lumpur (Malaysia), and Jakarta (Indonesia). The percentage is even higher in a number of Indian cities, including Chennai

FIGURE 11.33 A *favela*, or shantytown, in Rio de Janeiro, Brazil. Where states or municipalities provide little or no housing for the poor, people create their own. The roughly 750 favelas spread throughout Rio house a significant percentage of the city's population. In recent years, the city has extended basic services (postal addresses, schools, electricity, and running water) to many favelas, and residents have replaced shacks made of cardboard and scrap wood with more permanent brick and cinderblock structures, as a comparison of this photograph with Figure 6.27 reveals. *Courtesy of Arthur Getis.*

(Madras) and Kolkata (Calcutta). Crumbling tenements house additional tens of thousands, many of whom are eventually forced into shantytowns by the conversion of their residences into commercial property or high-income apartments. The Haitian earthquake of 2010 was especially devastating due to the large number of poorly constructed shacks in Port-au-Prince's squatter settlements.

No more than 20% of new urban housing in developing countries is produced by the formal housing sector; the rest develops informally, ignoring building codes, zoning restrictions, property rights, and infrastructure standards. Informal settlements house varying percentages of these populations, but for low-income developing countries as a whole during the 1980s and 1990s, only one formal housing unit was added for every nine new households—70% to 90% of all new households found shelter in shanties or slums. Peripheral squatter settlements, though densely built, may provide adequate household space and even water, sewers, and defined traffic lanes through the efforts of the residents. More often, however, overcrowding transforms these settlements into vast zones of disease and squalor subject to constant danger from landslides, fire, and flooding. The informality and often illegality of the squatter housing solution means that those who improvise and build their own shelters lack registration and recognized ownership of their homes or the land on which they stand. Without such legal documentation, no capital accumulation based on housing assets is possible, and no collateral for home improvement loans or other purposes is created.

Planned Cities

Some capital cities have been relocated outside the core regions of their countries, either to achieve the presumed advantages of centrality or to encourage more-uniform national development; examples include Islamabad (Pakistan), Ankara (Turkey), Brasília (Brazil), and Abuja (Nigeria) (see Chapter 9, p. 284). A number of developing countries have also created or are currently building new cities that are intended to draw population away from overgrown metropolises and/or to house industrial or transport centers.

The huge numbers of rural-to-urban migrants in China have strained its cities' capability to house them all. In Shanghai, the demand for housing has spawned hundreds of new apartment developments of multiple skyscrapers with names such as Rich Gate and Home of the Tycoons. The city has more than 4000 buildings 18 stories high or taller, far more than New York, and new satellite towns are planned and established in a short time. An hour north of Beijing is Sun City, a gated community with California-style houses; connected to Beijing by two six-lane superhighways, the area is scheduled for rapid development. Urban populations are expected to grow exponentially, so planning for new developments and towns in China continues apace.

Another Asian city, Bangkok, Thailand, is one of the most densely populated cities in the world, with an estimated population of some 10 million in the metropolitan area. It is a primate city; Thailand's second-largest city, Chiang Mai, has a population of less than half a million. In recent years, Bangkok has become known less for its palaces and temples than for its traffic-choked arteries, which severely impede travel by car or bus. In 2006, Thailand opened Suvarnabhumi, a major airport located about an hour outside of Bangkok. Linked to a seaport and other transport facilities, the airport is intended to become an air transport hub for Southeast Asia; it is planned to support 45 million travelers in its first phase, 100 million in phase three. The government is developing plans for a new city, Nakhon Suvarnabhumi, to be built in the vicinity of the airport. Planners envision it as a major new economic center for the country, containing pollution-free industries, warehouses, shops, and residences. The hope is that the new city

FIGURE 11.34 The Cyber Gateway Building in Hyderabad's Hitech City. The complex houses such firms as the multinational software companies Microsoft, IBM, and Toshiba, as well as such Indian companies as Wipro, which provides information technology services and product design. Hitech City also houses professional schools in business and information technology. © *Mehdi Chebil/Alamy.*

will help dilute the dense population of Bangkok and generate money for what is now primarily a low-income agricultural area.

Planning can also affect the fate of older cities experiencing huge population growth. Hyderabad, India, has a population of more than 5 million, which is expected to grow to 7.4 million by 2015. To cope with the growth, provincial officials have attracted international technology, pharmaceutical, biotech, and banking and insurance companies to planned suburbs (Figure 11.34). They directed funds into cleaning and "greening" the city, planting trees and creating parks and gardens. In addition, officials fought corruption and collected taxes via computer, opening transaction centers to make paying bills and banking simpler. The city now plans an international airport to rival Mumbai and Delhi. Hyderabad is not alone: examples of city planners trying to cope with growth, some more successfully than others, exist on every continent.

Summary of Key Concepts

- Cities developed in the ancient world under certain circumstances: in areas where there was a food surplus, social organization, a defensible situation, and a developing economy. Although there have been urban areas since ancient times, only recently have urban areas become home to the majority of people in industrialized countries and the commercial crossroads for uncounted millions in the developing world.

- All settlements growing beyond their village origins take on functions uniting them to the countryside and to a larger system of settlements. As they grow, they become functionally complex. Their economic base, composed of both *basic* and *nonbasic* activities, may become diverse. Basic activities represent the functions performed for the larger economy and urban system; nonbasic activities satisfy the needs of the urban residents themselves. Cities are marketplaces, centers of production, and centers of governmental administration.

- Systems of cities are reflected in the urban hierarchy and the rank-size rule. When a city is far larger than all others in the country, it is termed a primate city. Many countries have this dominant city as their main urban settlement, but there are only a few world cities, which dominate the global economy.

- Inside North American cities, urban areas often take on similar forms. At the core, the central business district has highest value and accessibility. Outside the CBD, lower-order commercial uses dominate. These patterns have inspired geographers to summarize urban form in the concentric zone, sector, multiple-nuclei, and peripheral models. The period following World War II brought massive changes in urban organization, with the decline and regeneration of the central city, accompanied by the rise and expansion of the suburbs. These changes have been accentuated by the tendency for urban dwellers to sort themselves by family status, social status, and ethnicity. In Western countries, these patterns are also influenced by governmental controls, which help determine land use.

- Urbanization is a global phenomenon, and the Anglo American models of city systems, land use, and social area patterns differ substantially from cities in the rest of the world, reflecting diverse heritages and economic structures. Western European cities differ from those in Eastern Europe, where land use reflects communist principles of city structure. Cities in the developing world are currently growing so quickly that they are unable to provide all their residents with employment, housing, safe water, sanitation, and other minimally essential services and facilities. In some cases, governments have been able to alleviate the situation somewhat by planning new cities or applying planning principles to rapidly growing older cities.

Key Words

basic sector 364	gentrification 379	rank-size rule 369
central business district (CBD) 370	hinterland 361	sector model 372
central city 362	megalopolis 375	site 363
central place theory 365	metropolitan area 362	situation 363
city 362	multiple-nuclei model 372	suburb 362
concentric zone model 371	multiplier effect 365	town 362
economic base 364	nonbasic sector 364	urban hierarchy 368
edge city 375	peripheral model 373	urban influence zone 367
gated community 383	primate city 369	urbanized area 362
		world city 369

Thinking Geographically

1. Consider the city or town in which you live or attend school or with which you are most familiar. In a brief paragraph, discuss that community's site and situation; point out the connection, if any, between its site and situation and the basic functions that it performed earlier or now performs.

2. Describe the *multiplier effect* as it relates to the population growth of urban units.

3. Is there a hierarchy of retailing activities in the community with which you are most familiar? Of how many and of what kinds of levels is that hierarchy composed? What localizing forces affect the distributional pattern of retailing within that community?

4. Briefly describe the urban land use patterns predicted by the *concentric zone, sector, multiple-nuclei,* and *peripheral* models of urban development. Which one, if any, best corresponds to the growth and land use pattern of the community most familiar to you?

5. In what ways do social status, family status, and ethnicity affect the residential choices of households? What expected distributional patterns of urban social areas are associated with each? Does the social geography of your community conform to the predicted pattern?

6. How has suburbanization damaged the economic base and the financial stability of the central city?

7. In what ways does the Canadian city differ from the pattern of its U.S. counterpart?

8. Why are metropolitan areas in developing countries expected to grow larger than many Western metropolises by the year 2015?

9. What are *primate* cities? Why are primate cities in the developing countries overburdened? What can be done to alleviate the difficulties?

10. What are the significant differences in the generalized pattern of land uses of North American, Western European, and Eastern European cities?

11. How are cities in the developing world influenced by their colonial pasts? If you had to create a model for land use in such cities as Mumbai and Bangkok, what essential elements would you incorporate?

CHAPTER TWELVE

Human Impact on the Environment

CHAPTER OUTLINE

Fishing boats stand anchored as a young girl from a nearby slum rummages through a garbage littered beach in Mumbai, India © *AP Images/ Rajesh Nirgude.*

Sailing home to California after competing in the Transpac sailing race in 1997, Captain Charles Moore came upon an enormous stretch of floating debris that is now known as the Eastern Pacific Garbage Patch. Located between Hawaii and Japan, the patch consists of rubbish trapped by the currents of the North Pacific Gyre, an area of heavy currents and gentle winds that keep the trash swirling in a giant whirlpool—"like a toilet bowl that never flushes," as one observer put it. A similar patch lies east of Japan, and together the two patches are known as the Great Pacific Garbage Patch (Figure 12.1). The gyres' spiral patterns draw in waste material from across the North Pacific Ocean, including coastal waters off East Asia and North America. Surface currents gradually move the floating debris toward the center, trapping it in the region. It can take as many as 5 years for a plastic water bottle that was carelessly discarded at a Los Angeles beach or that was washed down a storm drain and out to sea to reach the patch.

Estimates of the size of the Eastern Garbage Patch range from 700,000 square kilometers (270,000 sq mi) to double that number. That is, the patch is roughly either the size of Texas or twice as large.

Most of the trash comes from land-based sources. It is thrown or blown into the water from coastal settlements or washed into it through rivers, drains, and sewage pipes. About one-fifth is discarded from ships and oil platforms. Roughly 85% of the refuse in the patch is plastic, a lightweight, durable, and disposable commodity present in both advanced and developing countries. Plastic bottles and caps, plastic bags, six-pack rings, cups, bubble wrap, toothbrushes, fishing gear (nets, buoys, and lines), and innumerable bits of Styrofoam all inhabit the patch. The sun's ultraviolet rays make the plastic brittle, and waves break it into progressively smaller bits.

Millions of fish, birds, and sea turtles have died by mistakenly eating the trash or by becoming entangled in the patch's debris. On Midway Island, a major albatross rookery, for example, about 500,000 chicks are born each year. Forty percent of them die, starved to death with their bodies full of bottle caps, Lego pieces, and other plastic bits. An added concern is that the plastic absorbs toxic chemicals, such as DDT and polychlorinated biphenyls, from the seawater. Fish that feed on plankton absorb the chemicals, and when larger predators (fish, birds, or humans) eat the fish, the toxins are transferred to their own tissue, affecting the entire food chain.

The Great Pacific Garbage Patch is one of many examples that could have been selected to illustrate how people can affect the quality of the water, air, and soil on which their existence depends.

Terrestrial features and ocean basins, elements of weather and characteristics of climate, flora, and fauna constitute the building blocks of that complex mosaic called the *environment,* or the totality of things that in any way may affect an organism. Plants and animals, landforms, soils and nutrients, weather and climate all constitute an organism's environment. The study of how organisms interact with one another and with their physical environment is called **ecology.** It is critically important in understanding environmental problems, which usually arise from a disturbance of the natural systems that make up our world.

Humans exist within a natural environment that they have modified by their individual and collective actions. Forests have been cleared, grasslands plowed, dams built, and cities constructed. On the natural environment, then, has been erected a cultural environment, modifying, altering, or destroying the natural communities and processes that existed before human impact was expressed. This chapter is concerned with the interrelation between humans and the natural environment that they have so greatly altered.

Since the beginning of agriculture, humans have changed the face of the earth, have distorted delicate interrelationships within nature, and, in the process, have both enhanced and endangered the societies and the economies that they have erected. The essentials of the natural balance and the ways in which humans have altered it are not only our topics here but also matters of social concern that rank among the principal domestic and international issues of our time. As we shall see, the fuels we consume, the raw materials we use, the products we create, and the wastes we discard all contribute to the harmful alteration of the **biosphere,** the thin film of air, water, and earth within which we live.

ECOSYSTEMS

The biosphere is composed of three interrelated parts:

1. the *troposphere,* the lowest layer of the earth's atmosphere, extending about 9.5–11.25 kilometers (6–7 mi) above the ground

2. the *hydrosphere,* including surface and subsurface waters in oceans, streams, lakes, glaciers, or groundwater—much of it locked in ice or earth and not immediately available for use

3. the *lithosphere,* containing the soils that support plant life, the minerals that plants and animals require to exist, and the fossil fuels and ores that humans exploit.

FIGURE 12.1 The Great Pacific Garbage Patch is just one of five that may be caught in giant gyres in the Indian Ocean, the South Pacific, and the North and South Atlantic Oceans. More information about the garbage patch can be found on the Internet, including maps, photographs, videos, and satellite images. *Map: © Greenpeace.*

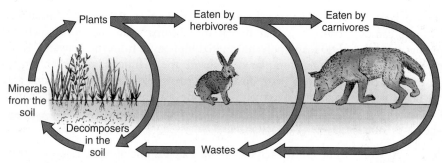

FIGURE 12.2 The supply of food in an ecosystem is a hierarchy of "who eats what"—a hierarchy that creates a food chain. In this simplified example, green plants are the *producers* (autotrophs), using nutrients and energy from the sun to make their own food. Herbivorous rabbits (*primary consumers*) feed directly on the plants, and carnivorous foxes (*secondary consumers*) feed on the rabbits. A food chain is one thread in a complex *food web,* all the feeding relationships that exist in an ecosystem. For example, a mouse might feed on the plants shown here and then be eaten by a hawk, another food chain in this food web.

The biosphere is an intricately interlocked system, containing all that is needed for life, all that is available for living things to use, and, presumably, all that ever will be available. The ingredients of the biosphere must be, and are, constantly recycled and renewed in nature. Plants purify the air, the air helps purify the water, and the water and the minerals are used by plants and animals and are returned for reuse.

The biosphere, therefore, consists of two intertwined components: (1) a nonliving outside energy source—the sun—and requisite chemicals, and (2) a living world of plants and animals. In turn, the biosphere may be subdivided into specific **ecosystems,** self-sustaining units that consist of all the organisms (plants and animals) and physical features (air, water, soil, and chemicals) existing together in a particular area. The most important principle concerning all ecosystems is that everything is interconnected. Any intrusion or interruption inevitably results in cascading effects elsewhere in the system. Each organism occupies a specific *niche,* or place, within an ecosystem. In the energy exchange system, each organism plays a definite role; individual organisms survive because of other organisms that also live in that environment. The problem lies not in recognizing the niches but in anticipating the chain of causation and the readjustments of the system consequent on disturbing the occupants of a particular niche.

Life depends on the energy and nutrients flowing through an ecosystem. The transfer of energy and materials from one organism to another is one link in a **food chain,** a sequence of organisms, such as green plants, herbivores, and carnivores, through which energy and materials move within an ecosystem (Figure 12.2). Most food chains have three or four links, although some have only two—for example, when human beings eat rice. Because the ecosystem in nature is in a continuous cycle of integrated operation, there is no start or end to a food chain. There are, simply, nutritional transfer stages in which each lower level in the food chain transfers part of its contained energy to the next higher-level consumer.

The *decomposers* pictured in Figure 12.2 are essential in maintaining food chains and the cycle of life. They cause the disintegration of organic matter—animal carcasses and droppings, dead vegetation, waste paper, and so on. In the process of decomposition, the chemical nature of the material is changed, and the nutrients contained within it become available for reuse by plants or animals. *Nutrients,* the minerals and other elements that organisms need for growth, are never destroyed; they keep moving from living to nonliving things and back again. Our bodies contain nutrients that were once part of other organisms, perhaps a hare, a hawk, or an oak tree.

Ecosystems change constantly whether people are present or not, but humans have affected them more than has any other species. The impact of humans on ecosystems was small at first, with low population size, energy consumption, and technological levels. It has increased so rapidly and pervasively as to present us with widely recognized and varied ecological crises. The **IPAT equation** is a helpful way of summarizing the different factors influencing the degree of human impact on the environment. The formula is written as I = PAT, where I (impact on the environment) is equal to P (population) multiplied by A (affluence or standard of living) multiplied by T (a technology factor).

The IPAT equation shows that growing populations and rising standards of living both contribute to greater strain on the environment. Technologies, however, can increase or decrease that impact. For example, with rising standards of living often come preferences for a cleaner environment; thus, pollution controls can be added to reduce environmental impacts. As awareness of environmental pollution has increased in developed countries, there has also been a tendency to shift polluting industries and waste disposal to poorer regions. Persons in poorer regions often have less control over the environment where they live and work and thus may be disproportionately exposed to the negative consequences of human effects on the environment. The environmental justice movement (see "Environmental Justice" in Chapter 9, pp. 306–307) has arisen to demand a clean, healthy environment for everyone. Some of the effects of humans on the natural environment are the topic of the remainder of this chapter.

IMPACT ON WATER

The world's supply of water is constant, and most of it is found in the oceans, where it is not available for direct human consumption. The system by which it continuously circulates through the biosphere is called the **hydrologic cycle** (Figure 12.3). In that cycle, water changes form and is purified or distilled through evaporation and condensation so that it is available with appropriate properties to the ecosystems of the earth. *Evaporation, transpiration* (the emission of water vapor from living things), and *precipitation* are the mechanisms

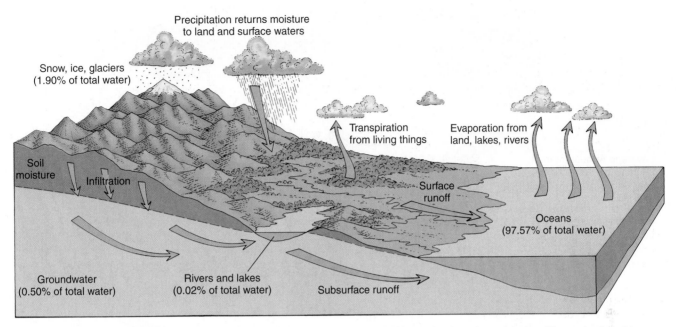

FIGURE 12.3 The hydrologic cycle. The sun provides energy for the evaporation of fresh and ocean water. The water is held as vapor until the air becomes supersaturated. Atmospheric moisture is returned to the earth's surface as solid or liquid precipitation to complete the cycle. Because precipitation is not uniformly distributed, moisture is not necessarily returned to areas in the same quantity as it has evaporated from them. The continents receive more water than they lose. The excess returns to the seas as surface water or groundwater. A global water balance, however, is always maintained.

by which water is redistributed. Water vapor collects in clouds, condenses, and then falls again to the earth. There it is reevaporated and retranspired, only to fall once more as precipitation.

People's dependence on water has long led to efforts to control its supply. Such manipulation has altered the quantity and quality of water in rivers and streams.

Availability of Water

Globally, fresh water is abundant. Enough rain and snow fall on the continents each year to cover the earth's total land area with 83 centimeters (33 in.) of water. It is usually reckoned that the volume of fresh water annually renewed by the hydrologic cycle could meet the needs of a world population 5 to 10 times its present size.

In many parts of the world, however, water supplies are inadequate and dwindling. The problem is not with the global amount of water but with its distribution (the average amount of precipitation an area receives) and reliability (the variability of precipitation from year to year). Regional water sufficiency is also a function of the size of the population using the water and the demands it places on the resource. The International Water Management Institute reports that, for the world as a whole, agriculture accounts for about 78% of freshwater use (Figure 12.4). Industry uses about 18%, and household and municipal use (water for drinking, bathing, watering lawns, and so on) accounts for the remainder. Since 1950, the acreage of land under irrigation has tripled, as have withdrawals of fresh water from streams, lakes, aquifers, and other sources. (An

FIGURE 12.4 Irrigation sprinklers in the Central Valley of California. Irrigation agriculture produces about 40% of the world's harvest from about 17% of its cropland. Usually, much more water is transported and applied to fields than crops actually require, using unnecessary amounts of a scarce resource. "Drip irrigation," which delivers water directly to plant roots through small perforated tubes laid across the field, is one method of reducing water consumption. © *Corbis RF.*

aquifer is a zone of water-saturated sands and gravels beneath the earth's surface; the water it contains is called *groundwater,* in contrast to surface waters, such as rivers and lakes.)

Scarcity is the word increasingly used to describe water supplies in parts of both the developed and developing world (Figure 12.5). More than 2 billion people—a third of the

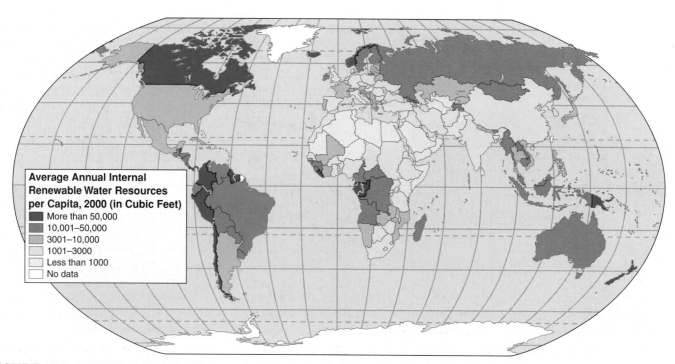

FIGURE 12.5 Availability of renewable water per capita. Renewable water resources are those available from streams, lakes, and aquifers. Although the United States has tremendous quantities of fresh water, it also uses tremendous quantities. Water consumption rises with population growth, increases in the standard of living, expansion of irrigation farming, and the enlarged demands of industry and municipalities that come with development. In a growing number of world areas, water is scarce, constraining sustainable development and requiring hard choices in the allocation of water among competing users. *Source: Student Atlas of World Geography, 3/e, John Allen, Map 50, p. 63. McGraw-Hill/Dushkin, 2003.*

world's population—live in regions facing a scarcity of water. Insufficient water for irrigation periodically endangers crops and threatens famine; permanent streams have become intermittent in flow; lakes are shrinking; and from throughout the world come reports of rapidly falling water tables and wells that have gone dry. According to the World Bank, chronic water shortages that threaten to limit food production, economic development, sanitation, and environmental protection already plague 80 countries. Ten countries in North Africa and the Middle East actually run a *water deficit:* they consume more than their annual renewable supply, usually by pumping groundwater faster than it is replenished by rainfall.

National data can mask water scarcity problems at the local level. A number of countries have major crop-producing regions where groundwater overpumping and aquifer depletion have led to serious water shortages and restricted supplies.

- In northern China, for example, irrigated farmland and urban and industrial growth are so depleting water supplies that for much of the year the Huang He (Yellow River) runs dry in its lower reaches before arriving at the Yellow Sea. More than 100 of China's large cities, most of them in the north, already have serious water shortages. Across much of northern China, water tables are dropping an average of 1 to 2 meters (3 to 6 ft) each year.

- In India, the world's second most populous country, the overall rate of groundwater withdrawal is twice the rate of recharge. In several northern states, including Haryana

and Punjab, the country's most important agricultural region, excessive water use is causing water tables to fall and wells to dry up.

- Lake Chad has been severely reduced in size by drought and the withdrawal of water from feeder rivers to irrigate agriculture. Once Africa's second largest lake, with a surface area of 25,000 square kilometers (9650 sq mi) in 1965, Lake Chad covered just 1500 square kilometers (580 sq mi) in 2005.

- Lake Chapala, the largest body of fresh water in Mexico, has lost about 80% of its intake water since the mid-1970s. The lake is fed primarily by the Rio Lerma, but almost all of the river's flow is now diverted for irrigation and industry. Mexico City and its suburbs extract water from their aquifers more than twice as fast as nature can replenish the water. As a result of removing so much groundwater, the city sank 9 meters (30 ft) during the 20th century.

In the United States, too, groundwater supplies are being depleted faster than they can be renewed in portions of Arizona, New Mexico, California, and Nevada. Demands upon the only significant source of surface water in the southwestern United States, the Colorado River, are so great that the stream often reaches the ocean (at the Gulf of California) as little more than a briny trickle. Aqueducts and irrigation canals siphon off its water for use in seven western states and northern Mexico. A number of western cities, including Denver and Santa Fe, have imposed mandatory restrictions on water use.

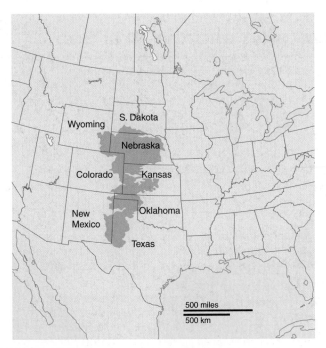

FIGURE 12.6 The giant Ogallala aquifer, the largest underground water supply in the United States, provides about one-fourth of all groundwater used for irrigation in the country. Depletion of the aquifer is most severe in its southern portion, where the Ogallala gets little replenishment from rainfall. Water tables have declined by 32 meters (100 ft) or more in many parts of north Texas. The capacity of the aquifer has decreased by about one-third since 1950.

The country's largest underground water reserve, the Ogallala aquifer, which supplies about 25% of all U.S. irrigated land, is being depleted three times faster than it is being replenished (Figure 12.6). Stretching from South Dakota to west Texas, the aquifer supports nearly half of the country's cattle industry, a fourth of its cotton crop, and a great deal of its corn and wheat. More than 150,000 wells now puncture the aquifer, pumping water for irrigation, industry, and domestic use.

The UN estimates that by 2015 nearly 3 billion people, or 40% of the projected world population, will live in water-stressed countries where it is difficult or impossible to get enough water to satisfy basic needs. Shortages of this indispensable resource pit developers against environmentalists, and users—agriculture, industry, and municipalities—against one another. Tensions are exacerbated in areas where two or more countries share a river system. The world's 263 transboundary rivers raise the risk of conflict over access to fresh water. Mexico, for example, is angered by U.S. depletion of the Colorado River before it reaches the international border; and by building dams and irrigating fields, Turkey and Syria have taken much of the water of the Tigris and Euphrates Rivers, reducing the amount of water available in downstream Syria and Iraq. India's diversion of a large portion of the Ganges River has left Bangladesh with water shortages.

Because the oceans contain a never-ending supply of water, some have looked to *desalinization* (cleansing seawater

of its salt and mineral content) to provide a technological solution to water shortfall. As long as the process is economically inefficient, however, it is unlikely to supply more than a small portion of humanity's needs. If in the future the costs fall far enough, desalinization could help augment domestic water supplies; it is doubtful that it could ever become cheap enough to provide water for agriculture.

Modification of Streams

To prevent flooding, to regulate the water supply for agriculture and urban settlements, or to generate power, people have for thousands of years manipulated rivers by constructing dams, canals, and reservoirs. Although they generally have achieved their purposes, these structures can have unintended environmental consequences, as discussed in Chapter 5. These include reduction in the sediment load downstream, followed by a reduction in the amount of the nutrients available for crops and fish; an increase in the salinity of the soil; subsidence; and dramatic declines in the populations of fish, such as salmon, that hatch in freshwater rivers, migrate to the ocean, and then return upriver to their place of origin to spawn (see "Blueprint for Disaster: Stream Diversion and the Aral Sea," pp. 398–399).

Channelization, another method of modifying river flow, is the construction of embankments and dikes and the straightening, widening, and/or deepening of channels to control floodwaters or to improve navigation. Globally, more than a half-million kilometers (310,000 mi) of river have been dredged and channelized. Many of the great rivers of the world, including the Mississippi, the Nile, and the Huang He, are lined by embankment systems. Like dams, these systems can have unforeseen consequences. They reduce the natural storage of floodwaters, can aggravate flood peaks downstream, and can cause excessive erosion.

Until 1960, the Kissimmee River in Florida twisted and turned as it traveled through a floodplain between Lake Kissimmee and Lake Okeechobee (Figure 12.7). The habitat supported hundreds of species of birds, reptiles, mammals, and fish. At the request of developers, ranchers, and farmers who had moved onto the wetlands and were disturbed by the tendency of the river to flood, the Army Corps of Engineers dredged the stream, turning 166 kilometers (103 mi) of meandering river into a straight, dirt-lined canal only 90 kilometers (56 mi) long. After the completion of the canal in 1971, the wetlands disappeared, alien plant species moved in, fish populations declined drastically, and 90% of the waterfowl, including several endangered species, vanished.

Channelization and dam construction are deliberate attempts to modify river regimes, but other types of human action also affect river flow. Urbanization, for example, has significant hydrologic impacts, including a lowering of the water table, pollution, and increased flood runoff. Likewise, the removal of forest cover increases runoff, promotes flash floods, lowers the water table, and hastens erosion.

Nevertheless, the primary adverse human impact on water is felt in the area of water quality. People withdraw water from

Blueprint for Disaster: Stream Diversion and the Aral Sea

In 1960 it was the fourth-largest inland sea in the world, covering an area of 27,000 square miles—larger than the state of West Virginia. Now the Aral Sea has less than half of its original surface area, and the volume of the water is only one-fourth of what it used to be. The level of the sea has dropped more than 18 meters (59 ft), and the sea has split into two: the Little Aral Sea in the north and the Large Aral Sea in the south.

One of the world's greatest human-induced environmental catastrophes, the shrinkage of the lake is just one result of diverting nearly all the water from its primary sources, the Amu Darya and the Syr Darya, to irrigate the agricultural fields of central Asia. These are some of the other consequences:

- As the water receded, it left behind thousands of square kilometers of polluted waste on the seabed. The rivers that feed it are contaminated by agricultural runoff and untreated industrial and municipal wastewater containing high levels of fertilizers, pesticides, heavy metals, and other toxic compounds. The Large Aral Sea is now considered a dead sea. Unable to survive in the salty, toxic water, all 20 known fish species have died out, and the commercial fishing industry has collapsed. Once a fishing port and popular resort, Müynoq is now more than 100 kilometers (63 mi) from the sea. Aralsk was once the main northern port for a sea that is now 80 kilometers (50 mi) away.
- Fierce wind storms whip up salty grit and toxic chemicals from the dried-up seabed and the land around it and deposit it on cropland hundreds of kilometers away, reducing the soil's fertility. Ironically, the agricultural crops for which the Aral Sea was sacrificed—mainly cotton and rice—are themselves at risk.

- Forests and wetlands upon which the region's animal life depend have been decimated. It has been estimated that three-quarters of the animal species in the basin have vanished.
- The health of the human population is threatened by the contaminated water, air, and soil. The incidence of such serious diseases as cholera, typhus, and cancers of the stomach and esophagus has increased significantly, as have respiratory system illnesses (asthma, bronchitis). High rates of miscarriages and birth defects prevail, and child mortality rates are among the highest in the world.

In an effort to save the Little Aral Sea, the World Bank and Kazakhstan government financed the building of a dam and a series of dikes on the Syr Darya. Since the completion of the dam in 2005, the level of the sea has risen, the surface area has expanded by some 30%, and fish stocks are being replenished.

Although the Large Aral Sea is still dying, efforts to save the Little Aral Sea show that it is possible to mitigate the harm people do to the environment.

---

lakes, rivers, or underground deposits to use for drinking, bathing, agriculture, industry, and many other purposes. Although the water that is withdrawn returns to the water cycle, it is not always returned in the same condition as it was at the time of withdrawal. Water, like other segments of the ecosystem, is subject to serious problems of pollution.

Water Quality

As a general definition, **environmental pollution** by humans means the introduction into the biosphere of wastes that, because of their volume, their composition, or both, cannot be readily disposed of by natural recycling processes. In the case of water, the central idea is that pollution exists when water composition has been so modified by the presence of one or more substances that either it cannot be used for a specific purpose or it is less suitable for that use than it was in its natural state. Pollution is brought about by the discharge into water

of substances that cause unfavorable changes in its chemical or physical nature or in the quantity and quality of the organisms living in the water. *Pollution* is a relative term. Water that is not suitable for drinking may be completely satisfactory for cleaning streets. Water that is too polluted for fish may provide an acceptable environment for certain water plants.

Human activity is not the only cause of water pollution. Leaves that fall from trees and decay, animal wastes, oil seepages, and other natural phenomena may affect water quality. There are natural processes, however, to take care of such pollution. Organisms in water are able to degrade, assimilate, and disperse such substances in the amounts in which they naturally occur. Only in rare instances do natural pollutants overwhelm the cleansing abilities of the recipient waters. What is happening now is that the quantities of wastes discharged by humans often exceed the ability of a given body of water to purify itself. In addition, humans are introducing pollutants, such as metals or synthetic organic substances, that take a very

1975 *EROS Data Center, USGS*

1987 *NASA*

1997 *EROS Data Center, USGS*

2005 *EROS Data Center, USGS*

long time to break down or cannot be broken down at all by natural mechanisms.

As long as there are people on Earth, there will be pollution. Thus, the problem is one not of eliminating pollution but of controlling it. Such control can be a matter of life or death. Waterborne pathogens and pollution kill millions of people (mostly children) each year. The people die from diarrhea and water-related diseases, such as cholera and typhoid. One column in Appendix 3 at the back of this book shows, by country, the percentage of the population with access to safe water.

The four major contributors to water pollution are agriculture, industry, mining, and municipalities and residences. It is helpful to distinguish between "point" and "nonpoint" sources of pollution. As the name implies, *point sources* enter the environment at specific sites, such as a sewage treatment facility or an industrial discharge pipe. *Nonpoint sources* are more diffuse and, therefore, more difficult to control; examples include runoff from agricultural fields and road salts.

Agricultural Sources of Water Pollution

On a worldwide basis, agriculture probably contributes more to water pollution than does any other single activity. In the United States, agriculture is estimated to be responsible for about two-thirds of stream pollution. Agricultural runoff carries three main types of pollutants: fertilizers, biocides, and animal wastes.

Fertilizers

Agriculture is a chief contributor of *excess nutrients* to water bodies. Pollution occurs when nitrates and phosphates that have been used in fertilizers and that are present in animal manure drain into streams and rivers, eventually accumulating in ponds, lakes, and estuaries. The nutrients hasten the process of **eutrophication,** or the enrichment of waters by nutrients. Eutrophication occurs naturally when nutrients in the surrounding area are washed into the water, but when the sources

(a) Before 1960

(b) After 1972

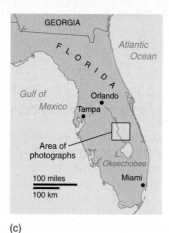

(c)

FIGURE 12.7 The Kissimmee River in Florida **(a)** before and **(b)** after the Army Corps of Engineers turned it into a straight canal 9 meters (30 ft) deep. The channelization largely eliminated wetlands, degraded bird and fish populations, and contributed to the deterioration of Lake Okeechobee and the Everglades. The federal goverment and the state of Florida have embarked on a long-term project to reestablish a natural flow of water to 69 kilometers (43 mi) of the river by returning it to a meandering path. You can check on the progress of the Kissimmee River Restoration Project on the Web. *(a) and (b) Courtesy of South Florida Water Management District.*

of enrichment are artificial, as is true of commercial fertilizers, the body of water may become overloaded with nutrients. Algae and other plants are stimulated to grow abundantly, blocking the sunlight that other organisms need. When they die and decompose, the level of dissolved oxygen in the water decreases. Fish and plants that cannot tolerate the poorly oxygenated water suffocate.

It has been estimated that, worldwide, this *accelerated* eutrophication affects half of all lakes and reservoirs in North America, Europe, and Southeast Asia, some 40% in South America, and 28% in Africa. Symptoms of a eutrophic lake are prolific weed growth, large masses of algae, fish kills, rapid accumulation of sediments on the lake bottom, and water that has a foul taste and odor.

High levels of nutrients from agricultural runoff are a primary cause of about 200 "dead zones" around the world, although sewage plants, storm water runoff, and air pollution also contribute the nitrogen and phosphorus that spur the explosive growth of phytoplankton and zooplankton, which die and sink to the bottom, and then are eaten by bacteria that use up the oxygen in the water. A dead zone is an area of oxygen depletion in which fish, crabs, and other aquatic creatures cannot survive. The world's largest dead zones include those in the Baltic Sea, the East China Sea, the Bay of Bengal, and the northern Gulf of Mexico off the coast of Louisiana (Figure 12.8). The zones, whose sizes vary from year to year, reach their peak during the summer months, as the water grows warmer and solar radiation increases, causing algal populations to bloom.

Biocides

The herbicides and pesticides used in agriculture are another source of the chemical pollution of water bodies. Runoff from farms where such *biocides* have been applied contaminates both ground- and surface waters. One of the problems connected with the use of biocides is that the long-term effects of such usage are not always immediately known. Dichloro-diphenyl trichloroethane (DDT), for example, was used for many years before people discovered its effect on birds, fish, and water plant life. Another problem is that thousands of these products, containing more than 600 active ingredients, are now in wide use, yet very few have been reviewed for safety by the Environmental Protection Agency (EPA). Finally, biocides that leach into aquifers can remain there long after the chemicals are no longer used. Thus, DDT is still found in U.S. waters even though its use was banned in the late 1960s.

Animal Wastes

A final agricultural source of chemical pollution is animal wastes, especially in countries where animals are raised intensively. This is a problem both in feedlots, where animals are crowded together at maximum densities to be fattened before slaughter, and on the factory-like farms where beef, hog, and poultry production is increasingly concentrated (Figure 12.9). American farms and large feedlots produce vast quantities of manure—nearly 3 billion pounds a day—but usually lack

(a)

FIGURE 12.8 The dead zone in the Gulf of Mexico off the Louisiana-Texas coast in 2007 covered roughly 20,500 square kilometers (7900 sq mi), similar to the size of New Jersey. More than 40% of the United States is drained by the Mississippi River and its tributaries, and each year the Mississippi washes more than 1.6 million tons of excess nutrients—chiefly nitrogen and phosphorus—into the Gulf of Mexico. The sources of the nutrients are fertilizer runoff, animal waste, industrial and sewage treatment wastewater, and air pollution. The nutrients stimulate the growth of algae, which eventually die, sink to the seafloor, and decompose, creating low oxygen (hypoxia) in the lower waters. When oxygen falls below 2 parts per million, the water cannot sustain sea life.

sewage treatment facilities. The main method for disposing of the waste is to put it into open lagoons (containment ponds) and then spray it onto surrounding fields as a fertilizer, from which it can leach into the water table and rivers.

The water pollution that occurs from spreading manure on land is suspected by many to be responsible for recent outbreaks of the microorganism *Pfiesteria piscicida* in North Carolina and the Chesapeake Bay and its tributaries. Dubbed the "cells from hell," these single-celled algae proliferate and become toxic when exposed to high levels of nitrogen and phosphorus, by-products of animal waste. The manure comes from the large poultry and hog farms of Maryland, Virginia, and North Carolina. *Pfiesteria* have killed millions of fish, and there is some evidence that the organism also sickens humans.

Other Sources of Water Pollution

As noted earlier, agriculture is only one of the human activities that contribute to water pollution. Other sources are industry, mining, municipalities, and residences.

(b)

FIGURE 12.9 An industrial hog-production operation in Ohio. (a) On factory-style hog farms such as the one pictured here, thousands of animals are fed and raised indoors in large, rectangular barns for the 4 or 5 months it takes them to grow to 250 pounds. **(b)** Feces and urine are washed through slots in the floor into pipes and trenches that carry the waste outdoors into holding pits known as waste lagoons. If released improperly, the waste pollutes both nearby soils and water with disease-causing pathogens and excess nutrients from the animal feed, particularly high concentrations of nitrogen and phosphorus. *(a) © Farm Sanctuary; (b) © Keith Meyers/New York Times Pictures/Redux Pictures.*

Industry

In developed countries, industry probably contributes as much to contamination of the water supply as does agriculture. Many industries discharge organic and inorganic wastes into bodies of water. These may be acids, highly toxic minerals, such as mercury or arsenic, or, in the case of petroleum refineries, toxic organic chemicals. The nuclear power industry has caused some water pollution when radioactive material has seeped from the tanks in which the wastes have been buried, either at sea or underground.

Such pollution can have a variety of effects. Organisms not adapted to living in contaminated water may die; the water may become unsuitable for domestic use or irrigation; or the wastes may reenter the food chain, with deleterious effects on humans. One of the most notorious pollution cases, which focused international attention on the dangers of industrial pollution, occurred in the village of Minamata in southwest Japan. From 1932 to 1968, a chemical plant that used mercury in its manufacturing process discharged tons of waste mercury into Minamata Bay, where it settled into the mud. Fish and shellfish that fed on organisms in the mud absorbed the mercury and concentrated it; the fish were in turn eaten by humans. More than 700 people died, and at least 9000 others suffered deformity or other permanent disability.

Mercury pollution comes not just from industrial wastewater but also from coal-fired power plants, waste incinerators, and chemical plants that pump mercury into the air. Much of the mercury returns to Earth, contaminating lakes and streams, where it accumulates in fish and shellfish. Canada, China, and Brazil are among the countries with areas of significant mercury pollution. In the United States, the EPA reports that virtually all of the country's lakes and rivers are contaminated with mercury, and 45 states have issued advisories on eating fish.

Among the pollutants that have been discharged into the water supply in the United States are **polychlorinated biphenyls (PCBs),** a family of related chemicals used as lubricants in pipelines and in a wide variety of electrical devices, paints, and plastics. During the manufacturing process, companies discharged PCBs into rivers, from which they entered the food chain. Several states have banned commercial fishing in lakes and rivers where fish have higher levels of PCBs than are considered safe. Although not all of the effects of PCBs on human health are known, they have been linked to birth defects, damage to the immune system, liver disease, and cancer. In 1977, the Environmental Protection Agency banned the direct discharge of PCBs into U.S. waters, but because they do not decompose readily, immense quantities of the chemicals remain in water bodies.

More recently, *percholate* and *vinyl chloride* have been implicated in the contamination of aquifers and wells. Percholate is the major component of rocket fuel; vinyl chloride is used to make plastic pipes, furniture, and upholstery. Drinking, bathing in, or cooking with the polluted water can cause liver cancer, nerve damage, circulatory problems, and skin lesions.

The petroleum industry is a significant contributor to the chemical pollution of water. Oceans and inlets are becoming increasingly contaminated by oil. Although massive oil spills like that from the tanker *Exxon Valdez* in 1989—which spilled about 42,000 tons of crude oil into Alaska's Prince William Sound, contaminating some 20,000 kilometers (12,400 mi) of pristine shoreline—command public attention, smaller spills routinely dump millions of gallons of oil into American waters each year. Over half the oil normally comes from oil tankers and barges, usually because of ruptures in accidents. Much of the rest comes from refineries, the discharge of tank flushings and oil-drenched ballast water from tanker holds, and seepage from offshore drilling platforms. The Gulf of Mexico, the site of extensive offshore drilling, is among the most seriously polluted major bodies of water in the world.

Acid precipitation (usually called acid rain), a by-product of emissions from factories, power plants, and automobiles, has affected the water quality and ecology of thousands of lakes and streams in the world. Because the precipitation is caused by pollutants in the air, it is discussed later in this chapter (see the section "Acid Rain," p. 406).

Many industrial processes, as well as electric power production, require the use of water as a coolant. **Thermal pollution** occurs when water that has been heated is returned to the environment and has adverse effects on the plants and animals in the water body. If the heated wastewaters are significantly warmer than the waters into which they are discharged, they can disrupt the growth, reproduction, and migration of fish populations. Many plants and fish cannot survive changes of even a few degrees in water temperature. They either die or migrate. The species that depend on them for food must also either die or migrate. Thus, the food chain has been disrupted. In addition, the higher the temperature of the water, the less oxygen it contains, which means that only lower-order plants and animals can survive.

Mining

Surface mining for coal, copper, gold, uranium, and other substances contributes to contamination of the water supply through the wastes it generates. Rainwater reacts with the wastes, and dissolved minerals seep into nearby water bodies. The exact chemical changes produced depend on the composition of the coal or ore slag heaps and the reaction of the minerals with sediments or river water.

Heap-leach gold mining, for example, involves pouring large amounts of cyanide onto piles of low-grade ore in order to extract the gold. Major mining companies practice this relatively new technique in many countries, among them the United States, Peru, Romania, Tanzania, and Indonesia. The companies dump massive amounts of the cyanide-laced waste into local rivers, contaminating the water. In addition to altering the quality of the water, the contaminants have secondary effects on soils, vegetation, and animals. Each year, for example, thousands of animals and migratory birds die in such western states as Arizona, Nevada, and California after drinking the cyanide-polluted water that has settled into ponds and lakes at gold mines.

A similar contamination of the water supply is occurring in the Amazon River and its tributaries, but with mercury rather than cyanide. Because mercury attaches itself to gold, an estimated half-million small-scale miners (called *garimpeiros*) in Brazil, Venezuela, and neighboring countries use the toxic liquid to separate gold from earth and rock. They pour mercury over the crushed ore they have dredged from riverbeds, press out the mercury with their hands, then burn the mixture to evaporate the rest of the heavy metal. The gold mining is estimated to send about 100 tons of mercury into the Amazon each year, poisoning the water and the fish in it, and another 100 tons into the atmosphere. Because it can take decades for concentrations to reach toxic levels, mercury pollution of streams is like a delayed-action time bomb, and thus the full effects of mercury poisoning in the Amazon Basin may not be known for many years. What is known, however, is that through absorption or inhalation a high percentage of miners have extremely high levels of mercury in their bodies and that they and others are exposed to mercury by eating fish.

Municipalities and Residences

A host of pollutants derives from the activities associated with urbanization. The use of detergents has increased the phosphorus content of rivers, and salt (used for deicing roads) increases the chloride content of runoff. Water runoff from urban areas contains contaminants from garbage, animal droppings, litter, vehicle drippings, and the like. Because the sources of pollution are so varied, the water supply in any single area is often affected by diverse contaminants. This diversity complicates the problem of controlling water quality.

Contaminated drinking-water wells have been found in many locations across the United States. Chemicals have reached groundwater by seeping into aquifers from landfills, leaking underground gasoline and fuel-oil storage tanks, septic tanks, and fields sprayed with pesticides and herbicides. The pollution of aquifers is particularly troublesome because, unlike surface waters, groundwater has a low capacity for purifying itself; it can remain contaminated for centuries.

Sewage can also be a major water pollutant, depending on how well it is treated before being discharged. This is not simply an environmental concern; it directly affects human health. Raw, untreated human waste contains viruses responsible for dysentery, polio, hepatitis, spinal meningitis, and other diseases.

Although municipal wastewater treatment is increasing in the most-developed countries, more than 90% of sewage in the developing world is discharged directly into waterways without treatment of any kind.

- A survey of 200 major Russian rivers shows that 80% of them are polluted by raw sewage and have dangerously high levels of bacteria and viral agents.
- Mexico City treats less than 10% of its wastewater, sending its sewage into rivers that irrigate farmland.
- Fully 70% of total surface waters in India are polluted, in large part because only about 200 of its more than 3000 cities have full or partial sewage-collection and treatment facilities. In New Delhi alone, some 7 million residents are not connected to the public sewage system.

Instead, open sewers—ideal breeding ground for mosquitoes that carry malaria and dengue fever—line the narrow lanes of slums, and although the water is unsafe for drinking, women use it to launder clothes, wash vegetables, and bathe their children.

Although sewage-treatment plants are common in the United States, only half of the American population lives in communities with facilities that meet the minimum goals set by the federal Clean Water Act. Aged sewage systems in 1100 cities still discharge poorly treated sewage into streams, lakes, and oceans. When the sewer system of Dade County, Florida, ruptures, as it does periodically, millions of gallons of raw sewage pour into the Miami River, which empties into Biscayne Bay in downtown Miami. Similarly, beaches along the Great Lakes are subject to contamination—and closure—when untreated sewage overflows into the lakes from aging wastewater treatment plants.

In many communities, special problems arise after heavy rains, when stormwater containing animal wastes, street debris, and lawn chemicals floods the sewers. As treatment plants become overloaded, both runoff and raw sewage are diverted into rivers, bays, and oceans. New York City alone has more than 500 storm water outlets that overflow in heavy rains, pouring some 65 billion gallons of untreated sewage (about 10% of the city's total sewage) into the Hudson River and Long Island Sound each year. But 1200 other cities in the East, Midwest, and Northwest also have sewage networks that are combined with the overflow systems for storm water.

Controlling Water Pollution

As the IPAT equation reminds us, technologies can help reduce the environmental impacts of growing populations and rising standards of living. Water pollution can be mitigated, although doing so requires the concerted effort of a variety of actors. Public education programs and environmental organizations foster concern over polluted water. In many communities, periodic manual clean-up efforts remove trash and debris from waterways, riverbanks, and beaches. Some companies have adopted "green" plans to eliminate or reduce their production of pollutants. Many countries have enacted water quality legislation, and many have entered into international agreements that have already begun to bear fruit (Table 12.1).

The most useful strategy for controlling water pollution is to avoid producing or releasing it into the environment in the first place. Industries can recycle or reuse materials that otherwise would be discarded into the waste stream. Communities can employ secondary or tertiary treatment of their sewage and recycle the sludge. They can also clean up leaking landfills and abandoned dumps. Legislation can ban the use of DDT, PCBs, phosphate detergents, and other toxins; it can also require the preservation and/or restoration of wetlands, which filter out sediment and contaminants. The use of double- instead of single-hulled oil tankers, mandated by MARPOL (Table 12.1), already has led to a significant decline in oil spills.

TABLE 12.1
Some Important International Agreements on Water Quality
1972: Great Lakes Water Quality Agreement between Canada and the United States; regulations to clean up the world's largest freshwater system
1973, 1978: International Convention for the Prevention of Pollution from Ships (MARPOL); since ratified by more than 150 countries; aimed at preventing and minimizing pollution from ships by oil, chemicals, sewage, garbage, and plastic materials
1976: Convention for the Protection of the Mediterranean Sea against Pollution; various measures designed to reduce water pollution
1990: London Dumping Convention; calls for an end to all ocean dumping of industrial wastes and plastic trash
2004: Stockholm Convention on Persistent Organic Pollutants; requires governments to eliminate or reduce releases of certain persistent chemicals, such as dioxin and PCBs

Once referred to as the sewer of Europe, the Rhine River is now much cleaner than it was in the 1970s and 1980s because of the International Commission for the Protection of the Rhine. The countries along the river have worked together to cut the quantities of pollutants such as nitrogen, phosphorus, lead, and ammonium entering the river and, eventually, the North Sea. They have also spent billions of dollars on wastewater treatment plants. Atlantic salmon have returned to the river after half a century when it was too poisonous for them to survive, and the populations of other fish have increased significantly.

The Mediterranean Sea is also on its way to gradual recovery. In 1976, when the 18 countries that border the sea signed the Convention for the Protection of the Mediterranean Sea against Pollution, all coastal cities dumped their untreated sewage into the sea; tankers spewed oily wastes into it; and tons upon tons of phosphorus, detergents, lead, and other substances contaminated the waters. Now many cities have built or are building sewage-treatment plants, ships are prohibited from indiscriminate dumping, and national governments are beginning to enforce control of pollution from land-based sources.

Because they are so diffuse, nonpoint sources of water pollution, such as agricultural and urban runoff, are more difficult to monitor and control than those from point sources. Again, the most useful tactic is to reduce the number and amount of pollutants before they reach water. Farmers and homeowners can be encouraged to apply less fertilizer, pesticides, and irrigation water to agricultural fields and lawns. Cities can separate storm sewers and municipal sewage lines to avoid overflow during storms. Regulations can be developed to lessen chemical runoff from mining and forestry. Although pollution control projects are expensive, the long-term costs of pollution are even higher.

In the United States, the federal government in 1972 took the lead in regulating water pollution with the enactment of the Clean Water Act. Its objective was "to restore and maintain the chemical, physical, and biological integrity of the nation's waters." Congress established uniform nationwide controls for each category of major polluting industry and directed the government to pay most of the cost of new sewage-treatment plants. Since 1972 such plants have been built to serve more than 80 million Americans, and industries have spent billions of dollars to comply with the Clean Water Act by reducing organic waste discharges.

The gains have been impressive. Many rivers and lakes that were ecologically dead or dying are now thriving. Once dumping grounds for all kinds of human and industrial waste, the Hudson, Potomac, Cuyahoga, and Trinity are among the rivers that are cleaner, more inviting, and more productive than before, and they now support fishing, swimming, and recreational boating. Similarly, Seattle's Lake Washington and the Great Lakes are healthier than they were in the 1980s. Efforts are underway to clean up the waters of Chesapeake Bay, the country's largest estuary, and to undo much of the damage that has been inflicted on Florida's Everglades by improving the water quality of the Kissimmee River and Lake Okeechobee.

IMPACT ON AIR AND CLIMATE

The **troposphere,** the thin layer of air just above the earth's surface, contains all the air that we breathe. Every day thousands of tons of pollutants are discharged into the air by cars and incinerators, factories and airplanes. Air is polluted when it contains substances in sufficient concentrations to have a harmful effect on living things.

Air Pollutants

Truly clean air has probably never existed. Just as there are natural sources of water pollution, so are there substances that pollute the air without the aid of humans. Ash from volcanic eruptions, marsh gases, smoke from forest fires, and wind-blown dust are natural sources of air pollution.

Normally, these pollutants are of low volume and are widely dispersed throughout the atmosphere. On occasion, a major volcanic eruption may produce so much dust that the atmosphere is temporarily altered. In general, however, the natural sources of air pollution do not have a significant, long-term effect on air, which, like water, is able to cleanse itself.

Far more important than naturally occurring pollutants are the substances that people discharge into the air. These pollutants result primarily from burning fossil fuels (coal, gas, and oil) and other materials. Fossil fuels are burned in power plants that generate electricity, in many industrial plants, in home furnaces, and in cars, trucks, buses, and airplanes. Scientists estimate that about three-quarters of all air pollutants come from burning fossil fuels. The remaining pollutants largely result from industrial processes other than fuel burning, the incineration of solid

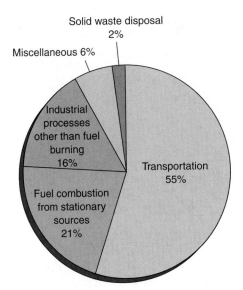

FIGURE 12.10 Sources of primary air pollutants in the United States. Primary air pollutants are materials that are emitted directly into the atmosphere in sufficient quantities to exert an adverse effect on human health or the environment. Transportation is the single-largest source of human-caused air pollution. The second-largest source is fuel combustion in stationary sources, such as power plants and factories. *Redrawn from Biosphere 2000, by Donald G. Kaufman and Cecilia M. Franz (NY: HarperCollins College Publishers, 1993, Fig. 14.3, p. 251).*

TABLE 12.2		
Major Sources of Primary Air Pollutants		
Type of Pollutant	**Symbol**	**Major Sources**
Carbon dioxide	CO_2	Combustion of fossil fuels
Carbon monoxide	CO	Incomplete combustion of fossil fuels, mostly in vehicles
Hydrocarbons	HC	Combustion of fossil fuels; petroleum refineries; petrochemical plants
Nitrogen oxides	NO_x	Transportation vehicles; power plants
Particulates	—	Automobile exhaust; oil refining; coal-fired power plants; farming and construction operations
Sulfur oxides	SO_x	Combustion of sulfur-containing fuels, especially coal

wastes, forest and agricultural fires, and the evaporation of solvents. Figure 12.10 depicts the major sources of air pollutants. Table 12.2 summarizes the major sources of six *primary* pollutants emitted in large quantities. Once they are in the atmosphere, these may react with other primary pollutants or with normal atmospheric constituents, such as water vapor, to form *secondary* pollutants.

Air pollution is a global problem. A recent study by the World Health Organization (WHO) concluded that more than 1.1 billion people live in urban areas with unhealthful air. Sulfur dioxide levels are considered unacceptable for some 625 million people in developing countries alone, and levels of smoke, dust, and other particulates are unacceptable for 1.25 billion people. Particularly at risk of breathing bad air are residents of such megacities as Mexico City, Cairo, Delhi, Seoul, Beijing, and Jakarta.

Like polluted water, dirty air kills people. According to the WHO, at least 3 million people die prematurely each year from illnesses caused by air pollution.

Factors Affecting Air Pollution

Many factors affect the type and the degree of air pollution found at a given place. Those over which people have relatively little control are climate, weather, wind patterns, and topography. These determine whether pollutants will be blown away or are likely to accumulate. Thus, a city on a plain is less likely to experience a buildup than is a city in a valley.

Unusual weather can alter the normal patterns of pollutant dispersal. A *temperature inversion* magnifies the effects of air pollution. Under normal circumstances, air temperature decreases away from the earth's surface. A stationary layer of warm, dry air over a region, however, will prevent the normal rising and cooling of air from below. As described in Chapter 4 (see Figure 4.11 and "The Donora Tragedy"), the air becomes stagnant during an inversion. Pollutants accumulate in the lowest layer instead of being blown away, so the air becomes more and more contaminated. Normally, inversions last for only a few hours, although certain areas experience them much of the time. Temperature inversions occur often in Los Angeles in the fall and Denver in the winter. If an inversion lingers long enough, over several days, it can contribute to the accumulation of air pollutants to levels that seriously affect human health.

The air pollutants generated in one place may have their most serious effect in areas hundreds of kilometers away, as atmosphere circulaton moves pollutants freely without regard to political boundaries. Thus, the worst effects of the air pollution that originates in New York City are felt in Connecticut and parts of Massachusetts. The chemical reaction that produces smog takes a few hours, and by that time air currents have carried the pollutants away from New York. In a similar fashion, New York is the recipient of pollutants produced in other places. Much of the acid rain that affects New England and eastern Canada originates in the coal-fired power plants along the lower Great Lakes and in the Ohio Valley that use extremely high smokestacks to disperse sulfurous emissions. Air pollution from China travels across the Pacific Ocean and ends up on the West Coast of the United States. And the coal-based industries in Russia and Europe produce sulfate, carbon, and other pollutants that are transported by air currents to the land north of the Arctic Circle, where they result in a contamination known as Arctic haze.

Other factors that affect the type and the degree of air pollution at a given place are the levels of urbanization, industrialization, and adoption of pollution control technologies.

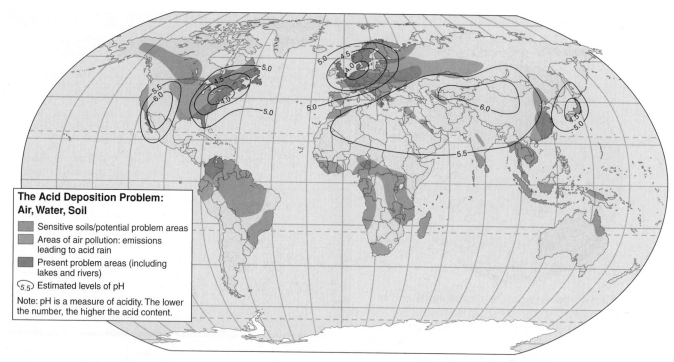

FIGURE 12.11 Acid precipitation: points of origin and current problem areas. Prevailing winds can deposit acid precipitation far from its area of origin. The acids in the precipitation harm or destroy soils, vegetation, aquatic life, and buildings. Occurring primarily in industrialized countries, acid precipitation has become a serious problem in many parts of North America, Europe, and Japan. *Source: Student Atlas of World Geography, 5th ed., John Allen, Map 65, p. 81. McGraw-Hill/Dushkin, 2008.*

Population densities, traffic densities, the type and density of industries, and home-heating practices all help determine the kinds of substances discharged into the air at a single point. In general, the more urbanized and industrialized a place is, the more responsible it is for pollution. Where burning for farmland improvement or expansion combines with rapidly expanding urban and industrial development—increasingly common in large areas of the developing world—widespread atmospheric contaminations results. For example, full-color satellite cameras regularly reveal a nearly continuous blanket of soot, organic compounds, dust, ash, and other air debris almost 3.2 kilometers (2 mi) thick that stretches across much of India, Bangladesh, and Southeast Asia, reaching northward to the industrial heart of China.

The sources of pollution are so many and varied that we cannot begin to discuss them all in this chapter. Instead, we will examine three types of air pollution and their associated effects.

Acid Rain

Although acid *precipitation* is a more precise description, **acid rain** is the term generally used for pollutants, chiefly oxides of sulfur and nitrogen, that are created by burning fossil fuels and that change chemically as they are transported through the atmosphere and fall back to Earth as acidic rain, snow, fog, or dust. The main sources of these pollutants are vehicles, industries, power plants, and ore-smelting facilities. When sulfur dioxide reacts with water vapor in the atmosphere, it becomes sulfuric acid, which is highly corrosive. Sulfur dioxide

contributes about two-thirds of the acids in the rain. About one-third comes from nitrogen oxides, transformed into nitric acid in the atmosphere.

Once the pollutants are airborne, winds can carry them hundreds of kilometers, depositing them far from their source. In North America, most of the prevailing winds are westerlies, which means that much of the acid rain that falls on the eastern seaboard and eastern Canada originates in 10 states in the central and upper Midwest (Figure 12.11). Similarly, airborne pollutants from Great Britain, France, and Germany cause acidification problems in Scandinavia.

Acid rain has three kinds of effects: *terrestrial, aquatic,* and *material.* The acids change the *pH factor* (the measure of acidity/alkalinity on a scale of 1 to 14) of both soil and water, setting off a chain of chemical and biological reactions (Figure 12.12). It is important to note that the pH scale is logarithmic, which means every step on the scale represents a factor of 10. Thus, 4.0 is 10 times more acidic than 5.0, and it is 100 times more acidic than 6.0. The average pH of normal rainfall is 5.6, categorized as slightly acidic, but acid rainfalls with a pH of 1.5 (far more acidic than vinegar or lemon juice) have been recorded.

Acid deposition harms soils and vegetation by acidifying soils and by coating the ground with particles of aluminum and toxic heavy metals, such as cadmium and lead. It kills microorganisms in the soil that break down organic matter and recycle nutrients through the ecosystem. Significant forest damage has occurred in the eastern United States, northern and western Europe, Russia, and China.

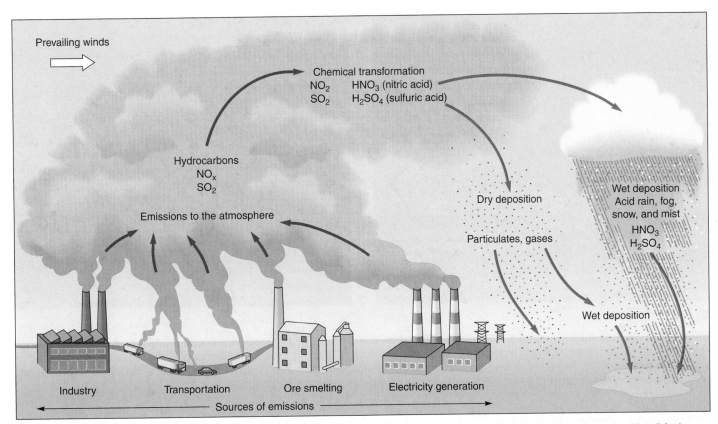

FIGURE 12.12 The formation of acid precipitation. Sulfur dioxide and nitrogen oxides produced by the combustion of fossil fuels are transformed into sulfate and nitrate particles; when the particles react with water vapor, they form sulfuric and nitric acids, which then fall to Earth. *Redrawn from* Biosphere 2000, *by Donald G. Kaufman and Cecilia M. Franz (NY: HarperCollins College Publishers, 1993, Fig. 14.5, p. 259).*

The aquatic effects of acid rain are manifold. The acidity of a lake or stream need not increase much before it begins to interfere with the early reproductive stages of fish. Also, the food chain is disrupted as acidification kills the plants and insects upon which fish feed. Acid rains have been linked to the disappearance of fish in thousands of lakes and streams in the United States, Canada, and Scandinavia and to a decline of fish populations elsewhere. On the verge of suffering from chronically high acidity are high-elevation streams, lakes, and ponds in the Sierra Nevada, the Cascade Range, the Rocky Mountains, and the Adirondacks.

The material effects of atmospheric acid are evident in damage to buildings and monuments. The acid etches and corrodes many building materials, including marble, limestone, steel, and bronze (Figure 12.13). Worldwide, tens of thousands of structures are slowly being dissolved by acid precipitation.

Photochemical Smog

While sulfur oxides are the chief cause of acid rain, oxides of nitrogen are responsible for the formation of **photochemical smog.** This type of air pollution is created when nitrogen oxides react with the oxygen present in water vapor in the air to form nitrogen dioxide. In the presence of sunlight, nitrogen dioxide reacts with hydrocarbons from automobile exhausts, industry, and natural sources to form new compounds, such

FIGURE 12.13 Damage due to acid deposition. The destructive effect of acid rain is evident on this old tombstone. Acidic fumes in the air, especially sulfuric and nitric acids, exact a heavy toll on buildings, monuments, and statues. Among the many structures that are slowly being destroyed by acid rain are the Lincoln Memorial and the Washington Monument in Washington, D.C., the Parthenon in Athens, Greece, and the Taj Mahal in Agra, India. © *The McGraw-Hill Companies, Inc./Photo by Louis Rosenstock.*

as **ozone.** The primary component of photochemical smog, ozone is a molecule consisting of three oxygen atoms rather than the two of normal oxygen. Warm, dry weather and poor

(a)

(b)

FIGURE 12.14 **Los Angeles (a) on a clear day and (b) when it is cloaked by photochemical smog.** When air over the city remains stagnant, it can accumulate increasing amounts of automobile and industrial exhausts, reducing afternoon sunlight to a dull haze and sharply lifting ozone levels. Mandates of the Clean Air Act and more-stringent restrictions on automobile emissions have resulted in reducing peak levels of ozone to a quarter of their 1955 levels. *(a) © Gregory Mancuso/Stock Boston; (b) © Robert Landau/Corbis Images.*

air circulation promote ozone formation. The hotter and sunnier the weather, the more ozone and smog are created. In general, therefore, more ozone is produced during the summer months than during the rest of the year.

Because the primary sources of the nitrogen oxides and hydrocarbons are motor vehicles and industries, photochemical smog tends to be an urban problem. The severity of the problem in any single area depends on climate, landforms, and traffic. Smog occurs around the world, affecting cities such as Ankara, Turkey; New Delhi, India; Mexico City; and Santiago, Chile. According to the World Bank, 16 of Asia's cities with the worst smog are in China.

Some 160 million Americans, or more than one-half of the U.S. population, live in or near areas that violate the federal standards for ground-level ozone that went into effect in June 2004. The warm, sunny climate and topography of California are particularly conducive to ozone pollution (Figure 12.14). California's valleys are encircled by mountains, which help hold air pollutants in the basins. When temperature inversions occur, the pollutants are effectively trapped, unable to escape to the stratosphere. And like their U.S. counterparts, more than half of all Canadians live in areas where ozone pollution can reach unacceptable levels. The region from Windsor to Quebec has the worst air quality (Figure 12.15). Approximately half of the region's ozone is generated locally; the other half comes from the Ohio Valley and the Cleveland and Detroit areas.

Photochemical smog damages both human health and vegetation. Chronic exposure to smog causes permanent damage to lungs, aging them prematurely, and is believed to increase the incidence of such respiratory ailments as asthma, bronchitis, pneumonia, and emphysema. Because children

have smaller breathing passages and less-developed immune systems than adults, they are especially susceptible to damage from the polluted air.

In addition to its effects on humans, ozone harms vegetation. Exposure over several days to ozone concentrations as low as 0.1 part per million damages trees, plants, and crops. Although smog originates in urban industrial centers, it can affect areas downwind from them. Damage associated with photochemical smog has been documented in forests downwind from Tokyo and Osaka in Japan; Beijing, China; Karachi, Pakistan; and Los Angeles, California, among other places.

Depletion of the Ozone Layer

Ozone, the same chemical that is a noxious pollutant near the ground, is essential in the stratosphere. There, approximately 10 to 24 kilometers (6 to 15 mi) above the ground, ozone forms a protective blanket called the **ozone layer,** which shields all forms of life on Earth from overexposure to lethal ultraviolet (UV) radiation from the sun. Mounting evidence indicates that emissions from a variety of chemicals are destroying the ozone layer. Most important is a family of synthetic chemicals developed in 1931 and known as **chlorofluorocarbons (CFCs),** including halons, carbon tetrachloride, and methyl chloroform. CFCs are found in hundreds of products. They are used as coolants for refrigerators and air conditioners; as aerosol spray propellants; as a component in foam packaging, home insulation, and upholstery; as fire retardants; and as cleaning agents. In liquefied form, they are used to sterilize surgical equipment and to clean computer chips and other microelectronic equipment. Also implicated in the depletion of the ozone layer is

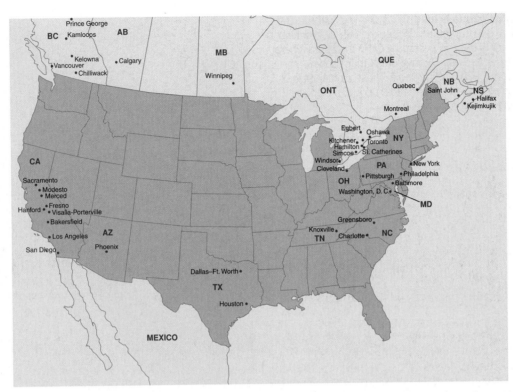

FIGURE 12.15 U.S. and Canadian cities most polluted by smog. The map shows only the 20 cities in each country with the highest levels of ozone contamination. Despite significantly reducing harmful emissions in recent years, the Los Angeles basin still has the worst ozone pollution in the United States in terms of the number of "bad air" days per year. However, some of the worst smog days in the country occur in Houston and Dallas–Fort Worth, Texas. In Canada, 10 of the 20 cities are in the Windsor-to-Quebec corridor, which is subject to cross-border pollution from the United States. *Source of data: American Lung Association, Environment Canada.*

methyl bromide, a pesticide used to sterilize soils and grain silos and to fumigate shipments of perishable goods.

After the gases are released into the air, they rise through the lower atmosphere and, after a period of 7 to 15 years, reach the stratosphere (Figure 12.16). There, UV radiation breaks the molecules apart, producing free chlorine and bromine atoms. Over time, a single one of these atoms can destroy tens of thousands, if not a potentially infinite number, of ozone molecules.

Each year, beginning in July, the atmosphere over the Antarctic starts to lose more and more ozone. In most parts of the world, horizontal winds tend to keep chemicals in the air well mixed. But circulation patterns are such that the freezing whirlpool of air over Antarctica is not penetrated by air currents from warmer Earth regions. In the absence of sunlight and atmospheric mixing, the CFCs and other gases work to destroy the ozone.

In 1985, researchers discovered what is popularly termed a "hole" (actually, a broad area of low-ozone concentrations) as big as the continental United States in the ozone layer over Antarctica, extending northward as far as populated areas of South America (Figure 12.17). The ozone depletion intensifies during August and September before tapering off in October as temperatures rise, the winds change, and the ozone-deficient air mixes with the surrounding atmosphere. A less dramatic but still serious depletion of the ozone shield occurs over the North Pole, and the ozone shield over the midlatitudes has dropped significantly since 1978.

A depleted ozone layer allows more UV radiation to reach the earth's surface. Increased exposure to UV radiation raises the incidence of skin cancer and, by suppressing bodily defense mechanisms, increases risk from a variety of infectious diseases. Because UV radiation also causes cell and tissue damage in plants, it is likely to reduce agricultural production. The most serious damage may occur in oceans. Increased amounts of UV radiation affect the photosynthesis and metabolism of the microscopic plants called phytoplankton that flourish just below the surface of the Antarctic Ocean. Phytoplankton form the base of the oceanic food chain and play a central role in the earth's CO_2 cycle.

The production of CFCs and other ozone-depleting substances is being phased out under the *Montreal Protocol on Substances That Deplete the Ozone Layer* of 1987, an international treaty that required developed countries to stop production and consumption of ozone-depleting substances after 1995 and to cease in developing countries by 2010. The Montreal Protocol spurred a rapid decline in CFC output. CFC use decreased 96% between 1986 and 2005, and the use of methyl bromide by 66%.

Even if all countries eventually comply with the Montreal Protocol, however, past emissions will continue to cause ozone degradation for years to come. The two most widely used forms of CFCs stay in the stratosphere, breaking down ozone molecules, for up to 120 years. Thus, full recovery of the ozone layer cannot be expected until the end of the 21st century.

FIGURE 12.16 How ozone is lost. CFCs and methyl bromide released into the air rise through the troposphere without breaking down (as most pollutants do) and eventually enter the stratosphere. Once they reach the ozone layer, UV rays break them down, releasing chlorine (from CFCs) and bromine. These elements, in turn, disrupt ozone molecules, breaking them up into molecular oxygen, and thus deplete the ozone layer.

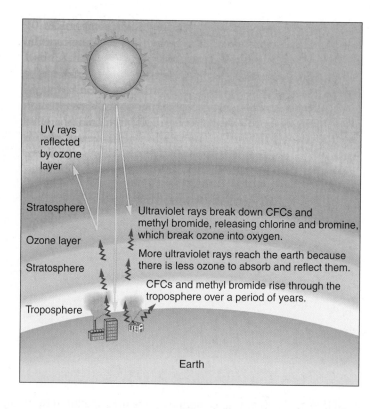

FIGURE 12.17 Ozone depletion over the Southern Hemisphere on September 16, 2003. The color scale below the image shows the total ozone levels. The pinks and purples indicate the areas of greatest ozone depletion. The area of significant depletion varies in size from year to year. In 2003, the hole grew to near record size, 29 million square kilometers (11.1 million sq mi). Although depletion of the ozone layer has been particularly severe over Antarctica, a decline in stratospheric ozone has also been observed over other parts of the world. © *National Centers for Environmental Prediction, NOAA.*

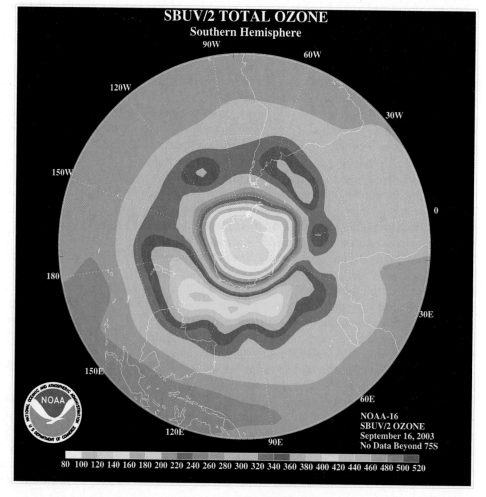

Controlling Air Pollution

A number of developments in recent years have given rise to the hope that people can reverse the decline in air quality. The total amount of lead added to gasoline has dropped worldwide by 75% since 1970. Several countries, both industrialized and developing, eliminated leaded gasoline from their markets. Many others reduced the lead content and/or introduced unleaded gasoline. The development is significant because exposure to the microscopic particles of lead that are emitted into the atmosphere when leaded gasoline is burned contributes to mental retardation, high blood pressure, and an increased risk of heart attacks and strokes.

As discussed earlier, the Montreal Protocol of 1987 called for global efforts to reduce the release of ozone-depleting substances in order to protect the ozone layer. The treaty has made a significant difference. The protocol and its amendments ban CFC production in industrial countries, and by 2005, total world production of CFCs and methyl bromide had fallen significantly. The drop has been most pronounced in the European Union and the United States. The production of CFCs actually has risen in China, India, and other developing countries, where it is still legal. There is good reason to believe that atmospheric concentrations of CFCs will fall slowly over the next several decades and that sometime between 2050 and 2075 stratospheric ozone levels will return to normal.

Another successful international accord is the 1979 Convention on Long-Range Transboundary Air Pollution, signed by 33 countries in Europe and North America and intended to reduce the emissions of nitrous oxides and sulfur dioxides. During the 1980s, air pollution in Europe was reduced as, for example, Austria, West Germany, Sweden, and Norway cut their SO_2 emissions by more than 50%. Emissions of nitrous oxides have proved more difficult to control.

Air pollution remains a serious problem in many developing countries, however, particularly those where major metropolitan areas are growing at explosive rates. In Mexico City and Santiago, Chile, for example, pollution exceeds WHO health standards 300 or more days per year. As noted earlier, China has 16 of the world's 20 most polluted cities, a situation that is not likely to improve in the near future as long as the country's economy continues to grow. By 2010, China surpassed the United States as the largest emitter of carbon dioxide. It is building an average of one new coal-fired power plant per week and, in another 20 years, will have millions more cars on the road.

The United States has made significant progress in cleaning up its air. A series of Clean Air Acts (1963, 1965, 1970, 1977) and amendments identified major pollutants and established national air-quality standards. After many years of debate, Congress in 1990 passed a Clean Air Act that represented the most sweeping legislation to date. It set forth goals to protect public health and the environment by reducing the amount of air pollutants that can be released, and it established a time table for reaching those goals. Major provisions call for

- reducing urban smog by setting limits on allow... of particulates and the concentration of ozone in u.
- using cleaner-burning fuels in the most polluted cities
- lowering nitrogen oxide and hydrocarbon emissions from motor vehicles
- requiring utilities to reduce their emissions of NO_x and SO_2

The country's air is cleaner now than it was when the first several Clean Air Acts were enacted, despite the fact that the population, economy, and number of vehicles have grown. Since 1985, emissions of lead have dropped 98%, of sulfur dioxide by 50%, and of carbon monoxide by 32%. Nevertheless, the air in many parts of the country still violates the public health standards.

Reaching the goals of the Clean Air Act will require reducing the type and volume of air pollutants from both stationary and nonstationary sources. A number of strategies can be employed to clean up stationary sources. Technological options include switching to cleaner-burning fuels; coal washing, which removes much of the sulfur in coal before it is burned; and removing pollutants from effluent gases in the smokestack by using scrubbers, precipitators, and filters. Another approach is to reduce energy consumption by using more efficient appliances, installing weatherstripping and insulation, and strengthening energy performance standards in the building codes for new buildings.

Reducing emissions from nonstationary sources—mainly motor vehicles of all types—can be accomplished in a number of ways. These include conforming to tighter tailpipe emission standards by retiring older automobiles, driving fuel-efficient automobiles, phasing out leaded gas, and implementing rigorous vehicle inspection programs. Catalytic converters have sharply reduced smog from vehicles. Travel can be made more energy efficient if a community is committed to rewarding those who carpool or use alternative means of transport, such as bicycles or mass transit.

IMPACT ON LANDFORMS

People have affected the earth wherever they have lived. Whatever we do, or have done in the past, to satisfy our basic needs has had an impact on the landscape (Figure 12.18). To provide food, clothing, shelter, transportation, and defense, we have cleared the land and replanted it, rechanneled waterways, and built roads, fortresses, and cities. We have mined the earth's resources, logged entire forests, terraced mountainsides, even reclaimed land from the sea. The nature of the changes made in any single area depends on what was there to begin with and how people have used the land.

Landforms Produced by Excavation

Although we tend to think of landforms as "givens," created by natural processes over millions of years, people have played and continue to play a significant role in shaping local

FIGURE 12.18 Human transformation of the land. Humans have altered much of the earth's surface in some way. The "almost pristine" areas, covered with original vegetation, tend to be too high, dry, cold, or otherwise unsuitable for human habitation in large numbers. They generally have very low population densities. "Partially transformed" describes areas of secondary vegetation, grown after removal of original vegetation. Most are used for agriculture or livestock grazing. "Almost fully transformed" areas are those of permanent and intensive agriculture and urban settlement; little or no original vegetation remains. *Source:* Student Atlas of World Geography, *5th ed., John Allen, Map 83, p. 99. McGraw-Hill/Dushkin, 2008.*

physical landscapes. Some features are created deliberately, others unknowingly or indirectly. Pits, ponds, ridges and trenches, subsidence depressions, canals, and reservoirs are the chief landform features resulting from excavations. Some date back to neolithic times, when people dug into chalk pits to obtain flint for toolmaking. Excavation has had its greatest impact within the last two centuries, however, as earth-moving operations have been undertaken for mining; for building construction and agriculture; and for the construction of transport facilities such as railways, ship canals, and highways.

Surface mining, which involves the removal of vegetation, topsoil, and rocks from the earth's surface in order to get at the resources underneath, has perhaps had the greatest environmental impact. Open-pit mining and strip mining are the most commonly used methods of surface mining. *Open-pit mining* is used primarily to obtain iron and copper, sand, gravel, and stone. As Figure 12.19a indicates, an enormous pit remains after the mining has been completed, because most of the material has been removed for processing.

Strip mining is increasingly employed in the United States to obtain coal; more coal per year now comes from strip mines than from underground mines. Phosphate is also mined in this way. A trench is dug, the material is excavated, and another trench is dug, the soil and waste rock being deposited in the first trench, and so on. Unless reclamation is practiced, the result is a ridged landscape (Figure 12.19b). In a variation of strip mining called *mountaintop removal,* the tops of

mountains are blasted off with dynamite to expose coal seams. Bulldozers push the mountaintops and slag waste into the valleys and streams below (see "Mountaintop Removal: Good or Bad?," pp. 414–415).

Landscapes marred by vast open pits or unevenly filled trenches are one of the most visible results of surface mining. Thousands of square miles of land have been affected, with the prospect of thousands more to come as the amount of surface mining increases. Damage to the aesthetic value of an area is not the only liability of surface mining. If the area is large, wildlife habitats are disrupted, and surface and subsurface drainage patterns are disturbed. In the United States, current law requires strip-mining companies to level the ridges and regrade the area, restore the soil, and replant grass or other vegetation. The law is not always obeyed.

Landforms Produced by Dumping

Excavation in one area often leads to the creation, via dumping, of landforms nearby. Both surface and subsurface mining produce tons of waste and enormous spoil piles. In fact, in terms of tonnage, mining is the single greatest contributor to solid wastes, with about 2 billion tons per year left to be disposed of in the United States alone. The normal custom is to dump waste rocks and mill tailings in huge heaps near the mine sites. Unfortunately, this practice has secondary effects on the environment.

(a)

(b)

FIGURE 12.19 **(a) An aerial view of the Bingham Canyon open-pit copper mine in Utah, said to be the largest human-made excavation in the world.** Since mining began at the site, approximately 15 billion tons of material have been removed, creating a pit more than 800 meters (2600 ft) deep and 4 kilometers (2.5 mi) wide at the top. The mine has yielded vast quantities of copper, gold, silver, and molybdenum. **(b)** About 400 square kilometers (154 sq mi) of land surface in the United States are lost each year to the strip mining of coal and other resources; far more is disrupted worldwide. On flat or rolling terrain, strip mining leaves a landscape of parallel ridges and trenches, the result of stripping away the unwanted surface material, or overburden. The material taken from one trench to reach the underlying mineral is placed in an adjacent one, leaving the wavelike terrain shown here. Besides altering the topography, strip mining interrupts surface and subsurface drainage patterns, destroys vegetation, and places sterile and often highly acidic subsoil and rock on top of the new ground surface. *(a)* © *Dr. Parvinder Sethi; (b)* © *Jim Richardson/Corbis.*

Carried by wind and water, dust from the wastes pollutes the air, and dissolved minerals pollute nearby water sources. Occasionally, the wastes cause greater damage, as happened in Wales in 1966, when slag heaps from the coal mines slid onto the village of Aberfan, burying more than 140 schoolchildren. Such tragedies call attention to the need for less potentially destructive ways of disposing of mine wastes.

Another example of the combined effect of excavating and filling on the landscape is the agricultural terrace characteristic of parts of Asia. In order to retain water and increase the amount of arable land, terraces are cut into the slopes of hills and mountains. Low walls protect the patches of level land.

Human impact on land has been particularly strong in areas where land and water meet. Dredging and filling operations undertaken for purposes of water control create landscape features such as embankments and dikes. In many places, the actual shape of the shoreline has been altered, as builders in need of additional land have dumped solid wastes into landfills. In the Netherlands, millions of acres of land have been reclaimed from the sea by the building of dikes to enclose polders and canals to drain them. Farming practices in river valleys have had significant effects on deltas. For example, increased sedimentation has often extended the area of land into the sea.

Formation of Surface Depressions

The extraction of material from beneath the ground can lead to **subsidence,** the settling or sinking of a portion of the land surface. Many of the world's great cities are sinking because of the removal of *fluids* (groundwater, oil, and gas) from beneath them. Cities threatened by such subsidence are located on unconsolidated sediments (New Orleans and Bangkok), coastal marshes (Venice and Tokyo), or lake beds (Mexico City). When the fluids are removed, the sediments compact and the land surface sinks. Because many of the cities are on coasts or estuaries and are often only a few feet above sea level, subsidence makes them more vulnerable to flooding from the sea and rising sea levels associated with climate change.

The removal of *solids* (such as coal, salt, and gold) by underground mining may result in the collapse of land over the mine. *Sinkholes,* or *pits* (circular, steep-walled depressions), and *sags* (larger and shallower depressions) are two types of landscape features produced by such collapse (Figure 12.20). If surface drainage patterns are disrupted, subsidence *lakes* may form in the depressions. Subsidence has become a more serious problem as towns and cities have expanded over mined-out areas.

As one might expect, subsidence damages structures built on the land, including buildings, roads, and sewage lines. A dramatic example occurred in Los Angeles in 1963, when subsidence caused the dam at the Baldwin Hills Reservoir to crack. In less than 2 hours, the water emptied into the city, resulting in millions of dollars' worth of property damage. The withdrawal of groundwater from beneath Mexico City has led to severe though differential subsidence. One of the reasons the 1985 earthquake in that city was so damaging was that subsidence had weakened building structures.

high risk of disruption by human activities. Although the 34 occupy only a small percentage of the world's land area, they house 75% of the world's most threatened mammals, birds, and amphibians, and 50% of all known higher plant species. In this section, we examine four major ways human activities modify animal and plant life and threaten to reduce biodiversity.

Habitat Loss or Alteration

The main cause of extinction has been the loss or alteration of habitats for wildlife. About three-fourths of all threatened species are affected by habitat degradation or loss. Agricultural activities (crop and livestock farming), extractive activities (logging and mining), and various forms of development (e.g., draining wetlands, clearing forests and grasslands for towns and cities) all modify or destroy the habitats in which plants and animals live. The destruction of the world's rain forests, the most biologically diverse places on Earth, is by some estimates causing the extinction of hundreds of plant and animal species every year.

As countries in Africa, Asia, and South America become more industrialized and more urbanized and expand their areas under cultivation, there will be an increasingly negative impact on wildlife. In Africa, wild animals are vanishing fast, in part the victims of habitat destruction. In Botswana, for example, 250,000 antelope and zebra died in a decade, disoriented by fences erected to protect cattle.

The tropical rain forests of Indonesia, home to such animals as the silvery gibbon and the orangutan, are being destroyed by logging, both legal and illegal; by the conversion of forests to plantations to grow trees for palm oil and paper production; and by surface mining for gold and zircon. The

FIGURE 12.20 A sinkhole in Guatemala City, Guatemala. Sinkholes form when the ground above an underground cavern suddenly collapses. They can be triggered by the lowering of the water table or by heavy rains that enlarge a crack in the cavern roof. Areas underlain by limestone, which is soluble in water, are particularly susceptible to the formation of sinkholes, as the many such depressions in Florida, Kentucky, Indiana, and Missouri attest. © Moises Castillo/AP Images.

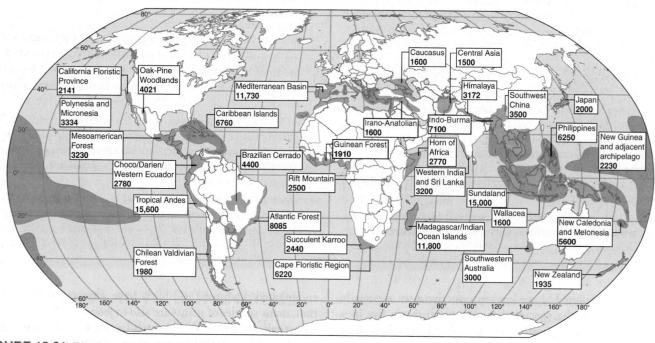

FIGURE 12.21 Biodiversity hot spots, Earth's biologically richest and most threatened ecosystems. Numbers indicate endemic (unique) species. Conservation International identified 34 of these critical habitats for plants and vertebrate animals. Each has a high number of species found nowhere else and has already lost at least 70% of its original vegetation. Some areas with high biodiversity, such as Amazonia and the Congo Basin, are not included on the map because most of their land area is relatively undisturbed. Notice that the hot spots are in areas that have been relatively isolated from other areas for a long time, either because they are islands or because they have special climatic conditions (e.g., Mediterranean or tropical). Source: Conservation International, 2008.

silvery gibbon lives only on the Indonesian island of Java, and between 80% and 90% of the orangutan population lives on the Indonesian island of Sumatra (Figure 12.22). Both species now are considered endangered. As selected animal species decline in numbers, balances among species are upset and entire ecosystems are disrupted.

A number of Arctic species are being affected by habitat alteration during the current warming trend. Springtime arrives in the Arctic a month earlier than it did a decade ago. As the amount of ice has declined, so have the populations of polar bears, walruses, and other ice-dependent marine mammals.

Habitat disruption characterizes developed as well as developing countries. Tidal marshes in the United States, for example, have been dredged and filled for residential and industrial development. The loss of such areas reduces the essential habitat of fish, crustaceans, and mollusks. The whooping crane has been virtually eliminated in the United States because the marshes where it nested were drained, and roads and canals brought intruders into its habitat. Its comeback, sought by breeding programs in the United States and Canada, is still uncertain.

Hunting and Commercial Exploitation

Another way in which people have affected plants and animals is through their deliberate destruction. We have overhunted and overfished, for food, fur, hides, jewelry, and trophies. In the past, unregulated hunting harmed wildlife all over the world and was responsible for the destruction of many populations and species. Beavers, sea otters, alligators, and buffalo are among the species brought to the edge of extinction in the

United States by thoughtless exploitation. Under protective legislation, their populations are now increasing, but hunting in developing countries still poses a threat to a number of species. In Central and West Africa, hunting rather than habitat destruction constitutes the main threat to some species.

Four African animals whose existence is threatened by hunting, most of it illegal, are the elephant, the rhinoceros, the mountain gorilla, and the hippopotamus.

- Prized for its ivory tusks, the African elephant has been ruthlessly slaughtered. Between 5 and 10 million of the elephants are estimated to have been alive in the 1930s, a number that declined to 1.3 million by 1979. Now, only 300,000 to 500,000 remain.

- The black rhinoceros, killed for its horn, is now an endangered species. The population has declined from nearly a million in sub-Saharan Africa a century ago to about 3500 today.

- All three subspecies of gorillas are endangered; the rarest of all is the mountain gorilla. About 700 mountain gorillas are believed to exist, most of them in national parks in the Democratic Republic of Congo, Uganda, and Rwanda (Figure 12.23).

- Since 1994, hunting has caused a precipitous decline in the population of the common hippopotamus in the Democratic Republic of the Congo, and the species is now ranked as vulnerable. The pygmy hippopotamus of West Africa was classified as vulnerable in 2000; by 2006, fewer than 3000 remained, and the species had become endangered, at risk of extinction.

The decline in the productivity of marine fisheries, discussed in Chapter 10, is due in large part to the widespread use of modern fishing technology, which has made hunting easier and more efficient. The technology includes the use of sonar, radar, helicopters, and Global Positioning Systems to locate schools of fish; more efficient nets and tackle; and factory trawlers to follow fishing fleets to prepare and freeze the catch.

According to the UN Food and Agriculture Organization, all 17 major ocean fishing areas in the world are now being fished at or above sustainable levels; 13 are in decline. The plundering of United States coastal waters has imperiled a number of the most desirable fish species, including haddock, yellowtail flounder, and cod in New England waters; Spanish mackerel, grouper, and red snapper off the Gulf of Mexico; halibut and striped bass off California; and salmon and steelhead in the Pacific Northwest.

Commercial fishermen from Japan, South Korea, Taiwan, and other countries use drift nets to capture squid, tuna, and salmon. The nets, which can stretch up to 65 kilometers (40 mi), have been called "curtains of death" because they are devastatingly effective, essentially scooping up all life in their path—not just the target species but also millions of nontarget fish, sea birds, turtles, and marine mammals. The World Wildlife Fund estimates that at least 60,000 dolphins, porpoises, and whales drown each year after becoming entangled

(a)   (b)

FIGURE 12.22 Two victims of habitat destruction and the demands an expanding population puts on land. Among the animals facing extinction in the wild are **(a)** the silvery gibbon and **(b)** the orangutan. Experts estimate that since 1975 the number of silvery gibbons has plummeted from about 20,000 to between 400 and 2000. The population of orangutans is believed to have been halved since the early 1990s. *(a) © Gerard Lacz/Animals Animals; (b) © Punchstock RF.*

FIGURE 12.23 The mountain gorilla (*Gorilla gorilla beringei*) is one of the world's most endangered primates. Although the gorillas live in national parks, their survival is not guaranteed. Both habitat destruction—the felling of trees for fuel and shelter—and illegal poaching have reduced their numbers. © *Getty RF.*

in fishing nets and other equipment. These accidental captures by crews fishing for other species are known as *bycatch;* they have significantly depleted the populations of many of the 80 species of the cetacean (fishlike) groups of sea mammals, critically endangering some of them.

Introduction of Exotic Species

A plant, an animal, or another organism (such as a microbe) that has been released into an ecosystem in which it did not evolve is nonindigenous (non-native)—an **exotic species.** An exotic species that causes economic or environmental harm is considered *invasive* (Figure 12.24). Human actions are the primary means of invasive species introductions.

The deliberate or inadvertent introduction of a species into an area where it did not previously exist can have damaging and unforeseen consequences. Introduced species have often left behind their natural enemies—predators and diseases—giving them an advantage over native species that are held in check by biological controls. The rabbit, for example, was purposely introduced into Australia in 1859. The original dozen pairs multiplied to a population in the thousands in only a few years and, despite programs of control, to an estimated 1 billion by 1950. Inasmuch as five rabbits eat about as much as one sheep, a national problem had been created. Rabbits became an economic burden and environmental menace, competing with sheep for grazing lands and stimulating soil erosion.

Invasions of exotic (also called *alien*) species have multiplied as the speed and range of world trade and travel have increased. In the United States alone, hundreds of harmful invaders have been discovered in recent years—harmful because they consume or outcompete native species. They include

- the Asian tiger mosquito, which was discovered in 1985 in a Japanese container of tires headed for a recapping plant in Texas and has since spread to 25 states; it carries a number of tropical viruses, including yellow fever, dengue fever, and various forms of encephalitis

- zebra mussels, first detected in Lake St. Clair, near Detroit, in 1985, which were released from ballast water from Eastern European ships and have spread rapidly to northeastern Canada, all the Great Lakes, hundreds of inland lakes, the Mississippi River and its tributaries; prolific reproducers, the mussels clog the underwater intake pipes of water treatment plants, power plants, and industrial facilities, smother native mollusks, and compete with algae-eating fish for food and oxygen

- the round goby, an aggressive fish that reached U.S. waters in 1990 in ballast chambers of ships from the Black and Caspian Seas and threatens to disrupt the Great Lakes' ecosystem

- the Asian gypsy moth, a voracious eater of trees and some crops, which arrived in Oregon, Washington, and British Columbia in 1991

- Africanized honeybees, more aggressive and venomous than European bees; they reached the southwestern United States in the 1990s after escaping from an experimental station in Brazil in 1957

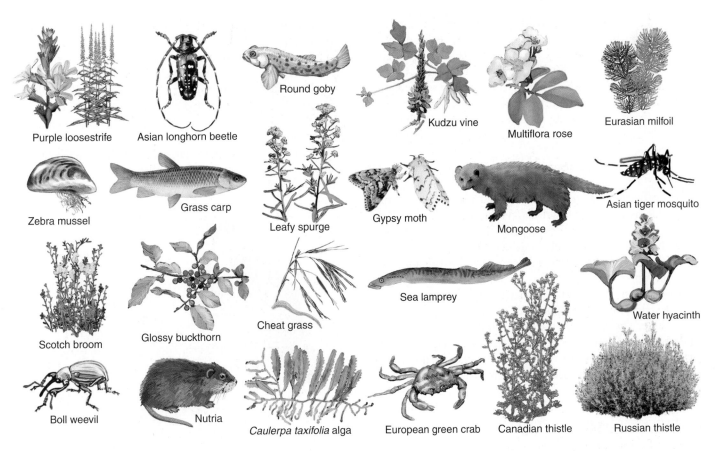

FIGURE 12.24 A few of the approximately 50,000 non-native species that have become established in North America over the past 300 years. At least 750 of these species cause significant environmental and/or economic damage. You can check on the Web to see if any of these exist where you live.

- the Asian long-horned beetle, which probably arrived in Brooklyn, New York, in wood pallets from China in 1996 and has since appeared in the Chicago area; it threatens species such as maple, elm, willow, and birch
- the emerald ash borer, an Asian beetle that arrived in wood packing material carried in cargo ships or airplanes; it was detected in Michigan in 2002 and within 5 years had spread to eight other states and Ontario, Canada, where it has killed millions of ash trees

In the United States, exotic species are second only to habitat loss as a cause of endangerment. About half of the species threatened with extinction in the country are in trouble at least partly because of them.

Plants and animals found on islands are particularly prone to extinction. Native plants and animals evolved in isolation, with few diseases or predators. Furthermore, because many island species occur on just one or a few islands, the loss of only a few individuals can be devastating to small populations. In the United States, Hawaii has more endangered species than any other state. Half of the islands' 140 native breeding bird species are now extinct, and of the 71 remaining, 32 are considered threatened. Bird declines were due both to habitat alteration—deforestation—and to such alien predators as tree-climbing rats, mongooses, and feral cats, dogs, and pigs.

Plants introduced to Hawaii include eucalyptus trees, ginger, and gorse. Miconia, a large-leaved plant, was brought in as a tropical ornamental. Outside the confines of a flowerpot, it grows to 50 feet or more, and its mammoth leaves (1 meter, or 3 ft, across) cast dense shade, killing native vegetation beneath it, promoting water runoff and erosion. Small colonies of these plants are scattered throughout the islands, and there is a massive eradication program underway in an attempt to curb its spread. The fear is that miconia might do to Hawaii what it has done in Tahiti, where it has replaced 70% of the native rain forest and is threatening 25% of the island's native wildlife species.

As this discussion indicates, introduced plants, as well as animals, can alter vegetative patterns. Some 300 species of invasive plants now threaten native ecosystems in the mainland United States and Canada. At least half were deliberately imported, including purple loosestrife, the melaleuca tree, Norway maple, and water hyacinth. These and other imports have arrived without their natural enemies and have spread uncontrolled, driving out native species.

An aquatic vine, hydrilla, imported into Florida from Sri Lanka for use in aquariums, was dumped into a canal in Tampa in 1951. Also known as water thyme, it has overgrown more than 40% of Florida's rivers and lakes and continues to spread rapidly. Transported on motorboat propellers and boat trailers, hydrilla has spread through the lakes and rivers of the South, as far west as California and as far north as Maine and the state of Washington. The plant creates dense canopies at the surface, interfering with swimming, fishing, and boating. The mats clog boat propellers and water intake pipes and reduce the amount of sunlight reaching the water bottom. By monopolizing the dissolved oxygen that fish and aquatic plants require to thrive, hydrilla reduces native diversity.

In an attempt at *biological control,* fighting an invader by importing a predator known to keep it in check elsewhere, Florida officials imported tilapia, a weed-eating fish, to solve the problems created by hydrilla. While the fish have done little to clear Florida waterways, they have driven out many types of native fish, especially large-mouth bass.

Disease-carrying microorganisms can also become invasive and do great harm. The Asiatic chestnut blight has destroyed most of the native American chestnut trees in the United States, trees with significant commercial as well as aesthetic value. The cause was the importation from China to the United States of some chestnut trees that carried a fungus fatal to the American chestnut tree but not to the Asiatic variety. Similarly, Dutch elm disease greatly reduced the number of American elms.

These are just a few of the many examples that illustrate an often ignored ecological truth: plant and animal life are so interrelated that when people introduce a new species to a region, whether by choice or by chance, there may be unforeseen and far-reaching consequences.

It is important to note, however, that not all introduced species are harmful. They are of little concern if they assimilate well and coexist with the native stock. Further, an import may become a problem in one area but not be highly invasive elsewhere.

Poisoning and Contamination

Humans have also affected plant and animal life by poisoning and contamination. In the last several years, we have become acutely conscious of the effect of insecticides, rodenticides, and herbicides, known collectively as *biocides.*

Some of the side effects of these biocides have been well enough documented for scientists to question their indiscriminate use. Once used, a biocide settles into the soil, where it may remain or may be washed into a body of water. In either case, it is absorbed by organisms living in the water, soil, or mud. If an organism is unable to excrete the biocide, its concentration within the animal continues to increase, a process called *bioaccumulation.* Toxins present in very small amounts in the environment can reach dangerous levels inside cells and tissues.

Food webs magnify the effect of toxins in the environment. When a predator eats a large number of plants or animals at a lower trophic level, the predator collects and concentrates the toxins from its prey. **Biological magnification** (also called **biomagnification**) is the accumulation of a

chemical in the fatty tissue of an organism and its concentration at progressively higher levels in the food chain. Zooplankton and small fish, for example, collect and retain the toxins from water, sediments, and organic debris. They are eaten in turn by small fish, shrimp, and clams, which build up higher concentrations of the toxins, as shown in Figure 12.25. The higher the level of a plant or an animal in the food chain, the greater the concentration of the poisons. The carnivores at the top of the food chain, large fish, fish-eating birds, and humans, can accumulate such high levels of the biocide that it adversely affects their health and reproduction.

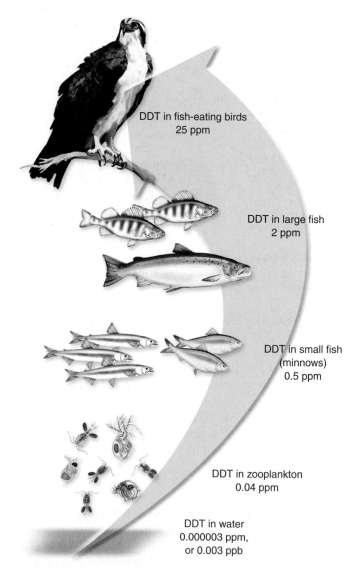

DDT in fish-eating birds
25 ppm

DDT in large fish
2 ppm

DDT in small fish
(minnows)
0.5 ppm

DDT in zooplankton
0.04 ppm

DDT in water
0.000003 ppm,
or 0.003 ppb

FIGURE 12.25 The bioaccumulation and biomagnification of DDT. The numbers are parts per million (ppm). Although the level of DDT in the water may be low, notice how the amount of DDT in the bodies of fish and birds increases as we go up the food chain. In this simplified example, birds at the top of the chain have concentrations of residues 50 times greater than small fish. Mercury, aldrin, chlordane, and other chlorinated hydrocarbons, such as PCBs, undergo magnification in the food chain. *Source: Cunningham, Cunningham, and Saigo,* Environmental Science, *7th ed. Boston: McGraw-Hill, 2003.*

One of the oldest and most dangerous pesticides is dichloro-diphenyl-trichloro-ethane (DDT). Hailed as a chemical miracle, DDT was first used during World War II as a delousing agent and to clear malaria-bearing mosquitoes from the paths of Allied troops. After the war, one of the first major undertakings of the World Health Organization was the Global Malaria Eradication Program, launched in 1955; its principal tool was DDT. Soon, tons of the pesticide were being used, both to combat disease and to increase agricultural yields, but within a few years two significant problems emerged: (1) biomagnification, or the increasing concentration of the chemical at higher levels of the food chain, and (2) insecticide resistance—the reproduction within a few years of mosquitoes that were immune to the poison.

The publication of Rachel Carson's *Silent Spring* in 1962 alerted the public to the devastating effect of the pesticide on birds and other wildlife. The chemical caused a decrease in the thickness of the eggshells of some of the larger birds, so that a greater number of eggs broke than normally would. Peregrine falcons, bald eagles, and brown pelicans were among the birds nearly made extinct by this disruption of the reproductive process. Although the use of DDT was banned in the United States in 1972, a number of countries, most of them in Africa, still use it. Because malaria is the biggest killer of children under age 5, and because DDT is one of the most effective insecticides against mosquitoes, the indoor spraying of DDT is supported by the World Health Organization and other agencies.

Meanwhile, other chlorinated hydrocarbon compounds have been developed and are in wide use. They include chlordane, aldrin, dieldrin, and dioxin. Because they do not break down easily, they accumulate in the bodies of animals in the food chain, thus affecting many nontarget organisms. The deaths of thousands of seals, Pacific sea lions, and Mediterranean striped dolphins are thought to be caused by accumulation of the chemicals.

The use of pesticides in the United States has increased steadily. According to the EPA, more than 2.4 million metric tons (5.3 billion lbs) containing hundreds of active ingredients are applied each year. The pesticides pollute water supplies, often contaminate the crops they are meant to protect, can cause allergic reactions, and sometimes sicken the farm workers who apply them. In addition, too often the pesticides are only temporarily effective.

Biocides may, in fact, exacerbate the problem their use is designed to eradicate. By altering the natural processes that determine which pests (insects, rodents, weeds) in a population will survive, biocides spur the development of resistant species. If all but 5% of the mosquito population in an area are killed by an insecticide, the ones that survive are the most resistant individuals, and they are the ones that will produce the succeeding generations.

There are now insects whose total resistance to certain pesticides has led some scientists to conclude that the entire process of insecticide development may be self-defeating. Despite the enormous growth in the use of biocides, crop loss to insect and weed pests has actually grown. According to

Department of Agriculture figures, 32% of crops were lost to pests in 1945; 40 years later, such losses had increased to 37%.

Biocides have also been known to increase problems by destroying the natural enemies of the intended target, leaving it to breed unchallenged. Examples include the tobacco budworm and the brown planthopper, which were relatively minor pests before intensive crop spraying destroyed rival pests.

Preserving Biodiversity

As people have become more aware of how their activities affect plant and animal life in often deleterious ways, public concern with the preservation of biodiversity has mounted. Ideally, the goal is to maintain diversity in all biomes, not just in the 34 hot spots identified in Figure 12.21. In the broadest sense, efforts are aimed at controlling or reducing the impact of the four main causes of endangerment: habitat loss or alteration, hunting and commercial exploitation, the introduction of exotic species, and the overuse of biocides. More narrowly, specific attempts tend to focus either on preventing the extinction of individual species or on preserving habitats that support maximum biological diversity. Governments, nongovernmental organizations, and other agencies and groups use a variety of methods to further their goals.

Legal Protection

Three of the many legal measures for preserving biodiversity are the following.

- *The UN Convention on Biological Diversity* (1992): an international treaty that by 2007 had been signed by 189 countries, its objective is for countries to develop national strategies for the conservation and sustainable use of biodiversity.

- *Convention on International Trade in Endangered Species* (1973): by 2007 signed by more than 160 countries, it regulates trade in living specimens of wild flora and fauna and the products made from some 700 threatened species. Due to its ban on international trade in elephant products—the most important being ivory—two African countries (Botswana and South Africa) have experienced a rise in their elephant populations.

- *The Endangered Species Act* (1973) is the most significant piece of biodiversity legislation in the United States. Among other things, it prohibits hunting or commercial harvesting of threatened or endangered species; prohibits importing them into or exporting them out of the United States; and can mandate protection of a habitat that is critical to the survival of a species. The act has saved several species—including the bald eagle, the peregrine falcon, and the American alligator—from possible extinction.

In addition, most countries have established national parks or other government-protected areas (e.g., refuges, nature preserves, marine reserves). Many, particularly in developing countries, attract significant numbers of ecotourists, who shoot with a camera rather than a gun.

Nongovernmental Organizations (NGOs)

Private organizations pursue a number of activities to preserve and protect species and habitats and slow the accelerating rate of species extinction. Among these NGOs are The Nature Conservancy, the World Wildlife Fund, The Wildlife Conservation Union, and Conservation International. The Nature Conservancy has joined with governments, private corporations, and indigenous people to purchase critical habitats. With branches in Africa, Asia, the Caribbean, and the Americas, it has undertaken projects in more than 30 countries and all 50 United States to preserve natural landscapes and the plants and animals they house. Greenpeace, established in 1971, has been actively involved in convincing world leaders to, among other things, ban commercial whaling, stop the destruction of ancient forests and the deterioration of oceans, and designate marine reserves in the Bering Sea.

A number of zoos, aquariums, and botanical gardens have breeding programs to save severely threatened species. Two species saved by captive breeding programs are the condor and the nene. Hunting and fragmentation of their habitat had reduced the wild population of California condors to less than 20 birds by 1987. All were captured and taken to the San Diego and Los Angeles Zoos to serve as breeding populations. By 2008, there were nearly 300 condors, about half of which had been released into the wild. Similarly, the number of the Hawaiian nene goose had fallen from the tens of thousands in the 1700s to less than 30 by 1950. They were bred in captivity, and the wild population now numbers more than 500.

SOLID-WASTE DISPOSAL

People have always been faced with the problem of ridding themselves of materials they no longer need or want. Prehistoric dwelling sites are located and analyzed by their *middens,* the refuse piles containing the kitchen wastes, broken tools, and other debris of human settlement. We have learned much about Roman and medieval European urban life by examining the refuse mounds that grew as hills in their vicinities. Modern societies differ from their predecessors in the volume and character of their wastes. As suggested by the IPAT equation, the greater a society's population and material wealth, the greater the amount and variety of its garbage. Disposing of the waste is a problem that each individual and each municipality must deal with.

Municipal Waste

The wastes that communities must somehow dispose of include newspapers and beer cans, toothpaste tubes and old television sets, broken refrigerators, cars, and tires (Figure 12.26). American communities face two major hurdles in disposing of these wastes: the sheer volume of trash and the toxic nature of much of it. Americans throw away more trash per person than any other country in the world, about 2 kilograms (4.5 lbs) per person per day. Solid-waste disposal costs are now the second-largest expenditure of most local governments. Americans generate more than twice as much waste per person as do Japanese and Europeans, four times as much as Pakistanis or Indonesians.

This volume of trash is the result of three factors—affluence, packaging, and population density. Craving convenience, Americans rely on disposable goods that they throw away after very limited use. Thus, although readily available substitutes are more economical, Americans annually throw out billions of baby diapers, razors, pens, and paper plates, cups, towels, and napkins. People in less affluent countries repair and recycle a far greater proportion of domestic products. In addition, nearly all consumer goods are encased in some sort of wrapping, whether it be paper, cardboard, plastic, or foam. One-third of the yearly volume of municipal trash consists of these packaging materials. Finally, with its relatively low population density, the United States has traditionally had ample space in which to dump unwanted materials. Countries with higher densities ran short of such space decades ago and have made greater progress in reducing the volume of waste.

FIGURE 12.26 Some of the 290 million tires Americans replace each year. Piles of scrap tires pose two major hazards: (1) they are breeding grounds for disease-carrying rodents and mosquitoes, and (2) they are fire hazards. If they catch fire, the piles can burn for a month or more, releasing thick black smoke and leaving behind a toxic, oily residue. In the last decade, markets for reuse of tires have expanded significantly. Some are exported abroad, some are retreaded, some are shredded and burned to generate electricity, others are shredded or ground to make mulch or rubberized playground equipment, and some are mixed with asphalt to pave streets. Nevertheless, most used tires are dumped, legally or illegally, in landfills or create nuisances in stockpiles. Although many states have enacted scrap-tire management programs, financed by a levy consumers pay when buying new tires, most scrap tires remain unused and unwanted. © *Don Kohlbauer/San Diego Union-Tribune.*

Although ordinary household trash does not meet the governmental designation of **hazardous waste**—defined as discarded material that may pose a substantial threat to human health or to the environment when improperly stored, transported, or disposed of—much of it is hazardous nonetheless. Products containing toxic chemicals include paint thinners and removers, old TV sets and computers, bleaches, oven and drain cleaners, used motor oil, and garden weed killers and pesticides (see "E-Waste," p. 424).

Countries use various methods of disposing of solid wastes; each has its own impact on the environment. Loading wastes onto barges and dumping them in the sea, long a practice for coastal communities, inevitably pollutes oceans. Open dumps on land are a menace to public health, for they harbor disease-carrying rats and insects. Burning the combustibles discharges chemicals and particulates into the air. In the United States, three methods of solid-waste disposal are employed: landfills, incineration, and recycling (Figure 12.27).

Landfills

Most U.S. municipal solid waste is deposited in *sanitary landfills*, where each day's waste is deposited in a natural depression or excavated trench, compacted, and then covered by a layer of soil (Figure 12.28). "Sanitary" is a deceptive word. Until recently, there were no federal standards to which local landfills had to adhere, and while some communities and states regulated the environmental impact of dumps, many did not. Even if no commercial or industrial waste has been dumped at

the site, most landfills eventually produce *leachate* (chemically contaminated drainage), liquids that pollute the groundwater when they leak from the landfill. Leachate forms when precipitation entering the landfill interacts with the decomposing materials. Thus, heavy metals are leached from batteries and old electrical parts, while organic chemicals drain out of leftover paint and other household products. Typical leachate contains a multitude of organic and inorganic chemicals, many of them poisonous. Environmental regulations now require that clay or plastic liners be used to protect groundwater supplies and that systems to extract water and methane be installed.

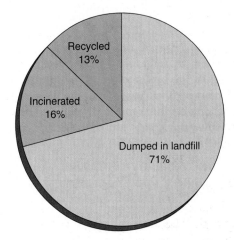

FIGURE 12.27 Methods of solid-waste disposal in the United States.

FIGURE 12.28 A sanitary landfill. Each day's deposit of refuse is compacted and isolated in a separate cell by a covering layer of soil or clay. Although far more desirable than open dumps, sanitary landfills pose environmental problems of their own, including potential groundwater contamination and seepage of methane and hydrogen sulfide, gaseous products of decomposition. By federal law, modern landfills must be lined with clay and plastic, equipped with *leachate* (chemically contaminated drainage from the landfill) collection systems to protect the groundwater, and monitored regularly for underground leaks—requirements that have increased significantly the cost of constructing and operating landfills.

E-Waste

It is the fastest-growing form of trash in developed countries, and you probably own several of the quickly obsolete devices that give rise to it. Electronic waste, commonly called **e-waste,** consists of discarded consumer electronic products used for data processing, telecommunications, and entertainment in private households and businesses. Those products include computers, computer monitors and printers, copiers, fax machines, cellular phones, television sets, VCRs, digital cameras, camcorders, BlackBerries, iPods, and the like. Because it is often cheaper and easier to buy a new device than to repair or upgrade an old one, millions of them are replaced each year. In the United States, the average cell phone is replaced after just 18 months, and the switch to digital television signals is generating a flood of junked TV sets.

Some of the components in electronics can be removed and recycled—glass, steel, aluminum, copper, and gold, for example. But the products also contain toxic metals more difficult to separate, including lead, arsenic, barium, selenium, cadmium, and mercury. If the products are not recycled properly, the chemicals inevitably will make their way from landfills and incinerators into the soil, air, and water.

According to the Environmental Protection Agency, the United States generates more e-waste than any other country. Because people are uncertain how to dispose of their electronic goods, particularly if the devices still work, an estimated 75% of the discards are stored in our closets, garages, offices, and warehouses. Nevertheless, more than 2 million tons of them enter U.S. landfills annually. Less than 15% are taken to recycling centers. By some estimates, 80% of e-waste collected for recycling actually is exported to countries such as China, India, Pakistan, Nigeria, and Mexico, where workers break them apart by hand to recover the steel, aluminum, copper, and gold. The child and adult laborers probably don't realize they are handling toxins that can damage their health and the environment.

In Guiyu, in the Guandong province of China, for example, thousands of scavengers who make their living this way are exposed to poisonous waste that creeps into their skin and lungs. The leftover plastics they burn or discard into rivers, irrigation canals, or onto fields along with other processing residues release toxics such as chlorine and dioxins into the air and create piles of contaminated ash, from which chemicals seep into the land and water. Guiyu's drinking water contains 2400 times the level of lead the World Health Authority considers hazardous, and its soil contains more than 200 times the lead threshold.

E-waste piles are accumulating around the world. Governments are beginning to draft legislation for the environmentally friendly disposal of this waste. In 2005, the European Union issued several directives addressing e-waste recycling and toxic-content problems. Among other things, the directives ban more than trace elements of six toxic substances, including lead, cadmium, mercury, and chromium-6, from most new electronic products; forbid disposing of untreated e-waste in landfills; and ban the export of toxic wastes. Additionally, they make the collection, recycling, and disposal of e-waste the responsibility of the manufacturers, to whom individuals may return electronic appliances. In contrast, by 2010 the U.S. EPA had not issued a clear set of goals and national guidelines to regulate e-waste, although six states had passed laws requiring individuals to recycle electronic waste. All such products must be taken to a recycler or to a municipal hazardous waste collection center.

Courtesy of Arthur Getis.

New York City's largest landfill, Fresh Kills on Staten Island, illustrates the problem. For more than half a century, trucks and barges daily carried approximately 11,000 tons (22 million lbs) of residential waste to the site. Opened in 1948 as a temporary, 200-hectare (500-acre) facility, Fresh Kills was not constructed to hold its contents securely. Located in an ecologically sensitive wetland area and adjacent to residential communities, it expanded to become a malodorous 1200 hectares (3000 acres) of decomposing garbage. Its four large mounds are as much as 70 meters (225 ft) high, taller than the Statue of Liberty. Every day thousands of gallons of leachate seeped into the groundwater beneath the landfill. Fresh Kills finally closed as a depository for municipal solid waste in 2001, although it temporarily reopened the same year to accept debris from the towers of the World Trade Center. Plans call for turning the site into the largest park in New York City, with sports fields, concert arenas, wildlife sanctuaries, and the like. The conversion will be technically complicated and will take years. Construction cannot be completed until the garbage decomposes, the mountains of trash settle, and the polluted water dissipates.

The closing of Fresh Kills made disposal of New York City's trash more complex and expensive. Sanitation trucks, tractor trailers, and railroads now carry about 70% of the waste out of state to landfills and incinerators in Pennsylvania, Virginia, South Carolina, Georgia, and Ohio. Many communities face similar problems in disposing of their solid waste. In 2003, for example, Toronto, Canada, began sending all of its trash to a town near Detroit, Michigan, after its own landfill closed and the city was unable to find a town in Ontario willing to be the site of a new landfill. Finding acceptable locations for landfills is a major problem because "Not in My Backyard" (NIMBY) protesters rise up in opposition nearly everywhere they are proposed.

The number of municipal landfills in the United States shrank significantly during the 1990s, falling from about 6500 in 1990 to fewer than 1800 in 2006. They closed either because they were full or because they could not comply with environmental regulations and were replaced by huge, regional landfills. In contrast to the United States, many Western European countries and Japan dispose of little of their municipal solid waste in landfills, relying instead on incineration and recycling.

Incineration

The quickest way to reduce the volume of trash is to burn it, a practice that was common at open dumps in the United States until it was halted by the Clean Air Act of 1970. Concern over air pollution also forced the closure of old, inefficient *incinerators* (facilities designed to burn waste), providing an impetus to designing a new generation of the plants. Municipal incinerators in the United States, mostly in the Northeast, burn about 15% of the national total of trash; Canada incinerates about 8%. Most municipal incinerators are of the waste-to-energy type, which use extra-high (980°C; 1800°F) temperatures to reduce trash to ash and simultaneously generate electricity or steam, which is sold to help pay operating costs.

A decade ago, incinerators were hailed as the ideal solution to overflowing landfills, but it has become apparent that they pose environmental problems of their own by generating toxic pollutants in both air emissions and ash. Air emissions from incinerator stacks have been found to contain an alphabet soup of highly toxic elements, ranging from *a* (arsenic) to *z* (zinc), and including, among other toxins, cadmium, dioxins, lead, and mercury, as well as significant amounts of such gases as carbon monoxide, sulfur dioxide, and nitrogen oxides. Emissions can be kept to acceptably low limits by installing electrostatic precipitators, filters, and scrubbers to capture pollutants before they are released into the outside air, although the devices add significantly to the cost of the plant.

A greater problem is created by the concentration of toxins, particularly lead and cadmium, in the ash residue of burning. Incinerators typically reduce trash by 90%; one-tenth remains as ash, which then must be buried in a landfill. In 1994, the U.S. Supreme Court ruled that the ash must be tested for toxicity and handled as hazardous waste if it exceeds federal safety standards. This means it must be disposed of in licensed hazardous waste landfills, which have double plastic linings, moisture collection systems, and tighter operating procedures than do ordinary municipal landfills.

Although the likelihood of pollution from incinerator by-products has sparked strong protest to their construction in the United States, they have become more accepted abroad. The seriousness of the air pollution and toxic ash problems, however, has aroused concern everywhere. In Japan, where more than three-fifths of municipal waste is incinerated, high atmospheric dioxin levels led the Ministry of Health in 1997 to strengthen earlier emission guidelines. Some European countries called at least temporary halts to incinerator construction while their safety was reconsidered, and increasingly landfills are refusing to take their residue.

Source Reduction and Recycling

The problems and costs associated with landfills and incinerators have spurred interest in two alternative waste-management strategies: source reduction and recycling. By *source reduction,* we mean producing less waste in the first place so as to shrink the volume of the waste stream and lower the monetary and environmental costs associated with landfills and incinerators. Manufacturers can reduce the amount of paper, plastic, glass, and metal they use to package food and consumer products. Since 1977, for example, the weight of plastic soft-drink bottles and of aluminum beverage cans has been reduced by 20% to 30%. Detergents produced in concentrated form and packaged in smaller containers require less water and less plastic to make, and because they are smaller, more of the plastic bottles can be shipped at the same time, reducing fuel usage and greenhouse gas emissions.

Another way to reduce the amount of waste needing disposal is by **recycling,** the recovery and reprocessing or reuse of previously used material into new products for the same or another purpose. Aluminum beverage cans usually are recast

FIGURE 12.29 Recycled tires used as mulch. Shredded tire bits can be used as mulch in gardens to help hold moisture in the ground. Although it doesn't enrich the soil with organic material, the mulch is clean and doesn't rot or attract termites, as wood mulch does. It can also be used around playground equipment, as shown here, because it doesn't accumulate dust or compact with use. *RubberStuff (R) Playground Safety Surface by ART. www.americanrubber.com.*

into new cans, for example, and glass bottles are crushed, melted, and made into new bottles. Old tires can be shredded and turned into rubberized road surfacing or used as mulch around playground equipment (Figure 12.29). Some communities collect leaves and other yard waste, which accounts for about 15% of the typical municipal waste stream, and turn it into compost. Recycling plastics is complicated by the many types of plastic containers in common use, which must be separated before being recycled. Recycled plastic can be converted into fiber for carpeting, playground equipment, insulation for clothing, and other products.

The widespread adoption of municipal recycling programs in the United States now diverts an estimated 25% to 30% of trash away from landfills and incinerators. The country currently recycles some 45% of the aluminum beverage cans, 48% of the paper, and 20% to 25% of the glass and plastic bottles entering the waste stream. Compared with other methods of solid-waste disposal, recycling has a relatively benign impact on the environment, despite the fact that it takes water, energy, and other resources to recover, process, and convert the materials into new products. Recycling saves natural resources by making it possible to cut fewer trees, burn less oil, and mine less coal. Because it typically takes less energy to make things out of recycled material than out of virgin materials, recycling saves energy. It also reduces the pollution of air, water, and land that stems from the manufacture of new materials and from other methods of waste disposal, and it saves landfill space for materials that cannot be recycled.

With all of these advantages, why isn't recycling more widely practiced in the United States? Japan and a number of Western European countries recycle a far greater proportion of their waste stream. Analysts have offered a number of explanations: (1) the cost of collecting the goods to be recycled, (2) fluctuations in market prices for commodities, and (3) the lack of a ready market for products manufactured from recycled material. Perhaps the most important factor, however, is that in the United States the price of energy historically has been low and the supply abundant, and the true monetary and environmental costs of making things from raw materials rather than recycled ones are hidden.

In less-affluent countries, where manufactured products are expensive but labor is cheap, recycling plays an important role in reducing the amount of solid waste. In many cities in developing countries, such as Manila (the Philippines), Phnom Penh (Cambodia), Cairo (Egypt), and Mexico City, thousands of poor people make a living sifting through the city's trash, looking for recyclable goods—tin cans, copper, wood, electronics, clothing, and the like—that they can sell to middlemen for businesses and industries (Figure 12.30). The wastepickers, or scavengers, play a vital role in reducing the amount of trash that must be compacted and covered with a fresh layer of dirt each day. It is estimated that in Indonesian cities, for example, wastepickers reduce total urban refuse by one-third.

Unfortunately, the environmental conditions under which wastepickers work are not good, and their life expectancy is considerably less than that of the general population. The health risks include injuries from accidents, infections from disease-carrying organisms, and exposure to gases that seep out of the layers of fermenting trash and to hazardous wastes such as dioxin and heavy metals.

Hazardous and Radioactive Wastes

The problems of municipal and household solid-waste management are daunting; those of treatment and disposal of hazardous and radioactive wastes seem overwhelming.

Hazardous Waste

As we have seen, the waste stream often contains highly toxic and hazardous materials that can harm human health and/or the environment. The terms *toxic* and *hazardous* frequently are used interchangeably, as we shall do here. More strictly defined, toxic waste is a relatively limited concept, referring to substances that are poisonous and can cause death or serious injury to humans and other organisms. *Hazardous waste* is a broader

Such wastes contaminate the environment in different ways and by different routes. Because most hazardous debris is disposed of by dumping or burial on land, groundwater is most at risk of contamination. In all industrial countries, at least some drinking water contamination from highly toxic solvents, hydrocarbons, pesticides, trace metals, and PCBs has been detected. Waste impoundments are also a source of air pollutants through the evaporation of volatile organic compounds. Finally, careless or deliberate distribution of hazardous materials outside of confinement areas can cause unexpected, but deadly, hazards. Although methods of disposal other than containment techniques have been developed—including incineration, infrared heating, and bacterial decomposition—none is fully satisfactory and none is yet in wide use.

Radioactive Waste

Every facility that either uses or produces radioactive materials generates *low-level waste*, material whose radioactivity will decay to safe levels in 100 years or less. Nuclear power plants produce about half the total low-level waste in the form of material from decommissioned reactors, used resins, filter sludges, lubricating oils, and detergent wastes. Industries that manufacture radio-pharmaceuticals, smoke alarms, and other consumer goods produce such wastes in the form of machinery parts, plastics, and organic solvents. Research establishments, universities, and hospitals also produce radioactive waste materials.

Because low-level waste is generated by so many sources, its disposal is particularly difficult to control. Evidence indicates that much of it has been placed in landfills, often the local municipal dump, where the waste chemicals may leach through the soil and into the groundwater. By EPA estimates, the United States contains at least 25,000 legal and illegal dumps with hazardous waste. As many as 2000 are deemed potential ecological disasters.

High-level waste can remain radioactive for 10,000 years and more; plutonium stays dangerously radioactive for 240,000 years. High-level waste consists primarily of spent fuel assemblies of nuclear power reactors—termed *civilian waste*—and waste generated as a by-product of the manufacture of nuclear weapons, or *military waste*. The volume of civilian waste alone is not only great but increasing rapidly, because approximately one-third of a reactor's rods need to be disposed of every year.

By 2008, more than 120,000 spent-fuel assemblies were being stored either indoors in the containment pools of America's commercial nuclear power reactors or outdoors in sealed containers made of steel and concrete, awaiting more permanent disposition (Figure 12.31). Thousands more are added annually. *Spent fuel* is a misleading term: the assemblies are removed from commercial reactors not because their radiation is spent but because they have become too radioactive for further use. The assemblies will remain radioactively "hot" for thousands of years.

FIGURE 12.30 Some of the estimated 80,000 wastepickers who make a living by scavenging the Promised Land dump in Manila, the Philippines, looking for items to resell. Metal, glass, plastic, paper, cloth, broken toys, and bits and pieces of machinery are all candidates. Wastepicking is an important source of income for many poor families, but the pickers, many of them women and children, usually work long hours in unhealthful conditions. Hundreds of people died here in July 2000, when the mountain of garbage, loosened by a week of monsoon rains, collapsed on their shantytown at the edge of the dump. © *Romeo Ranoco/Reuters.*

term referring to all wastes that pose an immediate or long-term human health risk or that endanger the environment. The discarded material, liquid or solid, contains substances that have one or more of the following characteristics: (1) ignitability (e.g., gasoline), (2) corrosiveness (e.g., strong acids), (3) explosiveness (e.g., nitroglycerine), (4) toxicity (e.g., PCBs).

The major producers of hazardous wastes are the chemical and petrochemical industries, mining, and electric generation. The potentially harmful wastes they generate include organic chlorine and phosphate compounds, heavy metals, and solvents. The EPA has classified more than 400 substances as hazardous, and currently about 10% of industrial waste materials are so categorized.

GEOGRAPHY
& *Public Policy*

Yucca Mountain

If the U.S. federal government had had its way, a long, low ridge in the basin-and-range region of Nevada would have become America's first permanent repository for the deadly radioactive waste that nuclear power plants generate. Despite years of study and planning, and the expenditure of billions of dollars on construction of the facility, however, opponents of the project appear to have prevailed, and Yucca Mountain has become a symbol of society's inability to solve a basic problem posed by nuclear power production: where to dispose of the used fuel. At present, no permanent disposal site for radioactive waste exists anywhere in the world.

In 1982, Congress ordered the Department of Energy (DOE) to construct by 1998 a permanent repository for the spent fuel of civilian nuclear power plants as well as vast quantities of waste from the production of nuclear weapons. Yucca Mountain in southern Nevada was selected as the site for this high-level waste facility, which was intended to store wastes safely for 10,000 years, until radioactive decay had rendered them less hazardous than they are today. Most of the waste would be in the form of radioactive fuel pellets sealed in metal rods; these would be encased in extremely strong glass and placed in steel canisters entombed in chambers 300 meters (1000 ft) below the Nevada desert. The steel containers would corrode in one or two centuries, after which the volcanic rock of the mountain would be responsible for containing the radioactivity.

Four areas of concern about the site emerged. First, the area is vulnerable to both volcanic and earthquake activity, which could cause groundwater to well up suddenly and flood the repository. Yucca Mountain itself was formed from volcanic eruptions that occurred about 12 to 15 million years ago; some geologists contended that a new volcano could erupt within the mountain. Seven small cinder cones in the immediate area have erupted in recent times, the latest just 10,000 years ago. In addition, a number of seismic faults lie close to Yucca Mountain. One, the Ghost Dance fault, runs right through the depository site. The epicenters of the 1992 and 2002 earthquakes at Little Skull Mountain were only 19 kilometers (12 mi) from the proposed dump site.

Second, rainwater percolating down through the mountain could penetrate the vaults holding the waste. Over centuries, water could dissolve the waste itself, and the resulting toxic brew could be carried into the groundwater under the mountain and then beyond the boundaries of the repository.

Third, the Yucca Mountain site lies between the Nevada Test Site, which the DOE uses as a nuclear bomb testing range, and the Nellis Air Force Base Bombing and Gunnery Range. Questions were raised about the wisdom of locating a waste repository just a few kilometers from areas subject to underground explosions or aerial bombardment.

Finally, opponents of the project pointed out that transporting high-level nuclear waste across the country is dangerous and irresponsible. Because each truck, barge, or rail car container would carry more radioactive material than was released by the atomic bombs used in World War II, breaching even one of them

(a)

(b)

FIGURE 12.31 (a) Highly radioactive spent-fuel rods are stored in water-filled pools at nuclear reactor sites. **(b)** Nuclear power plants whose storage ponds are full store nuclear waste in large, aboveground casks. *(a) © Getty RF; (b) Courtesy Office of Civilian Waste Management, Department of Energy.*

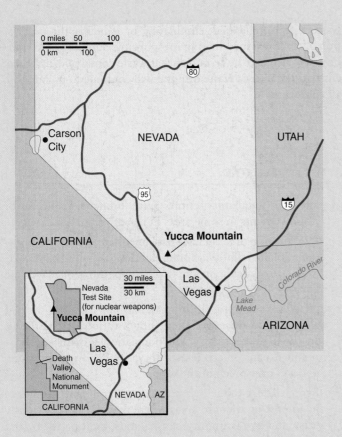

in an accident or a terrorist attack would be catastrophic. As one of Nevada's congressional representatives stated, "They could walk it, fly it, truck it, or send it here by rail. It doesn't make it any safer. This is an open invitation to terrorists around the world."

Despite these concerns, the Energy Department in 2002 recommended that Yucca Mountain be designated as the site for a national nuclear waste depository, a plan President Bush and Congress later approved. The project still faced substantial technical, legal, and political challenges, however, and the election of President Obama in 2008 brought construction of the depository to an end. Obama's budget eliminated almost all of the funding for the facility, the DOE withdrew its application for a license to build the depository, and a commission was appointed to devise a new strategy for permanent storage of nuclear waste.

Considering the Issues

1. What are the advantages and disadvantages of permitting nuclear power plants to operate when no system for disposing of their hazardous wastes exists?

2. Comment on the paradox that plutonium remains dangerously radioactive for 240,000 years, yet it might have been stored in a repository that was intended to safely hold wastes for only 10,000 years.

3. React to the fact that, even if Yucca Mountain opened, it would have been too small. It was designed to accept 77,000 tons of civilian and military wastes, but the radioactive waste that has accumulated already exceeds that amount.

4. Considering the uncertainties that would attend the irreversible underground entombment of high-level waste, do you think the government should instead pursue aboveground storage in a form that would allow for the continuous monitoring and retrieval of the wastes? Why or why not?

5. High-level waste is produced at relatively few sites in the United States. Low-level waste is much more ubiquitous; it is produced at more than 2000 sites in California alone. Which do you think should arouse greater public concern and discussion, high- or low-level waste?

Unfortunately, no country has yet solved the problem of how to safely dispose of the radioactive waste it already has, not to mention the added waste an expansion of nuclear power would produce. Until 1970, the United States, Britain, France, and Japan sealed wastes in protective tanks and dumped them at sea, a practice that now has been banned worldwide—although as late as 1993, Russia dumped 900 tons of waste into the Sea of Japan. Cardboard boxes containing wastes contaminated with plutonium have been rototilled into the soil, on the assumption that the earth would dilute and absorb the radioactivity. The Netherlands is reported to have incinerated some radioactive wastes at sea.

In the United States, much low-level radioactive waste has been placed in tanks and buried in the earth at 13 sites operated by the U.S. Department of Energy and 3 sites run by private firms. Millions of cubic feet of high-level military waste are temporarily stored in underground tanks at 4 sites: Hanford, Washington; Savannah River, South Carolina; Idaho Falls, Idaho; and West Valley, New York. Several of these storage areas have experienced leakages, with seepage of waste into the surrounding soil and groundwater. The most problematic may be the 177 tanks buried underground at the Hanford site. By the early 1990s, it had been determined that at least 66 of the giant tanks—some with a capacity of 1.1 million gallons—were leaking, and that about 1 million gallons had seeped into the soil, raising the fear that the highly radioactive waste had already reached underground water supplies and was flowing toward the Columbia River.

Many scientists believe that deep geologic burial is the safest way to permanently dispose of long-lived radioactive waste. This would involve packaging high-level solid and liquid wastes in containers that are buried deep underground. The United States has halted construction on its first permanent high-level waste repository in Nevada, (see "Yucca Mountain"). Finland has selected a site for its repository—the island of Olkiluoto—and Sweden is expected to do so soon.

Winning local support for a burial site is difficult, however, and as of 2009 attempts to do so in Britain, France, Switzerland, and Japan had not been successful.

Solid waste will never cease to be a problem, but its impact on the environment can be lessened by reducing the volume of waste that is generated, eliminating or reducing the production of toxic residues, halting irresponsible dumping, and finding ways to reuse the resources that waste contains. Until then, current methods of waste disposal will continue to pollute soil, air, and water.

Summary of Key Concepts

- We began this chapter with a description of the Great Pacific Garbage Patch. Captain Moore's first mate commented that the patch "is a reminder that there's nowhere that isn't affected by humanity."

- Humans are part of the natural environment and depend, literally, for their lives on the water, air, and other resources contained in the biosphere. But people have subjected the intricately interconnected systems of that biosphere—the troposphere, the hydrosphere, and the lithosphere—to profound and frequently unwittingly destructive alteration.

- All human activities have effects on the environment, effects that are complex and never isolated. An external action that impinges on any part of the web of nature inevitably triggers chain reactions, the ultimate consequences of which appear never to be fully anticipated.

- Efforts to control the supply of water alter both the quantity and the quality of water in streams, and structures such as dams and reservoirs often have unintended side effects. In many parts of the world, increased demand for fresh water has led to a lack of adequate supplies.

- Pollutants associated with agriculture, industry, and other activities have degraded the quality of freshwater supplies, although regulatory efforts have brought about major improvements in some areas in recent years.

- Combustion of fossil fuels has contributed to serious problems of air pollution. Some manifestations of that pollution, such as acid rain and depletion of the ozone layer, are matters of global concern.

- Activities such as agriculture and mining have long helped shape local landscapes, producing a variety of landforms. In the 20th century, world population growth and economic expansion accelerated the degradation of air, water, and soil over much of the world.

- People affect other living things—plants and animals—by importing them to areas where they did not previously exist, and by disrupting their habitats, hunting them, and using biocides to eradicate them. The greatest human impact is occurring in the tropical rain forests, where agriculture, industrialization, and urbanization are contributing to the extinction of hundreds of species a year.

- All the common methods of disposing of the wastes that humans produce release contaminants into the surrounding environment, providing further evidence of the fact that people cannot manipulate, distort, pollute, or destroy any part of the ecosystem without diminishing its quality or disrupting its structure.

Key Words

acid rain 406
biodiversity hot spot 415
biological magnification
    (biomagnification) 420
biosphere 393
channelization 397
chlorofluorocarbons (CFCs) 408
ecology 393
ecosystem 394

environmental pollution 398
eutrophication 399
e-waste 424
exotic species 418
food chain 394
hazardous waste 423
hydrologic cycle 394
IPAT equation 394
ozone 407

ozone layer 408
photochemical smog 407
polychlorinated
    biphenyls (PCBs) 402
recycling 425
subsidence 413
thermal pollution 402
troposphere 404

Thinking Geographically

1. Sketch and label a diagram of the *biosphere*. Briefly indicate the content of its component parts. Is that content permanent and unchanging? Explain.

2. How are the concepts of *ecosystem, niche,* and *food chain* related? How does each add to our understanding of the "web of nature"?

3. Draw a diagram of or briefly describe the *hydrologic cycle.* How do population growth, urbanization, and industrialization affect that cycle?

4. Is all environmental pollution the result of human action? When can we say that pollution of a part of the biosphere has occurred?

5. Describe the chief sources of water pollution. What steps have the United States and other countries taken to control water pollution?

6. What factors affect the type and degree of air pollution found at a place? What is *acid rain* and where is it a problem? Describe the relationship of *ozone* to *photochemical smog.* Why has the ozone layer been depleted?

7. What kinds of landforms has excavation produced? Dumping? What are the chief causes and effects of subsidence?

8. Briefly describe the chief ways that humans affect plant and animal life. What is meant by *biological magnification*? Why may the use of biocides be self-defeating?

9. What methods do communities use to dispose of solid waste? What ecological problems does solid-waste disposal present? How does the government define *hazardous waste,* and how is it disposed of?

10. What activities result in the production of high-level radioactive waste, and why is it difficult to dispose of?

11. Using the IPAT equation, discuss how the environmental impacts a society has vary from country to country.

PART FOUR

The Area Analysis Tradition

Gaul consists of three distinct regions, inhabited respectively by the Belgae, the Aquitani, and a people who call themselves the Celts. Variations in custom, language, and law distinguish these three peoples.

—Julius Caesar, *The Gallic Wars*[a]

Julius Caesar opened his 1st-century B.C. account of his transalpine military campaigns by observing that Gaul was divided into three regions. With that spatial summary, he gave to every schoolchild an example of geography in action. Caesar's report to the Romans demanded that he convey to an uninformed audience workable mental pictures of places they had never seen. He was able to achieve that aim by aggregating spatial data, by selecting and emphasizing what was important to his purpose, and by leaving out what was not. He was pursuing the geographic tradition of area analysis, a tradition that is at the heart of the discipline and focuses on the recognition of spatial uniformities and the examination of their significance.

The tradition of area analysis is commonly associated with the term *regional geography*, the study of particular portions of the earth's surface. Like Caesar, the regional geographer attempts to view a particular area and to summarize what is spatially significant about it. One cannot, of course, possibly know everything about a region, nor would "everything" contribute to our understanding of its essential nature. Regional geographers, however, approach a preselected earth space—a continent, a country, or some other division—with the intent of making it as fully understood as possible in as many facets of its nature as they deem practicable. It is from this school of area analysis that "regional geographies" of, for example, Africa, the United States, or the Pacific Northwest derive.

Because the scope of their inquiries is so broad, regional geographers must become thoroughly versed in all of the topical subfields of the discipline, such as those discussed in this book. Only in that way can area specialists select those phenomena that give insight into the essential unity and diversity of their region of study. Based on their topical knowledge, regional geographers frequently seek to delimit and study regions defined by one or a limited number of criteria.

Chapter 13 is devoted to the area analysis tradition. Its introductory pages explore the nature of regions and methods of regional analysis. The body of the chapter consists of a series of regional vignettes, each based on a theme introduced in one of the preceding chapters of the book. Because those chapters were grouped into three topical traditions—earth science, culture-environment, and locational, the separate studies demonstrate how area analysis is also part of topical (sometimes called "systematic") geography. They are examples of the regionalizing objectives of geographers who seek an understanding of their data's spatial expression. The step from these limited topical studies to the broader, composite understandings sought by the area analyst is both short and intellectually satisfying.

[a]*The Gallic Wars,* Julius Caesar, translated by John Warrington, 1955. New York: The Heritage Press.

Opposite page: Newlands Valley, Cumbria, in the Lake District of England. © *Digitalvision RF.*

economy and marketing practices. We dismiss—at that level of generalization—differences within the region based on slope, soil type, state borders, or characteristics of population. The boundaries of the Corn Belt are assumed to be marked where the region's internal unifying characteristics change so materially that different agricultural economies become dominant and different regional summaries are required. The content of the region suggests its definition and determines the basis of its delimitation.

Although regions may vary greatly, they all share certain common characteristics:

- Regions have *location*, often expressed in the regional name selected, such as the Midwest, the Near East, North Africa, and the like. This form of regional name underscores the importance of *relative location* (see Chapter 1, p. 7).

- Regions have *spatial extent*, recognized by territories over which defined characteristics or generalizations about physical, cultural, or organizational content are constant.

- Regions have *boundaries* based on the areal spread of the features selected for study. Since regions are the recognition of the features defining them, their boundaries are drawn where those features no longer occur or dominate. Regional boundaries are rarely as sharply defined as those suggested by Figure 13.2 or by the regional maps in this and other geography texts. More frequently, there exist broad zones of transition from one distinctive core area to another as the dominance of the defining regional features gradually diminishes outward from the core to the regional periphery. Linear boundaries are arbitrary divisions made necessary by the scale of world regional maps and by the summary character of most regional discussions.

- Regions may be *formal, functional, or perceptual*, as we saw in Chapter 1 (p. 13).

Formal (uniform) regions are areas of essential uniformity throughout in one or a limited combination of physical or cultural features. In previous chapters, we encountered such formal physical regions as the humid subtropical climate zone and the Sahel region of Africa, as well as formal (homogeneous) cultural regions in which standardized characteristics of language, religion, ethnicity, or livelihood existed. The frontsheet maps of countries and topographical regions show other formal regional patterns. Whatever the basis of its definition, the formal region is the largest area over which a valid generalization of attribute uniformity may be made. Whatever is stated about one part of it holds true for its remainder.

The **functional (or nodal) region,** in contrast, is a spatial system defined by the interactions and connections that give it a dynamic, organizational basis. Its boundaries remain constant only as long as the interchanges establishing it remain unaltered. The commuting region shown in Figure 1.10 retained its shape and size only as long as the road pattern and residential communities on which it was based remained unchanged.

FIGURE 13.2 Aachen, Germany, in 1649. The acceptance of regional extent implies the recognition of regional boundaries. At some defined point, *urban* is replaced by *nonurban,* the Midwest ends and the Plains begin, or the rain forest ceases and the savanna emerges. Regional boundaries are, of course, rarely as precisely and visibly marked as were the limits of the walled medieval city. Its sprawling modern counterpart may be more difficult to define, but the boundary significance of the concept of *urban* remains.

Not all regions are as rigorously and objectively structured as the formal and functional regions geographers devise and analyze. When regions have existed only in the perceptions of their inhabitants or the population at large, they are understandably called **perceptual (popular** or **vernacular) regions.** As composites of the mental maps of ordinary people, they reflect the areal identifications—the *sense of place*—of individuals and groups. As individual and group mental and emotional constructs, perceptual regions are more immediate and meaningful in the lives and behaviors of those who recognize them than are the more objectively-based regions of geographers.

- Regions are *hierarchically arranged*. Although regions vary in scale, type, and degree of generalization, none stands alone as the ultimate key to areal understanding. Each defines only a part of spatial reality.

On a formal regional scale of size progression, the Delmarva Peninsula of the eastern United States may be seen as part of the Atlantic Coastal Plain, which is in turn a portion of the eastern North American humid continental climatic region, a hierarchy that changes the basis of regional recognition as the level and purpose of generalization alter (Figure 13.3). The central business district of Chicago is one land use complex in the functional regional hierarchy that describes the spatial influences of the city of Chicago and the metropolitan region of which it is the core. Each recognized regional entity in such progressions may stand alone and at the same time exist as a part of a larger, equally valid territorial unit.

FIGURE 13.3 A hierarchy of regions. This is one possible nesting of regions within a *regional hierarchy* defined by differing criteria. Each regional unit has internal coherence. The recognition of its constituent parts aids in understanding the composite areal unit.

Such progressions may also reflect gradations in the intensity in spatial dominance of the phenomenon giving definition to the region. With particular attention to regions defined by the distribution of culture groups—but with application to regions delimited by other criteria—Donald Meinig suggested the term *core* to mean a centralized zone of concentration and greatest homogeneity of regional character. Areas in which the culture (or other defining feature) is dominant, but with less intensity and totality of development, he labeled *domains*. Finally, Meinig proposed the term *sphere* to recognize the zone of broadest but least-intensive expression of the regional character, where some of its defining traits are encountered but where it is no longer spatially dominant.

These generalizations about the nature of regions and the regional concept are meant to instill firmly the understanding that regions are human intellectual creations designed to serve a purpose. Regions focus our attention on spatial uniformities. They bring clarity to the seeming confusion of the observable physical and cultural features of the world we inhabit. Regions provide the framework for the purposeful organization of spatial data.

THE STRUCTURE OF THIS CHAPTER

The remainder of the chapter contains examples of how geographers have used the regional concept to organize their observations about the physical and cultural world. Each study or vignette explores a different aspect of regional reality. Each organizes its data in ways appropriate to its subject matter and objective, but in each, some or all of the common characteristics of regional delimitation and structure may be recognized. Each of the regional examples is based on the content of one of the earlier chapters of this book, and the page numbers preceding the different selections refer to the material within those chapters most closely associated with, or explained further by, the regional case study. As an aid to visualizing the application of the regional concept, the examples are organized by reference to the remaining three traditions of geography.

PART I: REGIONS IN THE EARTH SCIENCE TRADITION

The simplest of all regions to define, and generally the easiest to recognize, is the formal region based on a single, readily apparent component or characteristic. The island is land, not water, and its unmistakable boundary is naturally given where the one element passes to the other. The terminal moraine may mark the transition from the rich, black soils of recent formation to the parti-colored clays of earlier generations. The dense forest may break dramatically upon the glade or the open prairies. The nature of change is singular and apparent.

The physical geographer, although concerned with all of the earth sciences that explain the natural environment, deals at the outset with *single factor* formal regions. Many of the earth features of concern to physical geography, of course, do not exist in simple, clearly defined units. The geographer must make judgments as to appropriate boundary definitions in order to "regionalize" a particular phenomenon. A stated amount of received precipitation, the presence of certain important soil characteristics, the dominance in nature of particular plant associations—all must be decided on as regional limits, and all such limits are subject to change through time or by purpose of the regional geographer.

Landforms as Regions

(*See "Stream Landscapes in Humid Areas," p. 68.*)

The landform region exists in a more sharply defined fashion than such transitional physical features as soil, climate, and vegetation. For these latter areas, the boundaries depend on definitional decisions made (and defended) by the researcher. The landform region, on the other hand, arises—visibly and apparently unarguably—from nature itself, independent of human influence and unaffected by time on the human scale. Landforms constitute basic, naturally defined regions of physical geographic concern. The existence of major landform regions—mountains, lowlands, plateaus—is unquestioned in popular recognition or scientific definition. Their influence on climates, on vegetational patterns, and even on the primary economies of subsistence populations has been noted in earlier portions of this book. The following discussion of a distinct landform region, describing its constitution and its relationships to other physical features of the landscape, is adapted from a classic study by Wallace W. Atwood.

FIGURE 13.4 The Black Hills landform province.

FIGURE 13.5 The "Needles" of the Black Hills result from erosion along vertical cracks and crevices in granite. © *Getty RF.*

The Black Hills Province[a]

The Black Hills rise abruptly from the surrounding plains [Figure 13.4]. The break in topography at the margin of this province is obvious to the most casual observer who visits that part of our country. Thus the boundaries of this area, based on contrasts in topography, are readily determined.

One who looks more deeply into the study of the natural environment may recognize that in the neighboring plains the rock formations lie in a nearly horizontal position. They are sandstones, shales, conglomerates, and limestones. In the foothills those same sedimentary formations are bent upward and at places stand in a nearly vertical position. Precisely where the change in topography occurs, we find a notable change in the geologic structure and thus discover an explanation for the variation in relief.

The Black Hills are due to a distinct upwarping, or doming, of the crustal portion of the earth. Subsequent removal by stream erosion of the higher portions of that dome and the dissection of the core rocks have produced the present relief features. As erosion has proceeded, more and more of a complex series of ancient metamorphic rocks has been uncovered. Associated with the very old rocks of the core and, at places, with the sedimentary strata, there are a number of later intrusions which have cooled and formed solid rock. They have produced minor domes about the northern margin of the Black Hills.

With the elevation of this part of our country there came an increase in rainfall in the area, and with the increase in elevation and rainfall came contrasts in relief, in soils, and in vegetation.

[a]Adapted from *The Physiographic Provinces of North America* by Wallace W. Atwood. © Copyright, 1940, by Ginn and Company. Used by permission of Silver, Burdett & Ginn, Inc.

As we pass from the neighboring plains, where the surface is monotonously level, and climb into the Black Hills area, we enter a landscape having great variety in the relief. In the foothill belt, at the southwest, south, and east, there are hogback ridges interrupted in places by water gaps, or gateways, that have been cut by streams radiating from the core of the Hills. Between the ridges there are roughly concentric valley lowlands. On the west side of the range, where the sedimentary mantle has not been removed, there is a plateaulike surface; hogback ridges are absent. Here erosion has not proceeded far enough to produce the landforms common to the east margin. In the heart of the range we find deep canyons, rugged intercanyon ridges, bold mountain forms, craggy knobs, and other picturesque features [Figure 13.5]. The range has passed through several periods of mountain growth and several stages, or cycles, of erosion.

The rainfall of the Black Hills area is somewhat greater than that of the brown, seared, semiarid plains regions, and evergreen trees survive among the hills. We leave a land of sagebrush and grasses to enter one of forests. The dark-colored evergreen trees suggested to early settlers the name Black Hills. As we enter the area, we pass from a land of cattle ranches and some seminomadic shepherds to a land where forestry, mining, general farming, and recreational activities give character to the life of the people. In color and form, in topography, climate, vegetation, and economic opportunities, the Black Hills stand out conspicuously as a distinct geographic unit.

Dynamic Regions in Weather and Climate

(*See "Air Masses," p. 95.*)

The unmistakable and enduring clarity of the Black Hills landform region and the precision with which its boundaries may be drawn are rarely echoed in other types of formal physical regions. Most of the natural environment, despite its appearance of permanence and certainty, is dynamic in nature. Vegetations, soils, and climates change through time by natural process or by the action of humans. Boundaries shift, perhaps abruptly, as witness the recent migration southward of the Sahara. The core characteristics of whole provinces change as marshes are drained or forests are replaced by cultivated fields.

That complex of physical conditions we recognize locally and briefly as weather and summarize as climate displays particularly clearly the temporary nature of much of the natural environment that surrounds us, yet even in the turbulent change of the atmosphere, distinct regional entities exist with definable boundaries and internally consistent horizontal and vertical properties. "Air masses" and the consequences of their encounters constitute a major portion of contemporary weather analysis and prediction. Air masses further fulfill all the criteria of *multifactor formal regions*, though their dynamic quality and their patterns of movement obviously mark them as being of a nature distinctly different from such stable physical entities as landform regions, as the following extract from *Climatology and the World's Climates* by George R. Rumney makes clear.

Air Masses[b]

An air mass is a portion of the atmosphere having a uniform horizontal distribution of certain physical characteristics, especially of temperature and humidity. These qualities are acquired when a mass of air stagnates or moves very slowly over a large and relatively unvaried surface of land or sea. Under these circumstances surface air gradually takes on properties of temperature and moisture approaching those of the underlying surface, and there then follows a steady, progressive transmission of properties to greater heights, resulting finally in a fairly clearly marked vertical transition of characteristics. Those parts of the earth where air masses acquire their distinguishing qualities are called source regions.

Four major types of source regions are recognized: continental polar, maritime polar, continental tropical, and maritime tropical. Polar air masses are continental when they develop over land or ice surfaces in high latitudes; these are cold and dry. They are maritime when they form over the oceans in high latitudes. An air mass from these sources is cold and moist. Similarly, tropical air is continental when it originates along the Tropics of Cancer and Capricorn over northern Africa and northern Australia and is therefore warm and dry. It is maritime when it forms along the Tropics over the oceans, where it develops as a mass of warm, moist air. A single air mass usually covers thousands of square miles of the earth's surface when fully formed.

An air mass is recognizable chiefly because of the uniformity of its primary properties—temperature and humidity—and the vertical distribution of these. Secondary qualities, such as cloud types, precipitation, and visibility, are also taken into account. These qualities are retained for a remarkably long time, often for several weeks, after an air mass has traveled far from its source region, and they are thus the means of distinguishing it from other masses of air.

The principal air masses of the Americas, their source regions, and their paths of movement are shown in Figure 13.6.

Natural Resource Regions

(See "Coal," p. 124.)

The unevenly distributed resources on which people depend for existence are logical topics of interest within the earth science of geography. Resource regions are mapped, and raw material qualities and quantities are discussed. Areal relationships to industrial concentrations and the impacts of material extraction on alternate uses of areas are typical interests in resource geography and in the definition of resource regions.

Those regions, however, are usually treated as if they were expressions of observable surface phenomena—as if, somehow, an oil field were as exposed and two-dimensional as a soil region or a forested district. What is ignored is that most mineral resources are three-dimensional regions beneath the ground. In addition to the characteristics of an area that may form the basis for regional delimitations and descriptions of surface phenomena, regions beneath the surface add their own particularities to the problem of regional definition. They have, for example, upper and lower boundaries in addition to the circumferential bounds of surface features. They may have an internal topography divorced from the visible landscape. Subsurface relationships—for example, mineral distribution and accessibility in relation to its enclosing rock or to groundwater amounts and movement—may be critical in understanding these specialized, but real, regions. An illustration drawn from the Schuylkill field of the anthracite region of northeastern Pennsylvania helps illustrate the nature of regions beneath the surface.

The Schuylkill Anthracite Region[c]

Nothing in the wild surface terrain of the anthracite country suggested the existence of an equally rugged subterranean topography of coal beds and interstratified rock, slate, and fire clays forming a total vertical depth of 900 meters (3000 ft) at greatest development. Yet the creation of the surface landscape was an essential determinant of the areal extent of the Schuylkill district, of the contortions of its bedding, and of the nature of its coal content. A county history of the area reports, "The physical features of the anthracite country are wild. Its area exhibits an extraordinary series of parallel ridges and deep valleys, like long, rolling lines of surf which break upon a flat shore." Both the surface and the subsurface topographies reflect the strong folding of strata after the coal seams were deposited; the anthracite (hard) coal resulted from metamorphic carbonization of the original bituminous beds. Subsequent river and glacial erosion removed as much as 95% of the original anthracite deposits and gave to those that remained

[b]George R. Rumney, *Climatology and the World's Climates.* New York: Macmillan, 1968. Used by permission.

[c]By Jerome Fellmann.

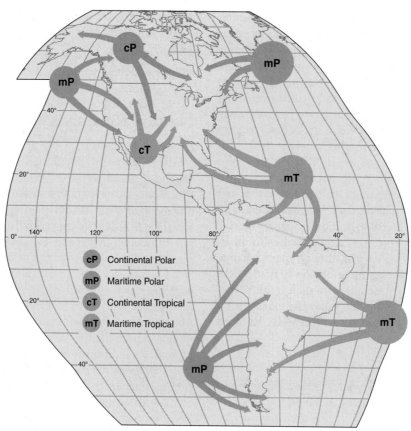

FIGURE 13.6 Air masses of North and South America, their source regions, and their paths of movement.

discontinuous existence in sharply bounded fields such as the Schuylkill [Figure 13.7], a discrete areal entity of 470 square kilometers (181 sq mi).

The irregular topography of the underground Schuylkill region means that the interbedded coal seams, the most steeply inclined of all the anthracite regions [Figure 13.8], outcrop visibly at the surface on hillsides and along stream valleys. The outcrops made the presence of coal known as early as 1770, but not until 1795 did Schuylkill anthracite find its first use by local blacksmiths. Reviled as "stone coal" or "black stone" that was difficult to ignite, anthracite found no ready commercial market, although it was used in wire and rolling mills located along the Schuylkill River before 1815 and to generate steam in the same area by 1830.

The resources of the subterranean Schuylkill region affected human patterns of surface regions only after the Schuylkill Navigation Canal was completed in 1825 [Figure 13.9], providing a passage to rapidly expanding external markets for the fuel and for the output of industry newly located atop the region. Growing demand induced a boom in coal exploitation, an exhaustion of the easily available outcrop coal, and the beginning of the more arduous and dangerous underground mining.

The early methods of mining were simple: merely quarrying the coal from exposed outcrops, usually driving on a slight incline to permit natural drainage. Deep shafts were

FIGURE 13.7 The anthracite regions of northeastern Pennsylvania are sharply defined by the geologic events that created them.

FIGURE 13.8 The deep folding of the Schuylkill coal seams made them costly to exploit. The Mammoth seam runs as deep as 450 to 600 meters (1500 to 2000 ft) below the surface.

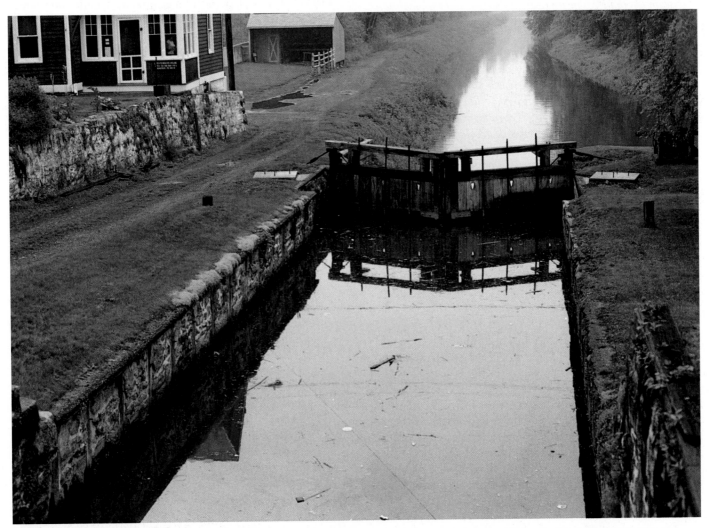

FIGURE 13.9 The Schuylkill Navigation Canal, like its counterpart Lehigh Canal, shown here, provided an outlet to market for the anthracite region's coal resources after 1825. © *Elizabeth J. Leppman.*

unnecessary and, indeed, not thought of, since the presence of anthracite at depth was not suspected. Later, when it was no longer possible to secure coal from a given outcrop, a small pit was sunk to a depth of 9 to 12 meters (30 to 40 ft); when the coal and the water that accumulated in the pit could no longer safely be brought to the surface by windlass, the pit was abandoned and a new one was started. Shaft mining, in which a vertical opening from the surface provides penetration to one or several coal beds, eventually became a necessity; with it came awareness of the complex interrelationships between seam thickness, the nature of interstratified rock and clays, the presence of gases, and the movement of subsurface water.

The subterranean Schuylkill region has a three-dimensional pattern of use. The configuration and the variable thickness of the seams demand concentration of mining activities. Minable coal is not uniformly available along any possible vertical or horizontal cross section because of the interstratification and the extreme folding of the beds. Mining is concentrated further by the location of shafts and the construction of passages, in their turn determined by both patterns of ownership and thickness of seam. In general, no seam less than 0.6 meter (2 ft) is worked, and the absolute thickness—15 meters (50 ft)—is found only in the Mammoth seam of the Schuylkill region.

Friable interstratified rock increases the danger of coal extraction and raises the costs of cave-in prevention. Although the Schuylkill mines are not gassy, the possibility of gas release from the collapse of coal pillars left as mine supports makes necessary systems of ventilation even more elaborate than those minimally required to provide adequate air to miners. Water is ever-present in the anthracite workings, and constant pumping or draining is necessary for mine operation. The collapse of strata underlying a river may result in sudden disastrous flooding.

The Schuylkill subterranean anthracite region presents a pattern of complexity in distribution of physical and cultural features and of interrelationships between phenomena every bit as great and inviting of geographic analysis as any purely surficial region.

PART II: REGIONS IN THE CULTURE-ENVIRONMENT TRADITION

The earth science tradition of geography imposes certain distinctive limits on area analysis. However defined, the regions that may be drawn are based on nature and do not result from human action. The culture-environment tradition, however, introduces to regional geography the infinite variations of human occupation and organization of space. There is a corresponding multiplication of recognized regional types and of regional boundary decisions.

Despite the differing interests of physical and human geographers, one element of study is common to their

concerns: that of process. The "becoming" of an ecosystem, of a cultural landscape, or of the pattern of exchanges in an economic system is an important open or implied part of nearly all geographic study. Evidence of the past as an aid to understanding of the present is involved in much geographical investigation, for present-day distributional patterns or qualities of regions mark a merely temporary stage in a continuing process of change.

Population as Regional Focus

(*See "World Population Distribution," p. 182.*)

In no phase of geography are process and change more basic to regional understanding than in population studies. The human condition is dynamic and patterns of settlement are ever-changing. Although these spatial distributions are related to the ways that people utilize the physical environment in which they are located, they are also conditioned by the purposes, patterns, and solutions of those who went before. In the following extract taken from the work of Glenn T. Trewartha, a dean of American population geographers, notice how population regionalization—used as a focal theme—ties together a number of threads of regional description and understanding. The aspirations of colonist-conquerors, past and contemporary transportation patterns, physical geographic conditions, political separatism, and the history and practice of agriculture and rural land holdings are all introduced to give understanding to population from a regional perspective.

Population Patterns of Latin America[d]

A distinctive feature of the spatial arrangement of population in Latin America is its strongly nucleated character; the pattern is one of striking clusters. Most of the population clusters remain distinct and are separated from other clusters by sparsely occupied territory. Such a pattern of isolated nodes of settlement is common in many pioneer regions; indeed, it was characteristic of early settlement in both Europe and eastern North America. In those regions, as population expanded, the scantily occupied areas between individual clusters gradually filled in with settlers, and the nodes merged. But in Latin America such an evolution generally did not occur, and so the nucleated pattern persists. Expectably, the individual population clusters show considerable variations in density.

The origin of the nucleated pattern of settlement is partly to be sought in the gold and missionary fever that imbued the Spanish colonists. Their settlements were characteristically located with some care, since only areas with precious metals for exploitation and large Indian populations to be Christianized and to provide laborers could satisfy their dual hungers. A clustered pattern was also fostered by the isolation and localism that prevailed in the separate territories and settlement areas of Latin America.

[d]From Glenn T. Trewartha, *The Less Developed Realm: A Geography of Its Population.* Copyright © 1972 by John Wiley & Sons, Inc. Reprinted by permission of John Wiley & Sons, Inc.

Almost invariably each of the distinct population clusters has a conspicuous urban nucleus. To an unusual degree the economic, political, and social life within a regional cluster centers on a single large primate city, which is also the focus of the local lines of transport.

The prevailing nucleated pattern of population distribution also bears a relationship to political boundaries. In some countries . . . a single population cluster represents the core area of the nation. In more instances, however, a population cluster forms the core of a major political subdivision of a nation-state, so that a country may contain more than one cluster. A consequence of this simple population distribution pattern and its relation to administrative subdivisions is that political boundaries ordinarily fall within the sparsely occupied territory separating individual clusters. In Latin America few national or provincial boundaries pass through nodes of relatively dense settlement [Figure 13.10].

. . . The spectacular rates at which population numbers are currently soaring in Latin America are not matched by equivalent changes in their spatial redistributions. Any population map of Latin America reveals extensive areas of unused and underutilized land. Part of such land is highland and plagued by steep slopes, but by far the larger share of it is characterized by a moist tropical climate, either tropical wet or tropical wet and dry. Such a climatic environment, with its associated wild vegetation, soils, and drainage, admittedly presents many discouraging elements to the new settler of virgin lands.

. . . [T]ropical climate alone is scarcely a sufficient explanation for the abundance of near-empty lands south of the Rio Grande. Cultural factors are involved as much as, if not more than, physical ones. One of the former is the unfortunate land-holding system that has been fastened on the continent, under which vast areas of potentially cultivable land are held out of active use by a small number of absentee landlords, who not only themselves make ineffective use of the land, but at the same time refuse to permit its cultivation by small operators. Because of the land-holding system, peasant proprietors are unable to secure their own lands, a situation that discourages new rural settlement. . . .

The changes now in progress in the spatial distributions accompanying the vast increase in numbers of people do not appear to involve any large-scale push of rural settlement into virgin territory. Only to a rather limited extent is new agricultural settlement taking place. Intercluster regions are not filling rapidly. The overwhelming tendency is for people to continue to pile up in the old centers of settlement in and around their cities, rather than to expand the frontier into new pioneer-settlement areas.

FIGURE 13.10 Basic settlement patterns of South America.
Population clusters focused on urban cores and separated by sparsely populated rural areas were the traditional pattern in Latin American countries. *Simon & Schuster, Inc. from the Macmillan College Text* Introduction to Latin America, *by Preston E. James. Macmillan College Publishing Company, Inc.*

Language as Region

(See "Language," p. 213.)

The great culture realms of the world (outlined in Figure 7.3) are historically based composites of peoples. They are not closely identified with nation, language, religion, or technology but with all these and more in varying combinations. Culture realms are therefore *multifactor regions*. Basic to cultural geography is the recognition of small regions of single-factor homogeneity that give character to their areas of occurrence and that collectively provide a needed balance to the sweeping generalizations of the culture realm.

Language provides an example of such small area variation, one partially explored in Chapter 7. The language families shown in Figure 7.19 conceal the regional dialect distinctions among the different official tongues of separate countries. These, in turn, ignore or submerge the language forms of minority populations, who may base their own sense of proud identity on their regional linguistic separateness. In scale and recognition even below these ethnically identified regional languages are those local speech variants frequently denied status as identifiable languages and cited as proof of the ignorance and the cultural deprivation of their speakers. However, such a limited-area, limited-population tongue contains all the elements of the classic culturally based region. Its area is defined, its boundaries are easily drawn, it represents homogeneity and majority behavior among its members, and it summarizes an areally distinctive cultural trait.

Gullah as Language[e]

Isolation is a key element in the retention or the creation of distinctive and even externally unintelligible languages. The isolation of the ancestors of the some quarter-million present-day speakers of Gullah—themselves called Gullahs—was nearly complete. Held by the hundreds as slaves on the offshore islands and in the nearly equally remote low country along the southeastern United States coast from South Carolina to the Florida border [Figure 13.11], they retained both the speech patterns of the African languages—Ewe, Fanti, Bambara, Twi, Wolof, Ibo, Malinke, Yoruba, Efik—native to the slave groups and over 4000 words drawn from them. Folktales told in the Gullah creole can be heard and understood by Krio-speaking audiences in Sierra Leone today.

Forced to use English words for minimal communication with their white overseers, but modifying, distorting, and interjecting African-based substitute words into that unfamiliar language, the Gullahs kept intonations and word and idea order in their spoken common speech that made it unintelligible to white masters or to more completely integrated mainland slaves. Because the language was not understood, its speakers were considered ignorant, unable to master the niceties of English. Because ignorance was ascribed to them, the Gullahs learned to be ashamed of themselves, of their culture, and of their tongue, which even they themselves did not recognize as a highly structured and sophisticated separate language.

In common with many linguistic minorities, the Gullahs are losing their former sense of inferiority and gaining pride in their cultural heritage and in the distinctive tongue that represents it. Out of economic necessity, standard English is being taught to their schoolchildren, but an increasing scholarly and popular interest in the structure of their language and in the nature of their culture has caused Gullah to be rendered as a written language, studied as a second language, and translated into English.

In both the written and the spoken versions, Gullah betrays its African syntax patterns, particularly in its employment of terminal locator words: "Where you goin' at?" The same African origins are revealed by the absence in English translation of distinctive tenses: "I be tired" conveys the concept that "I have been tired for a period of time." Though tenses exist in the African root languages, they are noted more by inflection than by special words and structures.

"He en gut no morratater fer mak no pie wid" may be poor English, but it is good Gullah. Its translation—"He has no more sweet potatoes for making pie"—renders it intelligible to ears attuned to English but loses the musical lilt of original speech and, more important, obscures the cultural identity of the speaker, a member of a regionally compact group of distinctive Americans whose territorial extent is clearly defined by its linguistic dominance.

Mental Regions

(*See "Mental Maps," p. 248.*)

The regional units so far used as examples, and the methods of regionalization they demonstrate, have a concrete reality. They are formal or functional regions of specified, measurable content. They have boundaries drawn by some objective measures of change or alteration of content, and they have location on an accurately measured global grid.

Individuals and whole cultures may operate, and operate successfully, with a much less formalized and less precise picture of the nature of the world and of the structure of its parts. The mental maps discussed in Chapter 8 represent personal views of regions and regionalization. The private world views they embody are, as we also saw, colored by the culture of which their holders are members.

Primitive societies, particularly, have distinctive world views by which they categorize what is familiar, and satisfactorily account for what is not. The Yurok Indians of the Klamath River area of northern California were no exception. Their geographic concepts were reported by T. T. Waterman, from whose paper, "Yurok Geography," the following summary is drawn.

The Yurok World View [f]

The Yurok imagines himself to be living on a flat extent of landscape, which is roughly circular and surrounded by ocean. By going far enough up the river, it is believed, "you come

FIGURE 13.11 Gullah speakers are concentrated on the Sea Islands and the coastal mainland of South Carolina and Georgia. The isolation that promoted their linguistic distinction is now being eroded by coastal development.

[e]By Jerome Fellmann.

[f]Source: T. T. Waterman, "Yurok Geography," *University of California Publications in American Archaeology and Ethnology* 16, no. 5 (1920): 189–93.

to salt water again." In other words, the Klamath River is considered, in a sense, to bisect the world. This whole earth mass, with its forests and mountains, its rivers and sea cliffs, is regarded as slowly rising and falling, with a gigantic but imperceptible rhythm, on the heaving, primeval flood. The vast size of the "earth" causes you not to notice this quiet heaving and settling. This earth, therefore, is not merely surrounded by the ocean but floats upon it. At about the central point of the "world" lies a place which the Yurok call qe'nek, on the southern bank of the Klamath, a few miles below the point where the Trinity River comes in from the south. In the Indian concept, this point seems to be accepted as the center of the world.

At this locality also the sky was made. Above the solid sky there is a sky-country, wo'noiyik, about the topography of which the Yurok's ideas are almost as definite as are his ideas of southern Mendocino County, for instance. Downstream from qe'nek, at a place called qe'nek-pul ("qe'nek-downstream"), is an invisible ladder leading up to the sky-country. The ladder is still thought to be there, though no one to my knowledge has been up it recently. The sky-vault is a very definite item in the Yurok's cosmic scheme. The structure consisting of the sky dome and the flat expanse of landscape and waters that it encloses is known to the Yurok as ki-we'sona (literally "that which exists"). This sky, then, together with its flooring of landscape, constitutes "our world." I used to be puzzled at the Yurok confusing earth and sky, telling me, for example, that a certain gigantic redwood tree "held up the world." Their ideas are of course perfectly logical, for the sky is as much a part of the "world" in their sense as the ground is.

The Yurok believe that passing under the sky edge and voyaging still outward you come again to solid land. This is not our world, and mortals ordinarily do not go there; but it is good, solid land. What are breakers over here are just little ripples over there. Yonder lie several regions. To the north (in our sense) lies pu'lekŭk, downstream at the north end of creation. South of pu'lekŭk lies tsi'k-tsik-ol ("money lives") where the dentalium-shell, medium of exchange, has its mythical abode. Again, to the south there is a place called kowe'tsik, the mythical home of the salmon, where also all have a "house." About due west of the mouth of the Klamath lies rkrgr', where lives the culture-hero wo'xpa-ku-mä ("across-the-ocean that widower").

Still to the south of rkrgr' there lies a broad sea, kiolaaopa'a, which is half pitch—an Algonkian myth idea, by the way. All of these solid lands just mentioned lie on the margin, the absolute rim of things. Beyond them the Yurok does not go even in imagination. In the opposite direction, he names a place pe'tskuk ("up-river-at"), which is the upper "end" of the river but still in this world. He does not seem to concern himself much with the topography there.

The Yurok's conception of the world can be summed up in Figure 13.12.

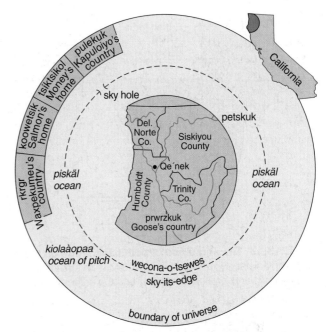

FIGURE 13.12   The world view of the Yurok as pieced together by T. T. Waterman during his anthropological study of the tribe. Qe'nek, in the center of the diagram, marks the center of the world in Indian belief. *Source: T. T. Waterman, "Yurok Geography," University of California Publications in American Archaeology and Ethnology 16, no. 5: 189–93, 1920.*

Political Regions

(*See "Boundaries: The Limits of the State," p. 284.*)

The most rigorously defined formal culture region is the national state. Its boundaries are presumably carefully surveyed and are, perhaps, marked by fences and guard posts. There is no question of a gradual transition zone or of lessening toward the borders of the basic quality of the regional core. This rigidity of a country's boundaries, its unmistakable placement in space, and the trappings—flag, anthem, government, army—that are uniquely its own give to the state an appearance of permanence and immutability not common in other, more-fluid culture regions. But its stability is often more imagined than real. Political boundaries are not necessarily permanent. They are subject to change, sometimes violent change, as a result of internal and external pressures. The Indian subcontinent illustrates the point.

Political Regions in the Indian Subcontinent[g]

The history of the subcontinent since about 400 B.C. has been one of the alternating creation and dissolution of empires, of the extension of central control based upon the Ganges Basin, and of resistance to that centralization by the marginal territories of the peninsula. British India, created largely unintentionally by 1858, was only the last, though perhaps the most successful, attempt to bring under unified control the vast

[g]By Jerome Fellmann.

FIGURE 13.13 The sequence of political change on the Indian subcontinent. British India was transformed in 1947 to the countries of India and Pakistan, the latter a Muslim state with a western and an eastern component. In 1971 Pakistan was torn by civil war based on ethnic and political contrasts, and the eastern segment became the new country of Bangladesh.

territory of incredibly complex and often implacably opposed racial, religious, and linguistic groupings.

A common desire for independence and freedom from British rule united the subcontinent's disparate populations at the end of World War II. That common desire, however, was countered by the mutual religious antipathies felt by Muslims and Hindus, each dominant in separate regions of the colony and each unwilling to be affiliated with or subordinated to the other. When the British surrendered control of the subcontinent in 1947, they recognized these apparently irreconcilable religious differences and partitioned the subcontinent into the second and seventh most populous countries on Earth. The independent state of India was created out of the largely Hindu areas constituting the bulk of the former colony. Separate sovereignty was granted to most of the Muslim-majority area under the name of Pakistan. Even so, the partition left boundaries, notably in the Vale of Kashmir, dangerously undefined or in dispute.

An estimated 1 million people died in the religious riots that accompanied the partition decision. In perhaps the largest short-term mass migration in history, some 10 million Hindus moved from Pakistan to India, and 7.5 million Muslims left India for Pakistan, "The Land of the Pure."

Unfortunately, the purity resided only in common religious belief, not in spatial coherence or in shared language, ethnicity, customs, food, or economy. During its 23 years of existence as originally conceived, Pakistan was a sorely divided country. The partition decision created an eastern and a western component separated by more than 1600 kilometers (1000 mi) of foreign territory and united only by a common belief in Allah [Figure 13.13]. West Pakistan, as large as Texas and Oklahoma combined, held 55 million largely light-skinned Punjabis with Urdu language and strong Middle Eastern cultural ties. Some 70 million Bengali speakers, making up East Pakistan, were crammed into an Iowa-sized portion of the delta of the Ganges and Brahmaputra Rivers. The western segment of the country was part of the semiarid world of western Asia;

the eastern portion of Pakistan was joined to humid, rice-producing Southeast Asia.

Beyond the affinity of religion, little else united the awkwardly separated country. East Pakistan felt itself exploited by a dominating western minority that sought to impose its language and its economic development, administrative objectives, and military control. Rightly or wrongly, East Pakistanis saw themselves as aggrieved and abused. They complained of a per capita income level far below that of their western compatriots, claimed discrimination in the allocation of investment capital, found disparities in the pricing of imported foods, and asserted that their exports of raw materials—particularly jute—were supporting a national economy in which they did not share proportionally. They argued that their demands for regional autonomy, voiced since nationhood, had been denied.

When, in November of 1970, East Pakistan was struck by a cyclone and tidal wave that took an estimated 500,000 lives, the limit of eastern patience was reached. Resentful over what they saw as a totally inadequate West Pakistani effort of aid in the natural disaster that had befallen them, the East Pakistanis were further incensed by the refusal of the central government to convene on schedule a national assembly to which they had won an absolute majority of delegates. Civil war resulted, and the separate new state of Bangladesh was created. [The sequence of political change in the subcontinent is traced in Figure 13.13.]

The country and nation-state so ingrained in our consciousness and so firmly defined, as displayed on the map inside the cover of this book, is both a recent and an ephemeral creation of the cultural regional landscape. It rests upon a claim, more or less effectively enforced, of a monopoly of power and allegiance resident in a government and superior to the communal, linguistic, ethnic, or religious affiliations that preceded it or that claim loyalties overriding it. As the violent recent history of the Indian subcontinent demonstrates, nationalism may be sought, but its maintenance is not assured by the initiating motivations.

PART III: REGIONS IN THE LOCATIONAL TRADITION

While location, as we have seen, is a primary attribute of all regions, regionalization in the locational tradition of geography implies far more than naming regions and mapping their boundaries. The central concern is with the distribution of human activities and the impact of those activities on the physical and cultural landscape.

In this sense, world regionalization of agriculture and of the soils and climates with which it is related is within the locational tradition. For practical and accepted reasons, however, such underlying physical patterns have been included under the earth science tradition. But the point is made: the locational tradition emphasizes the "doing" in human affairs, and "doing" is not an abstract thing but an interrelation of life and the environment on which life depends.

The locational tradition, therefore, encourages the recognition and the definition of a far wider array of regional types than do the earth science or culture-environment traditions. Any single pattern of economic activity or of cultural interaction invites the recognition of definable *formal regions*. The interchange of commodities, the control of urban market areas, the flows of capital, and the collection and distribution activities of ports are just a few examples of the infinite number of analytically useful *functional regions* that one may recognize.

Economic Regions

(*See "World Manufacturing Patterns and Trends," p. 347.*)

Economic regionalization is among the most frequent, familiar, and useful employments of the regional method. Through economic regions the geographer identifies activities and resources, maps the limits of their occurrence or use, and examines the interrelationships and flows that are part of the complexities of the contemporary world.

The economic region, examples of which were explored in Chapter 10, should be seen as potentially more than a device for recording what is in either a formal or a functional sense. It has increasingly become a device for examining what might or should be. The concept of the economic region as a tool for planning and a framework for the manipulation of the people, resources, and economic structure of a composite region first took root in the United States during the Great Depression years of the 1930s. The key element in the planning region is the public recognition of a major territorial unit in which economic change or decline is seen as the cause of a variety of interrelated problems, including population out-migration, regional isolation, underdevelopment, and poverty.

Appalachia[h]

Until the early 1960s, "Appalachia" was for most a loose reference to the complex physiographic province of the eastern United States associated with the Appalachian Mountain

[h]By Jerome Fellmann and Mark Bjelland.

FIGURE 13.14 This eastern Kentucky cabin is a reminder of economic and social changes in Appalachia. While traditional landscape features such as this log cabin remain, higher incomes, expansion of urban job opportunities, improved highway networks, and new communication technologies have reduced the poverty and isolation long associated with the region. © *Bob Douglas.*

chain. If thought of at all, it was apt to be visualized as rural, isolated, and tree-covered, as an area of coal mining, hillbillies, and folksongs [Figure 13.14].

During the 1950s, however, the economic stagnation and the functional decline of the area became increasingly noticeable in the national context of economic growth, rising personal incomes, and growing concern with the elimination of the poverty and deprivation of every group of citizens. Less dramatically but just as decisively as the Dust Bowl or the Tennessee Valley of an earlier era, Appalachia became simultaneously a popularly recognized economic and cultural region and a governmentally determined planning region.

Evidences of poverty, underdevelopment, and social crisis were obvious to a country committed to recognize and eradicate such conditions within its own borders. By 1960, per capita income within Appalachia was $1400 when the national average was $1900. In the decade of the 1950s, mine employment fell 60% and farm jobs declined 52%; the rest of the country lost only 1% of mining jobs and 35% of agricultural employment. Rail employment fell with the drop in coal mining. Massive out-migration occurred among young adults, with such cities as Chicago, Detroit, Dayton, Cleveland, and Gary the targets. Even with these departures, unemployment among those who remained in Appalachia averaged 50% higher than the national rate. Because of the departures, the remnant population—only 47% of whom lived in or near cities in 1960, as against 70% for the entire United States—was distorted in age structure. The very young and the old were disproportionately represented; the productive working-age groups were, at least temporarily, emigrants.

When these and other socioeconomic indicators were plotted by counties and by state economic areas, the maps revealed a coherent and clearly bounded region of economic distress [Figure 13.15]. It extended through 13 states from

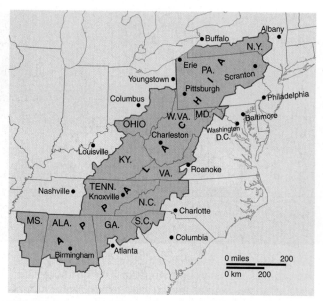

FIGURE 13.15 The boundaries of "Appalachia" as defined by the Appalachian Regional Commission were based on social and economic conditions influenced by political considerations, not topography.

Mississippi to New York, covered some 505,000 square kilometers (195,000 sq mi), and contained 18 million people, 93% of them white.

By 1963, awareness of the problems of the area at federal and state levels had passed beyond recognition of a multifactor economic region to the establishment of a planning region. A joint federal-state Appalachian Regional Commission was created to develop a program designed to meet the perceived needs of the entire area. The approach chosen was one of limited investment in a restricted number of highly localized developments, with the expectation that these would spark economic growth supported by private funds.

In outline, the plan was (1) to ignore those areas of poverty and unemployment that were in isolated, inaccessible "hollows" throughout the region; (2) to designate "growth centers" where development potential was greatest and concentrate all spending for economic expansion there; the regional growth potential in targeted expenditure was deemed sufficient to overcome charges of aiding the prosperous and depriving the poor; and (3) to create a new network of roads so that the isolated jobless could commute to the new jobs expected to form in and near the favored growth centers. Road construction would also, of course, open inaccessible areas to tourism and strengthen the economic base of the entire planning region.

In the years since the Appalachian Regional Commission was established, and in ways not anticipated, the economic prospects of Appalachia have altered. During the 1980s, new industrial jobs multiplied as manufacturing relocated to, or was newly developed in, the Appalachia portion of the Sunbelt. The new factory employment opportunities initially exceeded local labor pools, and former out-migrants returned home from cities outside the region, reestablishing a more balanced population

pyramid. At the same time, however, coal-mining jobs in the region plummeted and unemployment still remained above the national average. By the early 1990s, the Appalachian Regional Commission had committed more than $6 billion to the area, and over $10 billion more had come from other sources.

The commission's investments combined with changing perceptions of the region to fundamentally alter the 1960s picture of unrelieved depression. Extensive construction of highways, water systems, and sanitation facilities improved access to jobs and the quality of basic services for many residents of the region. Poverty rates declined and the gap in per capita income between Appalachia and the rest of the United States narrowed. Population flows stabilized and some parts of Appalachia became popular second home and recreational destinations.

Challenges remain. Some isolated areas of Appalachia were not served by the commission's projects. Mechanization of coal mining and the shift to cleaner coal from the western United States reduced employment in that sector. Manufacturing has been concentrated in metals, wood products, textiles, and apparel—all sectors badly hurt by global competition. Low-paying service sector jobs in the tourism industry have not made up for lost mining and manufacturing wages. In 2007, per capita income remained 20% lower in Appalachia than in the rest of the country. But instead of uniform social and economic distress, we see subregional contrasts between areas with relatively healthy economies and remaining areas of distress. In summary, the Appalachian Regional Commission's identification of an economically distressed region was a first step in creating focused economic development plans that improved the quality of life for many and created a more-diverse, stable regional economy.

Urban Regions

(See "Megalopolis," p. 375.)

Urban geography occupies a center stage position in the locational tradition of geography. Modern integrated, interdependent society on a world basis is urban-centered. Cities are the indispensable functional focuses of production, exchange, and administration. They exist individually as essential elements in interlocked hierarchical systems of cities. Internally, they display complex but repetitive spatial patterns of land uses and functions.

Because of the many-sided character of urbanism, cities are particularly good subjects for regional study. They are themselves, of course, formal regions. In the aggregate, their distributions give substance to formal regions of urban concentration. Cities are also the cores of functional regions of varying types and hierarchical orders. Their internal diversity of functional, land use, and socioeconomic patterns invite regional analysis. The use of both the formal region and functional region concepts is clearly displayed by the geographer Jean Gottmann, who, in examining the data and landscapes of the eastern United States at mid-20th century, recognized and analyzed Megalopolis. The following is taken from his study.

FIGURE 13.16 Megalopolis in 1960. The region was then composed of counties that, by U.S. census definition, were "urban" in population and economic characteristics. Much of the area is still distinctly "rural" in land use.

FIGURE 13.17 The "Pine Barrens" of New Jersey is still a largely undisturbed natural enclave in the heart of Megalopolis. Its preservation is a subject of dispute between environmentalists and developers. © *Elizabeth J. Leppman.*

Megalopolis[i]

The northeastern seaboard of the United States is today the site of a remarkable development—an almost continuous stretch of urban and suburban areas from southern New Hampshire to northern Virginia and from the Atlantic shore to the Appalachian foothills [Figure 13.16]. The processes of urbanization, rooted deep in the American past, have worked steadily here, endowing the region with unique ways of life and of land use. No other section of the United States has such a large concentration of population, with such a high average density, spread over such a large area. And no other section has a comparable role within the country or a comparable importance in the world. Here has been developed a kind of supremacy, in politics, in economics, and possibly even in cultural activities, seldom before attained by an area of this size.

Great, then, is the importance of this section of the United States and of the processes now at work within it. And yet it is difficult to single this area out from the surrounding areas, for its limits cut across established historical divisions, such as New England and the Middle Atlantic states, and across political entities, since it includes some states entirely and others only partially. A special name is needed, therefore, to identify this special geographical area.

This particular type of region is new, but it is the result of age-old processes, such as the growth of cities, the division of labor within a civilized society, the development of world resources. The name applied to it should, therefore, be new as a

[i]Jean Gottmann, *Megalopolis: The Urbanized Northeastern Seaboard of the United States.* Copyright © 1961. Twentieth Century Fund, New York. Reprinted with permission.

place-name but old as a symbol of the long tradition of human aspirations and endeavor underlying the situations and problems now found here. Hence the choice of the term Megalopolis, *used in this study.*

As one follows the main highways or railroads between Boston and Washington, D.C., one hardly loses sight of built-up areas, tightly woven residential communities, or powerful concentrations of manufacturing plants. Flying this same route one discovers, on the other hand, that behind the ribbons of densely occupied land along the principal arteries of traffic, and in between the clusters of suburbs around the old urban centers, there still remain large areas covered with woods and brush alternating with some carefully cultivated patches of farmland [Figure 13.17]. These green spaces, however, when inspected at closer range, appear stuffed with a loose but immense scattering of buildings, most of them residential but some of industrial character. That is, many of these sections that look rural actually function largely as suburbs in the orbit of some city's downtown. Even the farms, which occupy the larger tilled patches, are seldom worked by people whose only occupation and income are properly agricultural.

Thus the old distinctions between rural and urban do not apply here anymore. Even a quick look at the vast area of Megalopolis reveals a revolution in land use. Most of the people living in the so-called rural areas, and still classified as "rural population" by recent censuses, have very little, if anything, to do with agriculture. In terms of their interests and work they are what used to be classified as "city folks," but their way of life and the landscapes around their residences do not fit the old meaning of urban.

In this area, then, we must abandon the idea of the city as a tightly settled and organized unit in which people, activities, and riches are crowded into a very small area clearly separated from its nonurban surroundings. Every city in this region spreads out far and wide around its original nucleus; it grows amidst an irregularly colloidal mixture of rural and suburban landscapes; it melds on broad fronts with other mixtures, of somewhat similar though different texture, belonging to the suburban neighborhoods of other cities.

Thus an almost continuous system of deeply interwoven urban and suburban areas, with a total population of about 37 million people in 1960, has been erected along the Northeastern Atlantic Seaboard. It straddles state boundaries, stretches across wide estuaries and bays, and encompasses many regional differences. In fact, the landscapes of Megalopolis offer such variety that the average observer may well doubt the unity of the region. And it may seem to him that the main urban nuclei of the seaboard are little related to one another. Six of its great cities would be great individual metropolises in their own right if they were located elsewhere. This region indeed reminds one of Aristotle's saying that cities such as Babylon had "the compass of a nation rather than a city."

The description of Megalopolis in 1960 represents, as does any regional study, a captured moment on the continuum of geographic change. When that moment is lucidly described and the threads of areal character clearly delineated, the regional study serves as both a summary of the present and a prediction for the future. In the years since Gottmann described it, Megalopolis continued to develop along the lines he summarized. Urbanization proceeded, physically as well as functionally, to encroach upon the rural landscapes without regard for state boundaries or even the metropolitan cores that dominated in 1960. As then, new growth centers—becoming equivalents of central cities in their own right—were linked to the expanding transportation corridors, though now the lines of importance are increasingly expressways rather than railroads.

In the south, the corridors around Washington, D.C., are the Capital Beltway in Fairfax County and an extension from it westward to Loudoun County and Dulles Airport in Virginia and, to the north into Montgomery County, Maryland, the I-270 corridor. The Virginia suburbs focusing on Tysons Corner specialized in defense-related and information technology industries, and vast office building complexes and commercial centers are rapidly converting rural land to general urban uses. The Maryland suburbs emphasized health, space, and communications interests in their own new office, industrial, and commercial "parks" and complexes. Still farther to the north during the 1980s, in the "Princeton Corridor," a 42-kilometer (26-mi) stretch along Route 1 from New Brunswick to Trenton, New Jersey, huge corporate parks provided office and research space to companies relocating from the New York area and to new technology firms attracted by proximity to Princeton University. Morristown, New Jersey, and White Plains, in Westchester County, New York, were other similar concentrations of commercial, industrial, and office developments north and west of New York City. To the east, Stamford, Connecticut, with 150,000 daily in-commuters became by the late 1980s the headquarters center for major national corporations and had emerged as a truly major central city new on the scene in its present form since Megalopolis was first described.

Ecosystems as Regions

(See "Ecosystems," p. 393.)

A traditional though oversimplified definition of *geography* as "the study of the areal variation of the surface of the earth" suggested that the discipline centered on the classification of areas and on the division of the earth into regions. Considerations of organization and function were secondary and even unnecessary to the implied main purpose of regional study: the definition of cores and boundaries of areas uniform in physical or cultural properties. In our chapter reviews of the earth science, culture-environment, and locational traditions of geography, however, we have stressed that a more-dynamic view of the discipline recognizes that humans constantly exert discernible, changeable, and frequently adverse impacts on the physical environments they occupy. The landscape evidences of those human impacts are also subjects of regional study, though often their investigation requires or benefits from techniques different from the descriptive methodologies often associated with regional studies (see "Managing Ecoregions").

Newer research philosophies stress the need to study human and environmental interactions from the standpoint of *systems analysis*. That approach emphasizes the organization, structure, and functional dynamics within an area and provides for the quantification of the linkages between the things in space. The *ecosystem* or *biome,* introduced in Chapter 12, provides a systems-analytic concept of great flexibility that permits examination of the relationship between the environment and the biological realm, a relationship often impacted by human interventions. Because that relationship is structured, structure rather than spatial uniformity attracts attention and leads to new understanding of the region. The ecosystem concept, particularly, provides a point of view for investigating the complex consequences of human impact on the natural environment.

Much of our current appreciation of the Everglades ecosystem can be attributed to the evocative writings and tireless work of Marjory Stoneman Douglas. As a young newspaper reporter for the *Miami Herald,* she became impressed with the Everglades and in 1947 published a highly influential book, *The Everglades: River of Grass.* Along with other classics, such as *Silent Spring* by Rachel Carson, her book is one of the most important pieces of environmental writing. *The Everglades: River of Grass* was released the same year that the Everglades National Park was dedicated, and it helped reshape the American public's image of the Everglades region from that of an endless, dangerous, and useless swamp to that of a rich ecosystem filled with beauty and biological treasures. Notice how in this opening passage from her book, Marjory Stoneman Douglas evokes the unique regional character of the Everglades ecosystem.

GEOGRAPHY & *Public Policy*

Managing Ecoregions

Natural resource managers have long recognized that goals, plans, and standards need to be tailored to the local ecosystem. To better understand and manage the diversity of ecosystems, natural resource managers have adopted the regional concept by mapping ecoregions and establishing management strategies specific to each ecoregion. Ecoregions are areas of general similarity in ecosystems based on soils, landforms, land uses, and potential natural vegetation.

The U.S. Environmental Protection Agency, the U.S. Forest Service, and a variety of other state and federal resource management agencies have collaborated with their Canadian and Mexican counterparts to develop ecoregion maps for all of North America. The ecoregions have been mapped at four levels of detail or resolution, with the mapping of Level IV, the most detailed level, still in progress. At Level I, North America is divided into 15 ecoregions, including Arctic Cordillera, Tundra, Taiga, Hudson Plains, Northern Forests, Northwestern Forested Mountains, Marine West Coast Forests, Eastern Temperate Forests, Great Plains, North American Deserts, Mediterranean California, Southern Semi-Arid Highlands, Temperate Sierras, Tropical Dry Forests, and Tropical Wet Forests.

Different ecoregions have differing capacities and potentials and will respond differently to human-induced changes such as land clearance or pollution. Ecoregions are used by resource management agencies as a spatial framework for resource inventories, setting resource management goals, determining carrying capacities, and establishing biological criteria and water quality standards. For example, Minnesota has more than 12,000 lakes, which are treasured for their scenic, ecological, and recreational character. However, point and nonpoint sources of pollution have caused excessive growth of aquatic weeds and decreased water clarity on some lakes. Complicating matters, Minnesota's lakes vary widely in their natural conditions and vulnerability to pollutants. Lakes in the Northern Lakes and Forests ecoregion tend to be much clearer than lakes in the Western Corn Belt Plains ecoregion, so a one-size-fits-all management strategy wouldn't work well. Instead, the Minnesota Pollution Control Agency has selected reference lakes in each of seven ecoregions, so that typical "natural" conditions are known and can be used as a baseline for assessing degradation caused by humans.

Considering the Issues

1. In the interest of fairness, is it preferable to have the same set of pollution standards for the whole country? Or is it better that standards be based on how much pollution the local ecoregion can handle?

2. How might regulated cities and industries respond if they have to install more-expensive pollution controls just because they are located in a more-sensitive ecoregion?

The Everglades[j]

There are no other Everglades in the world.

They are, they have always been, one of the unique regions of the earth, remote, never wholly known. Nothing anywhere else is like them: their vast glittering openness, wider than the enormous visible round of the horizon, the racing free saltness and sweetness of their massive winds, under the dazzling blue heights of space. They are unique also in the simplicity, the diversity, the related harmony of the forms of life they enclose. The miracle of the light pours over the green and brown expanse of saw grass and of water, shining and slow moving below, the grass and water that is the meaning and the central fact of the Everglades of Florida. It is a river of grass.

More recent ecosystem conservation efforts have been carried forward by the South Florida Water Management District. It, too, describes the unique character of the Everglades region in its official publications and notes the landscape evidences of human impacts on the ecosystem.

It is a low place in a low land—with a towering stature. It supports an ecosystem teeming with an array of plants and animals as rich in diversity as the African savannas. The world's most famous wetland collects vast amounts of rainwater and shares it with an ever-growing urban population, filters and cleanses the water with the plants it nurtures, and captures potential floodwaters like a giant sponge.

It is the Florida Everglades—home to 68 threatened or endangered species, among them the Florida panther, the American crocodile, and the wood stork.

Not so long ago, but for a very long time, the Everglades was a pristine wilderness. Seasons came and went. Summer rains fell and often caused Lake Okeechobee to spill its waters over the natural southern shore and form a river.

The river spread over more than eight million acres, covering miles and miles, with a depth that ranged from a half-foot to two feet. It usually moved down the southern Florida

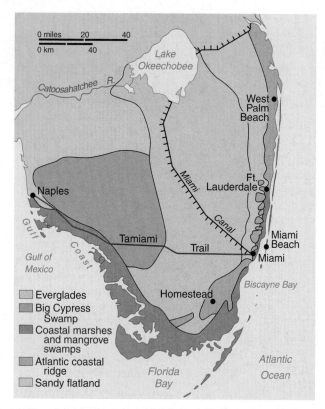

FIGURE 13.18 The Everglades is part of a complex of ecosystems stretching southward in Florida from Lake Okeechobee to the sea. Drainage and water-control systems have altered its natural condition.

FIGURE 13.19 Open water, saw grasses, and tree islands, all visible in this scene, constitute separate *biomes* of the Everglades, which is home also to a teeming animal life. *U.S. Fish & Wildlife Service; photo by Steve Farrell.*

peninsula, through a few outlets east and west, but mostly south to Florida Bay. Historically, it was a very slow river—flowing a quarter mile a day [Figure 13.18].

Native Americans living in and around the river called it Pahayokee (pah-HIGH-oh-geh), the "grassy waters." Englishmen saw a wide-open, green wet prairie and recalled the glades of their native countryside. They called this river, "Everglades," since it stretched as far as one could see [Figure 13.19]. Humans were there, but the impact of their presence was so minimal it was almost non existent. Over the last century, many more people came and the vibrant southern Florida ecosystem was altered to accommodate their needs. As the area grew, the Everglades shrank, its water controlled for human uses.

Today, the impacts to the Everglades are all too apparent. The great sheets of water once moving slowly across the expanse of the original Everglades, recharging the water table and providing flow to streams and rivers are now harnessed in canals. The natural timing of water ebbing and flowing as it crisscrossed the lower peninsula is now manipulated as it rushes through or stands behind manmade structures. Canals quickly drain the land into natural water bodies and are conduits for residential and agricultural runoff that pollute lakes, rivers, and estuaries.

Most of the expansive Everglades is divided into "Water Conservation Areas" that supply water to the lower east coast of southern Florida. The natural overland sheet flow so important to the ecosystem is interrupted. As recently as the 1930s, an estimated quarter million wading birds inhabited the Everglades. Today, those numbers have decreased by more than 90%. There were 2500 wood storks breeding in this vast wetland 40 years ago; but by 1990, these birds had dwindled to just 375.[k]

[k]South Florida Water Management District, *The Living Everglades: Overview.* http://glades.sfwmd.gov/empact/home/02_everglades/index.shtml, last accessed January 13, 2010.

Summary of Key Concepts

The region is a mental construct, a created entity whose sole function is the organization of spatial data. The scheme of that organization, the selection of data to be analyzed, and the region resulting from these decisions are reflections of the intellectual problem posed.

This chapter has not attempted to explore all aspects of the regional method. It has tried, by example, only to document its basic theme: the geographer's regions are arbitrary but deliberately conceived devices for the isolation of things, patterns, interrelations, and flows that invite geographic analysis. In this sense, all geographers are regional geographers, and the regional examples of this chapter logically complete our survey of the four traditions of geography.

Key Words

formal (uniform) region 436
functional (nodal) region 436

perceptual (vernacular, popular) region 436
region 435

regional concept 435

Thinking Geographically

1. What do geographers seek to achieve when they recognize or define regions? On what basis are regional boundaries drawn? Are regions concrete entities whose dimensions and characteristics are agreed upon by all who study the same general segment of earth space? Ask three fellow students who are not participants in this course for their definition of the "South." If their answers differed, what implicit or explicit criteria of regional delimitation were they employing? What type of region were they recognizing?

2. What are the elements or the identifying qualities shared by all regions?

3. What is the identifying characteristic of a *formal region*? How are its boundaries determined? Name three different examples of formal regions drawn from any earlier chapters of this book. How was each defined and what was the purpose of its recognition?

4. How are *functional regions* defined? What is the nature of their bounding criteria? Give three or four examples of functional regions that were defined earlier in the text.

5. The ecosystem was suggested as a viable device for regional delimitation. What regional geographic concepts are suggested in ecosystem recognition? Is an ecosystem identical to a formal region? Why or why not?

6. National, linguistic, historical, planning, and other regions have been recognized in this chapter. With what other regional entities do you have acquaintance in your daily affairs? Are fire protection districts, police or voting precincts, and zoning districts regional units identifiable with geographers's regions as discussed in this chapter or elsewhere in this book? How influenced are you in your private life by your, or others', regional delimitations?

Appendix 1

Map Projections

A map projection is a system for displaying the curved surface of the earth on a flat sheet of paper. No matter how one tries to "flatten" the world, it can never be done in such a way as to show all earth details in their correct relative size, shapes, distances, or directions. Something is always wrong, and the cartographer's task is to select and preserve those earth relationships important for the purpose at hand and to minimize or accept those distortions that are inevitable but unimportant.

If we look at a globe directly, only the front is visible; the back is hidden. To make a world map, we must decide on a way to flatten the globe's curved surface on the hemisphere we can see. Then we have to cut the globe map down the middle of its hidden hemisphere and place the two back quarters on their respective sides of the already visible front half. In simple terms, we have to "peel" the map from the globe and flatten it in the same way we might try to peel an orange and flatten the skin (Figure A.1). Inevitably, the peeling and flattening process will produce a map that either shows tears or breaks in

the surface or is subject to uneven stretching or shrinking to make it lie flat.

Of course, mapmakers do not physically engage in cutting, peeling, flattening, or stretching operations. Their task, rather, is to construct or project on a flat surface the network of parallels and meridians of the globe grid, or *graticule*. This can be done in a number of ways. Before discussing them, it is important to note that two types of circles appear on a globe's spherical grid. A **great circle** is formed on the surface of a sphere by a plane that passes through the center of the sphere. Thus, the equator is a great circle, and each meridian is half of a great circle. Every great circle bisects the globe, dividing it equally into hemispheres. An arc segment of the great circle joining them is the shortest distance between any two points on the earth's surface. A **small circle** is the line created by the intersection of a spherical surface with a plane that does *not* pass through its center. Except for the equator, all parallels of latitude are small circles. Different projections will represent great and small circles in different ways.

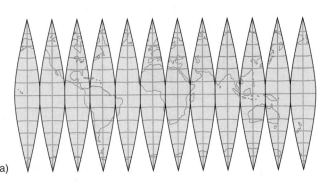

FIGURE A.1 **(a)** A careful "peeling" of the map from the globe yields a set of tapered gores, which, although individually not showing much stretching or shrinking, do not collectively result in a very useful world map. **(b)** It is usually considered desirable to avoid or reduce the number of interruptions by depicting the entire global surface as a single flat circular, oval, or rectangular shape. That continuity of area, however, can be achieved only at the cost of considerable alteration of true shapes, distances, directions, and/or areas. Although the Mollweide projection shown here depicts the size of areas correctly, it distorts shapes.

GEOMETRIC PROJECTIONS

Although all projections can be described mathematically, some can be thought of as being constructed by geometric techniques rather than by mathematical formulas. In geometric projections, the grid system is, in theory, transferred from the globe to a geometric figure, such as a cylinder or a cone, which, in turn, can be cut and then spread out flat (or *developed*) without any stretching or tearing (Figure A.2). The surfaces of cylinders, cones, and planes are said to be **developable surfaces**—cylinders and cones can be cut and laid flat without distortion, and planes are flat to begin with. In actuality, geometric projections are constructed not by tracing shadows but by applying geometry and using lines, circles, arcs, and angles drawn on paper.

Imagine a transparent globe with a light source located either inside or outside the globe. Lines of latitude and longitude (or of coastlines or any other features) drawn on that globe will cast shadows on any nearby surface. A tracing of that shadow globe grid would represent a geometric map projection. As Figure A.3 shows, the location of the light source in relation to the globe surface causes significant variation in the projection of the graticule on the developable geometric surface. An *orthographic* projection results from the placement of the theoretical light source at infinity. A *gnomonic* projection is produced when the light source is at the center of the globe. Placing the light at the antipode—the point exactly opposite the point of tangency, or point of contact between globe and map—produces a *stereographic* projection.

Cylindrical Projections

Suppose that we roll a piece of paper around a transparent globe so that it is tangent to (touching) the sphere at the equator. The line of tangency is called the *standard line* (or *standard parallel,* if it is a parallel of latitude); along it, the map has no distortion. Instead of the paper being the same height as the globe, however, it extends far beyond the poles. For a

gnomonic projection, we would place a light source at the center of the globe, and the light would project a shadow map upon the cylinder of paper. The result is one of many **cylindrical projections,** all of which are developed geometrically or mathematically from a cylinder wrapped around the globe.

Note the variance between the grid we have just projected and the true properties of the globe grid. The grid lines of latitude and longitude intersect each other at right angles, as they do on the globe, and they are all straight north–south or east–west lines. But the meridians do not converge at the poles, as they do on a globe. Instead, they are equally spaced, parallel, vertical lines. Because the meridians are everywhere equally far apart, the parallels of latitude have all become the same length. Although there is no scale distortion along the line of tangency, the equator, distortion increases with increasing distance away from it. The polar regions are stretched north and south as well as east and west, and their sizes are enormously exaggerated. The poles themselves can never be shown on a cylindrical projection tangent at the equator with a light source at the center of the globe.

The mathematically derived **Mercator projection** was inspired by the idea of a cylinder tangent at the equator. It is one of the most commonly used (and misused) cylindrical projections. Invented in 1569 by Gerardus Mercator, the Mercator projection was created to serve as a navigational chart during a time when European exploration of other parts of the world was at its height. The Mercator is the standard projection used by navigators because of a peculiarly useful property: a straight line drawn anywhere on the map is a line of constant compass bearing. If such a line, called a **rhumb line,** is followed, a ship's or a plane's compass will show that the course is always at a constant angle with respect to geographic north (Figure A.4). On no other projection is a rhumb line both straight and true as a direction.

Although it is an excellent navigational aid, the Mercator projection frequently has been misused in book or on wall maps as a general-purpose world map—misused because it gives grossly exaggerated impressions of the size of land areas away

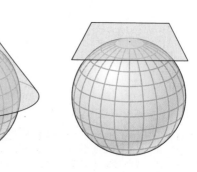

FIGURE A.2 Geometric projections. The three common geometric forms used in such projections are the cylinder, the cone, and the plane. One can think of making a map projection by imagining a transparent globe with a light source inside it and a sheet of paper touching the globe in one of the ways shown here. The globe grid and the outline of the continents would be silhouetted on the paper to form the map.

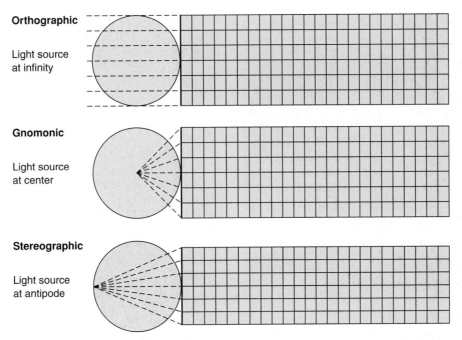

FIGURE A.3 **The effect of the light source location on *planar* surface projections.** Note the variations in the spacing of the lines of latitude that occur when the light source is moved. Completely different map grids would result from using a cylinder or cone as the developable surface.

FIGURE A.4 **Distortion on the Mercator projection.** A perfect five-pointed star was drawn on a globe, and the latitude and longitude of the points of the star were transferred to the Mercator map shown here. The manner in which the star is distorted reflects the way the projection distorts land areas. The enlargement of areas with increasing latitude is so great that a Mercator map should not be published without a diagram showing the varying scale of distance at different latitudes. The most significant property of the Mercator projection is that it is the only one on which any straight line is a line of constant compass bearing, or *rhumb line.* Although a rhumb line usually is not the shortest distance between two points, navigators can draw a series of straight lines between the starting point and the destination that will approximate the great circle route.

FIGURE A.5 **The Miller cylindrical projection** is mathematically derived.

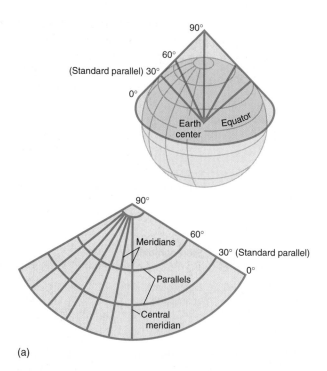

(a)

from the tropics. Notice on Figure A.4 that Greenland appears many times bigger than Mexico, when in fact it is only slightly larger, and that Alaska and Brazil appear to be about the same size; in actuality, Brazil is more than five times as large.

A number of cylindrical projections that are neither equal area nor conformal, such as the *Miller cylindrical projection* shown in Figure A.5, are often used as bases for world maps. The spacing between parallels of latitude on the Miller projection does not increase as rapidly toward the poles as it does on the Mercator, so there is less distortion of the size of areas in the higher latitudes. Although it retains no globe qualities, the Miller cylindrical is used in atlases and wall maps.

Conic Projections

Of the three developable geometric forms—cylinder, cone, and plane—the cone is the closest in form to one-half of a globe. **Conic projections,** therefore, often are used to depict hemispheres or smaller parts of the earth.

A useful projection in this category, and the easiest to visualize, is the *simple conic* projection. Imagine that a cone is laid over half the globe, as in Figure A.6a, tangent to the globe at the 30th parallel. Distances are true only along this standard parallel. When the cone is developed, of course, the standard parallel becomes an arc of a circle, and all other parallels become arcs of concentric circles. With a central light source, the parallels become increasingly farther apart as they approach the pole, and distortion is accordingly exaggerated.

One can lessen the amount of distortion by shortening the length of the central meridian, spacing the parallels of latitude at equal distances on that meridian, and making the 90th parallel (the pole) an arc rather than a point. Most of the conic projections that are in general use employ such mathematical adjustments. When more than one standard parallel is used, a *polyconic* projection results (Figure A.6b).

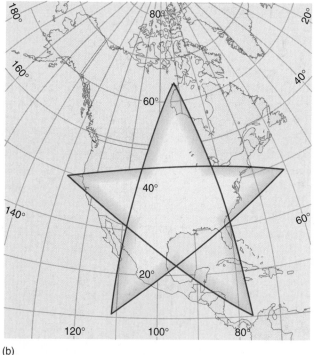

(b)

FIGURE A.6 **(a) A simple conic projection with one standard parallel.** Most conics are adjusted so that the parallels are spaced evenly along the central meridian. **(b) The polyconic projection.** The map is produced by bringing together east–west strips from a series of cones, each tangent at a different parallel. This projection differs from the simple conic in that the parallels of latitude are *not* arcs of concentric circles and the meridians are curved rather than straight lines. Although neither equivalent nor conformal, the projection portrays shape well. Note how closely the star resembles a perfect five-pointed star, unlike the star shown in Figure A.4.

Conic projections are widely used because they can be adjusted to minimize distortions and become either equal-area or conformal. By their nature, however, they can never show the whole globe. In fact, they are most useful for and generally restricted to maps of midlatitude regions of greater east–west than north–south extent. Many official map series use types of conic projections. The U.S. Geological Survey, for example, selected the *Albers equal-area conic projection*, shown in Figure A.7, for its *National Atlas of the United States of America.* It is an equivalent projection with very little distortion of shape even in an area as large as the United States.

Planar Projections

Planar (or **azimuthal**) **projections** are constructed by placing a plane surface tangent to the globe at a single point. Although the plane may touch the globe anywhere the cartographer wishes, the polar case with the plane centered on either the North Pole or the South Pole is easiest to visualize (Figure A.8a).

This *equidistant* projection is useful because it can be centered anywhere, facilitating the correct measurement of distances from that point to all others. For this reason, it is often used to show air navigation routes that originate from a single place. When the plane is centered on places other than the poles, the meridians and the parallels become curiously curved, as is evident in Figure A.8b.

Because they are particularly well suited for showing the arrangement of polar landmasses, planar maps are commonly used in atlases. Depending on the particular projection used, true shape, equivalency, or a compromise between them can be depicted. In addition, one of the planar projections is widely used for navigation and telecommunications. The *gnomonic*

(a)

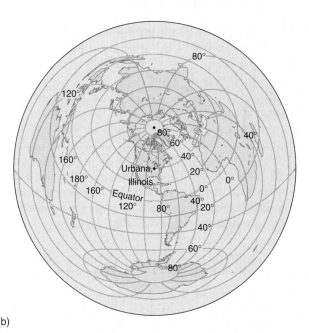

(b)

FIGURE A.8 (a) The planar equidistant projection. Parallels of latitude are circles equally spaced on the meridians, which are straight lines. This projection is particularly useful because distances from the center to any other point are true. If the grid is extended to show the Southern Hemisphere, the South Pole is represented as a circle instead of a point. **(b) A planar equidistant projection centered on Urbana, Illinois.** The scale of miles applies only to distances from Urbana or on a line through it. The scale on the rim of the map, representing the antipode of Urbana, is infinitely stretched. *(b) Copyright 1977, Brooks and Roberts. Used by permission.*

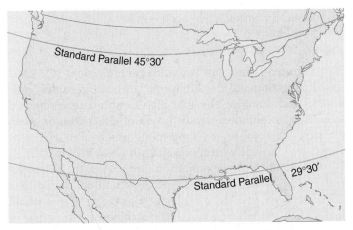

FIGURE A.7 The Albers equal-area conic projection, used for many official U.S. maps, has two standard parallels. All parallels of latitude are concentric arcs of circles, the meridians are straight lines, and parallels and meridians intersect at right angles. The projection is best suited for regions of considerably greater east–west than north–south extent.

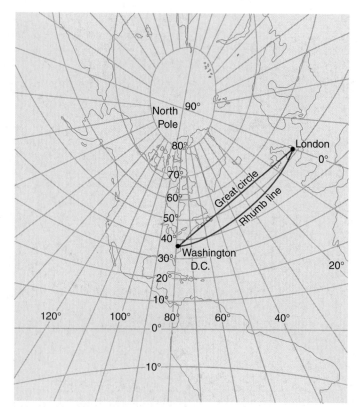

FIGURE A.9 **The gnomonic projection** is the only one on which all great circles appear as straight lines. Rhumb lines are curved. In this sense, it is the opposite of the Mercator projection, on which rhumb lines are straight and great circles are curved (see Figure A.4). Note that the distortion of shapes and areas increases away from the center point. The map is not conformal, equal-area, or equidistant.

planar projection, shown in Figure A.9, is the only one on which all great circles (or parts thereof) appear as straight lines. Because great circles are the shortest distances between two points, navigators need only connect the points with a straight line to find the shortest route.

MATHEMATICAL PROJECTIONS

The geometric projections we have just discussed can all be thought of as developed from the projection of the globe grid onto a cylinder, cone, or plane. Many projections, however, cannot be classified in terms of simple geometric shapes. They are derived from mathematical formulas and usually have been developed to display the world or a portion thereof in a fashion that is visually acceptable. Ovals are most common, but hearts, trapezoids, stars, butterflies, and other—sometimes bizarre—forms have been devised for special purposes.

One such projection is *Goode's Homolosine,* developed by the geographer J. Paul Goode as an equal-area projection for statistical mapping. Usually shown in its interrupted form, as in Figure A.10, it is actually a product of fitting together the

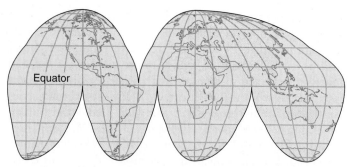

FIGURE A.10 **Goode's homolosine projection** is a combination of two different projections. It joins the sinusoidal and homolographic projections at about 40° North and South. To improve shapes, each continent is placed on the middle of a lobe approximately centered on its own central meridian. This projection can also interrupt the continents to display the ocean areas intact. *Copyright by the Committee on Geographic Studies, University of Chicago. Used by permission.*

Orthographic projection
centered on Washington, D.C.

FIGURE A.11 **The azimuthal orthographic projection** is formed by the projection of a hemisphere onto a plane, with the light source infinitely far away. It shows half the globe as it appears from deep space. An old projection, it was used by the Greek astronomer Hipparchus in the second century B.C. but probably was known earlier.

least distorted portions of two different projections (the sinusoidal projection and the Mollweide, or homolographic, projection) and centering the split map along multiple standard meridians to minimize the distortion of either land or ocean surfaces. This equal-area projection, which also represents shapes well, is widely used, especially in *Goode's World Atlas.*

One kind of planar projection (see p. A5), the *azimuthal orthographic,* was known to Egyptians and Greeks more than 2000 years ago. It shows a hemisphere of the earth as it would look if seen from deep space, thus matching a person's view of a globe (Figure A.11). Used mainly for illustration purposes, the orthographic is neither conformal nor equal-area. Shapes and areas are severely distorted, particularly near the edges, and directions are true only from the center point of the projection.

The azimuthal orthographic and Goode's projections show how projections can be manipulated or adjusted to achieve

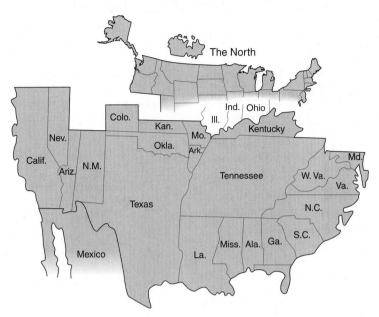

FIGURE A.12 Places mentioned in country music lyrics. In this map transformation, the United States is shown as it might look if the largest states were those most often cited in country music lyrics.

desired objectives. Since most projections are based on a mathematically consistent rendering of the actual globe grid, the possibilities for such manipulation are nearly unlimited. The map properties to be retained, the size and shape of areas to be displayed, and the overall map design influence the cartographer's choices in reproducing the globe grid on the flat map.

Some very effective projections are non-Euclidian in origin, transforming space in unconventional ways. Distances may be measured in nonlinear fashion (in terms of time, cost, number of people, or even perception), and maps that show relative space may be constructed from these data. One example of such a transformation is shown in Figure A.12.

Summary of Key Concepts

It is impossible to transform the globe into a flat map without distortion. Cartographers have devised hundreds of possible geometric and mathematical projections to display to their best advantage the variety of the world's features and relationships they wish to emphasize. Some projections are highly specialized and restricted to a single, limited purpose; others achieve a more-general acceptability and utility.

Key Words

azimuthal projection   A-5
conic projection   A-4
cylindrical projection   A-2

developable surface   A-2
great circle   A-1
Mercator projection   A-2

planar (azimuthal) projection   A-5
rhumb line   A-2
small circle   A-1

Appendix 2

Climate, Soils, and Vegetation

SOILS AND CLIMATE

Soil is one of the most important components of the physical environment. Life as we know it could not exist without it. Soils play an important role by storing and purifying water and are essential to plant, and thus animal and human, life.

Soil Formation

Soil can be defined as a layer of fine material containing *organic matter* (dead plant and animal material), *inorganic matter* (weathered rock materials), air, and water that rests on the bedrock underlying it. The physical and chemical disintegration of rock, called *weathering* (see Chapter 3), begins the process of soil formation. Weathering breaks down solid rock, ultimately producing finely fragmented mineral particles. These particles, together with the decomposed organic matter that comes to rest on top of them, are transformed into soils by water, heat, and the various living agents (such as bacteria and fungi) that decompose the organic matter. Soil formation is a dynamic process. The physical, chemical, and biological activities that produce it are constantly at work.

Although broad classes of soils extend over large areas of the earth's surface, the individual characteristics of soil in a given place may differ markedly over very short distances. Variation is due chiefly to the five major factors involved in soil formation.

1. The *geologic factor* is the parent (underlying) rock, which influences the depth, texture, drainage, and nutrient content of a soil.
2. The *climatic factor* refers to the effects of temperature and precipitation on soil. Temperature affects the length of the growing season, the speed of vegetation decay, and the rate of evaporation. Precipitation totals and intensity influence the type of vegetation that grows in an area and thus the supply of *humus*, decomposed organic matter.
3. The *topographic factor* refers to the height of the land, the *aspect* of a slope (which direction it faces), and the angle of slope. All of these affect the amounts of precipitation, cloud cover, and wind; temperature; and the surface runoff of water, drainage, and rate of soil erosion.
4. The *biological factor* refers to both living and dead plants and animals, which add organic matter to the soil and interact in the nutrient cycle. Plants take up mineral nutrients from the soil and return them to it when they die. Microorganisms, such as bacteria and fungi, assist in the decomposition of dead organic matter, whereas larger

organisms, such as ants and worms, mix and aerate the soil.
5. The *chronological factor* indicates the length of time the preceding four factors have been interacting to create a particular soil. Recall that soil formation is an ongoing but gradual process. Soils that have been forming for short periods of time retain many of the characteristics of their parent-materials. Soils that have been forming for long periods of time are more influenced by such soil-forming factors as climate and organisms.

Soil Profiles and Horizons

Over time, soils tend to develop into layers of various thicknesses. These layers, called **soil horizons,** differ from one another in their structure, texture, color, and other characteristics. A **soil profile** is a vertical cross section of the soil, from the earth's surface down into the underlying parent-material, showing its different horizons (Figure B.1).

- The surface layer, or *O-horizon* (O for *organic*), consists largely of fresh and decaying organic matter: leaves, twigs, animal droppings, dead insects, and so on.
- Beneath the O-horizon lies the fertile mineral-based *A-horizon,* representing topsoil. Plant nutrients abound, and biological activity and humus content are at their maximum. The humus helps give this horizon a dark color.
- Water percolating through the soil removes some of the organic and mineral matter from the bottom of the A-layer in a process called *eluviation* (outwashing), yielding the lighter-colored *E-horizon.*
- The material removed from the E-horizon is deposited in the *B-horizon,* or zone of illuviation (inwashing). Because it contains little organic matter, it is less fertile than the A-horizon. Depending on the types of minerals that have been deposited in this layer, it may be darker or more brightly colored than the E-horizon.
- The *C-horizon* is where weathering is slowly transforming bedrock into soil particles. The older the soil becomes, and the warmer and wetter the climate, the deeper and more discernible the C-horizon will be.
- The lowest layer, the unaltered bedrock, is designated the *R-horizon* (R for *regolith*). The designation is used only if the bedrock is within about 2 meters (6 ft) of the surface.

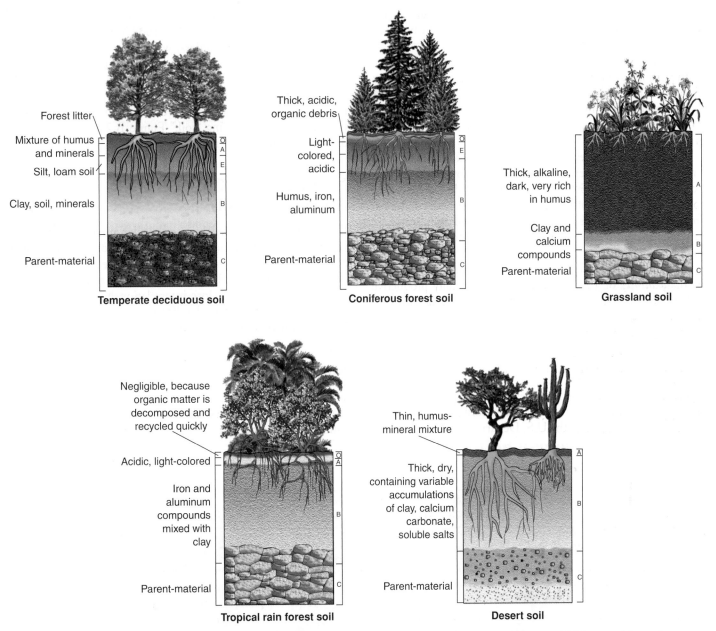

FIGURE B.1 Generalized soil profiles found in five major ecosystems. The number, composition, and thickness of the soil horizons vary depending on the type of soil. Not shown on these profiles is the lowest layer, the unaltered bedrock, or R-horizon. *Source: From Biosphere 2000: Protecting Our Global Environment, 3d ed. by Donald G. Kaufman and Cecilia M. Franz. (New York: HarperCollins Publishers, 2000), Fig. 16.3, p. 313.*

Soil Properties

The four major components of soil—minerals, organic matter, water, and air—interact to produce distinctive soils. **Soil properties** are the characteristics that enable us to distinguish one type of soil from another.

Soils contain both *organic* and *inorganic matter*. The latter, produced by weathering, consists of minerals, such as quartz, silicate clays, and iron and aluminum oxides. When weathering breaks down rocks into soil particles, the minerals are released to nourish plant growth.

Texture refers to the size of the mineral matter in the soil and is determined by the proportion of sand, silt, and clay particles. Sand is the largest particle type, followed by silt and then clay. The most agriculturally productive soil texture, called *loam*, is about 40% sand, 40% silt, and 20% clay.

Texture influences *soil structure*, which is defined by the way individual particles aggregate into larger clumps. The size, shape, and alignments of clumps affect the capacity of the soil to hold water, air, and plant nutrients.

Soils vary considerably in the *nutrients* they contain. These chemical elements—such as nitrogen, phosphorus, and

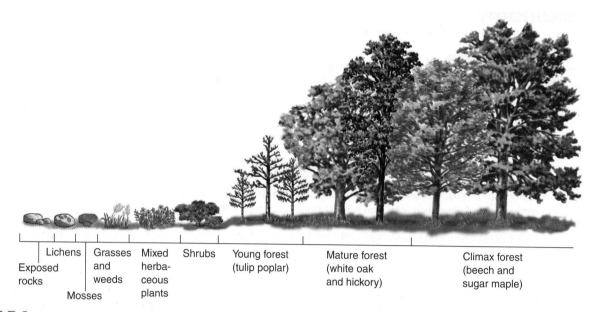

Exposed rocks   Lichens   Mosses   Grasses and weeds   Mixed herba-ceous plants   Shrubs   Young forest (tulip poplar)   Mature forest (white oak and hickory)   Climax forest (beech and sugar maple)

FIGURE B.3 An idealized plant succession in a temperate deciduous region. An increasing number of species are usually found at each stage of the succession. The particular species in any one location are determined by local differences in such factors as bedrock, elevation, temperature, sunlight, and rainfall. *Source: From* Biosphere 2000: Protecting Our Global Environment, *3d ed. by Donald G. Kaufman and Cecilia M. Franz. (New York: HarperCollins Publishers, 2000), Fig. 5.3, p. 86.*

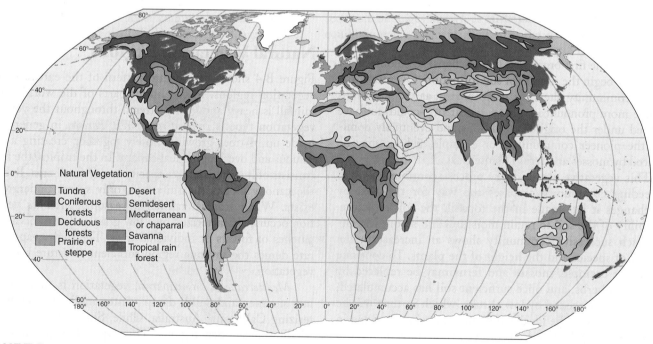

Natural Vegetation

Tundra
Coniferous forests
Deciduous forests
Prairie or steppe
Desert
Semidesert
Mediterranean or chaparral
Savanna
Tropical rain forest

FIGURE B.4 World map of natural vegetation.

America, and south-central Asia, the most prevalent type of vegetation is *prairie*, or *steppe*. These are extensive grasslands, usually growing on high humus content soils. When rainfall is higher in temperate areas, natural vegetation turns to *deciduous woodlands*. These types of trees, such as oak, elm, and syca-more, lose their leaves during the cold season.

Beyond temperate zones, in northerly regions that have mild summers and very cold winters, *coniferous forests* are com-mon. Evaporation rates are low. Usually, only a few species of trees predominate, such as pines and spruces. Still farther north, forests yield to *tundra* vegetation, a complex mix of very low growing shrubs, mosses, lichens, and grasses.

Appendix 3

2009 World Population Data

	Population mid-2009 (millions)	Births per 1000 Population	Deaths per 1000 Population	Rate of Natural Increase (%)	Projected Population (millions) mid-2025	Projected Population (millions) mid-2050	Projected Population Change 2009–2050 (%)	Infant Mortality Rate[a]	Total Fertility Rate[b]	Percent of Population of Ages <15	Percent of Population of Ages 65+	Life Expectancy at Birth (years), Both Sexes	Percent Urban	Percent of Population with HIV/AIDS, Adults Ages 15–49, 2007/2008	GNI PPP per Capita (US$) 2008	Population Density per Sq. Kilometer
WORLD	**6,810**	**20**	**8**	**1.2**	**8,087**	**9,421**	**38**	**46**	**2.6**	**27**	**8**	**69**	**50**	**0.8**	**$10,090**	**50**
MORE DEVELOPED	1,232	12	10	0.2	1,282	1,318	7	6	1.7	17	16	77	75	0.5	32,320	27
LESS DEVELOPED	5,578	22	8	1.4	6,805	8,103	45	50	2.7	30	6	67	44	1.0	5,170	67
LESS DEVELOPED (Excl. China)	4,246	26	8	1.7	5,329	6,666	57	55	3.1	33	5	65	43	1.4	4,910	58
LEAST DEVELOPED	828	35	11	2.4	1,151	1,657	100	80	4.6	40	3	56	27	2.9	1,230	40
AFRICA	**999**	**36**	**12**	**2.4**	**1,385**	**1,994**	**100**	**74**	**4.8**	**41**	**3**	**55**	**38**	**4.3**	**2,660**	**33**
SUB-SAHARAN AFRICA	**836**	**39**	**13**	**2.5**	**1,184**	**1,754**	**110**	**80**	**5.3**	**43**	**3**	**51**	**35**	**5.0**	**1,950**	**34**
NORTHERN AFRICA	**205**	**25**	**7**	**1.9**	**257**	**316**	**54**	**38**	**3.0**	**33**	**5**	**69**	**50**	**0.4**	**5,370**	**24**
Algeria	35.4	23	4	1.9	43.7	50.5	43	26	2.3	28	5	72	63	0.1	7,940	15
Egypt	78.6	25	6	1.9	99.1	122.3	56	19	3.0	33	5	72	43	—	5,460	79
Libya	6.3	24	4	2.0	8.1	9.8	56	18	2.7	30	4	73	77	—	15,630	4
Morocco	31.5	21	6	1.4	36.6	42.4	35	31	2.4	29	6	71	56	0.1	4,330	71
Sudan	42.3	33	11	2.2	56.7	75.9	80	81	4.5	41	3	58	38	1.4	1,930	17
Tunisia	10.4	17	6	1.2	12.2	13.9	34	19	2.0	25	7	74	66	0.1	7,070	64
Western Sahara	0.5	23	6	1.8	0.8	0.9	84	44	3.0	31	2	65	81	—	—	2
WESTERN AFRICA	**297**	**40**	**14**	**2.7**	**420**	**623**	**110**	**80**	**5.5**	**44**	**3**	**51**	**42**	**2.5**	**1,600**	**48**
Benin	8.9	41	9	3.2	13.8	22.0	146	89	5.7	44	3	56	41	1.2	1,460	79
Burkina Faso	15.8	46	14	3.2	24.8	40.8	159	89	6.0	46	3	57	16	1.6	1,160	58
Cape Verde	0.5	26	5	2.1	0.7	0.8	53	29	3.1	38	6	71	59	—	3,450	126
Côte d'Ivoire	21.4	37	14	2.4	29.9	43.7	104	100	4.9	40	2	52	48	3.9	1,580	66
Gambia	1.6	39	11	2.8	2.3	3.6	121	93	5.6	42	3	55	54	0.9	1,280	142
Ghana	23.8	31	10	2.1	32.2	45.2	90	50	4.0	40	4	59	48	1.9	1,430	100
Guinea	10.1	39	12	2.7	15.2	24.0	138	104	5.7	43	3	56	33	1.6	1,190	41
Guinea-Bissau	1.6	43	17	2.6	2.3	3.6	121	117	5.9	43	3	46	30	1.8	530	45
Liberia	4.0	40	10	3.0	5.9	8.8	124	99	5.8	44	3	56	58	1.7	300	36
Mali	13.0	43	15	2.8	18.6	28.3	117	110	6.0	45	2	48	31	1.5	1,090	10

	Population mid-2009 (millions)	Births per 1000 Population	Deaths per 1000 Population	Rate of Natural Increase (%)	Projected Population (millions) mid-2025	Projected Population (millions) mid-2050	Projected Population Change 2009–2050 (%)	Infant Mortality Rate[a]	Total Fertility Rate[b]	Percent of Population of Ages <15	Percent of Population of Ages 65+	Life Expectancy at Birth (years), Both Sexes	Percent Urban	Percent of Population with HIV/AIDS, Adults Ages 15–49, 2007/2008	GNI PPP per Capita (US$) 2008	Population Density per Sq. Kilometer
WESTERN AFRICA (continued)																
Mauritania	3.3	35	10	2.5	4.6	6.9	109	73	5.1	40	4	57	40	0.8	*2,000*	3
Niger	15.3	53	14	3.9	27.4	58.2	281	88	7.4	49	3	53	17	0.8	680	12
Nigeria	152.6	41	15	2.6	207.2	285.1	87	75	5.7	45	3	47	47	3.1	1,940	165
Senegal	12.5	39	10	2.9	17.9	26.1	108	61	5.0	43	2	55	41	1.0	1,760	64
Sierra Leone	5.7	40	20	2.0	8.1	12.4	119	89	5.2	42	4	48	37	1.5	750	79
Togo	6.6	35	8	2.7	9.3	13.2	77	91	5.1	41	3	61	40	3.3	820	117
EASTERN AFRICA	**313**	**40**	**13**	**2.6**	**455**	**682**	**118**	**76**	**5.4**	**44**	**3**	**51**	**22**	**5.6**	**1,030**	**49**
Burundi	8.3	36	15	2.1	11.2	14.8	79	120	5.4	41	3	49	10	2.0	380	298
Comoros	0.7	33	8	2.5	0.9	1.2	81	53	4.2	38	3	64	28	<0.1	1,170	302
Djibouti	0.9	30	12	1.9	1.1	1.5	70	67	4.2	37	3	55	87	3.1	2,330	37
Eritrea	5.1	38	10	2.9	7.4	10.8	113	58	5.3	42	2	58	21	1.3	630	43
Ethiopia	82.8	39	12	2.7	113.1	149.5	81	77	5.3	43	3	53	16	2.1	870	75
Kenya	39.1	39	13	2.7	56.5	83.8	115	67	4.9	42	2	54	19	7.4	1,580	67
Madagascar	19.5	38	9	2.9	28.4	42.3	118	70	5.0	44	3	59	30	0.1	1,040	33
Malawi	14.2	43	12	3.1	21.6	34.1	140	80	6.3	46	3	46	17	11.9	830	120
Mauritius	1.3	14	7	0.7	1.4	1.5	16	15.4	1.7	23	7	72	42	1.7	12,480	625
Mayotte	0.2	39	3	3.6	0.3	0.4	105	—	4.5	42	2	74	28	—	—	503
Mozambique	22.0	41	17	2.4	29.9	42.4	93	97	5.4	43	3	43	29	12.5	770	27
Reunion	0.8	18	5	1.3	1.0	1.1	31	8	2.5	27	7	76	92	—	—	324
Rwanda	9.9	41	16	2.5	14.5	21.8	121	62	5.5	44	3	48	18	2.8	1,010	375
Seychelles	0.1	18	8	1.0	0.1	0.1	37	12.9	2.2	23	8	73	53	—	19,770	191
Somalia	9.1	45	15	3.0	13.9	23.5	158	111	6.7	45	3	50	37	0.5	—	14
Tanzania	43.7	38	15	2.3	67.4	109.5	150	69	5.3	45	3	54	25	5.7	1,230	46
Uganda	30.7	47	13	3.4	51.8	96.4	214	76	6.7	49	3	50	13	5.4	1,140	127
Zambia	12.6	45	16	2.9	18.3	28.1	124	70	6.2	46	3	43	37	14.3	1,230	17
Zimbabwe	12.5	32	18	1.4	16.0	19.1	53	60	3.8	40	4	41	37	15.3	—	32
MIDDLE AFRICA	**125**	**42**	**14**	**2.8**	**189**	**306**	**144**	**95**	**6.1**	**45**	**3**	**51**	**41**	**2.5**	**1,650**	**19**
Angola	17.1	46	19	2.7	26.2	42.7	150	125	6.6	46	2	46	57	2.1	5,020	14
Cameroon	18.9	36	13	2.3	25.5	34.9	85	74	4.7	42	4	52	57	5.1	2,180	40
Central African Republic	4.5	38	19	1.9	5.5	6.5	45	106	5.0	41	4	45	38	6.3	730	7
Chad	10.3	43	17	2.6	13.9	20.5	98	106	6.3	46	3	47	27	3.5	1,160	8
Congo	3.7	36	13	2.3	5.3	7.8	113	75	5.3	42	3	53	60	3.5	3,090	11
Congo, Dem. Rep.	68.7	44	13	3.1	109.7	189.3	176	92	6.5	47	3	53	33	1.3	290	29
Equatorial Guinea	0.7	38	14	2.4	1.0	1.4	114	102	5.4	41	3	59	39	3.4	21,700	24
Gabon	1.5	28	10	1.8	1.9	2.5	68	55	3.6	37	4	59	84	5.9	12,270	6
Sao Tome and Principe	0.2	34	8	2.6	0.2	0.3	82	75	4.1	41	4	65	58	—	1,780	169
SOUTHERN AFRICA	**58**	**24**	**15**	**0.9**	**63**	**68**	**17**	**48**	**2.8**	**33**	**5**	**52**	**56**	**18.5**	**9,380**	**22**
Botswana	2.0	25	12	1.3	2.3	2.8	39	48	3.2	35	5	49	60	23.9	13,100	3
Lesotho	2.1	25	23	0.2	2.4	2.6	21	83	3.4	39	5	40	24	23.2	2,000	70

	Population mid-2009 (millions)	Births per 1000 Population	Deaths per 1000 Population	Rate of Natural Increase (%)	Projected Population (millions) mid-2025	Projected Population (millions) mid-2050	Projected Population Change 2009–2050 (%)	Infant Mortality Rate[a]	Total Fertility Rate[b]	Percent of Population of Ages <15	Percent of Population of Ages 65+	Life Expectancy at Birth (years), Both Sexes	Percent Urban	Percent of Population with HIV/AIDS, Adults Ages 15–49, 2007/2008	GNI PPP per Capita (US$) 2008	Population Density per Sq. Kilometer
SOUTHERN AFRICA (continued)																
Namibia	2.2	29	8	2.1	2.8	3.6	65	46	3.6	38	4	59	35	15.3	6,270	3
South Africa	50.7	23	15	0.8	54.5	57.4	13	45	2.7	32	5	52	59	18.1	9,780	42
Swaziland	1.2	31	15	1.6	1.5	1.7	48	85	3.8	35	4	46	24	26.1	5,010	68
AMERICAS	**920**	**17**	**7**	**1.1**	**1,063**	**1,205**	**31**	**18**	**2.2**	**26**	**9**	**75**	**78**	**0.6**	**23,380**	**22**
NORTHERN AMERICA	**341**	**14**	**8**	**0.6**	**395**	**481**	**41**	**6**	**2.0**	**20**	**13**	**78**	**79**	**0.6**	**45,890**	**16**
Canada	33.7	11	7	0.4	37.6	41.9	24	5.0	1.6	17	14	81	81	0.4	36,220	3
United States	306.8	14	8	0.6	357.5	439.0	43	6.6	2.1	20	13	78	79	0.6	46,970	32
LATIN AMERICA/ CARIBBEAN	**580**	**20**	**6**	**1.4**	**668**	**724**	**25**	**23**	**2.3**	**30**	**6**	**73**	**77**	**0.5**	**10,160**	**28**
CENTRAL AMERICA	**152**	**22**	**5**	**1.7**	**179**	**200**	**31**	**21**	**2.5**	**33**	**5**	**74**	**70**	**0.4**	**11,900**	**61**
Belize	0.3	27	4	2.3	0.4	0.5	56	18	3.1	39	5	73	51	2.1	6,040	14
Costa Rica	4.5	16	4	1.3	5.3	6.1	35	9.7	1.9	27	6	79	59	0.4	10,950	88
El Salvador	7.3	21	7	1.4	9.1	11.2	52	24	2.5	34	5	71	60	0.8	6,670	349
Guatemala	14.0	34	6	2.8	19.9	27.5	96	34	4.4	43	4	70	47	0.8	4,690	129
Honduras	7.5	27	5	2.2	9.8	12.4	66	23	3.3	38	4	72	49	0.7	3,870	67
Mexico	109.6	20	5	1.6	123.4	129.0	18	19	2.3	32	6	75	77	0.3	14,270	56
Nicaragua	5.7	26	5	2.1	7.1	8.2	44	24	2.9	38	4	71	58	0.2	2,620	44
Panama	3.5	20	4	1.6	4.3	5.1	47	15	2.4	30	6	75	64	1.0	11,650	46
CARIBBEAN	**41**	**19**	**8**	**1.2**	**46**	**49**	**19**	**34**	**2.5**	**28**	**8**	**71**	**63**	**1.1**	**—**	**176**
Antigua and Barbuda	0.1	17	7	1.0	0.1	0.1	26	*20*	2.1	28	7	73	31	—	20,570	199
Bahamas	0.3	17	6	1.1	0.4	0.5	33	11	1.9	28	6	72	83	3.0	—	25
Barbados	0.3	13	8	0.5	0.3	0.3	−8	*13*	1.8	22	12	77	38	1.2	—	653
Cuba	11.2	11	8	0.3	11.2	10.0	−11	4.7	1.6	18	12	78	76	0.1	—	101
Dominica	0.1	16	9	0.7	0.1	0.1	−10	*16*	2.3	29	10	75	73	—	8,300	96
Dominican Republic	10.1	24	6	1.8	12.0	13.4	33	32	2.8	33	6	72	64	1.1	7,890	207
Grenada	0.1	19	7	1.2	0.1	0.1	−8	*14*	2.4	29	6	74	31	—	8,060	308
Guadeloupe	0.4	17	7	1.0	0.5	0.5	21	6	2.4	23	12	79	100	—	—	240
Haiti	9.2	31	10	2.1	11.7	15.1	63	57	4.0	38	4	58	43	2.2	1,180	333
Jamaica	2.7	17	6	1.1	2.8	2.7	−1	26	2.4	30	8	72	52	1.6	7,360	246
Martinique	0.4	13	7	0.7	0.4	0.4	13	8	1.9	22	12	80	98	—	—	368
Netherlands Antilles	0.2	13	8	0.5	0.2	0.2	−7	13	1.9	22	10	76	92	—	—	254
Puerto Rico	4.0	12	8	0.4	4.1	3.7	−6	8.8	1.7	20	14	78	94	—	—	447
St. Kitts-Nevis	0.05	18	8	1.0	0.1	0.1	26	15	2.3	28	8	70	32	—	15,170	191
Saint Lucia	0.2	15	7	0.8	0.2	0.2	28	19.4	1.7	28	7	73	28	—	9,190	319
St. Vincent and the Grenadines	0.1	17	8	0.9	0.1	0.1	−13	17.6	2.1	29	7	72	40	—	8,770	283
Trinidad and Tobago	1.3	14	8	0.6	1.4	1.3	−4	26	1.6	24	7	69	12	1.5	23,950	260

Glossary

A

absolute direction   Direction with respect to cardinal east, west, north, and south reference points.

absolute distance   The shortest-path separation between two places measured on a standard unit of length (miles or kilometers, usually); also called real distance.

absolute location   (*syn:* mathematical location) The exact position of an object or a place stated in spatial coordinates of a grid system designed for locational purposes. In geography, the reference system is the global grid of parallels of latitude north or south of the equator and of meridians of longitude east or west of a prime meridian.

accelerated eutrophication   The overnourishment of a water body with nutrients stemming from human activities, such as agriculture, industry, and urbanization.

accessibility   The relative ease with which a destination may be reached from other locations; the relative opportunity for spatial interaction. May be measured in geometric, social, or economic terms.

acculturation   The cultural modification or change resulting from one culture group or individual adopting traits of a more advanced or dominant society; cultural development through "borrowing."

acid rain   Precipitation that is unusually acidic; created when oxides of sulfur and nitrogen change chemically as they dissolve in water vapor in the atmosphere and return to Earth as acidic rain, snow, fog, or dry particles.

activity space   The area within which people move freely on their rounds of regular activity.

adaptation   A presumed modification of heritable traits through response to environmental stimuli.

agglomeration   The spatial grouping of people or activities for mutual benefit.

agglomeration economies   (*syn:* external economies) The savings to an individual enterprise that result from spatial association with other, similar economic activities.

agricultural density   The number of rural residents per unit of agriculturally productive land. The measure excludes a region's urban population and its nonarable land from the density calculation.

agriculture   Cultivating the soil, producing crops, and raising livestock; farming.

air mass   A large body of air with little horizontal variation in temperature, pressure, and humidity.

air pressure   The weight of the atmosphere as measured at a point on the earth's surface.

alluvial fan   A fan-shaped accumulation of alluvium deposited by a stream at the base of a hill or mountain.

alluvium   The sediment carried by a stream and deposited in a floodplain or delta.

amalgamation theory   In human geography, the concept that multiethnic societies become a merger of the culture traits of their member groups.

anaerobic digestion   The process by which organic waste is decomposed in an oxygen-free environment to produce methane gas (biogas).

anecumene   *See* nonecumene.

animism   A belief that natural objects may be the abode of dead people, spirits, or gods who occasionally give the objects the appearance of life.

antecedent boundary   A boundary line established before the area in question is well populated.

aquaculture   Producing and harvesting of fish and shellfish in freshwater ponds, lakes, and canals or in fenced-off coastal bays and estuaries; fish farming.

aquifer   Underground porous and permeable rock that is capable of holding groundwater, especially rock that supplies economically significant quantities of water to wells and springs.

arable land   Land that is or can be cultivated.

Arctic haze   Air pollution resulting from the transport by air currents of combustion-based pollutants to the area north of the Arctic Circle.

area analysis tradition   One of the four traditions of geography, that of regional geography.

area cartogram   (*syn:* value-by-area map) A type of map in which the areas of the units are proportional to the data they represent.

arithmetic density   *See* crude density.

arroyo   A steep-sided, flat-bottomed gully, usually dry, carved out of desert land by rapidly flowing water.

artifacts   The material manifestations of culture, including tools, housing, systems of land use, clothing, and the like. Elements in the technological subsystem of culture.

artificial boundary   *See* geometric boundary.

assimilation   The social process of merging into a composite culture, losing separate ethnic or social identity, and becoming culturally homogenized.

asthenosphere   The partially molten, plastic layer above the core and lower mantle of the earth.

atmosphere   The gaseous mass surrounding the earth.

atoll   A near-circular low coral reef formed in shallow water enclosing a central lagoon; most common in the central and western Pacific Ocean.

azimuthal projection   *See* planar projection.

B

barchan   A crescent-shaped sand dune; the horns of the crescent point downwind.

basic sector   Those products or services of an urban economy that are exported outside the city itself, earning income for the community.

bench mark   A surveyor's mark indicating the position and elevation of a stationary object; used as a reference point in surveying and mapping.

bioaccumulation   The buildup of a material in the body of an organism.

biocide   A chemical used to kill plant and animal pests and disease organisms. *See also* herbicide, pesticide.

biodiversity hot spot   An area with an exceptionally high number of endemic species that is at high risk of disruption by human activities.

biological magnification   The accumulation of a chemical in the fatty tissue of an organism and its concentration at progressively higher levels in the food chain.

biomagnification   *See* biological magnification.

biomass   Living matter, plant and animal, in any form.

biomass fuel   Any organic material produced by plants, animals, or microorganisms that can be used as a source of energy through either direct burning or conversion into a liquid or gas.

biome   The total assemblage of living organisms in a single major ecological region.

biosphere   (*syn:* ecosphere) The thin film of air, water, and earth within which we live, including the atmosphere, surrounding and subsurface waters, and the upper reaches of the earth's crust.

birth rate   (*syn:* crude birth rate) The ratio of the number of live births during 1 year to the total population, usually at the midpoint of the same year, expressed as the number of births per year per 1000 population.

blizzard   A heavy snowstorm accompanied by high winds.

boundary   A line separating one political unit from another.

boundary definition   A general agreement between two states about the allocation of territory between them.

boundary delimitation   The plotting of a boundary line on maps or aerial photographs.

boundary demarcation   The actual marking of a boundary line on the ground; the final stage in boundary development.

butte   A small, flat-topped, isolated hill with steep sides, common in dry climate regions.

C

carcinogen   A substance that produces or incites cancerous growth.

carrying capacity   The numbers of any population that can be adequately supported by the available resources on which that population subsists; for humans, the numbers supportable by the known and utilized resources—usually agricultural—of an area.

cartogram   A map that has been simplified to present data in a diagrammatic way; the base normally is not true to scale.

cartography   The art, science, and technology of making maps.

caste   One of the hereditary social classes in Hinduism that determines one's occupation and position in society.

central business district (CBD) The center, or "downtown," of an urban unit, where retail stores, offices, and cultural activities are concentrated and where land values are high.

central city That part of the metropolitan area contained within the boundaries of the main city around which suburbs have developed.

central place A nodal point for the distribution of goods and services to a surrounding hinterland population.

central place theory A deductive theory formulated by Walter Christaller (1893–1969) to explain the size and distribution of settlements through reference to competitive supply of goods and services to dispersed rural populations.

centrifugal force In political geography, a force that disrupts and destabilizes a state, threatening its unity.

centripetal force In political geography, a force that promotes unity and national identity.

CFCs *See* chlorofluorocarbons.

chain migration The process by which migration movements from a common home area to a specific destination are sustained by links of friendship or kinship between first movers and later followers.

channelization The modification of a stream channel; specifically, the straightening of meanders or dredging of the stream channel to deepen it.

channelized migration The tendency for migration to flow between areas that are socially and economically allied by past migration patterns, by economic trade considerations, or by some other affinity.

chemical weathering The decomposition of earth materials because of chemical reactions that include oxidation, hydration, and carbonation.

chlorofluorocarbons (CFCs) A family of synthetic chemicals that have significant commercial applications but whose emissions are contributing to the depletion of the ozone layer.

choropleth map A map that depicts quantities for areal units by varying pattern and/or color.

circumpolar vortex High-altitude winds circling the poles from west to east.

city A multifunctional nucleated settlement with a central business district and both residential and nonresidential land uses.

climate The long-term average weather conditions in a place or region.

climax community An association of grasses, shrubs, and/or trees that is in equilibrium with the climate and soil of the site; the last stage of an ecological succession.

climograph A bar and line graph used to depict average monthly temperatures and precipitation.

cogeneration The simultaneous use of a single fuel for the generation of electricity and low-grade central heat.

cognition The process by which an individual gives mental meaning to information.

cohort A population group unified by a specific common characteristic, such as age, and who are treated as a statistical unit during their lifetimes.

commercial economy (*syn:* market economy) The production of goods and services for exchange in competitive markets where price and availability are determined by supply and demand forces.

commercial energy Commercially traded fuels such as coal, oil, or natural gas and excluding wood, vegetable or animal wastes, or other biomass.

Common Market *See* European Union.

compact state A state whose territory is nearly circular.

comparative advantage A region's profit potential for a productive activity compared with alternative areas of production of the same good or with alternative uses of the region's resources.

concentric zone model A model describing urban land uses as a series of circular belts or rings around a core central business district, each ring housing a distinct type of land use.

conformal projection A map projection on which the shapes of small areas are accurately portrayed.

conic projection A map projection based on the projection of the grid system onto a cone as the presumed developable surface.

connectivity The directness of routes linking pairs of places; all of the tangible and intangible means of connection and communication between places.

consequent boundary (*syn:* ethnographic boundary) A boundary line that coincides with some cultural divide, such as religion or language.

conservation The wise use or preservation of natural resources so as to maintain supplies and qualities at levels sufficient to meet present and future needs.

contagious diffusion The spread of a concept, a practice, or an article from one area to others through contact and/or the exchange of information.

continental drift The hypothesis that an original single landmass (Pangaea) broke apart and that the continents have moved very slowly over the asthenosphere to their present locations.

contour interval The vertical distance separating two adjacent contour lines.

contour line A map line along which all points are of equal elevation above or below a datum plane, usually mean sea level.

conurbation An extended urban area formed by the coalescence of two or more formerly separate cities.

convection The circulatory movement of rising warm air and descending cool air.

convectional precipitation Rain produced when heated, moisture-laden air rises and then cools below the dew point.

Convention on the Law of the Sea *See* Law of the Sea Convention.

coral reef A rocklike landform in shallow tropical water composed chiefly of compacted coral and other organic material.

core The nucleus of a region or country, the main center of its industry, commerce, population, political, and intellectual life; in urban geography, that part of the central business district characterized by intensive land development.

core area The nucleus of a state, containing its most-developed area, greatest wealth, densest populations, and clearest national identity.

Coriolis effect A fictitious force used to describe motion relative to a rotating earth; specifically, the force that tends to deflect a moving object or fluid to the right (clockwise) in the Northern Hemisphere and to the left (counterclockwise) in the Southern Hemisphere.

countermigration *See* return migration.

country *See* state.

creole A language developed from a pidgin to become the native tongue of a society.

critical distance The distance beyond which cost, effort, and/or means play an overriding role in the willingness of people to travel.

crude birth rate (CBR) *See* birth rate.

crude death rate (CDR) *See* death rate.

crude density (*syn:* arithmetic density, population density) The number of people per unit area of land.

crude oil A mixture of hydrocarbons that exists in a liquid state in underground reservoirs; petroleum as it occurs naturally, as it comes from an oil well, or after extraneous substances have been removed.

cultural convergence The tendency for cultures to become more alike as they increasingly share technology and organization structures in a modern world united by improved transportation and communication.

cultural divergence The likelihood or tendency for isolated cultures to become increasingly dissimilar with the passage of time.

cultural ecology The study of the interactions between societies and the natural environments they occupy.

cultural integration The interconnectedness of all aspects of a culture; no part can be altered without impact upon other culture traits.

cultural lag The retention of established culture traits despite changing circumstances rendering them inappropriate.

cultural landscape The natural landscape as modified by human activities and bearing the imprint of a culture group or society; the built environment.

culture A society's collective beliefs, symbols, values, forms of behavior, and social organizations, together with its tools, structures, and artifacts; transmitted as a heritage to succeeding generations and undergoing adoptions, modifications, and changes in the process.

culture complex An integrated assemblage of culture traits descriptive of one aspect of a society's behavior or activity.

culture-environment tradition One of the four traditions of geography; in this text, identified with population, cultural, political, and behavioral geography.

culture hearth A nuclear area within which an advanced and distinctive set of culture traits develops and from which there is diffusion of distinctive technologies and ways of life.

culture realm A collective of culture regions sharing related culture systems; a major world area having sufficient distinctiveness to be perceived as set apart from other realms in its cultural characteristics and complexes.

culture region A formal or functional region within which common cultural characteristics prevail. It may be based on single culture traits; on culture complexes; or on political, social, or economic integration.

culture system A generalization suggesting shared, identifying traits uniting two or more culture complexes.

culture trait A single distinguishing feature of regular occurrence within a culture, such as the use of chopsticks or the observance of a particular caste system; a single element of learned behavior.

cyclone A type of atmospheric disturbance in which masses of air circulate rapidly about a region of low atmospheric pressure.

cyclonic (frontal) precipitation The rain or snow that is produced when moist air of one air mass is forced to rise over the edge of another air mass.

cylindrical projection A map projection based on the projection of the globe grid onto a cylinder as the presumed developable surface.

D

database   *See* geographic database.

DDT   A chlorinated hydrocarbon that is among the most persistent of the biocides in general use.

death rate (mortality rate)   A mortality index usually calculated as the number of deaths per year per 1000 population.

decomposers   Microorganisms and bacteria that feed on dead organisms, causing their chemical disintegration.

deforestation   The clearing of land through total removal of forest cover.

delta   A triangular-shaped deposit of mud, silt, or gravel created by a stream where it flows into a body of standing water.

demographic equation   A mathematical expression that summarizes the contribution of different demographic processes to the population change of a given area during a specified time period: $P_2 = P_1 + B_{1-2} - D_{1-2} + IM_{1-2} - OM_{1-2}$, where P_2 is population at time 2; P_1 is population at beginning date; B_{1-2} is the number of births between times 1 and 2; D_{1-2} is the number of deaths during that period; IM_{1-2} is the number of in-migrants and OM_{1-2} the number of out-migrants between times 1 and 2.

demographic momentum   *See* population momentum.

demographic transition   A model of the effect of economic development on population growth. The first stage involves both high birth and death rates; the second phase displays high birth rates and falling mortality rates and population increases. Phase three shows reduction in population growth as birth rates decline to the level of death rates. The final, fourth, stage implies again a population stable in size but larger in numbers than at the start of the transition cycle.

demography   The scientific study of population, with particular emphasis on quantitative aspects.

density of population   *See* population density.

dependency ratio   The number of dependents, old or young, that each 100 persons in the productive years must, on average, support.

deposition   The process by which silt, sand, and rock particles accumulate and create landforms, such as stream deltas and talus slopes.

desertification   The conversion of arid and semi-arid lands into deserts as a result of climatic change or human activities such as overgrazing or deforestation.

developable surface   A geometric form, such as a cylinder or cone, that may be flattened without distortion.

devolution   The transfer of certain powers from the state central government to separate political subdivisions within the state's territory; decentralization of political control.

dew point   The temperature at which condensation forms, if the air is cooled sufficiently.

dialect   A regional or socioeconomic variation of a more widely spoken language.

diastrophism   The earth force that folds, faults, twists, and compresses rock.

dibble   Any small hand tool or stick used to make a hole for planting.

diffusion   *See* spatial diffusion.

distance   The amount of separation between two objects, areas, or points; an extent of areal or linear measure.

distance decay   The exponential decline of an activity or a function with increasing distance from its point of origin.

domestication   The successful transformation of plant or animal species from a wild state to a condition of dependency on human management, usually with distinct physical change from wild forebears.

doubling time   The time period required for any beginning total, experiencing a compounding growth, to double in size.

dune   A wavelike desert landform created by wind-blown sand.

E

earthquake   The movement of the earth along a geologic fault or at some other point of weakness at or near the earth's surface.

earth science tradition   One of the four traditions of geography, identified with physical geography in general.

ecology   The scientific study of how living creatures affect each other and what determines their distribution and abundance.

economic base   The manufacturing and service activities performed by the basic sector of the labor force of a city to satisfy demands both inside and outside the city and earn income to support the urban population.

economic geography   The study of how people earn a living, how livelihood systems vary by area, and how economic activities are spatially interrelated and linked.

ecosphere   *See* biosphere.

ecosystem   A population of organisms existing together in a particular area, together with the energy, air, water, soil, and chemicals upon which it depends.

ecumene   The permanently inhabited areas of the earth. *See also* nonecumene.

edge city   A distinct modal concentration of retail and office space situated on the outer fringes of a metropolitan area.

electoral geography   The study of the delineation of voting districts and the spatial patterns of election results.

electromagnetic spectrum   The entire range of radiation, including the shortest as well as the longest wavelengths.

El Niño   The periodic (every 3 to 7 or 8 years) buildup of warm water along the west coast of South America; replacing the cold Humboldt current off the Peruvian coast, El Niño is associated with both a fall in plankton levels (and decreased fish supply) and short-term, widespread weather modification.

elongated state   A state whose territory is long and narrow.

enclave   A territory that is surrounded by, but is not part of, a state.

endangered species   Species that are present in such small numbers that they are in imminent danger of extinction.

energy   The ability to do work. *See also* kinetic energy, potential energy.

energy efficiency   The ratio of the output of useful energy from a conversion process to the total energy inputs.

environment   Surroundings; the totality of things that in any way may affect an organism, including both physical and cultural conditions; a region characterized by a certain set of physical conditions.

environmental determinism   The view that the physical environment, particularly climate, molds human behavior and conditions cultural development.

environmental justice   The goal of providing healthy surroundings for all people, regardless of their skin color, level of poverty, or place of residence.

environmental perception   The way people observe and interpret, as well as the ideas they have about near or distant places.

environmental pollution   *See* pollution.

environmental racism   Any policy or practice that differentially affects or harms individuals, groups, or communities because of their race or color; the harm may be intentional or unintentional.

epidemiologic transition   Long-term shifts in health and disease patterns as mortality moves from high to low levels.

equal-area projection   *See* equivalent projection.

equator   An imaginary line that encircles the globe halfway between the North and South Poles.

equidistant projection   A map projection on which true distances in all directions can be measured from one or two central points.

equivalent projection   A map projection on which the areas of regions are represented in correct or constant proportions to earth reality; also called equal-area projection.

erosion   The result of processes that loosen, dissolve, wear away, and remove earth and rock material. Those processes include weathering, solution, abrasion, and transportation.

erosional agents   The forces of wind, moving water, glaciers, waves, and ocean currents that carve, wear away, and remove rock and soil particles.

estuarine zone   The relatively narrow area of wetlands along coastlines where salt water and fresh water mix.

estuary   The lower course or mouth of a river where tides cause fresh water and salt water from the sea to mix.

ethanol   Organic matter that has been fermented and distilled into alcohol; an alternative automotive fuel that, when blended with gasoline, forms gasohol.

ethnic cleansing   The killing or forcible relocation of one traditional or ethnic group by a more powerful one.

ethnicity   The social status afforded to, usually, a minority group within a national population. Recognition is based primarily on culture traits, such as religion, distinctive customs, or native or ancestral national origin.

ethnic religion   A religion identified with a particular ethnic group and largely exclusive to it.

ethnocentrism   The belief that one's own ethnic group is superior to all others.

ethnographic boundary   *See* consequent boundary.

European Union (EU)   An economic association established in 1957 of a number of Western European states that promotes free trade among member countries; often called the Common Market.

eutrophication   The enrichment of a water body by the addition of nutrients received through erosion and runoff from the watershed. *See also* accelerated eutrophication.

evapotranspiration   The return of water from the land to the atmosphere through evaporation from the soil surface and transpiration from plants.

e-waste   A popular name for discarded electrical or electronic products.

exclave   A portion of a state that is separated from the main territory and surrounded by another country.

exclusive economic zone (EEZ) As established in the United Nations Convention on the Law of the Sea, a zone of exploitation extending 200 nautical miles seaward from a coastal state that has exclusive mineral and fishing rights over it.

exotic species A plant, an animal, or another organism that has been deliberately or inadvertently introduced into an ecosystem in which it did not evolve; a nonindigenous species.

extensive agriculture A crop or livestock system in which land quality or extent is more important than capital or labor inputs in determining output. It may be part of either a commercial or a subsistence economy.

extensive commerical agriculture Extensive farming in a commercial economy; examples include large-scale wheat farming and livestock ranching.

extensive subsistence agriculture Extensive farming in a subsistence economy; examples include nomadic herding and shifting cultivation.

external economies *See* agglomeration economies.

extinction The elimination of all of the individuals of a particular species.

extractive industries Primary activities involving the mining and quarrying of nonrenewable metallic and nonmetallic mineral resources.

extrusive rock Rock solidified from molten material (magma) that has flowed from beneath the earth's surface onto it.

F

faults Breaks in rock produced by stress or the movement of lithospheric plates.

fault escarpment A steep slope formed by the vertical movement of the earth along a fault.

fiord A glacial trough whose lower end is filled with seawater.

floodplain A valley area bordering a stream that is subject to inundation by flooding.

flow-line map A map used to portray linear movement between places; may be qualitative or quantitative.

fold A bend or wrinkle in rock resulting from compression and formed when the rock was in a plastic state.

folk culture The body of institutions, customs, dress, artifacts, collective wisdoms, and traditions of a homogeneous, isolated, largely self-sufficient, and relatively static social group.

food chain A sequence of organisms through which food and materials move within an ecosystem.

footloose A descriptive term applied to manufacturing activities for which the cost of transporting material or product is not important in determining location of production.

Fordism The manufacturing economy and system derived from assembly line mass production and the mass consumption of standardized goods. Named after Henry Ford, who innovated many of its production techniques.

foreign direct investment (FDI) The purchase or construction of foreign factories and other fixed assets by transnational corporations; also the purchase of or merging with foreign companies.

formal (uniform) region A region distinguished by uniformity of one or more characteristics that can serve as the basis for an areal generalization and of contrast with adjacent areas.

form utility A value-increasing change in the form—and therefore in the utility—of a raw material or commodity.

forward-thrust capital A capital city deliberately sited in a state's frontier zone.

fossil fuel Any of the fuels derived from decayed organic material converted by earth processes; especially coal, petroleum, and natural gas, but also including tar sands and oil shales.

fragmented state A state whose territory contains isolated parts, separated and discontinuous.

frictional effect In climatology, the slowing of wind movement due to the frictional drag of the earth's surface.

friction of distance A measure of the retarding effect of distance on spatial interaction. Generally, the greater the distance, the greater the "friction" and the less the interaction or exchange, or the greater the cost of achieving the exchange.

front The line or zone of separation between two air masses of different temperatures and humidities.

frontal precipitation *See* cyclonic (frontal) precipitation.

frontier That portion of a country adjacent to its boundaries and fronting another political unit.

frontier zone A belt lying between two states or between settled and uninhabited or sparsely settled areas.

Fujita scale A scale for categorizing tornado intensity.

functional (nodal) region A region differentiated by what occurs within it rather than by a homogeneity of physical or cultural phenomena; an earth area recognized as an operational unit based on defined organizational criteria.

G

gated community A restricted-access subdivision or neighborhood, often surrounded by a barrier, with entry permitted only for residents and their guests; usually totally planned in land use and design.

gathering industries Primary activities involving the harvesting of renewable natural resources of land or water; commercial gathering usually implies forestry and fishing industries.

gender The socially created, not biologically based, distinctions between femininity and masculinity.

gender empowerment measure (GEM) A statistic summarizing the extent of economic, political, and professional participation of women in the society of which they are members; a measure of relative gender equality.

gene flow The passage of genes characteristic of one breeding population into the gene pool of another by interbreeding.

genetic drift A chance modification of gene composition occurring in an isolated population and becoming accentuated through inbreeding.

gentrification The process by which middle- and high-income groups refurbish and rehabilitate housing in deteriorated inner-city areas, thereby displacing low-income populations.

geocaching The pursuit of a cache using a GPS unit.

geodetic control data The information specifying the horizontal and vertical positions of a place.

geographic database In cartography, a digital record of geographic information.

geographic grid The set of imaginary lines of latitude and longitude that intersect at right angles to form a system of reference for locating points on the surface of the earth.

geographic information system (GIS) A configuration of computer hardware and software for assembling, storing, manipulating, analyzing, and displaying geographically referenced information.

geometric boundary (*syn:* artificial boundary) A boundary without obvious physical geographic basis; often a section of a parallel of latitude or a meridian of longitude.

geomorphology The scientific study of landform origins, characteristics, and evolutions and their processes.

geothermal energy Energy that is generated by harnessing the naturally occurring steam and hot water produced by contact with heated rocks in the earth's crust.

gerrymandering Dividing an area into voting districts in such a way as to give one political party an unfair advantage in elections, to fragment voting blocks, or to achieve other nondemocratic objectives.

GIS *See* geographic information system.

glacial till The deposits of rocks, silt, and sand left by a glacier after it has receded.

glacial trough A deep, U-shaped valley or trench formed by glacial erosion.

glacier A huge mass of slowly moving land ice.

globalization The increasing interconnection of all parts of the world as the full range of social, cultural, political, economic, and environmental processes and patterns of change becomes international in scale and effect.

Global Positioning System (GPS) A method of using satellite observations for the determination of extremely accurate locational information.

global warming A rise in surface temperatures on Earth, a process believed by some to be caused by human activities that increase the concentration of greenhouse gases in the atmosphere, magnifying the greenhouse effect.

globe grid *See* geographic grid.

globe properties The characteristics of the grid system of longitude and latitude on a globe.

GPS *See* Global Positioning System.

gradational processes The processes of weathering, gravity transfer, and erosion that are responsible for the reduction of the land surface.

grade (of coal) A classification of coals based on their content of waste materials.

graphic scale A graduated line included in a map legend by means of which distances on the map may be measured in terms of ground distances.

great circle A circle formed by the intersection of the surface of a globe with a plane passing through the center of the globe. The equator is a great circle; meridians are one-half a great circle.

greenhouse effect The heating of the earth's surface as shortwave solar energy passes through the atmosphere, which is transparent to it but opaque to reradiated longwave terrestrial energy. Also refers to increasing the opacity of the atmosphere through the addition of increased amounts of carbon dioxide, nitrous oxides, methane, and chlorofluorocarbons.

greenhouse gases Heat-trapping gases added to the atmosphere by human activities; carbon dioxide, chlorofluorocarbons, methane gas, and nitrous oxide.

Green Revolution The great increases in food production, primarily in subtropical areas, accomplished through the introduction of very high-yielding grain crops, particularly wheat and rice.

Greenwich mean time (GMT) Local time at the prime meridian (zero degrees longitude), which passes through the observatory at Greenwich, England.

gross national income (GNI) *See* gross national product (GNP).

gross national product (GNP) The total value of all goods and services produced by a country per year; also called gross national income (GNI).

groundwater Underground water that accumulates in aquifers below the water table in the pores and cracks of rock and soil.

gyre In oceanography, a large spiral oceanic surface current.

H

half-life The time required for one-half the atomic nuclei of an isotope to decay.

hazardous waste Discarded solid, liquid, or gaseous material that may pose a substantial threat to human health or the environment when it is improperly disposed of, stored, or transported.

herbicide A chemical that kills plants, especially weeds. *See also* biocide, pesticide.

hierarchical diffusion The process by which contacts between people and the resulting diffusion of things or ideas occurs first among those at the same level of a hierarchy and then among elements at a lower level of the hierarchy (e.g., small-town residents acquire ideas or articles after they are common in large cities).

hierarchical migration The tendency for individuals to move from small places to larger ones.

hierarchy of central places The steplike series of urban units in classes differentiated by both size and function.

high-level waste Nuclear waste that can remain radioactive for thousands of years, produced principally by the generation of nuclear power and the manufacture of nuclear weapons.

hinterland An outlying region that furnishes raw materials or agricultural products to the heartland; the market area or region served by a town or city.

homeostatic plateau The equilibrium level of population that can be supported adequately by available resources; equivalent to carrying capacity.

humid continental climate A climate of east coast and continental interiors of midlatitudes, displaying large annual temperature ranges resulting from cold winters and hot summers; precipitation at all seasons.

humid subtropical climate A climate of the east coast of continents in lower middle latitudes, characterized by hot summers with convectional precipitation and cool winters with cyclonic precipitation.

humus Dark brown or black decomposed organic matter in soils.

hunting-gathering An economic and social system based primarily or exclusively on the hunting of wild animals and the gathering of food, fiber, and other materials from uncultivated plants.

hurricane A severe tropical cyclone with winds exceeding 120 kilometers per hour (75 mph) originating in the tropical region of the Atlantic Ocean, Caribbean Sea, or Gulf of Mexico.

hydrologic cycle The system by which water is continuously circulated through the biosphere by evaporation, condensation, and precipitation.

hydropower The kinetic energy of moving water converted into electrical power by a power plant whose turbines are driven by flowing water.

hydrosphere All water at or near the earth's surface that is not chemically bound in rocks; includes the oceans, surface waters, groundwater, and water held in the atmosphere.

I

iconography In political geography, the study of symbols that unite a country.

ideological subsystem The complex of ideas, beliefs, knowledge, and means of their communication that characterize a culture.

igneous rock Rock formed from cool, solidified magma; may solidify beneath or at the earth's surface.

incinerator A facility designed to burn waste.

inclination The tilt of the earth's axis about 23½° away from the perpendicular.

Industrial Revolution The rapid economic and social changes in agriculture and manufacturing that followed the introduction of the factory system to the textile industry of England in the last quarter of the 18th century.

infant mortality rate A refinement of the death rate to specify the ratio of deaths of infants age 1 year or less per 1000 live births.

infrared Electromagnetic radiation having wavelengths greater than those of visible light.

infrastructure The basic structure of services, installations, and facilities needed to support industrial, agricultural, and other economic development.

innovation Introduction into an area of new ideas, practices, or objects; an alteration of custom or culture that originates within the social group itself.

insolation The solar radiation received at the earth's surface.

intensive agriculture The application of large amounts of capital and/or labor per unit of cultivated land to increase output; may be part of either a commercial or a subsistence economy.

intensive commercial agriculture Intensive farming in a commercial economy; crops have high yields and high market value.

intensive subsistence agriculture Intensive farming in a subsistence economy; the cultivation of small landholdings through the expenditure of great amounts of labor.

International Date Line By international agreement, the designated line where each new day begins; generally following the 180th meridian.

intrusive rock Igneous rock from magma that has hardened beneath the earth's surface and that has penetrated or been forced into or between preexisting rocks.

IPAT equation An equation relating the environmental impact of a society to the key issues of population, affluence, and technology.

irredentism The desire of a state to gain or regain territory inhabited by people who have historic or cultural links to the country but who now live in a neighboring state.

isochrone A line connecting points that are equidistant in travel time from a common origin.

isoline A map line connecting points of equal value, such as a contour line or an isobar.

isotropic plain A hypothetical portion of the earth's surface assumed to be an unbounded, uniformly flat plain with uniform distribution of population, purchasing power, transport costs, accessibility, and the like.

J

J-curve A curve shaped like the letter J, depicting exponential, or geometric, growth (1, 2, 4, 8, 16 . . .).

jet stream A meandering belt of strong winds in the upper atmosphere; significant because it guides the movement of weather systems.

K

karst topography A limestone region marked by sinkholes, caverns, and underground streams.

kerogen A waxy, organic material occurring in oil shales that can be converted into crude oil by distillation.

kinetic energy The energy that results from the motion of a particle or body.

L

land breeze Airflow from the land toward the sea, resulting from a nighttime pressure gradient that moves winds from the cooler land surface to the warmer sea surface.

landform region A large section of the earth's surface characterized by a great deal of homogeneity among types of landforms.

landlocked state A state that lacks a seacoast.

Landsat satellite One of a series of continuously orbiting satellites that carry scanning instruments to measure reflected light in both the visible and near infrared portions of the spectrum.

landscape The appearance of an area and the items comprising that appearance. A distinction is often made between "physical landscapes" confined to landforms, natural vegetation, soils, etc., and "cultural landscapes" (q.v.).

language An organized system of speech by which people communicate with each other with mutual comprehension.

language family A group of languages thought to have descended from a single, common ancestral tongue.

lapse rate The rate of change of temperature with altitude in the troposphere; the average lapse rate is about 6.4°C per 1000 meters (3.5°F per 1000 ft).

large-scale map A representation of a small land area, usually with a representative fraction of 1:75,000 or less.

latitude The angular distance north or south of the equator, measured in degrees ranging from 0° (the equator) to 90° (the North and South Poles).

lava Molten material that has emerged onto the earth's surface.

Law of the Sea Convention A code of sea law approved by the United Nations in 1982 that authorizes, among other provisions, territorial waters extending 12 nautical miles from shore and 200-nautical-mile-wide exclusive economic zones; generally referred to as UNCLOS.

leachate The contaminated liquid discharged from a sanitary landfill to either surface or subsurface land or water.

leaching The downward movement of water through the soil layer, resulting in the removal of soluble minerals from the upper soil horizons.

least-cost theory (*syn:* Weberian analysis) The view that the optimum location of a manufacturing establishment is at the place where the costs of transport and labor and the advantages of agglomeration or dispersion are most favorable.

levee In agriculture, a continuous embankment surrounding areas to be flooded. *See also* natural levee.

lingua franca Any of the various auxiliary languages used as common tongues among people of an area where several languages are spoken.

liquefied natural gas (LNG) Methane gas that has been liquefied by refrigeration for storage or transportation.

lithosphere The outermost layer of the earth, composed of the crust and upper mantle.

loam Agriculturally productive soil containing roughly equal parts of sand, silt, and clay.

locational tradition One of the four traditions of geography; in this text, identified with economic, urban, and environmental geography.

loess A deposit of windblown silt.

longitude The angular distance east or west of the prime (zero) meridian, measured in degrees ranging from 0° to 180°.

long lot A farm or other property consisting of a long, narrow strip of land extending back from a river or road.

longshore current A current that moves roughly parallel to the shore and transports the sand that forms beaches and sand spits.

low-level waste Hazardous material whose radioactivity will decay to safe levels in 100 years or less, produced principally by industries and nuclear power plants.

M

magma Underground molten material.

malnutrition Food intake insufficient in quantity or deficient in quality to sustain life at optimal conditions of health.

Malthus Thomas R. Malthus (1766–1834), English economist, demographer, and cleric, who suggested that, unless checked by self-control, war, or natural disaster, population will inevitably increase faster than will the food supplies needed to sustain it.

mantle The layer of earth between the crust and the core.

map projection A method of transferring the grid system from the earth's curved surface to the flat surface of a map.

map scale *See* scale.

marine west coast climate A regional climate found on the west coast of continents in upper midlatitudes, rainy all seasons with relatively cool summers and relatively mild winters.

market economy *See* commercial economy.

mass movement The downslope movement of earth materials due to gravity.

mass wasting *See* mass movement.

material culture The tangible, physical items produced and used by members of a specific culture group and reflective of their traditions, lifestyles, and technologies.

mathematical location *See* absolute location.

maximum sustainable yield The maximum rate at which a renewable resource can be exploited without impairing its ability to be renewed or replenished.

mechanical weathering The physical disintegration of earth materials, commonly by frost action, root action, or the development of salt crystals.

Mediterranean climate A climate of lower midlatitudes characterized by mild, wet winters and hot, dry, sunny summers.

megalopolis An extensive, heavily populated urban complex with contained open, nonurban land, created through the spread and merging of separate metropolitan areas; (*cap.*) the name applied to the continuous functionally urban area of the northeastern seaboard of the United States from Maine to Virginia.

megawatt A unit of power equal to 1 million watts (1000 kilowatts) of electricity.

mental map The maplike image of the world, country, region, or other area a person carries in his or her mind; includes knowledge of actual locations and spatial relationships and is colored by personal perceptions and preferences related to place.

mentifacts The central, enduring elements of a culture that express its values and beliefs, including language, religion, folklore, artistic traditions, and the like. Elements in the ideological subsystem of culture.

Mercator projection A true conformal cylindrical projection first published in 1569, useful for navigation.

meridian A north–south line of longitude; on the globe, all meridians are of equal length and converge at the poles.

mesa An extensive, flat-topped elevated tableland with horizontal strata, a resistant cap rock, and one or more steep sides; a large butte.

metamorphic rock Rock transformed from igneous and sedimentary rocks into a new type of rock by earth forces that generate heat, pressure, or chemical reaction.

metes-and-bounds survey A system of property description that uses natural features (trees, boulders, streams, etc.) to describe and define the boundaries of individual properties.

metropolitan area A large, functional entity, perhaps containing several urbanized areas, discontinuously built up but operating as a coherent economic whole.

migration The permanent (or relatively permanent) relocation of an individual or a group to a new, usually distant place of residence.

migration field An area that sends major migration flows to or receives major flows from a given place.

mineral A natural inorganic substance that has a definite chemical composition and characteristic crystal structure, hardness, and density.

ministate An imprecise term for a state or territory small in both population and area. An informal definition accepted by the United Nations suggests a maximum of 1 million people combined with a territory of less than 700 square kilometers (270 sq mi).

monoculture An agricultural system dominated by a single crop.

monotheism The belief that there is only one God.

monsoon A wind system that reverses direction seasonally, producing wet and dry seasons; especially describes the wind system of South, Southeast, and East Asia.

moraine Any of several types of landforms composed of debris transported and deposited by a glacier.

mortality rate *See* death rate.

mountain breeze The downward flow of heavy, cool air at night from mountainsides to lower valley locations.

multiple-nuclei model The idea that large cities develop by peripheral spread, not from one central business district but from several nodes of growth, each of specialized use.

multiplier effect The expected addition of nonbasic workers and dependents to a city's total employment and population that accompanies new basic sector employment.

N

nation A culturally distinctive group of people occupying a particular region and bound together by a sense of unity arising from shared ethnicity, beliefs, and customs.

nationalism A sense of unity binding the people of a state together; devotion to the interests of a particular nation; an identification with the state and an acceptance of national goals.

nation-state A state whose territory is identical to that occupied by a particular nation.

natural boundary (*syn:* physical boundary) A boundary line based on recognizable physiographic features, such as mountains, rivers, or deserts.

natural gas A mixture of hydrocarbons and small quantities of nonhydrocarbons existing in a gaseous state or in solution with crude oil in natural reservoirs.

natural increase The growth of a population through excess of births over deaths, excluding the effects of immigration or emigration.

natural landscape The physical *environment* unaffected by human activities. The duration and near totality of human occupation of the earth's surface assure that little or no "natural landscape" so defined remains intact. Opposed to *cultural landscape.*

natural levee An embankment on the sides of a meandering river formed by deposition of silt during floods.

natural resource A physically occurring item that a population perceives to be necessary and useful to its maintenance and well-being.

natural selection The process of survival and reproductive success of individuals or groups best adjusted to their environment, leading to the perpetuation of their genetic qualities.

natural vegetation The plant life that would exist in an area if humans did not interfere with its development.

neo-Malthusianism The advocacy of population control programs to preserve and improve general national prosperity and well-being.

neritic zone The relatively shallow part of the sea that lies above the continental shelf.

net migration The difference between in-migration and out-migration of an area.

niche The place an organism or a species occupies in an ecosystem.

nodal region *See* functional region.

nomadic herding The migratory but controlled movement of livestock solely dependent upon natural forage.

nonbasic sector The economic activities of an urban unit that supply the resident population with goods and services.

nonecumene (*syn:* anecumene) The portion of the earth's surface that is uninhabited or only temporarily or intermittently inhabited. *See also* ecumene.

nonfuel mineral resource A mineral used for purposes other than providing a source of energy.

nongovernmental organization (NGO) A group of people acting outside government and major commercial agencies and advocating or lobbying for particular causes.

nonmaterial culture The oral traditions, songs, and stories of a culture group along with its beliefs and customary behaviors.

nonpoint source of pollution Pollution from a broad area, such as one of fertilizer or pesticide application, rather than from a discrete source.

nonrenewable resource A natural resource that is not replenished or replaced by natural processes or is used at a rate that exceeds its replacement rate.

North and South Poles The end points of the axis about which the earth spins.

North Atlantic drift The massive movement of warm water in the Atlantic Ocean from the Caribbean Sea and Gulf of Mexico in a northeasterly direction to the British Isles and the Scandinavian peninsula.

nuclear fission The controlled splitting of an atom to release energy.

nuclear fusion The combining of two atoms of deuterium into a single atom of helium in order to release energy.

nuclear power Electricity generated by a power plant whose turbines are driven by steam produced by the fissioning of nuclear fuel in a reactor.

nutrient A mineral or another element an organism requires for normal growth and development.

O

offshoring The relocation of business processes and services to a lower-cost foreign location; the offshore outsourcing of, particularly, white-collar technical, professional, and clerical services.

oil shale Sedimentary rock containing solid organic material (kerogen) that can be extracted and converted into a crude oil by distillation.

ore A mineral deposit that can be extracted at a profit.

organic Derived from living organisms; plant or animal life.

Organization of Petroleum Exporting Countries (OPEC) An international cartel composed of 11 countries that aims at pursuing common oil marketing and pricing policies.

orographic precipitation The rain or snow caused when warm, moisture-laden air is forced to rise over hills or mountains in its path and is thereby cooled.

orthophotomap A multicolored, distortion-free aerial photographic image to which certain supplementary information has been added.

outsourcing (1) Producing abroad parts or products for domestic use or sale; (2) subcontracting production or services rather than performing those activities "in house."

outwash plain A gently sloping area in front of a glacier composed of neatly stratified glacial till carried out of the glacier by meltwater streams.

overburden Soil and rock of little or no value that overlies a deposit of economic value, such as coal.

overpopulation A value judgment that the resources of an area are insufficient to sustain adequately its present population numbers.

oxbow lake A crescent-shaped lake contained in an abandoned meander of a river.

ozone A gas molecule consisting of three atoms of oxygen (O_3) formed when diatomic oxygen (O_2) is exposed to ultraviolet radiation. In the lower atmosphere, it constitutes a damaging component of photochemical smog; in the upper atmosphere, it forms a normally continuous, thin layer that blocks ultraviolet light.

ozone layer A layer of ozone in the high atmosphere that protects life on Earth by absorbing ultraviolet radiation from the sun.

P

parallel of latitude An east–west line indicating the distance north or south of the equator.

PCBs Polychlorinated biphenyls; compounds containing chlorine that can be biologically magnified in the food chain.

peak value intersection The most accessible and costly parcel of land in a central business district and, therefore, in the entire urbanized area.

perceptual (vernacular, popular) region A region perceived to exist by its inhabitants or the general populace. It has reality as an element of popular culture or folk culture represented in the mental maps of average people.

perforated state A state whose territory is interrupted ("perforated") by a separate, independent state totally contained within its borders.

peripheral model A model describing metropolitan area land uses in the circumferential belt around a city; nodes on the belt are centers for employment or services, and residents of the developments on the belt lead their lives largely on the periphery of the city.

permafrost Permanently frozen subsoil.

perpetual resource A resource that comes from an inexhaustible source, such as the sun, wind, and tides.

pesticide A chemical that kills insects, rodents, fungi, weeds, and other pests. *See also* biocide, herbicide.

Peters projection An equal-area cylindrical projection developed by Arno Peters that purports to show developing countries in proper proportion to one another.

petroleum Oil and oil products in all forms, such as crude oil and unfinished oils.

pH factor The measure of the acidity/alkalinity of soil or water, on a scale of 0 to 14, rising with increasing alkalinity.

photochemical smog A form of air pollution produced by the interaction of hydrocarbons and oxides of nitrogen in the presence of sunlight.

photovoltaic (PV) cell A device that converts solar energy directly into electrical energy. *See also* solar power.

physical boundary *See* natural boundary.

physiological density The number of persons per unit area of agricultural land. *See also* population density.

pidgin An auxiliary language derived, with reduction of vocabulary and simplification of structure, from other languages. Not a native tongue, it is employed to provide a mutually intelligible vehicle for limited transactions of trade or administration.

pixel An extremely small sensed unit of a digital image.

place utility (1) The perceived attractiveness of a place in its social, economic, or environmental attributes; (2) the value imparted to goods or services by tertiary activities that provide things needed in specific markets.

planar (azimuthal) projection A map projection based on the projection of the globe grid onto a plane as the presumed developable surface.

planned economy A system of the production of goods and services, usually consumed or distributed by a governmental agency, in quantities and at prices determined by governmental programs.

plantation A large agricultural holding, frequently foreign-owned, devoted to the production of a single export crop.

plate tectonics The theory that the earth's crust consists of lithospheric plates that carry the continents and the ocean floor and float slowly on the plastic upper mantle, colliding with and scraping against one another.

playa A temporary lake or lake bed found in a desert environment.

Pleistocene The geologic epoch dating from 2 million to about 10,000 years ago during which four stages of continental glaciation occurred.

point source of pollution Pollution originating from a discrete source, such as a smokestack or the outflow from a pipe.

political geography The branch of human geography concerned with the spatial analysis of political phenomena.

pollution The presence in the biosphere of substances that, because of their quantity, chemical nature, or temperature, have a negative impact on the ecosystem or that cannot be readily disposed of by natural recycling processes.

polychlorinated biphenyls *See* PCBs.

polytheism The belief in or worship of many gods.

popular culture The constantly changing mix of material and nonmaterial elements available through mass production and the mass media to an urbanized, heterogeneous, nontraditional society.

popular region *See* perceptual region.

population density A measurement of the numbers of persons per unit area of land within predetermined limits, usually political or census boundaries. *See also* physiological density.

population geography The branch of human geography dealing with the number, composition, and distribution of humans in relation to variations in earth-space conditions.

population momentum (*syn:* demographic momentum) The tendency for population growth to continue despite stringent family planning programs because of a relatively high concentration of people in the childbearing years.

population projection A report of future size, age, and sex composition of a population based on assumptions applied to current data.

population pyramid A graphic depiction of the age and sex composition of a (usually national) population.

possibilism The philosophical viewpoint that the physical environment offers human beings a set of opportunities from which (within limits) people may choose according to their cultural needs and technological awareness.

potential energy The energy stored in a particle or body.

potentially renewable resource A resource that can last indefinitely if its natural replacement rate is not exceeded; examples include forests, groundwater, and soil.

precipitation All moisture, solid and liquid, that falls to the earth's surface from the atmosphere.

pressure gradient force Differences in air pressure between areas that induce air to flow from areas of high pressure to areas of low pressure.

primary activity The part of the economy involved in making natural resources available for use or further processing; includes mining, agriculture, forestry, fishing or hunting, grazing.

primary air pollutant Material, such as particulates or sulfur dioxide, that is emitted directly into the atmosphere in sufficient quantities to adversely affect human health or the environment.

primate city A country's leading city, much larger and functionally more complex than any other; usually the capital city and a center of wealth and power.

prime meridian An imaginary line passing through the Royal Observatory at Greenwich, England, serving by agreement as the zero degree line of longitude.

projection An estimate of future conditions based on current trends. *See also* map projection.

prorupt state A state of basically compact form that has one or more narrow extensions of territory.

proto-language An assumed, reconstructed, or recorded language ancestral to one or more contemporary languages or dialects.

proved (usable) reserves The portion of a natural resource that has been identified and can be extracted profitably with current technology.

psychological distance The way an individual perceives distance.

pull factor A characteristic of a region that acts as an attractive force, drawing migrants from other regions.

purchasing power parity (PPP) A monetary measurement that takes account of what money actually buys in each country.

push factor A characteristic of a region that contributes to the dissatisfaction of residents and impels their migration.

Q

quaternary activity Employment concerned with research, with the gathering or disseminating of information, and with administration, including administration of the other economic activity levels.

quinary activity A sometimes separately recognized subsection of tertiary activity management functions involving highest-level decision making in all types of large organizations. Also deemed the most advanced form of the quaternary subsector.

R

race A subset of human population whose members share certain distinctive, inherited biological characteristics.

radioactive waste Solid, liquid, or gaseous waste containing radioactive isotopes, whose half-lives can range from less than 1 second to millions of years; usually classified as low-level or high-level according to the amount and types of radioactivity in the substance.

rank (of coal) A classification of coals based on their age and energy content; those of higher rank are more mature and richer in energy.

rank-size rule An observed regularity in the city-size distribution of some countries. In a rank-size hierarchy, the population of any given town will be inversely proportional to its rank in the hierarchy; that is, the *n*th-ranked city will be 1/*n* the size of the largest city.

rate The frequency of occurrence of an event during a specified time period.

rate of natural increase The birth rate minus the death rate, suggesting the annual rate of population growth without considering net migration.

recycling The reuse of disposed materials after they have passed through some form of treatment (e.g., melting down glass bottles to produce new bottles).

redistricting The drawing of new electoral district boundary lines in response to changing patterns of population or changing legal requirements.

reflection The process of returning to outer space some of the earth's received insolation.

region In geography, an area of the earth that displays a distinctive grouping of physical or cultural phenomena or is functionally united as a single organizational unit.

regional autonomy A measure of self-governance for a subdivision of a country.

regional concept The view that physical and cultural phenomena on the surface of the earth are rationally arranged by complex but comprehensible spatial processes.

regionalism In political geography, minority group identification with a particular region of a state rather than with the state as a whole.

relative direction (*syn:* relational direction) A culturally-based locational reference, such as the Far West, the Old South, or the Middle East.

relative distance A transformation of *absolute distance* into such relative measures as time or monetary costs. Such measures yield different explanations of human spatial behavior than do linear distances alone. Distances between places are constant by absolute terms, but relative distances may vary with improvements in transportation or communication technology or with different psychological perceptions of space.

relative humidity A measure of the moisture content of the air, expressed as the amount of water vapor present relative to the maximum that can exist at the current temperature.

relative location The position of a place or an activity in relation to other places or activities.

relic boundary A former boundary line that is still discernible and marked by a cultural landscape feature.

religion A value system that involves formal or informal worship and faith in the sacred and divine.

relocation diffusion The transfer of ideas, behaviors, or articles from one place to another through the migration of those possessing the feature transported; also, spatial relocation in which a phenomenon leaves an area of origin as it is transported to a new location.

remote sensing Any of several techniques of obtaining images of an area without having the sensor in direct physical contact with it, as by air photography or satellite sensors.

renewable resource A naturally occurring material that is potentially inexhaustible, either because it flows continuously (such as solar radiation or wind) or is renewed within a short period of time (such as biomass). *See also* sustained yield.

replacement level The number of children per family just sufficient to keep total population constant. Depending on mortality conditions, replacement level is usually calculated to be between 2.1 and 2.5 children.

representative fraction (RF) The scale of a map expressed as a ratio of a unit of distance on the map to distance measured in the same unit on the ground (e.g., 1:250,000).

reradiation A process by which the earth returns solar energy to space; some of the shortwave solar energy that is absorbed into the land and water is returned to the atmosphere in the form of longwave terrestrial radiation.

resource *See* natural resource.

return migration (countermigration) The return of migrants to the region from which they had earlier emigrated.

rhumb line A line of constant compass bearing; it cuts all meridians at the same angle.

Richter scale A logarithmic scale used to express the magnitude of an earthquake.

S

Sahel The semiarid zone between the Sahara Desert and the savanna area to the south in West Africa; district of recurring drought, famine, and environmental degradation.

salinization The concentration of salts in the topsoil as a result of the evaporation of surface water; occurs in poorly drained soils in dry climates, often as a result of improper irrigation.

sandbar An offshore shoal of sand created by the backwash of waves.

sanitary landfill The disposal of solid wastes by spreading them in layers covered with enough soil or ashes to control odors, rats, and flies.

savanna A tropical grassland characterized by widely dispersed trees and experiencing pronounced yearly wet and dry seasons.

scale In cartography, the ratio between length or size of an area on a map and the actual length or size of that area on the earth's surface; map scale may be represented verbally, graphically, or as a fraction. In more general terms, *scale* refers to the size of the area studied, from local to global.

S-curve The horizontal bending, or leveling, of an exponential J-curve.

sea breeze Airflow from the sea toward the land, resulting from a daytime pressure gradient that moves winds from the cooler sea surface onto the warmer land surface.

secondary activity The part of the economy involved in the processing of raw materials derived from primary activities; includes manufacturing, construction, power generation.

sector model A description of urban land uses as wedge-shaped sectors radiating outward from the central business district along transportation corridors. The radial access routes attract particular uses to certain sectors.

secularism An indifference to or rejection of religion and religious belief.

sedimentary rock Rock formed by the accumulation of particles of gravel, sand, silt, and clay that were eroded from already existing rocks and laid down in layers.

seismic waves Vibrations within the earth set off by earthquakes.

self-determination The concept that nationalities have the right to govern themselves in their own state or territory, a right to self-rule.

shaded relief A method of representing the three-dimensional quality of an area by use of continuous graded tone to simulate the appearance of sunlight and shadows.

shale oil The crude oil resulting from the distillation of kerogen in oil shales.

shamanism A form of tribal religion based on belief in a hidden world of gods, ancestral spirits, and demons responsive only to a shaman, or interceding priest.

shifting cultivation (*syn:* slash-and-burn agriculture, swidden agriculture) Crop production of forest clearings kept in cultivation until their quickly-declining fertility is lost. Cleared plots are then abandoned and new sites are prepared.

sinkhole A deep surface depression formed when ground collapses into a subterranean cavern.

site The place where something is located; the immediate surroundings and their attributes.

situation The location of something in relation to the physical and human characteristics of a larger region.

slash-and-burn agriculture *See* shifting cultivation.

small circle The line created by the intersection of a spherical surface with a plane that does not pass through its center.

small-scale map A representation of a large land area on which small features (e.g., highways, buildings) cannot be shown true to scale.

sociofacts The institutions and links between individuals and groups that unite a culture, including family structure and political, educational, and religious institutions; components of the sociological subsystem of culture.

sociological subsystem The totality of expected and accepted patterns of interpersonal relations common to a culture or subculture.

soil The complex mixture of loose material, including minerals, organic and inorganic compounds, living organisms, air, and water, found at the earth's surface and capable of supporting plant life.

soil depletion The loss of some or all of the vital nutrients from soil.

soil erosion The wearing away and removal of soil particles from exposed surfaces by agents such as moving water, wind, or ice.

soil horizon A layer of soil distinguished from other soil zones by color, texture, and other characteristics resulting from soil-forming processes.

soil order A general grouping of soils with broadly similar composition, horizons, and weathering and leaching processes.

soil profile A vertical cross section of soil horizons.

soil properties The characteristics that distinguish types of soil from one another, including organic and inorganic matter, texture, structure, and nutrients.

solar energy Radiation from the sun, which is transformed into heat primarily at the earth's surface and secondarily in the atmosphere.

solar power The radiant energy generated by the sun; sun's energy captured and directly converted for human use. *See also* photovoltaic cell.

solid waste The unwanted materials generated in production or consumption processes that are solid rather than liquid or gaseous in form.

source region In climatology, a large area of uniform surface and relatively consistent temperatures where an air mass forms.

southern oscillation The atmospheric conditions occurring periodically near Australia that create the El Niño condition off the coast of South America.

spatial diffusion The outward spread of a substance, a concept, a practice, or a population from its point of origin to other areas.

spatial distribution The arrangement of things on the earth's surface.

spatial interaction The movement (e.g., of people, goods, information) between different places; an indication of interdependence between areas.

spatial margin of profitability The set of points delimiting the area within which a firm's profitable operation is possible.

special-purpose map *See* thematic map.

spring wheat Wheat sown in spring for ripening during the summer or autumn.

stage in life Membership in a specific age group.

standard language A language substantially uniform with respect to spelling, grammar, pronunciation, and vocabulary and representing the approved community norm of the tongue.

standard parallel The tangent circle, usually a parallel of latitude, in a conic projection; along the standard line, the scale is as stated on the map.

state (*syn:* country) An independent political unit occupying a defined, permanently populated territory and having full sovereign control over its internal and foreign affairs.

step migration A migration in which an eventual long-distance relocation is undertaken in stages, as from farm to village to small town to city.

steppe Treeless midlatitude grassland.

stratosphere The layer of the atmosphere that lies above the troposphere and extends outward to about 56 kilometers (35 mi).

stream load The eroded material carried by a stream in one of three ways, depending on the size and composition of the particles: (1) in dissolved form, (2) suspended by water, or (3) rolled along the streambed.

subduction The process by which one lithospheric plate is forced down beneath another into the asthenosphere as a result of a collision with that plate.

subnationalism The feeling that one owes primary allegiance to a traditional group or nation rather than to the state.

subsequent boundary A boundary line that is established after the area in question has been settled and that considers the cultural characteristics of the bounded area.

subsidence The settling or sinking of a portion of the land surface, sometimes as a result of the extraction of fluids, such as oil or water, from underground deposits.

subsistence agriculture Any of several farm economies in which most crops are grown for food, nearly exclusively for local consumption.

subsistence economy A system in which goods and services are created for the use of producers or their immediate families. Market exchanges are limited and of minor importance.

substitution principle In industry, the tendency to substitute one factor of production for another in order to achieve optimum plant location and profitability.

suburb A functionally specialized segment of a large urban complex located outside the boundaries of the central city.

succession A natural process in which an orderly sequence of plant species will occupy a newly established landform or a recently altered landscape.

superimposed boundary A boundary line placed over, and ignoring, an existing cultural pattern.

supranationalism The acceptance of the interests of more than one state, expressed as associations of states created for mutual benefit and to achieve shared objectives.

surface water Water that is on the earth's surface, such as in rivers, streams, reservoirs, lakes, and ponds.

sustainable development Economic development and resource use that satisfies current needs without jeopardizing the ability of future generations to meet their own needs.

sustained yield The practice of balancing harvesting with the growth of new stocks in order to avoid depletion of the resource and ensure a perpetual supply.

swidden agriculture *See* shifting cultivation.

syncretism The development of a new form of, for example, religion or music, through the fusion of distinctive parental elements.

syntax The way words are put together in phrases and sentences.

systems analysis An approach to the study of large systems through (1) segregation of the entire system into its component parts, (2) investigation of the interactions between system elements, and (3) study of inputs, outputs, flows, interactions, and boundaries within the system.

T

talus slope A landform composed of rock particles that have accumulated at the base of a cliff, hill, or mountain.

tar sand Sand and sandstone impregnated with heavy oil.

technological subsystem The complex of material objects together with the techniques of their use by means of which people carry out their productive activities.

technology An integrated system of knowledge and skills developed within a culture to carry out successfully purposeful and productive tasks.

tectonic forces The processes that shape and reshape the earth's crust, the two main types being diastrophic and volcanic.

temperature inversion The condition caused by rapid reradiation in which air at lower altitudes is cooler than air aloft.

territoriality The persistent attachment of most animals to a specific area; the behavior associated with the defense of the home territory.

territorial production complex In the economic planning of the former Soviet Union, a design for large regional industrial, mining, and agricultural development leading to regional self-sufficiency and the creation of specialized production for a larger national market.

terrorism The calculated use of violence against civilians and other symbolic targets in order to publicize a cause or to diminish people's support for a leader, a government, a policy, or a way of life that the perpetrators of violence find objectionable.

tertiary activity The part of the economy that fulfills the exchange function and that provides market availability of commodities; includes wholesale and retail trade and associated transportation, government, and information services.

thematic map (*syn:* special-purpose map) A map that shows a specific spatial distribution or category of data.

thermal pollution The introduction of heated water into the environment, with consequent adverse effects on aquatic life.

Third World Originally (in the 1950s), designating countries uncommitted to either the "First World" Western capitalist bloc or the Eastern "Second World" communist bloc; subsequently, countries considered not yet fully developed or in a state of underdevelopment in economic and social terms.

threatened species A species that has declined significantly in total numbers and may be on the verge of extinction; an endangered or vulnerable species.

threshold In economic geography, the minimum market needed to support the supply of a product or service.

topographic map A map that portrays the shape and elevation of the terrain, often in great detail.

toponym A place-name.

toponymy The place-names of a region or, especially, the study of place-names.

tornado A small, violent storm characterized by a funnel-shaped cloud of whirling winds that can form beneath a cumulonimbus cloud in proximity to a cold front and that moves at speeds as high as 480 kilometers per hour (300 mph).

total fertility rate (TFR) The average number of children that would be born to each woman if, during her childbearing years, she bore children at the current year's rate for women that age.

town A nucleated settlement that contains a central business district but that is smaller and less functionally complex than a city.

township and range system A rectangular survey system whose basic units of areas are the township and section; it identifies townships as being north or south of a particular baseline and east or west of a particular principal meridian. Townships are subdivided into square sections 1 mile on a side.

traditional religion *See* tribal religion.

tragedy of the commons The observation that, in the absence of collective control over the use of a resource available to all, it is to the advantage of all users to maximize their separate shares even though their collective pressures may diminish total yield or destroy the resource altogether.

transform fault A break in rocks that occurs when one lithospheric plate slips past another in a horizontal motion.

transnational corporation (TNC) A large business organization operating in at least two separate national economies.

tribal religion (*syn:* traditional religion) An ethnic religion specific to a small, localized, preindustrial culture group.

tropical rain forest The tree cover composed of tall, high-crowned evergreen deciduous species, associated with the continuously wet tropical lowlands.

tropical rain forest climate The continuously warm, frost-free climate of tropical and equatorial lowlands, with abundant moisture year-round.

troposphere The atmospheric layer closest to the earth, extending outward about 11 to 13 kilometers (7 to 8 mi) at the poles to about 26 kilometers (16 mi) at the equator.

truck farming The intensive production of fruits and vegetables for market rather than for processing or canning.

tsunami Sea waves generated when an earthquake, eruption, or underwater landslide abruptly moves the seabed, jolting the waters above.

tundra The treeless area lying between the tree line of Arctic regions and the permanently ice-covered zone.

typhoon A hurricane occurring in the western Pacific Ocean region.

U

ubiquitous industry A market-oriented industry whose establishments are distributed in direct proportion to the distribution of population (market).

underpopulation A value statement reflecting the view that an area has too few people in relation to its resources and population-supporting capacity.

unitary state A state in which the central government dictates the degree of local or regional autonomy and the nature of local governmental units; a country with few cultural conflicts and a strong sense of national identity.

United Nations Convention on the Law of the Sea (UNCLOS) *See* Law of the Sea Convention.

universalizing religion A religion that claims global truth and applicability and seeks the conversion of all humankind.

urban hierarchy The steplike series of urban units (e.g., hamlets, villages, towns, cities, metropolises) in classes differentiated by size and function.

urban influence zone An area outside of a city that is nevertheless affected by the city.

urbanization The transformation of a population from rural to urban status; the process of city formation and expansion.

urbanized area A continuously built-up urban landscape defined by building and population densities with no reference to the political boundaries of the city; it may contain a central city and many contiguous towns, cities, suburbs, and unincorporated areas.

usable reserves *See* proved reserves.

V

valley breeze The flow of air up mountain slopes during the day.

value-by-area map *See* area cartogram.

variable costs In economic geography, the costs of production inputs that change as the level of production changes. They differ from the costs incurred by agricultural or industrial firms that are fixed and do not change as the amount of production changes.

verbal scale A statement of the relationship between units of measure on a map and distance on the ground, as "1 inch represents 1 mile."

vernacular (1) The nonstandard indigenous language or dialect of a locality; (2) of or related to indigenous arts and architecture, such as a vernacular house; (3) of or related to the perceptions and understandings of the general population, such as a vernacular region.

vernacular region *See* perceptual region.

volcanism The earth force that transports subsurface materials (often heated, sometimes molten) to or toward the surface of the earth.

von Thünen model The model developed by Johann H. von Thünen (1783–1850) to explain the forces that control the prices of agricultural commodities and how those variable prices affect patterns of agricultural land utilization.

von Thünen rings The concentric zonal pattern of agricultural land use around a single market center proposed in the von Thünen model.

vulnerable species Species whose numbers have been so reduced that they could become threatened or endangered.

W

warping The bowing of a large region of the earth's surface due to the movement of continents or the melting of continental glaciers.

wash A dry, braided channel in the desert that remains after the rush of rainfall runoff water.

water table The upper limit of the saturated zone and therefore of groundwater; the top of the water within an aquifer.

weather The state of the atmosphere at a given time and place.

weathering The mechanical and chemical processes that fragment and decompose rock materials.

Weberian analysis *See* least-cost theory.

Weber model The analytical model devised by Alfred Weber (1868–1958) to explain the principles governing the optimum location of industrial establishments.

wetland A vegetated inland or coastal area that is either occasionally or permanently covered by standing water or saturated with moisture.

wind farm A cluster of wind-powered turbines producing commercial electricity.

wind power The kinetic energy of wind converted into mechanical energy by wind turbines that drive generators to produce electricity.

winter wheat Wheat planted in autumn for early summer harvesting.

world city One of a small number of interconnected, internationally dominant centers (e.g., New York, London, Tokyo) that together control the global systems of finance and commerce.

Z

zero population growth (ZPG) A situation in which a population is not changing in size from year to year, as a result of the combination of births, deaths, and migration.

zoning Designating by ordinance areas in a municipality for particular types of land use.